1 MONTH OF
FREE
READING

at

www.ForgottenBooks.com

By purchasing this book you are eligible for one month membership to ForgottenBooks.com, giving you unlimited access to our entire collection of over 700,000 titles via our web site and mobile apps.

To claim your free month visit:

www.forgottenbooks.com/free180049

ISBN 978-0-483-26836-4
PIBN 10180049

This book is a reproduction of an important historical work. Forgotten Books uses state-of-the-art technology to digitally reconstruct the work, preserving the original format whilst repairing imperfections present in the aged copy. In rare cases, an imperfection in the original, such as a blemish or missing page, may be replicated in our edition. We do, however, repair the vast majority of imperfections successfully; any imperfections that remain are intentionally left to preserve the state of such historical works.

TERCENTENARY MONUMENT.

IN

COMMEMORATION

OF THE

THREE HUNDREDTH ANNIVERSARY

OF THE

Heidelberg Catechism.

CHAMBERSBURG, PA.:
PUBLISHED BY M. KIEFFER & CO.
PHILADELPHIA: LINDSAY & BLAKISTON.
NEW YORK: A. D. F. RANDOLPH.
1863.

PREFACE.

THE Essays contained in this volume, having been specially prepared for the purpose by Reformed theologians of Germany, Holland, and America, in pursuance of arrangements previously made by the highest judicatories of the German Reformed Church in the United States, were read before a General Convention of the Church, held in Philadelphia, January 17–23, 1863, in honor of the Three Hundredth Anniversary of the Heidelberg Catechism. A full account of this Tercentenary Commemoration will be found in the History of the Convention which forms the introductory part of the book. The whole is now published under the supervision of the Committee of Arrangements, by Synodical order, and in conformity also with a resolution of the Convention.

LEBANON, PA.,
Ascension Day, May 14, 1863.

TABLE OF CONTENTS.

HISTORICAL INTRODUCTION.

By Rev. S. R. Fisher, D.D., and Lewis H. Steiner, M.D.,

SECRETARIES OF TERCENTENARY CONVENTION.

I.

PREPARATIONS FOR THE TERCENTENARY CELEBRATION.

The Tercentenary Celebration of the Formation and Adoption of the Heidelberg Catechism, observed by the German Reformed Church in the United States in the year A.D. 1863, in view of its bearings and results, may justly be regarded as no common event, and hence it is every way proper and desirable that some account of its origin and progress should be put upon record. It was this consideration, doubtless, that influenced the Tercentenary Convention, held in the city of Philadelphia in the month of January of that year, at which the Celebration was formally inaugurated, to direct its Secretaries to prepare a History of the Tercentenary movement from its beginning to its close, including letters and short sketches of the extemporaneous addresses and discussions of the Convention, which History shall form the Introductory Chapter to the Memorial volume. This History, in consequence of the early period of the year at which it is required to be prepared, cannot reach further than to the close of the Convention itself; and this probably is all that was contemplated in the instructions of the Convention, though an exact construction of the language would seem to require more.

Great events, it will be found, if facts are carefully traced out, generally owe their origin to some comparatively trivial circumstance, which, at the time, attracted but little attention. The Tercentenary Celebration of the Formation and Adoption of the Heidelberg Catechism, by the German Reformed Church in America, does not form an exception to this general rule. In the first volume of the work entitled "The Fathers of the German Reformed Church in Europe and America, by Rev. H. Harbaugh, D.D." the following language occurs at the close of his sketch of Frederick III.: "If the Reformed Church wishes still further to honor the memory of Frederick, it cannot do it in a more appropriate and better way than by laboring to make his blessed Heidelberg Catechism rise to new life and power in the hearts of its members. Should the Reformed Church in America feel desirous of reviving old memories, in grateful connection with the Palatinate prince and his zealous love for the Church, and seek fit occasion for such a pious purpose, we suggest the 300th anniversary of the year and day when he, with his own imprimatur, and with pious princely commendation, sent forth the Heidelberg Catechism into the churches and schools of his dominions—January 19, 1863. How appropriate! and what a blessing might such an occasion be made to the German Reformed Church in America!"* This was written early in the year 1857, and published soon afterwards. It was not, however, until about two years later that any formal movement was set on foot to carry out the suggestion here made. At the annual meeting of the Classis of Mercersburg, held in Huntingdon, Pa., in the month of May, 1859, a series of resolutions, bearing on the subject, was offered by the Rev. Dr. Philip Schaff, and adopted by the Classis. These resolutions read as follows:—

"*Resolved*, That Synod be respectfully requested to take preparatory steps, at its next meeting, towards a proper celebration of the Third Centennial of the formation and adoption of the Heidelberg Catechism, which will take place in 1863.

"*Resolved*, That it be recommended to Synod to order the preparation of a critical standard edition of the Heidelberg Catechism in the original German and Latin, together with a revised English translation and a historical introduction, to be published in superior style, as a Centennial edition, in 1863, of which the subsequent editions for ordinary use are to be a faithful reprint.

"*Resolved*, That it be also recommended to Synod, as another contribution towards such a centennial celebration, to order the preparation and publication of a Digest of the Minutes of Synod, presenting a complete, yet condensed, constitutional History of our Church in this country, from the first Synodical meeting in 1746 to the present time, and provided with full alphabetical indexes of persons and things for convenient reference."

These resolutions brought the subject to the attention of the Synod of the German Reformed Church in the United States, which met in Harrisburg, Pa., in the month of October, A.D. 1859. We accordingly find the following minute embodied in the published Acts and Proceedings of the Synod for that year:—

"The Classis of Mercersburg, as reported by the Committee on Minutes of Classes, requested Synod to take preparatory steps towards a proper celebration of the Third Centennial of the formation and adoption of the Heidelberg Catechism, which will take place in 1863. The request was acceded to, and the Rev. Henry Harbaugh, D.D., John W. Nevin, D.D., D. Gans, Thomas G. Apple, and Elder Goldsboro S. Griffith were appointed a committee to carry the object into effect.

---

* Lives of the Fathers, vol. i. pp. 230 and 231.

"The same Classis recommended to Synod to order the preparation of a critical standard edition of the Heidelberg Catechism in the original German and Latin, together with a revised English translation and a historical introduction, to be published in superior style, as a Centennial edition, in 1863. The recommendation was adopted, and a committee of seven, consisting of the Rev. Emanuel V. Gerhart, D.D., John W. Nevin, D.D., Henry Harbaugh, D.D., John S. Kessler, D.D., Daniel Zacharias, D.D., and Elders William Heyser and Rudolph F. Kelker, was appointed to carry the contemplated object into effect.

"The same Classis recommended to Synod, as another contribution towards such a centennial celebration, to order the preparation and publication of a Digest of the Minutes of Synod, presenting a complete yet condensed constitutional history of our Church in this country from the first Synodical meeting in 1746 to the present time. The recommendation was adopted, and a committee of seven, consisting of the Rev. Samuel R. Fisher, D.D., Henry Harbaugh, D.D., Benjamin Bausman, Joshua H. Derr, Prof. Theodore Appel, and Elders William Heyser and John Rodenmayer, was appointed to carry it into effect."

The committee last named in this minute has submitted no formal report to Synod. The subject intrusted to it, however, has received some attention; and although the contemplated Digest may not make its appearance during the Tercentenary year, yet it will, in all probability, follow in due course of time, and may still be considered as a product of the Tercentenary movement.

The committee second named submitted a report to the Synod held in Lebanon, Pa., in the month of October, A.D. 1860, which was received and adopted. This report reads as follows:—

"The committee appointed by the Synod of Harrisburg to prepare a Tricentennial Catechism beg leave to report progress.

"Synod has provided that the necessary expenses of the committee be defrayed from the proceeds accruing from the publication of the work. The work, however, cannot be published before the year 1863; and it is very doubtful whether these proceeds will do more than meet the expenses of publication. There is, accordingly, no provision made for the current expenses of the committee. The oldest editions of the Catechism in German and Latin, and other valuable resources, must be purchased. The committee must meet, perhaps frequently, in general session to prepare this work. We therefore request Synod to authorize its Treasurer to pay these necessary current expenses, the bills to be previously approved by the Trustees of Synod. Any books it may be necessary to purchase, the committee will place in the Library of the Theological Seminary."

At this same meeting Lewis H. Steiner, M.D., was added to the original committee.

We find no other report from this committee recorded in the Acts and Proceedings of Synod. The committee, however, attended to the work assigned them, and, as appears from announcements made at the Convention for the Tercentenary Celebration of the formation and adoption of the Heidelberg

Catechism, will have the work brought out in due form and elegant style, at the proper season.

The first-named committee, which may properly be called a Committee of Arrangements, to whom was committed the principal labor connected with the whole Tercentenary movement, applied themselves earnestly to the duties intrusted to them. The indefatigable chairman of the committee especially, from whose suggestion, doubtless, the whole enterprise originated, performed a vast amount of labor in bringing matters into proper shape, and in providing for carrying forward to a successful issue the several objects contemplated in the movement, for which he deserves the lasting gratitude of the Church. At the meeting of Synod, held in Lebanon, Pa., in the month of October, A.D. 1860, the committee submitted their first report. This report was received and amended. It was then—

Resolved, That the general plan proposed by the committee be accepted, and that the committee be instructed to carry out the several measures proposed.

The report, as amended, is as follows:—

" The committee appointed at the last annual Synod to take preparatory steps towards a proper celebration of the Third Centennial of the formation and adoption of the Heidelberg Catechism, in 1863, report—

" That they have had the matter committed to them under earnest consideration, and have come to the following conclusions in regard to it, which they respectfully present to the consideration of Synod:—

"1. Your committee believe that it is highly proper that the Church should suitably commemorate that great historical event.

"2. That a Convention of the whole Church should be held at some central place on the 19th of January, 1863, to be continued during as many days as Synod may determine.

"3. On this occasion Memoirs and Essays, prepared by persons previously appointed, should be read on subjects historically and theologically connected with the occasion, each one to be followed by a free discussion on the part of any or all present,—which discussion should be carefully reported; all of which may be collected, if it is thought proper, and published as a monumental volume.

"4. The whole celebration should also be turned to a practical account for the Church, by affording to every member of the Church, old and young, rich and poor, an opportunity to make a free-will offering to the Church. Synod should make arrangements, through the Classes, consistories, pastors, and parents, to bring clearly before every member, baptized and confirmed, the ground on which such an offering is regarded as proper on their part. The whole year should be allowed to the members to prepare their offerings. These free-will offerings should be gathered by each congregation previous to the meeting of Synod in October, and then presented with the names and sums of each donor. The result should be recorded in a book prepared for that purpose, to be preserved in the archives of the Church.

"5. The Synod in October, 1863, should be a General Synod of the whole Church. At its meeting the centennial occasion should be solemnly closed by appropriate services, and the amount contributed disposed of to the different benevolent objects and institutions of the Church in such proportion as Synod would regard wise and proper.

"6. Your committee submit the following list of subjects as proper to be handled in the way already indicated on that occasion:—

"1.) The city of Heidelberg.

"2.) The authors of the Heidelberg Catechism.

"3.) The Elector Frederick III.

"4.) The History of catechization in the Reformed Church, and its best practical use at the present time.

"5.) The confessional relations of the Heidelberg Catechism.

"6.) Melanchthon, and the Melanchthonian tendency in Germany.

"7.) The Theological System in which the Heidelberg Catechism rests, the theory of practical religion which it assumes, and the kind of religious life which it cultivates.

"8.) The fortunes of the Heidelberg Catechism in this country.

"9.) Swiss Reformers.

"7. The committee suggests to Synod, whether measures should not be taken to secure the consent of some theologians in Germany to furnish Essays on some of these subjects.

"8. Synod should take immediate measures to collect in Germany, as far as possible, for the use of such persons as it may appoint to prepare these papers, the literature by which they would be enabled to prepare their work from adequate and reliable sources. Such collection should afterwards be placed in the Library of the Theological Seminary.

"9. Finally, your committee would call the attention of Synod to the fact that the Western Synod has taken action which proposes a full co-operation with this Synod in the object in view, and suggests to Synod the propriety of adopting such measures as will complete a full union of both Synods in this movement."

The committee continued its labors during the year, and at the meeting of Synod held in Easton, Pa., in the months of September and October, A.D. 1861, submitted the following additional report, which was received and adopted, and the committee continued:—

"By the action of the last Synod the plan proposed for the proper commemoration of the tri-centenary of the formation of the Heidelberg Catechism, was accepted, and the committee instructed to carry out the several measures proposed. Accordingly your committee has been engaged during the year in making the arrangements necessary to secure execution of the plan. A correspondence has been opened with a number of eminent theologians in Germany and Switzerland, with a view of securing their co-operation in the way contemplated in the plan. There has not been sufficient time to hear from all. Hundeshagen of Heidelberg, however, and Dr. Ebrard of Speier, have already replied, highly approving of the object, and cheerfully promising contributions. We confidently expect favorable responses from others. As soon as we hear from all, and thus ascertain what subjects have been chosen by our brethren in the fatherland, your committee will take immediate measures to secure the requisite contributions from our own brethren at home. From the progress that has attended our efforts thus far, we feel encouraged to hope that all things will be ready for the success of the plan in due time. We have also the pleasure of informing Synod, that the Western Synod of our Church, at its last annual meeting, adopted the same plan, and appointed a committee to confer and co-operate with your committee in securing the end in view."

The final report of the committee was submitted to the Synod held in Chambersburg, Pa., in the month of October, A.D. 1862. It was received, taken up item by item, amended, and then adopted. The report, as adopted, reads as follows:—

"Your committee has continued during the year to attend to the work which Synod has committed to its care, and are happy to be able to report, that they have been successful in making the preliminary arrangements necessary to the solemn commemoration of the three hundredth anniversary of the formation of the Heidelberg Catechism.

"The necessary number of Essays and Memoirs, the reading and discussion of which are to constitute the main features of the Convention to be held on the 19th of January, 1863, have been secured. Eminent theologians in the fatherland have already sent on their contributions, accompanied with kind words of approval and encouragement, as Drs. Ebrard, Ullman, and Hundeshagen. Other contributions are promised, and still expected; those to whom the committee have written, but whose engagements were such as to prevent them from accepting the invitation extended, have declared their hearty approval of the object, expressed their interest in it, and assured us of their sympathy and communion in the spirit of the occasion.

"From a number of our brethren at home, we have also promises, that contributions shall be furnished in accordance with the plan heretofore approved by Synod. The committee have found warm and earnest co-operation in its labors in completing this part of its arrangements, receiving assurances of the warmest interest from all with whom their duties required them to correspond on the subject. It is believed that all arrangements necessary to make this feature of the commemoration interesting and profitable have been so far successfully made.

"It now yet remains for the Committee to propose to Synod some plan for carrying out the second feature of the commemoration. It is proposed to make the whole Tercentenary year an occasion for the presentation of free-will offerings on the part of every member in full communion with the Church. In order to effect this object, it is simply necessary to take such measures as will bring the matter, in a clear and earnest manner, before every Classis; through the Classes, before every charge and congregation; through each congregation, into every Sunday-school and family; and through these, to every member, every parent, and every child. To effect this object we present the following plan:—

"Each Classis is directed to hold a special meeting on or before the 25th of December, 1862, the object of which shall be to make all necessary preliminary arrangements to accomplish effectually within its bounds the objects in view. At this meeting the Classes shall attend to the following matters:—

"1. Provide for the representation of each charge by the pastor or pastors, and at least one lay-member from each congregation, in the Convention to be held January 19th, 1863.

"2. Take measures for bringing the nature of the commemoration before the people, in a general way, as early as possible in the year.

"3. Devise a definite and feasible plan or plans for bringing the grounds upon which a memorial free-will offering is expected, directly and definitely home to the mind and heart of all the adult members, and every child—

through the pastors, consistories, Sunday-school superintendents and teachers, and parents; that thus all, and especially children, may have the whole year before them in which to gather their offerings.

"4. Make such arrangements as will secure the special commemoration of the event contemplated in this Tercentenary year in each charge, in concert with all the charges in the Church. Where a charge is composed of several congregations, it is expected that there will be on such day a general meeting of all, in one of its central congregations. The day for this concert of commemoration shall be Trinity Sunday, being May 31, 1863. A discourse on the general subject ought also to be delivered in each congregation of such charges as are composed of more congregations than one.

"5. Require that each congregation make a full and regular register in two separate columns, one containing the names of the confirmed, and the other the names of the baptized and as yet unconfirmed, members, and place the sums contributed over against the name of each one. A copy of this congregational register must be furnished to Classis, that it may be able to present to the Synod in October, 1863, the names of all the donors, with their donations, within their bounds; which record will also, at the same time, be for posterity a full and accurate census of the Church as it stood in the memorial year.

"6. The Classes are requested to direct their pastors at all times, and on all proper occasions, publicly in the pulpit, and privately in families, to refer to this commemoration year, and use all diligence to spread the needed light on the subjects connected with it, that the zeal of the people may be awakened to its proper commemoration.

"7. In connection with the main features of the plan, and in such a way as shall not interfere with the concert of the celebration throughout the Church, the Classes, as well as pastors and congregations, will devise any measures for the benefit and success of the occasion, which shall in their view seem adapted to give it interest and render it edifying to all.

"8. Such members of the Church whom God has blessed with means, and who have intentions in any measure to include the Church among their heirs, should be encouraged to make this memorial year the occasion in which to secure such legacies to the Church by formal will.

"In all the endeavors to carry out the true purposes of this Tercentenary festival, so far as it pertains to the free-will offerings, several things should be particularly kept in mind.

"First of all, care should be taken to enlist the interest of EVERY ONE. Not a single man, woman, or child must be overlooked. The offering of a single penny from a poor child must be honored with the same sacred respect as the princely offering of hundreds and thousands of the rich. The opportunity of giving must be offered to all,—TO ALL.

"It must be clearly impressed upon the minds and hearts of all that this is not a collection of money *from* them, but an offering *by* them. It must be distinctly told to the people that it is a FREE-WILL OFFERING. It is not to be insisted upon that it is their *duty* to give, but that it is their *privilege* to give. They are invited to give only what their own willing hearts move them to give. The people must be exhorted to give what they do give from heartfelt gratitude in view of the good they have received from God by means of the Heidelberg Catechism and through the Church of the Heidelberg Catechism.

"The people should be reminded how by wholesome self-denial and prudent Christian economy, during this sacred memorial year, they may enjoy the blessed pleasure of making their free-will offering large and honorable. The young, and children especially, should be taught by their pastors and by their parents, that it is their reasonable and Christian duty to deny themselves, by their own will and consent, of some of those bestowments which they are wont to receive from kind parents, and which, though proper for them on ordinary occasions to enjoy, are not actually necessary, but may be dispensed with, so that the amount of their cost or vaĺue may be used to enlarge their free-will offerings. Not only may their offerings by this means be made more honorable, but the lesson which they will thereby learn may prove to them a wisdom and a benediction through all their after-life.

"On entering upon this Tercentenary Jubilee, the Church ought to consider well what it is undertaking, and endeavor to elevate its mind and heart to the greatness and grandeur of the occasion and the event which it proposes thus to honor. By entering upon it, the Church solemnly binds itself by all the memories of its own history, by all its professed love for its own symbolical standard, by all its obligation to sincerity in the offering of such a sublime festal service to God, and by its own self-respect, when thus solemnly acting in the presence and under the judging eye of the whole Christian world, to raise itself to a spirit and life in some honorable measure adequate to the occasion. Let the Church throw its devout, joyous, and zealous energies into all that it proposes to do in this festival year. Let it thus commend and endear to its children of coming generations the symbol which we shall soon hand over to their love and care, by its own example of attachment manifested in this grateful commemoration of its origin and history. It needs but the exercise of wisdom, zeal, and faith on our part, and that blessing of the divine Head of the Church which He will most surely vouchsafe unto us, to make this festival year an occasion of joy and strength to the Church, the good fruits of which may bless our children and children's children."

The Synod ordered thirty thousand copies of this report to be printed in tract form for gratuitous distribution,—ten thousand in the German and twenty thousand in the English language,—the expenses of which are to be defrayed out of the proceeds of the Tercentenary celebration. It also instructed each minister in the Church to read this report to his people from the pulpit.

The duty of choosing a place for holding the meeting of the Convention of the whole Church in January, 1863, was committed to the committee on the Tercentenary celebration, in conjunction with the committee of the Synod of Ohio and adjacent States, on the same subject. These committees announced at the proper time, through the papers of the Church, that the meeting would be held in the RACE STREET GERMAN REFORMED CHURCH, PHILADELPHIA, to commence on Saturday evening, January 17, 1863, at seven o'clock. They thus anticipated the time for opening the celebration proper, because the 19th of January fell on Monday, and in order to afford time for the necessary preliminary arrangements, and especially for the celebration of the Holy Communion of the Lord's Supper on Sunday.

At the same meeting of Synod, at which the final report of the committee was adopted, a memorial from a committee of the

Board of Trustees of Franklin and Marshall College, in relation to the completion of the full endowment of that institution, was laid before Synod. The subject was earnestly discussed, after which the memorial was referred to the committee on the Tercentenary Celebration, with instructions to propose a plan to meet the wants of the case. The committee subsequently submitted the following resolutions, as including the action necessary for the completion of the full endowment of the college, which resolutions were adopted :—

"*Resolved*, That the obligation, which Synod has already assumed by former action, of completing the endowment of the College by raising the sum of $30,000 still felt to be necessary for that purpose, is hereby acknowledged and renewed, and that, in the judgment of the Synod, this object ought to be accomplished during the tercentenary year; and since it is believed that there are those who desire particularly to remember the College endowment in their tercentenary free-will offering, all such shall be allowed to designate that as the object to which their contributions shall be applied.

"*Resolved*, That if, in the judgment of the College Board, the object of securing the entire amount needed may be promoted by agents, the permission of appointing one or more agents for that purpose is renewed; and the gifts thus secured during the tercentenary year shall receive record in like manner as all others, as tercentenary offerings."

At this meeting, also, the Rev. Dr. Philip Schaff submitted to Synod papers prepared by the Rev. Drs. Ullmann and Hundeshagen, of Germany, for the contemplated Tercentenary Celebration of the formation and adoption of the Heidelberg Catechism. The following resolutions were thereupon adopted :—

"*Resolved*, That these papers be placed in the hands of the committee on the Tercentenary Celebration of the Heidelberg Catechism, and that they be authorized to provide for the translation of these, and similar papers that may come into their hands, into the English language.

"*Resolved*, That the same committee be instructed to provide for the publication of all the memorial papers of the Tercentenary Celebration, in both the German and English languages.

"*Resolved*, That the ministers of the Church be requested to make earnest and suitable efforts to obtain subscribers for the proposed works, and forward them to the Chairman of the Tercentenary Committee on or before the 15th day of January next.

"*Resolved*, That this Synod, having received a certain number of essays from leading theologians of Germany, as contributions to the Memorial Volume of the Tercentenary year, return their most cordial thanks to those distinguished gentlemen severally, for the favor thus conferred by them on the German Reformed Church in this country, and order that a copy of the proposed Memorial Volume be respectfully forwarded to each of them, as a token of our affectionate regard.

"*Resolved*, That the Chairman of the Committee on the Tercentenary Celebration be instructed to forward this action to the authors of the several memorial papers referred to in it."

The several Classes promptly complied with the recommendation contained in the final report of the committee on the Tercentenary Celebration. They accordingly severally convened in special session, and adopted such measures as were deemed necessary to carry forward the particular objects contemplated in the movement. Arrangements were made for the appointment of delegates to the General Convention of the Church, and for bringing the whole subject before the members of the different churches and receiving their contributions to the several objects of benevolence. The result of these efforts up to the present time has been very favorable, and the prospects for the future are in every way highly encouraging. ·

The Committee of Arrangements, in carrying forward their work, necessarily had a considerable amount of correspondence with eminent men in Europe, which was, to a great extent, conducted through the Rev. Dr. Philip Schaff; and, as this very properly forms a part of the history of the enterprise, some extracts from the most important portions of it, expressive of the interest felt in the Tercentenary movement, are here inserted, as a fit close to this historical sketch :—

From the Rev. Dr. C. Ullmann, of Carlsruhe, formerly Professor of Church History in the University at Heidelberg.

"It afforded me real and truly great pleasure to learn that the glorious monument of faith, coming down to us from the most prosperous period of the Palatinate Church, whose worth has come to be so little appreciated by a great portion of our people, is still held in such high esteem on the other side of the ocean. I most heartily wish that the good object of the celebration may be successfully realized, and that it will not be materially interfered with by the civil troubles which have recently come upon the American people."

From the Rev. Dr. C. B. Hundeshagen, Professor in the University at Heidelberg.

"Your letter informing me that the German Reformed Church in the United States proposes holding a Tercentenary Celebration on the 19th of January, 1863, in honor of the Heidelberg Catechism, occasioned me great joy ; for it is an evidence of the vital attachment of the membership of the German Reformed Church of America, as well to the faith of their fathers, as to the country from which they derive their origin. This celebration, therefore, very properly has claims to a most lively interest on the part of German Christians ; and I am very thankful to the committee for the confidence reposed in me, which led them to take it for granted that such an interest would be felt by me. I accordingly announce to you with pleasure, that I am willing to prepare an essay to be read on that occasion. Among the various subjects proposed for discussion, I have chosen the first, namely: ' *The City and University of Heidelberg, with special reference to the Reformation-Period, and to the time of the Formation of the Heidelberg Catechism.*' "

In the letter accompanying the transmission of his essay, the following paragraph occurs :—

"The Lord grant unto the brethren in America a successful celebration, and inspire them with a fresh love for the precious treasure which the Reformed Church possesses in the Heidelberg Catechism. In several portions of Germany, also, the celebration will be observed. What will take place in this particular section of country, where the Heidelberg Catechism, since the year 1855, has in part been literally merged into the Union Catechism, I do not venture to predict."

This expression of interest in the Tercentenary Jubilee in America is only the more gratifying, coming as it does from the very city and university where the Heidelberg Catechism was prepared and published, and where in its early history it found its truest and ablest defenders against the assaults made upon it by its enemies.

From the Rev. Dr. Herzog, Professor in the University at Erlangen.

" God grant that the terrible war which desolates the United States may not interfere with this peaceful work. The last news which we have received is again favorable to the North.

" With the best wishes for the success of the coming festival, and for the Union itself, which is now so sorely afflicted, I remain yours, &c."

From the Rev. Dr. J. P. Lange, Professor in the University at Bonn.

"I can honestly assure you that I am thankful for the confidence reposed in me, which led you to invite me to prepare such an essay, and that I feel deeply interested in the celebration itself. As an evidence of this, I may refer to the fact that I have most heartily, and much to my own edification, taken part in two Reformation festivals in my native country. Several years ago I attended the Reformation festival on the Hunsrück (a mountain between Nahe and Moselle Rivers, on the western side of the Rhine), and about a year and a half ago that of the Principality of Meurs (in the Rhenish Province of Prussia). But, to my regret, I am compelled to say that the attention I have to bestow on my Biblical Commentary, in connection with

B

the various other duties which necessarily devolve upon me, will so occupy my time, as to prevent me from preparing the desired essay. Otherwise I should have chosen as the subject of an essay, '*The Development of the Reformed Doctrine of Election adapted to the Present Times*,' the materials for which are furnished in my Dogmatics; or prepared '*A Collection of Church Hymns, purely from the German Reformed Church*,' not in the interest of Confessionalism, but as an evidence that our Church is not deficient in this particular divine gift.

"I therefore ask you kindly to excuse me, and, at the same time, respectfully request you to communicate to the Convention, at the proper time, my best wishes and most cordial Christian greetings. May the Lord make the beloved German Reformed Church of America, and especially your Synod, more and more a joy-inspiring morning light in the West, and a bright token of the harmony of genuine confessional fidelity and Christian human charity; and to this end may the approaching festival be also abundantly blessed."

From the Reverend Dr. Ebrard, Erlangen, Germany :—

"I am most heartily willing to contribute my mite to the Tercentenary Celebration of the Heidelberg Catechism, and would prefer to adopt, as the subject of my essay, the tenth of the series proposed for discussion, namely, 'Melanchthon and the Melanchthonian Tendency in Germany,' because I hope to be able to prepare something at the earliest period on this subject. I purpose as soon as possible to enter upon the undertaking."

II.

PROCEEDINGS OF TERCENTENARY CONVENTION, WITH SKETCHES OF ADDRESSES.

In accordance with the announcement made by the Committee of Arrangements of the Eastern and Western Synods of the German Reformed Church, the clerical and lay delegates to the Tercentenary Convention assembled in the German Reformed Church, Race Street, Philadelphia, January 17, 1863, at seven o'clock P.M. It is proper to state that during the day the delegates, as they arrived from their distant homes, were welcomed to the houses of their brethren of the German Reformed and other Evangelical Churches of the city, and made the recipients of whole-souled Christian hospitality. The Christian greeting was as heartily received as it was offered. Brethren of one common mother, meeting to honor the memory of the sainted founders of their Church, to thank God for the inestimable blessing of a symbolical exponent of their faith which had kept them from the quicksands of error for three hundred years, and to exchange vows before entering upon another century of Christian duties and privileges, the countenances of all beamed with joy and happiness. It was an era in each delegate's life, and the privilege of having been a member of this Convention was felt to be a proud honor. All classes and conditions of life were represented in the laity: the judge had laid aside the ermine; the lawyer, his daily task of endeavoring to rectify man's relation to his brother; the statesman, the heavy duties which the necessities of the country imposed on him; the physician, his round of toil amid want and disease; the merchant had deserted his counter and ledger; the mechanic, the tools of his craft; and the farmer, the duties which even winter exacts from his industrious hands.

The church had been beautifully decorated with laurel wreaths and festoons, and presented quite a holiday aspect. On one side of the pulpit, encircled with a laurel wreath, was the date "1563," and on the other "1863," decorated in like style. The celebration of the Three Hundredth Anniversary was not only to be held with joyous hearts, but with all the external insignia of rejoicing and exultation. The German Reformed Church was being rejuvenated while it celebrated its early history, and one might pray that its future would be but an intensification of the vigor of its youth, and that in a green old age its highest glory should be the enlargement of the kingdom of God and the diffusion of peace on earth and good will to man.

The opening sermon was preached by the Rev. Samuel R. Fisher, D.D., of Chambersburg, Pa., on the words, "How shall we escape, if we neglect so great salvation?" (Heb. ii. 3.) The Rev. D. Zacharias, D.D., and the Rev. John Redbaugh, assisted in the services. At the same time, an opening sermon in German was preached in the Salem German Reformed Church, St. John Street, by Rev. Philip Schaff, D.D., from the words, " Remember them which have the rule over you, who have spoken unto you the word of God : whose faith follow, considering the end of their conversation : Jesus Christ, the same yesterday, and to-day, and forever. (Heb. xiii. 7, 8.)

On Sunday morning a sermon was preached by the Rev. John W. Nevin, D.D., of Lancaster, Pa., from the words, "Jesus Christ, the same yesterday, and to-day, and forever;" after which the members united in partaking of the Holy Sacrament of the Lord's Supper. The blest communion of the saints on earth with the sainted dead had been referred to by the speaker, and hearty thanks were not only offered to our Heavenly Father for the great goodness He had vouchsafed in feeding His servants, "through the holy mysteries, with the spiritual food of the most precious body and blood of His Son, our Saviour Jesus Christ, assuring them thereby that they were very members incorporate in the mystical body of His Son and heirs through hope of His everlasting kingdom, by the merits of His most blessed death and passion," but praises also were given for the privilege of participating in the blessed communion of God's saints, and "for the holy fellowship of patriarchs and prophets, apostles and martyrs, and the whole glorious company of the redeemed of all ages, who have died in the Lord and now live with Him for evermore."

On *Sunday evening* an essay on "The Organism of the Heidelberg Catechism" was read by the Rev. Thomas G. Apple, of Greencastle, Pa.

On *Monday morning*, January 19, the delegates assembled in the German Reformed Church, Race Street, at 9½ o'clock, and proceeded to organize the Convention for business. The Rev. B. C. Wolff, D.D., called the Convention to order, and moved that Rev. E. Heiner, D.D., be appointed President *pro tem.*, and the Rev. P. C. Prugh Secretary *pro tem.*, which motion was adopted.

After singing the 101st Hymn, the Convention was led in prayer by the Rev. B. C. Wolff, D.D.

On motion of William Heyser, Esq., the Committee of Arrangements of the two Synods was authorized to report officers for the permanent organization of the Convention. After some deliberation, the Committee reported the following nominations, which were unanimously adopted by the Convention :—

President.

Rev. JNO. W. NEVIN, D.D., Lancaster, Pa.

Vice-Presidents.

Rev. Samuel Helffenstein, D.D.................Gwynedd, Pa.
" B. C. Wolff, D.D...................................Mercersburg, Pa.
" Daniel Zacharias, D.D........................Frederick, Md.
Hon. John Cessna......................................Bedford, Pa.
Rev. Elias Heiner, D.D...........................Baltimore, Md.
" Joseph S. Dubs.................................North White Hall, Pa.
William Heyser, Esq................................Chambersburg, Pa.
Rev. John S. Kessler, D.D........................Allentown, Pa.
Hon. John W. Killinger............................Lebanon, Pa.
Rev. Moses Kieffer, D.D..........................Tiffin, Ohio.
" Isaac Gerhart...................................Lancaster, Pa.
Hon. G. C. Welker...................................Sunbury, Pa.
Wm. Mayburry, M.D......... ....Philadelphia, Pa.
Rev. Henry Willard................................Columbus, Ohio.
" J. Caspar Bucher.............................Mifflinburg, Pa.
" L. B. Schwarz.................................Boston, Mass.
Henry Leonard, Esq...............................Basil, Ohio.

Recording Secretaries.

Rev. S. R. FISHER, D.D............................Chambersburg, Pa.
LEWIS H. STEINER, M.D.........................Frederick, Md.

Corresponding Secretaries.

Rev. P. C. PRUGH...................................Xenia, Ohio.
" W. F. COLLIFLOWER.......................Jefferson, Md.

Treasurer.

G. S. GRIFFITH, Esq...............................Baltimore, Md.

The President, on taking the chair, addressed the Convention, in substance, as follows :—

"In view of the fact that my name appears on the Committee of Arrangements, it is proper for me to state that their action in nominating me for the position to which I am now called has been against my wish and without my consent. As it is now ratified, however, by the voice of the Convention, I, of course, accept the appointment as an honor, and thankfully acknowledge it at the same time as a pleasing evidence of your confidence and regard.

"The occasion which brings us together we all feel to be one of more than common interest and importance. We have been looking forward to it with anxious expectation for many past weeks and months. I have had my own fears, I own, for its success, in view especially of the distracted political state of the country. But since coming here these fears are happily dispelled. We all feel now that this Tercentenary Convention is no failure. The heart of the Church is here, and we have good reason to trust that the Spirit of God is here also, and that our coming together will be for the glory of God and the honor of His Church.

"No symbolical book was ever more worthy of having its origin and history commemorated in this way. It forms, we may say, the glory of the universal *Reformed Church*. It comes before us hallowed by the most precious memories and associations. It cannot be otherwise than both pleasant and invigorating to commune with its spirit.

"For ourselves, as a Church, much may be gained by renewing our communion, as we are here called to do, with the beginning of our own ecclesiastical life. In any case, it is wholesome to communicate thus in a living way with antecedent times. No form of existence in this world can be sound and vigorous that is not historical, rooted and grounded in the past. The single man, to be truly great, must remain bound through life to the memory and love of his childhood. So with all associations and communities of men; and so especially with religious organizations or Churches. No Church can deserve the name that is not a historical Church. It must have its right to exist in some charter handed down from the past; and to renounce its connection with this, is necessarily to become weak, and in the end to forfeit its title to consideration altogether. We claim to be a historical Church,—not an upstart sect of yesterday; we belong to the original necessity of Protestantism itself, whatever that may have been, and have the reason of our ecclesiastical being in the relations and circumstances of the period to which that great movement owes its birth. It is our duty, then, to cherish and cultivate a lively sense of our proper spiritual heritage in such view. Not to do so, can only be suicidal. Whether it be to hold fast ancient forms, or to unfold them into new shape, the condition of prosperity here remains always the same. We cannot *grow* in any way, except as we grow historically; that is, except as we abide in living union with our own root. Hence the importance of our present year of commemoration. Let us hope that it will serve to knit our sense of church existence with new force to what our Church was confessionally in the beginning, and thus make us strong for what may be the will of God concerning us in the future.

"Is it too much to hope, moreover, that this year of commemoration may tell auspiciously on the thinking and feeling of other historical Churches also in our land? Its object is in no sense sectarian or exclusive. We wish to quicken indeed our own denominational consciousness into new life; as knowing that without this it must ever be a heartless solecism for us to keep up our denominational existence at all. But we have no fear that by doing this in a truly historical way we shall be in any danger now of offending or repelling the proper denominational spirit of other Evangelical Churches. Rather what we need all round for mutual good understanding and sympathy among the Churches of the Reformation, is just such a revival of conscious interest in the history of the past as we are now seeking to promote. It is the unhistorical spirit, pre-eminently, which shows itself to be everywhere the spirit of schism and sect, while a sense for the historical leads naturally toward catholic unity and peace.

"It would be happy indeed if this Jubilee of the Heidelberg Catechism, which was once, in some sense, the common property and acknowledged bond of the entire Reformed Church, might serve to bring up again among our American Churches the old sense of this once familiar title, *Reformed;* as it served in the beginning to distinguish this general Confession or Communion from the other great section of the Protestant world, the Lutheran Confession. It is truly wonderful how even intelligent people in other branches of the Church have lost the historical force of the term, so as to fall frequently into the grossest blunders in speaking of our ecclesiastical relations. It would be much for the cause of true Church brotherhood—much for the interest of true historical Protestantism—if such ignorance or want of information could in any way be assisted toward a more just apprehension of Church genealogies and affinities, as they held in past times.

"In laying stress, however, on the family relationship of the *Reformed* Churches, we forget not the ties that join us at the same time, beyond all sister branches of this Confession, with the other great division of the general Protestant world. We have no wish nor mind to place ourselves in any sort of unfriendly antagonism to the Church which bears the venerated name of Luther. We are, of course, Reformed; we suppose that there was need for this form of Protestantism in the beginning, and that there is need for it still; and what we propose now is to assert and confirm our original character in such view. But, with all this, we do not for a moment imagine that our Communion carries in it the whole truth of Protestantism—much less the whole truth of Christianity. We believe that the Lutheran Church also belonged of right to the Protestant movement in the beginning, and that it has still a most important part to fulfil in the onward progress of this movement; and we sincerely desire that, in this country especially, it may have power to be true and faithful to its own proper historical vocation. Our own Church holds, we may say, both historically and constitutionally, a sort of intermediate position between the two great Protestant Confessions : we belong to the Reformed, but we are at the same time *German* Reformed, and in this way stand closely connected with the Lutheran Church, forming in fact a bond of communication between it and other Reformed Churches. This national relationship we have no wish to forget; and we may be very sure that our present effort to call up past memories and renovate old associations can have no tendency that way, but must work rather to promote the feeling of kindred interest and regard between our two German bodies. In this case, especially, the cause of union can never be advanced by concealing or forgetting our original occasions of difference. We cannot so far stultify ourselves as to imagine that these were at first without reason, and are therefore now of no force. On the contrary, we honor both Confessions in believing that the issues which divide them are real and great issues, and that they cannot be ignored or made of no account without great unfaithfulness to the whole cause of Protestant Christianity itself. No union founded on mere indifference here can deserve to be considered of any worth whatever. Only by understanding their original confessional differences, only by looking them steadily in the face and owning their importance, so as to surmount them at last in the way of a true inward conciliation and adjustment, can the two Churches, Lutheran and Reformed, ever come to a full legitimate union, such as shall prove a blessing to the world at large as well as to themselves. Such positive, and not simply negative, end of all confessional strife we desire with all our heart, and look upon our present celebration as being only favorable to it, and not in opposition to it in any way.

"Altogether, I congratulate you, Christian brethren and friends, on the circumstances of encouragement and hope in which, as a Church, we meet together at this time. The spirit of the occasion is full of promise, as it breathes also only peace and love; and I trust and pray that He who is the author of peace and the fountain of all righteousness may preside over our sessions and crown them with His blessing to the end."

With the view of having an accurate record of all the delegates present, the following resolutions, presented by Rev. John H. A. Bomberger, D.D., were adopted :—

"*Resolved*, That a committee, consisting of one member from each Classis represented in this Convention, be appointed to prepare a list of the delegates present, arranged according to the several Classes and pastoral charges to which they respectively belong, in the order of the Statistical tables of the Minutes of Synod.

"*Resolved*, That each pastor present be directed to furnish his name, with the names of the delegates from his charge, to the member of this committee belonging to his Classis. Lay delegates present without their pastor are requested to report their names to the committee separately. The committee consists of the Rev. J. Beck, East Pennsylvania Classis;

Rev. A. L. Dechant, Goshenhoppen; Rev. J. O. Miller, Zion; Rev. J. W. Santee, Maryland; Rev. D. W. Wolff, Lebanon; Rev. I. E. Graeff, Lancaster; Rev. A. G. Dole, East Susquehanna; Rev. C. H. Leinbach, West Susquehanna; Rev. J. G. Shoemaker, Clarion; Rev. D. O. Shoemaker, St. Pauls; Rev. I. G. Brown, Mercersburg; Rev. S. H. Giesy, Philadelphia; Rev. J. F. Busche, New York; and Rev. H. Williard, Synod of Ohio and adjacent States.

The committee reported a list of delegates, arranged according to the Classes and pastoral charges, on Thursday morning, which list, with corrections and alterations made afterward by the Secretaries, will be found appended to this Introduction as Appendix A.

On motion of Rev. E. Heiner, D.D., it was "*Resolved*, That all members of the German Reformed Church present at this Convention, whether supplied with credentials or not, be requested to take seats with the delegates, and that their names be registered with the same."

On motion of Rev. J. H. A. Bomberger, D.D., it was "*Resolved*, That the ministers of other evangelical denominations visiting this Convention be invited to take seats in the Convention, and requested to report their names to the Secretaries." In accordance with this resolution, the names of such ministers will be found collected together, at the end of this Introduction, in Appendix A. Some attended all the sessions, and others were only present at a single session.

The business necessary for the proper organization of the Convention being completed, the President announced that an Essay, prepared for the occasion by the Rev. Dr. Hundeshagen, of Heidelberg, Germany, would be read by the Rev. Prof. Thomas C. Porter, of Lancaster, Pa., by whom it had been translated from the German. The title of the Essay was, " The City and University of Heidelberg, with special reference to the Reformation-Period, and the Time of the Formation of the Heidelberg Catechism." Before the Essay was read, the Rev. Dr. Schaff gave a short account of the learned author.

This Essay was followed by the reading of another of the series, "The Elector Frederick III. of the Palatinate," prepared by the Rev. B. S. Schneck, D.D., of Chambersburg, Pa. The morning session was then closed with prayer, by Elder Wm. Heyser.

The Convention was opened, *Monday evening*, with singing, and prayer by the Rev. E. Heiner, D.D., and the attention of the members was invited to an Essay prepared by the Rev. Dr. Ebrard, of Erlangen, Germany—" Melanchthon and the Melanchthonian Tendency, and its Relation to the German Reformed Church." This was introduced by a few remarks concerning its author from the Rev. John W. Nevin, D.D., after which it was read by the Licentiate W. M. Reiley, Theological Tutor in the Seminary at Mercersburg, who had translated it from the German.

An opportunity was afforded to the members of the Convention to enter into a free discussion of the several topics brought to its attention by the Essays that had already been read. This was embraced by some, and sketches of their remarks are herewith given.

The Rev. W. C. Bennet, addressing the Chair, said :—

"Mr. PRESIDENT :—Under an All-wise, an All-seeing, and an All-superintending Providence, we are convened in this Tercentenary Convention. It is with profound gratitude to Almighty God and our ever-blessed Redeemer, that we have heard already, in connection with the proceedings and deliberations of this General Convention, a number of very excellent and learned essays on the adoption of our excellent Heidelberg Catechism three hundred years ago. It unquestionably should ever be remembered, however, that the origin of this glorious Reformation extended to the Middle Ages; the inward and the outward of all true Christianity ever being absolutely and inseparably connected.

"It has been repeatedly and confidently asserted that the glorious Reformation in Germany is a noble vine. A vine has not only branches, twigs, and buds, but also roots. The latter extended in many directions, in the hearts, the heads, and the lives of millions. The Holy Spirit helped them powerfully and believingly to pronounce with their hearts and their lips the Apostles' Creed, in their families and in their churches, from age to age. And thus all the friends and composers of the Heidelberg Catechism, at its adoption, were prepared to make and receive the Apostles' Creed as the soul and the life of the Heidelberg Catechism; a creed born in the Church as far back as the second century.

"In a certain sense, John Huss, who lived a hundred years before Luther, Calvin, Zwingli, Melanchthon, and a host of other Reformers, was emphatically a Reformed preacher. Let it ever be remembered that the Reformers did not make the Reformation, but that God and the Lord Jesus Christ made this glorious Reformation; and under these all-important circumstances, it appeared as the rising sun after a long and dreary night. Thus the Heidelberg Catechism also appeared in the Church as a bright morning star; a catechism not above the Holy Bible, but, in a certain sense, dictated by the Holy Spirit, and one which should ever be considered as a golden key to open up, in childlike simplicity, many precious truths of the Holy Bible, ever teaching that the God-man Christ Jesus is the Master and Centre of all true Christianity, and that not one or all of the Reformers should be elevated to this high position. That Christ, the God-man, lives in the souls and around the paths of all true believers, and under all circumstances, is the deepest and most mysterious doctrine of the Bible and the Catechism, which also ever make the Church our Heavenly Mother.

"Mr. President, let the heads of our families present to their children, as soon as they begin to read, the Catechism along with the Bible, so that the absolute importance of these precious books and their contents may be the more deeply impressed upon their hearts and memories, and that for many years after their parents may be in their graves. Let our prayers be, that such a state of things may exist throughout all ages, ministers and all others using these precious books, in all possible places. Amen!"

Rev. E. V. Gerhart, D.D. (President of Franklin and Marshall College), said:—

"Four essays have now been read. I desire to offer a few remarks upon the relation of the Augsburg Confession to the subjects discussed. It did not have so much reference to the view of Melanchthon as to the Zwinglian view of the Lord's Supper, to which it was antithetical. It was not the Confession of the *complete* Lutheran doctrine, but served to set forth the general faith of the Reformation in the German States. But it proved unsatisfactory. This became evident from the fact that the Augsburg Confession was altered in 1540, and the Formula Concordiæ was adopted in 1580. The altered Augsburg Confession was subscribed by Frederick III., by Calvin, Olevianus, and Ursinus. A fact was brought out this evening not known before, viz., that the altered Confession was so universally adopted that after a few years no copy of the original Confession could be found.

"Two tendencies sprang out of these movements. 1. A strictly Lutheran one, according to the 10th article. 2. A Calvino-Melanchthonian tendency. These acted and reacted upon each other in Germany, neither satisfying the general consciousness. They did not meet the wants of the Church. The unaltered Augsburg Confession did not even answer the demands of strict Lutherans. Hence the ferment of 1540–80. The Melanchthonian tendency was in substance the same as the Calvinian, and excited special animosity. It was called Crypto-Calvinism, charged with secretly advocating the Calvinistic view of the Lord's Supper. In this Melanchthonian view we have the very doctrine which the Reformed Church afterward held, *i.e.*, as to the substance of the doctrine. It was the Reformed doctrine, but not known under that name. The formation of the Heidelberg Catechism was the right development of this Melanchthonian style of thought, in regard to the Lord's Supper.

"Hence we have the result of a process going on in the mind of those portions of the Church involved in the movement, although the towering name of Luther overshadowed every other and gave its designation to this theory. So we have two different tendencies bearing the name of Luther. The essay read this evening shows the bitter conflict which arose between them.

"I look, then, upon the Heidelberg Catechism as the result of the formative period. It unites three tendencies : the Zwinglian, which lays special stress on the commemorative side of the Lord's Supper to the seeming disparagement of the other side; the Melanchthonian, which laid special stress on the communion side to the exclusion even of the commemorative; and the Calvinistic, which substantially agreed with the Zwinglian and Melanchthonian. The Lutheran tendency, rooted in the 10th article of the Augsburg Confession, continued to work also, and resulted in the Formula Concordiæ of 1580. A reaction was brought about in the Roman Catholic Church by the Reformation, which culminated in the Tridentine Decrees, 1545–1563. These three confessions, therefore—the Heidelberg Catechism, Form of Concord, and Tridentine Decrees—are analogous.

The Rev. Dr. Henry Harbaugh, of Lebanon, Pa., addressing the Convention, said :—"The essay of Dr. Ebrard just read discusses an important point—the influence exerted by Melanchthon on the Palatinate, and the Melanchthonian element as it entered into the formation and founding of the Reformed Church of the Palatinate under Frederick III., in 1563. The full extent and significance of this element, as it entered into that eventful period of the Reformation-history, has only during the last several decades come to be properly understood. The reason of this may be found in the more catholic spirit which has of late years characterized the study of that period of history.

" When the great Reformatory movement of the sixteenth century became unfortunately divided into the two great sections of the Lutheran and Reformed, the controversial spirit on both sides grew sharp and strong. In the heat of battle, preferences—we might say prejudices—became firmly set, and these were traditionally perpetuated from age to age. Being removed from the scenes of those early contests both by space and by time, we of the present day are in this respect in a favorable position for reviewing and perceiving the ruling elements which entered into the events of the times. It is difficult for us now to appreciate fully the strong traditionary feelings which then warped, if they did not even unconsciously darken, the minds of those who then contended with each other on both confessional sides. Even some of the Catechisms, and books of elementary religious instruction, were, we may say, rudely sharp and pragmatic, cultivating thus the spirit of sharp antagonism in the minds of the young, and perpetuating stern traditional prejudices in youthful minds, who could know but little of the points at issue.

In a passage in the catechetical work of De Witte—in many respects an excellent book—the catechumen is asked: 'Are the Papists properly called *Catholic*?' Ans. 'No: they are properly called *Kakolic*,'—playing upon a Greek word meaning *evil* or *wickedness*. We have also heard of an elementary religious book of that time in which the child is asked: 'Believest thou firmly that the Reformed hold six hundred and sixty-six errors in common with the Turks?' Ans. 'Yes; this I believe with my whole heart.' These are somewhat strong and extreme specimens; but they are still illustrative of the sharp antagonism in which the different Confessions stood toward each other, and show with what zeal it was sought to bias the minds of the age. In proportion as such traditional prejudices reigned, and as long as they reigned, it was, of course, impossible to take a calm and true view of the events in which they had their rise.

"With the dust of that great historical battle the partisan feelings of the age have in a great measure passed away, and men are prepared to look back and review the times with other eyes. The Reformed are now able to see the working of a great power in the bosom of Lutheranism, in which they discover not only a congeniality with what was precious to itself, but which actually became part of itself. Melanchthon, the author of the Augsburg Confession,—who at first stood fully with Luther in his views of the Lord's Supper,—was brought gradually to sympathize with, and at last substantially to adopt, the view of Calvin on this Sacrament, so that he incorporated it substantially in his amended edition of the Augsburg Confession of 1540, and, abandoning the view of Luther, or at least essentially modifying it, held and stated his views in a way which found hearty favor with the leading Reformed theologians.

"Besides,—what is a still more important fact,—the view of Melanchthon on the entire doctrine of the Lord's Supper took deep root, and extended itself widely and powerfully, in the bosom of the Lutheran Church itself. Such influence, in fact, did his views, as embodied in the tenth Article of the revised Augsburg Confession of 1540, obtain, that it became the ruling power in the Lutheran Church on German soil. This is evident from the fact that from 1540 to 1580 the altered Augsburg Confession entirely set aside the general use of the original Confession of 1530, so that when, in 1580, it was intended to republish the original Confession, no copy could be found to print from, and recourse had to be had to the original manuscript.

"The fact is, that the latest and most reliable investigations in history clearly show that Melanchthon was influenced by the Calvino-Reformed doctrine of the Lord's Supper, and he influenced the Lutheran mind largely, especially in the Palatinate, in favor of the same view: so that when the old Lutheran party rallied again, about the time when Frederick III. came into power in that Electorate, they were not able to·call back the general Lutheran mind from their tendencies toward and sympathy with the Reformed doctrine. Frederick III., with that deep insight which characterized him, wisely determined to embody these views in his Heidelberg Catechism. Melanchthon's influence had prepared the public mind for its favorable reception. The new Catechism came with welcome into the bosom which already had all aptitudes and longings for the views it embodies. Thus the Melanchthonian tendency in the Palatinate became the occasion, the basis, and the determining element from which rose the German Reformed Church of the Heidelberg Catechism. In brief, the Reformed Church influenced Melanchthon, and Melanchthon opened the way for the founding of the Reformed Church on what was before Lutheran ground.

" The historical facts on which this view of the rise of the Reformed Church of the Palatinate rests have been incontrovertibly established by such men as Dr. Ebrard, Dr. Heppe, Dr. Herzog, and others. Sudhof, in an article on the Heidelberg Catechism in Herzog's Real-Encyclopædie, and in his life of Ursinus and Olevianus, has vainly and ineffectually endeavored to controvert this view.

" Facts justify us, moreover, in believing that had the timid Melanchthon stood up firmly in maintaining the tendencies which his own influence had created, when these tendencies were again assailed by the old Lutheran party, the result might have been a full union of both sides of the Reformation on substantially the same confessional ground which the Heidelberg Catechism now represents. Who does not regret that so desirable a consummation was not realized? But Melanchthon was constitutionally timid. We may not blame that illustrious man : not more can be required of a man than is given him. He has been called a compromiser. We would not charge him with this. We attribute his silence to his timidity. · If, however, it should be thought true that the failure referred to has resulted from a compromising spirit, it is only another sad illustration of the fact, so often evident in history, that every endeavor to compromise the interest of fundamental truth must meet with sad and certain defeat.

"No feature of Reformation-history deserves more earnest study at the present time than this Melanchthonian tendency; and none gives better promise of pleasant and peaceful fruits to both the Reformed and Lutheran Confessions in their present status both in Europe and America."

The Convention having received an invitation to attend a concert of sacred music at Handel and Haydn Hall, on Tuesday evening, given by the Sunday-school of Christ Church (German

Reformed), it was resolved to accept the same, and hold its sessions on Tuesday in the morning and afternoon.

The evening session was then closed with prayer by the Rev. Thomas H. Leinbach.

At nine o'clock A.M on *Tuesday*, the session was opened with singing, and prayer by the Rev. D. Y. Heisler, of Bethlehem, Pa. The President announced the next Essay of the series to be that prepared by the Rev. Dr. Herzog, of Erlangen, Germany,—"The Swiss Reformers." This was introduced by some remarks from the Rev. P. Schaff, D.D., in reference to the German brethren whose Essays had already been presented to the Convention. He styled Dr. Hundeshagen the present proper successor of Olevianus,—one of the authors of the Heidelberg Catechism,—and spoke of Dr. Ebrard as one of the ablest theological writers of the present age, whose productions were not only known in his native land, but extensively known and well received in our own land. Dr. Herzog was a Swiss by birth, and especially well qualified, by his writings and studies, for discussing the labors of "The Swiss Reformers." He also referred to the several works which had proceeded from his pen and become authorities with theologians, and especially noticed the "Theological Encyclopædia," which is deservedly recognized as one of the most important scientifico-theological publications of the present age. The Essay was then read by the Rev. H. Harbaugh, D.D., by whom it had been translated from the German.

The Rev. John S. Kessler, D.D., of Allentown, Pa., addressed the Convention, in German, in relation to the Swiss Reformers. Being himself a native of Switzerland, he dwelt with much affection and pathos on the venerated Reformers of that country, and was listened to, by those who understood German, with the deepest interest.

The Convention then heard the Essay, "The Authors of the Heidelberg Catechism, Zacharias Ursinus, and Caspar Olevianus," which was read by its author, the Rev. Prof. Thomas C. Porter, of Lancaster, Pa.

The Rev. I. S. Demund, of Lancaster, Pa , addressed the Convention, expressing his high appreciation of the Heidelberg Catechism, which he regarded as next to the Bible, and decidedly the best book that has ever proceeded from mere human hands. We ought, accordingly, to treat it with due honor and respect. In his opinion, it is the grand central symbol of faith, around which all Protestant denominations will yet come to rally.

The Rev. Dr. Schaff stated that the Rev. Dr. Van Oosterzee, of Rotterdam, had been requested to prepare an Essay on "The Heidelberg Catechism in the Netherlands." A letter dated Leyden, Holland, December 27, 1862, which had just been received from the Rev. Dr. G. D. J. Schotel, explaining why Dr.

Van Osterzee could not accept the invitation, and accepting for himself the task of preparing the desired 'Essay, was read, and, on motion of the Rev. Dr. E. Heiner, was ordered to be placed in the records of the Convention.

The letter was written in French. The following is a translation :—

"My Dear Brother in Christ :—This morning my friend Dr. Van Osterzee, of Rotterdam, sends me your letter and asks me to write you for him. You are probably aware that the Curators of the University of Utrecht have called him to the Chair of Theology, and that he is so occupied, so charged with business, that it is an impossibility for him to undertake a history of the Palatinate Catechism. He requests that I should fill up the deficiency, —'the honor and advantage will be yours, my friend,' he writes ; and inasmuch as I am about publishing a Literary History of the Catechism, dedicated to Prince Frederick of the Pays Bas, it will be an easy matter to furnish the information desired by you. My book will appear January 19, 1863, and I have asked Dr. Ullmann, at Gotha, to give a sketch of the same in the *Theologische Studien und Kritiken.* I shall do myself the honor to send you next year, I hope by the 20th or 22d of January, the History of the Catechism in Holland, translated into your language. I hope, sir, that my sketches will be satisfactory to you.

"Accept the compliments of my friend Dr. Van Osterzee, as well as my own expressions of profound respect.

"G. D. J. Schotel. *Dr. of Letters,*
"Chevalier du Leon Nieulandais, formerly Reformed Pastor at Talbourg, now living in Leyden.
"Leyden, Holland, December 27, 1862."

The morning session was then closed with prayer by the Rev. A. G. Dole.

At three o'clock in the afternoon the Convention again assembled, and its session was opened with singing, and prayer by the Rev. Wm. K. Zieber, of Hanover, Pa.

The first Essay claiming attention was that furnished by the Rev. Dr. Ullmann, of Carlsruhe, Germany,—"Sketches from the History of the Heidelberg Catechism in the Land of its Birth." The reading of this Essay was prefaced by the simple statement from the Rev. Dr. John W. Nevin, by whom it had been translated, that the author was so well known to the German Reformed Church of this country, by his theological writings, that his name was sufficient to attract the attention of the members to whatever might proceed from his pen.

The following preamble and resolutions, offered by the Rev. E. Heiner, D.D., were unanimously adopted:-

"Whereas, Those eminent German divines, the Rev. Drs. Hundeshagen, Ebrard, Ullmann, and Herzog, have kindly furnished this Convention with very able papers, and most appropriate to the occasion of our Tercentenary celebration: Therefore

"*Resolved,* That this Convention has been highly gratified and pleased with the important and suitable Essays prepared by those learned and distinguished theologians and which have now been read before this body, so numerously represented from all parts of the German Reformed Church in the United States.

"*Resolved*, That our sincere and hearty thanks be tendered to these highly respected and greatly beloved brethren for their most valuable and deeply interesting contributions, and that the President of this Convention be requested to communicate the above action, and to make such further communications to them as he may deem most expedient and proper."

The President having announced remarks from the members as in order,—

The Rev. Dr. J. H. A. Bomberger addressed the Convention in relation to the Essay of the Rev. Dr. Ullmann:—

"There are two or three points of special interest for us, suggested by the able Essay just read, to which I beg leave briefly to refer. The *first* relates to that offensive last clause of the 80th answer of the Catechism. No one will deny its discordance with the prevailing mild, pacific tone of the Catechism. But neither will any deny that if the Protestant apprehension of the Romish doctrine of the mass be correct, then the mass is what the clause in question declares it to be. And fidelity to our past traditions requires us to hold fast to this view, though we may not proclaim it in such denunciatory terms. The *second* point refers to the influence of Melanchthonianism upon the theology, &c. of the Palatinate Reformed Church. This, we think, is being somewhat exaggerated, now that the fact of such influence is made out. And Dr. Ullmann, seems to me to have admitted as much. At any rate, whilst acknowledging the fact to some extent, it should be remembered that Zwinglianism entered largely into the composition of Melanchthon's system of faith. Indeed, he seems sometimes to lean more decidedly toward the views of the great and noble Swiss Reformer than to those of Luther himself. So that, traced to its primary source, the theology of the Palatinate flowed from a Zwinglian Melanchthonianism rather than from a Melanchthonian Lutheranism. The *third* point which must have attracted our notice is the intimate historical relation existing between the earlier catechetical system of our Church in this country, and the enjoined practice of the parent Church of the Palatinate."

These remarks were then followed by the reading of an Essay by the Rev. Thomas De Witt, D.D., of the Reformed Dutch Church, on "The Heidelberg Catechism in Holland and the United States." This Essay, in the absence of the author, was read by Dr. Lewis H. Steiner; and the Convention was dismissed, with the Apostolic benediction, by the Rev. D. Zacharias, D.D.

On *Wednesday* morning the delegates assembled with increasing zeal and enthusiasm. Notwithstanding the unpleasant weather—it was raining at times quite rapidly—there was a large attendance on the sessions of this day. The session was

c

opened with singing, and prayer by the Rev. John Külling, of Baltimore, Md.

A letter was read from the Rev. Isaac H. Reiter, Miamisburg, Ohio, which contained a mortuary record of the ministers of the German Reformed Church in the United States, containing the *date* of death and the *age* of each minister who had been transferred from the Church below to that above. This list of deaths was ordered to be incorporated with the proceedings of the Convention. It forms Appendix B of this Introduction. Mr. Reiter's letter is as follows:—

"MIAMISBURG, OHIO, January 17, 1863.

"BELOVED BRETHREN IN THE LORD JESUS CHRIST:—As a small contribution to the Tricentennial enterprise, I would hereby lay before the 'General Convention,' which is to assemble to-day in the city of Philadelphia, Pa., a list of the names of the deceased ministers of the German Reformed Church in the United States of America, arranged in alphabetical and chronological order, with *the date of the year* in which they died, and their *age* at the time of their death. I have used the utmost endeavors to make this list as nearly complete as possible, but, with all my efforts, I have not entirely succeeded, owing mainly to a want of the necessary documents, and to the tardiness of some of the friends of those deceased in replying to inquiries addressed to them. Hoping, however, notwithstanding its deficiencies, that it may in some degree aid to awaken hallowed memories of the past, to stimulate to grateful and benevolent activities in the present, and to lead to unreserved consecration and persevering fidelity and devotion to God and His Church in the future, I hereby submit this contribution to your consideration and favor, with the prayer for God's blessing upon it, and upon your deliberations as a General Convention of the Church.

"Yours in Christ,   ISAAC H. REITER."

The President read a letter from the Rev. D. Willers, Fayette, N. Y., expressing great interest in the purposes of this Convention, and regret that advancing age would prevent his attendance, and closing with some words of tender affection for the Heidelberg Catechism and the customs of the fathers of our Church in Germany and this country. The letter was ordered to be published in the Proceedings of the Convention. It forms Appendix C to this Introduction.

The Rev. John W. Nevin, D.D., read a portion of the "Introduction to the Heidelberg Catechism," prepared by him for the standard edition of this symbol. This paper was a sketch of the history and theological character of the Catechism with the cultus necessarily belonging to the same. Its reading occupied most of the morning session.

In this connection it is proper to state that the Synod of the German Reformed Church in 1859 appointed a committee, consisting of Dr. E. V. Gerhart, Dr. John W. Nevin, Dr. H. Harbaugh, Dr. J. S. Kessler, Dr. D. Zacharias, the Elders Wm. Heyser, and Rudolph F. Kelker, and Lewis H. Steiner, M.D., to prepare a critical edition of the Catechism in three languages—

German, Latin, and English—arranged in parallel columns. Dr. Nevin's article was the introduction to this edition, which it is intended shall be printed in the best modern style, an ornament to the house of every lover of the Church of his fathers. As it was desirable that a number of subscribers should be secured during the sessions of the Convention for copies of this Tercentenary edition of the Catechism, Dr. Steiner, in the name of the Committee, urged upon the members the importance of securing a copy of the publication as one of the memorial volumes of this great festival. It should be a matter of honest pride for every member of the German Reformed Church to have a copy of this elegant edition of the much-loved symbol. A large number of delegates manifested their interest by adding their names to the subscription-list.

The Convention then adjourned, and the session was closed with prayer by the Rev. Chas. F. McCauley, of Reading, Pa.

The afternoon session of Wednesday was opened with singing, and prayer by Elder G. S. Griffith, of Baltimore, Md. The time was occupied with an essay, "Creed and Cultus; with Special Reference to the Relation of the Catechism to the Palatinate Liturgy," read by its author, Rev. Henry Harbaugh, D.D., of Lebanon, Pa. The Convention adjourned after the reading was finished, and was dismissed with the Apostolic benediction by the President.

In the evening a session was held in German in the Salem Church, St. John's Street. It was opened with singing, and prayer by the Rev. P. Schaff, D.D. Dr. Schaff addressed the Convention, and with much earnestness and "Gemüthlichkeit" described the nature and object of the present Tercentenary Celebration of the Heidelberg Catechism. He also gave a short and succinct account of the Reformation in Switzerland and the Palatinate, and closed with a sketch of the German divines the Rev. Drs. Hundeshagen, Ullmann, Ebrard, and Herzog, with a summary of the contents of the Essays contributed by these brethren to the Tercentenary Convention.

Dr. Hundeshagen's Essay, "The City and University of Heidelberg," was read in German by Rev. John S. Kessler, D.D.; and the meeting was closed with singing, prayer by the Rev. Isaac Gerhart, and the Apostolic benediction by Rev. P. Schaff, D.D.

At nine o'clock on *Thursday* morning the Convention assembled in the Race Street Church, and the session was opened with prayer by the Rev. E. R. Eschbach, of Baltimore.

The Rev. Dr. Schaff offered a series of resolutions in reference to the publication of a Memorial volume, which were referred to a committee consisting of Rev. Drs. Heiner, Schaff, and Bomberger, and Elders Dr. J. McDowell and Joshua Motter.

Some business of minor importance being transacted, the

President announced the Essay, "The Genius and Mission of the German Reformed Church in Relation to the Lutheran and to those Branches of the Reformed Church which are not German," as in order; and it was accordingly read by its author, the Rev. Prof. T. Appel, of Lancaster, Pa.

The Rev. P. Schaff, D.D., having been called upon by the Chair to read an Essay which he had prepared, stated that it was too long to be read at this meeting, but that the substance of the Essay would be given in German at the evening meeting. (This Essay will appear in the German Memorial Volume.) He proposed on the present occasion to make some free remarks on

" *The Mission of the German Reformed Church in America, and the Significance of this Meeting with Reference to the same.*

" It is a striking coincidence that the most important meeting of the German Reformed Church in this country should take place during the most gloomy and trying period of our national history; when the fabric of our Union is shaken to the very base, and the battle-cry of civil war is resounding in our ears. This is not the first instance of a great undertaking conceived and executed in the midst of national excitement or calamity. Man's extremity is God's opportunity, and when man's pride is laid low in the dust, God is most ready to bless him. The University of Berlin, the literary metropolis of Germany and the pride of Prussia, was founded during a time of the greatest distress in Prussia, soon after the disastrous battle of Jena. Christ himself was born at a time when the house of David was lost in obscurity and the Jewish nation lay prostrate at the feet of a foreign and heathen conqueror. The Reformation appeared in the darkest hour of Papal tyranny. The Heidelberg Catechism is a work of peace, which originated at a time when theological wars raged most furiously, and when Melanchthon prayed to be delivered from the fury of divines. So it may be with our meeting. I look for great good out of this movement,—not only in the way of putting our Church intelligently before the other Churches of the land, but to the Church itself, to all her benevolent enterprises and literary institutions. It is the greatest meeting *we* have ever had,—the greatest that has been held in our Church for three hundred years. No occasion of similar significance can be enjoyed for one hundred years to come.

" And, now, *Christianus mihi nomen, Reformatus cognomen,* must be our motto. I am a Christian, and sympathize with every thing that is Christian. This is the spirit in which we commenced this meeting and intend to conclude it. Far be from us the spirit of bigotry or sectionalism. It is our pride to be German Reformed, but yet we know that this is only one portion of that city of God which, resting upon the rock of ages, reaches the heavens above with its pointed spires and turrets. How can we be inhabitants of that city without being residents of one of its many wards and houses? And our denominational location, our position, is decided by the grace and providence of God, which places us by natural and spiritual birth where we can do most good and labor with good faith. In this sense we are German Reformed; but we have no desire in this joyous celebration to promote any special private interest, but to advance the kingdom of our Lord and Saviour.

"It is felt by all that the Essays sent from across the ocean by our German brethren have been prepared in the same Christian, catholic spirit. They contain no unkind thrusts at Lutheranism, Calvinism, Methodism, or any other form of Christianity; they are cast in the Melanchthonian mould. Let us proceed in this spirit to the end of the meeting. We can best protect our own rights by religiously respecting those of our neighbors.

"I firmly believe in the peculiar mission of the German Reformed Church in this country. If we travel outside of this, we shall be thrown out on the stormy seas without captain and compass, and cannot justify our separate denominational existence. Each denomination has its separate mission, and should be true to itself. What is ours? If we understand this and act in accordance with it, from this meeting will issue new streams to make glad our Zion. Our mission is both theoretical and practical.

"I. THEORETICAL *Mission.*—This has reference to our theology. This is laid down, as to its leading genius and spirit, in the Heidelberg Catechism. A glance at a few of its peculiarities will show what our theoretical mission is.

"1. The Heidelberg Catechism is peculiarly *Christological.* And so our theology starts not from any abstract doctrine or precept, but from the living person of Christ,—the author and finisher of the new creation. What better starting-point can be desired than this most blessed fountain of our joys and hopes of everlasting life?

"2. The Heidelberg Catechism presents Christianity as a system of *life,* acting upon the whole man, transforming him into the blessed image of Christ. It proceeds from the vital union with Christ. It shows us the way to eternal life, and teaches us what is our only consolation in life and death. The first question is a precious pearl of catechetical literature,—the sum and substance of the whole Catechism. It puts our only comfort in the fact that we are not our own, but belong to Christ Jesus and are united to him in life and in death.

"3. The German Reformed theology must be *historical.* The Catechism is the result of no effort to strike out a new path of salvation or novel method of religious instruction. It only pro-

fesses to be an exposition or amplification of the three great
norms of the Christian : the Apostles' Creed, the Ten Commandments, and the Lord's Prayer. Thus it has a true historical
foundation, and hence it has outlived those methods of instruction which rest on a radical disregard for the wisdom and piety
of the past. We are not taught in it to set up a hostile spirit to
other denominations, but to love all, and do the duties which
our own position brings us.

"Living as I do at present in Puritan New England, and perfectly satisfied with my position,—being treated with the most
perfect kindness in the oldest and richest Seminary of our country,—still I must say that, with all my admiration for the excellencies and merits of the Puritan type of Christianity, I feel as
strongly convinced as ever that the German Reformed Church
has a special mission to accomplish, by virtue of the Christological and historical character of its thinking.

"But along with this historical element of our mission come
the churchly, liturgical, mystical, and contemplative elements,
all of which are very little felt in our age and country. Our
Christianity is apt to lose itself in a certain *busybodiness* and
outward mechanical routine, which may be right; but let us
recollect that while Martha was busying herself with the
practical affairs of life, Mary was commended by the Saviour
because of her *love*.

"II. PRACTICAL *Mission.*—A sound theology will not be indifferent to life. Theory and practice must go together, hand in
hand, for the glory of God, who made us for practical as well as
intellectual pursuits. Where can this union be better found
than in the Heidelberg Catechism? No one can charge it with
dryness. While a product of the study, it is also the product
of prayer. It could not have been produced except by men
who were practical Christians. Hence it has not only been used
as a book of instruction, but also one of devotion. Let us promote, as a Church, a deep, fervent, glowing, and truly Christ-
like type of practical piety, which lives and moves in Christ.

"In the next place, where is there a wider sphere of *domestic
missions* for any denomination (except the Lutheran) in this
country? Presbyterians, Methodists, Episcopalians, have tried
to raise German congregations, but, with a vast outlay, only
moderate success has been obtained. The reason is that this
work is providentially put in the hands of Churches who can
reach the German through the language and spirit of his home-
religion. And we are far behind other Christian Churches in
the land in this work, to our shame be it said. It is pleasant
to know that we are making of late some advance; and our
improvement should induce us to work on.

"But we must put our literary and theological institutions on
a broader and more stable basis if we should rightly fulfil our

theological and practical mission. To this idea we are but becoming awake. Other denominations have done much more to this end. Andover Seminary has an endowment of more than half a million of dollars, exclusive of the funds of Phillips Academy connected with it; and this the contribution of only a few individuals. One person gave one hundred and sixty thousand dollars in all. A donor, it is said, drew the money for his donation from bank in gold, and prayed over it for days on bended knees in his chamber, that God might bless it to the advancement of His own kingdom.

"How little we have done! and yet what grand results have been obtained! This very Convention is one of the fruits of these institutions which have resulted from our past liberality. Without the existence of our institutions, the Tercentenary Convention would never have been held.

"Let our meeting be made to mean something,—to announce that we intend to complete the endowment of our institutions and to carry out the grand designs of the German Reformed Church. A half-million of dollars should be raised during this Jubilee year in the Church, to be handed over to the Synod for apportionment among the various objects claiming our attention. Who will not give his dollars, hundreds, and thousands? I hope all will give, not so much from a sense of duty as from a feeling of *thankfulness*. This is the spirit of the Catechism, truly apostolic, truly Pauline; and, as the apostle himself expresses it in Romans xii., the brethren are urged to present their bodies a living sacrifice, holy, acceptable unto God, which is your reasonable service. In this spirit of thankfulness let us bring our offerings,—thankfulness to God for the blessings He has conferred on us in our Church and our Catechism.

"Then this year will be recollected as an important epoch, and as the brightest memorial year in our Church's history, long to be remembered by every son and daughter of the German Reformed Church."

The Convention was dismissed, after Dr. Schaff had finished his remarks, with the Apostolic benediction by the President.

The afternoon session was opened with singing, and prayer by the Rev. Isaac Gerhart, of Lancaster, Pa. The attention of the Convention was directed to an Essay, "The Relation of the Heidelberg Catechism to the various Confessions," which was read by its author, the Rev. E. V. Gerhart, D.D.

The President having announced that remarks from the members would be in order, the Rev. Joshua H. Derr addressed the Convention as follows :—

"I rise to make a few remarks on the general object of the Convention. The large numbers present at our sessions, and

the character of the Essays read before the Convention, have
made me feel hopeful of the future. All gloom and fear have
been chased away, and we shall now leave this meeting with
hope and joyous expectations.

"In all the Essays, one point seemed to me to have been
touched on but slightly, if at all. I refer to the analogy that
exists between the origin of the Catechism and the Apostles'
Creed. This is strikingly shown in the several circumstances
connected with the origin of both.

"1. The Creed was not formed at any one period of time, but
was the result of a continued evolution of the truths of Christian doctrine and faith, and reached its present form without a
trace of a polemic character marking its form and contents. So
the production of the Catechism was the result of time. Different forms of Catechisms had been proposed in the Reformation-period, specially prepared with reference to the different
errors of that period. The Heidelberg Catechism seemed to
grow out of the more perfected life of the German Reformed
Church, and to be freed also from taint of polemics. In this
way there seems to be a connection in the form of life and doctrine between it and the times of the apostles. This should
make us strong in our faith, as the analogy is so striking.

"2. The early Christians were made to suffer for their faith;
they were driven away from their homes, and thus their faith
was spread throughout all lands. Thus, also, the founders of
our Church were made to suffer, to live in poverty, and to undergo
banishment to other lands.

"The men in the sixteenth century who had any influence in
the formation of the Heidelberg Catechism seemed to have been
blessed with a special outpouring of divine grace. These circumstances require us to study with reverence the histories and
lives of the founders of our Church and the framers of our
Catechism.

"Some practical thoughts present themselves as flowing out
of these circumstances. 1. We ought to love the Catechism,
and show our love by using it in our families. 2. It should furnish the order, as well as the themes, of the preaching from our
pulpits. 3. We should rally around our institutions and do all
in our power to sustain them. 4. The claims of missions should
always be near our heart and command our warmest attentions.
5. In order to keep ourselves fairly before the world, we must
not only sustain our present weekly papers, but must have a
Review, through which the doctrines and usages of our Church
can always be presented to the world. 6. We should all try to
understand the sin of schism, and pray for the restoration
of the rent body of Christ. Is it too much to hope that the
irenical symbol, our Catechism, should be the rallying-point
for all?"

The session was closed with prayer by the Rev. Franklin W. Kremer, of Lebanon, Pa.

On *Thursday* evening the Convention met in Zion's German Reformed Church, Sixth Street above Girard Avenue, where the proceedings were conducted in German. The session was opened with singing, and prayer by the Rev. Thomas H. Leinbach.

The Rev. P. Schaff, D.D., delivered in a free way his Essay on the Heidelberg Catechism, treating in order of the Name, Origin, Authors, Adoption, Introduction, History, Theology, Value, and Use of the venerable symbol. After this, he made a practical application on the spirit, import, and probable effect of this Convention upon the promotion of the benevolent institutions and operations of the Church. He urged especially the importance of raising, from a spirit of true gratitude to God, in every congregation, Tercentenary contributions toward the promotion of the cause of Domestic Missions and Beneficiary Education, and for the more complete endowment of the Literary and Theological Institutions of the Church. If each communicant member of the German Reformed Church would only contribute one dollar, we should realize $100,000,—a sum not sufficient indeed to pay one-tenth of the expenses of this present civil war for a single day, but large enough to do an incalculable amount of good through the Church of Jesus Christ.

The older ministers present being called on for remarks, the Rev. Thomas H. Leinbach addressed the Convention, and spoke of his experience in catechetical instructions extending through more than forty years of his ministerial life. He hoped that this Jubilee would stimulate our ministers to increased zeal in the business of instructing the youth of the Church. He took leave of the Convention with some feeling remarks, referring to his advanced age, and prayed with heartfelt fervor that all would meet in the Church triumphant above.

The Rev. Isaac Gerhart, also one of the venerable Fathers of the Church, expressed his heartfelt joy that the Lord had spared his life to see this great Jubilee, and spoke with earnest enthusiasm of the strong and imperishable foundations which were furnished our Church in the doctrines of the Heidelberg Catechism.

After these addresses the Convention adjourned, and the session was closed with singing, and prayer by the Rev. B. S. Schneck, D.D.

During the session in Zion's Church, a number of the members having assembled in Race Street Church, they were called to order by one of the Vice-Presidents, and the meeting was opened with singing, and prayer by Rev. W. A. Good, of Reading, Pa.

The exercises of this meeting consisted in the reading of the Essay, "The Theological Seminary," by the author, the Rev. B. C. Wolff, D.D., of Mercersburg, Pa., and of the Essay, "The

Authority of the Heidelberg Catechism," by its author, the Rev. George B. Russell, of Pittsburg, Pa.

This meeting was then closed with prayer by the Rev. Joseph W. Santee, of Cavetown, Md., and dismissed with the Apostolic benediction by the Rev. B. C. Wolff, D.D.

On *Friday* morning the session was opened with singing, and prayer by the Rev. J. Casper Bucher.

The Essay, "The Theological System in which the Heidelberg Catechism rests, the Kind of Religious Life it cultivates, and the Theory of Practical Religion which it assumes," by the Rev. M. Kieffer, D.D., Tiffin, Ohio, was announced by the President as first in order. In the absence of the author, it was read by Lewis H. Steiner, M.D.

The Committee on Dr. Schaff's resolutions concerning the publication of the Tercentenary Essays reported through their Chairman, Dr. Heiner, a series of resolutions, which after sundry alterations were adopted, the first two being those proposed by Dr. Schaff. The resolutions are as follows :—

1. "*Resolved*, That the Essays prepared for this Convention, together with the Introductory Communion Sermon of the President of the same, be published in proper chronological and logical order, under the supervision of the Tercentenary Committee, as a Memorial volume of the General Convention of the German Reformed Church of the United States, held in Philadelphia from January 17 to January 23 inclusive, 1863.

2. "*Resolved*, That the Secretaries of the Convention be directed to prepare a History of the Tercentenary movement from the beginning to its close, including letters and short sketches of the extemporaneous addresses and discussions of the Convention; and that this History form the Introductory chapter of said Memorial volume.

3. "*Resolved*, That the Tercentenary Committee of Synod be directed to have the Memorial Volume stereotyped if they should deem such a measure expedient, to fix the price of the volume, and to give attention to its sale and general distribution.

4. "*Resolved*, That said committee on publication be directed to request such authors (the German authors excepted) as may have transcended the limits stated by the Committee of Arrangements to condense their articles so that they may not exceed thirty printed pages.

5. "*Resolved*, That a special committee of three be appointed to prepare a similar Memorial Volume in the German language, including the Minutes of the Convention, all the German Essays, a historical sketch of the Tercentenary movement, and a synopsis of the English Essays and Addresses. This Committee consists of Rev. P. Schaff, D.D., Rev. N. Gehr, and Rev. J. F. Busche.

6. "*Resolved*, That the members of the Convention and others interested in the publication be requested to send in without delay the number of copies desired for either one or both of the Memorial Volumes to the Chairman of the respective committees.

7. "*Resolved*, That three copies of the Memorial Volume be placed free of charge in the hands of each Essay-contributor, and that the profits, if any, arising from the publication of said volume, be handed over to Synod to be disposed of as it may think best."

It was also ordered that the Committee on Publication be directed to request a copy of the sermon preached at the opening of the Convention, Saturday evening, 17th inst., by the Rev. S. R. Fisher, D.D., for insertion in its appropriate place in the Memorial Volume.

The Essay "The Educational System underlying the Heidelberg Catechism" being announced as next in order, its reading was commenced by the author, the Rev. Daniel Gans, of Harrisburg, Pa., but was suspended in order to allow of the introduction of delegates from the Historical Society of the Presbyterian Church.

The Rev. Dr. P. Schaff introduced the Rev. S. J. Baird, D.D., and Samuel Agnew, Esq., who visited the Convention in the name and by the authority of the Historical Society of the Presbyterian Church.

The Rev. Dr. Baird said that he considered it a personal privilege to be permitted to communicate the salutations of the Presbyterian Historical Society to this Convention, and to bear the fraternal greetings of Westminster to Heidelberg. He would read the greetings which the Society he represented desired him to bear to the Tercentenary Convention. This he proceeded to do, and the paper is as follows:—

"PHILADELPHIA, January 23, 1863.

"MR. PRESIDENT AND REVEREND FATHERS AND BRETHREN:—It is with no ordinary emotions that we enjoy the privilege of tendering your Convention the fraternal salutations of the Presbyterian Historical Society. Our society embraces in its constituency all those branches of the Reformed Church in America which adhere to the standards of the Westminster Assembly. As a Church historical society we could not but regard with the profoundest interest the assemblage of your Convention, and recognize the signal and auspicious importance of the events which you celebrate. Ours is the only organized body in existence which embraces all branches of the Westminster Churches. And whether we regard the whole history of the past relations of the Reformed Churches, to which our labors as a historical society direct our attention, or the present state of feeling and sentiment in the several branches of the Church with which we are individually conversant and identified, we feel it to be at once our duty and privilege to offer you, in their name, as well as in our own, this heartfelt expression of congratulation and sympathy. Westminster tenders its fraternal greetings to Heidelberg.

"Nor on such an occasion do we apprehend that our appearance among those who do homage to the faith of Heidelberg can be regarded as, in any sense, unwarranted and intrusive. We recognize, indeed, your Churches as specially detailed by the King of Zion for the privilege and duty of bearing forward in the battle those standards which were emblazoned by the hands of Ursinus and Olevianus, and planted on the height of Zion's battlements by the illustrious Elector Frederick. But we, too, claim an interest in that faith and those formularies as our birthright inheritance from that mother Church of Scotland to which we trace our lineage. Although her old Confession was adopted three years before that of Heidelberg, she early and cordially accepted the latter as a faithful embodiment of the doctrine of Christ, and conceded to it an authority as unquestioned with her as in any branch of the Reformed Church. Nor can we fail to remember that when the hope of uniting the British Churches in the use of one set of formularies and one system of order induced the calling of the Westminster Assembly, its proceedings embraced a fraternal correspondence with the Churches of the Heidelberg Confession, and were conducted with their sanction and God-speed, and the fruits of its labors were hailed with their approval and vindication.

"Faithful to the sentiments of our fathers, we appear among you, with the assurance that if we realize emotions of peculiar veneration for the Assembly of Westminster, and cherish a peculiar affection for the formularies which we inherit from them, it is not that we have departed from the catholic sentiments of the age of the confessions; it is not that we love Heidelberg less, but Westminster more.

"In these days of tribulation, when the Lord seems preparing to arise and shake terribly the earth, when at the frown of His anger the pillars of our own beloved land are shaken, and men's hearts fail them for looking to those things which are coming upon the earth, we feel impelled to do what with propriety we may, to draw closer the bonds of fellowship between all those who belong to that kingdom which cannot be moved. Especially do we realize a desire to see relations of greater intimacy established between the various branches of that Reformed Church, which—one in the faith of its confessions—has been one in the spirit with which in all ages and lands it has cherished the principles of rational liberty and vindicated those rightful powers with which God has endowed the rulers of nations.

"Brethren, in the name of the Lord Jesus Christ we salute you. With you we look back, with subdued and grateful congratulations, to trace the vestiges of the past, and recognize the blessed results which, amid human weakness and imperfection, have been accomplished by the grace of God. With you we look forward with exultant joy to that day when the work of righteousness shall be peace, and the effect of righteousness, quietness and assurance forever. With you, we would humbly and courageously gird ourselves for the battle before us, keeping our eyes ever fixed on the folds of that blood-sprinkled banner whose pathway is victory and its rest glorious. We entreat God's blessing on your convocation, and His abundant grace to you and the Churches you represent. 'As many as walk by this rule, peace be on them, and mercy, and upon the Israel of God.'

"Yours in the bonds of the common faith.

"Signed in the name and by order of the Presbyterian Historical Society.
"SAMUEL J. BAIRD,
"*Corresponding Secretary.*"

Rev. Dr. Nevin, the President of the Convention, then replied in substance as follows :—"I feel no hesitation in responding to this greeting in the same cordial spirit with which it is tendered. The design of our celebration is not to cultivate a simply denominational feeling. Our strength consists in the cultivation and maintenance of a proper historical spirit, and hence we rejoice to extend the fraternal hand to the members of all branches of the Reformed Church. We are deeply convinced that it is only by the cultivation of such a historical spirit we can be brought into a more lively correspondence with these Churches. While we entertain none but kindly feelings to the great Lutheran Church, still our historical relations bind us more nearly to the Reformed Churches, and our prayer is, that this Convention may be instrumental in uniting us more closely to the sister branches of the one common stock."

On motion a committee, consisting of the Rev. Dr. J. H. A. Bomberger, Dr. P. Schaff, and Prof. Thomas C. Porter, was appointed to prepare a suitable reply to the Presbyterian Historical Society for its kind and Christian interest in the aims and proceedings of the Convention, which reply, as afterwards forwarded, is as follows:—

"PHILADELPHIA, March 13, 1863.

"REVEREND AND DEAR SIR:—The fraternal salutations of the Presbyterian Historical Society, so kindly conveyed by you to the recent Tercentenary Convention of the German Reformed Church, were peculiarly welcome. Deeply sensible as the Church is of the importance of the late Convention, not merely as a denominational jubilee, but as an occasion of great interest to evangelical Christianity at large, we see no reason for concealing our gratification at finding her convictions of that interest and importance shared by so influential and highly respected a society as that which you represent. The occasion was not only a novel one in the ecclesiastical annals of our country, but, by its special purpose and aims, is invested with great historical significance. And we have been cheered to find that significance fully appreciated by brethren so well qualified to estimate it.

"The Churches of the Heidelberg Catechism and of the Westminster Confession have good reason to feel themselves united by bonds of no ordinary tenderness and strength. Both by their external history, and by their inner constitution and economy, are they placed in close and vital relations to each other. And although the intimacy of these relations may have been more manifest and more frequently and cordially acknowledged during the period of their common earlier struggles than it has been since that time, why should it not be revived and cherished more warmly than ever? It is true that our respective Churches are not *twin*-sisters, chronologically; nor do they trace their nativity to the same geographical fatherland. But they are *sisters* still, and that in the closest sense. Not only are they thus related in being fellow-members of a 'holy nation,' the boundaries of whose abodes are not fixed by the narrow limits of earthly states and kingdoms, whose happy citizens cannot be sundered from their hallowed intercommunion even by the broader division-lines of divers nationalities and tongues. The Churches of the Heidelberg Catechism and of the Westminster Confession may claim a closer consanguinity than this. They spring from a common spiritual parentage, are offshoots of the same ecclesiastical stock. Not sisters-*in-law*, but such in *fact*, it is no wonder that they so often discern in each other the unmistakable lineaments of their common paternity, and, discerning these, feel mutually drawn together by strong inborn sympathy. Who shall chide them for cherishing that sympathy or yielding to its sacred attractions?

"Heidelberg and Westminster may be regarded as the most prominent representatives of the great and influential Reformed section of Protestant Evangelical Christianity. Their common parents in this view are Zürich and Geneva, in Switzerland. Though each, successively, embraced and illustrated the system held by both, with peculiar modifications, such as diverse nationalities and social influences would very naturally produce, in certain well-defined fundamental points they cordially harmonized, as they did not agree with other ecclesiastical and theological systems and their advocates. Heidelberg might not lay so much stress as Westminster upon minute definitions of the Divine decrees, but, with the Catechism of the Reformed Palatinate before her, the latter might well be persuaded that her German sister held and maintained all that was essential to evangelical orthodoxy on that subject. Westminster might seem to give less prominence than her elder sister to the Church as the body of Christ, and to the sacraments, but, with the noble confession of the Presbyterian divines of 1643 in her hand, Heidelberg could surely not accuse her English sister of apostasy from the faith of Geneva regarding the sacraments and the Church. In reference to ecclesiastical polity they have always been of one mind, theoretically and practically, and, so far as public worship is concerned, the best authorities agree in testifying to the unanimity in sentiment, and the almost unvarying uniformity of their usages. Mutually willing to wear any yoke which their common Lord and Master might impose, they cordially shared each other's strong aversion to the bondage of all human ordinances and devices. They began together in the spirit, and sought not to perfect themselves in the flesh.

"Conscious of this spiritual unity and affinity, how natural it was for the two Churches to regard each other with sincere affection, to maintain a cordial correspondence, and to be always ready to extend to each other the warm hand of efficient sympathy and help! Heidelberg, though by many years the older, did not despise her younger sister. Nay, there were none who rejoiced with more devout gratitude at the great event of Westminster than the members of the Reformed Faith throughout the Continent. It was a consummation long expected and desired. It was a harvest for which they had toiled no little. Much of the seed from which it sprang had either been sown by their own hands or had been obtained from their garners. That which they had sown they had scattered weeping. That which they furnished they had moistened with their tears. They had reason to rejoice in the happy result. Not in vain had the newly awakened friends of the gospel truth and gospel ordinances, forced to flee from cruel persecutions in England, been welcomed, as fugitives for Christ's sake, by their more fortunate brethren on the Continent. Both were profited by the fellowship thus providentially established, and the hearts and hands of all were cheered and strengthened by the sincere and lasting friendships thus formed. The earliest bonds which united Heidelberg and Westminster were wrought and cemented in the heat of fiery trials. Such bonds should rivet hearts closely and inseparably together. And so they did. For those bonds must, indeed, be strong and pure, which the rust of three centuries has not been able to corrode.

"Of the many offices of Christian kindness performed mutually for each other by the Churches we represent, and the memory of which is treasured in their early annals, we cannot stop to speak. You do not need to be reminded of them in detail. The children of the Palatines and the children of the Puritans will never forget the love their fathers bore to each other, nor the fraternal services mutually rendered in their successive seasons of trial. Neither will they forget or disclaim the motives and obligations under which those services place them, to cultivate among each other the most friendly relations and perpetually to cherish the most affectionate regard. The sacred memories to which we have adverted all strongly incite us to this. If we have sprung from a common root, if we do hold a common faith, if we are pervaded by a kindred spirit, if we are animated by a common zeal, if we have mutually shared like trials, successively cheering and succoring each other by deeds of true brotherly kindness and charity, then, indeed, the Churches of Heidelberg and Westminster should feel themselves united by close and indissoluble bonds; and then, too, it should be one of their constant aims to make the mutual charities and courtesies of their present and future fellowship ever harmonize with those of earlier times.

"It is one of the distinctive and commendable characteristics of the ecclesiastical posterity of Geneva, to 'contend earnestly' for what they hold to be 'the faith once delivered to the saints.' But for this very reason they cherish and exhibit the most 'perfect charity among themselves.' And for the pleasing and impressive illustration of this, furnished by the greetings of your society, we have cause to be grateful.

"It has been with sincere pleasure, reverend and dear sir, that we have thus endeavored to discharge the duty assigned us by the Tercentenary Convention of responding to the sentiment of your letter. On behalf of the Convention, permit us to convey through you its most Christian and fraternal salutations to the Presbyterian Historical Society, and to conclude in the language of John Knox, John Rutherford, John Craig, and others, addressed to Beza and the Reformed Churches of the Continent but three years short of three centuries ago. 'But we earnestly request you not to allow the friendly correspondence now commenced between us to die away. If you will diligently do this, we will endeavor to return to you the like favor. May the Lord Jesus prosper as long as possible the pious exertions of yourself and brethren for the increase of the Church of Christ. Farewell.'

"With sincere personal regard, very truly, yours, in the gospel,
"J. H. A. Bomberger,
"Thomas C. Porter,
"Philip Schaff,
"*Committee of the Tercentenary Convention.*"

The morning session was closed with prayer by the Rev. Dr. Samuel J. Baird, of the Presbyterian Church.

The afternoon session was opened with singing, and prayer by the Rev. Joseph W. Santee.

The Rev. Daniel Gans concluded the reading of his Essay, "The Educational System underlying the Heidelberg Catechism," which had been suspended during the morning session, by the reception of the delegates from the Presbyterian Historical Society.

The following resolutions, offered by Prof. T. C. Porter, were then adopted:—

"*Resolved*, That the Committee of Arrangements be instructed to present, in the name of the Convention, in case the profits arising from the sale of these books will warrant it, copies of the Triglott edition of the Heidelberg Catechism, and the Memorial volumes (English and German), to the University Library at Heidelberg; to the Libraries of the Theological Seminaries at Mercersburg, Pa.; Tiffin, Ohio; New Brunswick, N. J.; Andover, Mass.; Princeton, N. J.; Allegheny City, Pa.; Gettysburg, Pa.; Union Theological Seminary, New York City; and also to the Historical Society of the Presbyterian Church of the United States.

"*Resolved*, That copies of the Triglott edition of the Heidelberg Catechism be also presented to the Rev. Drs. Hundeshagen, Ebrard, Ullmann, and Herzog, of Germany, and the Rev. Dr. Van Osterzee, Professor at Utrecht, Holland, in addition to the Memorial volumes already provided for."

The Rev. Dr. J. H. A. Bomberger announced that he had received a letter from the Rev. Edward de Schweinitz, of the Moravian Church, expressing his regret that he was prevented from attending the Convention. On motion, Mr. de Schweinitz's name was ordered to be placed on the roll.

The Convention then adjourned, and the session was closed with prayer.

In the evening a session was held in Bethlehem German Reformed Church, which was opened with singing, and prayer by the Rev. D. Y. Heisler.

An abstract of the Rev. Dr. Ullmann's Essay was then read in German, by the Rev. L. B. Schwarz, of Boston, who also addressed the Convention, and instituted a comparison between the Heidelberg and the Rationalistic Catechisms.

The Rev. J. F. Busche, of New York, being called upon to address the Convention, said, " Though we have been listening to long Essays for some days, yet no one appears fatigued. The time has passed by so quickly that each member feels sad that this Convention cannot be prolonged. We have begun to feel our relation•to those great men of the Reformation whose history has been recalled by what we have heard. We have all felt as though we had seen and heard, in deed and in truth, the very authors themselves of the Heidelberg Catechism, and have gained the certain conviction that they were men of the deepest piety and faith, and hence were able to produce this incomparable Catechism,—more full and comprehensive, more definite and convincing, than any other. How well it reconciles differences in doctrine, particularly in that of the Lord's Supper, with such a true Melanchthonian spirit ! And this was the object of its publication by the pious Elector Frederick to the people of his dominion, and in it he was not disappointed. Can we ever tire of thinking of the manly and yet child-like faith with which he bravely defended his Catechism at the Diet of Augsburg, and with what Christian composure—more even than that possessed by Luther, with his ' Hier stehe ich, ich kann nicht anders, Gott helfe mir,' which might be interpreted as indicating fear— he stated his hope in the sure promise of Christ ' that what he might lose for His sake in this life would be restored to him a hundredfold in the next.'

"As an illustration of the effects of its teachings, I may mention the case of one I know. Born and educated in the Evangelical Church of Prussia, but somewhat under Lutheran influence, he had serious doubts in regard to the person of Christ. and His real presence in the Holy Eucharist. On coming to this country, he met the Heidelberg Catechism, and, through its clear and positive teachings on this point, all his doubts were removed, and he found it not only a cause of satisfaction to himself, but made it the text-book of his future teachings. By this symbol he was led to the German Reformed Church, and now shows his love for it by a diligent use of the same.

"Our Catechism is a norm of faith, as well as a work of faith. By it the whole Church, as well as a single individual, may be guarded from error and false doctrine. Hence it should be used, diligently and constantly, by parents and teachers, in our families, our schools, and our churches."

After Mr. Busche had closed his remarks, the Convention adjourned to meet at nine o'clock in the Race Street Church, and the session was closed with the Apostolic benediction by Rev. B. S. Schneck, D.D., and the singing of a Doxology.

During the session in Bethlehem Church, a number of the members held a session in the Race Street Church, which was opened with singing, and prayer by the Rev. Daniel Gans, of Harrisburg, Pa. The attention of the meeting was called to the reading of Essays by the Rev. B. Bausman, of Chambers-burg, on "Catechetics and Catechetical Instruction," and by the Rev. John H. A. Bomberger, D. D., on "The Fortunes of the Heidelberg Catechism in the United States."

At nine o'clock, the whole Convention having assembled, the exercises attendant upon its final adjournment took place. The large church was crowded with the members and others, drawn together by the solemn close of such an auspicious meeting. Each felt that the hour of parting was near at hand,—a parting which forbade the hope of meeting again on earth under like circumstances. The happy hours spent in reviewing the past history of the Church, and in recalling the self-sacrificing spirit of its fathers, would be a source of life-long pleasure : still it was necessary that these should come to an end, and that each member should use the strength and confidence he had acquired in the grand battle of life against sin and the wiles of the devil.

The Rev. Dr. Bomberger, in a short address, said: "That while he had enjoyed the rich intellectual and spiritual feast of the past week, still he had been anxious as to the practical results of our meeting. It was a special privilege to be the means of announcing to the Convention the first fruits of the Tercentenary,—the first manifestation of that thankfulness which we should all feel to God for the present Jubilee. He had just received a letter from the Rev. Dr. Samuel Helffenstein, sending his Christian greetings, regretting that he had been prevented by the infirmities of age from attending the Convention, but that he sent two bonds of $500 each, to be held in trust by the Race Street congregation,—the interest of the one to be given annually to the Widows' Fund, and that of the other to the cause of Beneficiary Education. He also had the pleasure of announcing the receipt of letters from two other members of the Church, who wished their names kept secret, containing donations of $1000 each, to special Church objects. Let these

D

instances be not singular, but the first indications of that generous liberality which should mark the Jubilee year."

On motion, it was ordered that a suitable reply be returned to the Rev. Dr. Helffenstein for his letter of greeting, with thanks for the example he has furnished the Church through his liberal donation.

The Rev. Franklin W. Kremer, of Lebanon, speaking of the effect of Catechization, addressed the Convention as follows :—

"MR. PRESIDENT :—The Essays to which we have listened during the progress of this Convention are admitted to be of a high order. For literary ability, historical research, and earnest piety, we hesitate not to say they are unsurpassed. A very flood of light has been shed by these Essays upon the origin, the character, the introduction into the Reformed Church, and the wide-spread influence of our venerable symbol, the *Heidelberg Catechism.* We feel still more than ever drawn toward this evangelical compendium of divine truth, and our hearts glow with gratitude to God for this invaluable treasure. It now remains for us, as ministers and lay-delegates, to labor and exert ourselves more than ever to more fully introduce among our entire membership, young and old, this incomparable summary of evangelical doctrines. Had we time, we might speak of the Catechism in the *family,* the *Sunday-school,* and in the *Catechetical Class.* We can now do little more than refer to the use that should be made of this book in these several departments.

"The family is not only the nursery of the State, but likewise of the Church. If good and loyal citizens are trained in well-regulated families, so all intelligent, pious, and useful members of the Church are trained in the same nursery.

"It will be our duty, therefore, on our return to our respective flocks, to recommend with new earnestness and zeal the instruction and indoctrination of our children and youth, and especially in the sacred enclosure of the family.

"Here it is that the mind and the heart should be preoccupied with the precious seed of the divine word. Every child should be required to commit to memory the Catechism, and parents should explain it to their children, as far as they may be able. It is very unfortunate that in many instances children are not required by their parents to commit any of the Catechism to memory before they attend catechetical lectures, preparatory to confirmation. And, in a general way, proper youthful nurture and training are very much neglected. Almost the entire work is left for the pastor to perform; and hence the limited success of *pastoral catechization.* Were the preparatory work properly attended to in the family, we would realize far more precious fruits from a complete process of religious training, including the efforts of the Sabbath-school and the catechetical class. Then we should have a far more intelligent, normal, and solid piety, and far more efficiency among the membership of the Church. Our children and youth would grow up like lovely plants in the rich soil of the Church, and Zion would appear truly lovely and beautiful. Then, too, would the spirit of benevolence be largely increased, and ample means would be seen flowing from every point into the different treasuries of the Church. God grant that these precious and desirable results may be soon realized, and, to this end, may His richest benediction rest upon this Convention."

The Rev. Prof. T. Appel made some remarks on the historical feelings excited by the Convention :—

" MR. PRESIDENT :—No doubt I simply express the general impression of this Convention when I say that we have been instructed and edified during the past week. It has been to us a season of refreshing and revival. For the time-being, we have not felt that our country is in a state of civil war. Our thoughts have turned away from scenes of bloodshed and carnage, and gone back to those bright periods of history in which the best and most cherished institutions of modern times took their rise. We have visited the fatherland, and communed with the spirits of Zwingli, Luther, Calvin, Melanchthon, with Frederick the Pious, and a host of others, who made their age luminous with their piety and good deeds. In such society as this, we have been enabled to exclude from our minds, for the while, the stormy and tempestuous present. For this we are thankful to God,—the giver of every good and perfect gift.

" We are now better prepared to understand the history and spirit of our own Church than we ever were before. Some things at least that seemed to be contradictory in our history have been satisfactorily reconciled during the present meeting. We used to be told that Zwingli was the father of the German Reformed Church; that it started with him in Switzerland somewhat in the same sense as the Lutheran Church started with Luther in Germany. But we could never look upon him with the veneration in which Luther was held by his followers, nor feel that he sustained such an intimate relation to us. Subsequently our attention has been directed to Germany as the proper home and birthplace of the German Reformed Church, and we have been told that it properly took its rise in connection with the formation of the Heidelberg Catechism. Then Calvin and the pious Melanchthon were held up as the spiritual fathers of the Church.

"There is, however, really no contradiction between these two accounts of the origin of the Church. The Reformed Church as a whole took its rise in Switzerland, and Zwingli is the father of all who hold in common the Reformed principle. But the Reformed movement did not appear as something fixed and settled from the beginning: it displayed a progressive tendency and showed itself susceptible of a true and healthy progress. When, therefore, it found a home in Germany proper many years after Zwingli's time, it had fully surmounted the Zwinglian platform and had arisen to a higher stadium in its progress. The old wall of separation between the sister Churches of the Reformation had in a great measure been broken down, and it was felt and acknowledged that there was a principle of unity as well as diversity in their general life. Would that no attempts had been made to build it up again! This progress toward a higher point of unity was due to the influence of Calvin and Melanchthon; and our own Catechism represents it more fully perhaps than any other Protestant Confession. Our own Church took its rise just when this spirit had become predominant over the old antagonism, and has embodied it for ages to come in the Catechism. This has been made to appear in the most satisfactory manner by the learned authors from Germany who have favored us on this festive occasion with their contributions.

"Under this view, D'Aubigné's History of the Reformation, so much read in this country, fails to give an adequate idea of our own or the Lutheran Church. It professes to be a History of the Reformation, not of Protestantism as such. It gives an account of the origin of the two great Protestant Churches and of their separation from each other, but says nothing of their subsequent organization, in which their true character came to light. · It has not yet told us any thing of the rise of the Reformed Church in the Palatinate, nor in any other part of Germany proper, and it most probably never will. This is a great defect in his book, and makes it fragmentary, one-sided, and imperfect. This deficiency, however, will be remedied, so far as our Church is concerned, by the Memorial Volume; and with it in our hands, we will know exactly where we stand.

"Having communed with the past, Mr. President, it might be profitable, if we had time, to look forward for a moment into the future. This occasion is elevated ground, upon which light from both the past and the future is shed. We shall never see such a celebration again. We could wish that such seasons might often occur. But before another celebration of this kind comes around we will have finished our work on earth, and our names will be forgotten or only remembered as they appear on the Minutes of Synod. Yet from this eminence we can cast a glance into the future and hear the footsteps of those who shall come after us and take our places in the Church of God. Here in this sacred place the next Centenary Celebration may be held. But the time has come for us to part; and to give these remarks a practical bearing, and with the view to perpetuate the historical feeling here awakened, I propose the following :—

"*Resolved,* That a Committee be appointed to consider the importance and propriety of establishing an Historical Society in the German Reformed Church, and to report at the next meeting of the Synod.''

This resolution was adopted. The Committee consists of the Rev. Prof. T. Appel, the Rev. Prof. Thomas C. Porter, and the Rev. Henry Harbaugh, D.D.

The members unanimously passed resolutions of thanks to the brethren of the Church in Philadelphia for their Christian kindness and hospitality, and to the Race Street Congregation for the chaste and beautiful festal decorations with which their church was adorned in honor of the Tercentenary.

The Rev. P. Schaff, D.D., addressing the Convention, said in substance:—

"In the Apostles' Creed, on which the doctrinal part of our venerable Catechism is based, we express our faith in God the Father, God the Son, and God the Holy Ghost, the one true and living God who made us, who redeemed us, and who sanctifies us. On the basis of this triune revelation of the triune God we believe the Holy Catholic Church, which rises far above all denominational and sectarian names and divisions. In the bosom of this Church of Christ we believe and enjoy the *Communion of Saints*, which knows no limits of time and space, and embraces the patriarchs, prophets, apostles, evangelists, martyrs, confessors, fathers, reformers, and all true believers of every nation, generation, and tongue.

> " 'The saints in heaven and on earth
> But one Communion make;
> All join in Christ, their living Head,
> And of His grace partake.'

"We have enjoyed in these days a rare feast of this blessed Communion, such as we never have before enjoyed, or perhaps shall not hereafter till we reach that far more glorious assembly of the Church triumphant in heaven, where all earthly divisions and distractions are resolved into eternal harmony. We have enjoyed communion among ourselves from every part of our Zion in this Western world. We have enjoyed communion with several of the most distinguished doctors of the mother Church in Europe, who have instructed and encouraged us through their valuable essays especially prepared at our request for this feast. We have enjoyed communion with the fathers and founders of our Church, who, though dead as to the flesh, still live with God and now surround us as a cloud of witnesses encouraging and guiding us from their heavenly home. All the great Reformers of the sixteenth century have passed before us in graphic pictures as they never did before: Luther, the Elijah of Protestantism, the humble monk, who from his quiet study at Wittenberg shook the world by the simple power of his faith; Melanchthon, the modest and conscientious, the meek and gentle, the mild and lovely disciple of John, the mediator between the Lutheran and Reformed Confessions, whose last care and prayer was for the unity of the Evangelical Churches; Zwingli, the honest and hardy son of the Swiss mountains,—those symbols of power and freedom,—whose chief object was to 'insert the pure Christ from the fountain of the Scriptures into the hearts of men;' Calvin, the exile from his native land for his faith, the great theologian, legislator, and disciplinarian, whose master mind and holy zeal for the glory of his sovereign Lord and free grace still control the most earnest and active portions of Protestant Christendom; Frederick III., confessedly the most pious and one of the wisest and best of all the princes of that rich period; Ursinus, who expressed his inmost life in the inimitable first question of his and our Catechism, and declared that he would not take ten thousand worlds for his conviction that he belonged to Christ for time and eternity; Olevianus, who, like his friend and fellow-author of the Catechism, sealed his faith by a pious death, his last word being a triumphant *certissimus* to the question whether he was assured of his salvation. These and others, heroes of faith, together with the stirring thoughts and events of that most eventful age, arose from the grave of history, and have spoken burning words of wisdom and counsel to us. But the Reformation itself rests upon Mediæval Christianity, and Mediæval Christianity upon Ancient Christianity, and the Christianity of the Fathers upon the Christianity of the Apostles, and the Apostles point us to Jesus Christ, the great Captain of our salvation, the ever-living Head of the whole Church, which is His body, the fulness of Him that filleth all in all.

"This is *historical* theology, this is *historical* Christianity, that holds communion and fellowship with Christ and His people in every age and every land. What rich treasures of thought and action, what inexhaustible resources of encouragement and enjoyment, are here opened up to us!

"The Tercentenary Convention now drawing to a close in this silent midnight hour forms an epoch in the history of our Church, a turning-point, the end of an old and the beginning of a new period. We have reaped a rich harvest of past labors and cares. Let it be also a seed-time for still richer harvests for our children and children's children. Let it be the fountain from which shall flow living streams to the glory of God and the advancement of His Church. Let us bury beneath this altar all our past animosities and controversies, and let us go forth as one body, one heart, and one soul, with renewed zeal and vigor, to do the work assigned us as individuals and as a Church in God's holy cause and service.

"What better thing can we do, after all, than labor, live, and die for Christ, who died for us? Kingdoms and empires rise and fall 'like the fabric of a vision that leaves no rack behind;' even our once proud and mighty republic is now shaken to its very base, and who can assure us that its former glory and power will ever return? Events passing from day to day in this the darkest period of our history strikingly illustrate the utter vanity of all earthly wisdom, power, and glory. But the kingdom of Christ outlives all changes and revolutions of history, which are ruled and overruled by an all-wise Providence for the progress and triumph of Christianity.

"Let us all thank God that we belong to the kingdom which cannot be shaken. And having been permitted to enjoy this festival in harmony and peace, though surrounded by the horrors of civil war, let us renew our vows, and manifest during the whole year and to the hour of death our heartfelt gratitude for the great salvation of our faithful Saviour Jesus Christ, who delivered us from our sins and misery and makes all things work together for our eternal happiness.

"Then we will act in the spirit of our venerated symbol, our children and children's children will bless us for this Tercentenary celebration, and it will be remembered even when we shall be gathered in to the glorious assembly of the first-born in heaven, where Christ shall be all and in all."

After the conclusion of Dr. Schaff's remarks, the Convention arose and sang the 201st Hymn:—

> "Amid a thousand snares I stand,
> Upheld and guarded by Thy hand;
> Thy words my fainting soul revive
> And keep my dying faith alive."

The members joined in repeating the Lord's Prayer with the President, who then pronounced the Apostolic benediction. The Doxology, "Praise God, from whom all blessings flow," was sung, and with it was closed the General Convention of the German Reformed Church in the United States, held in commemoration of the Three-Hundredth Anniversary of the formation of the Heidelberg Catechism.

A.

ROLL OF THE TERCENTENARY CONVENTION.

Classis of East Pennsylvania.

Rev. D. F. Brendle, Farmersville, Pa.
Laity.—Thomas Oberly, Daniel Boyer.

Rev. Isaac K. Loos, Mt. Bethel.
Laity.—Henry Raesly.

Rev. J. S. Herman, Kutztown, &c.
Laity.—Ezra Geismer, J. D. Warner.

Rev. John Beck, Easton.
Laity.—Michael Butz, W. H. Lawell, John J. Otto, James Hess, Jacob Rader, Anthony Zulich.

Rev. Levi K. Derr, Tamaqua.
Laity.—Jacob Schmauck.

Rev. D. Y. Heisler, Bethlehem, &c.
Laity.—George Steinmetz.

Rev. John Gantenbein, Kreidersville.
Rev. Joshua H. Derr, Allentown, &c.
Laity.—John Gross, Philip Williard, Paulus Wald (Theological Student).

Rev. J. W. Lescher (teacher), Wilkesbarre.
Rev. F. Strassner, Wilkesbarre, &c.
Laity—George P. Learn, Daniel Rambach.

Rev. Joseph H. Dubs, Allentown.

Classis of Lebanon.

Rev. George Wolff, Meyerstown.
Laity.—Peter Spangler, Jr., J. Coover, Levi Groh, Henry Tice, Cyrus Spangler, Thomas Bassler.

Rev. F. W. Kremer, Lebanon, 1st ch.
Laity.—W. D. Rauch, George D. Heilman, Joseph L. Lemberger.

Rev. H. Harbaugh, D.D., Lebanon, 2d ch.
Laity.—John Meily, Hon. John W. Killinger, Jacob Weidle, Esq., Jona. Raber.

Licentiate U. H. Heilman, Heilman Dale.
Rev. A. S. Leinbach, Reading, 1st ch.
Laity.—Hon. Daniel Young, D. Neff, Isaac McHose, A. F. Boas, Wm. Clewell.

Rev. C. F. McCauley, Reading, 2d ch.
Laity.—Isaac W. Levan, John Ermentrout, George K. Levan, Philip Zieber, William Graeff, Samuel Faust, Franklin C. Butz, George Shollenberger, George M. Ermentrout, Jacob II. Hain, Wittington R. Van Reed.

Rev. J. E. Hiester, Annville.
Laity.—William Fisher, William Ault, C. II. Killinger, Peter Forney, Henry B. Bodenhorn, John Philip Stein (Theological Student).

Rev. H. Wagner, Orwigsburg.
Laity.—Peter Albright.

Rev. T. II. Leinbach, Tulpenhocken.
Laity.—David Kintzler, Eli Klopp, II. Stump, Cyrus McCroll.

Rev. D. W. Wolff, Schuylkill Haven.
Laity.—Daniel Small.

Rev. Jacob D. Zehring, Bernville.
Laity.—Franklin R. Gerhart.

Rev. T. C. Leinbach, Womelsdorf.
Laity.—Henry Wiand, Joseph Conrad. David Gring, Sr.

Rev. Augustus L. Herman, Reading.
Rev. William A. Good, Reading.
Rev. A. Romich, Philadelphia.
Rev. II. Bokum (Chap. U. S. A.), Philadelphia.

Classis of Zion.

Rev. Jacob Sechler, Littlestown.
Laity.—John Hesson, David Schwartz, William Ritlent.

Rev. Jacob Ziegler, Gettysburg.
Laity.—Jacob F. Lower, Jacob Raffensberger, Jacob Rebert, Henry Lady.

Rev. W. C. Bennet, Boiling Springs.
Rev. Jacob O. Miller, York.
Laity.—William A. Wilt, William Stuck, William Gilberthorp, Henry Wiest, John Noss, John G. Noss and W. F. P. Davis (Theological Students).

Rev. E. II. Hoffheins, Abbottstown.
Laity.—Charles Rebert, John A. Hoffheins.

Rev. Daniel Gring, Shrewsbery.
Laity.—Dr. Joseph Coblentz, David Gring.

Rev. T. P. Bucher, Gettysburg.
Laity.—John Slyder, F. E. Vandersloot.

Rev. A. R. Kremer, Mechanicsburg.
Laity.—Peter Stambaugh, Jacob Myers.

Rev. William K. Zieber, Hanover.
Laity.—Henry Wirt, Henry C. Schriver, Edgar Slagle, Daniel J. Albright, Emanuel Thomas, II. M. Schmuck, Titus S. Eckert.

Rev. Henry Mosser, Landisburg.
Laity.—Jacob Ritter.

Rev. Samuel Phillips, Carlisle.
Rev. D. Ernest Klopp, Blain.
Laity.—George Ickes, Jeremiah Hench.

Licentiate W. M. Reily, Mercersburg.
Rev. Jacob Kehm, East Berlin.
Laity.—George Julius, Aaron Spangler, Jesse Eppleman, John Myers, Andrew Ferrence.

Rev. F. W. Vandersloot, York.
W. D. Lefevre (Theological Student), Pleasant Grove.

Classis of Maryland.

Rev. D. Zacharias, D.D., Frederick City.
Laity.—Dr. Lewis H. Steiner, Frederick Zumpstein, H. Getzendanner (Theological Student).

Rev. E. Heiner, D.D., Baltimore, 1st ch.
Rev. E. R. Eschbach, Baltimore.
Laity.—G. S. Griffith, Jacob Yeisley.

Rev. J. S. Foulk, Baltimore, 2d ch.
Laity.—John Rodenmayer, Jacob King.

Rev. John Kuelling, Baltimore, 3d ch.
Laity.—Louis Blaufusz.

Rev. William F. Colliflower, Jefferson.
Rev. J. W. Santee, Cavetown. '
Laity.—George Harbaugh.

Rev. Jesse Steiner, Walkersville.
Rev. John G. Fritchey, Taneytown.
Laity.—John Feeser, Jacob Shriner, Joshua Crawford, Jno. W. McAllister, William A. Fritchey.

Rev. Henry I. Comfort, Mechanicstown.
Rev. John H. Wagner, Hagerstown.
Laity.—Frederick Humrickhouse, William Levy, David Zeller.

Rev. John M. Titzel, Emmittsburg.
Laity.—Joshua Motter.

Rev. Henry Wissler, Manchester.
Rev. E. T. C. Boehringer, Norfolk.

Classis of Philadelphia.

Rev. J. H. A. Bomberger, D.D., Race St. C.
Laity.—Charles Wannemacher, D. McWilliams, Charles Santee, Dr. T. Ingram, David Correll, William Beecher, John Wiest, Dr. William Maybury, John G. Alberger, S. H. Bibighaus, George Doll, John Hinckle, George Dodd, Philip Horn, George Priest, William G. Graver, Jacob Y. Dietz, Gilbert L. Lentz, William Howell, A. Holland, George Butz, Dr. D. S. Gloninger, A. L. Kaub.

Rev. J. G. Wiehle, Salem's ch., Philadelphia.
Rev. N. Gehr, Zion's ch., Philadelphia.
Laity.—Henry Euler, Elias Derr, Levi Johnson, Enos Bossert, Nicholas Wetzel, August Feldmann, Philip Renneisen.

Rev. S. G. Wagner, Böhm's church.
Laity.—Jesse Frantz, George Scheetz.

Rev. P. Seibert Davis, Norristown.
Laity.—William Earnest, Reuben Schall, David Schall.

Rev. S. H. Giesy, Christ church, Philadelphia.
Laity.—Charles N. Brock, Thomas F. Brock, A. H. Van Haagen, Philip F. Fry, William C. Ewing, Charles W. Arney.

Rev. J. G. Neuber, Bethlehem ch., Philadelphia.
Laity.—John W. Huber, Christian Wahl, George Gelbach, John Doelph.

Rev. Jacob Dahlman, West Philadelphia.
Laity.—Wilhelm D. Gross, Christian Gross, Jacob Klemm, George Muth.

Rev. W. G. Hackman, Kulpsville.
Laity.—John Weber, Aaron Drake, Joseph Proctor.
Laity.—Abraham Taney, S. Vincent.

Rev. Alfred B. Shenkle, Trappe.
Rev. Charles W. Shultz, Camden, N. J.
Rev. N. S. Aller, Pleasantville, Pa.
Laity.—John Garner.

Rev. C. Lukens, Frankfort, Pa.
Rev. R. R. Schmidt, Glassboro', N. J.
T. J. Seiple (Theological Student), Freeland.

Classis of Mercersburg.

Rev. J. Rebaugh, Middleburg and Clearspring.
Laity.—James R. Cushwa, Stephen Kroh, Abraham Ditto, John McLaughlin, Daniel Zeller.

Rev. Walter E. Krebs, Waynesboro'.
Laity.—John W. Coon, David B. Russel, Jerome Beaver, Levi C. Kepner.

Rev. C. F. Hoffmeier, McConnellsburg.
Rev. Jacob Hassler, Martinsburg.
Laity.—Anthony S. Morrow.

Rev. Isaac G. Brown, Mercersburg.
Laity.—Dr. John McDowell, Joseph Fuss, Herman Hause.

Rev. Thomas G. Apple, Greencastle.
Laity.—George Cook, A. B. Wingerd.

Rev. B. Bausman, Chambersburg.
Laity.—William Heyser, Sr., Bernard Wolff, George R. Colliflower, John B. Cook.

Rev. A. S. Vaughan, Shippensburg.
Laity.—Hon. Henry Ruby, Moses Conner.

Rev. Henry Heckerman, Bedford.
Laity.—Hon. John Cessna, George Oster.
Laity.—Peter Ewalt, Shellsburg.

Rev. George R. Zacharias, Strasburg.
Laity.—William Bossert.

Rev. N. E. Gilds, St. Clairsville.
Laity.—Jacob Walters.

Rev. W. R. H. Deatrich, Grindstonehill.
Laity.—Dr. E. Hartzell, Henry L. Miller, Dr. W. J. Maxwell, Jacob S. Wertz, C. B. Weldy.

Rev. J. W. Love, Waterstreet.
Laity.—Frederick Hyle, Benjamin Cross.

Rev. G. C. Seibert, Ph. D., Chambersburg.
Rev. B. S. Schneck, D.D.,   "
Rev. S. R. Fisher, D.D.,   "
Rev. Philip Schaff, D.D., Mercersburg.
Rev. B. C. Wolff, D.D.,   "

Classis of Goshenhoppen.

Rev. J. S. Kessler, D.D., Allentown.
Rev. P. S. Fisher, Tohickon, &c.
Laity.—Peter Solliday, Aaron Gerhard, Jacob Scholl, Daniel Oehl, Dr. Charles Everhart, David Appenzeller, William Schlichter, Isaac Gerhard, Jacob Hange, Samuel Leidy, Sr., Samuel Leidy, Jr.

Rev. Samuel Hess, Hellertown, Pa.
Rev. N. S. Strassburger, Pottstown, &c.
Laity.—Henry Fink, David B. Mauger, Lewis Marsteller, Franklin W. Gerhart.

Rev. A. L. Dechant, Keeler's, &c.
Laity.—Daniel Hunsicker, T. L. Hoffmeier, Daniel Smith.

Rev. David Rothrock, Durham.
Laity.—Solomon Anders, John L. Boyer, Henry Stover, Isaac Summer, Daniel A. Welder.

Rev. R. A. Van Court, Falkoner Swamp.
Laity.—Frederick Stauffer, Isaac F. Yost, E. Miller, Levi Lefever, Henry Stauffer, Jones Huber, Benjamin Tyson, Wm. Fox, Esq., S. M. K. Huber (Theological Student).

Rev. G. W. Aughinbaugh, Riegelsville.
Laity.—Tobias Worman, N. Wolfinger, Oliver Worman.

Rev. William G. Engel, Hill Church.
W. M. Landis (Theological Student), Centre Valley.
Laity.—Dr. P. G. Shive (Hilltown), Leidy L. Gerhart (Doylestown).

Classis of New York.

Rev. John F. Busche, New York.
Laity.—George F. Augustine.

Rev. O. T. Lohr, Elizabeth City, N. J.
Rev A. Schroder, Bridgeport, Conn.
Rev. Lewis B. Schwarz, Boston, Mass.
Rev. C. A. Hoehing, New Brunswick, N. J.
Matthew Schaible (Theological Student), Newark, N. J.

Classis of Lancaster.

Rev. A. H. Kremer, Lancaster, 1st ch.
Laity.—George H. Bomberger, John May, Philip Bausman, Dr. Samuel Welchans, Abraham Fishel, John B. Roth, Edw. J. Zahm, Jacob Bausman.

Rev. I. S. Demund, St. Paul's church, Lancaster.
Laity.—George Spurger, John II. Pearsol, Amos Hoffmeier, Christian Gast, H. H. W. Hibshman (Theological Student).

Rev. Isaac E. Graeff, Millersville charge.
Laity.—Philip Arndt.

Rev. George Kurtzman, Middletown.
Rev. Daniel Gans, Harrisburg.
Laity.—Daniel W. Gross, J. B. Thomson, Daniel E. Muench, I. M. Kelker, Charles F. Muench.

Rev. Martin A. Smith, Hummelstown.
Laity.—A. W. Milleisen, A. Mader, Martin Schaffner, Peter Heckert.

Rev. Frederick A. Gast, New Holland.
Laity.—John Sausman, Albert Sutton.

Rev. William T. Gerhard, Manheim.
Laity.—W. J. Fraser, J. W. Shenk, A. Etneier, Joseph Doebler, John Brion, Emanuel Keener, Henry Gray.

Rev. John V. Eckert, New Providence.
Laity.—Daniel Lefever, Samuel Hersh, Daniel Helm.

Rev. John Naille, Elizabethtown.
Laity.—John Klopp.

Rev. Daniel Hertz, Ephrata.
Laity.—Isaac Bushong, Henry Heller, Christian S. Hoffman, Henry Stauffer, Benjamin Swartz.

Rev. Prof. T. C. Porter, F. and M. C., Lancaster.
  "   E. V. Gerhart, D.D.,   "
  "   Professor Theodore Appel,   "
  "   John W. Nevin, D.D.,
  "   Isaac Gerhart,   '
  "   Albert Helffenstein, Sr., Shamokin.
  "   John G. Wolff, Maytown.
Laity.—John Hollinger.

Classis of East Susquehanna.

Rev. C. A. Rittenhouse, Mount Zion.
Rev. William Goodrich, Bloomsburg.
Licentiate Samuel Transeau.
Laity.—Joseph Mertz.

Rev. D. B. Albright, Paradise.
Laity.—David Eshbach, Levi Linn, Charles Hottenstein, David Derr.

Rev. Albert G. Dole, Milton.
Laity.—Colonel W. H. Frymire, Levi Balliett, A. Straub.

Rev. Lucian Cort, Sunbury.
Laity.—Hon. G. C. Welker.

Rev. John W. Steinmetz, Danville.
Laity.—David Diehl.

Rev. Henry Hoffman, Berwick.
  "   Henry Losch, Shamokin.
  "   Henry S. Bassler, Berrysburg.
Laity.—Daniel Heckert, George Negly, Henry Clouser, David Seiler, Samuel Buck.

Rev. Ephraim Kieffer, Lykens Valley.
Laity.—Philip Moyer, Simon Sheetz, John Williar.

Rev. N. E. Bressler, Armstrong Valley.
Rev. Isaac F. Steely, Mahontongo.
Laity.—Henry Roast, Jefferson Steely, Aaron Brown, Simon Weary, D. Weary, Samuel Weary.

Rev. Jared Fritzinger, Mahony.
Laity.—William A. Haas.

Classis of West Susquehanna.

Rev. J. Casper Bucher, Mifflinburg.
 "   Adolph B. Caspar, Middle Creek.
 "   Charles H. Leinbach, Lewisburg.
Laity.—Abraham Brown, Michael Brown, Michael Fichthorn, Joseph Negley, Solomon Ritter, J. A. Mertz, Jacob H. Brown, Samuel Zeller.

Rev. Israel S. Weisz, Mifflinburg.
Laity.—George Kleckner, George Gutelius.

Rev. William H. Groh, Boalsburg.
Laity.—J. H. Keller, William Keller, Peter Hoffer, Daniel Fleischer, James Osman.

Rev Henry C. Heyser, Liverpool.
Laity.—Jacob Mirriam.

Rev. John K. Millet, Nittany.
Laity.—J. C. Kryder, J. M. Kryder.

Rev. David G. Klein, Bellefonte.
Laity.—J. Hoffer, C. Glassner.

Rev. A. R. Hottenstein, Selinsgrove.
Laity.—Levi Swarm, John Hilbish, William Motz, Edward Bossler.

Classis of Clarion. •

Rev. C. A. Limberg, Luthersburg.
 "   J. G. Shoemaker, Curlsville.
Laity.—Jacob Brinker.

Rev. J. S. Shade, Petersburg.
Laity.—Daniel Bostaph.

Rev. F. Wise, South Bend.
Laity.—William G. King.

Rev. H. Daniel, Red Bank.
 "   C. R. Dieffenbacher, Kittanning.
 "   E. D. Shoemaker, Charlesville.

Classis of St. Paul.

Rev. David B. Ernst, Saegertown.
 "   Abner Dale, Mercer Mission.
 "   D. O. Shoemaker, Fairview.
Laity.—D. L. Kramer.

Rev. L. D. Leberman, Meadville.
" H. F. Hartman, West Greenville.
" L. J. Mayer, Clarksville Mission.
" G. B. Russell, Allegheny City.

Synod of Ohio.

Rev. Peter C. Prugh, Xenia,   Ohio.
" Henry Williard, Columbus,   "
" J. McConnell, Stoutsville,   "
" D. W. Kelly, Shelby,   ''
" J. Rinehart, North Lima,   "
Laity.—Henry Leonard, Basil,   "

Rev. E. E. Higbee, Pittsburg, Pa.
Laity.—W. E. Schmertz, Bernard Wolff, Jr., T. C. Craig, D. S. Dieffen
bacher, T. Kæmmerer, J. Sheets, J. Carr.

Rev. Christian C. Russell, Latrobe, Pa.
Laity.—G. F. Kiehl, M. Soxman.

Rev. A. B. Koplin, Elk Lick, Pa.
" F. A. Edmonds, Berlin,   "
Laity.—J. Musser.
" Frederick Fox (Theological Student, Cinn.).

Rev. D. H. Reiter, Stoystown,   Pa.
" C. Cort, Altoona,   "
" Geo. H. Johnson, Somerset,   "
Laity.—H. L. Baer.
" A. Beam, Jenner ⋈ Roads, "
" E. H. Dieffenbacher (F. & M. Col.).

Ministers of other Evangelical Denominations.

Rev. J. M. Olmstead, D.D.,   Presbyterian.
" H. E. Spayd,   "
" Jonathan Edwards, D.D.,   "
" Mr. Baker,   ''
" L. Olmstead,
" H. Bielefeld,
" David Malin, D.D.
" John U. Günther,
" W. E. Schenck, D.D.,
" M. B. Grier,
" John W. Grier,
" F. Hendricks,
" W. W. Latta,
" F. W. Porter,
" Samuel J. Baird, D.D.,
" James Clark, D.D.,   "
" James H. Baird,   "
" W. J. Mann, D.D., Evangelical Lutheran.
" E. Hutter,   "
" Joseph A. Seiss, D.D.,   "
" M. Sheeleigh,
" Charles P. Krauth, D.D.,   "

Rev. J. S. Reninger, Lutheran.
" Jacob Dahlman, Reformed Dutch.
" Charles Becker,   "
" E. S. Porter, D.D.,   "
" J. T. Cooper, D.D., United Presbyterian.
" W. W. Barr,   "
" Wesley Kenney, Methodist Episcopal.
" W. G. Robinson,   "
" Charles Cook, D.D.,   "
" A. Atwood,   "
" G. W. Smiley, Evangelical Reformed.
" Dr. G. O. Glavis, Evangelical Alliance.
Rt. Rev. Alonzo Potter, D.D., Protestant Episcopal.
Rev. K. Goddard, D.D.,   "
" E. De Schweinitz, Moravian.

B.

LIST OF DECEASED MINISTERS

OF THE

GERMAN REFORMED CHURCH,

WITH THEIR AGES AND DATE OF DEATH.

By Reb. Isaac H. Reiter, Miamisburg, Ohio.

	When they died.	Their age at death.		When they died.	Their age at death.
A.			Brown, D.D., John............	1850	78
			Bibighaus, D.D., Henry......	1851	74
Antes, Henry........................	1755	...	Bonnell. W. Wilson............	1850	41
Alsentz, John George...........	1769	...	Bayer, J. A......................	......	...
Alleborn, Jacob..................	......	...	Buettner, Ph. D., J. G.......	......	...
Aurandt, John Dietrich.......	1831	71	Brücker, Peter.................	1854	28
Altermatt, J. B..................	......	...	Bear, Jacob.....................	1855	44
Althouse, John..................	......	...	Becker, D.D., Jacob C.......	1858	68
Albert, John E..................	1856	...	Baumunk, John.................	1858	33
B.			**C.**		
Boehm, John Philip...........	1749	...	Chitara, Ludwig...............	1790	...
Bartholomæus, Dominicus...	1759	...	Christman, Jacob.............	1810	65
Bechtel, John..................	1777	87	Comingoe, Bruin Romcas...	1842	...
Brandmiller, John............	1777	73	Cares, John.....................	1843	32
Bucher, John Conrad.........	1780	50	Carey, Joel.....................	1849	35
Boehm, Charles Lewis........	1786	...	Crooks, David..................	1858	47
Boos, William..................	......	...	Carroll, Andrew...............	1857	73
Becker, D.D., Christian L....	1818	62			
Blumer, Abraham..............	1822	85	**D.**		
Beecher, Jacob.................	1831	32			
Boyer, Jacob....................	......	...	Dorstius, G. H.................	......	...
Begeman, Augustus L. W....	......	...	Dillenberger, John Jacob...	......	...
Boetticher, F. W...............	......	...	Du Bois, Jonathan............	1774	...
Brunner, Martin...............	......	...	Dallicker, Frederick.........	1799	61
Beussel, Herman	1849	...	Dubbendorff, Samuel........	1800	..

E

	When they died.	Their age at death.		When they died.	Their age at death.
Dechant, John Peter.............	1824	42	Helfrich, John Henry........	1810	77
Dieffenbach, Jacob..............	1825	41	Hoffman, Daniel.................		...
Dechant, Jacob William........	1832	48	Hauck, William....................		...
Dieffenbach, Henry.............	1838	...	Hiester, William.................	1828	58
Dreyer, John H...................	1840	72	Hillegas, John...................	1828	28
Dieffenbacher, Jacob F.........	1842	40	Helffenstein, Jonathan........	1829	45
Descombes, Jacob..............	1845	48	Hautz, Anthony.................	1830	72
			Hoffman, James.................	1834	74
E.			Hoffmeier, John Henry......	1838	78
			Helffenstein, Charles.........	1842	61
Ernst, John......................	1804	60	Hinsch, Lebrecht L............	1842	...
Eisenberg, Peter.................	1804	...	Hangen, Jacob W...............	1843	38
Evans, Nathan...................	1848	26	Hendel, Jr., D.D., William.	1846	78
			Herman, D.D., Frederick L.	1848	86
F.			Herman, Frederick............		...
			Hiestand, Henry..............		...
Frankenfeldt, Theodore.......	1757	...	Helfrich, John.................	1852	57
Faber, John Theobold.........	1788	50	Hoffeditz, D.D., Theodore L.	1858	75
Faber, John Christopher......	1796	65	Hassinger, David.............	1858	61
Felix, John.......................		...	Hoffeditz, T. C. W............	1859	40
Faust, Benjamin.................	1832	35	Heffelfinger, David............	1860	45
Faber, John Theobald........	1833	62			
Fries, Yost Henry..............	1839	62	**I.**		
Funk, Henry....................	1855	39	Ingold, John William........		...
Fisher, Richard Adams.......	1857	51	Ibecken, Herman G...........	1844	43
			Irvine, Matthew..............	1857	40
G.					
Goetschius, John Henry......	1740	...	**K.**		
Gross, John Daniel.............	1793	...	Kidenweiler, Rudolph........	1762	...
Gerber, John....................		...	Knaus, Charles.................	1830	...
Gueting, George Adam........	1812	71	Knoebel, Hartman.............		...
Gobrecht, John C..............	1815	82	Kieffer, Daniel G. H...........		...
Gloninger, Philip..............	1816	29	Koch, Henry....................	1845	50
Gebhard, John Gabriel........	1826	77	Keller, Abraham.............	1852	42
Geistweit, George..............	1831	70	Keller, John...................	1852	...
Graves, Dietrich................	1833	70	Kessler, Christian............	1855	33
Gobrecht, John.................	1834	57	Keyes, N. A....................	1857	50
Gerber, J.........................	1840	...	Keller, Jacob B................	1858	33
Giesy, Henry....................	1845	88	Kooken, John R...............	1862	47
Gerhardt, John Henry........	1846	64			
Geiger, Jacob....................	1848	55	**L.**		
Guldin, John C.................	1863	...			
			Lange, Charles.................	1768	...
			Lischey, Jacob.................	1781	....
H.			Leydich, John Philip........	1784	69
			Lupp, Ludwig.................	1798	65
Heger, John Frederick........	1720	...	Lentz, Andrew.................	1812	....
Hock, John Jacob..............	1737	...	La Ros, Joseph................		31
Hochreutner, John Jacob.....	1748	...	Long, David....................	1832	30
Henop, Frederick L............	1784	...	Lerch, Daniel B..............		....
Helffenstein, John C. A........	1790	42	La Ros, Jacob.................	1845	89
Hendel, D.D., William.........	1798	...			

	When they died.	Their age at death.		When they died.	Their age at death.
M.			Rahauser, Daniel	1847	...
			Rike, John	1855	28
Martin, ———		...	Reber, Joel L.	1856	40
Müller, Frederick Casimir		...	Reinecke, John	1859	70
Miller, John Peter	1796	81			
Mann, ———	1831	...	**S.**		
Muck, David	1838				
Miller, Henry		...	Schertlein, John Ferd	1740	...
Middlekauff, Solomon S.	1845	26	Steiner, John Conrad	1762	56
Moschop, F. G.		...	Stapel, Casper Michael	1763	...
Mayer, D.D., Lewis	1849	66	Schwope, Benedict	1771	...
Mertz, David	1849	86	Steiner, Conrad	1782	...
Miller, John C.	1851	25	Suther, Samuel	1788	66
Mahnenschmidt, John Peter	1857	84	Schlatter, Michael	1790	74
			Stock, Philip		
N.			Stoy, William	1801	75
			Senn, Jacob	1818	42
Nevelling, John W. G.	1844	94	Stahlschmidt, John C.	1829	90
Neal, Benjamin T		...	Schaffner, Henry B	1830	...
Netcher, Francis	1857	33	Sanders, John L.	1840	...
			Staehr, Samuel	1843	...
O.			Strickland, George	1844	33
			Shade, Jacob B.	1846	29
Oehl, John Jacob	1780	...	Swigert, Peter	1846	31
Otterbein, William	1813	87	Scholl, Jacob	1847	50
Osborn, Truman		...	Stahley, Stephen	1850	...
			Stump, Frederick R.	1850	36
P.			Stump, William	1851	29
			Sonnedecker, Henry	1851	59
Pernisius, Paul Peter		...	Stem, Franklin D.	1851	....
Pauli, Philip Reinhold	1815	73	Stump, Adam	1856	40
Pomp, Nicholas	1819	85	Shearer, David	1857	75
Porter, Louis R.	1834	...	Strassburger, John A.	1860	63
Plassman, Frederick W.	1848	32	Smaltz, John H.	1861	68
Pauli, William	1855	64			
Pomp, Thomas	1852	...	**T.**		
			Toberbiller, Frederick	1738	....
R.			Torsihius, Peter Henry	1740	....
Rothenbühler, Frederick	1766	40	Templeman, Conrad	1761	74
Reiger, John Barth.	1769	62	Theus, ———	1775	....
Riess, Jacob		...	Troldenier, George	1800	46
Rauch, Christian Henry					
Rahauser, Jonathan	1817	53	**U.**		
Reiter, William	1826	27			
Rassman, Henry	1832	79	Ungerer, John J		....
Runkel, John William	1832	84			
Reighley, Charles		...	**V.**		
Rice, Henry L.	1837	41			
Rauch, Ph. D., Frederick A.	1841	85	Vock, Ludwig Ferd		...
Rudy, John	1842	...	Vandersloot, Fred. W.	1831	58
Reily, James Ross	1844	56	Van Dyke, Hamilton	1834	30

	When they died.	Their age at death.		When they died.	Their age at death.
Van Linge, Jacob...............	1845	...	Weyberg, Samuel..............	1833	60
Vandersloot, Fred. E...........	......	...	Wack, John Jacob.............	......	...
			Wack, Casper	1839	87
W.			Webb, William C...............	1849	37
			Winebrenner, Christian......	1858	...
Wuert, John Conrad...........	1744	...	Wack, George..................	1856	80
Weiss, George Michael.........	1762	...	Weisz, George.................	1859	66
Wirtz, John Conrad............	1763	...			
Witner, John George..........	1779	...	**Y.**		
Wallauer, George...............	......	...			
Weikel, John H....,.............	1781	...	Young, Daniel.................	1831	35
Waldschmid, John.............	1786	62	Young, Andrew S.............	1848	37
Weyberg, D.D., Casper D.....	1790	...			
Welmer, Jacob..................	1790	...	**Z.**		
Winkhaus, John Herman.....	1793	35			
Wagner, Daniel.................	1810	60	Zufall, John	1769	...
Willy, Bernhard F.............	1810	...	Zulich, John....................	1821	...
Weber, John William..........	1816	81	Zeiser, J. Nicholas............	1840	...
Wiestling, Jacob H............	1826	33	Zerbe, Henry K................	1846	33

C.

LETTER OF REV. DIETRICH WILLERS.

FAYETTE, NEW YORK, January 9, 1863.

To " The General Convention of the German Reformed Church," Phila-delphia.

REVEREND AND DEAR FATHERS AND BRETHREN:—I congratulate you upon the highly important object of your meeting, the Celebration of the Tercentenary Anniversary of the existence of the Heidelberg Catechism.

I am sorry that I cannot be in your midst. My advancing age will not permit me in the midst of winter to undertake this journey. But be assured I am in spirit with you, and participate in your deliberations. May you all enjoy the presence of our Lord Jesus Christ!

In addressing you, I am not about to give a description of Frederick III., called the Pious, as he well deserved, the Elector of the Palatinate, nor of Caspar Olevianus and Zacharias Ursinus, the compilers of the Heidelberg Catechism, whose names have descended with renown to posterity; nor of the city of Heidelberg and its University near the delightful shores of the Neckar; nor of the history of the origin and progress of the Catechism and its translation into Hebrew, ancient and modern Greek, Latin, Low Dutch, Spanish, French, English, Italian, Bohemian, Polish, Hungarian, Arabic, and Malay, besides the numerous German editions; nor will I write about its introduction in the heart of Germany, Bremen, Switzerland, Hungary, Poland, France, England, Scotland, and particularly in the Netherlands. All this has been done by far abler pens than mine by our great divines on both sides of the Atlantic, and will be spread before the General Convention during its sessions. It is my intention only to write concerning the intrinsic value of the Catechism.

The intrinsic value of our Catechism has not been diminished by the lapse of time. It met with opposition at the beginning from the Church of Rome and from our sister Church the Lutheran, on account of its views on the Lord's Supper. The Arminians opposed it because they supposed they discovered there that which it did not contain—the doctrine of predestination. Emperors, kings, princes, arrayed themselves against its propagation. Men of learning and erudition in Church and State opposed its leading doctrines. Theologians, ecclesiastical writers, as well as courtiers, used their influence, through published books and pamphlets, either to suppress or diminish the influence of the Heidelberg Catechism. Those that wore the crown, the purple, and the mitre, endeavored to overthrow its influence by edicts, menaces, and the power of the sword. But all was in vain. God was on our side. The Elector-Palatine, Frederick III., trusted in God and in the promises of His Lord and Saviour Jesus Christ, as he affirmed before the emperor and the assembled princes. He defended his Catechism on account of its agreement with the word of God, and made this defence with such force that August of Saxony, in the Imperial Assembly, cried out, with enthusiasm, "Fritz, you are more pious than all of us put together!"

What a beautiful illustration was this pious prince of the good which can be accomplished by men in high position when influenced by religious principles! Their influence may not only extend over countries, but even over continents. They are suns dispersing light and warmth over the whole earth,—beacons throwing their light far out upon the sea. The Catechism, thus favored by the adoption and influence of princes and potentates, was carried by our fathers to this Western Hemisphere,—the garden of the world. Persecution had only aided in its propagation. As boisterous waves fall powerless for harm against the rock-bound shore, and only make it thereby more prominent, so persecution left the Catechism unharmed, although it directed the attention of the religious world to its beauty and simplicity. To-day you celebrate its Tercentenary victory, and, you must confess, "Victories are easier to be celebrated than to be won." The preparation for a victory often requires centuries, and the wheels of time accomplish what seem to be numberless revolutions before the object is attained.

The intrinsic value of the Catechism is specially seen in the precious doctrines it contains. It is a mine surcharged with precious metals. We do not always see the shining metal on its surface, but, on examining the interior with the lamp of faith, we find how beautifully it displays the doctrines of salvation; and frequently the same are seen swimming on the surface like costly merchandise. There are answers in our Catechism far surpassing in beauty those in any other symbolical book: such, for instance, as the 26th, 27th, and 54th. The language approximates that of inspiration as it was employed by prophets and apostles. The very faith and spirit of the apostolic age breathe in these answers. However more learned we may be than our fathers, we must confess that they had more faith in a, Divine Providence, more confidence in their Redeemer, and a higher idea of the Church than we of the present age possess. Had we the faith of the fathers of the Reformation, our Church would receive greater blessings from above. When we read the answers referred to, we see a faith, in all its splendor and ardent love for the Saviour, such as Paul shows in Romans viii. 38, 39. In Ursinus and Olevianus there was an apostolic faith,—the same invincible faith that dwelt in Martin Luther when he said, before entering Worms, "And if there were as many devils in the city as tiles upon the roofs, yet would I enter."

The first answer contains the marrow of the whole Christian religion, the doctrine of redemption, which is the centre of Christianity; the consoling doctrine of preservation, and the comforting assurance through the Holy Spirit of our everlasting salvation, the care of the heavenly Father for all Christians, extending even to every hair of our head; Christ as. Lord, Master, and Sovereign over our body and soul. Indeed, the whole blessed Trinity is here unveiled as an essential part of our religious belief. Divine Providence is so explained in the Catechism that the Christian can rest assured that, at all times and in all places, he stands under the control of his heavenly Father, through Christ his Saviour. The 54th answer is like a tower for our protection and a bulwark for our defence against all powers of earth and all assaults of hell. The Son of God is Lord and Sovereign over His Church; He gathers it as a hen gathers her brood under her wings; He defends it by His gospel and spirit; He is a living wall around His people, an impregnable bulwark; He preserves them to Himself, preserves believers in body and soul. Out of the whole human race He chooses His Church, and even from the beginning to the end of the world He chooses its members to everlasting life, agreeing in true faith, and every Christian must believe that "I am and forever shall remain a living member thereof." With such a prop, relying on such an anchor, the true believer can never be lost. This doctrine is worth more than all the wealth, and possessions, of the world.

The Heidelberg Catechism was a common bond, uniting the different branches of the German Reformed Church, encircling those who held to the doctrines of Calvin and Zwingli; a belt encompassing large portions of the globe,—Germany, Switzerland, France, Poland, Hungary,—and of sufficient elasticity to take in our land. Well may it be called a Church-Confession. Though neither Arminian, nor Predestinarian, nor Pelagian, nor Episcopalian, nor Puritan, yet if we take the word Reformed in its most extended sense, as including all Protestant Churches who differ from Dr. Martin Luther on his views on the Eucharist, they may all subscribe to *its* doctrines and teachings. The Catechism of Luther, besides, is somehow connected with the Heidelberg Catechism, since the latter really breathes a Melanchthonian spirit in accord with the Augsburg Confession, to which the Elector Frederick III. subscribed, and to which also Calvin gave his signature when at Strasburg. The Catechism may be received by those of different shades of belief, the Arminian finding support in the 37th, 40th, and 42d questions, the Predestinarian in the 1st and 54th, and the Pelagian in the 87th (which excludes all from the kingdom of salvation who do no good works) and the 89th (where the free will of man is brought into exercise). The Episcopal Church finds satisfactory nourishment in the doctrine of the Father, Son, and Holy Ghost (laid down in Questions 7, 8, 120, 59, 29, 30, 60, and 91), in the doctrine of the Sacraments and the Ten Commandments. As the Puritans profess to follow the pure word of God, they can find this in the Heidelberg Catechism, since all the doctrines rest on the Holy Scriptures. Well may it be called a Biblical Catechism, as its authors labored to have no other foundation for its doctrines save the words of holy writ. The Catechism, so far as its doctrines are concerned, may be said to have as its motto—The word of God, the whole word of God, and nothing but the word of God. It places no reliance on vague and uncertain traditions as such. It allows no change in its doctrines, unless they should be shown contradictory to the word of God. This was the spirit of the Elector-Palatine, the pious Frederick III., when before the Diet at Augsburg (vide Nevin on the Catechism, page 66), he said, "As for his Catechism, it was all taken from the Bible, and so well fortified with marginal proof-texts that it had not yet been overthrown, and he had good hope never would be in all time to come. If any one could show it wrong from the Holy Bible, which he now held in his hands, he was ready to hear him, great or small, friend or foe." It seems as though the Elector had been animated with the prophetic spirit, and had seen through the veil hiding the future, when he exclaimed, "He had good hope it never would be overthrown in all time to come." The Catechism is to-day your Tercentenary guest, and in the very recital of its victories it says to you, "Welcome, companions of my victory, welcome to the festival and all its blessings!"

Wherever the German Reformed Church plants her standard, wherever the footprints of her confessors shall appear, the Catechism must be found. As long as the German Reformed Church shall endure (and I both hope and believe its doctrines will stand until the end of the world, until the sand-glass of time has run out, and the morning of the Resurrection has arrived), so long will the Heidelberg Catechism be known, and will spread its Church life and light over grateful millions, who have been brought through its instructions to the green pastures of everlasting life.

The Catechism begins with the lowest state of man and advances to his highest earthly glory. After showing that the Christian's greatest comfort is in Christ (Question 1), it descends to a consideration of the depth of human depravity, treating of the purity of the original creation of man, his apostasy and departure from God, his alienation from God, and the necessity of regeneration—of a new creation in Christ Jesus. Whilst it shows man in the deep gulf of human misery, it also assists him out of the same, through the glorious doctrine of regeneration in Christ Jesus. Faith in the promises of God is required, and also in the meritorious services of the Redeemer, and it gives the catholic undoubted Christian faith in the words of the Apostolic Confession, which may be called the root, germ, and development of a Christian's faith. The doctrine of Father, Son, and Holy Ghost is then explained: The Father is the source and foundation, so to speak, of the Holy Trinity,—the Creator, Preserver, and Governor; the Son, coequal with the Father in nature, is the Mediator between God and man,—our Redeemer; the Holy Ghost is the Bearer (*Träger*) of all divine blessings to the Church. Justification by faith is the cardinal doctrine of the whole book,—salvation by grace, not by good works. Faith is worked in us by the Holy Spirit, through the gospel, and is confirmed by the holy Sacraments.

Our Symbol tells us what God does, but draws no line marking out where divine agency ceases and human efforts begin. The Sacraments are "holy, visible signs and seals," and they really give what they signify. Good works flow from Christian faith as a river from its source. The tree implanted into Christ, the sweet root of Jesse, must bring forth blossoms and fruits. The Christian, assisted by the Holy Ghost, can fulfil the Ten Commandments and every commandment by love to God. He loves to commune with God, and prayer is the genuine sign of his piety; and in no form can he express his spiritual and temporal wants better than in that prayer of all prayers,—The Lord's Prayer.

This is the beautiful division of our Catechism: 1, man's misery; 2, man's redemption; 3, man's gratitude to God for his deliverance from misery through the performance of good works. As a spiritual hymn has it: "Durch Dich bin Ich erst Mensch geworden, Mein Leben wird verklärt durch Dich." The Evangelical Lutheran Catechism begins with the Ten Commandments,—shows man what he ought to do before he has been granted power to do it. The Heidelberg Catechism closes with the Ten Commandments and prayer, which duties the Christian can perform after having obtained the pardon of his sins through Christ, being adopted into the divine family as a royal son or daughter of God. Thus our Catechism is adapted for the instruction of believing catechumens. These express confidence in the Redeemer already in the first answer. They are considered there as belonging to Him. The Church brought them to Christ. They were initiated into His holy Church with all her blessings. In Holy Baptism they became the property of the Holy Trinity. They were brought from the arms of an earthly father to those of the heavenly Father,—to the bosom of the Redeemer; from the nourishing breast of an earthly mother to that of the Church, where the blessed gifts of the Holy Spirit abound.

The Heidelberg Catechism is suited to the greatest divine, and at the same time to the simplest, honest soul. Well could some of our old theologians use it as a text-book in the instruction of their students of divinity; for therein may the greatest theologian make thorough researches as to the doctrines of the Creation and Preservation of man, of the divine government and redemption through Christ, of the Church and her Sacraments. All the essential doctrines of Christianity are contained in its pages. And the fathers of our Church were moved by the right spirit when, at the Synod of Mifflinburg in 1828, they compelled our Professors of Theology to say in their oath "that they in their accepted office would adopt and maintain, as the foundation of all instruction, the inviolable, divine authority of the Holy Scriptures, and the truth of the doctrine of the Heidelberg Catechism in its essence." This makes our Symbolic book a theological text-book in our German Reformed Seminary on this side of the ocean. That our confessional Standard contains one polemical question (80), and yet another (44) failing in proper explanation, this is no matter for surprise when we consider the imperfection of all human labors under the sun.

The Catechism breathes a conciliatory and pacific spirit. It takes a middle course, on the doctrine of the Lord's Supper, between the views of Zwingli and Luther, has a Melanchthonian character, and labors particularly to promote the best feelings of friendship and love, yea, even of union, between the German Reformed and Lutheran Churches agreeing in the Augsburg Confession. That Jesus Christ is really present *in* the Lord's Supper,—this is a doctrine in which German Reformed and Lutherans can unite.

Our Symbolical Book is adapted to all grades and conditions of life. Potentates, kings, and princes have been educated in its blessed doctrines, sitting at the feet of pious teachers, even as peasants and day-laborers and "them of low degree." It has a home in the icy regions of the north and under the burning sun of the south. Taking its origin in the east, it has followed the apparent course of the king of day over to the west. It has travelled from the Weser to the Seine, from the Alps and Apennines to the Rocky Mountains of America and the golden shores of California.

At this Tercentenary Celebration every minister should labor to revive the family customs of our venerated fathers. When divine service was closed, the children were questioned at home as to the text and contents of the sermon, and were examined in their Catechism. Besides their parochial schools during the week, they had a parochial school at home. Blessed custom! May it not be revived? The Catechism must receive its first support in the family, if it shall prosper in the Church. We have our Sunday-schools; but the books of the Sunday-School Union do not cultivate the Church-spirit of our denomination. We want a Sunday-school library for ourselves, and we want a love for the Catechism inculcated in the hearts of the young. Besides the Heidelberg Catechism, we have a Catechism for Sunday-schools, by Rev. Dr. P. Schaff, based on the same, which will be of excellent service if carefully used. The same may be said of Dr. Nevin's book on the Heidelberg Catechism. The Bible, Catechism, and Hymn-Book should be used in all our families, and then all will be well.

Finally, let us show, during the year, our duty to the Church, in free-will offerings. We have reason to be thankful to the Church, which, by the Bible and Catechism, has led us to the Saviour. If all portions of our Church would give according to their ability, we should be able to establish a new Professorship in our Seminary, and to aid largely in the cause of Domestic and Foreign Missions, and thus we could propagate the Catechism by our offerings.

Our Catechism has been an unspeakable blessing to the Church for three hundred years. New countries have not been conquered under its influence, but millions of souls have through it been conquered for Christ their Mediatorial King, and before we begin the journey of another century with our Catechism—a journey the end of which none of us shall see—let us mark well the advice of the Psalmist (xlviii. 12, 13): "Walk about Zion, and go round about her: tell the towers thereof. Mark ye well her bulwarks, consider her palaces; that ye may tell it to the generations following."

Wishing you all the blessing of the Most High God on your Convention, I remain, with due respect and love, your friend and brother,

D. WILLERS

OPENING SERMON.

By REV. SAMUEL R. FISHER, D.D.
CHAMBERSBURG, PA.

OPENING SERMON.

By Rev. Samuel R. Fisher, D.D., of Chambersburg, Pa.

" How shall we escape, if we neglect so great salvation?"—HEB. ii. 3.

THE inquiry of the text is one of deep interest and solemnity. It addresses itself to every class and condition of men, who come within the reach of the influences of the gospel. It applies to them, not only as individuals, but also in their collective and associated capacity, whatever particular form that may assume. Hence it is peculiarly applicable to us, in the circumstances in which we are at present assembled. We have come together, as the representatives of the German Reformed Church in the United States, for the purpose of inaugurating the series of solemnities, the observance of which has been ordered by her highest judicatories, in honor of the adoption and publication of the Heidelberg Catechism, which took place just three hundred years ago, in the Palatinate, under the authority of the Elector Frederick III.

The text naturally suggests three points, which may profitably engage our attention, though briefly, at the present time:—

I. *The great salvation, which we as a Church enjoy.*

II. *The duty devolving upon us in view of this great salvation;* and

III. *The consideration with which the observance of this duty is enforced.*

I. The first point, then, to which our attention is invited, is, *The great salvation, which we as a Church enjoy.*

The term *salvation*, in its most common acceptation, as used in the gospel, means deliverance from a state of sin and its consequences, and restoration to the enjoyment of the peace and favor of God. In the text, it does not refer so much to this salvation itself, as to the peculiar facilities possessed for arriving at a knowledge of its nature and our absolute need of it, and appropriating its special provisions to our own particular cases. That this interpretation is correct, will appear from a brief consideration of the context.

In the chapter immediately preceding that of the text, the apostle dwells upon the superiority of Christ, as a messenger sent from God, above every one who had appeared before him in a similar capacity. In view of this superiority, he infers, in the chapter before us, the duty of giving the more earnest heed to the things which we have heard, lest at any time we should let them slip; and then, by way of enforcing this duty, he refers to the fact, that the word spoken by angels (that is, by the prophets and teachers of the Old Testament dispensation) was stead-fast, and every transgression and disobedience received a just recompense of reward, and, in view of it, proposes the solemn inquiry of the text: "*How shall we escape, if we neglect so great salvation ?*"

The question naturally arises, What are the particular ingredients which constitute the great salvation which we as a Church enjoy? In reply to this question, I remark:—

1. In the first place, that we are favored with all the blessings and privileges of the gospel, which are enjoyed, in common, by all Christian denominations in this highly favored, though at present greatly afflicted, land. We have the means of grace in rich and glorious abundance. We have the Bible in our possession to read and examine for ourselves. It is translated into a language which all our people understand. We are furnished with a variety of facilities for arriving at a proper knowledge of its contents, in the way of commentaries and books of instruction and devo-

tion. We enjoy God's holy Sabbaths, with all the blessings and privileges, which are peculiar to them in a Christian land. We are favored with the instructions of a stated ministry, with the administration of the holy sacraments, and with all the means of grace, legitimately belonging to the Church as instituted by God. In this respect, we are highly favored, as much so as any other member of the great sisterhood of Christian Churches.

2. In the second place, I remark, that we possess in the Heidelberg Catechism, as the only symbolical book of recognized authority in the Church, a summary of the Christian faith of singular excellence and worth. Other Churches have their symbols of faith. These are by no means destitute of their excellencies. There are, however, certain features about the Heidelberg Catechism, which lead us to prefer it above every other symbol of faith.

We admire the deep earnest tone which underlies its whole construction. It seizes fast hold upon the spirit, and fails not to inspire every earnest mind with feelings and sentiments of deep devotion. The reader feels, in perusing it, that he is grappling with solemn realities, in which he himself has a special personal interest.

To us it is a strong recommendation of the book, as a system of religious instruction, though this has been made a ground of objection by some, that it invariably recognizes the catechumen as being in the Covenant and Church of God. Most other books of a similar character deal with catechumens as though they were outside of the Church, and impart their instruction with a view to induce them to enter it, and prepare them for enjoying its privileges. The Heidelberg Catechism, however, regards the catechumen as already in the Church by baptism, and deals with him as one recognizing and desiring to claim and enjoy the privileges of this relation. The system of Christianity which it recognizes is accordingly what is technically called the educational system. It regards Christianity, in its distinctive features, as a growth, which has its commencement, in the

case of the children of Christian parents, in early childhood, and, under a proper religious training, gradually
develops itself until, as the child attains to the years of
accountability, it feels induced under its influence to come
forward and claim for itself the privileges which belong to
its relation to the Church. This is fully in accordance with
such divine precepts as bear directly upon the duties of
Christian parents towards their children. "Train up the
child in the way he should go; and when he is old he will
not depart from it." "And, ye fathers, provoke not your
children to wrath; but bring them up in the nurture and
admonition of the Lord."

But, in addition to all this, no one of correct principles
can fail to honor the Heidelberg Catechism for its peaceful
and truly catholic spirit. Whilst it shuns not to give special prominence to all the cardinal doctrines of the gospel,
such as the fall of man and consequent depravity of human
nature, the utter hopelessness and helplessness of man in
his fallen condition, the necessity of regeneration, and of
repentance and faith in the Lord Jesus Christ in order to
salvation, the intimate union of believers with Christ, the
vicarious nature of the atonement, the true, real spiritual
character of the sacraments, and the necessity of good
works, in reference to which all evangelical Christian
denominations are agreed, it carefully avoids all those non-
essential points in regard to which different opinions prevail, and at the same time expresses itself, even in respect
to the cardinal doctrines of Christianity, in such a way as
not to furnish any real ground of offence to any truly
candid mind. In but a single instance does it indulge in
the use of seemingly harsh language; and that is when,
speaking of the Romish mass, it pronounces it an accursed
idolatry, which phraseology itself, history tells us, was not
in the Catechism as originally composed, but was introduced for certain local reasons some time after its adoption.
In this respect it presents a striking contrast to the spirit
which pervades the great body of the earlier symbols of

6

the Christian faith in the Protestant Churches, and which not unfrequently express themselves in harsh terms, and sometimes even invoke the curse of God upon those who differ from their teachings. The prevailing spirit of the Heidelberg Catechism is truly catholic. Whilst it makes no compromise with sin or any of the enemies of righteousness, it breathes a spirit of peace and good will to all who profess to love the Lord Jesus Christ.

The possession of such a symbol of faith must be regarded by us as no small boon, for which we are under special obligations to the Great Head of the Church.

3. In the third place, I remark, as still another ingredient entering into the great salvation which we as a Church enjoy, that God, in His providence, has been pleased to continue us in existence as a branch of His militant Church, during a period of three hundred years, and to preserve unto us our precious symbol of faith intact even unto the present day. It is true, that in the fatherland our mother Church has, through political influences, become to a great extent merged into a general ecclesiastical organization, known as the Evangelical Church, and that even in this country, the little vine which was transplanted hither some one hundred and thirty years or more ago, is still, from various causes not necessary to enumerate, a comparatively small branch; yet we are gratified to know that of late years what remains of the Church in the fatherland has become greatly revived, and is beginning to assume and assert its distinctive life and character with peculiar power and force; and none of us are ignorant of the progress which our Church in this country has made in the last quarter of a century, and of the special tokens of promise which now distinctly mark her future.

Some years ago, also, there was a strong tendency in the German Reformed Church, especially in this country, to depart more or less from her original landmarks, and to throw aside her distinctive customs and usages, under the mistaken notion that they were clogs to her true spiritual

F

7

prosperity. A powerful reaction, however, has taken place, and, in the face of much opposition from some misguided ones who were once within, and from more without, she has been gradually returning to her original and legitimate position as a Church, and, as a consequence, her precious symbol of faith, the Heidelberg Catechism, is receiving more and more its proper honor, and the customs and usages of the Church are becoming more and more restored, and the prospects are most favorable to a full and hearty return to all the rights, immunities, privileges, and distinctive features which belong to us as a branch of the Church of Jesus Christ.

Surely, in view of all the favors conferred upon us as a religious denomination, to which we have thus briefly referred, we have every reason to regard the privileges we at present enjoy as constituting in our case *a great salvation*, which is the point it was our purpose to illustrate.

II. The second point claiming our attention, as suggested by the text, is, *The duty devolving upon us, as a Church, in view of this great salvation.*

The text supposes that it is possible to neglect the great salvation to which it refers, and hence it itself embodies one of the most solemn forms of warning against the consequences of such neglect. A failure to appreciate this salvation according to its intrinsic merits, and to improve it to the purposes for which it has been conferred, constitutes this neglect, and the fact that a solemn warning is presented against the sad consequences of it, necessarily implies an obligation to attend to the opposite duty, as this is the only method by which such neglect can be avoided. What, then, is the duty of the German Reformed Church in view of the great privileges it enjoys?

1. I remark, in the first place, that we as a Church are under special obligations, if we will properly meet the requirements made at our hands, to use every appropriate means in our power to make our people more fully acquainted with the nature of the privileges we enjoy as a

Church, so that they may appreciate them more highly, and be prompted to give all diligence to turn them to proper and profitable account. This is one of the great objects contemplated in the Tercentenary celebration of the adoption of the Heidelberg Catechism, the series of solemnities connected with which we are engaged in inaugurating. The provision which has been made for the reading of essays and memoirs bearing upon the history and genius of the Heidelberg Catechism, and for the discussion of such topics relating to the origin, distinctive character, progress, and interests of the German Reformed Church, as they may suggest, looks decisively in this direction. To the same effect also are the plans and measures which have been adopted by the Synods and the several Classes, for the purpose of bringing the objects contemplated in the Tercentenary movement prominently before our people. Hence it has been directed that a special sermon shall be preached by each pastor to his people, on a specified Sunday, relating to the history and character of the Heidelberg Catechism, and the same subject is to be repeatedly brought to their attention during the year in different appropriate forms. Not only the pastors, but consistories also, and Sunday-school superintendents and teachers and parents, are to be enlisted in this important work. If these several plans shall be faithfully carried out, one of the particulars entering into the duty devolving upon us as a Church will be fully met.

2. This, however, does not, by any means, cover the whole of the obligations resting upon us as a Church, in view of the special privileges we enjoy. We must not rest satisfied with merely enlightening our people as to the several topics which are to constitute the particular subjects of discussion and consideration during the year before us; but we must seek to elevate their standard of piety, and to enlist their energies and efforts in the promotion of vital godliness, and the general advancement of the interests of the Redeemer's kingdom. The sermons to be preached

9

and the addresses to be delivered, as well as the prayers to be offered, if they shall be attended to in the spirit contemplated in the very appointment of the present year of special solemnities, are all intended to contribute to the promotion of this great and important end. It is felt that our people not only need to be instructed in the history, doctrines, and usages of our Church, and thus be led to form an intelligent attachment for them, but also to have awakened in them a tone of deep piety and entire consecration to the service of God. Unless this is specifically aimed at as an object to be, in a great measure, attained by the different religious observances which are to take place during the present festival year, we shall come short of the duty devolving upon us as a Church, in view of the signal privileges we enjoy.

3. But even this, in connection with what precedes it, does not entirely exhaust our duty as a Church in the highly favored circumstances in which we are placed. We are not only to seek to spread intelligence and promote a spirit of deep-toned piety among our people, but we must also strive to awaken in them feelings of true thankfulness to God for the great mercies we enjoy, such as shall manifest themselves in the entire consecration of their property, as well as their hearts and lives, to the service of their Redeemer. Hence it is wise, as well as highly proper, that, in the arrangements entered into for the purpose of carrying forward the observances of the present festival year, special provision has been made for soliciting the free-will offerings of the people to the cause of the Redeemer, and thus to afford them an opportunity to manifest their feelings of thankfulness by contributing to the various objects of benevolence. The privilege is to be extended to all, and yet the offering is expected to be free. None are to be overlooked, but nothing is to be done by constraint. This is the true spirit in which to solicit the gifts of benevolence. The objects claiming remembrance are many and various; still, those who may not be able or willing to give to all

are to be at perfect liberty to select for themselves the particular objects to which their gifts shall be appropriated. It should, however, whilst every one is to be left to his own free choice as to whether he will contribute or not, be a special object aimed at in the labors of the present year, to make every one not only feel it to be his duty, but also to claim it as his privilege, to give. In this way should we as a Church, if we will manifest a becoming spirit of thankfulness, by a united and general effort during the year before us, erect a monument of gratitude to God, worthy of the occasion, and that shall stand as a praiseworthy example to coming generations.

Our limits will not allow us to dwell further upon the particular duty devolving upon us as a Church in view of our great privileges. What has been said must suffice, and has been designed to be merely suggestive rather than exhaustive.

III. It remains yet to attend briefly to the consideration with which the observance of this duty is enforced; and this, it must be admitted, is the strongest possible.

If as a Church we are faithful in carrying out the objects contemplated in the present Tercentenary movement, we may confidently expect the most happy consequences to result to us as a branch of the true Church of Jesus Christ. The movement is one which, we are fully persuaded, if carried forward in its legitimate spirit, cannot fail to meet with the approbation of God; and with His approbation resting upon our efforts, we have every thing hopeful to expect. If we strive earnestly, not only to make our people better acquainted with the history and genius of the German Reformed Church, and with its peculiar doctrines and customs, and thus lead them to appreciate them more highly and cherish them more warmly, but also seek diligently to promote among them a spirit of fervent piety and entire consecration to the service of God, and elicit their benevolent activities in the way of free, liberal, and general contributions to the cause of Christ, we shall most cer-

11

tainly continue to live, and prosper as a Church. We shall not only increase in numbers, but also in influence and power for good. Our people will become intelligent, devout, active, and efficient servants of the living and true God. They have as strong intellects and as warm hearts as any other class of society, and all that is needed to make them powerful for good, is to bring them under proper influences. We have, then, every thing to gain, as a Church, from the faithful discharge of the duties devolving upon us in view of our distinguishing privileges and mercies.

But this is not all that is embraced in the consideration enforcing the faithful observance of our duty as a Church. A failure to discharge this duty must be disastrous to us. This view of the case is set forth, in the strongest possible terms, in the inquiry of the text. If those who lived under the Old Testament dispensation and failed to improve the comparatively scanty privileges they enjoyed, met with their just recompense of reward, how shall we escape, who are so highly favored in point of privileges, if we neglect so great salvation? Escape, in case of neglect, is wholly impossible. Our ruin is inevitable. We may drag out a sickly existence, as a denomination, for some time to come, but our eventual entire overthrow will most certainly occur. Our doom is sealed. Destruction must most assuredly overtake us.

Better also, we may still add, that we had never vowed, than that having vowed we should fail to pay. Better that we had never enjoyed our distinguishing privileges, than that having enjoyed them we should fail to appreciate and improve them. Better that we had never resolved to enter upon the solemn observances of the festal season before us, than that having entered upon them we should fail to carry . them out in their true spirit and meaning. Our privileges increase our responsibilities, and our condemnation is correspondingly aggravated when these responsibilities fail to be faithfully met.

Let us, then, dear brethren, one and all, assembled as we

12

are for the purpose of inaugurating the series of solemnities, the observance of which has been assigned us as a
Church during the coming year, enter upon them under a
deep sense of their importance and of the great responsibility which they involve. Let us endeavor to impress
ourselves with a consciousness of our insufficiency by our
unaided powers to carry forward successfully the work
committed to our hands; and let us look earnestly and confidently to Him from whom all our help must come, for His
constant presence, guidance, and assistance in all the duties
that shall devolve upon us. If we enter upon and carry
forward the work before us in this spirit, there is no ground
to fear that our labor of love shall be lost. Our hearts,
as individuals, shall be cheered, and strengthened, and
blessed; and our Church shall indeed arise and shine, the
glory of the Lord being truly risen upon her.

13

UNDYING LIFE IN CHRIST.

By PROF. J. W. NEVIN, D.D.
LANCASTER, PA.

UNDYING LIFE IN CHRIST.

By Prof. J. W. Nevin, D.D., Lancaster, Pa.

" Jesus Christ the same yesterday, and to-day, and forever."—HEB. xiii. 8.

THE text looks immediately to what goes before, though not just in the way implied by our common English version. This seems to refer the previous exhortation to the example of those who were still living, as teachers and rulers in the Church, and whose life is there characterized as having its aim or end in Christ, who is always the same. But the reference in the original is plainly not to these, but to former teachers and rulers—among them the blessed martyrs Stephen and James—men who had continued steadfast in their faith to the last, and were now gone to inherit its rewards; so that it would give the meaning better to say: "Remember them which have had the rule over you; who have spoken unto you the word of God; whose faith follow, considering the issue of their conversation or life;" that is, fixing your attention on the fact that they held the beginning of their confidence steadfast unto the end. Then it follows as an independent proposition: "Jesus Christ is the same yesterday, and to-day, and forever;" the full meaning of which, in its relation to the affecting exhortation going before, can be more easily felt than expressed, while it becomes the occasion at once also for the solemn caution in the next verse: "Be not carried about with divers and strange doctrines." The force of it in both directions will come more fully into view as we go on to consider now the great subject itself which it offers to our contemplation—THE SAMENESS, CONSTANCY, AND ABIDING PERPETUITY OF CHRIST, IN CONTRAST

17

WITH THE MUTABILITY AND VANITY OF THE WORLD IN EVERY
OTHER VIEW.

We say, of the world in every *other* view; because it is as
belonging to the world, and forming part of its life, that
our Lord Jesus Christ is here exhibited for our consideration. It is, indeed, only in virtue of His divine nature that
He possesses the "power of an endless life," to such extent
as to be the same yesterday, to-day, and forever; but still
it is not of His divinity separately considered that the text
must be understood to speak, but of His divinity rather
as joined with His humanity in the constitution of His
Mediatorial Person, through which He became joined at
the same time with our general human existence, and incorporated thus into the life and being of the world. It is not
of the Word, as "the same was in the beginning with God,"
that this declaration of unchanging sameness is made, but
of the *Word made flesh;* not of the Son of God, considered
simply in His eternal generation, as born of the Father before all time—"by whom also He made the worlds"—but
of the Son of God, born of the Virgin Mary, by the power
of the Holy Ghost, into the very bosom of His own creation,
so as to become the deepest principle of its history through
all time. It is the Man, Christ Jesus, who, in the midst of
this ever-rolling, ever-changing system of things which we
call the world, stands forth sublimely to the gazing admiration of faith as "the same yesterday, to-day, and forever."

The general relation which Christ holds to the world in
this view is twofold. He is in Himself what the world is
not, and has no power ever to be aside from His person;
but He is this, at the same time, not for Himself simply, but
for the world also, which is thus brought to find in Him its
own last end and only perfect sense. What is a relation
thus of opposition and contrast, in one view, becomes everywhere, in another view, a relation at the same time of inward correspondence and agreement. Both aspects of the
case must be taken together, to make our apprehension of
it in any way complete.

18

I. There is such a relation of opposition and correspondence, in the first place, between Christ and the world regarded *as a mere system of nature*. This is the nearest and most immediate view we can take of the general sense of the text.

It belongs to the very idea of what we call nature, that it should be subject everywhere to fluctuation and change. Things in this form are what they are not, by standing still, but by being rather in a perpetual flow. They come and go, appear and disappear, continually, in the same instant; and such stability as they may seem to have in any case is never the sameness exactly of the same things, but the same show only of different things that follow each other in restless succession. Such constancy as the world has in this form is its inconstancy. Its very being, we may say, is an everlasting ceasing to be; like the image thrown from the face of a mirror, which holds only in the vanishing process of its own perpetual reproduction, through each following moment of its apparent duration.

In this broad view, the fleeting, transitory character of the world is not simply represented to us in the more outward, palpable changes that are always taking place in the course of nature. These indeed are fraught with lessons of wisdom on the subject, which only the most careless can fail to consider and lay to heart. The rolling seasons and circling years are here full of instruction. Flowing brooks and changing forests, the flowers of spring and the colored leaves of autumn, all have a voice to remind us that the "fashion of this world passeth away." All around us, and all within us, viewed in such merely physical light, is adapted to force home upon us the thought that the world of nature is vain, and our own life, as comprehended in it, all the while hastening to an end. It is a perpetual round throughout of repetition and change, in which the whole creation may be heard falling in with that old burden of the Preacher: "Vanity of vanities; vanity of vanities; all is vanity." But it is not simply in these outward changes of form and state, we say, that the unsubstantial, unabiding character of the world, as we now have it under consideration, challenges our most thoughtful regard. For an earnestly reflecting mind, it is something which is felt to reach far beyond such appearances, and to enter into the universal constitution of nature itself.

As compared with its more ephemeral forms of existence, we sometimes think of the earth itself as abiding forever, and talk of its everlasting hills and mountains and seas; but in truth there is no room, philosophically speaking, for any such distinction as this; and when we are brought to commune more closely with the life of nature, we are made to feel that it carries with it really no force. The clouds are no more fleeting in their substance than the rocks; the flowers are of no more evanescent constitution than the everlasting hills. Nay, it is in the contemplation precisely of these apparently enduring forms of creation, that the deeply meditative spirit comes to its most overwhelming and affecting sense of the emptiness and nothingness of the world in itself considered; since the more we consider them the more all are felt to be apparitional only, phenomenal merely, and not substantial; signs and shadows, which have their proper truth not so much in themselves as in things that lie beyond them in another order of existence altogether.

In this view it is that the visible earth and heavens are so frequently employed, in the Old Testament, to represent, in the way of contrast, the eternal and immutable nature of God. "Before the mountains were brought forth," says the Psalmist, "or ever thou hadst formed the earth and the world, even from everlasting to everlasting, thou art God." All sink into insignificance before Him, and become as nothing over against His power. "By the word of the Lord were the heavens made, and all the host of them by the breath of His mouth." In all their visible grandeur they are but the outward manifestation of His invisible will, to which they owe their being every moment, and which is something infinitely greater and more enduring than themselves. "Lift up your eyes to the heavens," God says by the Prophet, "and look upon the earth beneath; for the heavens shall vanish away like smoke, and the earth shall wax old like a garment, and they that dwell therein shall die in like manner; but my salvation shall be forever, and my righteousness shall not be abolished." And again, more generally: "All flesh is grass, and all the goodliness thereof as the flower of the field: the grass withereth, the flower fadeth; because the Spirit of the Lord bloweth upon it: surely the people is grass. The grass withereth, the flower fadeth; but the word of our God shall stand forever."

But the word of the Lord, which is opposed in this way to the transitoriness of the world, is nothing less in the end, according to St. Peter (1 Pet. i. 25), than the word of the gospel itself; and in this character again it is, as we know, no outward declaration or command simply proceeding from Jehovah, but the personal Word, the divine Logos, which in the fulness of time became man for us men and for our salvation, in the person of our Lord and Saviour Jesus Christ. "All things were made by Him," we are told, "and without Him was not any thing made that is made;" and so of Christ Himself it is said, with reference to what He was for the world thus before He became man: "He is the first-born of every creature; for by Him were all things created that are in heaven and that are in earth, visible and invisible, whether they be thrones, or dominions, or principalities, or powers; all things were created by Him, and for Him; and He is before all things, and by Him all things consist."

We need not be surprised, then, to find the full force of this relation ascribed in the New Testament to our Saviour Jesus Christ, the incarnate Son of God, in the very same terms that are used to represent it in the Old Testament as holding of the infinite Jehovah Himself. What He was for the world before He became man, the

21

fountain of its life, the foundation of its being, that He continued to be also after He became man; the work of the new creation taking up into itself in this way the work of the old creation, so as to be only the fulfilment, in a higher sphere, of its original purpose and sense. Because He was the first-born of the natural creation thus (Col. i. 15–18), He became also the " beginning, the first-born from the dead," the principle of the resurrection; because all things were made by Him, and for Him, He became also the head of His body, the Church, "that in all things He might have the pre-eminence." It is as the Maker of the worlds, upholding all things by the word of His power (Heb. i. 2, 3), that, after He had by Himself purged our sins, He sat down on the right hand of the Majesty on high. In which view also the sacred writer does not hesitate to apply to Him (Heb. i. 8–12) such strong language as this: " Thy throne, O God, is for ever and ever. Thou, Lord, in the beginning hast laid the foundation of the earth; and the heavens are the work of Thy hands. They shall perish, but Thou remainest; and they all shall wax old as doth a garment; and as a vesture shalt Thou fold them up, and they shall be changed: but Thou art the same, and Thy years shall not fail." So, after His resurrection, we hear Him proclaiming Himself to St. John in the vision of Patmos: " I am Alpha and Omega, the beginning and the end, which is, and which was, and which is to come, the Almighty."

Thus is Christ in His human character itself—the Son of Man who is at the same time the Son of God—over against the whole world of nature in every other view, the same yesterday, to-day, and forever. The ages come together in His person. He is before all things, and by Him all things consist. They change, but He remains in the midst of them always the same; for through all their changes He lives and works, upholding them by the word of His power. Their mutability serves, in this way, to enforce the thought of His abiding constancy; their vanity points continually

22

to the fulness of immortal life in His person. But the relation is not one of mere outward comparison and opposition. As thus different from the world, Christ is at the
same time, as we have seen, in the most profound sense
one with the world. He is the principle, the original and
fountain, of its whole first creation; and in this character
He has entered still more deeply into its life through the
mystery of the incarnation, so as to be now the principle
within it of all that is comprehended in the idea of the
second creation. In this twofold view, then, He may be
said to redeem the world from its inherent vanity, and to
make over to it the power of His own glorious immortality.
There is such a thing, we know, as the glorification of
nature itself through union with His person, causing it to
pass forever beyond the conditions of vanity and change to
which it is subject in our present state. The body of
Christ Himself was glorified in this way when He rose from
the dead; the bodies of His people, we are told, shall hereafter be made glorious in like manner; and there is to be
at the last, in some way which we cannot now understand, a glorification also of the whole natural creation—
new heavens and a new earth (2 Pet. iii. 13)—resulting
from the victorious headship of Him who is the Alpha and
the Omega, the first and the last, the beginning and the
ending, of its universal being and life. And may we not see
how the assurance and sense of all this for faith must go to
invest even the world as it now stands with the freshness
and beauty of a new perennial life, such as it can never
possibly have in any other view? If it be in the power
of mere poetry and art, so to raise the perishable forms
of nature into the sphere of the ideal that they shall
become there in a certain sense immortal, how much
more may it not be possible for religion to make all things
luminous with the glow of a still higher immortality, by
joining them with the thought of God, and the undying,
everywhere present grace and truth of Jesus Christ!

II. This relation of Christ to the world, however, comes

into still clearer view when we ascend from the sphere of mere physical existence into the sphere of *humanity and history*, where nature shows itself joined with self-conscious mind, and the world stands sublimated to its highest sense in the free personality of man.

The mutable, perishing character of the world in this superior order of its existence is adapted to affect us with a sense of its vanity, far beyond all that we feel in considering the mere changes of nature. These last are in full harmony with the constitution to which they belong. It lies in the very conception of nature that it should be made up of endless parts and subsist by endless revolution and change. That is the law of its being, which shows it at once to be created for something beyond itself, in whose presence it is required always to vanish and pass away. But it belongs to the conception of mind that it should not thus vanish and pass away; that it should bring unity into the manifold; that it should fix the fleeting forms of sense in firm and stable duration. In the spirit of man, past and future are brought together in the power of the present—the transitoriness of time surmounted in the apprehension of the infinite. He was made, we are told, in the image and likeness of God, to be the head of the natural world and to exercise lordship over it in every lower view— to be in it and of it through his bodily organization, and yet to be above it at the same time through his intelligence and reason, disclosing within himself a new and higher order of life altogether. He was formed for immortality, and all his powers and capacities point to such glorious destination. In his life the past should not be lost and left behind, but should perpetuate itself always in each succeeding portion of time; and there should be for him, properly speaking, no death. For such an existence as his, the very thought of death is something unnatural, violent —nothing less, in truth, than the most tremendous contradiction. And, as the life of the individual man should be thus full and enduring, there should be a correspond-

24

ing harmony and deathless unity also for the life of the race. History should be but the concord of ages, meeting together in the solution of the same grand problem of humanity. Nation should join hand in hand with nation, and each generation live itself forward continually into the life of the next, to carry out and complete, in one universal sense, the true idea of a reign of truth and righteousness upon the earth.

But how different from all this, alas! do we find to be now the actual state of this higher human creation! Sin has entered into the world, and death by sin; and so death has passed upon all men, for that all have sinned. That which was formed to be the region of undying life in the world's constitution has become itself the region of mortality and change; in common with the lower nature around him, man is made subject to a vanity which was not originally his own; and it is this subjection precisely which, more than all else for the contemplative spirit, causes the whole world to seem empty and vain. That the grass should wither, and the flower fade, is no matter for sorrowful surprise; it belongs to their nature to come and go in this way; but that all flesh should be *like* grass, and the glorious estate of man as the flower of the field —that may well be a cause for sadness and lamentation. That a life formed for immortality should be found continually breathing itself out like a vapor that appeareth for a little time and then vanisheth away; that there should be room at all to resemble it in this way to the most evanescent things around us—this indeed is something over the thought of which it is not unnatural even to shed tears of grief. Well might the Psalmist exclaim: "Lord, make me to know mine end, and the measure of my days, what it is; that I may know how frail I am. Behold, Thou hast made my days as an handbreadth, and mine age is as nothing before Thee: verily, every man at his best state is altogether vanity. Surely every man walketh in a vain show; surely they are disquieted in vain: he heapeth up riches, and knoweth not who shall gather them."

This vanity reaches forth, at the same time, into the universal history of the race. It has made it to be frag-mentary, disjointed, and to a great extent fearfully cha-otic. It spoils the brotherhood of nations, and breaks the unity of ages and generations. Life is carried forward from period to period, it is true, with some sort of memory and tradition; but it is a shadowy bond at best which thus connects the present with the past, and such as proves for the living in the end only a ghostly communion with the dead. "One generation passeth away, and another gene-ration cometh," like the leaves of the forest, or as shadows that chase each other over the autumnal plain. It is the old wail of Moses, the man of God: "Thou turnest man to destruction; and sayest, Return, ye children of men. For a thousand years in Thy sight are but as yesterday when it is past, and as a watch in the night. Thou carriest them away as with a flood; they are as a sleep: in the morning they are like grass which groweth up. In the morning it flourisheth, and groweth up; in the evening it is cut down, and withereth." In this order of mere nature, those who have gone before us into the other world can be thought of only as having been gathered into Sheol, the land of dark-ness, forgetfulness, and silence; and when it is asked: "Your fathers, where are they? and the prophets, do they live forever?" the one same answer must ever be, the ques-tion itself reverberated from the hollow sides of the tomb.

In contrast, now, with all this, Jesus Christ stands out to the vision of faith as the same yesterday, to-day, and for-ever. He is so not simply as God, but also as man. The general vanity of the race extends not to His person. As He was without sin Himself, He could not come under the power of death except by His own free consent; and then it was, as we know, not that He might remain in the grave or see corruption, but that death itself should be destroyed and swallowed up of victory, through His glorious resurrec-

26

tion. In all the time of His humiliation upon the earth He could say: "Before Abraham was, I am;" and now that He reigns exalted at the right hand of God, it is but the full revelation of the majesty that lay hid in His person in the manger and upon the cross, the bursting forth again of the glory which He had with the Father before the foundation of the world. His goings forth are from of old, from everlasting; and of His kingdom and righteousness there shall be no end.

But what we need most to understand and consider is, that in all this He is not simply distinguished from our general human life in every other view, but comprehended in it also in such way as to be for it at large what He is for Himself. His relation to it in this way is more intimate, more profound, and more comprehensive than that of its natural root in the first Adam. He is within it the principle and centre of a new creation, in the bosom of which the power of the old curse is found to be broken, the law of sin and death abolished and brought to an end. There is no condemnation now to them that are in Christ Jesus. They are redeemed from the vanity of this dying world; they have passed from death unto life. Old things for them have passed away, and all things have become new. They belong even here to an economy or order of existence which transcends entirely the whole constitution of nature, the whole reign of Satan, the god of this world; in virtue of which they may be said to be sharers already of Christ's immortality, as they are destined also to reign with Him hereafter eternally in heaven. "In Him was life," we are told—life in its fontal, self-existent form; "and the life became the light of men"—was not simply the origination of their natural being, but passed over into them also as the incorruptible "word of God which liveth and abideth forever." "Because I live," the Saviour says, "ye shall live also." "Fear not; I am the first and the last: I am He that liveth, and was dead; and, behold, I am alive for evermore, Amen; and have the keys of hell and

27

of death." He is not simply the proclaimer here of an outward doctrine—a truth or fact holding beyond His own person—but the actual destroyer of death, who thus brings life and immortality to light by bringing them to pass, and so causing them to be where otherwise they could have had no place whatever. "I am the resurrection and the life," we hear Him saying—the whole power and possibility of these things for the human world: "he that believeth in me, though he were dead, yet shall he live; and whosoever liveth and believeth in me shall never die."

Holding such relation to the world, it is easy to see how Christ becomes for the life of humanity, regenerated in this way, such a power of unity in space and continuity in time as it cannot possibly have under any other form. As the deepest principle of it, He must be at the same time the most comprehensive bond of its organization in every view.

The new creation shows itself wider, thus, than all distinctions, whether of nature or from sin, that belong to the old. It joins in one the most distant nations of the earth, and tunes into harmony the physical differences and moral discords of the whole human race. "He is our peace," says St. Paul; here again not in a merely outward way as a teacher of peace, but as being Himself such a new organization of our universal human life, as, by carrying it beyond all these occasions of difference and schism to its last ground in God, causes the sense of them to be overwhelmed by the feeling of that better and far more glorious common existence, in the power of which they are thus neutralized and brought to an end. "He hath made both one"—it is said of the Gentile and the Jew—having abolished in His flesh the enmity, to make in Himself of twain one new man—so making peace; and came and preached peace to you which were afar off, and to them that were nigh. For through Him we both have an access by one Spirit unto the Father. So universally: In Christ Jesus "there is neither Jew nor Greek, there is neither

28

bond nor free, there is neither male nor female; but Christ is all and in all."

And what He is for all coexistent states and conditions of the race in this way, He is also for its successive generations in time. As He joins the nations together, so does He bind the ages into one; imparting to them, as it were, a simultaneous being in the unity of His own glorious life.

So, even in the Old Testament, the relation of the righteous to God is represented as their refuge and escape from the vanity of the world, by which they must otherwise be swept away as with an overwhelming flood. They are housed in Him securely through the ever-rolling course of years, according to that grand declaration of the ninetieth Psalm: "Lord, Thou hast been our dwelling-place in all generations." Even in Sheol the patriarchs are not dead; have not become a memory only or a name; have not vanished into Sadducean vacuity and night. They live still, in virtue of their living union with God. Hence the force of our Saviour's argument: "As touching the resurrection of the dead, have ye not heard that which was spoken unto you by God, saying, I am the God of Abraham, and the God of Isaac, and the God of Jacob? God is not the God of the dead, but of the living."

Now, however, in Christ the power of this unseen life is made to be something far more full and real for believers than it was before. The Old Testament saints had their hidden abode in God, indeed, only through Him as the everlasting Word; but it was in anticipation always of what was necessary to make their life in this form actual and complete, namely, the coming of Christ in the flesh; and so stood in the character of hope rather than in that of present, satisfying fruition. "These all died in faith," we are told (Heb. xi. 13, 39, 40), "not having received the promises, but having seen them afar off. Having obtained a good report through faith, they yet received not the promise; God having provided some better thing for us, that they without us should not be made perfect." Abraham

29

accordingly, in that uncompleted state, looked joyfully for the day of Christ (John viii. 56); and he saw it, and was glad. But the Word, which was only coming before, has now actually come; that eternal life which was with the Father has been manifested through the mystery of the Incarnation; and, being joined to it and made one with it, by the power of faith, all true Christians have in it an immortality of existence that reaches through all time. They are said to be *in* Christ; and the life which they live in the flesh is not so much their own as that which is lived into them, through the Spirit, from His undying person. "We are in Him that is true," says St. John, "even in His Son Jesus Christ: this is the true God and eternal life." To be so taken up into Christ is itself to be taken out of the vanity of this perishing world, and to be made superior to its revolutions and ages. In Christ, the dead still continue to live. This itself—and no simply outward state in any other view, whether in hades or heaven—is the true conception of their immortality. It is such an immortality, moreover, as includes in it the full power of the resurrection. "For if we believe that Jesus died and rose again, even so them which sleep in Jesus will God bring with Him." Our life now, on either side of the grave, "is hid with Christ in God; when Christ, who is our life, shall appear, then shall we also appear with Him in glory." (Col. iii. 4.)

We believe, then, in the "communion of saints," as reaching not only to those who yet live, but to those also who have died in the Lord. When the question is now asked: "Our fathers, where are they? and the prophets, do they live forever?" the answer is no longer a doleful echo simply sounded back upon us from their tombs, but a voice from heaven rather, saying: "Blessed are the dead which die in the Lord from henceforth: yea, saith the Spirit, that they may rest from their labors; and their works do follow them." We will not worship them; we may not invoke their intercession and help, as we might be glad to do if

they were still with us here on the earth; but neither will
we consent to think of them as elysian shadows only,
dwelling beyond the clouds, and in no farther communication with the Church below. They are with us still, not in
memory alone—not as having a mere fictitious immortality
in our minds, through the recollection of their words and
deeds—but as having their common home with us in Him
who is the same yesterday, and to-day, and forever. We
are come, in Him, to no necropolis simply, no voiceless city
of the dead; but "unto the city of the living God, the
heavenly Jerusalem, and to an innumerable company of
angels; to the general assembly and church of the first-
born, which are written in heaven, and to God the Judge
of all, and to the spirits of just men made perfect." We
join in waking, active worship, around the throne of God,
with the glorious company of the apostles, the goodly fellowship of the prophets, and the noble army of martyrs, as
well as with the holy Church throughout all the world. And,
at this time especially, may we not be allowed to say that
we join in worship also with the founders and spiritual
heroes of our own Reformed Zion, the end of whose conversation we are now called upon to consider, that we may be
stirred up afresh to follow their faith? Is it too bold a
thought, that in the midst at least of that "great cloud of
witnesses" with which we are surrounded from all ages in
the heavenly world, the spirits also of such men as Luther
and Zuingli, the stern Calvin and the meek Melancthon,
Olevianus and Ursinus, and that great and good prince
whose name still lives for us embalmed and enshrined in
the Heidelberg Catechism as Frederick the *Pious*, may
even now be looking down upon us with kindred sympathy
and delight, and taking part in these devotional solemnities
as their own? What is the narrow chasm of three hundred
years for the Spirit of Jesus Christ, whose wonder-working
province it is to overcome all separations both in time
and space? What are whole centuries of death, in Him
who is the true Life; the Alpha and Omega of God's crea-

tion; the vanquisher of the curse that lay upon the world through sin; who holds in His hand now the keys of hades and the grave; and in whom, thus risen from the dead and made head over all things to the Church, His saints have their common habitation and home through all generations?

III. Once more: Jesus Christ is the same yesterday, to-day, and forever, as being the *absolute fountain of all truth and reason* for men, so that there can be neither certainty nor stability in the intellectual world, under any view, except as it is ruled, ordered, and actuated everywhere from His presence and by His Spirit.

So much lies at once in the character which belongs to Him as the everlasting WORD. He is, in this view, as we have already seen, the beginning or principle, and so of course the universal reason also, of the whole creation. He is the thought of God, which finds utterance in the general constitution of the world; and He is the source at the same time of all the power of thinking in a created form, by which it is possible for this thought to be in any measure perceived or understood. It enters into the very conception, however, of all such created and dependent reason, that it should be in itself liable to error, and so exposed to variation and change; and this is a liability which, in such a world as ours, must necessarily run into all sorts of actual aberration and lapse from the truth. To these imperfections and disorders, then, whether proceeding from the weakness of nature or the power of sin, Christ stands opposed as the original, independent Logos, with whom there is "no variableness nor shadow of turning;" while He offers Himself to us, at the same time, as being here again, the only proper and sufficient complement of our wants, and the principle of all true light within us, both for this world and for that which is to come.

This vanity of our intellectual and moral life is, of all vanities to which we are subject, in some respects the most mournful and sad; for it meets us just where we know

32

there ought to be solid and stable duration—namely, in the region of *ideas*, whose very office it is to surmount the fleeting forms of sense, and to hand themselves forward in spiritual force from one generation to another. We find ourselves confronted with it, however, from all sides, through every age of the world. The thinking of men, even more than their outward working and walking, has been for the most part only what the Psalmist calls a vain show.

Even in the sphere of Christianity itself, we find no end to the differences and flowing changes of human thought. This is owing largely, of course, to the blinding and corrupting influence of sin; but it is the result in part also of what we may style the necessary limitations of our nature itself, making it impossible for us to see truth by ourselves in an absolute and universal way. Our particular thinking is comprehended always in the more general thinking which surrounds us; and this, again, moves and changes from one age to another, according to the general law of our human life. For our present state, in this way, it would seem that there can be no absolutely stationary apprehension even of Christian doctrine itself; since to be stationary is to be dead, and only that which moves has life. We know it to be a fact, at all events, that Christianity, from the beginning, has been a world of thought ever in motion, whose uniformity and continuance have been maintained only through vast oppositions and never-ceasing changes of form and aspect. The same truths have turned themselves in new phases to the contemplation of the world, age after age. Doctrines have had their history; confessions, their appointed times and spheres; churches, their different tasks and successive missions. All has come down to us through perpetual commotion and change.

But, in the midst of all this fluctuation, Christ Himself, the fountain of Christianity, remains ever the same. Even the change from the Old Testament to the New, vast revolution as it was, changed not the identity of Him who was equally the soul and the life of both. After His incarnation, He was still the angel which had been with the Jewish Church before in the wilderness; and for eighteen centuries, now, He has never forgotten for a moment His promise to be in the midst of the Church in its Christian form, through all ages, on to the end of the world. In this view He is not simply *one* in Himself, over against the manifold and the successive, as exhibited in the historical movement of Christianity beyond His own person, but He is one also for what is thus outside of Himself, a principle of unity for the Church, and the power that binds and holds it together in true catholic wholeness through all ages, making it to be still, in spite of all partial and temporary discords, the home of His Spirit, and as such, for the world at large, the only "pillar and ground of the truth."

Standing in this universal sameness of Jesus Christ, then, we will not desire on the present occasion to limit and bound our Christian sympathies by any merely partial ecclesiastical lines. Our Tercentenary Jubilee is indeed, in one sense, a denominational festival, which has for its object the new intonation of our old denominational history and life. We believe that the Reformed Church had a vocation to be, and to speak forth the confessional word that was in her at the beginning; and we cannot see that the time has come for this word to be either withdrawn or hushed into indifferent silence. Rather it seems to us, that if Protestantism itself be still necessary, then must it be for the interest of Protestantism, and so of universal Christianity also, that the great issues by which it was divided within itself at the first, should not now be thus passively surrendered and given up, but that they should be rather so maintained still, as to compel, if possible, their conciliation and settlement in a truly inward way. Only so can we hope for the catholicity or wholeness of positive faith in distinction from the pseudo-catholicity of merely negative and hollow unbelief. We are, therefore, still Reformed, and we may add also *German Reformed*. We glory, as of old, in the Heidelberg Catechism, and we are here met to festoon with wreaths of evergreen the memory of the fathers to whom it stands indebted for its origin and birth three hundred years ago. All this we willingly confess. But God forbid that we should do this now in any spirit of mere sectarian bigotry and exclusiveness, or that we should so hold our feast as to nourish and strengthen in ourselves the feeling that we alone are the Lord's people, and that beyond our confessional life there is no room to conceive either of a true Christianity or a true Church.

We mean by our solemnity, certainly, no such wickedness and folly as that. On the contrary, we will try to make this commemoration an occasion rather for cultivating in ourselves the sense of Christianity in its widest and most universal form. We will not dare to make our Catechism the full and whole measure of Christ. We will not stop short in our faith with either Luther or Calvin; we will not put our ecclesiastical fathers, whether in Switzerland or Germany, in the place of Him who "holdeth the seven stars in His right hand, and walketh in the midst of the seven golden candlesticks," and who alone is the first and the last, the beginning and the ending, of the new creation as of the old, the same yesterday, to-day, and forever. Through all human confessions, we will look to Him who is before and beyond them all, as the one glorious object of the universal Christian creed, in union with whom the Church also remains always and everywhere one—the fulness of Him that filleth all in all. This emphatically is that faith of the fathers who have gone before us, which we are now called upon and here solemnly pledge ourselves to follow — considering the end of their conversation — in opposition to all "divers and strange doctrines." With them, as with St. Peter of old, we say, now and evermore: "To whom shall we go, Lord, but unto Thee? Thou hast the words of eternal life; and we believe, and are sure, that Thou art the Christ, the Son of the Living God!"

35

We close with a few general conclusions of vast practical account suggested by the whole subject.

1. *Jesus Christ is Himself the truth and reality of the Gospel,* which He came into the world to proclaim. It is not a message of salvation simply published by Him in an outward way, "as God at sundry times and in divers manners spake in times before unto the fathers by the prophets:" it is the revelation of redemption and life for men immediately in His own person. His incarnation—the act of His coming in the flesh—was itself redemptive, and may be said to have included in itself, from the beginning, all that was needed for the full salvation of the world. It formed the true mediation between God and man, and served to bridge over the awful chasm which before separated earth from heaven. What we call the atonement in its more special sense, as wrought out by His sufferings and death, was nothing more, after all, than the irresistible, inevitable movement of the incarnation itself out to its own necessary end. Once in the world as He was in this way, there was for Him no other outlet from the burden of its curse, save that which was offered to Him by the accursed death of the cross: He must suffer in order that He might through the resurrection enter into His glory. All, however, lay in His being "born of a woman, and so made under the law, to redeem them that were under the law, that we might receive the adoption of sons." The atonement and resurrection were but the outworking energy of that eternal life which was manifested in Him when the Word became flesh. His coming into the world was at once the real bringing into it of a new order of existence, a form of life higher than all that was in the world before, which then could not remain bound to His single person, but was made to flow forth from Him, through His resurrection Spirit, as the power of a new creation in the Church also, for the benefit of His people through all ages.

This is the true, distinctive conception of Christianity, as we have it graphically set forth in the Apostles' Creed; and

36

in this sense, accordingly, we say of Christianity that it is
made and constituted literally by the constitution of
Christ's person; that it is thus not a doctrine primarily,
nor a rule of life, but a grand historical fact; and that He
is in such view the root and principle of it from beginning
to end. He is not simply the occasion of it, or the cause
of it, or the origin and commencement of it in the common sense of these terms, but He is, in the very constitution of His person itself, as the "second Adam who is the
Lord from heaven," what we may call the seminal or fontal
source of the universal new creation in this form. Christianity starts genetically from no confession, no catechism,
no outward creed—nay, with all reverence be it spoken,
not even from the Bible itself—but only and alone from
that bright Morning Star, "the root and the offspring of
David," of whom it is said, "When Thou tookest upon
Thee to deliver man, Thou didst not abhor the womb of
the Virgin; when Thou hadst overcome the sharpness of
death, Thou didst open the kingdom of heaven to all
believers."

2. *Truth,* thus, in its highest form for man is *identical with
life,* and is something to be reached and possessed only
through *living communication with the life of Christ.* As the
everlasting Word, He is the source both of the reason which
is in things universally, and also of the reason by which
alone it is possible for them to be understood. By His incarnation, more fully still, He is the revelation of God's
mind and will immediately in the sphere of our rational
nature itself. This revelation is no outward shining simply
in the way of precept or doctrine, but the light that streams
directly from what He is in His own nature and being; and
for this reason, also, it is not something to be apprehended
on the part of men by mere thought and reflection, but
must ever have for its vehicle into their minds the very
power of that heavenly life itself to which it belongs, and
apart from which, indeed, it has no reality or truth whatever.
Thus, it is not the light of Christ that is represented in the

37

Gospel, as communicating life to the world; but, on the contrary, "the *life* that was in Him," we are told (John i. 4), "became the light of men." Hence we hear the Saviour Himself saying: "I am the Light of the world; he that followeth me—makes himself one with the living Spirit of my person—shall not walk in darkness, but shall have the light of life." So St. Paul: "Ye were once darkness, but now are ye light in the Lord." To know Christ is to be in Christ; to have part in His grace in any way, is to have part in His personal being. And hence it is that all forms of His grace, the benefits which He accomplishes for His people, are spoken of so commonly not as outside gifts merely, the result of His ministerial teaching or working, but as inhering actually in His own life. "I am the resurrection and the life;—I am the light of the world;—I am the way, the truth, and the life;—I am the living bread which came down from heaven; he that believeth on me, believeth not on me, but on Him that sent me; and he that seeth me seeth Him that sent me;—He is our peace;—He is made of God unto us wisdom, and righteousness, and sanctification, and redemption:" such is the characteristic tenor of this whole glorious Gospel of the blessed God, in speaking of its own power of salvation for the children of men. ▪ All is not only from Christ, and by Him, but in Him and through Him also, as the first-born from the dead, "the beginning of the creation of God" in this new form. "God hath given to us eternal life; and this life is in His Son."

3. Being in this way the only true light, the beginning and foundation of the whole gospel, Jesus Christ must be Himself, of course, the *great argument always of the truth of the Gospel, and of His own presence by means of it in the world.* That is the nature of light: it demonstrates itself in demonstrating other things around it; and so the last proof of it in the end is only the evidence which in the first place streams forth from itself. How shall any one prove the existence of the sun, except by what the sun shows itself to be, shining in the heavens and illuminating the whole

natural creation of God? So does the Sun of Righteousness, in this new creation of which we now speak, authenticate and declare itself to be what it is, by the very fulness of its own indwelling light, with which it floods and irradiates all other things. How shall that which is itself the deepest and most comprehensive manifestation of truth in the world be rendered clear and sure by any demonstration from beyond itself? The self-revelation of God in Christ is for men the truth of all truth, the light of all light; and if known at all effectually, it must be known in and by Christ alone. Here emphatically the word holds good: "In Thy light we shall see light." This is that knowledge of which St. John speaks: "We KNOW that we are of God, and the whole world lieth in wickedness: we KNOW that the Son of God is come, and hath given us an understanding, that we may KNOW Him that is true; and we are in Him that is true, in His Son, Jesus Christ. This is the true God and Eternal Life."

4. From all this it follows that *the only true and sure way of Christian knowledge for us, at all times, is that Christological method of studying Christ and His gospel, which is set before us in the old pattern of the Apostles' Creed.* It must be so, both for practical purposes and for the ends of theological science. The art of growing in grace, and in the saving knowledge of our Lord Jesus Christ, holds especially in the habit of regarding His person with the steady contemplation of faith; for in doing so, more than in any other way, our darkness is illuminated, our affections are purified, our will is made strong; and beholding His glory, as the Apostle has it, we are transformed into the same image, from glory to glory, as by the Spirit of the Lord. But what we wish just now to insist upon more especially, is the necessary application of the same canon to the science of Christian divinity, whose object it is to expound and set forth theoretically the universal sense of the Gospel. If Jesus Christ be for Christianity what we have now seen that He is, the sum and substance personally of its whole constitution, then is

it at once plain that Christianity never can be understood or preached to full purpose, except under that historical view in which it is exhibited to us in the actual movement of His own theanthropic life and work. Our theology can never begin successfully from any other centre than that of the Incarnation; there can be no safe footing for our speculative constructions of doctrine, beyond that which is offered to us immediately in the fact of the hypostatical union, regarded as the actual basis of the new creation to which it belongs. What is the real principle of Christianity itself must be for us the real principle also of its whole apprehension and representation. We must think ourselves into it everywhere, from that living, concrete ground, or else we shall have for our thoughts, in place of it, a metaphysical abstraction only, that will not deserve to be considered true Christian theology at all. It will not do to build here on any philosophical dogma or hypothesis outside of Christ. It will not do to build, or rather to dream of building, even on the Scriptures themselves, outside of Christ; for in Him alone all the promises of God are Yea and Amen; and it is the very spirit of Antichrist to say, that they can ever be the word of God truly for any man's thought or reason, except *through* the acknowledged presence of the Word made flesh. The order is, Christ first, then the Bible; and not the Bible first, then Christ. "On this rock," our Saviour says, in answer to St. Peter's memorable confession, "I will build my Church;" and that confession, let it be well considered, is but the germ of the Apostles' Creed, as we find it afterwards unfolded with necessary development in the ancient Church.

And now, then, it is no gain, we may be well assured, but an immense loss rather, that this old order of thought has grown strange to so much of our modern theology, and that so much of our theological thinking—and along with this, unhappily, so much of our pulpit teaching—has come to move in another construction of Christianity altogether. No one who considers it properly can help feeling it to be

40

an ominous fact, that the Creed has fallen in our time so largely into disuse and neglect. It argues a falling away, unquestionably, from the old stand-point of Christian observation—which we know at the same time to be the only one, if Christ Himself be real, that can be considered either true or safe. Let it sink deeply into our minds, brethren in the ministry especially, that all right Christian theology, in the very nature of the case, must be Christological theology; and that all right Christian preaching must be also Christological preaching; and that, being so, both must be cast prevailingly in the mould of the original Christian Creeds, which are all here of one signification and sense, since in no other form is it possible to deal with the facts of Christianity in a truly Christological way.

5. One more thought, and I have done. The end of all Christian worship—the end of all Christianity for man—is *living fellowship and communion with God through His Son Jesus Christ*. What we all need, as we have seen, is not just good doctrine for the understanding, or good direction for the will, or good motives for the heart, but the power rather of a new life, which, proceeding from God and being inserted into our fallen nature, may redeem us from the vanity of this present evil world, and make us to be in such sort "partakers of the divine nature" that in the end we may be counted worthy to have part also in the resurrection of the dead. This life we can never have directly for ourselves. God hath given it to us, we are told, only in His Son; and if we are to have part in it at all, therefore, it can be only in the way of derivation from His person. It is plain, at the same time, that this derivation can never be parted from its original source in Christ, so as to become for any one his own separate property and possession. "I live," St. Paul says, "yet not I, but Christ liveth in me; and the life which I now live in the flesh, I live by the faith of the Son of God, who loved me, and gave himself for me." The life of the Christian

41

thus requires to be nourished and fed continually from that same immortal spring out of which it has taken its start in the beginning; in signification of which, accordingly, the "washing of regeneration," as it is called, is to be followed constantly to the end by the use of that other sacrament which is called the "communion of the body and blood of Christ," as showing by what aliment alone it is at last that this new existence is maintained in our souls. What the sacrament before us thus signifies and seals for our faith is the inmost meaning of Christianity, and the one great object, as we have said, of all true Christian worship.

We are here to-day, Christian brethren, in circumstances well suited to remind us of our common vanity. We are here to commune with the past, long buried, though not forgotten; and in doing so we are powerfully reminded how rapidly our years also are passing away. We shall never meet again, from all parts of the land, as we have been brought together on this joyful but yet solemn occasion. Many of us will soon be gone to join those of our own generation, whose familiar forms, still fresh in our memory, seem to flit before us, even now, amid the solemnities of this hour; and it will not be long till all who are here shall have been swept away, in like manner, into the oblivious gulf of ages. For "we all do fade as a leaf;" "our days are as an handbreadth, and our age is as nothing before God." "As for man, his days are as grass, and as a flower of the field, so he flourisheth; for the wind passeth over it, and it is gone, and the place thereof shall know it no more." And now to this private vanity, which belongs to every one of us, must be joined the sense of that public political misery, by which the earth is made to tremble beneath our feet, and the very heavens above us seem ready to collapse in one universal crash of ruin over our heads. But in the midst of all these crushing and confounding thoughts, oh, what a word is that—dying brethren in the undying Christ—which, *through* these sacramental symbols

42

of His broken body and shed blood, speaks now to our faith from His own lips!—"Whoso eateth my flesh, and drinketh my blood, hath eternal life; and I will raise him up at the last day. As the living Father hath sent me, and I live by the Father, so he that eateth me, he shall live by me. This is that bread which came down from heaven; not as your fathers did eat manna, and are dead: he that eateth of this bread shall live forever." It is the word of Him who is the Amen, the faithful and true witness, the beginning of the creation of God, and the first-begotten of the dead. Let us respond to it, from the fulness of our hearts, one and all, "Lord, evermore give us this bread."

"And now, unto Him that loved us, and washed us from our sins in His own blood, and hath made us kings and priests unto God and His Father; to Him be glory and dominion for ever and ever. *Amen.*"

43

THE

CITY AND UNIVERSITY OF HEIDELBERG,

WITH SPECIAL REFERENCE TO THE PERIOD OF THE REFORMATION
AND THE TIME WHEN THE HEIDELBERG CATECHISM
WAS PRODUCED.

By DR. C. B. HUNDESHAGEN,

PRIVY CHURCH-COUNCILLOR AND PROFESSOR OF THEOLOGY IN HEIDELBERG.

TRANSLATED BY REV. PROF. T. C. PORTER, A.M., LANCASTER, PA.

CITY AND UNIVERSITY OF HEIDELBERG,

WITH SPECIAL REFERENCE TO THE PERIOD OF THE REFORMATION AND THE TIME WHEN THE HEIDELBERG CATECHISM WAS PRODUCED.

By Dr. C. B. Hundeshagen,

PRIVY CHURCH-COUNCILLOR AND PROFESSOR OF THEOLOGY IN HEIDELBERG.

Translated by REV. PROFESSOR T. C. PORTER, A.M., Lancaster, Pa.

AMONG the territorial divisions into which the German Empire fell, there was none, at the close of the Middle Ages, which had become so enlarged, wealthy, and prosperous as the land ruled over by the Princes Palatine. Their original domain, "the so-called Chur-Pfalz," or Electoral Palatinate, lay along the fertile banks of the Neckar and the Middle Rhine, reaching out from both streams, here to a greater and there to a less distance, into the interior. The other possessions of this princely house were isolated and remote. Chief among them was the Upper Palatinate, now included in the kingdom of Bavaria, with its cities, Amberg and Neuburg. The capital of the Electors was Heidelberg, picturesquely situated at the junction of the valley of the Neckar with that of the Rhine. On a steep hill overlooking the city rose their famous castle. In 1386, Rupert I., with a spirit full of enthusiasm for science and art, had founded the University, which is one of the oldest in Germany. He bestowed on it great rights and liberties, as well as ample revenues, and cherished it with care until the day of his death, in 1390. From that time it grew in reputation as a seat of learning. Besides the main Electoral line, there were also collateral branches of the princely family, who governed smaller portions of the Palatinate territory under the title of "Palsgraves," or Counts Palatine, and were distinguished from each other by the names of the cities in which they resided,—Amberg and Neuburg, Zwei-brücken and Simmern.

When, in the struggle of Luther against Rome, the summons of the gospel had resounded far and wide, not a single country inhabited by the German race remained wholly unmoved by that event. But here and there it was a long while before the purer confession gained a decisive victory over ancient error; yea, decades of years passed by in certain places before the people were allowed to enjoy the blessings of an existence acknowledged by their rulers, a settled mode of divine worship and comprehensive ecclesiastical institutions. Among the last to be thoroughly renovated by the new spiritual leaven was the Electoral Palatinate.

True, indeed, movements of the kind had been felt on her soil in the very dawn of the Reformation. Shortly after the publication of his celebrated theses, Luther was sent, in April, 1518, as a commissioner, by the superiors of his Order, to a meeting of Augustinians in the convent at Heidelberg. Their business being ended, according to the custom of the age, a disputation was held, at which Luther put up theses and stood forth in their defence. This disputation excited a lively interest: many teachers and students of the University, and people of all classes, attended as hearers. The appearance of the bold Reformer, and his powerful words, left a deep impression: several young theologians, who at a later period came out as champions of the Reformation in Southern Germany, received then their first impulse. The new doctrine soon after began to gain a permanent foothold in a few districts. Some of the knights Palatine, among whom was the famous Franz von Sickingen, gave it protection in their territories. So, too, did the Palsgrave Lewis II. of Zwei-brücken, who abolished the mass and introduced a Lutheran order of worship. But yet the Reformation failed to find either an intellectual centre or influential political support. The former, which countries like Saxony and Hesse possessed in their universities, Wittenberg and Marburg, was wanting in the Electoral Palatinate. The University of Heidelberg stood from its origin in the closest connection with the Romish Church. The Pope, who as early as 1385 consented to its establishment, in a special bull, was, and continued to be, in its eyes, the highest authority. As regards ecclesiastical jurisdiction, it was subject to the Bishop of Worms, its spiritual advowee. Dotations from the Pope and church-endowments furnished the most considerable portion of its revenue. Not only were the teachers of theology required to be ordained clergymen and to live in celibacy, but, from the year 1439, the Cathedral of the Holy Ghost was united to the University, and, as the result, no fewer than twelve professors, as canons of that establishment, were fettered to the interests of the hierarchy by the enjoyment of handsome benefices and the possession of increased rights and liberties. At the time of the Reformation, the University had already outlived the bloom of the first century and a half of its existence. Its intellectual life was confined to the barren exercises of the scholastic philosophy and theology now falling into decay. The teachers were more concerned about the maintenance and enlargement of their privileges than the adoption and diffusion of new elements of culture. Between the years 1523 and 1533, it is true, the celebrated philologists, Hermann von dem Busche, Simon Grynæus, and Jacob Ulicyll exerted a quickening influence. These men had been called, in order to revive at Heidelberg the study of classical antiquity, which had formerly thriven under the care of Rudolph Agricola and Conrad Celtes. But the prevailing spirit was against them, and in a brief while, one after the other, they forsook the Palatinate University. Thus, as a whole, with but few exceptions, it stood decidedly antagonistic to the Reformation. The consequences soon became apparent: the students deserted in large numbers and flocked to Wittenberg and the neighboring Tübingen. In the year 1526, the rector complains that the attendance at the University was falling away on account of the spread of Lutheran opinions, that there were more teachers than students, and hence that every effort should be made to put down the innovation.

The evangelical cause found also no solid support in the ruler of the Palatinate. From the year 1508 to 1544, the reins of government rested in the hands of the Elector, Lewis I. He did not, indeed, belong to the unconditional opponents of the Reformation; nay, he was even favorably inclined toward it in a certain degree, and on several occasions showed his disapproval of violent measures against Luther and his followers. At the Diet of Worms he had come out boldly on the side of the Reformer, and in 1532 had taken an active part in the conclusion of the religious treaty at Nuremberg. But actual sympathy with the new movements did not harmonize with his natural disposition, which preferred peace and quiet in his own house as well as in the empire. When, therefore, the two young teachers Brenz and Billican, in 1522, made an attempt in Heidelberg to expound the New Testament after the manner of Luther, they were silenced on account of the uproar caused by it among the other theologians of the University. In the territories of the knights, however, the Elector permitted what he could not prevent, and held to his position of moderate Catholicism till the day of his death. The successor of Lewis was his aged brother Frederick II. By reason of a long life full of change and adventure, and his close personal connection with the house of Hapsburg, he had hitherto taken but little interest in the religious questions of the age. In the mean while the doctrines of the gospel had so spread among the people of the Palatinate, that it was plain the new Elector could not put them down by force. His nephew, the strong-minded Otho Henry, had already, in 1542, introduced Lutheranism into the

Neuburg portion of the Palatinate, and had also joined the league of Smalkald. For this step he had been driven from his land and subjects by Charles V. and the Duke of Bavaria, and was now living at the court of Heidelberg. Yet here he only labored the more zealously to influence his uncle in favor of the evangelical cause. On the 28th of March, 1545, the Elector applied to Melanchthon for counsel. But before his advice concerning church-measures in the Palatinate was carried out, the impatience of the people outran the hesitation of the prince. On Sunday, December 20, 1545, as the mass was about to be celebrated in the Church of the Holy Ghost at Heidelberg, the whole assembly began to sing with loud voice the hymn, *"Es ist das Heil uns kommen her,"* composed by Spreter of Kotweil, and long in use among the signals of the Reformation. Anxiously did the Elector now hasten to follow the course marked out by public opinion. He decreed a new order of worship, and, at the Christmas festival of 1545, the Holy Supper was administered according to the evangelical mode in the chapel of the castle, and received, not by himself, it is true, but by his consort, a niece of the emperor, and the attendants of the court. On the 3d of January, 1546, the same thing was done in the Church of the Holy Ghost for a large assembly of the people.

By this act, the greatest of the German Electorates, headed by its prince, took at length a decided stand in favor of the Reformation. But the event occurred at an exceedingly critical period; for scarcely had a year and a half gone by, when the league of Smalkald, formed by the evangelical princes and estates of Germany for the defence of Protestantism against the emperor, fell to pieces, in consequence of the battle of Mühlberg, fought April 25, 1547, and its members were obliged to feel the weight of the imperial anger. Frederick, too, although not a member, but only a supporter, of the league, came in for his share of hard words. Unlike John Frederick 'of Saxony, he was not, indeed, deprived of his Electoral dignity, but the progress of the Reformation in the Palatinate suffered a severe check. He could not escape the necessity of enforcing the law relating to faith and worship, published by the emperor,—the so-called *Interim*, notwithstanding it led to the restoration of popery. Clergymen who resisted the impeperial edict were immediately deposed. Still, when, in the monastery of the Franciscans at Heidelberg, after the sermon, the prior began once more to celebrate mass in the presence of Frederick, who appeared there in princely pomp, many of the congregation, and some of them persons of distinction, withdrew. Among the students and younger teachers of the University, indignation at this relapse into a custom that had just been abandoned was lively and general. The University as a whole, however, stood yet on the side of the papacy, and when the great majority of its members, in spite of the fine threatened by the rector, refused to join in the Corpus-Christi procession on the 20th of June, 1549, and styled the order of the rector an impious mandate, and the procession an idolatrous profanity, an appeal was made to the government for protection against "the rebellious youth." For four years the Palatinate remained under the heavy pressure of the Interim, until the Elector Maurice of Saxony had curbed the dangerous encroachments of the emperor and wrested from him the treaty of Passau. Only then did the courage of Frederick begin to revive. After the conclusion of the religious peace at Augsburg, in 1555, he expressed a more positive sympathy with the evangelical cause, and on the 11th of November of the same year opened, in the old convent of the Augustins at Heidelberg, the so-called Sapienz-Institute, for the education of preachers. He also issued orders for the introduction of a new ecclesiastical system, and in 1556 afforded an asylum in his dominions to those professors of the faith who had been driven from England by the persecutions of Queen Mary. Three days before his death, on the 26th of February, 1556, he, together with his wife and forty persons of the court, partook of the Holy Supper in both kinds.

Hailed with joy and confidence by the evangelical portion of his subjects, whose favorite he had long been, the palsgrave Otho Henry now ascended the Electoral throne. Under this prince, who was distinguished in every respect, the Reformation in the Palatinate went forward with new vigor. As early as March, 1556, he issued a decree that for the future nothing but the pure doctrines of the gospel should be preached in the land, and that all papal and *interimistic* superstition should be put away. The ecclesiastical system projected in the time of his predecessor was pushed on to completion. The persons intrusted with this work were the court-preacher Michael Diller, the Heidelberg pastor and professor Henry Stoll, and the superintendent Dr. John Marbach, invited from Strasburg for the purpose. In the summer of the same year there followed a special visitation of the churches of the whole country, that occupied a period of seven weeks. The Electoral commission, which acted in the matter, drew up a report not favorable in all its particulars. It states that in many places the people were not in the habit of attending church, or at most but few of them, and for this cause catechetical instruction had to be discontinued; indeed, that many of the laity, and those, too, who regarded themselves as particularly intelligent, held the holy sacraments in low esteem. It is easy to see that such demoralization among the people was a result of the long continuance of a vacillating policy in ecclesiastical affairs. The report of the visitors gave rise to a series of plans for the thorough renovation of the Church of the Palatinate, by the founding of schools, by the introduction of better arrangements in the University so as to train up well-qualified ministers, and by the careful management of church-property, so that the pastors would not be reduced by the pressure of want to the condition of peasants.

This praise must be awarded to the excellent Otho

53

Henry, that he entered with full spirit upon the execution of these plans. A church-court (*Kirchenrath*), consisting of two clergymen and an equal number of lay members, was instituted, to exercise a general supervision over the ecclesiastical interests of the country. But the chief and most earnest care of the Elector was to reanimate the life-less University, and by a reform of the faculty of theology to secure a supply of evangelical preachers, for lack of whom the Palatinate was still suffering in the highest degree. He, therefore, energetically devoted himself to the work. A written scheme, drawn up by Philip Melanch-thon, in 1545, at the request of Frederick II., was the basis upon which he proposed to build. In 1557, Melanchthon, who was brought into the neighborhood of Heidelberg by the religious conference at Worms, received an invitation from the Elector to pay him a visit, and, during the ten days between the 20th and 31st of October, communicated to the noble prince a great deal of valuable counsel in regard to the important measure. Through the changes thus effected by Otho Henry, the University, which had hitherto been accustomed to pride itself on its ancient rights and immunities, lost much of its corporate independence. The controlling influence of the Elector was felt from this time forth, especially in the appointment of professors. Its great privileges had been productive of so little good for so long a period, that the resumption of them by the state could not but result to its advantage. In no other way was the regeneration of its inner life and spirit possible. In the plan of reorganization there is everywhere manifest an effort to harmonize its course of instruction with the reformation that was taking place in the Church. The Elector, in his preface to the new constitution, says of the faculty of theo-logy, that "it is not supported, ordered, and provided for in such a manner as accords with the plain teachings of the holy gospel, which the eternal, merciful, gracious God, for the sake of His dear Son, has again revealed and made clear in these last times;" also, "that the salaries, in the

54

present years of scarcity, are too small to obtain suitable lecturers (*Legenten*)," and hence he "felt himself bound, by reason of the official obligations resting upon him as Elector, to remove these defects." And, in truth, the decay of the faculty was only too evident. At that time it consisted of but two professors, whose instructions were attended by a very insignificant body of students. One of them was Henry Stolo, favorably inclined to the doctrines of the Reformation; the other, Matthew Keuler, an avowed papist, who, because, by his own confession, unwilling either to put away his concubine or to marry her, was compelled to vacate his chair in the University. Now the faculty was to consist of three ordinary or regular professors. "All of them shall maintain such a walk as becometh Christians, and by no means busy themselves with useless, knotty questions, fanciful opinions, intricate sophisms, or prolix digressions and overstrained comments, but expound the text with care and judgment, illustrate it, if necessary, with approved writings and brief extracts, solve doubts that may arise in the most skilful manner, and leave every thing else to the *scholastics* and their *readers* (*Legentes*) and followers; as to doctrine and ceremonies, they must abide by the Augsburg Confession and its Apology, together with the new church-order." "For the support and strengthening of the true doctrine and religion of Christ, the annual sum of 1200 florins shall be appropriated to such adults who, already well versed in the sciences, may be willing to apply themselves earnestly to the study of theology, so that able preachers and ministers of the divine word may be thus secured."

By these measures the Church and University of the Electoral Palatinate were delivered from the unsettled condition in which they had so long been, and fully organized according to a general plan. But, in carrying it out in all its details, a vast deal yet remained to be done, and some of the most formidable difficulties only came clearly into view when the magnanimous Otho Henry, after a brief reign of three years, was snatched away by an unexpectedly sudden death on the 12th of February, 1559.

A retrospective glance shows us that the lateness of the Reformation in the Palatinate afforded the people time for a gradual transition from the old faith to the new. But this, on the other hand, brought with it the serious disadvantage that the first organization of its ecclesiastical affairs occurred just at the period when the struggle of German Lutheranism against the growing influence of Calvinism was raging with the greatest violence, so that the Church of the Electoral Palatinate could not avoid being entangled in all the vicissitudes of the conflict.

During the years in which the Evangelical Church of Germany was taking shape under the moulding power of the Augsburg Confession of 1530, no organization of the kind existed as yet in the Palatinate. But just as Frederick II.—and after him Otho Henry—began the work, the quarrel between the school of Melanchthon and the strict adherents of Luther in regard to the doctrine of the Lord's Supper produced a division into parties which extended throughout the whole of Germany. To which side the two Electors inclined is evident in the simple fact, that, from the year 1545, Melanchthon was their confidential adviser in all measures of reform. When, therefore, the Church of the Palatinate placed itself upon the basis of the Augsburg Confession, that version of it was, of course, chosen which best accorded with these circumstances,—viz.: the one altered by Melanchthon, who, in 1540, undertook the task of amending the original, especially in the article on the Lord's Supper, so as by this means to bring about a better understanding between the adherents of Luther and the Swiss Reformers. The expression, in the version of 1530, which says that the body and blood of Christ are really present *under* the form of bread and wine, in that of 1540 he had so changed as to read, that *with* the bread and *in* the wine the body and blood of Christ are really communicated; he also struck out the positive rejection of the opposite doctrine. With this Confession of 1540 fully agrees the following declaration concerning the Holy Eucharist in Otho Henry's church-order of 1556: —"The Supper of Christ is a sacrament and divine symbol, in which Christ, really present, offers and communicates to us with bread and wine His body and blood." In this same instrument there is also found no trace of exorcism in connection with baptism; nor is there any indulgence shown toward the retaining of images in churches, as in Saxony and elsewhere. On the contrary, as was the case in all Reformed communities, their removal is earnestly enjoined, and Otho Henry in person advocated the measure when opposition to it had created a disturbance among the citizens of Heidelberg. In harmony with the endeavor to bring about a better state of feeling between the parties at variance upon the doctrine of the Lord's Supper, the Elector not only suffered men who were notoriously in favor of the Swiss view to remain in his neighborhood, but even gave them places in the University and high offices in the state. Finally, the conduct of the Palatine princes toward the members of the Calvinistic churches of foreign lands fully corresponds with the spirit of Melanchthon and his school. Scarcely had the first half of the sixteenth century expired when these churches and their congregations in England, France, and the Netherlands were exposed to bloody persecution. Multitudes of persons, young and old, were put to death; whilst others, compelled to abandon home and country, sought refuge in Protestant Germany. But in not a few of the strictly Lutheran states the spirit of bigotry prevailed to such a degree that the strangers, under the name of "Sacramentarians," either met with an extremely cool reception or were driven away with merciless severity. In certain cases the hatred against them was so strong that the martyrdom of these Sacramentarians was styled "a martyrdom of the devil." Far different was their experience in the Palatinate. Inspired by warm Christian sympathy, Frederick H. and Otho Henry gave free admission to the fugitives. Men of talent among them received employment in the University of Heidelberg, and, when the number of the exiles increased, they were allowed the privilege of forming themselves into congregations after their own pattern. All this taken together shows that the Evangelical Church in the Electoral Palatinate deviated in many points of doctrine and practice from the strictly Lutheran Churches in the rest of Germany, and based its polity upon different principles. Under the influence and counsels of Melanchthon it assumed from the first a kind of middle position between Luther on the one side and Zwingli and Calvin on the other. It was difficult, however, to maintain this middle position with firmness. Those who thought and felt with Melanchthon, or the so-called "Philippists," were accused by the strict Lutherans of a secret leaning toward Calvinism, and, for this reason, were regarded with greater hostility, almost, than the real Calvinists themselves. They were generally forced to acknowledge that, in spite of their peaceful bearing, all hope even of the slightest concession from the opposite party had to be given up. The cruelty exhibited in the cases mentioned above also tended to deepen the feeling of estrangement, and the two branches of the Reformation springing from Luther continued to diverge more and more. Princes who—like the noble Otho Henry, Lutheran as he originally was—were accustomed always to look at the common interests of Protestantism and measure its wants from a higher point of view, could not but lose all respect for a movement which seemed to live only by theological quarrels and the putting down of every thing in the Church that differed from its own standard. Compared with the spirit of Lutheranism thus dwarfed and crippled, that of the Reformed Church now stood in bold contrast. For a long time established in German Switzerland, and just then presided over by such venerable men as Henry Bullinger and Peter Martyr Vermili, its golden age began with the settlement of Calvin in Geneva, by the moulding power of whose creative intellect it took, in a few decades of years, the form of the Evangelical Church of Western Europe. A *Church* in a much fuller sense of the word than the Lutheran, the consciousness that all its energies were needed in the work of social regeneration prevented an undue predominance of theological doctrine, and kept within bounds the polemical tendencies of the mere school. By her practically peaceful spirit in the midst of controversy, by her unshaken faith under heavy trials and bloody persecutions, by her brilliant array of great scholars and men of marked character both among the clergy and laity, she could not but awaken admiration in minds not clouded with prejudice, even in those parts of Germany originally Lutheran. The Palatine Electors saw, moreover, that if the University of Heidelberg was to enter upon a successful career, and not sink down again into the bondage of a dry, barren scholasticism, they must not look to the philosophical circles of the fatherland only, when selecting professors to fill up gaps in the various faculties, but have regard also to the rich intellectual forces then available in Reformed Protestantism abroad. In 1557, so many distinguished foreigners had already come to Heidelberg, that the mind of Melanchthon was filled with anxiety,—and not without good reason; for, after his death in 1560, the Reformed party acquired new strength. A final transition to this side was an event confidently anticipated, here and there with concern, but in other places with joyous hope.

The decisive step was at length taken by Otho Henry's successor, Frederick III., of the Simmern line of the Palatine house, and the formation of the *Heidelberg Catechism* was the chief act by which the adoption of the Calvinistic creed was fully consummated.

Without going into detail, it is enough to say here that the new Elector devoted himself to his grand work with rare conscientiousness and fidelity. He is, beyond dispute, the greatest ruler of whom the Protestant Church of the Palatinate can boast, and, as regards piety and loyalty to the faith, is a shining example of an evangelical prince.

His leanings toward the Reformed Confession began rather early. As a pensionary of France, he was brought into close relations with the people of the West, and his son John Casimir was permitted to reside at the French court until the family succeeded to the Electoral dignity. By this intercourse with France, Frederick was placed in a position to understand the value of the movements there set on foot for the development of the Reformation. Hence, as soon as he came into power, men of the Reformed party, like the Frenchman Francis Hotoman, and the Strasburger Jacob Sturm, appeared at his court on business relating to church-affairs. The nature of the matters discussed on this occasion, and the direction in which Frederick's mind was then already moving, may be inferred from a letter written by Hotoman to Bullinger in Zurich, and dated Heidelberg, March 16. He says, "I cannot tell you any thing new yet, because I am waiting to see what a certain country will bring forth. God grant a propitious hour to the birth! Calvin, Farel, Beza, are filled, at these prospects, with the brightest hopes for the future. But the ultimate decision depends upon the strength and influence of the several parties who surround the new Elector. Hence my talk shall be of them."

During the early years of the reign of Frederick III., a remarkable body of eminent men, differing from each other in many respects, had been brought together in Heidelberg, partly as members of the University and partly as officers in Church and State. Some of them were natives of the Palatinate, whilst others, especially the theologians, had been invited from abroad or had come hither of their own accord,—a few in the time of Otho Henry, but most of them since the accession of Frederick. As regards their relations to religion and the Church, they form three or four distinct groups,—Lutherans, Philippists, and Reformed,—who are again subdivided into Zwinglians and Calvinists. At the head of the Lutheran party stood Tilemann Hesshus, born at Wesel. He had taken a degree in Wittenberg, and Melanchthon, without being well acquainted with his character, had given him a recommendation, in January, 1558, to the chancellor of the Palatinate, Minkwitz; in consequence of which he not only obtained the first place in the faculty of theology, but was also appointed general superintendent and member of the church-council (*Kirchenrath*). His bitter and disgraceful quarrel with Klebitz soon gave reason for regret that such an extremely violent zealot should have been called to such an important position. In Paul Einhorn of Nordlingen, whom Frederick had put into the second theological professorship in March, 1559, Hesshus found an active coadjutor; but he did not remain long in Heidelberg. At the court, the Lutheran cause was advocated by the court-judge (*Hofrichter*) Erasmus of Venningen, a man of great personal dignity and honorable bearing, but withal fanatical in his religious views. In the same class must be ranked also Otho Henry's chancellor, Von Minkwitz, who, on account of his wealth, office, and skill in public affairs, wielded an extensive influence. Finally, in the territories of the knights, where, as is well known, the Reformation struck root far earlier than in the rest of the country, the attachment to the doctrines of Luther was very strong among the clergy, the nobles, and the people.

To the group of the Melanchthonians or Philippists belonged Henry Stoll, or Stolo, a native of the Palatinate. From 1526 he was a pastor in Heidelberg, and in his later years a professor in the University at the same time. In 1556 he had already reached the age of sixty-seven, having adhered faithfully to the evangelical confession through all its varying fortunes. Highly beloved on account of his peaceable character, and esteemed for his eloquence in the pulpit, he died in 1557, while superintendent in Heidelberg. But the chief strength of the Melanchthonians lay in Michael Diller, formerly prior of the Augustinian convent, and after that preacher in Speier. Thrice banished from this free city by command of the emperor, he went in 1548 to the canton of Basel, but in 1553 was employed by Otho Henry as court-preacher, and in 1556 accompanied him to Heidelberg, where in 1570 he died, leaving behind him an enviable reputation. Closely allied with him were three counts of the house of Erbach. Count George, who had received his religious education at Geneva under Calvin himself, was invested by Frederick with the highest dignity in his gift, that of grand steward of the household (*Grosshofmeister*), and his brothers, Eberhard and Valentine, were like him prized as able and conscientious servants of the state. The chancellor of Frederick, Christopher Probus, a native of the Palatinate, held similar opinions in regard to theology and the Church. He was distinguished for administrative ability and the large extent of his legal and general culture.

As decided Zwinglians may be named the secretary, Stephen Zierber, a relative of Melanchthon; the eminent teacher of law, Christopher Ehem; and the Brandenburger, William Klebitz, deacon in the Church of the Holy Ghost. The most prominent leader of the party, however, was Thomas Erastus (*Liebler*), a Swiss, who in 1558 entered the service of Otho Henry as family physician and professor of medicine, and since then had risen to great influence. In Erastus remarkable natural gifts were united with a fiery zeal, and he was one of those persons who everywhere find adherents and seek after them. In theological matters he was well versed, and for this reason was made a member of the church-council (*Kirchenrath*). Against Hesshus he took a bold and open stand, and went to considerable trouble in order to bring men of his own way of thinking into the faculty of theology, and that, too, not without success.

Called to Heidelberg as extraordinary professor in 1557, and thus, in advance of Hesshus, the earliest to appear on the stage in the armor of Calvin, was Peter Boquin, former prior of the Carmelite monastery in Bourges. Driven from France on account of his religious faith, he preached for a while to a congregation of French exiles in Strasburg, and from thence came to the Palatinate. The next strong pillar of the Calvinistic party was Wenceslaus Zuleger, a Bohemian by birth, who had studied theology and jurisprudence in Geneva. So highly was he esteemed by the Elector Frederick, that in 1560 he appointed him, then only twenty-nine years of age, president of the church-council, over the heads of the older members. One of the first acts of Zuleger in his new office was to invite to Heidelberg a man who soon took a very prominent position in the Church of the Palatinate,—Caspar Olevianus. Born at Treves, Olevian studied jurisprudence at Bourges, and afterward theology at Geneva under Calvin, and at Zurich under Bullinger and Peter Martyr. In 1559 he returned to his native city, and began to preach there the evangelical doctrine. This led to a sharp collision with the Catholic clergy, which ended with his being thrown into prison. Freed from his bonds by the interposition of the Palatine prince in January, 1561, he was yet condemned to banishment. Before the close of the year he accepted the post of teacher in the Sapienz-College at Heidelberg. Soon after he was transferred to the third theological professorship, and thence, in a short time, to the pulpit and a place in the church-council. In all the measures of reform projected by the council he took a lively interest, and by his great ability and zealous labors won the entire confidence of the Elector. Early in 1561, Emanuel Tremellio, a learned Italian who had come over to the Reformed Church in Switzerland, was appointed to the chair vacated by the Lutheran, Paul Einhorn, as Professor of Old Testament exegesis. About the same time, Peter Dathenus, a Netherlander of Ypern, became tutor to the princes, and not long after, a member of the church-council. But in the month of September, 1561, the theological faculty acquired one of its most distinguished ornaments in Zacharias Ursinus, a native of Breslau. For seven years a favorite disciple of Melanchthon, he had, during a second residence in Zurich and Geneva, shown a decided leaning to the doctrines of Calvin and entered into close fellowship with Peter Martyr. The aged Reformer, having received an invitation to a professorship in Heidelberg, recommended in his own stead the young Ursinus, who by his extensive learning and unwearied diligence in the twofold office of rector of the Sapienz-College and professor of theology, as well as by his quiet, peaceable spirit, soon rose high in public esteem. In the few years following, the Calvinistic party was increased by the arrival of Lambert Pithopäus of Deventer, Francis Junius of Bourges, Daniel Tossanus of Mompelgard, and Girolamo Zanchi of Alzano.

The calling in of so many strangers created some dissatisfaction. But the object of the Elector—which was to reorganize the Church after the Reformed pattern—could not be attained in any other way. The views of the men thus brought together in Heidelberg did, indeed, differ in regard to many important matters. For example, the desire of Olevianus to introduce the Calvinistic form of church government was shared by none of the other parties, and his plan only found support from the strict disciples of the school of Geneva. By the Zwinglian Erastus it was violently assailed. But in opposition to extreme Lutheranism, which by the overbearing conduct of Hesshus had lost all credit, Melanchthonians, Zwinglians, and Calvinists united as one man; and from this union, through the joint labors of Ursinus and Olevianus, sprang a common formula of faith, given to the world in January, 1563,—the HEIDELBERG CATECHISM.

64

THE SWISS REFORMERS.

By DR. HERZOG,

ERLANGEN, GERMANY.

TRANSLATED BY H. HARBAUGH, D.D., LEBANON, PA.

THE SWISS REFORMERS.

By Dr. Herzog, Erlangen, Germany.

Translated by H. Harbaugh, D.D., Lebanon, Pa.

WHAT place have the Swiss Reformers in a collection dedicated to the memory of the Heidelberg Catechism? True, this work has also been valued and used as it deserves in the Swiss Church, not only in German but also in French Switzerland, and is still in use in several cantons. But the Swiss theologians have in no way had part in its formation. Still, the production of this distinguished doctrinal work is nevertheless to be traced back to an impulse which proceeded from the Swiss Reformers. With this book, Germany has returned with usury that which it had received from Switzerland. It may, therefore, be allowed a Swiss theologian to express the thanks of his fatherland for this divine gift from Germany, by here presenting to his readers a brief sketch of the fathers and founders of the Swiss Church, which may at the same time be regarded as a witness of that unity in the Spirit, which binds together all Reformed Churches.

When we speak of Swiss Reformers, we do not wish to imply that they were all of Swiss origin: on the contrary, the majority of them were immigrated friends. Œcolampadius was by birth a Palatine (from Weinsberg, which became part of Wurtemberg in 1504); Berthold Haller, the Reformer in Bern, was a Swabian; Erasmus Ritter, Reformer in Schaffhausen, was a Bavarian; Leo Juda, the friend and assistant of Zwingli, was an Alsatian. Of those men who introduced and founded the Reformation in French Switzerland, only Viret is a Swiss by birth, from

Orbe in the canton of Vaud: strictly speaking, even he cannot be called a Swiss, since Vaud was only in the later years
of his life joined to Switzerland. The same is true of the
other actors in French Switzerland; since in the case of all
these countries the rise of the Reformation, and their union
with Switzerland, are cotemporaneous. In the fact that so
many foreigners are found among the Swiss Reformers, we
may see reflected a peculiarity of Swiss life in general,
without which the prominent position which this country
occupied in the Reformation of the sixteenth century
could not well be explained. The geographical position
of Switzerland, connected with the susceptibility of the
nationality of the Swiss people, and their aptness for cultivation, furnish the ground of its living rapport with the
adjoining countries, whence also it received manifold elements of cultivation and living incitement: it became,
namely, an asylum for those who were persecuted for the
sake of the gospel. Eminent men from Germany and
France found in Switzerland spheres of activity, or could
secure such, from whence they could send back a salutary
influence upon their fatherland.

It is, however, always worthy of notice, that the man on
whom depended the whole movement, who gave it the
direction which it has since maintained, and which others
have prosecuted, was by birth a Swiss; and it is not to be
denied, whatever may be said to the contrary, that Zwingli
developed himself into a Reformer independently of Luther.
In the early part of his public life, the religious falls somewhat behind the humanitarian and political forces, in his
activities. Yet even in the first years of the sixteenth
century he had received words from the lips of his teacher,
Thomas Wittenbach, which fell like a gleam of light into
his soul,—namely, that the death of Christ is the only ran-
som for the sins of men. These words, more immediately
designed to refute a writing of the Bishop of Basel in the
year 1503, and uttered in an academic disputation, led the
keen-sighted young man to look upon monkery and the

Catholic sacraments, from that time forth, with somewhat different eyes. The same Wittenbach was accustomed to say that the time was not far distant when the philosophical theology (in the stiff forms of which his own instructions moved) would be set aside, and the old doctrines of the Church, as they are laid down in the Scriptures and in the works of the Fathers of the Church, would be restored. Such and similar expressions were seed-thoughts, which afterwards brought forth rich fruits.

Animated by a desire to read the New Testament in the original, Zwingli in the year 1513 began the study of the Greek language. In the two following years he turned more decidedly away from the philosophy and theology of the wranglers, as he says, and made up his mind that he must let all that alone, and seek to learn the mind of God purely from His own simple word. "Then I began to beseech God for His light, and the Scripture became much more easy to me." (Works, ed. of Schultz & Schulthess, i. 79.) His connection with Erasmus, which began about this time, served him not only in his humanistic studies, but through Erasmus his attention was also called to a fundamental error of the Catholic religion,—namely, that which consisted in seeking salvation of creatures. A Latin poem of Erasmus on the invalidity and perversity of saint-worship, as practised in the Roman Church, deeply impressed his mind in regard to this point. His opposition to the worship of saints connected itself in his mind most immediately with the idea of God as the absolute causality, and the only source of all salvation. Thereupon he had a conversation with Capito, in Einsiedeln, in the year 1516, when both of these men agreed that the papacy must be overthrown. But neither in Glarus nor in Einsiedeln did he assume a directly polemical position. In opposition to the idolatrous worship of Mary, of which Einsiedeln was the centre for Switzerland and adjoining countries, he insisted that Christ is the only Mediator. He appeared polemically when he aided in silently removing the inscription, "Here is full absolution from guilt and punishment for all sins," from the church in Einsiedeln, when he commanded the nuns in the abbey, instead of singing the customary matins, to read the New Testament, and allowed them even to leave the convent. There can, therefore, be no doubt of the fact that Zwingli was not turned into the track of the Reformation by Luther. On the other hand, it lay in the nature of things that the appearing of Luther involuntarily inspired him with courage, and also rendered the people of Zurich receptive toward the Reformation. In general, Zwingli only appeared as Reformer, with full decision, after his call to Zurich: there he found the δος μοι που ϑω—the place on which to stand.

With other Swiss Reformers, as, for instance, with Œcolampadius, we find more of Luther's influence, and greater dependence on him. Œcolampadius, as he himself acknowledges, in a work published in 1519 (Canonis Indoct.), had his attention called to Luther originally through his Sermons on the Ten Commandments, which appeared prior to 1517. The effect of this work upon his pious mind was thenceforward to make Christ appear more glorious, the gospel holier to him, so that, setting aside all self-sufficiency, he ascribed all good to Christ, to himself little, yea, nothing. The rising of Luther against Tetzel, which followed, confirmed Œcolampadius in his good opinion of this dauntless man of God. From that time forth he acknowledged that he had learned of Luther that our righteousness consists in the forgiveness of sins. (Bucer to Myconius, April 23, 1534.) As Brigitta monk, he expressed himself in plain words—which his friends against his will made public—in favor of Luther; and in his work on Confession, which he had written in the convent of Altenmünster, he celebrated anew Luther's great merits. Calvin, independent as he stands before us, was fully conscious of his dependence on his great predecessor, and expressed himself to that effect. "Multum illis debemus omnes," he was accustomed to say. This calls to mind the words of Wellington in regard to Napoleon I.: "We must all learn from him." In his doctrine of the Lord's Supper he sought to reconcile the truth which lay at the foundation of the Lutheran doctrine, with the positions settled through the Swiss Reformation, and subscribed the Augsburg Confession in the sense in which its own author had explained it; that is, he subscribed this confession as it stood in the edition of the year 1540. In his publication against Pigius, 1543, he openly declared that through Luther's service and labor the purity of the gospel had at that time been again restored. To Bullinger he expressed himself (Nov. 25, 1544) that he would still acknowledge Luther as a servant of Christ, even though he should denounce him (Calvin) as a devil. This, as is well known, was not to be feared. It is reported that Luther, on the appearance of Calvin's Treatise on the Lord's Supper, should even have said, "If Œcolampadius and Zwingli had from the beginning expressed themselves in like manner, they would never have fallen into such extended disputations." These words, reported by Petzel in his narrative of the sacramental controversy, be they authentic or not, in either case, as J. Müller (The Evang. Union, p. 328) says, correctly express what is substantially the true state of the case.

In every effort to secure merit for ourselves, the first condition is to acknowledge the merit of those who have gone before us. This the Reformers of Switzerland did; and even in the heat of the unhappy sacramental strife they did not forget it. It is not to be disputed that they conducted themselves in that controversy with much more propriety than their renowned opponent. The fact that they, notwithstanding all their agreement with him, still held substantially to their own course, resulted from various causes. Above all, the reformatory problem was far-reaching, and neither by Luther nor his cotemporaries was it on all sides perfected; so that work enough still remained for others. Then, also, not all spirits are formed after one and the same type; and our Reformers had their own peculiar spiritual individuality; they had followed a peculiar process of development: this exerted a moulding influence on their conception of Christianity, on their theological and churchly activity. The character of the people from whom our Reformers proceeded, and the nation in which they wrought, are here also to be considered. In relation to the reigning differences with Luther and his disciples, our Reformers held forth the principle—which was, it is true, at that time altogether new—that those differences do not set aside and destroy the harmony in essentials, and hence should not disturb peace and fellowship between both these Churches. Luther, on the contrary, on account of the bad temper in which·he found himself since the Wittenberg disturbances, committed the great mistake of exalting the article concerning the Lord's Supper into a fundamental article, and of denying to the Swiss Reformers, who deviated from it in their teaching, all claims to a Christian faith. How faithfully his adherents followed him herein is satisfactorily known. That principle, however, which was set forth by our theologians, has in the later civilized world carried off the palm of victory.

Regardless of all that, down to the present day, has been offered in the way of objection, we may with all correctness contend that in reference to the *formal* principle of the Reformation, the authority of the Holy Scripture, an essential agreement exists between our Reformers and those of the Lutheran Church. Though Zwingli and Œcolampadius, in their discussions of the relation between the Word and Spirit, sometimes express themselves in a way which might induce the belief that too much room is made for subjectivity, they are still separated by a deep chasm from the fanatics of that time; and the boldest explanations of Œcolampadius in regard to this matter evidently accord with Augustinian principles. Just as these principles find their limitation and relative rectification through others of the same teacher, so the same rule holds good in regard to Œcolampadius, and also to Zwingli.

The exegetical labors of both these men, among which those of Œcolampadius on the Old Testament have even received from Gesenius flattering acknowledgment, show in the most decided way their estimation of the written word. In general, a very strong impulse was given to Scripture explanation, and even to criticism on the text, which proved a healthy check and balance to the later Protestant scholastics. The substance of what Zwingli and Œcolampadius have said in regard to the relation of Scripture and Spirit, we can comprehend in the proposition, that the written word of God can be understood and explained only through the same Spirit by whom it was originally dictated. Calvin has the credit of having placed this matter in its true light. He who has explained all the books of the New Testament, with the exception of the Apocalypse, as also the greatest number, and those the most important, of the Old Testament, and that in such manner and way that his commentaries are still a pattern of correct exegetical symmetry, and in which all the elements of healthy biblical explanation accord,—he has also established the proper relation of Scripture and Spirit (in the Institutes, book i. chap. vii.); he has introduced into the Protestant theology, if not the idea, still the doctrine, of the witness of the Holy Ghost, which only later (in the seventeenth century) was taken up into the sphere of the Lutheran theology. This witness of the Holy Spirit he has apprehended and described in its essence, its significance and extensive bearings, with accustomed clearness, circumspection, and profound insight, and has accurately defined the boundaries beyond which fanaticism begins.

Still, if on the one side our Reformers have been charged with a fanatical over-estimate of the subjective spirit, and a depreciation of the written word of God, the opposite charge has been made against them from the other side, as though they had adhered to a slavish dependence upon the letter of the word, and had sought to impress this stamp upon their Churches. This was associated with tradition:

and it was held that our Reformers in principle occupied in reference to it an altogether different position from Zwingli. It was therefore contended that the Lutheran principle in regard to the Scripture was only negatively regulating, in this sense, that every thing not directly contrary to Scripture must be allowed its force and value. The Swiss Scripture principle was regarded as a positive one, in the sense that every thing which could not be shown as directly contained in Scripture must be rejected. This was more particularly so defined that Luther was content to regard the so-called middle matters, which in the Scriptures are neither commanded nor forbidden, as without obligation, whilst the Swiss rejected them. This distinction, however, does not hold good. Zwingli, for example, to whom mostly reference is made, does not wish absolutely to reject the command concerning fasting, although no explicit word of Scripture is found enjoining it, but desires to leave fasting to each one's free will. (In his work on Liberty concerning Meats. Works, i. p. 12.) He wishes, first, only a diminution of the many Catholic holy days. (Works, i. p. 317.) In the beginning he did not wish the convents unconditionally abolished, at least not for such as, on account of poverty and sorrow of life, remained inmates of them; only they shall have no other rules than the rules of Christ. When organs were set aside, with which in Zurich for a time all singing was suspended, Zwingli stood on the ground that all this was not easily reconcilable with Scripture. The same holds true of the images, which were regarded as wholly forbidden in Scripture. Besides, Zwingli was careful that the people, before the images (the Lay-Bibles) were taken from them, should be properly instructed. In the same spirit he expressed himself against the radical abrogation of infant baptism, because no express word of Scripture excludes this baptism. Thus, he set forth the principle that where there is no clear word of God there is room left for a certain freedom. In the preface of his Liturgy of the Holy Supper, he remarks, in relation to the "accompanying" ceremonies, "Herein every Church has its own opinion." So also he retains much of the old ritual in that Liturgy. He defended the making of the cross, also the mass-dress of the priests; he also at first retained the covering of the head, which has since been set aside even in the Catholic Church. (De Canone Missæ Epicheresis, Op. iii. p. 111.) Not Zwingli, but a certain party, which in the same work (loc. cit. p. 119) he opposes, was anxiously wedded to the letter: "God has not designed to bind us to outward circumstances. The outward order is in our power. Christ celebrated the Supper in a room or hall; Paul, in a temple in the presence of a large assembly, &c. Above all ought we to guard ourselves against the spirit of small strife; for here the word holds good, 'Knowledge puffeth up, but charity edifieth.'" In general, Œcolampadius was of the same mind. Very beautifully and correctly does he say, in his Pastoral Letter of 1527, "The human traditions we may in part reject, in part follow; in so far as faith and love are not prejudiced, there is no danger at hand if even the fundamental sense of the Holy Scripture is not fully rendered. Hence we must not on account of such matter raise strife, or disturb charity." The French, it is true, were more rigorous; but Calvin soon receded from his first puritanical severity, which had induced him in 1538 to resign his position in Geneva, because the council, at the instance of the Bernese, restored again the use of the baptismal fonts, and unleavened bread in the great Church festivals; nor would he, in 1538, have resigned his place on account of these matters, if he had not recognized in these innovations an encroachment of the State and a violation of the rights of the Church.

As regards the *material*, or *material* principle, of the Reformation, even a superficial glance at the writings of our Reformers shows that they with all force and decision taught "forgiveness of sins and salvation by faith in Jesus Christ, and that it is not to be found in the satisfaction and merits of works." (Words of Œcolampadius, in his Disputation held in Basel, 1523.) They were therefore charged, as well as Luther and the theologians of his Church, by the Catholics, that they designed to abrogate all works. Great as is the agreement in this respect between the Reformers on both sides, it is nevertheless clear that the Swiss manifest a tendency peculiar to themselves.

Catholicism rose historically from the corruption of the Christian consciousness through the elements of the Jewish and the heathen religion, which, conquered by Christianity, in that way perpetuated their life in the bosom of Christianity itself. If Catholicism were to be fundamentally conquered, it would be necessary to attack it at both these points. Hence the Reformation problem took form according as the Jewish-Catholic or the Pagan-Catholic was most directly taken as the point from which to make the onset. Whilst Luther directed his attack more immediately against the Jewish phase or feature of Catholicism, and accordingly protested against the Catholic idea of sanctification by works, and placed justification by faith in the foreground, Zwingli, taking his position in the idea of God's absolute causality, and holding to only one source of salvation, lifted his voice more immediately against the Catholic deification of creatures. Both of these men aimed at establishing the truth that men are made partakers of salvation through the pure grace of God in Christ. Both wished to solve the question, through what means man's attainment of salvation is mediated. In this endeavor Zwingli went back to the objective idea of God,—not, however, led by the speculative interest to learn what God in Himself is; but he would learn what God is for us,—for us who desire to be certain of salvation. The question in which Zwingli felt fundamental concern was, not how all that is was determined through the absolute causality of God, but this: how man, in his consciousness, determined through his need of salvation and atonement, stands related to God as to the only source of salvation. Zwingli put the question thus: Who saves man, God or the creature? whilst with Luther the question is, much rather: What at, or in, man saves him, faith or works? This difference manifests itself clearly in the manner in which both these men were drawn into their polemical course,—Luther through the abuses of indulgences, that is, through the extreme judaizing righteousness by works; Zwingli through the idolatrous abomination of saint-worship, against which, in his explanation of the concluding words (Works, i. pp. 266–301), he directly presents the proposition that God works all things in us,— that we are nothing except through His will. Hence he comprehends the catholic disorder in general under the one point of view which regards it as a darkening of the Christian consciousness before God, the only source of salvation. In this the other Swiss Reformed theologians in general are in agreement with him. Hence the mass is throughout represented as idolatrous; hence, also, Farel treats justification by works itself as something idolatrous, in the theses which he set forth at Basel, 1524: "Whoever hopes to be saved and justified by virtue of his own works and merits, and not through faith, he exalts himself, and, blinded by unbelief, makes himself God." So very severely was, what is matter of subjectivity, referred to the objective.

With Zwingli, the principles which pertain to *absolute predestination* are chiefly connected with this same mode of view. For Zwingli was—what, moreover, has only again become known within the last several decades—a strict predestinarian, and has expressed his supralapsarian views in even stronger terms than Calvin, who actually regarded Zwingli as having gone too far in regard to this dogma. The other Swiss Reformers, as is known, also adhered to this doctrine, and this in the supralapsarian sense; so Bullinger, who did not, it is true, in his confession, the Second Helvetian, suffer this dogma to come forward in its highest aspect. Also Peter Martyr, and others. More mildly than the rest did Œcolampadius express himself, holding fast only to the kernel of the matter, in the

reply which he wrote to the question addressed to him in
1530 by the Waldensian George Morel: "Our salvation
comes from God, our ruin from ourselves." But the other
Swiss Reformers, as well as Œcolampadius himself, were
primarily led, in the formation and carrying out of this
doctrine, by a speculative interest. With Calvin this is so
clearly not the case that it is unnecessary here to speak of
the matter. Nor is this the case with Zwingli. True, his
predestination hangs together with his idea of God, and is
an efflux of the same; but that with which he most immediately concerns himself is to exclude human merit, that he
may show that the salvation of man is the work of divine
grace. It is also to be kept in view that the positions of
Zwingli on predestination have no pantheistic background.
However much he follows Picus of Mirandula, whom he
had already studied in Glarus, in holding forth prominently
the absolute causality and immanence of God in the world,
so much on the other side does he hold fast to the transcendence and free personality of God.

From the same view of Catholicism above illustrated
flowed the original Swiss *doctrine of the Lord's Supper*, as we
find it in Œcolampadius and Zwingli. Only when so viewed
can the one-sidedness, incompleteness, and relative incorrectness of this presentation of the doctrine be explained.
As, namely, on the Lutheran side there had not been in
this respect a sufficiently decided break with Catholicism,
this had to be supplied, if the mission of the Reformation
was not, in an essential point, to remain unfulfilled. Thus
there came into existence a form of doctrine which fully
cleared out, it is true, the Catholic leaven, but at the same
time shot beyond the mark, in lowering the Lord's Supper
at last to a mere act of profession, by which its significance
as a means of grace for the communicant himself was more
or less sacrificed; and this was in another form again a
Catholicizing error. When Luther says that the fundamental evil of the mass consists in this, that through it
something is to be given to God instead of something

78

being received from Him, something similar finds place in
that doctrinal view: first of all there is, of course, a testimony to be given to the congregation; before the congregation, and then further before God, a confession of faith in
the atoning death of Jesus is to be made. It is, moreover,
not to be overlooked that Zwingli and Œcolampadius did
not stop short in this form of the doctrine. Even in their
earliest writings on this subject we find sympathies, and in
the later ones more than mere sympathies, with a view
which ascribes to the Lord's Supper the value of a means
of grace, by which it is taught that a self-communication
of the exalted Saviour to the believing soul is effected
according to John vi. This form of doctrine, we may say,
Œcolampadius had practically realized, when, in the Church
agenda prepared by himself in 1529, it was ordered that
the Lord's Supper should be celebrated in rotation monthly
in each of the four principal churches in Basel; so that to
this day a celebration of the Lord's Supper is conducted
every Sunday in one or other of the principal churches.
This would have no meaning if the Lord's Supper were
merely an act of profession. As regards the particulars of
this doctrinal view, Œcolampadius has given the tropical
explanation of the words of institution more correctly than
Zwingli. Starting out with the fact that in Aramaic the
copula are not found, and, further, following analysis,—
as when we say of an image of Calvin, This is Calvin,—he
placed the trope in the word "body," a mode of interpretation which, in general, Luther has sanctioned, when not
used in reference to the Lord's Supper. Calvin has the
honor, in regard to the Lord's Supper also, of having perfected, illustrated, rectified, and brought to consummation
the Reformed form of doctrine. With this it is not said
that his representation stands above all fault, especially in
what relates to his view of the working of the glorified
humanity of Christ in the participant; but the excellency
of his mode of teaching on this point consists in the fact,
that, with all his adherence to the Reformed type of doc-

trine, he assigned to the matter of profession its place of proper subordination to the symbolical interpretation, and placed the self-communication of Christ in the foreground, by which he suffered the essential in the Lutheran doctrine, which, as we have said, Zwingli and Œcolampadius also knew, to come to its full right; on which account many members of the Lutheran Church of that period, and later, even down to our time, have decidedly agreed with him.

The assertion has been made, that there is in the Reformed Church, as distinguished from the Lutheran and Catholic, an original tendency toward the *separation of Church and State*, which tendency would naturally have to be traced back to the impulse which proceeded from the Swiss Reformers. By this some design to express a censure ; others intend it as praise. This is not the place to discuss this question theoretically; but we must only say this much: that to the Swiss Reformers, as also to the Lutheran, a separation in the sense in which it has since been attempted, and in part realized, lay remote from their minds, in the same way as did the idea of that religious freedom which stands therewith connected. Zwingli had even no idea of any kind of independence and self-dependence of the Church; rather he lets it disappear entirely in the State; he makes no effort in any way to obtain for it a separate position. The council of two hundred in Zurich passes for him as Synod; and he will know absolutely nothing of a church discipline administered by the Church itself. To Œcolampadius, on the contrary, belongs the merit of setting forth the independence and self-dependence of the Church, in part theoretically, and in part also practically, at least in the particular of church discipline, the realization of which he zealously sought to bring about. This is only the more meritorious as in this respect he stood over against Zwingli, and even in Basel fell upon manifold opposition, which placed unconquerable obstacles in the way of the full realization of his principles. Very worthy of consideration are the words which he wrote to his friend Zwingli in reference to church discipline :—"Insupportable as anti-christ does the government become, when it robs the Church of its respect: Christ has not said, if he will not hear, tell it to the government, but, tell it to the Church." In this respect, among the Reformers of German Switzerland, Œcolampadius approaches most nearly to those of French Switzerland. Among the last, as to this tendency, Calvin stands forth prominently. In the Institutes he has treated at length, and in a very positive manner, of the independ-ence and self-dependence of the Church; but in practice he has contented himself with an incomplete application of his principles, as he himself says, taking into considera-tion the troublous circumstances of the times. Into the foreign Churches which were forming under his influence he ever infused principles, and breathed a spirit, which, under the co-operating influence of peculiar historical cir-cumstances, have provided for many of these foreign Churches a greater independence and self-dependence than was to be found in Geneva itself.

All our Reformers were anxiously concerned to bring about a *reformation in morals;* for it is known to every one how very much the morality of all classes of the people had degenerated, up to the end of the Middle Ages, in all the countries of European Christendom, and how even the ecclesiastics, the lower as well as the higher, and up to the very highest, seem to have been intent, through their own example, to goad on the people to contempt for moral laws. The Reformers kept this condition of things firmly in view. As they were decidedly dogmatic, so they were also strictly practical. They made Christianity to be felt as a principle of true renewal and regeneration for the general life of the people, as well as for individual life. They set in motion a force which still lives on, and which especially in the age of the Reformation brought forth the most blessed fruits. We have here not merely Geneva in our eye, where the transformation was specially marked, so that Farel confessed that he would rather be the last in

81

Geneva than the first elsewhere,—for here the contrast with the previously prevailing dissoluteness appeared especially striking,—but the same is true, in a greater or less degree, of all the other cantons that became Reformed, where no such heroic measures had been plied as in the fearfully corrupt Allobrogian town. But such a moral purification of the general life could not, in the existing circumstances, be effected unless the state would lend its castigating arm; and the fact that the state interested itself in the moral practices of the people, is, in a great measure, owing to the constant urging of the Reformers.

In this respect, as in general in every thing which belongs to the founding and confirming of the Reformation in the different Reformed Churches of Switzerland, we have occasion to admire the manifold wisdom of God (πολυποίκιλος σοφία, Eph. iii. 10), which located each one in exactly that place *where he might find the field of labor which was best adapted to his peculiarities.* In regard to this, a few words in conclusion.

Among the Reformers of German Switzerland there was none so well fitted to introduce the Reformation as Zwingli. This we may confidently assert without undervaluing the rest. Œcolampadius, it is true, possessed important gifts and knowledge, but he lacked the courage to take the initiative,—that energetic propulsion for which Zwingli is distinguished. The same is true of the other Reformers of French Switzerland, who, besides, lacked the other gifts and knowledge necessary to such a prominent position. On the other hand, there was no canton so well adapted to become the birthplace of the Swiss Reformation as the canton Zurich. Here there was no man in any way cele-- brated to take up the gauntlet against the Reformer; no university stood forth as shield-bearer of the old church-affairs. The diocesan bishop resided in distant Constance, whose personality, moreover, just at that time did not command much respect. Besides this, the people of Zurich, on account of their spiritual susceptibility, on account of their courageous character mostly, we may say, were predisposed toward accepting and carrying' through the Reformation. The aptitude for the Reformation had extended in Zurich into the highest circles; and thus Zwingli found among the most influential members of the government men who entered in the most zealous manner into his views, and rendered him the most important aid in his endeavors to realize them. We may take any view we please theoretically in regard to the relation of Church and State, this much is certain, that in the then existing circumstances it was of the most decided significance for the success and spread of the Reformation that it was first taken up at a definite point in the peculiar national life, that is to say, in the State organism. In this way it was able at that time to become a historical power. Moreover, Zwingli, beyond all others, was fitted to advance the spread of the Reformation. He united unwearied activity, inexhaustible energy, with great versatility and knowledge of human nature. It is not to be denied that he did not always lay hold of the right means for the attainment of his end. The gospel was not to be helped to victory by the civil sword. On the bloody field of Cappel, on the 13th of October, 1531, he suffered for his error, and expiated it through the bloodthirsty vengeance of the Catholic cantons. His words, that the firm position of the Reformation could only be secured by the shedding of blood, he fulfilled in a different sense from what he intended, by his death, and in so far his death is certainly a martyr's death. From that time forth, as the Catholic Church was spreading by the reaction, new conquests were not to be expected; it was now necessary to provide for the securement of what had been won, to confirm, purify, and firmly establish it. This was the mission of Bullinger, which he also fulfilled in an excellent manner,—better than Zwingli, whose gifts belonged to another intellectual sphere, could have accomplished it. Bullinger united much firmness and perseverance with wisdom and prudence, and with special love in his treatment of men. He represented well his office in its relation to the Church abroad, exerting, namely, a most decided influence upon the puritanical opposition which was forming itself in England. In theology he occupies a far less prominent position than Zwingli; but the Zwinglian ideas appear in him clarified, brought back to their .proper measure, and made more fruitful for the Christian community.

The same man who in so fortunate a manner introduced the Reformation in Zurich would in Basel certainly have soon spoiled every thing, and dug away the ground from under his own feet. The people of Basel, although susceptible of cultivation, and not at all unreceptive toward the Reformation, were still not possessed of that elastic plasticity which belonged to the Zurichers, and which made that people capable of becoming the basis upon which Zwingli carried out his plans. In addition to this, the Catholic Church in Basel was well represented, partly by the Bishop of Uttenheim, who also inspired personal respect, and partly by the University and the many learned men connected with it,—above all, by Erasmus, which last had only the more power to prevent a truly evangelical Reformation as he had declared himself in favor of a moderate Catholic Reformation, by which, according to the judgment of many, he appeared in some measure to meet the demands of the times. Œcolampadius was the man, in these circumstances, everywhere to hit the right vein, and to conduct himself in accordance with the existing state of things. He contented himself at first with a very modest position; outwardly small results did not weary his patience. He knew how to suit himself to the circumstances, to accommodate himself to the divine hand, and to await His help, without compromising the truth or dishonoring himself. His gift of popular presentation enabled him to work upon the mass of the citizens in whom the Reformation had its proper root; his scientific cultivation fitted him as academic teacher; and excellently well did he use the professorship committed to him, to carry forward the struggle in the academic department. Thus, we know that his disputations in 1523, his lectures on Isaiah in 1523 and 1524, did certainly assist in the introduction of the Reformation as much as any of his sermons. Nor in Bern would Zwingli have been in his proper place. Here all the indulgence of Berthold Haller was needed, in order that the hand might not be withdrawn from the work. He had to endure what even Œcolampadius would have found hard to bear; and yet on this uncultivated soil he obtained the victory for the Reformation earlier than this was accomplished in the learned and renowned university city of Basel.

The Reformation of French Switzerland, which proceeded from Bern, was a more than adequate remuneration for the injury suffered by German Switzerland in consequence of the battle of Cappel. Among the French Reformers Calvin stands out by far most prominently. However, this man, in so many respects celebrated, would nevermore have been fitted to break the way for the Reformation, and to introduce it. For this he was by nature far too timid and unsocial. He loved quiet and retirement, that he might give himself up undisturbed to his researches; and it is well known that he was only by force retained in Geneva, through Farel, who threatened him with the wrath of God if he did not, in a time of so great need, give his aid to the gospel in Geneva. Farel was the right man to break up this hard fallow ground. For this was needed his *furia francese*, by which we by no means deny that he often transcended the bounds of that which is allowable and proper, and lost sight of the preacher of the gospel. Calvin, on the other hand, was fitted, by all his peculiar gifts, to render service in the second period of the Reformation,—that is, at the time when it became necessary to establish, regulate, and carry forward what had been won. He was a powerful organizer for the Church, in the administration of its discipline, and powerful in the systematizing of its doctrinal conceptions. The theological labors of Zwingli stand related to those of Calvin in the same way as the strugglings of the manifold ideas of a gifted youth do to the labors of a ripe man, who, without ignoring his youth, seizes the substantial ideas which so struggled, holds them fast, sets them in order, dresses them out, winnows and further improves them. In a general way, among all the Reformers Calvin stands absolutely first. Luther exceeded him in geniality, but he stands far beneath him in all that relates to the power of comprehending religious truth, and its logical, systematic arrangement and representation. That Calvin, through his theological labors as well as through his personal inworking upon the foreign Churches, has exerted a far-reaching influence, need here only be stated.

The two men who composed the Heidelberg Catechism, pupils of the Swiss Reformers and personal friends of Calvin, Bullinger, and others, have continued their work on German soil, and have so firmly established it on this soil that it has, until the present day, victoriously outlived the assaults of opposing confessionalism, and has rendered to the Reformed of German tongue, in all lands, that help which may be expected from a work founded on God's word, through living, believing erudition.

MELANCHTHON,

AND

THE MELANCHTHONIAN TENDENCY IN GERMANY, AND ITS RELATION TO THE REFORMED CHURCH.

By DR. EBRARD,

ERLANGEN, GERMANY.

TRANSLATED BY REV. W M. REILY, A.M., MERCERSBURG, PA.

MELANCHTHON,

THE MELANCHTHONIAN TENDENCY IN GERMANY, AND ITS RELATION TO THE REFORMED CHURCH.

By Dr. Ebrard, Erlangen, Germany.

Translated by W. M. REILY, Tutor in the Theological Seminary at Mercersburg, Pa.

§ I.

INTRODUCTION.

MELANCHTHON, the greatest of the learned coadjutors of Luther in the Reformation of Saxony, is rightly claimed by the Reformed Church, beside Zwingli and Calvin, as the third of her Reformers, and especially as the founder of the German Reformed Church. It is true he was identified from the first with the Lutheran reformatory movement. It is true, also, that Zwingli had already exerted a powerful influence upon Southern Germany, of whose importance but few at present form a correct conception.* It is further true that the first developing activity of the Reformed ·Church on the Rhine (particularly in the Palatine Electorate under Frederick III.) is to be attributed in a great measure to the agency of decided disciples of Calvin.† But Zwingli's

---

* Zwingli's writings spread just as rapidly and extensively as those of Luther, in Swabia, Franconia, Bavaria, and the Alsace. Thus, for example, it is an established fact that, immediately after its publication, in Nürnberg alone three hundred copies of his "Auslegung der Schlussreden" (July, 1523) were sold. Distinguished men of Nürnberg, like *Albert Dürer*, were zealous, decided, and steadfast adherents of Zwingli, in respect to the doctrine of the Lord's Supper.

† Cf. Sudhoff's Ursinus und Olevianus. (Elberfeld.)

original influence in Swabia and Franconia was soon undermined through the Lutheran controversy on the Lord's Supper, and the feeble remnants remaining in the Tetrapolis (Strasburg, Memmingen, Constance, and Lindau) were all afterward assimilated to Lutheranism, and connected themselves with the federation of the Augsburg Confession; whilst the influence of Melanchthon and his pupils, which was at home in the Palatinate and there prevailed from the beginning, passed over and associated itself with that of Calvin. And, in fine, the rest of the German Reformed Churches which afterward sprang up in opposition to the exclusive Lutheranism circumscribing itself in the Form of Concord, are in reality nothing else than Melanchthonian elements, which were violently thrust out of the Lutheran Church; which, however, with their separation from the latter and connection with the Reformed Church, naturally experienced the new and moulding influences of Calvinism.

By reason of this historical position of Melanchthon, especially on account of the influence which, through his pupil Ursinus,* his theology exerted upon the composition of the Heidelberg Catechism, it is no more than right that, in its Tercentenary Celebration, a grateful glance should be directed to Master Philip, and a share of our attention be devoted to the relation which he and his school sustained to the Reformation on its Reformed side and the Reformed Church.

§ II.

MELANCHTHON AS OPPOSED TO ZWINGLI.

Originally, when Luther and Zwingli were engaged in controversy, Melanchthon took a decided stand on the side of Luther, and was as little prepared as he to concede the doctrinal claims of Zwingli. The Zurich Reformer, so fre-

---

* Cf. *Gillet*, Crato von Craffstein und seine Freunde. (Frankfort on the Main.) Part i. pp. 6–9.

quently and so badly misunderstood, correctly laid down as his fundamental thesis, that the Lord's Supper is not a *repetition*, but a *memorial*, of the death of Christ.* It was with this antithetical reference that he used the word "memorial;" and according to his view, its meaning is not limited to a dry mental commemoration, as opposed to a living embracing and possessing, but it implies the deepest and most earnest activity of faith in reference to the atoning death of Christ, as the central object of faith. Pertaining to the words of institution, he had from the beginning, and on a good exegetical basis, satisfied himself that what is mainly intended is a believing reference back to the death of Christ.† The Saviour does not speak of a body which He presents in the bread, but of His body which He gave over to death for the forgiveness of sins, and of His blood which He poured out. Zwingli's whole method of viewing the contents of faith, which was pre-eminently an objective one,—that is, his making not so much *our* faith *in* the work of Christ, as the historical work of *Christ* itself, the doctrinal centre,—constrained him to consider the sacramental signs and transactions not so much abstractly or in reference to what they are in themselves, as in their direct and chief reference to the great centre of our religion, viz., Christ Himself, thus as things whose value consists in this alone, that they point to Him. From the start he was led mainly to oppose the error, that the sacraments, in contradistinction to Christ, had any independent value, or that they were intended in their way to complete the sacrifice and work performed by the Saviour. When Zwingli spoke of the body and blood of our Lord, which the communicant received, he contemplated, of course, the *true* and *real*, *i.e.*, the *historical* body and blood of Christ. The body offered on the cross, and the blood there shed, are, in

* Schlussrede, xviii. 1523.

† Cf. his Auslegung Schlussrede, xviii. Opp. Zwinglii, ed. Schuler et Schulthess, vol. i. p. 234.

the sacraments as in the word, made over to the believer, so that he participates in the benefits of Christ's sacrifice. Here it did not occur to Zwingli to discriminate between the mystical union, that bridal relationship of the soul to its Lord, the life-union of the centre of the believer with the person of Christ,—a union which, it is true, is not one of space, but one which transcends all limitations of space, and yet is in the highest sense of the word real, —and believing on Christ.* He did not bring out prominently and emphasize the fact that in the Holy Supper a life-union with the person of Christ is realized, because with him this was presupposed in the idea of faith; and when Luther, through a false exegesis, wanted to force upon him the assertion that the bread was, or contained, the *glorified* body of Christ, and that the *physical* or *oral manducation* of this body effected the *forgiveness of sins*, Zwingli withdrew only the more decidedly to his original fundamental maxim: that in the Lord's Supper we are concerned with the *crucified* body of Christ, and the believing remembrance of Christ's *death*, as the sole ground of pardon.

As Luther viewed faith on its subjective side,—*i.e.* the faith of the individual as opposed to the Church as an institution,—and at the same time had his attention directed to the fanatical sects of that day, he had a presentiment, if not a clear conception, of the necessity of a counterpoise to a subjectivism which overleaped itself. And this seemed to him to be met in "the sacrament of the altar," regarded as it was in the Middle Ages, where the Church, it was supposed, as a power standing above the individual, confers a benefit upon each member, which could not be obtained independently of it, in virtue of a personal faith alone; thus a benefit which is specific, in itself unattainable by faith, still conveying an actual bless-

* For proof of this, see my "Dogma v. h. Abendmahl, u. seine Geschichte. (Frankfurt.) Vol. ii. p. 88 ff. et pp. 103–109.

ing only to the believer, yet something with which he is supplied only by the Church. Luther (1520, de captiv. Bab.) stripped the medieval doctrine only of the scholastic theologoumenon of Lanfranck, viz.: only the properties of the bread and wine remain. At the same time he adopted the doctrine received from Cardinal Cambray:* that the substances of the bread and wine remained; still the substances of the glorified body and blood of Christ were united with these, and together with them, in precisely the same way, were eaten and drunk physically and orally. This theory Luther never abandoned.† He did not refer the Lord's Supper primarily to the death of Christ, but to a union with the glorified Saviour, which he regarded as a union of our *body* with Christ's glorified body. With this cherished theory he came to the words of institution, and interpreted them in its favor. They had a figurative meaning, of course, but his explanation of them was quite artificial. Confining his attention, it may be said, exclusively to the first four words, *this is my body*, he assumed that a synecdoche was here employed, so that of the indefinite subject, *what I hold in my hand*, it is said, "it" (as to one of its ingredients) "is the body of Christ," without at the same time disclosing the fact that, so far as the other ingredient is concerned, it was bread. It is just as if one were to say, *this is beer*, whilst it is a *mug containing beer.*

---

* As Luther himself tells us. Opp. (ed. Fen.) ii. fol. 262 b.

† During the transactions of the Wittenberg Concordia, he inserted in his Instruction the following, as Melanchthon termed it, clear and succinct "summa" of his views on the subject:—"The body of Christ is truly eaten in and with the bread, so that *what the bread effects and suffers, the body of Christ effects and suffers;* thus it is distributed, masticated, and swallowed." When the attention of modern Lutherans is directed to this expression, they would evade its force by saying that it is obscure. But, on the contrary, it is remarkably perspicuous; and when Luther undertook to present his views "in summa," he certainly knew what he was about to say. But those who explain it as an assertion of only momentary significance, which finds its corrective in others, expose themselves still more; for in his *Kl. Bek. v. Abendm.* (1544) Luther *literally repeats* this statement as the last expression of his convictions in reference to the doctrine of the Lord's Supper.

But Luther overlooked the fact that such breviloquences occur only where the hearer expects, or is accustomed to find, a particular kind of material in a particular kind of vessel. And when he further taught that the body of Christ, invisibly present in the bread, is exhibited as a sign and seal of pardon, two things were forgotten: one, that an invisible substance cannot be a sign and seal; the other, that there is no causal relation between the forgiveness of sins and the oral manducation of the body of Christ. And when, finally, he taught that unbelievers also received the body of Christ in a physical way as a sign of pardon, he forgot that he thus destroyed his own conception of a sign and seal, and that the glorified body of Christ is a living organic one, which could in no wise be and enter where Christ's Spirit was not present.

Now, untenable and full of contradictions as was this residuum of the medieval doctrine of transubstantiation, which Luther retained, it was originally adhered to with zeal by Melanchthon. This was owing in part to the moulding influence of Luther, as also to Melanchthon's own pious deference toward all the teachings of the Church which did not evidently conflict with the doctrine of justification by faith. He did not look upon the sacraments as sacrificial ceremonies which atoned for sin,* but as the *signs* of that forgiveness of sin, which was procured through the only sacrifice of Christ.† Yet he did not regard the bread as a sign of the crucified body of Christ, but held that the glorified body of Christ, invisibly present in the bread, to be eaten in the ordinary physical way, was a sign of grace and of pardon, resulting from the sacrifice of Christ on the cross, and now applied to the individual communicant.‡

---

* Loci of 1521. De partic. mensæ.—Nec participatio mensæ justificat, sed fidem confirmat. In his Com. on the Epis. to the Romans: Non remittit noxam manducatio corporis Domini.

† Loci. De Signis. Baptismus nihil est, participatio mensæ Domini nihil est, sed testes sunt και σφραγιδες divinæ voluntatis erga te. Nostra imbecillitas *signis* erigitur, ne de misericordia Dei inter tot insultus peccati desperet.

‡ Quam non potuit dubitare Gedeon, quin victurus esset, cum tot signis con-

He further regarded Lanfranck's theory of transubstantiation as an adiaphorous human theologoumenon, but not as an absurdity. The presence of the glorified body of Christ and oral manducation, however, he held as indispensable and essential articles of faith.* Not only did he thus express himself in disapproving of Carlstadt,† but also zealously espoused the cause of Pirckheimer and Luther in opposition to Œcolampadius and Zwingli. The doctrine of the Swiss theologians seemed to him insipid and absurd, and he called them vain babblers (ματαιολογους).‡ He held, further, that the body of Christ, whilst it was not necessarily ubiquitous, could be everywhere present at pleasure.§ A very considerable impression was made upon his mind by certain passages in the Church Fathers, especially Hilarius and Chrysostom, from which he thought it evident that the early Church taught the doctrine of the local presence and oral manducation. Yet at the same time doubts must have arisen in his mind; for in letters to Justus Jonus and Aquila we find him saying that he had disputed much, but modestly, with Luther in regard to the Lord's Supper (cum multa timide disputassem), but that he was overpowered by the firmness with which Luther maintained his convictions.|| Moreover, for two whole years (1526–28) he sought an opportunity to express himself publicly in

---

firmatus esset, tam dubitare tu non debes, quin misericordiam consecutus sis, ubi evangelium auderis, et evangelii σφραγιδας acceperis : baptismum et *corpus domini et sanguinem.* Precisely as a "miraculum" is the sacrament a signum misericordiæ. See De Signis.

* Letter to Hess. 1520. Equidem sententiam de transubstantione haud gravatim amplector, sed inter articulos fidei non temere numeraverim. Verum corpus Christi manducare, fidei articulus est, quocunque tandem modo sacrosanctum corpus figuram panis induat. (Corp. Ref. i. p. 145.)

† See *Galle.* Versuch einer characteristik Melanchthons als Theologen (Halle, 1845), p. 366 ff.

‡ Letter to Gerbel, 1528, Corp. Ref. i. p. 974.

§ Letter to Balthasar, 1528 (Corp. Ref. i. p. 948). Et quod quidam disputant, Christi corpus non *posse* in multis locis esse, id non satis probant.

|| Corp. Ref. i. p. 913 ad p. 964.

favor of Luther against the Swiss doctors. At last he wrote quite a friendly private letter to Œcolampadius,* in which he expresses frankly, but with all possible calmness, his objections to his view. These are based upon the words of Christ: "Lo I am with you alway, even to the end of the world;" and those of the Apostle Paul: "The bread which we break, is it not the communion of the body of Christ?" It is evident that if he had proceeded consistently on this ground he would have been led to Calvin's doctrine of a living union of the centre of the individual's being with the living person of Christ, and not to Luther's doctrine of consubstantiation and oral manducation. But, weak, dependent, and timid as he unfortunately was, he allowed himself on the occasion of the recess of the Imperial Diet at Spires (1529), where the Swiss theologians were proscribed as sectarians who gainsaid the sacraments of the true body and blood of Christ, to be led strenuously to oppose the efforts making to form an alliance of the Swiss and the Tetrapolitans with the Protestant princes;† and thereupon he proceeded to write against the Sacramentarians, and prepare on the subject his publication Sententiæ Veterum Scriptorum de Cœna Domini. Then followed the invitation of Philip of Hesse to the Conference at Marburg, which, as might be supposed, was equally unwelcome to Melanchthon and Luther. Like the latter, Melanchthon regarded as weak and foolish the desire for peace and unanimity on the part of the Swiss theologians.‡ And in the year 1530, reiterating Luther's unjust animadversions against the Swiss, he reproached them with the

---

* To be found in *Galle*, p. 382. He could here say with truth, Seis autem, me hactenus magis exortitisse spectatorem hujus fabulæ, quam actorem. Et multas graves habui causas, cur non admiscuerim me tam odioso certamini.

† Letter to Camerarius (Corp. Ref. i. p. 1068), and those to Baumgartner (the same, pp. 1069 and 1077). Mori malim, he writes, quam societate Cinglianæ causæ nostros contaminari.

‡ Letter to Agricola, 1529. Magnopere contenderunt, ut a nobis fratres appellarentur. Vide eorum stultitiam. (Corp. Ref. i. p. 1108.)

assertion, that their whole system was unscriptural, and that in none of their writings did they make mention of justification by faith.* True to this position, he sets forth the doctrine of the Lord's Supper in the Augsburg Confession in a form which did not confine itself to the doctrine of consubstantiation, but included that of transubstantiation.†

§ III.

MELANCHTHON ABANDONS LUTHER'S DOCTRINE OF THE LORD'S SUPPER.

AFTER the Diet of Augsburg and the religious peace of Nürnberg, Melanchthon was relieved from certain perplexities arising from his politico-ecclesiastical relations, Now we find him possessed of sufficient reflection and candor to subject the sacramental dogma to a new investigation; and all at once the correct principle again recurs to him. As early as 1530 (Nov. 9), Bucer writes to Schwebel that "Melanchthon stated that he would be satisfied with him, if only it were acknowledged that Christ is present in the supper, not in the bread, and present to the soul, not to the body."‡ About the same time Melanchthon received the Dialogos of Œcolampadius, in which his Sententiæ Veterum is answered, and where the author proves that the Fathers called the bread and wine αντιτυπα. Melanchthon certified to Luther himself that this production made an abiding

---

* Letter to Martin Gürlitz, 1530 (Corp. Ref. ii. p. 25). "Agnovi quam nullam habent Christianam doctrinam. . . . Nulla est mentis fidei justificantis in omnibus Zwinglianorum libris." Melanchthon must have given these *libri* a very superficial perusal.

† That the true body and blood of Christ are truly present in the Supper under the *form* of bread and wine. It is worthy of note that the Romish or Catholic doctrine of the Lord's Supper is given in literally the same language in some of the modern ultramontane Catholic Catechisms (*e.g.* the one recently introduced in the Palatinate of the Rhine). At the Diet of Augsburg (1530) a number of the Protestant princes raised objections to that form of stating the doctrine, and effected so much, that in the Latin edition the offensive words "under the form" were omitted.

‡ Centuria Epistolarum ad Schwebelium. Biport., 1597, p. 150 f.

impression upon him.* Bucer's idea of a life-union of the person of Christ with the soul of man became apparent to him in its true light. This was the old truth to which he himself had originally attached so much importance, viz. that it is the will of Christ to be with us, and, as Melanchthon adds, "to take up his abode within us."† Accordingly, with him the salient point of the sacramental dogma consisted no longer in the union of the glorified body of Christ with the bread, and His blood with the wine, for the purpose of oral manducation, but in the internal union of the person of Christ ("vivi Christi," "totius Christi," as he was wont to say) with the psychical centre of man. As a necessary consequence, the bread and wine became the signs and seals of an inner spiritual transaction. But this his awe for Luther did not permit him to acknowledge, except privately, in letters to a few intimate friends.‡ He contented himself with setting forth the *principle*, which of itself would inevitably lead to these consequences. This principle was embodied in the formula which constantly occurs in his own writings and in those church orders and liturgies which originated under his influence (*e.g.* those of Mecklenburg, and the Palatine Electorate, under Otho Henry, and many others), in the words, "Christ assures us in His supper that it is His will *to be with us* truly and really, *to dwell in those who are converted*, and make them partakers of all His gifts and benefits." Melanchthon was

---

* Corp. Ref. ii. 217.

† In Dec. 1532, Melanchthon writes to Rothmann thus: Fatendum est, Christum adesse vere *et verbo et signo,* cum eo utimur . . . . Adesse vere dicunt Christum in cœna (as opposed to, in pane) quod nihil habet incommodi. In the *Expli. Sym. Nic.* he writes thus: Hæc sumtio est testimonium et pignus, quod Filius Dei sit *in sumentibus,* nec tantum adsit in illa sumtione, sed habitet in iis . . . . ut sit pignus *assiduæ* præsentiæ et efficaciæ in credentibus. Deplorandum est, papistas tantum dicere de *præsentia in pane* et prorsus tacere de *præsentia* assidua in credentibus.

‡ *E.g.* to Brentz, June, 1535; and here he is very cautious: he observes that most of the proof-passages from the Fathers explain this mystery *typically and tropically.*

the better satisfied with this newly-gotten conviction, after Luther's conduct in his interview with Bucer, which led to the conclusion of the Wittenberg Concordia. Here Luther stated that he would be content if only it were conceded that "bread and wine were signs, with which at the same time Christ's body and blood were received;" nay, if only it were taught, with the Mühlhauser Confession, that Christ is the food of the believing soul, and that our souls are fed by faith on the crucified Saviour, so that He lives in us and we in Him.

§ IV.

THE FORMATION OF A MELANCHTHONIAN SCHOOL.

Although Melanchthon had actually abandoned Luther's doctrine of the Lord's Supper, he had not sufficient courage openly to renounce it. During the transactions in reference to the Concordia, he allowed himself to be sent to Cassel by Luther with the above-mentioned Instruction, in which the doctrine of a literal mastication of Christ's body is retained. Instead now of insisting upon his own views, which were the opposite of what was here expressed, and of declining to serve as a messenger in the circumstances, as he should have done, he contents himself with thus writing to Camerarius: "Ask me not in reference to my own view; for I was merely the messenger of some friends." Likewise it was not owing to the personal service of Melanchthon, so much as to the power of the truth itself, and the force of circumstances, that after the Wittenberg Concordia the view of Melanchthon spread in Germany, and a Melanchthonian or Philippistic school was formed. It originated in the Tetrapolis and Swabia. The authors of the Swabian Syngramma, in which Œcolampadius was so violently assailed, were not able to conceal the fact that a doctrinal theory entirely at variance with that of Luther lay hidden in formulas sounding much like his own. In plain terms is the doctrine stated by Brentz, in his *Landescatechismus*, that "the Holy Supper was not designed to

feed and satisfy the body, but to afford nourishment to the
soul, for the conservation of spiritual benefits conferred
upon us in baptism and appropriated by faith, and hence
it is rightly called *spiritual* meat and drink." Just at this
time (1539–41) it providentially happened that Calvin had
been driven to what, next to Strasburg, was the most important of the four upper German cities (the Tetrapolis).
This was the man who, independently of Bucer and
Melanchthon, was led to the correct and in all respects
consistently developed sacramental doctrine, holding that
in the words of institution our Lord was speaking concern-
cerning His *crucified* body and *shed* blood; yet, according to
His words in John vi. and John xvi., a real participation in
the fruits of His death was not possible without a real participation in His *living person.* We must be united, as the
branch to the vine, to the ascended Saviour, through the
Holy Ghost, in a manner purely supernatural and tran-
scending all limitations of space, so that "by possessing
Christ we may partake also of all His benefits." In the
Lord's Supper, the renewing of the already existing life-
union, and hereby the new appropriation of pardon once
for all secured by the death of Christ, are sealed to the
believer through the visible signs and pledges. In accordance with the divine injunction, the physical man receives
from the hand of the minister the natural food and drink,
wherein is sealed to him the spiritual nourishment of the
inner man, through Christ, the living bread from heaven.
This doctrine Calvin, without fear of man or concern as to
consequences, openly acknowledged, and fairly and fully
unfolded, during the transactions in reference to the Concordia in Switzerland, 1536–37. Afterward, in his Institutes, and especially in his tract *De Cœna*, he expressed
it just as distinctly, at the same time developing and establishing it. When he appeared before the conferences in
an official capacity, *e.g.*, as the Duke of Lüneberg's delegate to Hagenau, Worms, and Regensburg, he entered
upon such terms of cordial intimacy as was due his col-

leagues in the great work of the Reformation. Still, he did not hesitate a moment to send his *De Cœna* to Luther, for whom he entertained the highest regard. The latter had previously sent Calvin a Christian greeting through Bucer, and informed him that he had read his Institutes with unusual pleasure (singulari cum voluptate);* and, now again accepting the *De Cœna*, he expressed himself as altogether pleased with it.† At this time Calvin was held in high esteem throughout Germany, having received from the Protestant theologians at Regensburg the honorable title of "the theologian;" and, as his works were extensively read, a large number of the divines of Northern Germany became acquainted with this fairly and fully developed doctrine of the Lord's Supper, a doctrine which by Melanchthon was carefully kept from the light and barely alluded to. But at last, perceiving the decided friendship existing between Luther and Calvin,‡ Melanchthon became possessed of courage sufficient to come out more openly with his views on the subject. To his immediate pupils he, likely, had disclosed his views in full, whilst with ordinary friends he is not merely *silent*, as hitherto, in reference to a local presence of the body of Christ in the bread, but expressly and decisively denies it.§ In his publications also he speaks of the Lord's Supper as a sealing of the spiritual indwelling of Christ in the believer, in a manner which leaves no doubt as to his actual opinion. In the *Examen Ordinandorum* (a book possessed of symbolical

---

* Calvin (to Farel, Nov. 29, 1539) expresses joy on account of this salutation and message from Luther through Bucer, and adds: Dam reputa, quid illic de eucharistia dicam! Cogita Lutheri ingenuitatem.

† Non inepte judicat his scriptor.

‡ Melanchthon tells us of Luther: Calvinus magnam gratiam iniit,—"Calvin stood in great favor with Luther." (See Henry, Leben Calvins, ii. p. 267.)

§ Letter to Brentz, June 12, 1535, where he rejects the physica conjunctio panis et corporis.—Letter to Veit Dietrich, Oct. 25, 1543: Miror, tot sæculis homines doctos non cogitasse discremen inter agens liberum et rem inanimatam Christus tanquam agens liberum *adest actione* institutæ; post actionem non vult esse incluses pani.

authority, and to which subscription was made obligatory
in the Churches of Pomerania, the Saxon Electorate,
Mecklenburg, and other countries), Melanchthon says, "As
we partake of the Holy Supper (in qua sumtione), the Son
of God is really and truly present, and assures the believer
that He applies to him His merits and benefits, and that for
our sake He assumed human nature, in order that He
might make us members of His own body, incorporated
into Him through faith, and washed and made clean by His
blood." This language he almost literally repeated in the
article of Worms, 1537; and, if possible, his opinion is expressed still more clearly in his *Explicatio Symb. Nic.* (1556),
in which he says, "This participation (in the bread and
cup) is a *testimony and pledge* that the Son of God is *in those
participating* (not in the bread), and this not only during the
act, but that He abides in them. . . . The Supper was instituted as a pledge of the constant and effectual (assiduæ et
efficaciæ) presence of Christ in the *believer;*" and adds that
it is to be regretted that the Papists always speak of a
presence of Christ in the bread, but are entirely silent
concerning the abiding presence of Christ in believers.
With equal frankness and decision did he express himself
against the doctrine of the ubiquity of Christ's body, in
his objections to Osiander De Inhabitatione Dei in Sanctis
(1551).

§ V.

MELANCHTHON'S DOCTRINE CONCERNING THE LORD'S SUPPER ECCLESIASTICALLY SANCTIONED.

It is not surprising now, in view of the reputation of
Melanchthon as a Reformer, and his influence as a professor of divinity, that a numerous school of theologians
embracing his views should be formed throughout Germany.
This took place during the two decades between the conclusion of the Wittenberg Concordia and the renewal of the

sacramental controversies (1536–1556).* But now it was most natural for the question to be constantly arising, what sanction could be claimed for this mode of teaching the doctrine of the Lord's Supper in the Protestant Church of Germany, the Church of the Augsburg Confession. It is true, the tenth article of this confession, in its antithesis, was directed against the Zwinglian, and not against the Calvino-Melanchthonian, sacramental doctrine, but in its thesis, in both the German and Latin edition, it excluded the latter as well as the former.† If thus the Augsburg Confession of 1530 prevailed as in all respects normal, the Melanchthonian doctrine of the Lord's Supper could certainly find no room for an ecclesiastically sanctioned existence in Germany. But such was not the case. At the convention of the Smalcald Federation (Feb. 1537), met with a view to the council about to be held, Luther presented a declaration of faith, in which he set forth the doctrine of the Lord's Supper in a form which allowed sufficient room for the Melanchthonian view of the subject.‡ Amsdorf, it is true, urged him to alter the wording in favor of a more decidedly Lutheran phraseology (such as is found in the Articles of Smalcald). But the articles thus amended *were dropped*, to be taken up again by the rigid Lutheran party a long time after Luther's death, and clothed with the importance of a symbolical book. The proceedings of the council came to a sudden and unex-

---

* It is with the greatest injustice that Heppe so perverts these historical facts, as though the Melanchthonian theory, as opposed to the genuine Lutheran, was the more original, "the old Protestant one." The truth of the matter is that at that time a clear conception of the minute difference between Luther and Calvin was had by but a few ; that to this difference Luther himself attached but little practical importance, and, accordingly, that Calvin's doctrine would naturally spread, carried forward by the force of its own truth and aided by Melanchthon's doctrinal publication, and would remain uncontroverted.

† De cœna Domini docent, quod corpus et sanguis Christi adsint et *distribuantur* vescentibus (not credentibus) in cœna Domini: et improbant secus docentes.

‡ That the body and blood of Christ are received *with* the bread and the wine. See the original in Heppe, Confes. Entwickelung der alt prot. Kirche, p. 86 ff., Gesch. d. deutsch. Protestantismus, i. p. 167.

pected close. In its stead a religious conference was to be held on the soil of the German Empire. This was attended upon, as before stated, by Calvin himself, as delegate from the Duke of Lüneberg, 1540–1541. The Protestant imperial deputies presented before this conference *a new and improved edition of the Augsburg Confession,*—as they called it, the "enriched or amended" Augustana. In this edition, Melanchthon,—in Luther's presence, with his knowledge and approval,—in entire accordance with the spirit and meaning of the Wittenberg Concordia, set forth the article pertaining to the Lord's Supper in literally the same form in which Luther himself had expressed it in the original sketch of the Smalcald Articles.* So far from objecting to it on account of this emendation, the imperial deputies and Protestant theologians, even Calvin himself, subscribed it, and presented it to the emperor at Worms and at Regensdorf as the confession of the Church. In 1557, at the Council of Frankfort-on-the-Main and the Colloquium at Worms, it was reconfirmed as the confession of the Church, and firmly adhered to against the strictures of the Jesuits, who would have the Augsburg Confession of 1530 alone regarded as possessing proper authority. And this edition of the Confession was not only authorized in this legal and abstract way, but it also passed over into the Churches and was practically adopted by them. Thus, in 1554, it was incorporated into the church-order and agenda of the Palatinate under Otho Henry; in 1549, in the Corpus Misnicum, the doctrinal formulary of the Saxon Electorate; in 1573, in the *Corpus Doctrinæ* of Ansbach Baireuth, and others. Moreover, the state of the Church was by no means such that this amended confession existed as a second kind of confession beside the older one of 1530, as if there existed Churches of the unaltered by the side of Churches of the altered confession. On the contrary, the

---

* De cœna Domini docent, quod *cum* pane et vino vere exhibeantur (the *distribuantur* is avoided) corpus et sanguis Christi vescentibus in cœna Domini.

original text of 1530 was not even reprinted during the interval between 1541 and 1580. The amended edition *had entirely displaced the older*, so that, in the year 1560, the Elector of Hesse, as also Chemnitz (Judic. de Controv. quibusdam, p. 7), could say that "the text of 1540 alone was used in the churches and schools," was in *omnium manibus*, and *plerisque ignota et vix unquam visa fuerit prima editio.* The fact is, that the original text of 1530 was not only entirely out of print, but also had to such an extent disappeared, that when the Elector August of Nassau, in 1580, wished to have it reprinted, he sought in vain for a copy, and eventually found himself necessitated to pray the Elector of Mayence to send him the original manuscript, which had been handed over to him at Augsburg (1530) and was now filed in the royal archives.

From these facts, now, we must be careful not to make improper inferences. As we have seen, it is altogether false to assert that the Melanchthonian sacramental theory was the one originally maintained by the Protestants of Germany. Nay, it is a well-established and evident fact that Luther's doctrine of consubstantiation, local presence in the bread and wine, and oral manducation, was the originally prevailing* doctrine and conviction of the Lutheran Church, and of Melanchthon himself. And it is none the less false to assume that between 1541 and 1553, with the amended text of the Augustana, Melanchthon's doctrine concerning the Lord's Supper was the one alone prevalent, and that with the text of the so-called *Invariata* the genuine Lutheran sacramental doctrine disappeared. For how otherwise could it happen that within a single decade the entire powerful party of the Flacians should be formed? Did they spring like mushrooms out of the ground? And how was it possible for them to

---

* The somewhat different view of the Swabians, and the Zwinglian tendency of Philip of Hesse, are not denied. But the former were not conscious of their divergence from Luther, and the latter did not make his known.

come off victorious over the Melanchthonian school, and crush it, if the masses of the population in general had not adhered to the pure Lutheran doctrine and were disposed so to continue? But in the reception of the amended text (1541) the Protestant deputies had no idea of any thing else but that *they* would relinquish the genuine Lutheran doctrine. Luther himself, at that time, expressed himself as pleased "that the Confession stood firm." And when Dr. Eck declined to accept the amended text as being fairly authoritative, he met with the rejoinder, "that no material or substantial alteration had been made." The sole intention in the modification of the tenth article was *that it might, according to the sense of the Wittenberg Concordia, be made possible for the Tetrapolis to subscribe the Confession, and thus, with the other Protestant powers, as an organization having one faith, press forward with their cause in opposition to both Emperor and Pope.* For this reason the doctrine of the Lord's Supper was expressed in a form which in no wise conflicted with the genuine Lutheran theory, nor yet with that of Bucer, Calvin, and Melanchthon, without, however, bringing out either to a full expression. The natural consequence of this was, that the Calvino-Melanchthonian doctrine of the Lord's Supper came to be tolerated, yea, it may be said, was likewise sanctioned, by the Church in the strictly Lutheran parts of Germany; but absolutely false is the assertion of Heppe, that it was the exclusively sanctioned doctrine. And a further consequence was, that the Melanchthonian school and tendency could make unresisted advances and become widely spread.

§ VI.

THE HOSTILITY TO THE SCHOOL OF MELANCHTHON.

So successful was the propagation of this Melanchthonian school after the death of Luther, not only becoming so widely spread, but evincing also such an inteusive force, that the adherents of the genuine Lutheran doctrine of the Lord's Supper began to fear that the latter would be forgotten, and their own existence as a party cease. The Upper German cities—viz.: Strasburg, Memmingen, Constance, and Lindau—were Reformed in thé sense of the Tetrapolitana and Mühlhusiana; *i.e.* in the sense of Bucer and Calvin. In Swabia the original view of Brentz* prevailed, which plainly differed widely from that of Luther. Thoroughly Reformed influences co-operated in the Reformation of Hesse (Lambert von Avignon, 1526). This was also the case in Zweibrücken (Schwebel and Fliesbach, 1524). In the Electoral Palatinate, as early as Otho Henry, just as many genuine Calvinists, like Erastus and Boquinus, as Melanchthonians, *e.g.* Diller, were prominent and active, both in high ecclesiastical councils and in the professorial chairs, whilst the ultra-Lutheran Hesshus could not gain a foothold. Here, indeed (in the reign of Frederick II., 1544), the earliest Reformatory movements took place under specifically Melanchthonian auspices; and Melanchthon has the credit of reforming the University of Heidelberg (1536). And when the venerable Archbishop of Cologne, Hermann Count of Wied-Runkel, had the "Cologne Reformation" elaborated, through Melanchthon, in 1543,† the order of worship thus introduced did not succeed even in that city, and had to succumb to the power of the Papacy. Duke William IV., however, introduced it into Jülich-Cleve-Berg, and with it the clearly-expressed sacramental doctrine of Calvin and Melanchthon,‡ and thus it exerted a normal influence upon all the countries along the Rhine. More than this, the adherents of the genuine Lutheran doc-

---

* Which must be distinguished from Brentz's later rigid Lutheranism.

† He had undertaken an Erasmian Reformation in 1530, which, however, was unsuccessful, and with which Luther rightly found much fault.

‡ That the Lord extends and makes over to us His flesh and blood *with* the visible signs, bread and wine, not for the nourishment of the natural and temporal, but for the nourishment of the spiritual and eternal, life.

trine of the Lord's Supper had to see the day when Melanchthon's Examen Ordinandorum, in which the formula of the
doctrine of the Lord's Supper was so shaped as not only to
allow and encourage, but to require, the adoption of the Melanchthonian theory, was formally introduced and stamped
with the character and mandatory authority of a Church
formulary, in the very cradle of the Reformation, in the
Electorate of Saxony, and so, afterward, in Pomerania,
Mecklenburg, part of the territory belonging to Brandenburg, and many other countries. Nearly all the confessions of the particular state Churches contained the Melanchthonian doctrine as expressed in the Examen Ordinandorum. Thus the *Conf. Saxonica* which prevailed in the
Saxon Electorate, Brandenburg, Ansbach Baireuth, Mans-
feld, Stolberg, Pomerania, Prussia, Wurtemberg, and
Strasburg, and was approved in the Palatine Electorate,
Hesse, and Bremen. So also the *Concordia Francofurdensis*
(1542), the Church Order of *Cassel* (1539), that of Swabian
Hall (1543), and many others. Now the zealous followers of
Luther began to feel that the conflict going on was one for
existence. The theory hitherto only tolerated threatened
to become prevalent and to displace every rival doctrine.
Then, with the zeal of despair and with the fanaticism
of a cause which could not employ fair and reasonable, but
only violent, measures, they began that well-planned and
stubborn contest (1553–1577) which brought many a pang
to the heart of the noble but despondent Melanchthon, and
saddened the whole later period of his life. This is not
the place to set forth the particular stadia and various
events of this conflict. They are easily gathered from any
Church history.* Two facts, however, should be stated.
One, that these zealots did not, as Heppe asserts, set up a
new doctrine, for they adhered with fidelity to the original

---

* A fresh and comprehensive insight into the subject, particularly in
reference to the Crypto-Calvinistic controversies, is afforded by the admirable
work of Gillet: Crato von Craffstein und seine Freunde.

one of Luther and of the Augsburg Confession (1530); but they did adopt a new standard of what was right and allowable; for by their conduct* they put an end to the tolerance which, since 1541, had been justly conceded to the Melanchthonian school. The other fact is, that they succeeded in putting down the Melanchthonian tendency and doctrine, as unsanctioned in the federation of the Augsburg Confession. This was the case in the Saxon Electorate, Lower Saxony, Brandenburg, Wirtemberg, and Strasburg; and in other sections they forced the Melanchthonian element out of the Church of the Augsburg Confession, as in the Electoral Palatinate, Zweibrücken, Solms, Wied, and, later, also in Bremen (about 1590) and Hesse (in 1604),† and in this way occasioned the formation of the *German Reformed State Churches.*

---

* As when they overawed the Melanchthonian tendency in the Electorate of Saxony, which was there openly unfolded and ecclesiastically sanctioned, and then, too, represented what they had thus overawed as Calvinism clandestinely foisted in upon the Church. And again, when they universally ignored and denounced as apostasy the measures of concession and conciliation based on the Wittenberg Concordia, and represented the amended Augustana as merely a private production,—nay, as a felony of Melanchthon.

† The difficulties in the Palatinate are so intimately associated with the history of the origin of the Heidelberg Catechism, to which subject one of the accompanying articles is devoted, that it is unnecessary to give it any further notice here. In Bremen, where *Hardenberg,* a pupil of Melanchthon, represented and defended the views of his teacher, the Flacians were originally victorious (1561). But in the year 1562 a reaction took place, when the Flacians were banished. Occupying the Melanchthonian confessional stand-point, they used at first exclusively the amended Augustana and the Frankfurt Recess; but afterward (1571), in order to set up a secure palisade against Flacianism, they added the *Conf. Saxonica* and Melanchthon's *Corpus Doctrinæ.* About 1590, the Heidelberg Catechism was introduced, and henceforth Bremen was regarded as a Reformed Church. This example serves to show us how such churches were gradually forced over into the Reformed Church. (Cf. Kohlmann: "Welche Bekentniss Schriften haben in der ref. Kirche Bremens Geltung?") Only in Schleswig-Holstein, Braunschweig-Wolfenbüttel, and Nürnberg was the original confessional position of Melanchthon of 1541–1543 maintained, but in such a way that, whilst they shunned the Form of Concord, they did not permit themselves to be thrust out of the Church of the Augsburg Confession.

But here, finally, is a point to which special attention must be given,—viz.: what attitude did Melanchthon himself assume at the beginning of these hostilities? Without prejudice to this honored and illustrious man, we are permitted to say on this subject that his timidity and solicitude resulted in much harm. First to be mentioned are his timorous concessions during the Interim of Augsburg and Leipzig, by which he undermined his influence for all subsequent time; for at that time he yielded to the Papal demands in reference to public worship to such an extent that his concessions not only reached the utmost limit of the morally admissible, but, in truth, here and there exceeded it. Thus he put deadly weapons into the hands of the hostile Flacians, who always alluded to this weakness when it was found expedient to undermine the influence of Melanchthon in a Protestant community. Equally unfortunate was it, when the zealots began their campaign with a dishonorable assault upon a band of English refugees, who were compelled to leave their homes on account of fidelity to their creed, that Melanchthon did not *at once* courageously enter the lists in behalf of oppressed truth; for here his testimony would have had effect. The more Flacianism advanced, the more timorously did Melanchthon withdraw. As *Præceptor Germaniæ*, it was incumbent upon him vigorously to controvert the consubstantiation theory with biblical arguments. But instead of this he satisfied himself by undertaking to smother the fire of the conflict where it had burst into flames by the recommendation of unionistic doctrinal formularies.* In vain did Calvin repeatedly urge him to come out for once with a public statement of his con-

---

* Cf. the *Formula Concensus*, by which, at the Colloquium of Worms (1557) he wished, with unjustifiable concessions, to conciliate the Flacians, and only provoked the Wirtembergers, who were opposed to this party. Also his "Gutachten in der Pfälzer Wirren," which was equally unsuccessful, &c. Also Gillet i. p. 149.

victions.* In vain was he appealed to by his disciples, persecuted as Calvinists (Gillet i. p. 129). The more carefully he avoided every such statement, the more boldly did the hostile party venture forward, until eventually they made Melanchthon himself the object of their attacks (Gillet i. 131 ff.), and they had reason to believe that he would only the more certainly remain silent. Thus, weary of the *rabies theologorum*, he died, leaving his own school to decline and certainly to disappear; whereas by a bold and candid testimony at the proper time he might without doubt have secured for it, if not a ruling, at least a tolerated position in the Church of the Augsburg Confession. Still, no more can be required from any one than has been committed to him. However, the want of courage on the part of Melanchthon contributed to bring it about, that the fragments of his school soon found it necessary to take refuge in the Reformed Church.

His differing from Luther in respect to the doctrine of predestination and free will, exerted no influence upon this course of development. For only during the Swiss controversy (1558) did he come forward with a few theses expressive of his peculiar view. It is true his enemies took advantage of this conduct to convict him of heresy; yet it can by no means be said that the relation of his school to the Reformed Church was at all determined by his indefinite theory of a co-operation of the free will in conversion. For in respect to the dogma of predestination the Reformed Church agreed with Melanchthon's enemies, the Flacians. Both adhered to this doctrine as held by the Reformers, which, if possible, was more sharply expressed by Luther than by Calvin, and which the former zealously maintained until the close of his life.† Thus the Philippists could not

---

* See the passages in question in *Sudhoff's* Theol. Handbuch zur Auslegung des Heidelberger Katechismus (Frankfurt), p. 388.

† A few years before his death, Luther wrote to Capito that if he were to recall his productions, the work De Servo Arbitrio would be the last. The assertion that the doctrine of absolute predestination is not an original Pro-

have been prompted by their preferences in this direction to attach themselves to the Reformed Church. It was solely on account of the Calvino-Melanchthonian doctrine of the Lord's Supper, for which since the year 1560 there was neither room nor license in the Church of the Augsburg Confession. After entering the federation of the Reformed Church, they could not fail gradually to imbibe the rigid predestinarian principles which here prevailed. In their new ecclesiastical home they did not venture forward with the highly important and fruitful germs of a Melanchthonian development in this respect, no more than they would have dared to do so in their former position with the Melanchthonian doctrine of the Lord's Supper. In conclusion, when these germs were transplanted, although in hampered circumstances, into the Form of Concord, adherence to the doctrine of predestination became an indispensable condition of connection with the Reformed Church. Accordingly, Hesse, Bremen, and the Palatinate were represented in the Synod of Dort, 1618, and the Bremen theologians subscribed, though with bleeding hearts, the resolutions of that body. Thus, so far as the doctrine of the Lord's Supper is concerned, the Reformed Church has to thank Magister Philippus for nothing which it could not have received clearer and better from the hands of Calvin; whilst in respect to the doctrine of election it were well if she would let it appear that the current of Melanchthonian theology, which passed over into her bosom, was not, in God's providence, directed thither in vain.

---

testant nor the original Reformed one, but was first introduced into the Reformed Church by Calvin, is, if possible, more preposterous than that the Lutheran doctrine of the Lord's Supper was not the original Protestant one, but was foisted in upon the Lutheran Church by the Flacians. Cf. Jul. Müller: Lutheri de Predestinatione et liberi Arbitrii Doctrina.

´SKETCHES

FROM THE

HISTORY OF THE HEIDELBERG CATECHISM IN THE LAND OF ITS BIRTH.

By DR. C. ULLMANN,
CARLSRUHE, GERMANY.

TRANSLATED BY J. W. NEVIN, D.D, LANCASTER, PA.

SKETCHES

FROM THE HISTORY OF THE HEIDELBERG CATECHISM IN THE
LAND OF ITS BIRTH.

By Dr. C. Ullmann, Carlsruhe, Germany.

Translated by PROFESSOR J. W. NEVIN, D.D., Lancaster, Pa.

I CHEERFULLY accept the invitation with which I have
been honored, to furnish a contribution to the Tercentenary
Jubilee of the Heidelberg Catechism, which my brethren
of the Reformed Confession have it in mind to hold on
the other side of the ocean. In doing so, my studies direct
me to the historical side of the subject. I propose, however, no full history of the Catechism. Should this be
attempted anew, after all of the sort that has been given to
the world before, with a view to more full and thorough
detail, it would require a work for which the intended
Memorial Volume would offer no sufficient room, while I
should myself also have neither the time, nor yet the necessary material, for its preparation. For, strange to say,
though of easy historical explanation, the University library
of the very city in which the formulary received its being,
famous as it is for its other treasures, is not only not rich,
but positively poor, in resources for the history of the Catechism; and otherwise also, unfortunately, the land of its
birth has preserved but little for this purpose. Looking
away from any such object, then, I hope still to do some
service, if with the means at my command I try to illustrate
some leading facts from the history of the Catechism, particularly in its native country, and with this furnish also a
short account of its modern fortunes, which may not be
without interest for fellow-confessionists living at a dis-

115

tance. In this view the present sketch will consist of two principal parts: in the first four sections I will treat mainly of the causes which gave the Catechism its great authority and powerful influence in the Church of the Palatinate, as well as of the controversies to which it gave rise; in the last two I will endeavor to show how, in the course of the present century, it came into disuse in its native land, but finally has found here also again what may be called a new restoration to life and power.

I.

THE RELATION OF FREDERICK III. TO THE HEIDELBERG CATECHISM.

If ever a book has been of pervading signification for the ecclesiastical life of a people, the Heidelberg Catechism was so for the Church of the Palatinate. It gave to this Church principally her original character, and formed the central power of her development for nearly three hundred years; it may be said to have been the most active leaven of her life within, and her highest renown without, the most vigorous and most admired, but at the same time most violently assaulted, product of her womb.

The deepest and most enduring ground of this significance of the Catechism must be sought, undoubtedly, in its whole *inward* constitution. It was, above all, the essential scripturalness of its contents, the admirable distribution of its matter, the pithy sententiousness of its language, and the deep earnestness of conviction it breathes in every word, which caused the book to carry with it at once its own authority and weight. If we take only the first question concerning the "only comfort in life and in death," in which itself we have the marrow and spirit of the entire Catechism—what all has it not wrought! For how many has it not been the living sum of their heart's belief, and the fondest utterance of their mouth's confession, their guiding star in life, and their consolation on a dying bed!

116

And all this, only through its indwelling, triumphant power of Christian truth and assured faith, by which these few lines rank with the highest and best that have ever appeared, under any form, in the sphere of evangelical doctrine and Christian profession.

Such properties must have secured credit for the Heidelberg Catechism under any circumstances, and did in fact give it vast influence far beyond the bounds of its native land. At the same time, however, it is usual, with works of this sort, for *historical* and *personal* considerations to co-operate powerfully in strengthening their influence; and that such was the case also with the Heidelberg Catechism admits of no doubt. Only there was a difference in this respect between it and the Catechism of Luther, where the person of the author, who was the most honored father of the Reformation, and at the time in the full zenith of his life and power, threw directly into the scale quite as much weight as the inward worth of the publication itself.

The Heidelberg Catechism, it is known, had two authors, Zacharias Ursinus, professor of theology, and Caspar Olevianus, preacher at Heidelberg. Both were excellent, highly respectable men, distinguished each in his way,—the one by thorough theological learning, the other by his practical talent and glowing zeal for evangelical truth. They were both, however, posthumous sons only, and not fathers, of the Reformation, both at the time extraordinarily young and comparatively but little known, both, moreover, of only recent settlement in the land for which the Catechism was immediately designed;* and the undertaking, besides, proceeded in the last instance not from themselves, but from one who, as their superior, called them to it and made it their charge. Wonderful now as it must ever remain, not only that a work of such unity should have been composed by *two*

---

* Olevianus was called to Heidelberg in 1560, Ursinus in 1561. The composition of the Heidelberg Catechism fell at farthest within the year 1562, since it appeared from the press as early as January, 1563.

authors, but yet much more that two such *young* men, of whom the one numbered less than twenty-eight, the other only twenty-six years, should have been prepared to produce any thing so solid, rich, and complete—all goes still to show that it could not be the persons of *these* men which gave the matter importance, as the person of Luther did in the case of his Catechism.

On the contrary, we are met, in the case of the Heidelberg Catechism, with another personal presence of the most conspicuous order. This is the sovereign under whom it appeared, the Elector Palatine Frederick III. Of him, then, and his position with regard to the Catechism, we have now more particularly to speak.

Frederick III. was a prince of rare order, whose clear understanding, blameless manners, unshaken fidelity, and restless activity for the welfare of his subjects, gained for him the respect of his own and of later times. It was not in these things, however, with all their worth, that his most peculiar and honorable distinction lay, but in this rather, that with him, as with few earthly monarchs, the prince and the Christian were so intimately joined together that the one cannot be thought of without the other. Piety formed the ground-tone and the ruling trait of his character—a piety which was plain and unpretending in its utterances, but which at the same time proclaimed itself so decidedly in his whole being and action as to make itself irresistibly felt by every one who came near him. Above all, it was not simply an indefinite, sentimental piety, but bore a sharply marked Christian stamp, and exercised a vigorous power over the entire life of the prince as well as of the man. "Lord, as Thou wilt!"* was the Elector's motto. The expression of the Lord's will lay for him, at the same time, in the Holy Scriptures, in which his whole

---

* "*Herr, nach deinem Wille!*" The theme also of a fine spiritual song, which he composed in his old age. See, in regard to it, my Essay in the *Theol. Stud. u. Krit.*, 1861, 3.

faith was most deeply and firmly rooted; and as he endeavored with full earnestness to form not only his own life, but also the public order both in Church and State, according to this rule, his measures took necessarily of themselves, in the circumstances, a reformatory character. History recognizes in him the chief Reformer of his land, and shows how he exhibited, as such, the most energetic activity, along with the noblest spirit of a witnessing confessor.

But this prince stood not in a merely outward relation to the Heidelberg Catechism, such as other rulers may have held to new ecclesiastical arrangements within their territories: his connection with it was as intimate and close as it could possibly be in his position. The reformation of his land was for him the highest object of his life, and the main part of this reformation work was in his view the Catechism. He himself had conceived the project of it, and selected the men for its execution; he himself also superintended this execution, and even applied his own hand at last personally to the work. He was, moreover, when heavy dangers threatened it at the outset, its first champion; and in the presence finally of death itself, it received still his joyful testimony, as the unchanging expression of his Christian faith.* On all sides, the book is as inseparably interwoven with Frederick's personal convictions as with his whole governmental action.

And this relation it was then also that imparted to the Catechism from the historical and personal side, beyond all else, the consecration which has attended it through all centuries, and which, in conjunction with its inward excellence, has ever commended it anew to the piety of successive generations. It was the peculiar consecration that belongs to such writings as are at the same time *acts*, and as need to be considered essential parts of the inmost life and highest aims of some personal character, which just

---

* In his will, which is printed in Struve's *Pfalz. K. Historie*, pp. 275–292. The passages that refer to the Catechism occur pp. 280 and 291.

in this way has made itself ·felt effectually also in the development of a grand spiritual whole.

It must be of interest for us now to know. what view this prince *himself* had of his task, in the establishment of the Catechism. And we are not without utterances on this point from his own mouth. To appreciate these properly, however, we must consider the matter somewhat more closely in its general connection.

It is known that when Frederick III. succeeded to the government of the Palatinate in 1559, the Reformation was already far advanced in this land, but that its ecclesiastical condition was at the same time unsettled and distracted in the highest degree. The residence city, Heidelberg, in particular, had become a sort of rendezvous for all the leading parties which were then in the Protestant Church—the more rigid Lutherans, Melanchthonians, Zwinglians, and Calvinists; and among these the extreme sections especially contended with one another frequently in the most scandalous style. Frederick himself, in the beginning, aimed at conciliation. But when his attempt to make peace, by the dismissal of the hottest champions and the help of the famous "Judgment" he had procured from Melanchthon on the main matter of controversy (the doctrine of the Lord's Supper), failed to accomplish its purpose, he yielded himself, especially after the Diet of Naumburg in 1561, more and more to the *Reformed* side— an inclination which may have been promoted by the progress of his own thinking, as well as by the prevailing influence of the Calvinistic theologians around him, who had greater attraction for him than the more blunt-mannered Lutherans. As he did not mean, however, by any means, to be a follower of Calvin, but always declared rather his steady veneration also for Luther, and acknowledged afterward, as before, the Augsburg Confession as modified by Melanchthon, his position may be characterized as that of a mild Melanchthonian Calvinism, foreshadowing the idea of confessional union. It was not in his mind to oppose the Lutheran Confession in general, but only to hold himself evangelically free and independent over against certain Lutheran peculiarities in the doctrine of the Lord's Supper.

In these circumstances, Frederick, in virtue of his princely right of reformation and his inward call to it, determined to bring order and unity into the distracted Church of his land. And, since all turned here first upon *doctrine*, while doctrine again in the form of public confession makes itself known and felt chiefly through the *catechism*, this became necessarily the point toward which, more than any other, the eye of the reforming prince must be directed. But just in this department, now, the condition of things in the Palatinate was so circumstanced that it could in no wise satisfy his wishes. Some of the ministers used the Catechism of Luther, some that of Brentz, while others, again, compiled their own directories, or else made use of none at all. In many places, besides, the catechization of the young was altogether neglected, while in others it was badly attended.* Along with the difference of doctrine, there prevailed thus, at the same time, disorder, wilfulness, and want of discipline; and if Frederick was to bring this unbecoming, unhealthful state of the Church to a full end, while yet his religious convictions as they then stood would not allow him to have recourse to either Luther's Catechism or that of Brentz as a manual to be universally enforced,† there remained no other alternative for him but to form a *new* Catechism, and then to adopt all proper measures for securing its actual and general use.

That this was the object and purpose of Frederick, in

---

* See Dr. C. SCHMIDT, in the publication, very instructive on this subject, entitled: *Der Antheil der Strasbürger an der Reformation in der Kurpfalz.* Strasburg, 1856. Introduction, pp. 23 and 24, and elsewhere.

† Before this—and as late, indeed, as Oct. 1559—Frederick had directed the preceptor of his son, the young Prince Christopher, to instruct him according to Luther's Catechism. See VIERORD'S *Gesch. der Ref. in Baden*, b. 1, p. 458.

the preparation of the Catechism, is clearly stated by himself in his order for its introduction, dated the 19th of January, 1563.* Proceeding here, if not expressly in so many words, yet most decidedly in spirit and sense, from the fundamental idea of a Christian State, in which the government is to be considered as charged with the highest moral and religious interests of the people, he declares it to be a main part of the office and trust committed to him by God, "not only to maintain a discreet, upright, and virtuous walk before his people, but also and principally to guide and bring them more and more into the genuine knowledge and fear of the Almighty, and of His life-giving word as the only foundation of all virtues." The arrangements adopted for this purpose by his ancestors—the reference was mainly, no doubt, to the Church order of Otho Henry—had not borne the "hoped-for and desired" fruit; and it was not enough, therefore, to renew them, but pressingly necessary to undertake an "improvement" and to "make further provision." To this belonged, above all, that the youth should be held in the schools and churches to the "pure and uniform doctrine" of the Holy Gospel; and since there was wanting, for such purpose, a "fixed, sure, and harmonious" catechism, in order to do away with all "incorrectness and unlikeness," he had now, with the counsel and co-operation of the whole theological faculty, also of all the superintendents and prominent ministers of the land, provided and set up a summary of the Christian religion out of God's word, "whereby henceforth not only the youth may be piously instructed and kept also of one mind in such Christian doctrine, but the preachers and schoolmasters themselves, likewise, may have a settled form and measure how they shall conduct themselves in the instruction of the young, and not make daily changes,

---

* Printed in NIEMEYER's *Collectio Conf. in eccles. ref. publicatarum*, pp. 390, 391; where from p. 392 the Heidelberg Catechism in its original form (German), and from p. 428 the Latin translation of it, are to be found

or bring in contrary doctrines, according to their own pleasure."

It was not, thus, any improvement in the mode of instruction, or the like, that Frederick chiefly aimed at with his Catechism, but he had his eye in it, above all, on what was for him the most vital and fundamental of all Church interests, *unity of faith* and *harmony of doctrine* in firm, well-assured order; and in this view all pains were taken also to make the book the inalienable common property of the Church, and to secure for it, as such, a living interest with all its members. True, the Catechism was not imposed beforehand upon the ministers as an unchangeable, absolutely binding rule of faith; for, according to the consistorial instructions of the year 1564, every minister and school teacher, before entering on his office, must have the Catechism, as well as the general Church service, submitted to him, with the question: "Whether he could approve it, or what he found in it to censure?"* And while it was enjoined on the two church counsellors, who had the direction of the Synodical meetings held in every Classical district in May, to exercise any animadversion they might find needful in the sphere of doctrine, they had at the same time this charge: that, "if any one had a doubt to present in regard to some points of the Catechism or Church service, he shall be kindly encouraged to make it known, and be kindly heard and conferred with in regard to it."† But, with all this, it was, on the other hand, quite as decidedly required of the church council to see that the congregation "be instructed and taught with true, sound, godly, prophetical and apostolical doctrine, and not with human dreams and notions," and that for this purpose especially the most diligent use should be made of the Catechism in its proper meaning and sense. To every minister, more-

---

* See the Church Service of the Palatinate in the *Evangel. Kirchenordnungen* of RICHTER, b. 2, p. 277.

† Ibid. p. 280.

over, entering on his office, must be handed, along with the service-book, the Catechism, with the charge to "inculcate it diligently upon young and old;" and to bring in " no sort of novelty, contrary to it, either in doctrine or ceremony."*

It was plainly, thus, the design of Frederick that the Catechism, though not an absolutely binding rule of *faith* —which he recognized in the Bible only—should be, nevertheless, a firm and abiding *norm of doctrine;* and such a norm of doctrine, moreover, as might not only be a bar negatively against all arbitrary divergencies and innovations, but much more a treasure of positive and actual truth also for the Church, which, being made to live in the mind and heart of the teacher himself, should flow over from him into the very life also of the congregation. And since this looked not only to the young, but to the *whole* congregation, embracing all ages, other arrangements were adopted for securing the object in such broad view, which will be noticed in the following section.

II.

CHURCH READING OF THE CATECHISM, SERMONS AND ACADEMICAL LECTURES UPON IT.

The object of making the Heidelberg Catechism a true people's book for the Palatinate, and investing it with fresh interest and authority for the entire community through every period of life, might be consulted in different ways; and we find that in fact no proper means for the purpose was overlooked.

In the first place, the Catechism was regularly *read* throughout, in prescribed sections, before the congregations. The *Kirchenordnung* of the Palatinate† directs in

---

* See RICHTER, b. 2,pp. 277, 278, and 284.

† The Kirchenordnung, which contains also the Catechism and the Agenda, must be distinguished, as the more general, from the special Kirchen*raths*-

regard to this as follows:—"Firstly, inasmuch as the old folk have grown up in Popery without the Catechism, and readily forget the articles of the Christian religion, it is considered necessary that on all Sundays and Festivals, in villages and country towns, likewise also in the cities, before the sermon, the minister shall read before the people clearly and understandingly a portion of the Catechism, so as to go over the whole in *nine* Sundays." Then the divisions are given, as they are to be read successively on nine Sundays, closing for the tenth with the "sentence in which every one is reminded of his calling."*

In the next place, the Catechism was placed in close connection with the *preaching;* and this in two ways. First, it was directed that the preachers should, on every suitable occasion, refer to the Catechism, and bring in passages from it to confirm and enforce their own declarations; or, as the Inspection Order† has it, they shall not only teach the Catechism to young and old, but must, "as often as the text allows, with special earnestness and diligence quote it, adopt its language, and, as it were, season their sermons with it, in order that the manifold usefulness of it may be the more seen and felt, and the book be made the more clear, pleasant, and comforting to the people." Secondly, however, the Catechism must be formally and fully explained in the preaching, forming thus— without prejudice to God's word as the ultimate authority —its regulating object and canon. This was the properly so-called *Catechetical Preaching.*

---

ordnung. The first is of the year 1563, the second of the year 1564, both from Frederick III. The Kirchenordnung is found in RICHTER's work, pp. 257–275.

* See RICHTER, p. 260.

† This Inspection Order, originated by Frederick III., and afterward (in the middle of the seventeenth century) brought out anew by Charles Louis, is printed in an anonymous book, containing much valuable old matter, entitled: "*Die neueste Relig. Verfassung und Relig. Streitigkeiten der Reformirten in der Unterpfalz.*" Leipz. 1780, pp. 58–72. The passage here quoted is found on page 61.

On this the Kirchenordnung expresses itself thus :*—
" Moreover, on every Sunday afternoon, at such hour as
may be appointed for every place, *catechetical preaching*
shall be held, in such wise that the minister, after the
hymn, shall first say the Lord's Prayer, and call upon God
for the right understanding of His word; then read the
Ten Commandments understandingly before the people;
after which he shall examine the catechetical class; . . .
and, when the questions have thus been answered in the
presence of the congregation, he shall then go on to
expound simply and briefly some following questions, so
as to preach over the whole Catechism *at least once every
year.*"

What is here sketched only in its ground features took
afterward a more definite form. In the first edition, the
Heidelberg Catechism had no numeration of the questions.
Subsequently, not only was this introduced, but a division
of it was made also into fifty-two Sundays, to suit the catechetical preaching. The first trace of this division is found
in a copy of the Catechism which is incorporated with the
Kirchenordnung that appeared as early as November 15,
1563, at Mosbach: after the year 1573 it appears in separate editions of the work itself. In the beginning, moreover, the order called for a blending of catechization and
preaching in the afternoon service: first some questions
were asked and answered, and then a short exposition followed on the part of the minister. In time the catechization fell away, and there remained only the preaching on
the proper catechetical lesson.†

The origin of such catechetical preaching seems to
belong to the Palatinate, and to fall in with the rise of the
Heidelberg Catechism. If we suppose a foreign source,
we might think in particular of the Calvinistic mother

* RICHTER, p. 261.

† Even in the agenda incorporated with the *Kirchenordnung* of 1563 we
have a special forcible *prayer*, to be used "after the preaching of the Catechism." It is found in RICHTER's work, b. 2, p. 267.

Church in Geneva. But, although the Catechism of Calvin was divided according to Sundays, the Genevan Church ordinances of 1561 know nothing of catechetical preaching for grown persons, but require only the use of the Catechism for children;* and at the Synod of Dort, 1618, the Genevan divines even expressly declared themselves opposed to such preaching, because they held the method of question and answer to be the only one suitable in this sphere.† On the other hand, along with the spread of the Heidelberg Catechism went hand-in-hand the practice also of catechetical preaching, on the Lower Rhine, for instance, and in Holland; while in the Palatinate it continued, age after age, a fixed institution, organically wrought into the universal life of the Church.‡ When, in the year 1777, the rumor spread in Holland that some of the ministers in the Palatinate were seeking to do away with these sermons, the Classis of Amsterdam appealed on the subject with concern to the ecclesiastical council at Heidelberg, but received from this body in return, with thanks for their fraternal interest, an assurance that put their fears to rest.§ So the matter stood on to the beginning of the present century. I myself have heard catechetical sermons, in the Church of the Holy Ghost at Heidelberg, by the departed church counsellor Abegg, of whose peculiar and edifying character some general impression, at least, remains with me to this day.

The efficiency of the catechetical preaching was promoted principally by the fact, that from time to time a

---

* See the *Ordonnances eccl. de Génève* in RICHTER, b. 1, pp. 342–353; and on the point in hand, pp. 345 and 351.

† As is more particularly shown in an article on the Heidelberg Catechism by PLITT, published in the *Stud. u. Krit.* for 1862.

‡ How far it prevailed also beyond the Reformed Church I am not able to say. Professor PALMER speaks of it frequently (in his *Homiletics* and *Catechetics*, as also in Herzog's *Real-Encyclop.* vii. pp. 446–452), as a thing of general custom in the age of the Reformation; but he gives no instances in detail.

§ Rel. Verf. der Reformirten in der Unterpfalz, pp. 123 and 124.

public trial was instituted to see how far they had produced proper fruit.*   At the Classical meetings, the whole
congregation at times—young and old, male and female—
were subjected, for this purpose, to a searching examination on the Catechism, by ministers appointed for the
service; and the result of it was not only declared to the
pastor in his "*censure*," but published also by the inspector,
from the Lord's table, to the congregation itself, whether
for praise and encouragement or for blame and admonition.   Moreover, at least under Frederick IV.,† the con-
ferring of the right of citizenship and permission to marry
were made dependent on the ability of the parties to repeat
the principal portions of the Catechism.

All goes to show how the Heidelberg Catechism was
regarded in the Palatinate as the immovable foundation
of the whole Church life.   It stands forth practically as the
proper *congregational confession:* for the minister, to whom
it offered itself always as the measure of doctrine; for the
people, on whom it was continually urged and enforced as
the common scriptural chart of salvation for the whole
Church.   If the catechism should be, as Nitzsch strikingly
remarks,‡ "a test of public doctrine and public confession,
a foundation for the general or common working of Christianity," there was no want of care in the Palatinate to
make this true of the Heidelberg Catechism.

We have here, however, still a third matter to notice.
To explain and keep alive the Catechism, the ministers
themselves must be suitably imbued with a thorough scientific knowledge of its contents; and for this there was no
more judicious means than *academic lectures.*   Printed
works, such as Olevianus had already furnished in his *Firm
Ground of Christian Doctrine*, could not serve the same pur-

* Rel. Verf. der Reformirten in der Unterpfalz, pp. 92 and 93.
† By an order of the year 1694. See VIERORDT's *Gesch. d. Reform. in
Baden*, ii. p. 17.
‡ System of Christian Doctrine, ⸹ 2.

pose; for there could be no certainty of their general use. Ursinus, accordingly, as principal of the Sapienz-College, with the first introduction probably of the Catechism, opened a course of lectures upon it in the Latin language, which he continued to repeat annually there till the year 1577. Out of this grew his well-known catechetical work, which went through several editions (Neustadt, Geneva, Leyden), and was enlarged afterward by David Pareus.* In the same way, we know, Henry Alting's solid commentary on the Catechism was based upon such lectures, held by him in the first half of the seventeenth century at Heidelberg.† We may assume, therefore, that a standing order had place here; and we have in fact the testimony of a work already referred to,‡ of the year 1780, that formerly lectures had been delivered in the Sapienz-College daily on divinity, and "especially on the Heidelberg Catechism." How late this regulation had continued, it might be hard to determine; most probably not beyond the middle of the eighteenth century. As long, however, as it lasted, it was a principal means, undoubtedly, for giving the Catechism a fast hold on the life of the Church, as it served to show also the extraordinary importance which was attached to the book in its native land.

All that we have now brought into view in this section shows, in the clearest manner, how in the Church of the Palatinate pains were taken in every way, and from all sides, to give the Catechism active power and force, as the one harmonious and abiding ground of Christian faith and confession, through all the layers of society. We may doubt if any other Catechism has ever had as much done for it in this respect as is found to have been done for the Heidelberg Catechism.

---

* ALTING, *Hist. Eccles. Palat.* p. 196.
† See the Preface to this work in the Amsterdam edition of 1646.
‡ Rel. Verf. der Reformirten in der Unterpfalz, p. 237.

III.

THE EIGHTIETH QUESTION.

A peculiar feature in the history of the Heidelberg Catechism is offered to our view in its *eightieth question.* This it
was especially which called forth attacks upon it, from
different sides, and at times even threatened its continued
use in the Church of the Palatinate; which, however, only
served again to increase and strengthen the zeal of the
Reformed in its favor. Our purpose here is, neither to
blame, nor yet to justify what can admit of no full defence:
we wish only to explain the origin and course of the
matter; although this of itself must involve also a judgment.

The eightieth question occurs in connection with those
which treat of the Lord's Supper, and is intended to state
the difference between it and the Popish mass. The difference is given thus: "The Lord's Supper testifies, that we
have full forgiveness of all sins by the one sacrifice of Jesus
Christ, which He Himself has once accomplished on the
cross; and that by the Holy Ghost we are ingrafted into
Christ, who with His true body is now in heaven, at the
right hand of God His Father, and is to be there worshipped. But the mass teaches that the living and the
dead have not forgiveness of sins through the sufferings of
Christ, unless Christ is still daily offered for them by the
priests; and, further, that Christ is bodily under the form
of bread and wine, and is therefore to be worshipped in
them." So far the matter would have been without difficulty; it is an altogether objective representation of the
opposite doctrines, in which the strongest Catholic, even if
he might object somewhat to the form, could find nothing
as to substance wrongful to his own confession. But now, at
the close, came a consequence, drawn from the statement
going before, which cut deeper, and was felt to be a just
occasion for offence. The words follow: "and thus the

130

mass at bottom is nothing else than a denial of the one sacrifice and passion of Jesus Christ, and an accursed idolatry." And with these words it is that the subject here before us is concerned.

There is first a question of criticism belonging to it to be solved. The historian of the Palatinate Church, Struve,* affirms, on the authority of the learned Alting,† that in the first edition of the Heidelberg Catechism the *entire* eightieth question was wanting. This supposition, however, is erroneous, as D. L. Wundt has already made clear enough by referring to copies of the edition, yet extant, in which the question is to be found.‡ In itself, besides, it would not be likely that, with the strong opposition of Frederick III. to Popery and Catholicism, so weighty and significant a point as the relation between the Lord's Supper and the mass should have been passed over, in the new formulary, with entire silence. For the prince otherwise improved every opportunity to express this opposition openly, both in doctrine and worship. But, although the whole question is not thus an addition to the original text, the conclusion of it just quoted is so without a doubt; and this itself again appears to have been brought in, not at once, but in two different gradations, marking a corresponding progress of polemical zeal. First there was only the proposition: "the mass is at bottom nothing else than a denial of the one sacrifice and passion of Jesus Christ;" then came afterward the last and strongest clause: "and an accursed idolatry."

There is found in Heidelberg—the property once, probably, of the Ministerial Association of the place—an interleaved copy of "Köcher's Catechetical History of the Reformed Church, Jena, 1794." Here, in a side note to page 251, made with a lead pencil by some unknown but seem-

---

* Pfälzische Kirchenhistorie, p. 141.
† Hist. Eccles. Palat.
‡ Magazin für pfälz. K. Gesch. ii. pp. 112 and 113.

ingly competent hand, the affair is explained in the following manner: "There is no doubt but that in *one* year, namely, 1563, three editions of the Heidelberg Catechism were published at Heidelberg, or rather some leaves were printed twice, as, for example, fol. 55, on which occurs the famous eightieth question. In the first edition the concluding words, so offensive to the Catholics: 'so that the mass is, &c.,' were not present at all. The termination of the Council of Trent in this year, in which the Protestants generally were anathematized in certain of their doctrines, occasioned the Elector Frederick III. to have the words added: 'so that the mass is at bottom nothing else than a denial of the one sacrifice and passion of Jesus Christ.' But inasmuch as, after this second edition or variation also, still other provocations which had been passed at the Council of Trent became known, out came in the same year 1563 a third edition, making the appendix to the eightieth question still more harsh, as it now stands. I have had both the two last editions in my hands, and have gone over them carefully. The last is my own." So far the unknown annotator, who supports his view, besides, with some other observations; among them this one deserving notice, namely, that the Elector Frederick III. had himself put his thoughts of the Council of Trent on paper, and that the manuscript, six sheets long, in which he had belabored the Assembly with his own hand, was still to be seen in 1789.

This representation, which has to do not so much with three different *editions* of the Catechism belonging to the year 1563, as with a double *reprint* rather of only a single leaf (fol. 55) in the otherwise unchanged original edition,*

---

* The work *"Relig. Verfassung der Ref. in d. Unterpfalz"* (Leipzig, 1780) gives, pp. 119–122, a view substantially the same with this, only that it supposes the first two editions of the Catechism to have been *wholly destroyed.* This, of course, is conceivable; but it is hard to see why a whole edition should be destroyed, when it concerned only a short addition to a single passage, for which the reprint of a single sheet—nay, of a single leaf—would have been abundantly sufficient.

I am the more inclined to receive as right, inasmuch as it is essentially confirmed by the before-named D. L. Wundt, a good judge in matters of this sort.* He himself had likewise the so-called second edition, which belonged to the Ministerial Association of Heidelberg, before his eyes, and mentions also that it had at the close the following words: "What was overlooked in the first print, in particular fol. 55, has now been added by command of his Electoral Grace."

According to this documentary evidence, then, the polemical addition must be referred at once to Frederick III. himself; and as he was accustomed often, and even in his official acts, to use against Catholic doctrines and usages such terms as "abomination" and "idolatry," and stronger expressions still,† the thing is altogether internally probable. Even the milder Otho Henry himself had previously allowed a similar word in regard to the mass, in the Kirchenordnung established by him in the year 1556.‡ How much more must the far more decided Frederick feel himself impelled this way! As regards, moreover, the connection with the *Council of Trent*, it is something also altogether credible. Only a short time before its close in 1563, in its 21st and 22d sessions, on the 16th of July and the 17th of September, 1562, the council had taken up again the subject of the Lord's Supper, and had not only affirmed, in the most decided terms, transubstantiation, the adoration of the host, the sacrifice of the mass, the withdrawal of the cup from the laity, the use of the Latin language in the mass, and what else goes with all this, but had laid strong anathemas besides on all who refused to receive these determinations as true. This was exactly the time when the Heidelberg Catechism, whose introductory order is dated the 19th of January, 1563, was going through the press; and it is quite

---

* In his *Magazin* already referred to, p. 113.

† As, for example, on Confirmation, in the Kirchenordnung, p. 277, RICHTER.

‡ The expression ran: "From all this it is clear that there is much error and *idolatry* in the Popish mass." See STRUVE's *Pfälz. K. Historie*, p. 52.

conceivable that Frederick received his first knowledge of the last weighty decrees of the council—which could not fail to be repugnant to him in the extreme—after the first impression of his Catechism was already struck off, but was at once excited by it to meet the Catholic anathemas with a similar game on his own side, which he did, then, first with some moderation, but afterward, provoked perhaps by further information, in the roughest manner, outbidding even the hard word of his predecessor. Thus would we have here offence against offence, the violent retaliation of a single prince against the solemnly quiet, but none the less wounding, damnatory judgment of a whole vast Church assembly—a trait from the image of an age involved in sore conflicts, which we cannot be pleased with, but which, as things then stood, it is not hard for us to understand.

One bent only on defence may, indeed, say: The conclusion of the eightieth question was nothing more than the necessary consequence of the Reformed stand-point, over against the Catholic adoration of the host; but what is a matter of conviction, if there is to be any true religious freedom, it must be proper also to express; and Frederick did this just in the language of a time which was everywhere straightforward, and that shrank not, also, from what was sharp and severe. But, with all this, we are bound to distinguish always, where and for whom any thing is spoken. It holds differently with a dogmatic compend and with a book for the young and for the people at large. For the last the eightieth question went in its polemical sharpness too far, and even in the rough dialect of its age cannot be fully excused.

Frederick, indeed, when he ordered the offensive addition, had no thought whatever of a confessionally divided population, or even of a puritanic state in the modern style; what he had in his mind rather was a united Evangelical Reformed people, whose political and ecclesiastical constitution should be of one mould. And if it had turned out and remained so, the matter would not have been of so

134

much consequence. But there remained Catholics in the Palatinate; nay, there came in Catholic rulers again, with a full restoration of the Catholic worship in its strictest form. And then, of a truth, the concluding clause of the question became a serious thing; being justly open to reproach as an uncalled-for and gratuitous offence, while it served as a welcome occasion also for assailing the Reformed Church generally, and even for seeking its overthrow.

IV.

ASSAULTS UPON THE HEIDELBERG CATECHISM—ITS VINDICATION AND ESTABLISHMENT IN AND ALONG WITH THE PALATINATE CHURCH.

In the existing state of religious parties, it was to be expected that the Heidelberg Catechism would be vigorously attacked from its first appearance. So it happened in fact: first on the strong Lutheran side. Hesshus, whom the Elector had dismissed on account of his intemperate zeal for Lutheranism—the *exul Christi*, as he chose to style himself—issued forthwith a "*True Warning*," in which nearly every leading doctrine was contradicted, with the addition of a special tirade besides on the "fanaticism of bread-breaking in the Lord's Supper." Next appeared the more respectable combatant Matthias Flacius, with his "*Refutation of a small Calvinistic Catechism*," also in the year 1563. The Wirtemberg theologians Brentz and Jacob Andreä came out with sharp censures; Laurentius Albertus, a preacher on the Rhine, endeavored to fortify the cities Spire and Worms against the virus of the new doctrines; and even the Melanchthonian divines at Wittenberg put forth a decidedly unfavorable "judgment"—a fact which goes against the idea that the Catechism was only a transcript of the Melanchthonian scheme of doctrine.* Nay, the matter

---

* Among the damaging opponents of the Catechism is to be mentioned also a certain Francis Balduin, a renegade to the Roman Church, who resided in France. See ALTING, *Hist. Eccl. Pal.* p. 192. STRUVE, p. 144.

did not stop with the theologians simply, and their battles with the pen; the princes, who had so much to do in those times with Church affairs, also took it in hand. The Lutheran neighbors of Frederick, in particular, the Elector Wolfgang of Zweibrücken, Duke Christopher of Wirtemberg, and the Margrave Charles II. of Baden, expressed their earnest concern for his apostasy from the Lutheran faith, and its consequences. Against those who assailed the Catechism with the pen stood forth in its defence the Heidelberg theologians, in particular Ursinus, who had been so largely concerned with its preparation; who was supported, however, by the whole theological faculty, in an apology published in the year 1564. To meet the princes, Frederick himself came forward as the manly champion of his own work. He did so, above all, as is well known, after other occasions, at the Diet of Augsburg in 1566, with such effect that he not only gained the highest praise from the princes for his personal piety and honesty, but secured, with the Catechism, freedom also for his whole reformatory work;* so that he was subject to no further molestation. Here it was especially that the illustrious prince not merely saved his Catechism, but by his readiness for every sacrifice, even to parting with life itself, in its behalf, consecrated it with that inward sanction of whose significance we have spoken before.

Stronger, more persistent, and more effective than these Lutheran attacks was the opposition of the *Catholics*. On this side the whole book was repulsive; but the eightieth question operated perpetually as a special provocation. Here also the hostility to it soon took a very practical form, inasmuch as nothing less was proposed than its suppression and destruction. Literary combatants, indeed, presented themselves here also, as Koppenstein in the year 1621, and

---

* ALTING says: "Decretum: etsi Palatini electoris peculiaris sit sententia de S. Coena, non tamen propter istum dissensum damnandum aut a societate Augustanæ Confessionis excludendum esse." *Hist. Eccl. Pal.* p. 202.

Rittmayer in the beginning of the eighteenth century; but what was done in the way of actual interference, mainly under the influence of the Jesuits, was more important. The utterance of a Catholic dignitary reveals the temper which prevailed in this respect in high circles. When the army of the League, under Tilly, had taken Heidelberg, in the year 1622, the Pope's nuncio Montorio, in his report to Rome, spoke of it as a cause for joy that in the same city from which the norm of the Calvinists, the Heidelberg Catechism, had proceeded, "the holy mass henceforth would be celebrated, and the true faith spread abroad."* And when in the year 1685 the Catholic line Pfalz-Neuberg succeeded to the government of the Palatinate, the war against the work, especially after Lenfant came out in 1688 with his book, "*The Innocence of the Heidelberg Catechism*,"† assumed a continually more and more earnest character, until at length the third Catholic Elector, Charles Philip, was prevailed upon, in the year 1719, to attempt its suppression altogether.

For a long time previously it had been insisted that a book using such strong language against the Catholic doctrine, in a land of mixed religious confessions, and under Catholic rulers, was wholly unallowable; and when now in the year 1719 a new edition of the Heidelberg Catechism appeared, bearing the Elector's coat of arms on the title-page, with the words underneath, "*By order of his Electoral Serene Highness*," and a notification of the "*Electoral Privilege*," the thing was held up to the prince as an outrage upon his person and dignity not to be endured. The consequence was that on the 24th of April, 1719, he issued several orders, in virtue of which all copies of the Heidelberg Catechism containing the eightieth question—and there were no others—were to be forthwith confiscated, none to be given out under a penalty of ten florins,

---

* See VIERORDT, Gesch. d. Ref. in Baden, ii. p. 169.

† The work was written in the French language, and had the title: *L'Innocence du Catéchisme de Heidelberg.*

and the use of the book thenceforward generally in churches and schools to be severely punished. This, in connection with other oppressions, especially the violent transfer of the Church of the Holy Ghost in Heidelberg, led to an active controversy, in which foreign Reformed powers, with England and Prussia at their head, came vigorously to the help of their brethren in the Palatinate; while the clergy stood up, perseveringly at least, if not always with as much resolution as could have been wished, for the same cause, at home.*

The ruling points insisted upon in the controversy by the Reformed—aside from the easily explained circumstance of the Electoral coat of arms and privilege†—were in substance as follows. The eightieth question contains no condemnation of persons, but only of doctrine; but if Catholics may condemn Protestant doctrines, as in the Tridentine decisions and elsewhere, Protestants cannot consistently be refused the same right in regard to Catholic doctrines. On Reformed principles, the adoration of the host, particularly beyond its sacramental use, could not be looked upon as any thing else than idolatry; it is an error of public worship, which is more dangerous than an error of the understanding, and should it be forbidden to speak of it as it appears, there would be no real freedom of religion and conscience; for it belongs to this, necessarily, that one should be allowed to confess his convictions and their consequences before all men. But now, by imperial pacification and decree, especially since the Peace of Westphalia, religious freedom was as fully assured to the Reformed Church as to the rest of the alliance of the Augsburg Confession, and the Heidelberg Catechism was one of the most generally received symbols of the Reformed, the con-

---

* The entire controversy is given at large, with interesting public papers, in STRUVE's *Pfalz. K. Historie*, pp. 1368–1468.

† The whole affair could be referred to the bookseller, who was a Catholic, and seems simply to have followed a standing usage.

fessional basis in particular of the Church in the Palatinate. She could not, then, be required to change it. Nay,
she had no right .to do so if she would, since the Catechism belonged, as their common property, to all the Reformed Churches. Should she still do it, however, notwithstanding this, it would be only to confess that she had
been teaching before something scandalous, untrue, and
disgraceful. These representations—assisted, it is true, by
other more telling motives—gained at last their end. By
an Electoral rescript of the 16th of May, 1720, in the first
place, the Catechism was conditionally allowed again, and
soon after its freedom was in practice fully restored.*
From this time on there was no renewal of direct hostility
against it, although here and there an occasional war-cry
was lifted up, on the part particularly of the Jesuits, and
in other respects the Reformed Church in the Palatinate
had often to contend with heavy difficulties and straits.

While battle was thus maintained for and against the Heidelberg Catechism, particularly in its native land, from the
time of its first appearance, it ran a victorious course of *acknowledgment,* such as few other books of the sort have had,
throughout a large portion of the Christian world. A speaking evidence of this appears at once in the numerous *translations* which in long succession fell to its lot. Not only was it
soon translated into the dead languages, as into the Latin—
on order from the Elector—by Joshua Lagus and Lambertus
Pithopäus, into Greek by the celebrated philologist Syl-
burg, and by some one even into Hebrew itself: there
were versions of it also, far and wide, into living tongues
—Dutch, French, English, Italian, Spanish, Polish, Hunga-

---

* I cannot understand how *Niemeyer*, in the preface to his edition of the
Reformed Confessions, p. 61, allows himself to say: "From this time on
the hard expressions in the eightieth question were left out or softened." I
have before me an edition of the Catechism which was printed 1736, at
Heidelberg, "after collation with old copies," and here the eightieth question
stands in full. But this edition falls within the reign of Charles Philip; for
his death did not take place till 1742.

rian, Modern Greek, Arabic, Singalese. But the high estimation of the Catechism appears still further from the
fact of its wide *reception* and use. The Synod of Wesel
ordered its use in 1568, that of Embden in 1571; in
Switzerland it was introduced, particularly in Bern, St.
Gall, and Schaffhausen; so along the Lower Rhine—Hesse,
Brandenburg, Anhalt—and in Hungary; with the Dutch
it travelled into their colonies—as, for example, to the
Cape of Good Hope; with the Reformed emigration from
the Old World over to the Free States of America; and,
even where it came not formally into use, as in the Reformed Churches of France and England, it was dignified,
at least, with the highest honor and respect. It is known,
moreover, that it was declared to be of symbolical
authority by the Synod of Dort in 1618; and altogether
it would be hard to name any one else of the numerous
Reformed symbols whose confessional authority has been
so widely felt and acknowledged as that of the Heidelberg
Catechism.*

All this, however, reacted necessarily on the estimation
in which the formulary was held by its native Church,
causing it to appear more precious always in her eyes.
If it had been in the beginning the fountain-head of her
inward life, it became pre-eminently besides, in the course
of time, her outward honor and pride, the most powerful means by which she made her influence felt on other
Churches, and the most effectual bond of her fellowship with the holders of the Reformed faith, generally,
in Germany and throughout the world.† Nay, it came to
something yet more than this. The public *legal* rights,

---

* The only one to be compared with it in this view would be the *Second
Helvetic Confession*, which, however, in the nature of the case could not come
into the same popular use.

† With reason ALTING, in his *Hist. Eccl. Palat.* p. 191, says of the Kirchenordnung of Frederick III. and the Catechism: "Hæ bases erant ac funda-
menta Ecclesiæ Palatinæ, hæc vincula conjunctionis ejus cum aliis Ecclesiis,
Gallicis, Helveticis, Belgicis." But this holds mainly of the Catechism.

also, of the Reformed Church in the Palatinate depended on the Heidelberg Catechism. When these were restored to her by the Peace of Westphalia,* she not only regained her church property, but, above all, had secured to her at the same time the right of pursuing her ends in the way of her own original church order. One most essential part of this order, however, was the Heidelberg Catechism; and the right thus guaranteed to her of using it untrammelled and unabridged was specially appealed to, in fact, against the proposed oppression of Charles Philip. But the right of living according to her own order involved for the Church, at the same time, the duty of doing so; and this duty extended itself, of course, to what was the weightiest arrangement in the original church system of the Palatinate, the use, namely, of the Heidelberg Catechism, and a continued adherence to its principles. Only as the Church remained true to this duty could she lay claim properly to its corresponding right.

Thus, all things wrought together, causing the Heidelberg Catechism to take deep and strong root in the Church of the Palatinate: the inward excellence of the book itself and outward arrangements in its favor, threatening assaults and their successful repulse, motives of piety and grounds of legal right. For nearly three hundred years it was seen lifted up as the standard of this Church, with such authority as has hardly been exercised by Luther's Catechism over any Lutheran land. The time came notwithstanding, however, when even in the Palatinate itself it was cast aside like an antiquated piece of ancestral furniture, and given up freely and without force.

---

* See *Instrument. Pacis Westphal.*, art. iv. §§ 5, 6, 19; art. v. § 31.

V.

DOWNFALL OF THE HEIDELBERG CATECHISM IN THE PALATINATE.

On till toward the close of the eighteenth century the Heidelberg Catechism stood in full force, for all religious instruction, within the Reformed Church of the Palatinate. From that time its credit begins to wane; the sphere of its use grows continually smaller, and scarcely thirty years pass before it is banished from church and school altogether. The causes and the course of this revolution it cannot be without interest now to consider.

All conceivable arrangements, as we have seen, were devised from the first for upholding the credit of the Heidelberg Catechism in the Church of the Palatinate. Still the Reformed Church in general always held itself somewhat more free than the Lutheran in regard to the authority and use of symbolical books. She had, for example, no sworn engagement. Her care thus was rather for the inward habit and posture of the clergy in regard to received doctrines and their authority. Now, there was not wanting in the Palatinate also, through all this time, a specific confessional spirit. But inasmuch as it had been kept up mainly through the tradition or present sense of wrong suffered under Catholic government, and out of rivalry with the Lutherans, it came to possess a very external character. There was much jealousy—and often, indeed, with good cause — for ecclesiastical rights and privileges, but, along with this, the utmost indifference for the most part toward all that pertained to the proper life of the Church.

For it was now the time also when *Rationalism* was gaining more and more general sway in Germany. This way of thinking, which had no measure for the things of religion other than common understanding and moral utility, and which in its fancied illumination looked down

142

with contempt on the theological darkness of previous centuries, gained entrance also, of course, into the Palatinate. Here, however, it soon found itself at wide variance with the Heidelberg Catechism, which proved offensive to it, we may be sure, not simply by its characteristic *theology*, but by the whole positive tone of its *faith*—its evangelical doctrine in general. There was no longer any living point of contact with it, and so no power to understand it. This inward estrangement was followed then by outward renunciation, still more readily than this happened with similar cases in the Lutheran Church—not simply because there was among the Reformed in general a greater amount of freedom in such things, but because in the Palatinate particularly there prevailed at the time such a laxness of church government as had place perhaps nowhere else.

The Heidelberg theologians, in the second half of the last century—J. Wundt (†1771), Büttinghausen (†1786), Heddäus (†1795), and others—stood not yet, indeed, in open opposition to the symbolical church doctrine; they sought only to soften it to a universalist sense. But they were far enough, at the same time, from espousing the cause of positive Christianity with any such faith and courage as in the neighboring land of Swabia had been displayed in its behalf by Bengel and Oetinger, or, later, by Storr and his followers. Many students besides from the Palatinate attended the universities of Northern Germany—Halle and Jena particularly—and brought home with them neological views, which, meeting there no firm spiritual barrier, soon spread themselves far and wide. An advanced representative of this tendency appears, toward the close of the last and at the beginning of the present century, in the person of the highly-gifted and widely-active pastor and church-counsellor J. F. Mieg, of Heidelberg, who was in his time the most influential Reformed minister in the Palatinate. To him is due mainly the new Palatinate Hymn-Book, which made its appearance in 1785, and in which we have already a spirit most decidedly opposed to that of the

Heidelberg Catechism. This same spirit, however, in its unhindered progress, must necessarily seek to make an end also of the other religious formularies which had been produced by the early life of the Church. There came in a great liturgical waywardness, under the influence of which the old Scripture-fraught services were exchanged for other prayers and forms—those in particular of Zollikofer; and finally the destructive movement reached also the richest legacy from the hands of Frederick the Pious, the Heidelberg Catechism.

In this case, nevertheless, it is necessary to distinguish two different spheres of instruction, that for children and that preparatory to confirmation. For the instruction of children, with some exceptions, the Heidelberg Catechism in its shortest form was retained till the time of the Union, when it was entirely done away with, having at first no other substitute than a manual of Scripture sentences. In the most important department of religious teaching, on the other hand, that preparatory to confirmation, it had long before gone into disuse, both in its smaller and larger forms; universally, we may say, after the general prevalence of Rationalism at the close of the last century.* In place of it, use was made of what were called pastoral manuals; each pastor formed for himself, as he thought best, his own rule or plan of instruction; and it may easily be supposed that these productions, according to the theology of the pastors, would not only differ much among themselves, but be also of very different worth. Such a pastoral manual was the "Guide to Religious Instruction for Children of Tender Age," which had the Heidelberg

---

* Traces of the actual setting aside of the Heidelberg Catechism, and of a still wider disposition that way, appear as far back as 1780 in a work of that year on the ecclesiastical condition of the Reformed in the Lower Palatinate, pp. 126, 127. According to what is stated there, the Catechism must have been much more strictly retained in the cities than in the country. The author himself is willing to allow its symbolical authority, but would prefer having a different manual of instruction.

pastor Amadeus Böhme for its author, about the year 1790, and passed afterward frequently through the press. It acquired great credit, and soon came into pretty general use for schools and classes preparing for confirmation.* What its character was, however, we may see at once from the first question: "What is God?" Answer: "The first cause of all things.' Compare *this* first question with the first of the Heidelberg Catechism concerning the "only comfort in life and death," and there cannot be a moment's doubt as to the relation between the old, which was to be given up, and the new, which was to be substituted in its place. A weak, spiritless fabrication of the day, instead of a work of solid historical force and power; and, along with this, instead of the order which Frederick III. had established in this sphere, almost total church dissolution!

There were still, however, among the Palatinate ministers of the time, earnest and pious men also, who were sorely pained with this state of things, and were not afraid to express their feelings in regard to it. Among these is to be named above all J. F. Abegg, professor of theology finally, and pastor of the Church of the Holy Ghost in Heidelberg, as the noblest representative of the Reformed spirit in the Palatinate during the first half of the present century.† For this worthy man the Heidelberg Catechism precisely, which he followed in his teaching from 1794, had proved the richest mine of Christian knowledge and the entrance to scriptural truth. He wrote also, in the year 1806, an article in the Studien of Daub and Kreuzer, in which he pays it a handsome tribute, and indicates at the same time what was then the existing state of things, in a very characteristic manner.‡ Abegg assumes here that the

---

* What is here said is given partly from my own recollections, and partly from communications kindly made to me by older ministers in the Palatinate.

† He died 1840. See my *Character of Abegg* in the Theol. Stud. u. Krit., 1841, pp. 515–551.

‡ See the work for 1806, ii. pp. 112–140. The article is on the *Means of Religious Culture in the Protestant Church.*

clergy were under an historical and legal obligation to use the Catechism with fidelity, though not blindly, and portrays with affectionate interest the merits of the book, "whose utterances express so powerfully and triumphantly the confident feelings of the pious." Then he comes, however, on the question: How, after all, the better membership of the Church might stand affected toward the Catechism? This he had taken all pains in various ways to understand, and seemed always, he says, to hear this answer: "Take not from us the book of trust and love, the friend and comforter of our fathers! Though it have already something of an old-fashioned look, and may seem to favor also some worn-out notions, still thrust it not away! . . . Every other, compared with it, is for us a stranger; to this our hearts open with confidence and love, and in communion with it find their nearest approach to Jesus Christ, the author and finisher of our faith."

From all this, two things become very plain: first, that at this time (about 1806) there were ministers, probably quite a number of them, who had already either given up the Heidelberg Catechism altogether, or at least were strongly inclined to do so; secondly, however, that among those "who belonged still in reality to the Church" were found also not a few who clung to it with affection and good faith and would not hear of its being set aside. But, as time went on, the number of these last declined, the voice of piety died away, and the reigning spirit of the age became too strong not to fulfil its course at last in the entire abrogation of the Catechism.

VI.

REVIVAL OF THE HEIDELBERG CATECHISM IN NEW FORM.

In the year 1803, the Palatinate east of the Rhine was incorporated into what was known soon after as the Grand Duchy of Baden. The Reformed part of its population came in this way into the composition of a state, in which on the Protestant side the Lutherans formed a considerable majority; and there arose now very naturally, along with the wish for the closest possible political union, a desire to effect also an ecclesiastical conjunction of the two Protestant Confessions. The excellent Grand Duke Charles Frederick—led, however, not by state policy alone, but also by an upright evangelical heart devoted with fatherly inte_ rest to the welfare of his country—took the preparatory steps for the purpose; and under his second successor, Grand Duke Louis, with the co-operation of a General Synod convened for this end, the union of the Lutherans and the Reformed in Baden into *one* evangelical Protestant Church was in the year 1821 actually carried into effect. This is not the place to consider the worth of that fact: we confine ourselves at present to its bearing in particular on the Heidelberg Catechism.

Inasmuch as the Union in Baden was not simply one of church government, but looked to *doctrine* also, along with worship and constitution, and for this a set form was framed at large in regard to the main matter of difference, the Lord's Supper, there could be, of course, no further use of the two Confessional Catechisms, either Luther's or that of Heidelberg—at least not in their original form. They were, indeed, along with the Augsburg Confession, recognized still, in "their heretofore acknowledged normative character," as symbolical books of the United Church;* but as "forms of instruction in church and school" they were expressly and formally put out of use.† It would be wrong, however, so far at least as the Heidelberg Catechism is concerned, to make the Union alone responsible for its being set aside. We have seen that the Reformed in the Palatinate had themselves already turned their back almost entirely on their Catechism. The Union only gave the force of law and regulation here to what was already

---

* Unionsurkunde, ? 2.

† Unionsurkunde. App. 4, ? 3.

an existing fact. It is not, in this case at least, then, to be charged with the throwing away of an ancestral inheritance of faith. On the contrary, looking at the matter rightly, we must say rather that by it first the foundation has been laid for a movement once more in the opposite positive direction. And this in the following manner.

The committee appointed by the consolidating General Synod on the subject of a manual of instruction (*Lehrbuch-Commission*), among the most conspicuous members of which were found the Heidelberg theologians Daub and Schwarz, had most decidedly, as the whole theological character of these worthy men of itself implied, *this* conception of the Union, that it was not simply to dispose of the existing doctrinal differences by declaring them indifferent and so setting them aside, but must before all present and establish something positive. "Not in the indefinite," they say in their report, "not in an indifferentistic nothing, is the Union to complete itself, but on the ground of positive, evangelical, churchly Christianity." It was proposed, accordingly, to provide a manual of instruction, in which "the Augsburg Confession held in common, and the Confessional Catechisms belonging severally to the two Churches, that of Luther and the Heidelberg, should flow together and work in conjunction." In this sense also the General Synod framed their resolution. They proposed to have a Catechism which should be formed "on the ground of the previous Catechisms," and which should possess—as the Heidelberg did so decidedly—the "character of a confessional book."*

No Catechism of this sort, however, was at once produced. On the contrary, from circumstances which it would carry us too far here to explain, a manual was brought in from the year 1830, in which precisely the

---

* The fullest information in regard to the whole matter may be had from the transactions of the Baden General Synod of 1855, according to official report, Carlsruhe, 1856, i. pp. 195–339. In regard to the particular point here noticed, see pp. 210–215.

qualities now described were plainly *not* to be found, and which, besides lacking all church spirit, was also neither fully scriptural nor truly popular. But this formulary was not able to maintain its ground. Even from its first appearance it met sharp opposition, on the part of at least a small number of faithful ministers; and in the course of the following twenty years, during which a cheering revival of Christian life and Church feeling took place in our land also, the disposition to reject it became continually stronger and more general, till it was found to be finally an acknowledged, urgent necessity to have the whole matter in some way changed.

It came to pass thus—since a simple restoration of the old Catechisms was out of the question, as implying nothing less than a dissolution of the Union—that there was a return once more to the thought of their being worked up into a real *United Catechism*, of truly historical foundation and force. This thought had in the mean time found much discussion and favor also outside the sphere of official Church management; various attempts had been made, in a literary way, to provide what was felt to be called for; and in that part of the former Electoral Palatinate which now belongs to Bavaria, the lead had been actually taken, as early as the year 1854, with the ecclesiastical introduction of a Catechism composed in this spirit.* A number of Diocesan Synods of the land, besides, had begun to move in the same way, which the whole condition of the Church seemed now clearly to warrant and recommend. In these circumstances, the authorities of the Evangelical Church in Baden addressed themselves to the subject with great readiness, and the result was a formulary, which, being submitted to a General Synod convened in the summer of 1855, was, after some slight alterations, almost unanimously adopted.

---

* See in regard to it the article of Chief Counsellor *Mühlhäusser*, entitled: Union Catechisms, in the Theol. Stud. u. Krit. 1861. pp. 341 seq.

This Catechism embraces now what may be considered the substance of the Heidelberg, and this indeed to a good extent more fully and exactly than the free reproduction adopted in the Palatinate of the Rhine. The glorious first question appears there unchanged, as a matter of course. But the whole disposition and division also rest on the Heidelberg Catechism, and are so carried out as to omit none of its more pithy and choice questions. The changes rendered necessary by the incorporation of the leading points of Luther's Catechism, and by the stand-point of the Union, or the advanced development of theology, as well as the modifications required on other grounds, have been made with conscientious care; and the language, which both in the Heidelberg Catechism and in that of Luther is so distinguished for its truly popular and solid force, has been with sparing hand subjected to alteration, only in those places where it seemed to be absolutely needed. Every unprejudiced person—so we trust—will allow that in this book the Heidelberg Catechism in the main is renewed and restored to life again for its native land, as far as the idea of its organic interfusion with the Lutheran and our whole present church state could in any way possibly permit.

The result of this Catechism has been, thus far, all that could be wished. Its introduction took place without difficulty; and it may be particularly mentioned that older people in the Palatinate were sensibly affected when they again heard the well-remembered words which they had learned in their youth, on the "only comfort in life and in death." Abroad, the book was not only very favorably received in a literary view, as by Nitzsch, for instance, in an extended notice,* but it has already made a conquest also in the ecclesiastical world of which we may be sincerely glad. In our kindred, though in many respects also more advanced, Church of Prussia on the Rhine, it was received

---

* Deutsche Zeitschrift. Jahrg. 1857, pp. 5 ff.

first among the manuals whose use was held to be under church sanction; and when measures were taken afterward to have a formal Union Catechism prepared for the province, it was used as the basis for this new formulary, which differs from ours now, accordingly, in no material respect.*

With all this, the new Catechism will not fail to meet opposition in coming years, to which existing relations also may be expected to give additional force. Then will the *Union itself*, however, be put to the test in the Church of Baden. It will appear how much of positive Christianity and church life it is able to carry and preserve, and whether, if found wanting in such view, it can be still in any way maintained. But, in any event, the Catechism has at least found a place of preservation in the Church of the Rhine, which, if God will, shall remain sure.

---

* See Mühlhäusser, as before, pp. 351 and 368.

BRIEF HISTORY

OF THE

HEIDELBERG CATECHISM IN THE NETHERLANDS.

By DR. G. D. J. SCHOTEL,

KNIGHT OF THE NETHERLAND ORDER OF THE LION, IN LEYDEN, HOLLAND.

TRANSLATED BY H. HARBAUGH, D.D., LEBANON, PA.

A BRIEF HISTORY

OF THE

HEIDELBERG CATECHISM IN THE NETHERLANDS.

By Dr. G. D. J. Schotel,

KNIGHT OF THE NETHERLAND ORDER OF THE LION, IN LEYDEN HOLLAND.

Translated by H. HARBAUGH, D.D.

I venture to furnish a brief sketch of the history of a book which deserves to be regarded as one of the most remarkable productions of the human spirit to be found in the whole history of Christian literature. No book has exerted a more important influence upon the fortunes of whole kingdoms and nations. It was the basis of freedom to respectable ecclesiastical confederacies,—a leader and guide under the fiercest persecutions,—a source of consolation and encouragement in prisons, on scaffolds, and in the midst of martyr-fires. It was a book most highly prized for reading and instruction in private and public assemblies, in schools and families. Violently assailed, but manfully defended, it maintained its ground amid all the revolutions of states. It was translated into almost all ancient and modern languages, poetically rendered into verse, republished in countless editions, explained, paraphrased, amplified and regarded by thousands as the "crown of the Holy Scripture," as the "portal to the knowledge of God," as a "gift of God," as a "fountain of living water;" whilst some also pronounced its authors "men who, like the apostles, had been filled with the Holy Ghost."

This book is called the *Palatinate* or *Heidelberg Catechism*, after its fatherland the Palatinate, and its birthplace

Heidelberg. The Palatinate, so rich in memories for the Netherlands, gave a hospitable reception to thousands who had escaped the wrath of the Inquisition and the hands of the bloodthirsty Duke of Alba. In like manner did its Prince Palatine, with his family, for many years find friendly shelter and a safe asylum in the Netherlands. Heidelberg with its University was the cradle and nursery, the nurse and instructress, of that long list of worthy men who stood forth in our fatherland as preachers of the gospel; and their emigrated and banished professors, ministers, and citizens, during the Thirty Years' War, also found homes, protection, and nourishment in the Netherlands.

At almost the same moment when the light of the Reformation was kindled in Germany, it could also be seen to dawn forth in the Netherlands; and those who longed for the spiritual morning of the new life—whether that longing had been awakened by the reading of the mystic and ascetic writings of that day, or through the study of the Holy Scriptures—greeted it with inexpressible joy. When the Reformers had published their ideas concerning doctrine and life, and their works had been distributed by thousands even in the Netherlands, others also opened their eyes to the light, and fraternal assemblies began to be held, where they mutually encouraged, edified, and comforted one another as those storms were approaching which already raged over Germany, and now also began to threaten the fatherland.

What in Germany the Emperor was not able to accomplish, that the Duke and Count attempted in his Netherland States,—to smother in the germ the seed which had just been scattered, forcibly to destroy with the sword and consume with the flames the rising heresies. But in vain. As the phœnix from his ashes, there arose from every funeral-pyre, and every stream of blood, new confessors; and hundreds forsook kindred and friends and all they possessed, to seek liberty of conscience in Germany and England;

and when Philip began to swing his bloody scourge, when the Inquisition had instituted its bloody tribunal, when spies crept through the land to betray and arraign, when the sword was stained still more deeply with blood, the flames began to burn more fiercely, and the graves opened still more wide to swallow up the living, those who had already left their fatherland were followed by hundreds of thousands more; and not only in London, but also in Emden, Bentheim, Dantzic, Hanau, St. Lambert, Frankfort, Schönau, Cleves, Cologne, Neuss, Stade, Aachen, Hamburg, Goch, Buderich, Wesel, Embden, Denlaken, Emmerich, Rees, Gennep, and in other places, congregations of Netherland refugees were established.

To these thousands belonged a man who has for three hundred years been by some deeply despised, and by others extravagantly praised, Peter Dathenus, whom we recognize as a man who was ardent but not always judicious, zealous but not always cautious, learned but not always wise. He was born at Cassel, in Belgium, early became a monk, and entered the convent of the Carmelites at Ypern. Having become acquainted with the doctrines of the Reformation, and much interested in them, he soon left his convent and went to London, where he established himself as book-publisher. Here, coming in contact with the most prominent leaders of the Reformation, he burned with zeal to dedicate his powers to the advancement of the great cause, and hence devoted himself to the ministry. Compelled after the death of Edward to leave England, he roved about in Germany, and was at length located as minister at Frankfort-on-the-Main. When the Netherland refugees were there also deprived of religious freedom, he presented himself before Frederick III. of the Palatinate, who took him under his protection, showing him many favors, especially in this, that he vacated for the scattered Netherlanders the old convent of Frankenthal, at Worms, that they might locate there and without molestation enjoy their worship in the Netherland language.

Peter Dathenus was the minister and the soul of this new congregation, which daily increased in numbers. This congregation was conducted according to the Church Agenda which De Lasky had prepared in England, which John Untenhoven had translated into the Dutch language, and according to the extracts made from it by Martin Micronius or Martin Klein. In their religious instruction they used, besides the large Catechism of De Lasky, also the small Catechism of Micronius; and in the brief examination into the faith of those who intended to approach the Lord's Supper, they used an extract from the small Catechism of Micronius. But when the Liturgy and Catechism of the Palatinate were introduced, the congregation at Frankenthal also received them; and it is likely that they used the edition of this Catechism which had appeared in Emden in 1563, to which were added some forms of prayer. Some ascribe this translation to Dathenus, but without sufficient ground. Perhaps he may have made use of the Emden translation, which did not materially differ from his own; perhaps he improved that translation. However this may be, the translation made by him appeared in 1566, which, with the exception of unimportant changes in single words, is entirely the same which is still in use in the Reformed Church of the Netherlands. This translation is, however, far less successful than the Latin, and later the idea was entertained of perfecting a new one; but no one ventured to assume this labor, perhaps from reverence for the symbolical character which the translation of Dathenus had attained, and from fear that the work, while it might

ment to the old, be rejected by the majority. Not all the Reformed congregations in Germany followed the example of Frankenthal; and in East Friesland the Catechism of De Lasky, or the so-called Catechism of the country, could never be supplanted by the Heidelberg Catechism.

The most of the congregations in the Netherlands introduced it at once, especially as it was included at the end of the translation of the Bible, after the New Testament; and the Psalms rendered into metre by Dathenus, in the same way as the Catechism of Calvin in the Walloon churches of the Netherlands; that having the metrical Psalms of Marot and Beza appended. To this must be added the fact, that the largest number of the ministers, even when they had not been educated at the Heidelberg University, had still spent a longer or shorter time in Heidelberg, and many of them stood in intimate friendly relations with the theologians of the Palatinate.

Still, in the beginning of the Reformation the congregations were not bound to make use of the Heidelberg Catechism. The Synod of Wesel, 1568, and of Emden, 1570, although, through the influence of Netherland theologians, they urgently recommended it, nevertheless allowed the congregations in this respect full liberty.

The Synod of Dordrecht, 1574, believing that the unity of the Reformed could be promoted through this book of instruction, enjoined the introduction of it in all churches and schools of the Netherlands,—a resolution which was soon after confirmed, on their solicitation, by a decree of the Prince of Orange, and the States-General.

The following Synods at Dordrecht, 1578, and at Middelburg, 1581, passed a resolution of the same import; and the National Synod at the Hague, 1586, expressly decreed that the ministers everywhere should explain briefly the Heidelberg Catechism in the afternoon service in such a way as to get through it once every year. Thus, accordingly, the Catechism was firmly planted on an ecclesiastical and civil foundation, and, with the exception of Gouda, everywhere introduced in churches and schools.

At first, subscription to the Catechism was not thought of. This was first done in consequence of a resolution of the Synod at the Hague in 1586, which resolution was reiterated by the Synod at Middelburg, 1591, and was gradually endorsed by the remaining provinces. This was, however, done with great lack of uniformity, and it not unfrequently met

159

with opposition; yea, in some places the subscription does not seem to have at all been consummated.

Before the close of the sixteenth century, there were men in the Reformed Church of the Netherlands who could not agree with several doctrines of the Heidelberg Catechism, as Tyes Sybrantsz, at first minister in the St. Jacob's Church in Utrecht, and later in Meudenblik; Casper Yansz Coolhaes, minister in Leyden; Hermann Herberts, minister in Dordrecht and Gouda; Derok Volckertsz Coornhert, a noted author and poet; Cornelius Wiggertsz, minister in Hoorn; and James Arminius, professor in Leyden. By their teaching and writing they wrought great confusion in the Church. Ardent was the war of the pen. It rained controversial pamphlets, in which different parties defended their views. In vain did the Government attempt to reconcile the contending parties. At last it was concluded to submit the controversy to a National Synod, which was accordingly held in Dordrecht in 1618–19. It condemned the Remonstrants or Arminians, declared the Catechism to be a symbolical book agreeing with the word of God, and enjoined that all ministers, professors of theology, and instructors of youth, should subscribe it.

Herewith the Heidelberg Catechism had reached the highest honor which a human production can attain. It was sanctioned by the representatives of the entire Reformed Church, covered over with words of praise, and declared to be a symbolical book; which declaration was at that time confirmed by the sovereign of the land, in 1651 by the State Assembly, and anew in 1694. How completely the Netherlanders were taken up with this book may be seen from the many hearty eulogies preserved in countless writings, and which are often in such measure extravagant that even the Palatine theologians had to acknowledge that the Netherlanders exceeded them by far in reverence for their Catechism. They spoke of it as a work divinely inspired by the Holy Ghost, and regarded it as having the same authority as the Holy Scriptures. "In the

Heidelberg Catechism," they said, "is contained the complete divine doctrine in a small compass; the Holy Scriptures is a rule and standard of doctrine in so far as it is
explained in the sense set forth in the Catechism; the
Holy Scriptures must be interpreted according to the
direction of the Heidelberg Catechism." All such-like
declarations, which we might increase to hundreds, certainly proceeded from ministers of the Reformed Church,
but are not declarations of the Church; nor was it the
most noted and learned ministers that thus expressed
themselves; but these eulogies for the most part dropped
from the lips or escaped from the pen in the heat of controversy. The States-General called it only a platform of
unity, which is to be understood and explained according
to the contents of the Divine Scriptures, with which also
it would be found in full agreement. So thought also
Ameseus, Voetius, Maresius, Brakel, Smytegelt, Lampe,
D'Outrein; yea, all expounders of this book. "The Catechism," said they, "is by no means to be regarded equal in
value with the Divine Word." "We do not hold the Catechism as a rule according to which the instruction must
regulate itself, for in this light we regard only the Holy
Scriptures. It is an empty fear that the Catechism may
ever be regarded as a canonical book; for from the pulpit,
and even in the Catechism itself, we are taught otherwise."

During the sixteenth century the Remonstrants still
warred against the Catechism, and ministers also arose in
the bosom of the Reformed Church who declared themselves opposed to some of its doctrines. To the first
belonged Hugo Grotius and Batelier. Grotius, in two of
his publications, expressed himself unfavorably toward the
Catechism, but was answered as he deserved by Andrew
Rivet; whilst Batelier entered into an ardent pen-contro-
versy with Voetius. Episcopius, also, and Abraham Heydanus mixed in with the strife. Among those in the
bosom of the Reformed Church who set themselves in
opposition to the Catechism were Adrianus ·Coerbach,

Balthaser Bekker, a Cartesian and minister in Franeker, and Ponhaan van Hattem. Bekker was—some think unjustly—charged with teaching false doctrine in his book of Instruction on the Catechism; and Van Hattem was arraigned on account of his Spinozian views expressed in his Treatise on the Catechism, and deposed.

Very numerous are the editions of the Catechisms issued in the course of the sixteenth and seventeenth centuries. The first were printed in Emden, Frankenthal, Ronean, Norwich, and London, and introduced secretly,—and also in the Netherlands, but these appeared without the name of the printer or the place where issued. Thus, for instance, it was published by Herman Schenckel in Delft, 1567, who was in the following year punished by death. The first one who ventured to place his name on the title-page was John Packts, printer, in Leyden.

In the oldest editions there is no variation in the general features. It may, however, be observed that in the revisions sometimes the German, sometimes the Latin, edition was followed; and, since the German editions of the Catechism vary in the texts, it is not a matter of surprise that these are also found in the Netherland translations. There appeared in Antwerp, 1580, an improved edition of the translation of Dathenus provided with new proof-texts, and enlarged by the addition of the Psalms rendered into metre by Marnix of Aldegonde. This edition was prepared by Casper van der Heyden or Heydanus, one of the most remarkable men on the arena of the Church in the sixteenth century,—a man of extensive biblical knowledge and approved piety. This edition is followed in all subsequent reprints.

In the sixteenth and seventeenth centuries there was no want of commentaries on the Catechism. The oldest, and those always very highly esteemed, are the *Exegemeta sive Commentaria in Catechisie Religiones Christianæ,** first published

---

* By Jeremiah Bastinging, minister in Antwerp and Dordrecht.

in 1588, afterward also in 1590, and translated into the Netherland language by Henry van der Corput, minister in Dordrecht. This Exegemeta was followed later by the Commentaries of Philip Lansbergen, earlier minister at Antwerp and at Goes; Henry Willemsz Brandt; Ruardus Aeronius, minister in Schiedam; Sybrandus Lubberti, professor in Franeker; John Becius, minister in Dordrecht; John Beildsnyder; John Coccejus, professor in Leyden; Henry van Diest, professor in Deventer; Antonius Hulsius, professor in Leyden; Melchior Leydekker, professor in Utrecht; John Martinius, and Christianus Schotanus, professor in Franeker. All these were written in Latin; whilst Amielius Calemborg, George de Mey, Balthasar Bekker, Pontiaan van Hattem, and other ministers, published explanations of the Catechism in the Netherland language. Festus Homminus, professor in Leyden, also published a translation of the Commentary of Ursinus. Later, this translation, with appendices by John Speljardus, was reissued; it was finally, in 1726, again published, in an improved and enlarged form, by John van der Honert, professor in Leyden.

Great is the number of *Sermons* on the Catechism which have appeared, both in the Latin and Netherland language, many of which have been a great many times republished. Worthy of notice are those of Emilius van Calemborg, Floris de Bruin, Cornelius Gentman, Henry Groenwegen, and especially those of David Knobbe, minister in Leyden, Peter van Hagen, minister in Amsterdam, Franciscus Redderus, minister in Rotterdam, Casparus Sibelius, minister in Deventer. They were, with some exceptions, for the most part more adapted to make the public acquainted with the various doctrinal views of the Reformed Church than with the doctrine of the gospel, and were in general dry, sterile, scholastic discussions. Their authors were especially unwearied in endeavors to defend the Reformed doctrine against all earlier and later heretics; and the same was also done in the numerous books of Instruction in the

163

Catechism which at that time appeared. They wished to make the children early acquainted with the various views of the Arians, Pelagians, Catholics, Remonstrants, Mennonites, Lutherans, Hattemites, and others, and place them in a condition to answer them. After the Voetician and Coccejian controversies had created confusion in the churches, and the minister party was attacked, the books of instruction, as also the sermons, were written either in a Voetician or a Coccejian spirit.

In the Latin schools the Latin translations of Beza and Pithopæus were used; and in the Greek schools the Greek translation made in 1648, by order of the States, and also that of Sylburgius, were in use.

Thus, in the seventeenth century the Catechism was the only book of instruction in church, school, and family. No village was so small, no farm so remote, that it did not find entrance to it. It was to be found in every manner of form, at the end of all Bibles and Psalm-books; and whoever wished could obtain it, explained, paraphrased, confirmed, with or without marginal notes, in full and abridged, and in every known language.

But not only in the mother-country was it the only religious book of instruction (all others were enlargements, paraphrases, explanations, and compendiums of the Catechism), but also in transmarine colonies no other was known; and the ministers were careful that it should be translated into the languages of the countries which acknowledged the sovereignty of the States-General. In this way it was translated into the Arabian tongue by Professor Jacob Golius, who also had the book printed at his own expense. William Konyn translated it into the Senegalian language; Sebastian Danokaerts, minister in Amboyna, and Georgius Henricus Werndly, into the Malayian, and others into the Greek language.

Cornelius Coons also translated it into English, and Martin into French, for use in schools. Truly could one of our poets say, "It was understood in all languages."

Yea, it was not only translated into all languages, but a number of times rendered into verse, and sung. In this way was it rendered in Latin by Franciscus Plante, and in the Netherland language by Samuel Ampfing John Dakerius, John Bagelaar, Constantia Eusebia, Andrew Anduersen, Peter van Gand, and others: even as late as the close of the last century it was rendered into rhyme by Peter Francis Halma, and Jonas Andrew Repelaer, in the same language.

But never did the Heidelberg Catechism see a more glorious period than during the first half of the eighteenth century. To no one was the care of a congregation or the instruction of youth intrusted until he had first, by the subscription of his own name, acknowledged its authority as a symbolical book. There was no instruction imparted wherein it was not explained, no church in which sermons on it were not preached, no school in which it was not used for instruction, no family in which it was not committed to memory. Scholars and poets, ministers and teachers, vied with each other in expanding it, abridging it, writing books of which it was either the basis or the guide. No work written upon it was allowed to be published which had not first been ecclesiastically approved. There was no Netherlander, from the head of the Republic down to the humblest day-laborer, who was not required publicly to declare that the doctrines of this book agree with the word of God, and that it comprehends every thing that is necessary unto salvation, before he could be received as a member of the Church. He that did not agree with its teachings, and in accordance with them enter the Church, could neither hold office nor position in the State. Yea, it was at one time made a subject for consideration in the States-General whether it was not highly necessary to refuse all applications for offices, even those in villages the duties of which are discharged only on the public street, from all those who had not publicly professed the Reformed faith; and the children of the Catholics, if they did not wish to be excluded from the public instruction, had, like all others, to commit the Heidelberg Catechism to memory. Thus was the Catechism adhered to, if possible, more firmly than ever. It was regarded "as the richest legacy of the forefathers;" "with it would stand or fall the Church of the Netherlands."

Woe to him who ventured to attack it, or preach a doctrine which deviated from that of Ursinus, or from the Church in which it was received! Then it became apparent that the blood of the forefathers still rushed fiery through their veins, and that in the matter of intolerance they had not yet degenerated from the spirit of those who had gone before. This was experienced by Bekker and Van Hattem, Becius, the Hebraens (Hebreen), the Shorists, and whatever other names they bore,—the heretics of the seventeenth and beginning of the eighteenth century. This, too, Venema, Van der Os, Van der Marck, Klunau, Ten Sage, Ten Broek, and many others, were to experience later. But the ecclesiastical proceedings which were conducted against them show that there was yet many a one who from abhorrence to blind ecclesiastical faith contended for tolerance and freedom of speech; for Ten Broek, Ullman, Van der Marck, and Venema did not stand alone, but found strong confederates among the most learned and renowned men of their time; and how many there were who were prepared, though not always actively, to fall upon and destroy the sickly mysticism which began to appear daily more visibly, and here and there grew into a perfect fury, is shown by the process against Schortinghuis, and the Nykirkisch disturbances.

We would too far transcend the limits allowed us, should we attempt to enter upon a circumstantial consideration of the ecclesiastical discussions which prevailed during the eighteenth century in regard to some doctrines of the Heidelberg Catechism. They related, namely, to the Sabbath, the satisfaction of Christ for all sinners, the Lord's Supper, our natural proneness to hate God and our neighbor, and

166

were carried forward with that ardor which characterized all ecclesiastical controversies in the Netherlands. Whilst these and other dissensions created confusion in the Churches, and it rained anew controversial and uncharitable pamphlets, some moderate theologians were engaged in publishing sermons and commentaries on the Catechism, which were, it is true, more tolerant than those of the seventeenth century, but still largely partook of a controversial character, of the nature of apologies for the Reformed system of doctrine, and written in the Voetician or Coccejian spirit.

Among the sermons on the Catechism which in this period are favorably distinguished may be mentioned those of Bernard Smytegelt, minister in Middelburg, and those of John van der Kemp, minister in Dirksland. Both are highly practical, have been very frequently republished, and are still read among the people, especially those of Van der Kemp. The other collections of sermons were nearly all written in the Voetician or Coccejian spirit, vanished soon after their appearance, had but few readers, and never became generally known. The catalogue of these writings is very large, and our space does not allow us to speak of them. We may mention D'Outrein, Köcher, and Van Alpen.

Favorable mention, on account of the practical tendency of their catechetical writings, may be made of Matthew Gargon, minister in Vliessingen, Simon Molenaar, minister in Vlaerdingen, John D'Outrein, minister in Dordrecht and Amsterdam, Justus Vermeer, and of the Professors Hermann Alexander Röell, John van der Honert, and Albert Schulteus. Among the commentators of the Heidelberg Catechism in the eighteenth century, the first rank belongs to the moderate Coccejian minister John D'Outrein, a pupil of Vitringa, Professor at Franeker. After the example of his renowned teacher, he sought to effect a desirable change in the mode of preaching as it then prevailed, and, instead of the dry, sterile, pointless, emotionless, and tasteless preaching, which was full of learning but without application, he sought to bring upon the pulpit the pure truths of the gospel, and to enforce the practice of true piety. One of his works* was translated into the French, English, German, Portuguese, and Malay languages; others were at various times republished. His catechetical work with the title: *Het Goude Kleinood van de Leer der Waarheid, die naar die Godsaligheit is, vervattet in den Heidelb. Catech. nader uitgebreidt, opgeheldert en betragt*, was also nine times reprinted, translated into German, by renowned poets celebrated in verses, and by his cotemporaries praised to the skies. I nowhere find that this commentary met with any opposition in Holland, but that the German translation prepared by Frederick Adolph Lampe, professor in Utrecht, was violently assailed by Esdr. Henr. Edsardus, of Hamburg,† chiefly on account of one word which had evidently been a misprint crept into the text through the carelessness of the translator.

How highly this work was prized in Germany may be learned from the testimonies drawn from the Heidelberg Catechism, and D'Outrein's Commentary on that Catechism, in regard to some doctrinal views of the German Evangelical Protestant Church in general, and in regard to the proposed reformation of their cultus by the General Synod of Baden in the year 1843 in particular, presented for the hearty consideration of the clerical members of the Diocesan Synods of Baden assembling in the year 1846, by John Hormuth, Evangelical Protestant minister in Altlassheim. The compiler, taking the best Holland edition of John D'Outrein (that of 1770), compares his explanations of doctrinal points with the documents which formed the original articles of the Baden Union, and shows how much these last deviate from the Confessional books and the teachings of the Reformed Church, and that they are composed in the spirit of the Lutheran Church. In our father-

---

* Korte Schets der Godlyke Waarheden. †Bibl. Brem. Cl. ii. p. 378.

land the *Goude Kleinood* itself also belongs to the literary history of the Catechism. It is antiquated, and, as it embodies the Coccejian spirit, it is not held in high estimation by the orthodox. For a long time, however, it was the hand-book of the earnest Coccejians.

The catechetical works of John van der Honert, professor in Leyden, a zealous Coccejian and true champion against the errorists of his time, are less read, and are merely intended for the study of the learned. Besides the Treasure of Ursinus, which we have already mentioned, and a work on the Catechism, he also wrote a Preface to the Netherland translation of Johann Rodolphus Rodolphi *Catechesis Palatina in usum auditorii sui illustrata.*

The *Explicatio Catechesis Heidelb.* of Herman Alexander Röell did not meet the general expectation based upon his fame for great learning. It is confused, obscure, and incomplete. Better are the *Lucubrationes in Catechismum Palatinum* of Peter van der Hoeke, and the *Dictata* of Professor Albert Schulteus, translated by John Bazeuth, minister in Dordrecht.

In the eighteenth century the Heidelberg Catechism still continued to be used as a book of instruction in schools, and no less large than in the seventeenth century was the number of little books prepared according to the scheme of the Catechism, and published for the young. Religious instruction was, nevertheless, in a sorrowful condition, and for the most part was left in the hands of the school-teachers. The children learned little beside the dogmas of the Church, and those in their controversial aspects, but not the least in regard to morals.

At the close of the eighteenth century a commencement was made to bring about an improvement in religious instruction. Books of instruction were published which did not only contain the doctrine of faith, but also the principles of morals, and that were at the same time adapted to serve the purpose of imparting instruction in biblical history, which had been so long neglected in the schools.

169

The events which followed on each other in wonderfully quick succession,—the misery which the revolution of 1795 brought in its train, and which affected also our father-land,—the oppressive chains which were laid upon civil and moral liberty,—the heavy offerings of property and blood which were repeatedly demanded, filled all hearts to such a degree that room was left for no other thoughts than those pertaining to the misery of the fatherland and their own personal tribulations, and all other interests had to vanish before those of the present moment. What a host of writings on tolerance and brotherly love could not effect was brought about by the common sorrow,—frater-nal union. The controversies which for years had wrought confusion in Church and State were forgotten, and when here and there a faint echo of them was still heard, it soon died away. Opinions and utterances which before had set the Church in fire and flame, and were condemned by ecclesiastical tribunals, were not even noticed,—or were heard, discussed, and answered with forbearance. The wall of partition which had been erected between the different ecclesiastical parties tottered, and gradually fell to pieces. Even toward the Roman Catholics was the brotherly hand extended; and when the controversial points were still touched on in the handling of the Catechism, it was no longer done in the spirit of the fathers. After the restora-tion in 1813, tolerance was the key-note in all that was discussed and resolved upon by the prince and his coun-sellors. It held the first place in the assemblies of the nobles, and in the convention which met to organize the ecclesiastical interests which had been thrown into con-fusion by the French supremacy when the Church lost its independence, and it shone forth in the new Constitution, by which the old was renewed to suit the spirit of the times, but in which especially the State was granted more influence over the Church than was before the case.

By this Constitution the symbols of the Netherland Church were not set aside; even the preaching on the)

Heidelberg Catechism was prescribed, and subscription to it required. This, however, was not done by professors of theology, rectors, and other teachers, as previous to 1795, but only by those who, after having stood an examination, were admitted into the office of the public ministry. These were not required to subscribe themselves in the way of promise that they would preach the doctrine of the confession of faith, the Heidelberg Catechism, and the canons of the Synod of Dordrecht, explain them faithfully, and declare that these in all points agree with God's word, but only that the doctrines which agreeably to the word of God are comprehended in the received formularies by unanimity of the Netherland Reformed Church, were by them sincerely received and heartily believed, that they would faithfully teach and advance them, and that they confirm this by the subscription of their names.

In the year 1835, when the Separatistic disturbances aroused the Church from its deep sleep, it was discovered (was it intentional, or accidental?) that there is an ambiguity in the expression "agreeably to the word of God;" and one explained this expression so as to mean that they believed the doctrines and the formularies because they (*quia*), the other in so far as they (*quatenas*), the third as those which (*quippe*), agree with the word of God; and when the Synod was earnestly asked for a definite explanation of the controverted expression, it declared, after careful consideration, that it was not its privilege to accede to this request, because such declaration transcended the limits of their privilege. This was merely a plausible pretext; for if the Synod had the right, by royal permission, to amplify or change the Constitution, it also possessed the right to furnish an explanation of several words in an article of the Constitution. The true reason was anxiety for the rest and peace of the Church; for whatever explanation they might have given, it could only have become the source of bitter disunion. In 1841 the applicants went further, and asked for the abrogation of the new and the restoration of the old subscription formulary, adopted in 1618–19. The Synod declined satisfying this request, but now gave a more definite explanation of the subscription formulary: "that it was not sufficient to adhere to this or that truth contained in the formulary-article, but that in general the doctrines prescribed therein, as they, according to their substance and spirit, constitute the substance and principal contents of the Reformed Confession of Faith, are to be received by the ministers of the Reformed Church." Here it remained; and the *theologiæ candidati* still subscribe the formulary prescribed in 1816, without definitely knowing to what it obligates them, whilst the Separatists subscribe the old one prescribed by the Synod of Dordrecht, in which the doctrinal formularies are explained as agreeing with the word of God.

The Catechism in the Netherlands, as before the new, organization, was still explained from the pulpit on Sunday afternoon; but soon complaints were heard here and there that the catechetical sermons were poorly attended. Some attributed this to the Catechism itself, which, as it was thought, the congregation did not wish any more to hear; but the Synod properly judged that this evil lay rather at the door of the ministers and their handling of the Catechism in the pulpit, and admonished them to exercise more care in their catechetical sermons. Since then nearly thirty years have passed, during which this matter of the Catechism has not been mentioned either by the congregation, the Consistory, or the Synod. The congregation went on attending upon the catechetical sermons more or less regularly according as they were conducted; the Synod continued to exercise care that they were regularly held, till in 1861 it came to the conclusion that the obligation to hold the catechetical sermons did no longer exist, and resolved to leave it to the free choice of the ministers whether they would preach on the Catechism or not. This, however, created opposition in such measure that Synod

172

was necessitated the following year to recall this resolution, and anew to make the catechetical sermons obligatory.

In the Netherlands, sermons on the Catechism are preached to this day. Some explain it word for word; others take the questions as motto, and preach in a free way upon the truth contained in them. Explanations and sermons on the Catechism are also still published.

Toward the end of the eighteenth, and in the nineteenth century, appeared the Commentaries of H. Ferre, C. Brinkman, Bartholomew Outboter, minister in Wonbragge, John Carel Salier, professor in S. Hertogenbosch, Peter Cartenius, professor in Amsterdam, of which the last-named especially is still held in high estimation by the Separatists; further, those of Gerard Benthen Reddingen, minister in Arsen, F. Liefsting, minister in Rauwerd and Ecrnsun, T. van der Linden, minister in Kantus, S. H. Koorders, minister in Maarsen; also the Guides of Reddingen, of Maslin, minister in Bern, and the catechetical sketches of Scheffer, minister in Leyden, were used by the ministers in the preparation of their sermons on the Catechism. As a general thing, the Catechism was very highly prized in our fatherland by the Orthodox; and the Liberals, although they did not fully agree with its teachings, still regarded it as a venerable memorial of the hoary past.*

---

* See Geschiedenis van den Oorsprong, de Invoering, en Lotgevallen van den Heidelbergschen Katechismus, door G. D. F. Schotel, Phil. Theol. Mag. Litt., Doctor. uistend predikant van Tillburg te Leyden, Ridde van der Nederl. Leeuw. Amsterdam, by W. H. Kerberger, 1863. 374 Bladzyde.

FREDERICK III.

ELECTOR OF THE PALATINATE.

By B. S. SCHNECK, D.D ,

CHAMBERSBURG, PA.

FREDERICK III., ELECTOR OF THE PALATINATE.

By B. S. Schneck, D.D., Chambersburg, Pa.

I.

INTRODUCTION.

AMONG the "spoils" which the spirit of ancient prophecy promised to the Redeemer, belong also the "great" and the "strong" (Isa. liii. 12). And at no time do we behold so large a portion of this class becoming decided disciples of Jesus as during the pentecostal days of the Reformation.

After a long period of night and gloom, the clear, bright sunlight of the blessed gospel arose with cheering beams upon Germany, and a new day dawned in the history of Christ's kingdom on earth. It was then, under the movings of the Spirit of the Lord, that children were really born unto Him like the "dew of the morning." And among these "children" there were those who were among the "great" and the "strong" of the earth.

A line of German princes, the best and noblest of that select class, were raised up as guardians and defenders of the Reformation. Accessible as their consciences were to evangelical truth, their hearts were soon favorably inclined, and the positions which they occupied enabled them to operate effectively against the opposing influences of the Emperor, Charles V.

Germany had long ceased to be a political unit, such as it was in the days of Frederick Barbarossa. It was cut up into a number of separate governments; and the princes had already come into possession of considerable independent power, which in certain circumstances they could bring to bear against the Emperor himself. Hence we

177

behold in the history of the Reformation this interesting, and in its way singular, spectacle: on the one hand an Emperor, a decided opponent of the Reformation, who left no effort untried to crush out Protestantism; and on the other an array of German princes, faithful friends, strong protectors, and zealous guardians of the Reformation, ready to introduce it and further its progress in their dominions to the utmost, in spite of all expostulations and threats from Emperor or Pope.

In glancing at these evangelical princes of the Reformation-period more in detail, we behold a galaxy of magnificent and most engaging characters. Look, for instance, upon those three princes of Saxony:—the noble, the universally esteemed, the sagacious and conscientious Frederick the Wise (1486–1525), the earliest protector of Luther in the darkest days of his trials; next, John, surnamed the Constant, the brother of Frederick (1525–32), who, with the living faith and firmness of the Christian, remained true to the cause of the Reformation till his death, and was instrumental in accomplishing a great work by establishing, as well as disseminating, the pure gospel in his dominions; and, finally, the gentle and devotedly pious John Frederick, who became a martyr of the Reformation after the battle of Mühlberg, in 1547, bearing the terrible calamity in the spirit of the primitive confessors.

And then, turning your eye away from these Saxon princes, you behold at their side the imposing figure of the impetuous and energetic Landgrave Philip of Hesse, with heart and soul wrapped up in the Reformation, not only forthwith introducing it into his own country (1526), but by his political sagacity and dexterity laboring with might and main to obtain for it political existence and acknowledgment elsewhere, in order that a foothold might be secured to the renovated Church in the future.

Take a glance at another picture. It rises up before you from the more southerly portion of Germany. It is a prince, also, and, mentally and morally, head and shoulders taller than his predecessors. For he is not only, like these, a protector and promoter of the Reformation, nor merely its witness and representative before the Emperor and the world, but he is himself a Reformer, richly endowed with all the attributes of head and heart for so important a mission. It is Prince Frederick III. of the Palatinate. What those Saxon princes and that young prince of Hesse were to the young *Lutheran* Church, that, and much more, Frederick III. became to the *Reformed* Church. He is not merely a protector and promoter, nay, he is the founder, of the Reformed Church in Germany, and as such his form looms up before us in grave and exalted proportions. So pure and true, so eminently devout, and so fully animated by the Spirit of Jesus Christ is he, that scarcely any one of those Lutheran princes can be regarded as his equal.

The confessional position on which the Reformed Church stands at this day was not eliminated and prepared by others for him. On the contrary, he was personally active and aided in the work himself, and then defended it, in 1566, before the assembled princes of the Empire, with an assurance of faith and a Christian heroism that not only challenge our admiration, but force on the mind the conviction that he was indeed a star of the first magnitude and of the brightest lustre in the constellation of Christian confessors.

And now that the Reformed Church in the New and in the Old World gives expression to her joy, as she does this day by her Tercentenary Festival, and in view of the elevated and sweetly evangelical doctrinal position of the Heidelberg Catechism, remembering what a treasure was committed to her three centuries ago, she is simply fulfilling a debt of gratitude and filial love by remembering in this connection Frederick III., through whom, by God's favoring mercy, that venerable symbol to which she adheres with unswerving devotion was called into being.

II.

FREDERICK III. TO THE BEGINNING OF HIS REIGN.

Frederick III., surnamed the Pious, was born in Simmern in 1515. The possessions of his father, Count Palatine John II., lay westward from the central province
of the Rhine, between the Neuse and Moselle. In addition to the beautiful valleys between these streams, he
possessed a large portion of the picturesque mountains
of that region. His son Frederick was, as a matter of
course, educated in the Roman Catholic faith, to which the
father was zealously attached. He received his education at the courts of the Cardinal of Lorraine, the Bishop
of Liége, and the Emperor Charles II. Amid these surroundings not a breath of evangelical air was permitted to
be felt, and hence the young count could not fail to give
himself up to the only system of faith which was professed by those in whose society he moved. God had
endowed him with high and noble qualities both of head
and heart, a clear and vigorous understanding, a sound
judgment, and great moral earnestness. His conscience was
as active as his head was clear; and, as he had no difficulty on the one hand in perceiving the wrong, so he felt it to
be on the other his conscientious duty to protest against it.
And hence it may be said that he was a Protestant in his
conscience before he was one in his faith. But the Protestant conscience was soon followed by a Protestant faith.
The young prince had seen, as well in Metz as in Liége,
the voluptuous and immoral life of the higher orders
of the clergy, and had besides heard the doctrine of "good
works" preached up as the sole ground of salvation, according to the system of the Roman Church. This contradiction between the preaching and the practice of the
priesthood made him pause, and awakened in his mind
the first doubts in regard to the doctrine of the merits
of so-called good works. In order to satisfy his mind on

180

the subject he had, whilst yet at Liége and the court of Charles V., sought counsel from that eminent evangelical preacher, Albert Hardenberg, and the celebrated Reformer of the Netherlands, John de Lasky. From them he received, as it would seem, his first religious impressions, although the circumstances in which he was placed prevented him from taking a decided stand at that time. Western Europe was threatened by the Turks. The wild sons of Mohammed swept like a hurricane from the East through Hungary, and threatened the very heart of Christendom in Germany. Then it was that Frederick, obeying the loud call to arms, went forth to meet the archenemy on the field of battle. And nobly, honorably, did he distinguish himself there.

On the successful termination of the war and his safe return he was united in marriage with the Margravine Maria von Anspach, a pious princess of the Protestant faith. Her example and influence led him to the final step in favor of the evangelical faith.

Frederick was then Governor of the Upper Palatinate, that portion of country bordering on the Bohemian forest. His moderate income and the cares of a large family of children, whose training gave him much concern, had the effect to deepen his serious impressions, and to drive him in fervent prayer and supplication to the throne of his heavenly Father. A most sad and deeply painful family affliction, which befell him at this time, served as an additional means to lead him to seek help and consolation from God. A beloved son, whilst attempting to cross the Eure, near Bourges, in France, fell into the stream, and was drowned. A young man, seeing the perilous condition of the boy, threw himself into the water for his rescue. But in vain: the young man himself escaped with difficulty a similar death.

This calamity, which occurred in 1556, was overruled for good in another way. Between the young man referred to, who in that perilous situation had vowed to God that if his life were spared he would preach the blessed gospel of Christ in his own country, and the sorrowing father who wept over his lost boy, a bond of friendship was established never to be broken, and resulted in large blessings to the Reformed Church. That young man was Caspar Olevianus, of Treves, in Germany. He was then twenty years of age.

Shortly after this sudden bereavement of Frederick, his honored father lay on his dying bed. The son had ere this become a decidedly evangelical Christian. Through his unwearied instructions and entreaties, he had succeeded in gaining over the father to clearer views of the evangelical faith. And when the venerable sire departed this life in a living faith in the Lord Jesus, resting with full assurance on His merits (1557), his son was called to experience indeed a new source of sorrow, but he was permitted at the same time to rejoice in the death of that father as a fellow-heir of immortal glory and blessedness.

After governing for two years the hereditary possessions of his father, Otho Henry, his uncle, dying without issue, Frederick succeeded (1559) to the Electoral throne of the Rhenish Palatinate. He had now attained a vigorous age, and was a man of great knowledge and experience in temporal as well as spiritual things. But the best of all was that he was a firm and decided Christian, whose faith had stood well the test of affliction, and who had grown up to the stature of a vigorous disciple, full of joy and hope in his Saviour. From all his antecedents it was reasonable to expect that he would, "as a most benevolent, courteous, and pious prince, endeavor conscientiously to promote the glory of God and the welfare of his subjects to the best of his ability.'

182

III.

FREDERICK AS A REFORMER.

The condition in which Frederick found the Church in the Palatinate was by no means encouraging. It was trembling with commotions, and the abominations of excited theological controversy had usurped even the sacred desk. Roman Catholicism had indeed been abolished, but amid the storm of fury which had been conjured up by the fanatical ultra-Lutheran Hesshus, the tender plant of evangelical faith and piety could not thrive. At first Frederick attempted by gentle means to reconcile the contending parties. But when Hesshus still continued to rave and bluster against the "Zwinglian devil," and when Klebitz paid back his antagonist in the same hard coin, until the feud had become a public scandal, the Elector at once interposed, by suspending both belligerents from office and ordering them out of the country. This energetic course on the part of the Elector had indeed an immediate effect so far as the restoration of peace was concerned, but it did not restore the Church from its condition of uncertainty and fluctuation to security and permanence. Three parties existed in the Palatinate Church at the time: the extreme Lutheran, the extreme Calvinistic, and between these the Melanchthonian party. This last party was anxious to effect a compromise on the points of difference held by the two extreme parties just named.

The Elector was necessitated to make a decision in favor of only one of these tendencies, if he wished to do any thing decisively toward the consolidation of the Church. His mind had already been made up to this course, and hence (in 1559) he sent his private secretary, Stephan Zierler, with an autograph letter to Melanchthon at Wittenberg, that eminent son of the Palatinate, requesting his views in regard to the organization of the Church and the best means of settling questions at issue. Under date of

Nov. 1, 1559, Melanchthon expressed his views to the Elector at length. It was one of the last acts of his life,—he died in April of the following year,—an act by which, in the eventide of his pilgrimage, he rendered the most beautiful tribute of gratitude to *that* country in which the sweetest pleasures of his childhood had been enjoyed. The tenor of his counsel in the matter bears the impress of the mild and peaceable spirit of that great and good man, notwithstanding the anathemas which were fulminated against him by those who pretended to be more Lutheran than Luther himself. In regard to the administration of the Lord's Supper, he advised an adherence simply to the words of the apostle (1 Cor. ix. 16): "The bread which we break, and the cup which we bless, is it not the communion of the body and blood of Jesus Christ?" He further advised the Elector *to adhere to a fixed doctrinal position, and that he should call to his aid, from the Churches of various countries, learned and pious men to take into consideration questions of controversy.*

The closing portion of this counsel was, indeed, not followed; but when the Dukes of Gotha and Weimar, both sons-in-law of the Elector, visited him with their Lutheran court-preachers, Mörlin and Stössel, in the spring of 1560, and proposed a theological disputation to the Elector, he acceded to the proposition, and the celebrated professor at Heidelberg, Peter Boquin, was chosen to represent the Reformed side. He took the position, that "the true substance of the true body of Christ was indeed received in the sacrament, but not in a corporeal way, nor by all, but alone by believers through faith." Boquin triumphed; for he was on the side of truth. The Elector was more firmly than ever resolved to establish the Reformed doctrine in the Palatinate. After he had thus come to a decision himself, he lost no time in organizing the Church according to the Reformed doctrinal position. This he did with energy and zeal, and would not allow himself to be moved from his convictions of truth either by the hue and cry of a few

Lutheran zealots, or by the letters of Prince John Frederick of Gotha and Duke Christopher of Würtemberg. The attacks of the former he met with silence and pity; to the remonstrances of the latter he replied by letters which evinced that he knew full well what he was about, and that he was acting only in obedience to that which he believed and knew to be the truth. As early as the 12th of August, 1560, he issued a proclamation, in which he required every minister to subscribe to the expression of views by Melanchthon. Those who refused were dismissed from office,—which was the lot of a considerable number. Their places were supplied by ministers of the Reformed Church, mostly refugees from the Netherlands, France, and the German territories. Among the most distinguished of those newly appointed were Caspar Olevianus and Zacharias Ursinus. The former, like Calvin, had studied law. But the vow made amid the waves of the Eure gave a new direction to his after-life. He went to Geneva, and became a pupil of Calvin and a devoted friend of Theodore Beza. William Farel exacted a promise from him that he would preach the gospel in his native city of Treves. In 1559 this promise was redeemed, and with favorable results. An Evangelical Church was founded there, which increased from day to day. At this juncture Archbishop John V. arose, and by force of arms and starvation conquered Treves, banished the Protestants, and cast Olevianus and other prominent leaders of the movement into prison. Only through the earnest efforts of the Elector Frederick and other Protestant princes were they released from their confinement by paying a fine and at once leaving the city. The Elector now called Olevianus, as court-preacher and professor, to Heidelberg. Ursinus was a native of Breslau, in Silesia. He was a warm friend and admirer of Melanchthon. But on this very account the ultra-Lutherans looked upon him with suspicion. They rendered his life burdensome in his native city, where he held the post of rector in the Elizabethan Gymnasium. For the sake of peace he turned his back upon Breslau and went to Zurich. From here he was called by the Elector to the theological professorship at Heidelberg.

Olevianus and Ursinus soon became the principal organs of the Elector in renovating the Palatinate Church. They stood side by side, like Luther and Melanchthon, one being the complement of the other. Olevianus, a pupil of Calvin, and withal a practical and energetic man, was not so profoundly learned, but an able preacher, and possessing administrative and governing talents of a very high order. Ursinus, a pupil of Melanchthon, was rather unpractical and without any preaching talent, but a close student, a man of varied stores of knowledge, great clearness of mind, and a good University teacher. The same divine providence which placed Melanchthon by the side of Luther in Wittenberg is visible also in placing Ursinus by the side of Olevianus in Heidelberg. In addition to these two master-spirits, many others were called to Heidelberg, among whom were Emanuel Tremellio, a native of Italy, and Peter Dathenus.

More important, however, than these appointments—at least so far as a direct effect upon the *people* was concerned —was the change which Frederick now undertook in the outward forms of worship. The remains of Romish peculiarities were banished,—altars, pictures, crucifixes, and the like. So, too, the sounds of the organ were hushed, and the Latin chants were abolished. Instead of these, German hymns were sung by the whole congregation to the praise of God.

If it is objected that Frederick went too far in some of these reforms, in that he seems to have ignored the significance of art in the kingdom of God, it should not be forgotten that he was not impervious to the spirit of the age in which he lived, any more than others, but was borne on the flowing tide of opposition against all kinds of images and ceremonial worship. The abhorrence against Catholic "idolatry" led many a sincere Christian heart to the extreme of an ultra-puritan hatred of legitimate art. To purify the worship of God from all remains of a papal age was, however, a merely *negative* work, which had no power of itself to renovate the Church. To effect this, something *positive* is required. The weeding out of the old tares must be succeeded by the implantation of a new seed.

IV.

THE HEIDELBERG CATECHISM.

Frederick III. was fully aware that in order to a thorough reformation it was not enough to tear down, but to build up also; not the weeding process only, but the planting process,—not the removing of the old only, but also the laying of new foundations,—were requisite. Hence he had, with commendable forethought, determined to provide the Church of the Palatinate with *a new and solid doctrinal basis*. But why a *new* basis? it might be asked. The Elector had good grounds for not adopting any of the existing confessional books. There were, as we have seen, Lutheran and Calvinistic elements at hand in the Palatinate Church, and they were at war with each other. By adopting either of the old symbols, the Elector would have given offence to the other party. The great matter was, therefore, to reconcile and unite the old parties. To accomplish this, a new symbolical book was demanded. But to attain this end such symbol must be of an irenical character,—must present the pure truths of the Bible without obtruding the sharp corners of polemics, and draw from the doctrinal controversies of the past the precious metals of truth, which alone are of permanent value. Accordingly, Frederick III. in 1562 commissioned Olevianus and Ursinus with the preparation of a Catechism of the Christian religion, which should serve as a Confession of Faith and doctrinal basis of the Reformed Church of the Palatinate.

Such is the origin of the *Heidelberg Catechism*. The Elector himself took the liveliest personal interest in the work, which, more than any thing else, lay near his heart, and upon which he constantly and freely bestowed his aid and counsel. He made several changes in the plan with his own hand, and in the second edition the eightieth question was added at his instance, the answer to which concluded with the words: "so that the mass, at bottom, is nothing else than a denial of the one sacrifice and sufferings of Jesus Christ." But when, about that time, the Council of Trent promulgated its anathema against all who would not acknowledge the mass to be of divine authority, the Elector used every effort to suppress the previous edition, and added the clause which pronounces the mass "an accursed idolatry." Before the close of the year 1563, the Catechism was published in the form in which it has ever since appeared.*

We see from this that his whole heart was engaged in the work, and hence it may justly be regarded as *his* work. As soon as the Catechism was finished, Frederick called together at Heidelberg a *Synod* composed of the superintendents and principal pastors of the Palatinate (December, 1562), for the purpose of examining and reviewing the Catechism, and, in case of approval, to give to it their ecclesiastical sanction. The Synod met, examined, and sanctioned it. In January, 1563, the Elector caused it to be published in Latin and German, with an ever-memorable *preface* drawn up by himself. "It is the sacred duty of princes," he says in this preface, "not merely to be mindful of the *temporal welfare* of their people, but also to see to it that they are instructed in the knowledge of God, and imbued with due and becoming reverence for His holy word." He then expatiates upon the efforts of his predecessors in reference to the Palatinate Church and the neglected and confused condition of the schools, in which

* Leben der Väter u. Begr. der Ref. Kirche. VIII. Theil. Von K. Sudhoff, pp. 108, 109.

Catechisms had hitherto been used according to the whims of the teachers, and in this way argues in the most forcible manner in favor of the introduction of the new Catechism, whose sole use in churches and schools he earnestly recommends. "We exhort and earnestly command," he continues, "that you will gratefully receive this Catechism or method of instruction, which is designed for the promotion of God's glory and the good of our subjects and the salvation of your souls. And, moreover, that you will duly impress upon the minds of the young, both in schools and churches, and upon the people generally from the pulpit, a proper understanding of its teachings, and that they will profess and live according thereto; fully assured, that if our children are early and faithfully instructed and trained according to God's holy word, the Almighty will bestow reformation of life and conduct, and thus dispense temporal and eternal blessings upon them." The Catechism soon had an extensive circulation. Three editions were called for in the same year. The questions and answers in these editions follow each other in unbroken succession, without division or number. The proof-passages from the Bible are cited in the margin, and refer simply to the *chapters*. It was not till 1573—ten years later—that it was divided into fifty-two sections or Sundays, and furnished with specific references.

Much might be said in regard to the character and value of this Catechism; but this is foreign to the subject in hand. Let it suffice, therefore, to say that it is the common confession of faith and text-book of the entire German as well as Dutch Reformed Church from the Palatinate to the Netherlands, and from the Netherlands to the United States of America. It combines German heartsomeness with theological acumen and clearness, biblical simplicity with evangelical power and fulness. "It is deserving," says a Lutheran historian of Germany in our own time,*

---

* Dr. J. Henry Kurtz, Lehrbuch d. Kirch-Geschichte. Third ed. p. 490.

"of the estimation in which it is held not only by the Reformed in Germany, but in other countries also." Thousands upon thousands have been told by it "what is their only comfort in life and death," and it will tell the same to thousands upon thousands in coming generations, until the militant Reformed Church, meanwhile resting upon that platform, shall be gathered into the great triumphant Church of her Lord in heaven!

V.

FREDERICK AS A DEFENDER OF HIS WORK.

The commotion which the Catechism occasioned throughout Germany was extraordinary. The high-toned Lutheran theologians, with Hesshus (now of Bremen) as leader, at once opened with a violent attack upon it. He sent forth into the world his "Warning," and was followed by the celebrated champion Matthias Flacius, with his "Refutation of the Calvinistic Catechism of Olevianus." The duty of meeting the attacks of these and other theologians devolved upon the excellent Ursinus, and in the capacity of a *defender* he proved himself to be a worthy pupil of his master Melanchthon.

Not only the theological world, however, but the Lutheran princes, became alarmed. The brother-in-law of Frederick, Margrave Charles II. of Baden, the Duke Christopher of Würtemberg, and Count Wolfgang of Zweibrücken, jointly addressed Frederick in two several letters in the months of May and July, 1563, in which they direct his attention to the danger of excluding himself from the compact of the Peace of Augsburg. But all this did not move him. Conscious of acting in the fear of God, he regarded not the frown of man. Nor was he willing that his Catechism should be submitted to the judgment of the Evangelical States of the Empire, to obtain thus a legal sanction for it,—a measure which the princes referred to had urged upon him. Failing in this, they proposed a theological discussion. This, too, was resisted by Frederick for a long time, because, as he said, he did not wish to have any thing to do with these captious theologians. At length, however, he yielded the point during a personal interview at Hilsbach with Duke Christopher.

The debate was held in April, 1564, in the convent at Maulbron, near Bretten, the birthplace of Melanchthon. Olevianus, Ursinus, and Boquin, the professors at Heidelberg, accompanied their prince. On the other side were John Brentz, the Chancellor James Andreä of Tübingen, and other divines, with Duke Christopher. Besides these, a number of secular counsellors were in attendance from both sides. These last were to keep the peace, if unhappily "the theologians should act unseemly toward each other"! The question proposed was again the Lord's Supper. Andreä and Ursinus were the chief disputants. The Würtembergers intrenched themselves behind their favorite dogma of the *ubiquity* of *Christ's body*, which had been brought forward four years ago at Stuttgart as a result of the so-called "*communicatio idiomatum.*" It was, to be sure, very easy to unite this doctrine of the ubiquity with Luther's position of "*in, with, and under;*" but the question to be decided was, whether this doctrine of the ubiquity itself was founded in Holy Scripture, or whether it was merely a human invention. The debate continued a whole week. When the third day was reached with no better prospect of coming to a result than at the start, Frederick was heard to say, "I am not yet tired of the debate; for I came here to learn, and I want to learn my whole life-long." But when the debate had continued an entire week without any advance toward harmony of views, it was resolved to separate. Previously, however, "on Tuesday, the 18th day of April, toward morning, just as the clock struck the hour of three" (so reads the history), "Frederick subscribed his name to the views held by him on the subjects in controversy, as these were drawn up by himself on the previous night. Duke Christopher did the same. The conference then separated, without having arrived at any results." Alas! what a commentary on the imperfection and weakness of man, even in his best estate, that the very *feast of communion and fellowship* should become an apple of discord and disunion!

By previous arrangement, the proceedings of this conference were not to be published. As, however, *then* as *now* each party claimed the victory, full reports were soon issued and spread broadcast over the land. The fires of theological controversy received fresh fuel and raged more fiercely than before. Controversial books and tracts followed each other in quick succession. Mutual animosities increased. The peace of the Church was disturbed.

The Emperor Maximilian II. ascended the throne in 1564. He clearly saw the consequences threatening the peace of his empire from the commotions produced by this Reformation in the Palatinate. In the persuasion that God only has rightful authority over the consciences of men, he was disposed at first to abide faithfully by the terms of the "Religious Peace" of 1555. But the question arose, whether Frederick III. was still entitled to the claim of being a confederate under the Augsburg Confession. To these the "Religious Peace" secured full liberty in matters of religion, whilst "Calvinists" were excluded from this privilege. True, Frederick had, at a meeting of the Protestant princes in Naumburg, subscribed the Confession of Augsburg. But, in the estimation of Roman Catholics and high-toned Lutherans, the publication of the Heidelberg Catechism was an apostasy from that "Confession" and an adoption of Calvinism, and, consequently, it was held that Frederick had forfeited his rights under the Peace of 1555.

There were not wanting those who insisted upon the exclusion of Frederick from the Articles of Peace. The papal nuncio was specially active in the matter. Roman Catholic and Lutheran princes made common cause with him, and did all in their power to incite the emperor against Frederick. In the estimation of many, the Electoral dignity was already regarded as a foregone conclusion, and the hard lot of John Frederick of Saxony* was believed to be in store for Frederick. All kinds of rumors were afloat on this subject, especially in view of the dangers which threatened him in the Imperial Diet which was to meet at Augsburg in 1556. So threatening did the danger appear, that his brother, Count Richard of Simmern, earnestly besought him not to attend the Diet. But to this advice he would not yield. There are yet on record two letters which he wrote on that occasion to his anxiously concerned brother. They bear a noble testimony not only to his unshaken confidence in God and his Christian heroism, but also to his manly courage in standing up before the world as a witness for Jesus. How rare are such examples of decided, witness-bearing piety among the great and noble of this world!

"There may be danger in store for me at the Diet," he wrote; "but I have a comforting hope and trust in my heavenly Father, that He will make me an instrument of His own power for the confession of His name in these latter days, not in word only, but also in deed and verity, before the Roman empire of the German nation, as did my late brother-in-law, John Frederick of Saxony, of blessed memory. I presume not, indeed, to compare myself with my honored relative; yet I do know that the same God from whom he derived his strength still liveth, and can easily uphold me, insignificant as I am, and even if it should come to the shedding of blood,—an honor for which, if my God and Father should be pleased so to use me, I could never be sufficiently thankful in time or in eternity."

In this spirit of the witnesses of the earliest ages Frede-

---

* In the battle of Mühlberg he was defeated and taken prisoner by the Emperor Charles V., and condemned to death, but was afterward pardoned. He was deprived of his Electoral dignity, however, and continued a captive in the emperor's camp for five years.

rick went to the Diet, accompanied by his son John Casimir. His position was a most trying one. The Imperial Vice-Chancellor Zasius now arose before the assembled princes, and read a lengthy and severe accusation against Frederick, closing with the distinct imperial command, that the Elector should remove all Calvinistic ministers and teachers from the Palatinate, and to conform to the Augsburg Confession in every respect; otherwise he should be deprived of all the privileges guaranteed to him by the terms of the "Religious Peace." The Elector withdrew for a short time, and then returned to his place with his son John Casimir, bearing the Bible and the Augsburg Confession. These, under God, were to be his weapons of defence.

His reply to the charges was brief, bold, clear, convincing, and overwhelming. When reviewing the charge of having fallen away from the Augsburg Confession, he reminded the emperor that in matters of faith and conscience he could acknowledge but one Master, even the Lord of lords and King of kings. In regard to the charge of Calvinism, he said he could testify before God that he had never read Calvin's books, and hence could not know precisely what was meant by Calvinism. On the other hand, he had signed the Augsburg Confession, as a number of the princes present could testify, and he still held the same faith as then. He moreover challenged any one who could convict him of having done aught to show his departure from that faith, to come forward and testify against him. "As regards my Catechism," he said, in conclusion, "I believe it to be so well fortified with proofs from the Bible, that it has not been, and I believe will not be, overthrown in all time to come. If, however, any one can show it to be wrong by proofs from this Bible which I now hold in my hands, I am ready to hear and answer him from out of that holy book. Meanwhile, I trust in your majesty's gracious forbearance. Should this, nevertheless, not be granted to me, I shall still comfort myself with the

194

certain promise which my Lord and Saviour Jesus Christ has made to me and all His saints, that whatever I may lose for the honor of His name will be restored to me an hundredfold in the world to come."

This noble testimony of the pious prince made an overpowering impression upon the assembly. The silence of death reigned during the delivery and after the close of his address. All were struck with amazement. Not a few were in tears. It was felt that *a Christian hero* stood before them, whose strong tower was God, whose weapon of defence was God's holy word. As he thus stood forth in and for Christ, many felt their own inferiority in the comparison. When he had finished, the eyes of all were silently fixed upon him. Only the Bishop of Augsburg murmured something about the eightieth question of the Catechism, the answer to which calls the mass an "accursed idolatry." But no one heeded him, for just at this point Augustus of Saxony approached Frederick III., and exclaimed, tapping him on the shoulder, "Fritz, thou art more pious than the whole of us!" And at the close of the session the Margrave of Baden said to the princes, "Why trouble ye the Elector? He has more piety than all of us together."

The victory over the machinations of his enemies was complete. And when the emperor finally submitted the question, whether the Elector Frederick III. should be regarded as an ally of the Augsburg Confession, the members of the Diet replied, that he was sound in the faith according to the essentials of this standard, and, as regarded the article of the Eucharist, whilst he showed some variation from that confession, they believed in the possibility of coming to a satisfactory understanding with him on that point; but in no event should he be excluded from the terms of the "Religious Peace."

Frederick now returned unmolested to Heidelberg. Stories of his having been imprisoned, and even beheaded, had already been spread over the town. The joy at seeing him safe and sound in their midst was, therefore, the more heartfelt and universal. The day after his arrival he attended the preparation service for the Holy Communion in the Church of the Holy Ghost. Olevianus officiated on the occasion. The Elector grasped his hand in the most cordial manner, and exhorted him to continue steadfast in the faith of the Saviour. The congregation were deeply moved at this impressive scene, and many a heart overflowed with joy for having such a prince. And well might they rejoice and thank God; for it is rarely that princes are found of the same elevated piety and decision of Christian character as this Elector of the Palatinate. He has become a shining witness and confessor for the truth as it is in Jesus, without shedding his blood. The Reformed Church may justly be proud of *such* a man. Even the Emperor Maximilian seems to have been favorably impressed toward him at the Diet; for in 1570, when on his way to Spires, Frederick had the honor of entertaining the emperor at Heidelberg. When about to leave, Frederick presented his imperial guest with a copy of the Bible in the Spanish language, with these words: "The treasures of all wisdom and knowledge are contained in it, namely, that heavenly wisdom by which only emperors, kings, and princes are directed how to govern wisely and well." Maximilian received the book kindly; nay, more, he promised to read it diligently.

VI.

FREDERICK'S EFFORTS TO ADVANCE THE CHURCH INTERNALLY.

Frederick III. not only maintained the cause of the Church in the face of the Emperor and the State, but was ever concerned for its growth and welfare. We have already seen his diligence in calling pious and learned men from abroad to Heidelberg. The revenues from the monasteries and convents which had been abolished, he did not apply to his own use, as was the wont of other princes, but set aside the entire amount for the use of the Church and of schools, and added from his own purse the sum of twenty-four thousand florins. He took special pains in the establishment of good schools. Thus, he enlarged the *pædagogium* at Heidelberg, and endowed it with the income of an abolished foundation elsewhere. The *Collegium Sapientiæ* at Heidelberg was also increased, so that in place of twenty seminary students seventy were sustained. A portion of the property belonging to monasteries he appropriated to the erection of hospitals and orphan-houses. And, above all, he watched with assiduous care that the gospel in its purity should be preached to the people, and the Catechism diligently expounded and impressed upon them on every Sabbath afternoon.

The introduction and exercise of a wholesome constitution and church discipline devolved upon Olevianus. He had already in 1560 requested Calvin to send him the ecclesiastical laws of Geneva. On receiving them, Olevianus prepared and endeavored to introduce a discipline which should be independent of the temporal power. But it was some time before he succeeded. When, however, in 1567, the Englishman Withers, on taking his theological degree, defended the thesis, "that the minister is in duty bound, in connection with his consistory, to carry out Church discipline, and, if necessary, to pronounce even upon *princes* the sentence of Excommunication," a powerful impression was produced, not only on the members of the University, but also on the court and the whole city. The subject was fully discussed *pro* and *contra*, and not without much acerbity of feeling. The Elector himself became deeply exercised on the subject, and was moved to take a decided stand in favor of the views of Olevianus. In 1570 he promulgated the decree, which ordered all congregations to appoint consistories ("*Presbyterien*"), to whom should be committed the independent exercise of church discipline. These consistories or presbyteries were called *censors*. They were, however, not chosen by the congregations, but

197

were appointed by a higher Church judicature. This measure proved most salutary for the Palatinate Church.

As might have been expected, the introduction of a new Church government called forth violent opposition, and estranged many excellent men from Olevianus. Among these were such men as Sigismund Melanchthon, (a nephew of the Reformer, who was then professor of Natural Science), the Chancellor Probus, and especially the excellent physician Thomas Erastus. The latter was suspected of Arianism, and remained suspended from church privileges for several years, without being proved guilty of the charges alleged against him.

As in his case, so also was discipline brought to bear upon others who came under suspicion of the same heresy, and, it must be acknowledged, in a manner at once harsh and extremely severe. This was the case in regard to the pastor of a church in Heidelberg, Adam Neuser, Pastor Suter of Feudenheim, Pastor Vehe of Kaiserslautern, and Inspector Sylvanus of Ladenberg, who were accused of being in consultation with the embassador of Transylvania, with a view of taking refuge in that asylum for Arians and Socinians. Suter, Sylvanus, and Vehe were imprisoned in Heidelberg, July 15, 1570, and Neuser fled the country. The Consistory pronounced the prisoners guilty of blasphemy. The jurists, however, hesitated to pronounce sentence against them. But their hesitation was cut short by Frederick himself, who banished Suter and Vehe and ordered Sylvanus to be executed. This order was carried into effect in the public square of Heidelberg, on the 23d of December, 1572. The Genevan *auto da fé* was thus reenacted in Heidelberg. Frederick HI. honestly believed that he was acting for the glory of God when he signed the death-warrant of Sylvanus; and yet in what contrast does it stand to that noble declaration made and defended by him at Augsburg in 1566, "that in matters of faith and conscience man is accountable to God only"! But let us not judge him too severely. He, too, paid a tribute to the weakness of human nature in that form which the spirit of the age demanded.

VII.

FREDERICK'S INTEREST IN THE WELFARE OF NEIGHBORING CHURCHES.

Frederick HI. did not restrict himself merely to the Church of the Palatinate, but took a lively interest in the prosperity of neighboring Churches.

He lived at a time when the Protestants of France and the Netherlands were persecuted unto death by Roman Catholic governments, during the bloody period of Bartholomew's night in Paris and the murderous reign of Duke Alba. From both these countries hundreds upon hundreds came, as exiles, to the adjoining Palatinate. Frederick kindly received and aided them in their distress. They were for the most part a skilful and industrious people, and hence they proved a blessing to the country in which they settled. This was especially the case in Heidelberg, the valley of Franconia, Schönau, and St. Lambert, where large numbers of them found a home. If Frederick's own kindness of heart had not prompted him to assist these poor sufferers, his second wife, the former Countess of Neuenar, and sister-in-law of Count Egmont,* would doubtless have encouraged him to such deeds of Christian charity. It is not strange, therefore, that he should deeply sympathize with every passing event in France and the Netherlands. The news of the terrible slaughter in Paris in 1572 (Bartholomew's night) filled his soul with horror and amazement. Without a moment's delay he called out an army to the aid of the Huguenots in France, with John Casimir, his favorite son, as commander-in-chief. His efforts were crowned with glorious success. His army was victorious, and aided the Huguenots in obtaining peace. Another son of Frederick fought and fell in the battle between the

---

* Executed at Brussels in 1568.

Netherlands and Spain. On hearing the sad tidings, Frederick consoled himself with the reflection that his son had died on a bed of honor, inasmuch as he was engaged in the cause of God and religion.

So also he took a lively interest in the formation of the Reformed Church in the Lower Rhine. Among other evidences of this, the simple fact may here be adduced, that he commissioned his court-preacher, Dathenus, to the first Synod held in Wesel in 1568, who became its president, and in other ways essentially contributed to the organization of the Reformed Church in that country.

VIII.

FREDERICK'S CHARACTER AND DEATH.

Amid such indefatigable activity, Frederick gradually advanced to old age. Some of the children by his first marriage, as well as their mother, had departed this life. Like many an aged sire before and since his time, he began to feel a greater degree of loneliness as his pilgrimage drew to a close. When informed of the death of Maximilian II., which took place in October, 1576, he exclaimed, "Verily, as a sexagenarian prince, I also am weary of life, and would say, with Simeon, 'Lord, now lettest Thou Thy servant depart in peace,' if I had only first been permitted to converse with the young emperor, and to have seen my young prince Louis once more before my death, in order that I might communicate with both in reference to the religious condition of the country."

This last wish was not realized. Two weeks after the emperor's death, the good and noble Elector was also called to his reward. When he felt his end approaching, he drew up his last will with his own hand, in which he embodied a full and thorough confession of his faith. In this faith, he said, he expected to appear with joy before the judgment-seat of Christ.

To those who stood around his dying bed, he said, "I

have lived long enough for you and the Church; I am now called to a better life. I have done for the Church all I could; but my power was limited. God, who can do all things, and who has cared for His Church before I was born, liveth and reigneth in heaven still, and will not forsake us; nor will He allow those prayers and tears which I have offered up in this chamber upon my knees for my successor and the Church, to be without a blessing." To his court-preacher he said, "The Lord may call me hence whenever it pleaseth Him; my conscience is at peace in the Lord Jesus Christ, whom I have served with all my heart. I have been permitted to see that in all my churches and schools the people have been led away from men and directed to Christ alone." And again, "I have been detained here long enough through the prayers of God's people; it is now time that I should be gathered into the true rest with my Saviour." He then requested Tossanus to read to him the thirty-first Psalm and the seventeenth chapter of the Gospel of John, the former commencing with:

"In Thee, O Lord, do I put my trust; let me never be ashamed: deliver me in Thy righteousness. Bow down Thine ear to me; deliver me speedily; be Thou my strong rock," &c.

And the latter containing that great prayer of the Son of God, sometimes called the Intercessory Prayer:

"These words spake Jesus, and lifted up His eyes to heaven, and said, Father, the hour is come," &c.

After this, he once more engaged in fervent, audible prayer, then sunk, gently and full of joy, into the embraces of death. It was the 26th of October, 1576.

Frederick III. is in every respect the model of a Christian prince, and as such he is one of the most engaging characters of the sixteenth century. His religious convictions were clear and well grounded. He was able to give a reason of the Christian hope that was in him. His faith was not a mere traditional one. His was the faith of a living, personal experience,—a faith that "purifies the heart and works by love," and which was interwoven with his very life and being. And hence his faith was life and divine power in him. His external life was but a faithful mirror of the light and power of God *in* him. He was a tender husband, a good father, an excellent ruler. The pre-eminent characteristics in his politics were his *prayers for his people.* Just because his whole exterior life and outward actions flowed forth from the harmonious unity of an internal life of faith is it, that such a quickening and pleasing impression is made upon us in the contemplation of his character. Before God he was like a little child: before man he was a hero. Thus we behold him at the Diet of Augsburg beaming with the brightest lustre of a Christian confessor in behalf of the truth. Surrounded by many enemies, some of them waiting for his ruin, he stands up unappalled before the emperor and the world, and witnesses "a good confession" of his faith. It was a great deed which Frederick then and there performed; it was a deed of Christian heroism,—a deed which will never be forgotten in the history of the Christian Church, and will command the admiration of coming generations, especially in the Reformed Church.

Not only his appearance at the Diet of Augsburg, however, but his whole life and all his activities are of the greatest significance to the German Reformed Church. He is, in the full sense of the word, *its founder and father.* She rests, next to God's holy word, upon the Heidelberg Catechism as her foundation. And this Catechism, as we have seen, owes its existence to Frederick III. He examined, supplemented, published, and afterward defended it before the emperor and the representatives of the whole German empire. And hence a large share of the untold blessings which have been experienced by thousands, and will be experienced, we may hope, by thousands in the future, are due, under God, to this most excellent prince.

And now that the German Reformed Church, after the

lapse of three hundred years, feels called upon to record her gratitude to God for this invaluable and precious treasure, she cannot, and dare not, forget the Elector of the Palatinate, Frederick III., who was the chosen instrument in the hands of God to present and commit it to her trust. So long as this Catechism shall tell an immortal soul what is its only comfort in life and death, so long will the memory of Frederick III. continue to live, and his name be called "blessed," even to the latest generations.

203

THE

AUTHORS OF THE HEIDELBERG CATECHISM.

By REV. PROF. T. C. PORTER, A.M.,

LANCASTER, PA.

THE AUTHORS OF THE HEIDELBERG CATECHISM.

By Rev. Prof. T. C. Porter, A.M., Lancaster, Pa.

WHEN standing in the presence of any grand work of art, be it a painting, a statue, or a Gothic cathedral, after the first glow of admiration has passed away, a desire springs up to know something about its origin, the powers and forces that produced it,—in a word, the personal history of the man or men who conceived the idea and embodied it thus in a permanent form. The same is true also of works that belong particularly to the sphere of the spirit,—such as poems, systems of philosophy, and confessions of faith. In this view, the early creeds of the Christian Church stand on a level with the highest creations of human genius. And among the monuments of the kind that have come down from the age of the Reformation, none occupies a more honorable place than the Catechism of the Palatinate.

The authors of this celebrated symbol did not, indeed, play a part so conspicuous in the eyes of the world as the original Reformers. For that they came too late upon the stage of action. Before they were born, the Augsburg Confession had appeared, and Zwingli had perished on the fatal field of Cappel. While they were yet boys at school, Luther had ceased from his labors; and when they had reached the years of mature manhood, Melanchthon and Calvin were drawing to the close of their earthly career. But the mantles of these mighty prophets fell upon no worthier shoulders. As faithful and eminent servants of God, they well deserve grateful respect and veneration.

both for what they were in themselves and for what they have accomplished.

ZACHARIAS URSINUS was born in the city of Breslau, the capital of Silesia, on the 18th day of July, 1534. His father, Andrew Baer, although of patrician descent, had become poor, and was then serving as domestic tutor in the family of a wealthy citizen. Of course the son received his own name, Baer, at the baptismal font, but afterward changed it, according to the fashion of the learned men of the time, into the more sonorous corresponding Latin title, Ursinus. The possession of more than usual talent began to reveal itself very soon in an extraordinary quickness of perception, united with a strong love of knowledge. These natural gifts were carefully fostered by his father, and gained him so many friends that in 1550, at the early age of sixteen, he was sent to the University of Wittenberg, the means for his support being furnished by the senate and merchants of his native city. Here, during a period of seven years, he sat as a scholar at the feet of Melanchthon; and when the latter set out for the memorable religious conference, held in 1557, at Worms, Ursinus went with him. Provided with the necessary funds by the senate of Breslau, and a flattering testimonial from his friend and teacher, the young theologian had resolved to travel abroad for his own improvement. In his circular Melanchthon describes him as a young man of respectable extraction, endowed by God with a gift for poetry, of upright and gentle manners, worthy of the love and praise of all good men. "He has lived in our academy," he continues, "about seven years, and has endeared himself to everybody of right feeling among us by his sound erudition and his earnest piety toward God." The object of his pilgrimage is said to be, to make himself acquainted with the wise and good of other lands; who are asked to receive him in such a manner as his learning and his modesty deserve. From Worms Ursinus proceeded to Heidelberg, Strasburg, Basel, Lausanne, and Geneva.

During a brief sojourn in each of these places he became acquainted with some of the most distinguished leaders of the Reformation, and seems to have left a very favorable impression in regard to his character and abilities. Calvin presented him with a full copy of his works, as a token of esteem. From Switzerland he passed on, through Lyons and Orleans, to the city of Paris, where he spent some time in the study of French and Hebrew. Thence he went back again to Switzerland, and tarried a while at Zurich, where he enjoyed the confidence and friendship of Bullinger and Peter Martyr. On his return to Wittenberg, in September, 1558, he received a call from the authorities of Breslau to a professorship in the St. Elizabeth Gymnasium. This post he accepted, and soon won an enviable reputation as a teacher. But it was not long before a difficulty arose, which brought his labors in the service of his native city to an abrupt close. Just then the whole Lutheran Church in Germany had begun to be convulsed by its second fierce theological war concerning the doctrine of the Lord's Supper. The high-toned orthodox party, headed by Westphal and Hesshus, hated and persecuted the followers of Melanchthon, under the name of Philippists, Sacramentarians, or Crypto-Calvinists. Every town or community was divided. Breslau formed no exception. The feud ran high, and Ursinus, on account of his visit to the Reformed Churches in Switzerland and his close intimacy with Melanchthon, became an object of suspicion. Under these circumstances, he published a small tract in his own defence,—his first theological production. Its views of the Holy Eucharist agree with those of Melanchthon, who bestowed on it expressions of the warmest praise, and addressed a pacific letter to the people of Breslau, which was followed by a momentary lull in the strife. But it soon broke out afresh with increased violence. Ursinus, who, like his great master, had a gentle nature, averse to quarrels and inclined to peace, made up his mind to withdraw. This event was no doubt hastened

by the death of Melanchthon, which occurred on the 19th
of April, 1560; for on the 26th of the same month he
handed in his resignation. The magistracy would gladly
have retained him, in spite of the clamor of his enemies;
but his purpose to seek a more quiet sphere of action was
not be shaken. "A martyr to the holy cause of peace," a
voluntary exile from the home of his youth, he turned his
face toward the south. To one who asked whither he
would go, he said, "I am well content to quit my
country when it will not tolerate the confession of truth,
which I cannot with a good conscience renounce. Were
my excellent preceptor, Philip, still alive, I would betake
myself to no one else than him. As he is dead, however,
my mind is made up to turn to the Zurichers, who are in
no great credit here, it is true, but whose fame stands so
high with other Churches that it cannot be obscured by
our preachers. They are pious, great, learned men, in
whose society I am disposed to spend the remainder of
my days. As regards the rest, God will provide." His
faithful friend, John Crato, filled the purse of the poor
scholar, and on the 3d of October he reached Zurich.
Here he attached himself to the amiable Peter Martyr,
under whose guidance he continued to pursue his theological studies during the winter. In the summer following, Martyr received a call to Heidelberg from the
Elector Frederick III. The aged Reformer, not willing
to exchange his peaceful retreat for an arena of labor and
strife, had already, in July, declined an invitation from
Bishop Jewel to return to England. The present invitation he also declined, for the same reason, but warmly
recommended Ursinus in his stead. After some negotia-
tion, the call was extended to the younger theologian, and
accepted; not, however, without fear and trembling. His
heart was deeply moved, and he did not conceal his
anxiety from his friends. He clearly foresaw the conflicts
and trials that awaited him. He thought himself over-
rated by the men of Heidelberg, and once gave utterance

to the words, "Oh that I could remain hid in a corner!
I would give any thing for shelter in some quiet village."
But yet, like a true Christian, he obeyed the voice of duty,
and in the month of September, 1561, in the twenty-
eighth year of his age, was appointed principal of the
"*Collegium Sapientiæ,*" or divinity-school of Heidelberg.
The next year he had the degree of doctor conferred upon
him, and began to deliver theological lectures in the university.

Having brought Ursinus to the theatre of their joint
labors, let us now turn to his colleague.

CASPAR OLEVIANUS, born in the city of Treves, on St. Lawrence's day, August 10, 1536, and baptized in the church
of St. Lawrence, was descended from a wealthy and esti-
mable family of burghers. His father, Gerhard von der
Olewig, was master of the guild of bakers, a member of
the senate, and public treasurer. His mother, Anna, was
the daughter of a rich butcher, Antony Sinzig, also master
of his guild. The signs of promise which the boy gave
awakened the highest hopes in the minds of his parents,
and made him the favorite of his maternal grandfather.
It was determined to educate him in the science of the
law. After passing rapidly through several lower schools,
he entered the college of St. Germain. Here he met
with an aged priest, whose holy life and earnest religious
teachings left the deepest impression upon his youthful
heart, and were held ever after in grateful remembrance.
He taught that the children of God in all ages, even in
the times of the Old Dispensation, possessed in the pro-
pitiatory sacrifice of Jesus Christ their only comfort in
life and death. His pupil confesses, with joyful emotion,
that then there was kindled within him a spark of true,
saving knowledge, which glowed more and more, until it
illumined his whole soul. The piety of this venerable
father of St. Germain shone the brighter because of the
almost universal immorality and corruption which prevailed among the clergy of Treves. At the early age of

fourteen, Olevianus was sent to Paris to finish his classical studies, and afterward, to the celebrated law-schools of Orleans and Bourges. In these places there existed at that time many zealous friends of the Reformed faith, who worshipped in secret, with whom, like Calvin before him, he became associated, without, however, fully surrendering himself to the power of the truth. But while in Bourges, in 1556, an event occurred which changed the whole course of his life. One day, as he was walking on the bank of the Eure along with the son of the Elector Frederick III., then Palsgrave of Simmern, they fell in with a party of young German noblemen who had been drinking deeply. A proposal was made by some voice in the crowd to cross the river in a boat lying hard by. All of them at once rushed into it, and begged the prince to go with them. He did so, against the earnest remonstrances of Olevianus, whose fears proved to be well founded; for in the middle of the stream the boat was overset and every soul drowned. In a vain attempt to rescue his companion he himself was placed in extreme peril, and only saved by a servant of the prince, who pulled him out in mistake for his master. When struggling in the water, he made a solemn vow to God that, in case he should be delivered and called to the work, he would preach the gospel in his fatherland. He now devoted himself to the study of the Holy Scriptures. After taking the degree of doctor of laws, he returned home; but the practice of his profession had lost all its charms. Clearer and clearer in his inward ear sounded the divine call. In order to fulfil his vow and fit himself for the work of the sacred ministry, he resorted to Geneva, and sat for some time under the teachings of Calvin. After a brief sojourn at Zurich with Bullinger and Peter Martyr, he came to Lausanne to enjoy the counsels of Beza, with whom he formed an ardent and enduring friendship. Here the eloquent Farel, the indefatigable enemy of the priests, persuaded him to abandon his studies, and go back to his native city, to lift up there the standard of the Reformation.

Among the better class of the burghers of Treves, the cause of the gospel had for years been making silent progress. By their influence, Olevianus was now, in 1559, appointed head-master of the Bursa, an endowed school. In his new office he soon found an unexpected opportunity for beginning the great work which lay nearest his heart, and that without going beyond the direct line of his duty. A text-book on dialectics, already in use, from the pen of Melanchthon, and filled with passages of Scripture, afforded him abundant material through which to communicate to his pupils, along with worldly wisdom, a knowledge of the way of salvation by Jesus Christ. But an active temperament and the weight of his solemn vow did not long suffer him to confine his efforts to so narrow a sphere. He desired to reach the whole body of his countrymen. The light of truth which irradiated his own soul was not to be hid under a bushel. He accordingly issued a public notice, inviting his fellow-citizens to listen to a discourse at the Bursa, on St. Lawrence's day, between the hours of eight and ten in the morning. It was, indeed, a hazardous undertaking; but he well knew where to look for strength, and that many of the first men of the city were secretly in favor of reform. The sermon was preached on his twenty-fourth birthday, in the presence of a large concourse of people, of every rank and condition,—men, women, children, servants, and high officials in church and state. With arguments drawn from the Holy Scriptures, he vigorously attacked the doctrine of the mass, the worship of saints, religious processions, and other practices of the Romish Church. An extraordinary excitement followed this bold stroke. The adherents of the old faith had him arraigned before the assembled magistracy. The result of the trial was, that whilst for some special reason he was forbidden to impart religious instruction at the Bursa, except in the Latin language, the privilege was granted him, to preach the word of God in the vernacular tongue in the church of St. James, which belonged to the city. News of what had occurred in his capital soon reached the ears of the Elector, who was then absent in Augsburg. He at once despatched some of his councillors to investigate the affair. Olevianus was cited to appear before them. In union with the evangelical party among the burghers, he presented a paper in which they claimed protection under the Religious Peace of Augsburg, on the ground that they had adopted the Confession. The Catholic clergy denied the claim, and accused them of being Calvinists. On the 25th of August, Olevianus was again summoned before the electoral deputies, and again forbidden to preach. Planting himself on the Imperial Recess and the regular call which he had received from his congregation, he refused to obey. All attempts to silence him proved unavailing. His flock had increased to six hundred members, and was growing daily. The church of St. James became too small for the multitude of his hearers. Aid was sought from abroad, and the palsgrave Lewis of Zweibrücken, to use their own phrase, "loaned" them another preacher, by the name of Flinsbach. But the tide of opposition rose higher, and the crisis drew near.

The Elector, who was at the same time an archbishop and held supreme jurisdiction in ecclesiastical as well as civil affairs, took the alarm, hurried home, raised an army in the rural districts, and marched against the city, into which he rode, attended by an advanced guard of one hundred and seventy troopers. He told the friends of the gospel that the Peace of Augsburg could afford them no shelter, because Treves was not expressly mentioned in the treaty, and hence was not a *free* city, and could not introduce the Reformation without the consent of its spiritual lord. Might prevailed over right. Large numbers of the burghers were punished with heavy fines and cast into prison. At length they were released from their bonds, but condemned to perpetual banishment. The neighboring

214

Protestant princes, who had strongly interceded in their behalf, gave the homeless ones a warm welcome to their own territories. The Jesuits were now called in to complete the work of destruction. Since then, Treves has continued to be Roman Catholic, and has lately gained no little celebrity as the city of the "Holy Coat." To this very day an annual procession is held on Whitmonday, called the Olevian Procession, in order to thank God for her deliverance from the heresy of Olevianus. But, in spite of all this persecution, the good seed has not wholly perished even there. A thriving evangelical congregation may be found worshipping every Sabbath in the ancient basilica, in answer to the fervent prayers of their exiled brethren of the sixteenth century.

In common with his fellow-sufferers, Olevianus had subscribed a written oath, in which all claims for future redress were renounced, but with the full understanding that this act should not be construed in any way to his prejudice as a true minister of the gospel on the basis of the Augsburg Confession. When he affixed his signature, he made the solemn declaration three times, both before and after: "I here publicly testify, in the presence of God, my heavenly Father, and in the presence of my Saviour Jesus Christ, and in the presence of the whole company here assembled, that I have preached the Holy Gospel and the word of God purely, and according to the contents of the Augsburg Confession, by which confession and belief I yet stand, and by the help of divine grace will continue to stand."

His release from the prison of the archbishop was due mainly to the powerful intercession of the Elector Frederick III. of the Palatinate, who, in January, 1561, offered him an asylum in Heidelberg, where he was first employed as a teacher in the " *Collegium Sapientiæ*," or divinity-school, thence transferred to the third theological professorship in the university, and not long after appointed court-preacher and member of the church-council.

The situation of the Palatinate at this period was peculiar. The Reformation, which in other countries had gone
forward with rapid strides, had made but slow progress
under the rule of his predecessors, when Frederick III.
came into power, on the 12th day of February, 1559, at the
ripe age of forty-four. A man of large and varied expe-
rieuce, he exhibited in his character a rare combination
of excellent qualities. He was at once energetic and prudent, firm and mild, zealous and tolerant, and sincerely
pious without a shade of bigotry. Both he and his wife,
Mary of Ansbach, were warmly devoted to the evangelical
cause; and the chief object of his life seemed to be to promote above all things the spiritual and everlasting welfare
of his people. But his plans of reform soon encountered a
very formidable obstacle in the great diversity of religious
views and practices which prevailed at the court, in the
university, and everywhere throughout the land. In order
to remedy the evil and pave the way for unity and harmony, he conceived the happy idea of framing a catechism
which would serve both as a standard of faith and a book
of instruction in the church and in the school. For the
latter purpose the Augsburg Confession was not at all
adapted. The mind of the Elector was no doubt led to this
determination by the attempt of the old Lutheran party,
under the leadership of Hesshus, then general superintendent of the churches, to carry out their measures
with a high hand. Be that as it may, he selected, after
mature deliberation, as the men best fitted to execute his
noble design, Zacharias Ursinus, who had already distinguished himself in the theological controversy against
Hesshus on the doctrine of the Lord's Supper, and Caspar
Olevianus, who had won his favor and admiration by
eloquence in the pulpit and the practical skill he had displayed as a member of the church-council. The result
justified the wisdom of his choice.

Both were comparatively young, the one in his twenty-
eighth and the other in his twenty-sixth year. At first

glance this might be regarded as a serious objection, and under ordinary circumstances would perhaps be; but in that era of universal awakening, when the souls of men were stirred in their inmost depths, the intellectual faculties appear to have been quickened and endowed with unwonted vigor and strength, so that the acquisition of vast stores of learning and the development of talent and genius at an early age were by no means uncommon. Calvin was only twenty-six when he published his Institutes, and Melanchthon scarce twenty-four when he gave to the world his celebrated *Loci Communes.* At the feet of these same great masters, after a thorough previous training in the schools, Ursinus and Olevianus had studied with honor. Young as they were, they had travelled much and seen much, and, more than all, had passed through the fiery ordeal of persecution and felt the chastening influences of disappointment and sorrow.

Both were Germans, born and reared on German soil, the one in the extreme eastern and the other in the extreme western portion of the fatherland,—in Breslau and in Treves. Heidelberg at that time could boast of a brilliant circle of older, foreign divines, of no mean ability and fame, who had found their way thither from Italy, Switzerland, France, and the Netherlands, to fill high places in the Church and in the university. *They* could not by mere accident have been overlooked. The Elector, no doubt, saw that his own countrymen would stand in closer, living connection with the movements of the Reformation in Germany, and possess a better knowledge of the religious wants of the people.

Both rested, like Frederick himself, upon the basis of the Augsburg Confession, then the common symbol of Protestantism in the whole German empire. But the form of this symbol, to which they held, was not the first version of 1530, but the so-called *Variata* of 1540, altered by Melanchthon in the article on the Lord's Supper.

Notwithstanding these points of agreement, they differed

widely in other respects. Their natures were very unlike. In Olevianus there dwelt a spirit of lofty enthusiasm and hope,—an untiring energy which no reverses could quench or daunt. He excelled as a popular orator, and well knew how to stir the heart and move the springs of action. His talent for organization was admirable, and in the field of the Church and social life he strove to carry out the principles of reform to their full extent. His proper sphere was the outer world. Ursinus, on the other hand, had a temperament strongly inclined to melancholy. He was prone to look upon the dark side of things. Of a sensitive and retiring disposition, he shrank from personal contact with his fellow-men. A profound thinker, he loved the quiet seclusion of the student's chamber, where, by the subdued glow of the midnight lamp, he could hold silent communion, through the medium of books, with the wise, the great, and the good of all ages. Although a consummate master of the dialectic art, he preferred the peaceful arena of the written page to the stormy theatre of public debate. But these differences were not antagonistic, irreconcilable. Like polar opposites, they exerted a mutual attraction, which ended in a higher concord. The character of the one theologian was an exact counterpart to that of the other.

Such were the men to whom Frederick intrusted the important task of preparing a formulary of faith. Just what, and how much, each of them contributed to the work, it would be very hard, if not impossible, to determine. It seems, however, to have proceeded from the pen of Ursinus and to have been cast in the mould of his mind. In the language of an eminent critic, "The Catechism is no cold workmanship of the rationalizing intellect. It is full of feeling and faith. The joyousness of a fresh, simple, childlike trust appears beautifully and touchingly interwoven with all its divinity. A rich vein of mysticism runs everywhere through its doctrinal statements. A strain of heavenly music seems to flow around us at all times while we listen to its voice. It is moderate, gentle, soft, in one word, *Melanchthonian*, in its whole cadence; the fit echo and image thus, we may fairly suppose, of the quiet, though profoundly earnest, soul of Ursinus himself." According to a passage in a letter of Olevianus to Bullinger, the authors drew their material from many sources. The age abounded in catechetical literature, and they were greatly indebted to the previous labors of Lasky and Calvin in this sphere. But their work is not borrowed in any sense, nor modelled after any other. It stands as an organic creation. It does not spring from the school of Geneva, nor from that of Zurich, but flows rather from the Augsburg Confession, and its production may be considered as the crowning act, in which the Melanchthonian tendency among the friends of that Confession became complete. The result was, the birth of the *German* Reformed Church.

Whilst the Catechism was hailed with unmingled joy and admiration by the other Reformed Churches of Europe, its appearance awakened anger and hatred among the members of the orthodox Lutheran party in the German empire. They looked upon it as an apostasy from the true faith. Its calm tone and its mild and peaceful spirit only provoked them the more. The winds of strife were let loose upon it from various quarters. The first to sound the note of alarm, in his "True Warning," was Tilemann Hesshus, the old adversary of the Heidelberg divines. He was soon followed by Flacius Illyricus, a man of great learning, but a bitter partisan, in his so-styled "Refutation of the Calvinistic Catechism of Olevianus," published in 1563. The storm was gathering. At length the Lutheran theologians of Würtemberg put forth a voluminous censure, in which eighteen questions of the Catechism were charged with containing heresy. An answer to this assault was drawn up by Ursinus, in the name of the united theological faculty of Heidelberg, which vindicated the Catechism in so able a manner that its authority in the Palatinate was more firmly established than ever. Not yet satisfied, Duke

Christopher of Würtemberg, on the strength of their long and intimate friendship, took the Elector himself to task for his unorthodox conduct, and urged upon him the appointment of a conference, at which the points in dispute might be thoroughly discussed and settled. This conference was held at Maulbronn in the month of April, 1564. The two princes appeared, each surrounded by his leading divines. On the side of Frederick, the chief speaker was Ursinus; on that of Christopher, James Andreä, Chancellor of the University of Tübingen. The questions debated were—1. Is the body of Christ in all places? and, 2. Must the declaration, This is my body, be understood literally as the words sound? The discussion lasted five days, and then broke off abruptly, each party, as usual, claiming the victory. The breach only grew wider, and the battle continued to rage. Replies and rejoinders flew thick and fast, and the whole theological atmosphere became electric. In the next year, 1565, came out the "Declaration and Confession of the Theologians of Tübingen on the Majesty of the Man, Christ;" and then the answer from Heidelberg, in 1566, "Solid Refutation of the Sophisms and Cavils of the Würtemberg Divines." During all this fierce struggle, the peace-loving Ursinus was compelled to take the post of champion in the front rank. How much his soul was pained is evident from his words to Bullinger: "In this battle I have received a wound from which I will not recover as long as I live." Meanwhile the Catechism found great favor at home. It was taught in the schools, preached from in the churches, and lectured on in the university.

In the summer of 1566 the Palatinate was visited by the plague, and Heidelberg suffered terribly from its ravages. The court withdrew, the doors of the university were closed, and nearly all the pastors of the city abandoned their flocks and fled. Among the few who remained, in the spirit of true heroism and self-sacrifice, to minister to the sick and dying, were Olevianus and Ursinus. On this occasion the former wrote a small tract, entitled "Thoughts with which a Christian should console himself for the Loss of his Brethren," and the latter, another, under the name of "Preparation for Death."

After the signal triumph of the Elector at the Imperial Diet of 1566, where an attempt was made by his enemies to bring down upon him the wrath of the emperor and thrust him beyond the pale of the Religious Peace of 1555, on the ground that he had deserted the basis of the Augsburg Confession, the fires of ecclesiastical controversy began to burn dim. Olevianus believed that the propitious season had now arrived for carrying out his plans of church-reform in the Palatinate. Toward this end he had toiled with unwearied zeal as a member of the church-council, which exercised supreme control over ecclesiastical affairs. As early as 1564 he had matured a system of church-polity, of the presbyterian type, strictly fashioned after the order and discipline of the Church of Geneva. But he had yet to learn that to make systems of government is a far easier thing than to put them into practical operation.

Two difficulties of no ordinary magnitude stood in his way. In passing over from the old order to the new, the Churches of the Reformation in many places had fallen, to a greater or less extent, under the dominion of the state. And, since it is not in human nature to part willingly with power once enjoyed, Olevianus would have made but little progress, if the Elector Frederick had not been accustomed to look more to the will of God and the eternal welfare of his subjects than to his own personal aggrandizement. As it was, not a few of the civil dignitaries were secretly hostile or indifferent to the scheme.

The other difficulty lay in the social condition of the people. Under the old order, the Romish priests had everywhere winked at the corruption of the public morals. Vicious practices and crimes, not within reach of the secular tribunals, were treated as trivial offences, or lightly punished. The fact that a man was an adulterer, a drunk-ard, a thief, or a liar, did not debar him from the enjoy-ment of church-privileges. The same laxity continued to exist after the dawn of a purer day. Indeed, in some re-spects it was worse for the time-being. All social revolu-tions are attended by excesses, and here the liberty of the gospel was mistaken for a license to sin. Relieved from the yoke of papal bondage, men were disposed to fight against all spiritual restraint and discipline as tyrannical and unjust. A letter from Ursinus to Bullinger affords a glimpse into the state of things in Heidelberg at this period. He says, "God has indeed delivered us from idolatry, but there follows after an unspeakable laxity of morals, a profaning of the name of God, the Church, the pure doctrine, and the sacraments."

It is not to be wondered at, therefore, that the introduc-tion of a system of church-polity like that of Olevianus should awaken opposition. A spark only was needed to kindle it into a blaze, and that spark was furnished by George Withers, an Englishman, who had come to Heidel-berg to apply for a degree in theology. The theses which he proposed had reference to church-discipline and excom-munication, and, being a rigid Calvinist, he maintained, in the discussion, the authority and right of the ministers and presbyters of a church to exclude "even a prince" from the Holy Supper, in case he should be guilty of any gross violation of the moral law.

This step produced a stir among the divines of Heidel-berg. The matter was largely debated,—at first in an amicable spirit, and then with warmth and passion. Men began to take sides. All the disciples of Calvin rallied around Olevianus, whilst the opposing party was headed by Thomas Erastus, an eminent Swiss physician, who had studied at Basel, Padua, and Bologna, and had been invited to a chair in the university on account of his wide-spread reputation. Here he travelled beyond the bounds of his legitimate calling, to meddle in the theological disputes

222

of the day, and gathered about him a band of followers, the chief of whom were Neuser, Sylvanus, Willing, Xylander, Simonius, and Sigismund Melanchthon, a nephew of the great theologian. The position which Erastus now assumed was, that the whole government and discipline of the Church should be left in the hands of the civil authorities. Rudely tearing asunder the ties of former friendship, he attacked Olevianus with savage bitterness and pertinacity, but soon discovered that his assaults made no impression upon the Elector, in whose favor and confidence his adversary continued to stand, high and secure. His next endeavor was to excite odium against him among the Reformed theologians of other countries, and, through them, indirectly to influence the court of Heidelberg. He looked principally to Zurich, where his own views of church government and discipline prevailed. In his letters to Bullinger, he attributes to Olevianus the most dishonorable motives, speaks of his inordinate ambition, and rings the changes on his baseness, cruelty, and violence. He calls him "a pope" (*summus episcopus*), and his associates, Zuleger and Zanchius, the one "a Sylla," and the other "a downright fool." On the contrary, he extols the virtues of his own followers. Neuser, who led a notoriously loose life, is a good and pious man; and all the rest are spoken of in the same flattering strain, although most of them were either immoral in their habits or heterodox in their religious sentiments. This constant stream of abuse and misrepresentation had its effect upon Bullinger, who at length sent to the Elector an earnest remonstrance against the introduction of a Calvinistic church-polity. Frederick laid the matter before his theologians, and requested them to draw up an opinion concerning the true doctrine of the Holy Scriptures in regard to church-discipline. In answer to the request, Ursinus, as their common organ, prepared an elaborate statement, in which he argues with irresistible force that the exercise of spiritual power on the part of ministers of the gospel flows logically from the doctrine

223

of the keys, as set forth in the eighty-second, eighty-third, eighty-fourth, and eighty-fifth questions of the Heidelberg Catechism.

Erastus, however, did not yield, nor abandon his sinking cause. His tongue and pen kept on as busy as ever. But his diatribes were no longer heeded, and Olevianus was going on quietly in his chosen path, when an unexpected blow fell with crushing weight upon the head of his antagonist. The Emperor Maximilian had called a meeting of the imperial diet at Spires. Thither the Elector went, in obedience to the summons, and, whilst there, made the discovery that Adam Neuser and John Sylvanus, two of the principal supporters of Erastus, had been for some time carrying on a treasonable correspondence with the Turks, then the terror of all Europe. Neuser saved himself by flight, and found his way to Constantinople, where, if report be true, he turned atheist and died by a horrible disease, similar to that which destroyed King Herod. Sylvanus was arrested and tried, both on the ground of treason and of heresy. It came to light that he was infected with the poison of Arianism, and had written a blasphemous libel against the Holy Trinity and the Person of Jesus Christ. After a long confinement in prison, he was condemned, and publicly beheaded in the market-place at Heidelberg.

This sad event had a powerful effect upon the mind of the Elector. He at once gave his decided approval to the plans of Olevianus, and in 1570 actually instituted presbyteries, consisting of ministers and elders, to whom, under the title of *censors*, the discipline of the Church was committed. Loud and fierce were the cries of indignation now uttered by the enemies of good order and sound morals. They styled the presbytery a Spanish Inquisition, and said that the ordinance requiring all persons to report their names before coming to the Table of the Lord (*Anmeldung*) was no better than Popish confession and absolution. Two natives of Switzerland, Thomas Maderus and Dr. Grynæus, having for some reason been debarred from the Holy Communion, the anger of Bullinger was excited to such a degree that he wrote to Beza a letter filled with the severest charges and complaints against Olevianus. Beza replied, and said, in defence of his friend, that, "after a long and intimate acquaintance of many years, he had never seen in him any trace of haughtiness, ambition, or love of intrigue."

In the face of determined opposition and the lukewarmness of the court, the university, and a large portion of the people, the church-polity of Olevianus continued to work its way with slow but steady progress, and had already begun to yield good fruits, when the wise and pious Elector Frederick HI. was gathered to his fathers, on the 26th day of October, 1576. This appears from a passage in the funeral sermon of Tossanus. He says: "Every one must acknowledge that there now exists in Heidelberg, and in the entire Palatinate, order, quietness, and a Christian-like state of affairs, very different from what it has been in past years."

The bright prospect was now suddenly overshadowed by a gloomy eclipse. Lewis, the son and successor of Frederick, was a devoted adherent of the old Lutheran party, and his chief aim and delight seemed to be to tear down all that his father had built up. The Heidelberg Catechism was put under ban, and the university, the churches, and the schools were immediately purged of all persons who would not subscribe to the new order of things. Among the first victims was Olevianus. Not only deprived of his place in the church-council, but forbidden to teach, preach, or write, he was also held for some time a prisoner within the walls of the city. At length he was released through the earnest intercession of Lewis von Sain, Count of Wittgenstein, late high-steward at the court of Frederick, and brought by him, in 1577, to his ancestral seat at Berleberg, in order, as he wrote, "to instruct his sons in Christian doctrine, the languages, and the useful arts, and along with this also to preach."

Ursinus, quiet and retiring though he was, fared little better. He too was forced to seek another field of labor, which he happily found at Neustadt on the Hardt. Prince John Casimir, the second son of Frederick, had received, by an agreement of the family, a small but very fertile territory in the Palatinate of the Rhine, and made Neustadt, the principal town, his capital. Here, unmolested by his brother Lewis, he extended a warm welcome to the Reformed clergy and professors who had been expelled from Heidelberg. He established, moreover, an institution of learning, under the title of *Casimirianum*, or Casimir Academy; and to a professorship in this institution Ursinus was called in November, 1577.

His health had been seriously impaired by long confinement and incessant mental toil. He was subject to distressing attacks of hypochondria. But yet he sought no rest, resolved, like a true hero in the battle of life, to persevere unto the end. Over the door of his study a visitor could read the words,—

> Amice, quisquis huc venis,
> Aut agito paucis, aut abi,
> Aut me laborantem adjuva,—

which mean, "Friend who comest hither, be brief, or go, or aid me whilst I toil." As a result of his lectures, duing this period, he has left behind a " Commentary on Isaiah." His great work, " An Exposition of the Heidelberg Catechism," also claimed no meagre share of his time and attention; and when, in June, 1580, the old Lutheran party issued the celebrated Formula of Concord, the final goal of their development, he felt himself bound in conscience to answer its open attacks upon the Reformed faith, in a masterly critique, entitled "Christian Animadversions upon the Book of Concord."

Soon after, his physical powers began to fail. He grew weaker and weaker, until at length, on the 6th day of May, 1583, he passed from the conflicts and trials of earth to the rest of the Church triumphant in heaven. Francis Junius, who stood beside him in his last hours, speaks in glowing terms of his joyful faith, inward peace, and full assurance of salvation. His body was buried in the choir of the church at Neustadt, and on the monument erected to his memory by his colleagues was inscribed the simple but true epitaph, "A great theologian, a vanquisher of erroneous doctrines touching the Lord's Supper and the Person of Christ, a powerful speaker and writer, an acute philosopher, a wise man, and a strict teacher of youth."

Not much more than half a year after the death of Ursinus, the Elector Lewis V. also departed this life. "He vanished," in the language of another, "like a transient cloud" (*transiens nubecula*), and with him the reign of Lutheranism in the Palatinate. The foundations which Frederick IH. had laid, in such a solid manner, with the assistance of Ursinus and Olevianus, still stood unshaken. The regency came into the hands of Prince John Casimir, who restored the exiled Reformed clergy and professors, as far as possible, to their old places; and Frederick IV., the son of Lewis, when he reached the years of manhood, continued the good work begun by his grandfather, thus fulfilling the prophetic words uttered by that noble prince on his death-bed: "*Lutz wirds nicht thun; mein Fritz wirds thun.*" •

Meanwhile, Olevianus had found free and unfettered scope for his activities as a professor, preacher, and church reformer, in the domains of the excellent and learned Count Lewis of Wittgenstein. The fruits of his lectures on the Holy Scriptures, delivered in 1578, he embodied in his Commentaries on St. Paul's Epistles to the Romans, the Galatians, the Philippians, and the Colossians. But the main theological work, upon which he labored with special care, was a treatise on the "Covenant of Divine Grace;" and he may justly be regarded as the founder of that school of theology which afterward rose to such high fame and influence in the person of John Cocceius of Bremen. The largest portion of his time and energies, how-

227

ever, was devoted to the business of practical church-reform. With indefatigable zeal he visited the churches, held conferences with the clergy, removed abuses, introduced discipline, and toiled in every way for the thorough establishment of his favorite presbyterian system of church-polity. And in the course of a few years he had the satisfaction of beholding his efforts crowned with complete success. In 1584 he left Berleberg and settled in the neighboring town of Herborn, where he died of dropsy on the 15th day of March, 1587.

His will, written during his last illness, affords striking evidence of his Christian character and faith. After commending the Palatinate, and the reigning families of Wittgenstein, Nassau, and Solms, to the grace of God, and liberally providing for the support of his mother and sister, he concludes thus: "Herewith I also commend my body and soul to my beloved God, Father, Son, and Holy Ghost, through the one eternal High Priest, relying upon His gracious covenant and promise that He will to all eternity be my God and the God of my seed, and that He will never deal with me in anger, as He has sworn to me in His oath. Is. liv. 10." When dying, the question was put to him by Alsted: "Dear brother, are you beyond doubt certain of your salvation in Christ?" Laying his hand meekly on his breast, he breathed out his spirit with the word "*Certissimus!*" His remains were deposited in the church at Herborn, and Theodore Beza bewailed the loss of his friend in a Latin poem of great elegance and beauty.

CREED AND CULTUS:

WITH SPECIAL REFERENCE TO THE RELATION OF THE HEIDEL-
BERG CATECHISM TO THE PALATINATE LITURGY.

———————

By H. HARBAUGH, D.D.,
LEBANON, PA.

CREED AND CULTUS:

WITH SPECIAL REFERENCE TO THE RELATION OF THE HEIDELBERG CATECHISM TO THE PALATINATE LITURGY.

By H. Harbaugh, D.D., Lebanon, Pa.

OUR Saviour carries forward in His Church, and by her ministrations, His threefold remedial office of Prophet, Priest, and King. These offices, which existed in the Old Testament economy in separate persons, were united and fulfilled in Him; and by Him they are perpetuated in His body, the Church, in which He lives on in His fulness, as the perennial source of grace and salvation to all men.

As in Christ, so in His Church, prophet, priest, and king are not three separate offices, but one office in a threefold form. They are all embodied in one and the same Christian minister. Their functions unite in his ministrations in every complete divine service. He is a prophet in his pulpit teaching, a priest in the altar service, and a king in the exercise of the power of the keys. The Church fulfils its functions only as it carries forward in its bosom this threefold ministration in unity and symmetry. In the due use of this threefold function consists its true, free, and proper cultus.

Thus the Church must ever embrace in its remedial activities the threefold interest of Creed, Ritual, and Government, as these find expression in Confession or Catechism, Liturgy, and Code of Laws. Hence, Church History is made up of doctrine, worship, and government; and these three, like the divine offices of prophet, priest, and king which underlie them, are one. They complement and energize one another. They must be consistent with

231

each other. There must ever be an inward harmony between them. As one is honored, all are honored; as one suffers, all suffer with it.

It may be easily shown, from the history of the Church, that a failure to use these three functions in its ministrations, each in its due degree and proportion, has always wrought evil tendencies and produced disastrous results in the general cultus of the Church. Previous to the Reformation the prophetic office had not its full, free honor and exercise; when, as a consequence, the priestly office grew arrogant, and the kingly tyrannical. Since the Reformation, in the Protestant Church the tendency has been the other way. The prophetic office has been plied beyond its proportion, while the priestly and kingly have suffered corresponding undervaluation, neglect, and tacit dishonor.

When the Church falls back in the due exercise of either of these offices, those which are unduly plied in consequence will themselves ultimately suffer, — on the principle that a disease in one vital organ of the body, though it may for a time throw the pressure of a forced activity upon others, will at length reduce all to its own level of weakness and morbid action. Hence it will be found that those branches of the Church which start out without Liturgy start out also without Catechism; and those which lose their Liturgy in a gradual neglect of the proper priestly function, in the same process of defection, also suffer their Catechism to fall into disuse; whilst the kingly function, at the same time, loses its nerve and vitality. The use and honor of the Creed in the priestly office of worship is the measure of its use in the prophetic office; the use of the power and virtue of the keys in the priestly office of binding and loosing, in the liturgical absolution, is the measure of their honor and power in the kingly functions of discipline and government. What God has joined together for good, man cannot sunder without evil.

In the history of our holy religion, as exhibited in the Old Testament and the New, the prophetic office ever points toward, sets forth, and defines the priestly and kingly offices, determines their character, demands their proper exercise, detects deviations, and presents the test for discrepancies and inconsistencies. The creed of a Church must ever perform the same service. Its worship "in spirit" must ever be a worship "in truth,"—that is, according to a true ritual,—as well as a worship "decent and in order;" and both of these interests can only be properly directed and conserved by its prophetic or teaching function. Creed determines worship and discipline. As is the Catechism, so is the Liturgy and so is the Government.

The relation which the kingly office, as represented in government, sustains to the prophetic and priestly offices, is intimate and important. It is required to stand in full consistency and harmony with the other two offices by a necessary law of relation. This part of the general subject we must, however, here pass by; devoting our present discussion to the relation which the prophetic and priestly offices sustain to each other.

Confining our inquiry to the Reformed Church, and taking the Heidelberg Catechism as its doctrinal standard, we propose to exhibit and explain the relation which this standard sustains to its correlative department of ritual; or to show what kind of cultus and worship is required by, and consistent with, the Heidelberg Catechism.

We shall have to begin with a historical inquiry. With what kind of cultus and worship was the Heidelberg Catechism originally associated in the bosom of the Palatinate Church, to which it owes its origin?

The Heidelberg Catechism and the Palatinate Liturgy rose together out of the same reformatory movement in the Palatinate under Frederick III. The want of a settled faith, which led to the production of the Catechism in 1563, called forth in the same year the Liturgy which it was designed should provide for and represent the worship of the Church as the Catechism did its doctrine, and be, as Göbel says, "a part of it." Hence the Heidelberg Catechism was printed in full in the Liturgy as a part of it, and is variously referred to in its rubrics. Much of its language is also embodied in its offices, in the way of free allusion; and the second prayer for the Service of the Lord's Day is compiled of the very language of the Catechism, as found in its answers expository of the Lord's Prayer. This Liturgy was the guide of worship in the Palatinate, so far as it was Reformed, for nearly two centuries: editions of it, some with slight changes, having been published in 1567, 1585, 1587, 1601, 1655, 1685, 1704, 1724, 1763.

In his preface to the Liturgy, dated at Mosbach, November 15, 1563, the Prince Frederick III. informs us that as he had, the previous January, published a Catechism to promote purity and uniformity in doctrine among his subjects, so now, in order that the same end might be attained "as regards the Ceremonies, the administration of the Holy Sacraments, and other Church Services," in which hitherto not a little diversity had been felt and found, he had now, "through his most prominent Theologians, Superintendents, Ministers, and other pious, learned men and counsellors, caused a Liturgy to be prepared and printed, according to which form the ministers shall uniformly regulate themselves in the preaching of the word, the administration of the Holy Sacraments, and other services. We require, accordingly, herewith, of all and each of you, and graciously enjoin upon you, that you be stirred up to receive our Liturgy and follow the same with earnest industry." To Olevianus was intrusted the preparation of this work, some time in the year 1562. A Synod, composed of the superintendents and the most prominent ministers, carefully reviewed it in all its particulars. The preparatory work of Olevianus met with decided favor in the Synod. Several timid ones, who were still inclined to vacillate, received no countenance. Only the offices for the administration of Baptism and the Lord's Supper were somewhat abridged.* On the 25th of October, 1563, Olevianus was enabled to write to Bullinger that the Liturgy was finished, had received the approbation of the prince and his council, and was then in press.

It does not appear that any copies of the first edition of this Liturgy are now extant. Dr. Daniel, in his Codex Liturgicus, gives the Palatinate forms from the edition of 1585. "Collata est editio anno 1585 typis excusa," is his note, vol. iii. p. 65. Dr. Ebrard says he has in his possession a copy of the edition of 1585, and also an exact reprint of the same published in 1704. From this it would appear that neither of these prominent Liturgists had access to the original edition of 1563, though the edition of 1585 is an exact reprint of it. This edition of 1585 was in use in the Palatinate Churches till 1601; when it was again issued by the Prince Palatine Frederick IV., "who, at the instance of his counsellors and principal theologians, after it had been in a few places improved and explained,† ordered it to be republished." In the reign of Prince Palatine Charles, when "but very few copies could any longer be had," he ordered it to be "printed anew;" from which words we may judge that it was an exact reprint, not of the edition of 1585, but of the "improved" edition of Frederick IV. This edition of Prince Charles bears date January 29, 1684.

Thus far the changes in the successive editions are slight. In the later editions, however, the original work seems to have been subject to more important changes. In comparing these—as, for instance, the copies known in this country—with the parts given by Daniel from the edition of 1585, we find that some rubrics are omitted, some enlarged, some changed. In the opening of the

---

* C. Olevianus and Z. Ursinus, by Lic. K. Sudhoff, pp. 124, 134, 135. See also the letter of Olevianus to Bullinger, pp. 483–485.

† "An etlichen wenigen Orten verbessert und erklärt."

regular Lord's Day service, the old greeting—"Grace, peace, and mercy," &c.—is omitted; the Lord's Prayer is placed after the Confession and Absolution, whereas in the original the general prayer immediately succeeds. In the Baptismal Service an important rubric is omitted; two introductory paragraphs are added; and, what is far more important, that old prayer which in old editions alludes to the Flood and to the passage of the children of Israel through the Red Sea as prefiguring Holy Baptism (as in our New Liturgy, p. 204) has this part omitted, which changes the entire character of the prayer. In the sacramental services important rubrics are omitted, and other changes made. The services for the sick and dying are very much changed. This will answer as a specimen of these changes. No doubt a comparison of the rest of the offices would reveal similar ones.

In the formation of the Palatinate Liturgy, considerable use was made of the Netherland Liturgy. During the reign of Frederick III., 1559–1576, the Heidelberg Reformers of that time, Ursinus, Olevianus, and Tremellio, stood in cooperation with De Lasky, who had prepared a Liturgy for the Netherland congregation in London, 1550, and which was afterward published in an abridged form by Martin Micronius, at Emden, "for the Netherland congregations in Christ." This work of De Lasky, itself based on a Liturgy prepared in 1549 by Polanus, pastor of the Walloon Church in Strasburg, became also the basis of the Liturgy which, at the establishment of the Reformed Church of the Netherlands, was constructed by Dathenus, 1566, adopted for the use of the Netherland Churches, at the Synod of Wesel, 1568, and at the Synod of Emden, 1571, for the use of Churches of the Lower Rhine, which was also gradually introduced, and is still in use. Owing to the relation in which De Lasky stood to the Reformers of the Palatinate,[*]

---

[*] Geisen, in his "History of the Reformation in Heidelberg," shows, says Dr. Ebrard, that De Lasky "also exerted a certain influence on the formation of the Heidelberg Catechism."

Dr. Ebrard thinks that from 1560 forward his Liturgy may have exerted an influence on the cultus of the Palatinate, which at that time does not seem to have had a Liturgy of its own, and states that reference was had to it and use made of it in the formation of the Palatinate Liturgy, and adds that the Palatinate Liturgy "is at bottom only a re-modelling of the Netherland Liturgy." Use was, however, also made of Calvin's Genevan Liturgy of 1543,* though, in form, only to a limited extent.

To what extent the Netherland Liturgy is used in the Palatinate appears from a comparison. The Baptismal Service, as a general whole, and even also in single parts, agrees verbally with that of the Netherland, but it is fuller. The Form of Preparation for the Lord's Supper is new, and is wanting in the Netherland Liturgy. The Form for the Administration of the Lord's Supper agrees word for word with that of the Netherland Liturgy, taken from the abridgment of Micronius. The Confession does not follow the text of the Netherland Liturgy, but that of the French. The Absolution and prayer after the sermon are new. The prayer which in the Netherland Liturgy comes after the weekday sermon is here found as the prayer after the afternoon sermon. The prayers before and after cate-chetical instruction are new. The Netherland prayer after the principal sermon is here found as Prayer for a Day of Prayer, but in an abridged form. The Morning and Even-ing Prayer are identical with those of the Netherland Lit-urgy; the first enlarged. The Form for Marriage is the same as that in the Netherland Liturgy, only somewhat abridged. The Forms for the Visitation of the Sick, the Dying, and the Prisoners are new, as also is the Form for the Burial of the Dead.

The fact thus brought to light by Dr. Ebrard that the Palatinate Liturgy has prevailingly a Dutch or Netherland

---

* Max Göbel. Geschichte des Christl. Lebens in der Rheinisch-Westphä-lischen evangelischen Kirche. Vol. ii. p. 121.

origin, in connection with the additional fact that Calvin's Liturgy was also made use of in its construction, explains an important peculiarity of it,—namely, its somewhat heavy, stiff, didactic features, and its deficiency in liturgical glow and devotional warmth. In these features it differs in a marked manner from the spirit of the Heidelberg Catechism, as all acknowledge, just as the rigid Calvinistic scholasticism of the so-called Commentary of Ursinus differs from the free, warm, practical, devotional fervor of the Catechism itself. Hence, even in the Palatinate, it has long since gone out of use, as having the radical defect which characterizes all liturgies produced from the stand-point and in the spirit of the old Calvinism.

The Palatinate Liturgy makes full provision for all the services of the Church, and in its rubrics points out distinctly and definitely how the newly reformed public worship shall be conducted. Dr. Ebrard says that in the preparation and introduction of this Liturgy Frederick III. has not made any substantial change in the worship of the Palatinate, but rather enriched than simplified the divine service.* It is necessary to present, as briefly as possible, the contents of this Liturgy, that we may have before us a picture of the Churches as they worshipped in the Palatinate. This Liturgy is divided into four parts.

I.

OF DOCTRINE.

Under this head it furnishes us the matter indicated by the following subdivisions:—

1. Regulation for sermons, whence they are to be derived, and what end they are to hold in view. Here

---

* "His (Lutheran) successor Ludwig VI., in his Agenda of 1577, left the service as simple as he found it. . . . In the Palatinate, therefore, there was in the beginning no difference between the Reformed and Lutherans: the cultus of the Lutherans was from the beginning as simple as that of the Reformed."—*Ebrard's Praktische Theologie*, p. 258.

we are taught that all sermons are to be drawn from the canonical Scriptures, but that the order of the Catechism shall be followed by the ministers in their preaching.

In the Preface to the first edition it is ordered: "The ministers shall not of themselves undertake to explain any book of the Holy Scriptures without the counsel and previous knowledge of their Superintendents, who shall then see to it that the books of the New Testament, which are most profitable to the common·people and most edifying to the Churches, are in preference presented and explained on Sundays." There is added, says Daniel, in the edition of 1585, in which the same order· is repeated, what approaches more nearly to the Lutheran customs: "Otherwise, generally, the Sunday Gospels, as they are called, shall remain. Still, the people shall be reminded what the gospel is, and that the same is to be found in Paul no less than in the Evangelists."

2. General introduction to all sermons. Here the minister is instructed always to begin thus :—

"Grace, peace, and mercy, from God the Father, and His beloved Son Jesus Christ, our Lord, and the fellowship of the Holy Ghost, be with us all. Amen."

Or thus :—

"The grace of our Lord Jesus Christ, the love of God, and the fellowship of the Holy Ghost, be with you all. Amen."

Then follows an "Exhortation to prayer, to be used occasionally by the Minister before the sermon, especially on Weekdays." This occupies the same place, and is to the same purpose, as the address which introduces the Confession of Sin in the Lord's Day Service of the Provisional Liturgy. It closes with the Lord's Prayer.

3. Regulations for preaching on Sundays. A sermon shall be preached on every Sunday morning at eight o'clock, in all cities, towns, and villages, which, as all other sermons, shall not exceed an hour in length: the sermon shall be introduced by one of the forms prescribed

239

as above, and closed by a prayer designated. A catechetical discourse shall be delivered every Sunday afternoon. So important was this service regarded that, " in larger towns and cities, where two sermons are delivered in one afternoon," before the beginning of the first sermon, and after singing and prayer, "the Summary of the Catechism, together with the texts of the five principal parts, shall be distinctly read to the people, when half an hour shall be employed in explaining several questions of the Summary," after which the youth shall be examined on the questions explained. "In the other service, to be held toward evening, the principal points of Christian doctrine contained in the Catechism shall be explained somewhat more fully and in detail, for the benefit of the adults and the aged. The introduction shall be the same as in the case of other sermons, namely, the prescribed greeting, singing, and prayer." The conclusion shall be made with the prayer provided for the catechetical service. "In the country, however, where only one service is held in the afternoon, the youth shall assemble at the second ringing of the bell, to be *examined* and *catechized;* when this has been done, the bell shall be rung the third time, that the whole congregation may come together. Then, as an introduction, after singing and prayer, the Summary of the Catechism, together with the texts, shall be read; after which half an hour may be spent in explaining several questions." The service shall be concluded "with the usual prayer."

4. Sermons on Weekdays. In every city or large town, two sermons shall be preached during the week, namely, on Wednesday and Friday; and in villages, one on Wednesday, or some other suitable day. German Psalms and Hymns shall be sung both before and after sermon; and the service shall be concluded "with the particular prayers designated under the proper head."

5. The first Wednesday of every month shall be observed as a special day of prayer, when " both young and

old, men and women, and servants, shall, as far as possible, meet together according to the special proclamation
made." A suitable sermon shall be delivered; "before
and after the sermon, penitential Psalms shall be sung,
and the service shall then be closed with the prayer designated for such occasions."

6. Sermons on Festivals and Holy-days. "On Christmas
and the day following, the basis of our salvation, namely,
the Incarnation of the eternal Son of God, and the personal union of the two natures in Christ, shall be explained, together with the benefits flowing to us therefrom, as all this is contained in the Second Part of the
Catechism." On the Sunday between Christmas and New
Year, being the time when new elders are elected, a
sermon shall be preached on the duties of the elder's
office. On Easter-day and the Monday following, the history of the resurrection of Christ shall be the subject of
the sermon; it shall also be shown how His resurrection
is related to our own. In order that the history of Christ's
resurrection may be better understood, and that the people
may derive more profit therefrom, ministers shall begin to
explain the history of the sufferings and resurrection of
Christ on the Sunday *Invocavit*,—which is the first Sunday
in Lent,—and continue until Easter. On the Festival of
the Ascension, the minister shall preach on the ascension
of Christ, His sitting at the right hand of God, and His
coming to judge the quick and the dead. On Whitsuntide and the Monday following, the second chapter of
the Acts of the Apostles shall furnish the subject of
preaching.

7. Morning and Evening Service. "In all the larger
towns, on all weekdays, the people shall be assembled
every morning, and, without singing, have a chapter of the
sacred Scriptures distinctly read to them, the substance
of which, together with such of the principal doctrines
therein contained as are most profitable for comfort, exhortation, and instruction, shall be briefly and simply

241

pointed out. This shall be followed by the regular Morning Prayer in connection with the Lord's Prayer; the whole service not to be extended much over half an hour."

"In like manner, every evening, the minister shall conduct a similar service at a suitable hour, reading a chapter, explaining and improving it as above, and concluding with the Evening Prayer, in connection with the Lord's Prayer."

8. On the afternoon of the day preceding the administration of the Lord's Supper, a sermon shall be delivered on the benefits and the right observance of the same. At the same time also a true Christian self-examination shall be instituted, according to the directions which the minister shall find in the Catechism, and in the formulary for administering the Lord's Supper. On this occasion the Evening Prayer for the day may be omitted.

9, 10. The Catechism and Catechization. Here the nature and use of a Catechism, and the reasons for diligently catechizing the young, are carefully explained. In addition to the catechetical services to be held every Sunday afternoon, it is also directed "that 'in all villages and smaller towns, on all Sundays on which the Lord's Supper is not celebrated, the minister before the sermon shall distinctly and clearly read from the pulpit several questions of the Catechism, so that the entire Catechism may be publicly read at least twice in each year."

11. Then follows a synopsis of the Heidelberg Catechism, in twenty-five questions and answers, under the three heads of Sin and Misery, Our Deliverance from Sin, and the Gratitude due to God for our deliverance.

12. Passages of Holy Scripture, whereby every one may see, in any station, age, or condition, what his calling requires him to do. These passages are arranged under the heads of Kings and Princes; Councils, Officers, Counsellors, and Judges; Subjects; Ministers, Elders, and Deacons; Hearers; Schoolmasters, Schoolmistresses, and Scholars; Married persons in general; Husbands, Wives, Parents,

Children, Masters and Mistresses, Servants and Handmaids; the Aged and the Young; the Rich and the Poor; closing with General Passages.

II.

OF PUBLIC PRAYER.

After a rubric directing that "before the Morning Sermon, especially on Sunday, Holy-days, and Fast-days, the following prayer *shall be* used," the full service for the Lord's day is given. After the greeting,—Grace, peace, and mercy, &c.—the opening prayer includes the following parts:—Confession of sin, followed by petitions for pardon, sanctification, and for grace rightly to understand and appropriate the word of God, closing with the Lord's Prayer. Then follows the sermon. After the sermon follow the Confession and Absolution, introduced by this rubric: "On Sundays, after the Morning Sermon,* the minister shall say:—

"Beloved in the Lord:—Since in the commandments of God we see, as in a glass, how great and manifold our sins are, on account of which we deserve temporal and eternal punishment, let us heartily confess the same to our faithful Father.

"Therefore say with me thus:—

"I, a poor sinner, confess before Thee, my God and Creator, that I have grievously and in manifold ways sinned against Thee, not only by gross outward sins, but much more through inward natural blindness, unbelief, doubts, despondency, impatience, pride, covetousness, secret envy, hatred, malice; these, and other sinful affections, which Thou, my Lord and God, seest in me, and which, alas! I cannot with sufficient humility deplore, I repent of

---

* In the edition of 1724 the words "and especially after the preparatory Sermon" are here thrown in; which may indicate that at that time the original habit of using the Confession and Absolution invariably in *every Sunday service* had already begun to be set aside.

and bewail before Thee, and heartily beseech Thee for Thy mercy through Thy beloved Son Jesus Christ. *Amen.*

"Then shall the Minister announce to the believing the forgiveness of sins, and to the impenitent the judgment of God, saying:—

"Hearken now unto the sure comfort of the grace of God, which, in His Gospel, He promises to all believers.

"Thus saith the Lord Jesus Christ (St. John iii. 16): God so loved the world, that He gave His only begotten Son, that whosoever believeth in Him should not perish, but have everlasting life.

"Unto as many of you, therefore, as abhor themselves and their sins, and trust that, through the merits of Jesus Christ alone, they are all forgiven them, and have resolved more and more to die unto sin, and to serve the Lord in true holiness and righteousness: to them, because they believe in the Son of the living God, I announce, by the command of God, that they are released in Heaven from all their sins, as He has promised in His holy word, through the perfect satisfaction of the most holy passion and death of our Lord Jesus Christ. *Amen.*

"But unto as many among you as have still pleasure in their sins and shame, or continue in sin against their conscience, I announce, by the command of God, that the wrath and judgment of God abides upon them, and that all their sins are retained in Heaven; and that they cannot be released from eternal damnation, unless they be converted.

"Inasmuch as we now doubt not that we and our prayers are sanctified by the sufferings of Jesus Christ, and acceptable before God, let us heartily call upon him, and say:—

"Our Father, who art in heaven, &c."

This Confession and Absolution is then followed by the "Prayer for Sunday Morning after the Sermon," for which two forms are given, either of which may be used. The first prayer contains the following parts in a kind of collect form:—Thanksgiving for bodily and spiritual mercies;

petitions for the benefits to be derived from the word of God; for the civil authorities; for the fruits of the earth; for all men, especially for persecuted brethren, and for all in affliction. The second prayer is an enlargement of the successive petitions of the Lord's Prayer. Both prayers conclude with the Lord's Prayer. Then the minister says: "Praise the Lord in your singing." After the singing the minister pronounces the Benediction: "The Lord bless thee, and keep thee," &c.

This part of the Liturgy then proceeds to furnish the following forms:—The prayer to be used after the sermon on the Catechism; two prayers to be used after the sermon on weekdays; a prayer for special days of Fasting and Prayer. Then follow the prayers for the Festival days of the Church-year; prayer for Christmas after the sermon; prayer for New-Year's day; prayer for Good Friday; prayer for Easter after the sermon; prayer for Ascension day after the sermon; prayer for Whitsuntide after the sermon; two prayers for the daily Morning and Evening Service.

III.

OF THE ADMINISTRATION OF THE HOLY SACRAMENTS.

1. HOLY BAPTISM.*

The children shall be brought to the church to be baptized. The most suitable time for the administration of

---

* The grounds on which the baptism of children is claimed are given in rubrical introductory remarks. This does not properly belong to our present discussion. It may, however, be noticed that the children of Christian parents are regarded as comprehended in the promises of the covenant in which the parents themselves stand, referring to Acts ii. 38, 39; hence "Holy Baptism, as the assuring sign and seal of this covenant, shall be communicated to them, and they thus be distinguished from the children of unbelievers." It is held that, by virtue of this Christian birth in the covenant, they as well as the parents receive the Holy Ghost, who implants faith in the heart. This is evidently based upon the idea of "infant faith" as advocated at an early period by Calvin (Henry's Life of Calvin, vol. i. p. 83) and by a number of Reformed theologians, and later very ably by Stapfer in his System of Theology. Thus it is held that, having the Holy Ghost by virtue of the

this sacrament is Sunday, Holy-days, or at times in the week when the congregation is assembled. Care shall be taken that those presenting themselves as sponsors shall not be light and frivolous persons.

It is most of all important that the views of the nature and efficacy of Baptism which underlie and reign in this baptismal service should be here exhibited. What efficacy is attributed to the sacramental mystery* may be best seen from the prayer which immediately precedes the sacramental act, together with the one that immediately follows. The first will show in what state the child is regarded as being before its baptism, what it is believed to need, and what is expected and desired in its behalf in the "mystery of baptism." The prayer is as follows:—

"O Almighty, everlasting God, who, according to Thy

---

parental covenant (and a latent faith, or faith in possibility and aptitude), all of which the sacrament of Baptism ratifies and confirms, baptism cannot be denied them, according to Acts x. 47. (In which reference to Acts, however, two facts are overlooked: First, that the passage refers to adult subjects; and, Secondly, that they were Gentiles upon whom the Holy Ghost had come *extraordinarily*, breaking through into the Gentile world, in pentecostal character and efficacy. So much St. Peter asserts in the next chapter, where he "rehearsed the matter from the beginning" to the brethren of the circumcision in Jerusalem, saying that "the Holy Ghost fell on them, *as on us at the beginning.* Then remembered I the word of the Lord, how that He said [before the day of Pentecost, and in reference to it], John indeed baptized with water; but ye shall be baptized with the Holy Ghost. Forasmuch then as God gave them the gift *as He did unto us,*" &c. Acts xi. 1–4 and 15–17. It was not, therefore, the ordinary giving of the Holy Ghost, as by Baptism, but His extraordinary coming, as on Pentecost.) It further holds that on the same ground children are not the smallest portion of the Christian Church (or community, "Gemeine"), which Church (Gemeine), with all its members, is redeemed by the blood of Christ, and sanctified " with the washing of water (durch das Wasserbad) by the word. Eph. v. 26. For these and other reasons, it is clear that the little children should by no means be excluded from Baptism."

* This word, as applied to Baptism, occurs several times in the Service. This of itself speaks volumes, and is satisfactory evidence that its view of the sacrament is fairly beyond the reach of any scheme which makes it *merely* confirmatory of a grace already received, or promissory of one to be received in future.

246

strict judgment, didst punish the unbelieving and impenitent world by the Flood, but in Thy great mercy didst save
believing Noah: and didst overthrow Pharaoh with all his
host in the Red Sea; but didst lead Thy people Israel
through on dry ground: whereby this Baptism was pre-
figured; through Thy boundless mercy, we beseech Thee,
look graciously upon this, Thy child; by Thy Holy Spirit
engraft it into Thy Son Jesus Christ, that it may be buried
with Him in His death, also arise with Him in a new life,
in which following Him daily it may cheerfully bear its
cross, cleave to Him with a true faith, a steadfast hope, and
fervent charity, that for Thy sake it may gladly forsake this
life, which at best is nothing but a death, and appear at the
last day without terror before the judgment-seat of Christ
Thy Son; through the same our Lord Jesus Christ Thy Son,
who with Thee and the Holy Ghost, one God, liveth and
reigneth forever. *Amen.*"*

---

* This prayer is substantially contained in the baptismal service of Leo
Juda, 1523, Daniel Codex Liturg. vol. iii. p. 109; also in Zwingli's Zurich
Liturgy, 1525, Daniel Codex Liturg. vol. iii. p. 112; also in the English Book
of Common Prayer, 1547, Daniel Codex Liturg. vol. iii. p. 446. The first part
of the prayer is entirely changed in the later editions of the Palatinate Liturgy:
when it was first changed, we have no means of ascertaining at hand.

The same year in which Leo Juda prepared his "Toufbüchli," appeared
also "Das Taufbüchlein verdeutscht durch D. Martin Luthern, 1523," in
which this prayer is also found substantially. See Walch's ed. of Luther's
Works, vol. x. columns 2628, 2629; and again, col. 2624, 2625. Daniel, in his
Codex Liturgicus, vol. ii. p. 192, has the following note in relation to the
prayer, and its history:—

"Claussen p. 803, 827 censorium supercilium adversus totam orationem
distringit 'dies wenig glücklich gewählte Gebet—ein Beispiel geschmackloser
Typik enthält eine gekünstelte Parallelisirung des Taufwassers mit der
Sündfluth und dem rothem Meere.'

"Fatetur Vir Doctus, jam Tertullianum de Bapt. c. 9 similia protulisse:
fatendum erat totam orationem ex sacra scriptura haustam esse 1 Pet. iii. 20,
21; 1 Cor. x. 1, 2. Quod ad antiquam ecclesiam, quin integra oratio, occurrat,
vehementer dubito: certum est, ecclesiam Romanum hodie nullatenus eam
adhibere."

With the judgment of Claussen few would agree. The charge of "geschmackloser Typik" must lie primarily against St. Peter and St. Paul!

What is meant by the destruction of the unbelieving and impenitent world by the Flood, and the saving out of it of Noah and his family,* the overthrow of Pharaoh and his host in the Red Sea, and the safe bringing through of God's people,—as prefiguring this sacramental mystery,—cannot be misunderstood. The subject of baptism, it is believed and taught, will be rescued from the perishing world by being transferred into the ark of Christ's Church, and thus be "saved by water: the like figure whereunto, even baptism, doth also now save us;" it is believed and taught that as Israel, passing the Red Sea, was transferred from the Egypt-ward to the Canaan-ward side, and thus divided from their enemies, so in baptism we are delivered from the old state of bondage and the pursuit of our old enemies, sin and the devil, and have our feet firmly placed on the vantage-ground of deliverance, where, though there be still a long and weary road to travel, and enemies to harass, the cove-nant-pillar now turns its bright-shining side toward us and its dark-frowning side toward our old enemies, at the same time moving on before us and dividing between us and them.

What they regarded as the state of the child after the sacramental mystery had been accomplished in its behalf, and what they believed was bestowed on it and confirmed to it through and in Holy Baptism, may be seen from the prayer immediately following upon the act of Baptism. It runs thus:—

"Almighty, merciful God and Father, we render Thee praise and thanks, that, through the blood of Thy beloved Son Jesus Christ, Thou hast forgiven us and our children all our sins, and through Thy Holy Spirit hast received us as members of Thine only-begotten Son, and thus also as Thy children, and hast sealed and confirmed to us all this† by Holy Baptism; we also beseech Thee, through the same Thy beloved Son, that Thou wouldst at all times govern this

---

* 1 Pet. iii. 20, 21 ; 1 Cor. x. 2.
† "This grace," in later editions.

child by Thy Holy Spirit, that it may be brought up in a Christian and godly way, and grow and increase in the Lord Jesus Christ, that it may confess Thy Fatherly goodness and mercy which Thou hast shown to it and us all, live in all righteousness under our only Teacher, King, and High-Priest Jesus Christ, valiantly war against and prevail over sin, the devil, and his entire kingdom,* and exalt and praise Thee, and Thy Son Jesus Christ, together with the Holy Ghost, the only true God, forever. *Amen.*"

In this prayer the fact is recognized that through Baptism the child has received the forgiveness of sin, has been received as a member of Christ, made the child of God; all of which has been sealed and confirmed to it by Holy Baptism. Standing thus in the grace of Christ, it is asked, not that it may be brought into, but that it may be brought up in, a Christian and godly way; not that it may be united with Him, but that it may "grow and increase in the Lord Jesus Christ." And so on, in all the rest of the prayer, it is assumed that the child stands now in grace, from which vantage-ground it is to "confess God's fatherly goodness and mercy," live righteously under the benefits of Christ's prophetic, priestly, and kingly offices, war successfully against, and overcome, all its enemies, and exalt and praise God forever.

In another part of the service, speaking of the obligations that rest on us as baptized persons, it is said, "We promise God the Father, Son, and Holy Ghost, that by His grace we will acknowledge and confess Him alone as our only true and living God, call upon Him alone in all need, and live as obedient children, as this new birth requires," which must be followed by a conversion of the entire life.†

---

* A clear allusion to Question 127, Heidelberg Catechism.

† This conversion is set forth in substantially the language of Questions 88, 89, 90, of the Heidelberg Catechism, where conversion, as being in the Third Part of the Catechism, presupposes the regeneration, which belongs to Part Second.

It is further taught that when a baptized person falls into sin through weakness, he shall recall his baptism, and by it arouse himself to seek forgiveness of Christ, "and firmly believe that, for the sake of Christ's shed blood, those sins shall nevermore be remembered before God, inasmuch as Holy Baptism is an undoubted witness that we have an everlasting covenant with God, and that we are baptized in the living fountain of the everlasting mercy of the Father, and the most holy Passion and death of Jesus Christ, through the power of the Holy Ghost."*

2. THE LORD'S SUPPER.

It is directed that the Lord's Supper shall be administered in the larger towns at least once a month, and in villages once in two months, and in either case always on Christmas, Easter, and Whitsuntide. As the edification of the Church may require, it is Christian and right to celebrate it oftener. The minister shall always give notice of the solemnity a week previous, exhorting the congregation to prepare for it; also that they may meanwhile instruct such of their children as are to receive the sacrament for the first time, that they may be presented on the following Saturday, or on some previous suitable day, to the minister, that he may further direct them.

On Saturday before the Holy Communion the Preparatory Service shall be held, according to the form prescribed for that occasion. On this occasion, also, those who are for the first time to commune shall be presented at the altar to make confession of their faith. They shall recite the Creed, the Ten Commandments, and the Lord's Prayer,

---

* In accordance with this, the parents and sponsors, at the close of the service, are exhorted "to remind it, when it shall arrive at the age of understanding, that, by the reception of this divine covenant sign and seal of Holy Baptism, it did publicly, in the presence of God, of His holy angels, and the Christian Church, renounce the devil and the world, with all their works and lusts, and give and obligate itself to the Lord, to serve Him throughout its whole life in holiness and obedience to His holy gospel."

and be questioned from the Catechism in regard to the Lord's Supper. Such as are not able to repeat all these, on account of backwardness, shall have them repeated to them by the minister, after which they shall with the rest make confession of them.

Then the minister reads before the congregation a form of examination and confession in questions, including the three general points treated of in the Heidelberg Catechism. 1. Confession of sin and misery. 2. Profession of faith in the deliverance promised in the gospel. 3. Promise to put away all sin and lead a Christian life. To each of these points, suitably enlarged, and presented in the question-form, the communicants are required to respond with an audible YES. Then the minister says —:

"All who now find all this in their hearts must not doubt, that through the holy Passion and death of Christ they already have the forgiveness of all their sins, and shall certainly continue to have the same so long as they persevere in these purposes, even though there be yet many infirmities remaining in them, which by the same Passion and death of Jesus Christ are also covered: in view of which, let every one who from his heart desires this say—*Amen*.

"Kneel down, and pray as the Lord has taught us:

"Our Father, who art in heaven, &c."

Then the benediction is pronounced. It is added, in a closing rubric, that "if the circumstances of the congregation make it necessary, and time permits, the minister shall yet instruct the people in the principal points of religion, from the Summary of the Catechism. This he shall also do in the plainest and simplest way possible in his sermons, both in connection with the Preparatory Service and that of the Holy Communion. Should any one have any private matter of concern upon his mind, in regard to which he would desire to speak with his minister, the opportunity shall be afforded him."

In the "Form for celebrating the Holy Supper," the rubric directs that on those days when the Lord's Supper is celebrated, a sermon on the death of Christ and in reference to the Lord's Supper shall be delivered, in which shall be treated of the institution, order, occasion, benefit, and fruit of the Holy Supper; and in this sermon the minister shall study brevity, on account of the Service which is to follow, in which the Supper is also further explained. Before the Service is read, the Prayers appointed for Sunday shall be offered.

Having seen in the Office of Baptism how firmly this Liturgy holds the doctrine of sacramental grace, we may expect a priori to find the Office of the Lord's Supper consistent therewith, and hence the assuming of this fact would seem to be the fundamental canon for its true and consistent interpretation. The fact, moreover, that the great controversy in regard to the Lord's Supper—not merely between the Lutherans and the Reformed, but as it reigned more especially in the bosom of Lutheranism itself between the "true Lutheran party," as they were called, and the Melanchthonian tendency—became the direct and main occasion of the founding of the Palatinate Reformed Church, may account for any caution and conservation in the statements characterizing this Office of the Holy Eucharist.

Hence it is that in the exhibition of the nature and efficacy of the Sacrament in this office, evident and great care is taken not only to give no countenance to what the Reformed movement was combating in the Roman Church, but also to keep as far as possible away from the views of those in the Lutheran Church who persisted in extreme statements—whatever they may have regarded as the truth underlying them—over against the Swiss and Calvinistic theologians, as well as Melanchthon and those who sympathized with what is called the Melanchthonian tendency, out of which, beyond doubt, sprang the Reformed Church of the Palatinate.* Hence the idea of

---

* Western Germany, and, above all, the Palatinate of the Rhine (also Hesse), which had been won over to the Reformation more by Melanchthon's than by

sacramental grace is less prominently brought out here than in the Baptismal Service; and thus quotations might easily be made from this Service which would seem, in an isolated form, to favor the memorialistic theory of the Lord's Supper, just as the Heidelberg Catechism could be quoted to the same purpose, if its system, as it lies in its three divisions or parts, and its ground-tone, were ignored. This would, however, in either case be unfair, and unworthy of any one making serious inquiry into the subject.

The true Reformed doctrine of the Holy Supper, as held by Calvin, Melanchthon, the authors of the Heidelberg Catechism, Ursinus and Olevianus, and as exhibited in all the reigning symbols of the Reformed Church, lies in and pervades this Service as its muscles and its life-giving blood. A few quotations from central parts of the service will sufficiently justify this remark.

In the Preparatory Service the communicant is assured, and encouraged to believe, "that Christ now again by His Holy Supper, as with certain letters and seals, confirms, by the operation of the Holy Ghost in his heart, to each·one among them in particular, the salvation which He has promised and bestowed upon him once in Holy Baptism." He is also assured that by His Holy Supper "the Lord Jesus Christ Himself does, with His crucified body and shed blood, by the operation of the Holy Ghost, feed and nourish his hungry and contrite heart and weak soul unto eternal life, as certainly as he receives from the hand of the minister and eats and drinks with his mouth the holy bread and cup of the Lord in remembrance of Him."

In the prayer which immediately precedes the consecration of the elements, occurs also this passage —"Merciful God and Father, we beseech Thee, that *in this Holy Supper,* in which we celebrate the glorious remembrance of the

---

Luther's influence, shared also in Melanchthon's views of the Lord's Supper. As regards cultus, it remained free from puritanism, and throughout homogeneous with the Lutheran Church.—*Ebrard's Dogmatik,* vol. i. p. 54.

bitter death of Thy dear Son Jesus Christ, Thou wouldst so operate in our hearts through Thy Holy Spirit, that we, in true confidence, may surrender ourselves more and more to Thy Son Jesus Christ, that our weary and contrite hearts may be *nourished and quickened by His true body and blood, even by Him, true God and man,* the only heavenly bread, through the power of the Holy Ghost, so that we may no more live in our sins, but He in us, and we in Him."

The bread was given with the words: "The bread which we break is the communion of the body of Christ." The wine with the words: "The cup of blessing which we bless is the communion of the blood of Christ." In the edition of 1585: "The body of our Lord Jesus Christ, given unto death for you, strengthen and preserve you in faith unto eternal life." "The blood of our beloved Lord Jesus Christ, shed for your sins, strengthen and preserve you in faith unto eternal life." The concluding prayer is introduced with the words: "Beloved in the Lord, inasmuch as the Lord has now, at His table, fed our souls, let us together give thanks and praise His name." This has a strong objective tone.

The sacramental doctrine of this Office is that of a spiritual real presence of Christ, and a real communion, on the part of him who worthily partakes, with the life of Christ Jesus, by the power of the Holy Ghost; which view the Reformed Church of the Palatinate held in common with the primitive Church, and in harmony with the views of Calvin and Melanchthon. It holds that the sacramental mystery is effected, not as the Roman Church held, by the pronunciation of the words of institution, but by the efficacious union with the elements of the Holy Ghost,—which union, constituting the consecration, is effected by "the powerful benediction of the Holy Ghost upon the elements of bread and wine,"—and that it is by the power of the same Holy Ghost, dwelling at the same time both in Christ and in the communicant, as the true Spirit of Christ, that His life, in the communion of His Body and Blood, is communicated to His people. This is the doctrine of the Heidelberg Catechism, of which this Liturgy is the companion. In Question 76 we are taught that in the Holy Supper we are "more and more united to His sacred body by the Holy Ghost, who dwells both in Christ and in us,"—so "that we live and are governed forever by one Spirit, as members of the same body are by one soul." In Question 79 it is said that we are "really partakers of His true body and blood, by the operation of the Holy Ghost." In Question 80 it is affirmed that the Lord's Supper testifies to us "that we by the Holy Ghost are ingrafted into Christ." Thus the Holy Ghost mediates Christ and the Sacrament, and also the communicant and the Sacrament,—His union with the Sacrament, and our union with Him through the Sacrament. The presence of the Holy Ghost, as Christ's Spirit, in the Sacrament, makes Christ's presence spiritual and real in the sacramental transaction; and the presence of the Holy Ghost at the same time in us makes it spiritual and real to us,—makes it the mystery and means of our communion with the life of Christ, as at once concealed and revealed in the sacramental mystery of His Body and Blood.

IV.

OF OTHER CHURCH CUSTOMS AND SERVICES.

This part begins by making provision for the Festival and Holy-day services. It is directed that "Holy-days shall be observed in the same manner as Sundays." Besides Sundays, "Christmas with the day following, New-Year's day, Easter with the day following, Ascension day, and Whitsunday with the day following, shall be regularly observed." Suitable services for these holy-days are prescribed, the preaching regulated, and appropriate prayers provided.

That the Reformed Church carried its reformatory measures also into the Church-year is well known. Though disposed to set aside more of its details than the Lutheran

Church, yet it never let go its hold of the fundamental parts of it. The Swiss Reformed Church, in this respect, in the Reformation of Worship, proceeded with great conservatism. The fundamental points in the Church-year were from the very first firmly retained. The Liturgy of Basel, 1539, directs that Christmas, Easter, Ascension day, and Whitsuntide shall be celebrated. Although it states that "many holy-days are not to be praised," it yet adds, "that the services, the exalted virtues, and the blessedness of the Virgin Mary, the holy Apostles, John the Baptist, and the beloved Martyrs, may be celebrated earnestly and unchanged, in the preaching of the divine word, on the days assigned to them in the Calendar, since early prayer and preaching are held every day."*

The Ulmer Order of Church Service, prepared under the influence of Œcolampadius, Blaurer, and Bucer, in 1531, favors the abrogation of holy-days and festivals, on the ground that they have been made to serve superstition and luxurious indulgences, but recommends, meanwhile, that the ministers hold service on those days, and use them in such a way as shall have a tendency to improve the people and call them back from superstition.

The desire to purify these Festivals from their abuses led the early Reformed Liturgies to confine the celebration of the prominent festivals to a single day. The Hessian Liturgy of the year 1526 directs that, "Besides the Lord's Day no Festivals shall be celebrated except only these: the Birth of Christ, His Circumcision, the Epiphany, the Presentation of Christ in the Temple, the Annunciation of the Incarnation of the Word of God, the Resurrection on the first day of Easter, the Ascension, the first day of Whitsuntide, the Visitation of the blessed Virgin Mary." In regard to the commemoration of John the Baptist—on which day his Birth, as well as his Beheading, is to be had in remembrance—the Holy Apostles and Evangelists, and the Martyr

---

* Alt's Kirchen-Jahr, pp. 456, 457.

St. Stephen, it is indeed appointed "that immediately after the morning service a public sermon is to be delivered," but it is also immediately added, "which being done, they go to their labors in the name of the Lord."

The later Hessian Liturgy of the year 1566, on the other hand, ordains that "Christmas with the day following, the Circumcision, the Epiphany, the Purification, the Annunciation, Easter with the day following, the Ascension, Whitsuntide with the day following, the day of John the Baptist, and the Visitation, shall be celebrated the same as Sunday, by refraining from worldly labor. On the Apostles' days, Magdalene, Michael, the conversion of St. Paul, Maundy-Thursday, Good Friday, and on the *third* day of the three principal Festivals, only an early service is to be held."* From these facts it is clearly seen that much of what was at first merely tolerated, and even in part discountenanced (only, however, on the ground of its prevailing abuse), was gradually reinstated, from conviction, as a proper part of the cultus.

"In the course of time, the practice of the Swiss and German Reformed Churches assumed a fixed and uniform order, according to which the following Festivals were included by both in their Church-year. 1. Christmas, celebrated during two days, with a preparatory vesper-service on Christmas-eve. 2. New-Year, with a vesper-service the evening before as the close of the year. 3. Palm-Sunday: Maundy-Thursday (celebrated only by a weekday service) and Good Friday. 4. Easter, celebrated two days. 5. Ascension day. 6. Whitsunday, two days. 7. Trinity Sunday. To this was added the day on which the Fall Communion was held; the yearly great Fast-day; the Harvest Festival, and the Reformation Festival.

"Besides this, it is to be noticed that already the older Liturgies, in regard to the liturgical prayers for the single Sundays, distinguish the seasons of the Epiphany, the Passion, Easter, Whitsuntide, and the last one from the

---

* Alt's Kirchen-Jahr, p. 456.

Fall Communion to Christmas. To this must also be added the practice, introduced at a later period, of celebrating the four weeks before Christmas as the Advent season, and of beginning a new Church-year with the first Sunday in Advent."*

Dr. Strauss, in his work on the Church-year, speaking of the Evangelical Church-year as it now stands in its best sense, says, "As regards the Reformed Church, it started out holding to its celebration in common with others, and has also in a great measure returned to it." He also adds, that where this has not yet been wholly done, there is a growing disposition in that direction.

Dr. Alt says that at present the Reformed Churches of Switzerland and Germany have a Church-year quite similar to what he calls the German Evangelical Church-year,—the Church-year, namely, as it has unfolded itself in its best form in the bosom of Protestantism. This point has not been violently attained, but is a result reached by a regular progress, carrying along with it the full convictions, mind, and heart of the Church.

"In the time of the Reformation," says Dr. Herzog, "the great Christian Festivals were everywhere retained in Switzerland, except in Geneva, where, however, their solemn observance was soon again restored. In most of the cantons, besides the principal Christian Festivals, there were also celebrated days of Mary, the Apostles, and Saints; but they were very soon set aside: only the Annunciation has continued to this day in Bern, Waadt, and Aargau. Till very lately Good Friday has received no commemoration corresponding with the sacredness of the day; the reason of this was, that the day immediately preceding it, Maundy-Thursday, or Passion-Thursday, was celebrated as the true holy-day. In the most recent times, however, ecclesiastical action has been taken in regard to this point, which has resulted very favorably to the day. At present Good Friday is honored as a principal holy-

---

* Alt's Kirchen-Jahr, pp. 456, 457.

day in the whole of Reformed Switzerland, with the exception of the canton Glarus. In 1860 the first general celebration of the day took place, and, according to reliable report, everywhere with much solemnity and great earnestness. In all places, except in the canton Bern, the Lord's Supper is connected with it. In the canton Waadt a churchly commemoration of the day had been resolved upon, and introduced immediately before the outbreak of the Revolution of 1845, which the Revolutionary times swept away; but on the 21st of January, 1861, the Great Council of that canton declared Good Friday as a principal holy-day."

A Hymn-Book, "for use in Public Worship in the Reformed Churches of the Hessian and Hannauian Palatinate, and other neighboring countries, published at Marburg, 1746," contains, together with the Heidelberg Catechism and most commonly used liturgical forms, "the Gospels and Epistles for every Sunday, as also for the great Festivals, and other Festivals, and Apostles' days, throughout the whole year. To which are added, at the request of many, the prayers drawn from the Epistles (the Collects) for the promotion of Worship." The Gospels, Epistles, and Collects are all printed at length. This same book substantially, but "enlarged," was published in this country by Christopher Saur, of Germantown, Pa., in 1763. It is stated on the title-page that this book is "at present altogether used in the Reformed Churches of the Provinces of Hesse, Hannau Palatinate, and Pennsylvania, as well as other adjoining countries." It contains also the Heidelberg Catechism, the Gospels, Epistles, Collects, and Prayers. We have before us the second edition.

In the German Reformed Church of America the principal Festival days of the Church-year have from the beginning been honored in the same measure and after the same manner as in the fatherland. During the first quarter of the present century, contemporaneously with the introduction of the English language, the customs of our forefathers were in danger of suffering some damage in this as in other respects. In the last two decades, however, a strong reaction has taken place; and there is at present in the German Reformed Church of America a healthy and growing respect for all the sacred Festivals of the Church-year.

The other Offices comprehended in this fourth part, as having a less central significance in cultus, need not here be particularly described. Directions are given concerning Psalmody and the minister's dress; a form for the Annunciation and Administration of Marriage; for the Visitation of the Sick; Prayers for the Sick and Dying; an Office for the Administration of the Lord's Supper to the Sick; Directions for the Visitation of Prisoners; and a Burial Service.

Necessary additional forms, as for the Ordination of Ministers, Elders, and Deacons, and for the Excommunication and Restoration of such as had violated the Discipline of the Church, were supplied in 1655 from the Netherland Liturgy.*

From this necessarily brief and general sketch of the Reformed cultus and worship as it was established and conducted in the Palatinate Church, we may form some conception of that rich and genial bosom of religious powers in the midst of which its members, old and young, learned and unlearned, rich and poor, were nurtured from day to day, from week to week, and from year to year, in the family, school, and congregation. Their cultus, as diligently plied in teaching, worship, and discipline, was an all-pervading, steady, every-day nurture and power around them. When we transfer ourselves into the midst of the religious activities of that age and country, we seem to be passing into a new, peculiar world of religious

---

* Max Göbel, Geschichte des Christlichen Lebens, &c., vol. ii. p. 121.

educational influences. There is nothing fitful, nothing wilful, nothing irregular, nothing left to individual caprice. How substantial, orderly, earnest, are all their religious ordinances and arrangements! The authority of the Church is honored, the office of the holy ministry respected. Faith in God's covenant is implicit, and the holy sacraments are believed to bestow what they represent. Doctrine is carefully guarded and diligently inculcated in the family and school, in the pulpit, and in the catechetical exercises. Discipline is vigorously administered and humbly honored. Worship is engaged in with reverence, sincerity, and godly delight. Christianity is with them not a fancy and a feeling merely, but a substantial, renovating, and nourishing power for the whole life. A religious element and atmosphere embosom every earnest interest of life, and pervade every circumstance and condition of society. How prominent, in all these religious activities, was the part acted by the Heidelberg Catechism and the Palatinate Liturgy!

Before we proceed to delineate more specifically the cultus which lies in, and underlies, this Liturgy, and show its consistency with the scheme of doctrine and worship which the Catechism unfolds, it is necessary to exhibit briefly the fundamental principles of a true Christian cultus.

Great mischief has arisen from the habit of comprehending under the idea of cultus only worship and service,—only that which we are required in religion to do toward God. This is not its basis, but only its result,—its fruit. Cultus has its basis in what God does to us; by which it is made possible to us to bring Him worship and service. Cultus, as the word implies, is God's spiritual husbandry, His nurture, cultivation, care, tending, and attending of His covenanted children, as the plants of His grace. It is the love of God, the grace of Christ, the communion of the Holy Ghost, brought to us, the Church's grace-bearing soil beneath us, all its motherly ministrations around us and its constant communications from heaven upon us, as being itself the kingdom and the power and the glory of heaven on earth,—the tabernacle of God with men,—at once the mother that begets us, the house that shelters us, the family that nurtures us, the home in which our hearts centre, and the beginning of that heaven for which it prepares and fits us.

Cultus, then, goes before what we do to God. It is before any Christian life in us; it makes us Christians, giving us the life of grace. We are its object, not its producing cause. What we receive of God is cultus; what we give forth to Him, as the fruit of its operations, is worship.*

The object of cultus is to bring God and man together in the most intimate and complete communion. It has its beginning, therefore, properly after the Fall. In his paradisaic state, man, yet in the full possession of God's image in which he was made, responded fully to God in purity and grateful love. In him were no obstructions to obscure the full reflection of the divine purity and love. All above him, between him and his divine prototype, was medium for open communion; all beneath him found him to be the true mediator through whom it could present free and full expression of the meaning and purpose of its creation. Man was the image of the Highest above him, the microcosm of the macrocosm beneath him. What more was needed? What more could have been? Worship was there; but no special cultus was needed to call it forth. All was in its normal state and relations, and all activities of man were spontaneous devotion. God was all, and in all.

The Fall spoiled all this original order, and made a remedial institution necessary, and with it came divine cultus for the restoration of man, with its promise, its

---

* See Mercersburg Review, vol. vi., 1854, pp. 573–600; also vol. vii. pp. 116–136; where we have exhibited this subject at some length.

covenant union with God through grace, establishing, confirming, and communicating its grace to man through sacred persons, in sacred places, at sacred times, and by means of sacred things.

In the Old Testament, as operative through sacred persons, cultus centred in the high-priesthood; as operative in sacred places, it had its centre in the Holy of Holies; as operative in sacred times, it centred in the great day of Atonement; as operative in sacred things, it centred in the mercy-seat. Head and centre of all sacred persons, places, times, and things, stood the high-priest vicar in office for God in His remedial purposes,—the priestly central office,—toward which the prophetic and kingly offices looked, and to which they were subordinate. From him, through sacred persons, places, times, and things, God's gracious communications and endowments extended out, by beautifully arranged and gradatory subordinated attenuations, toward, and upon, and over, and into all sacred persons, places, times, and things; forming thus a gracious heavenly presence, power, and love for the cultivation of all who came into its sphere, and evoking corresponding responses of worship from all blessed by its grace, manifesting itself in acts, words, and lives of devotion, gratitude, and praise. What God did to them was the basis and cause of all that they did to Him. *His* cultus called forth *their* worship.

All this was shadow and type of better things to come. The Head of the New Testament cultus is "the Apostle and High-priest of our profession, Jesus Christ," "who is set on the right hand of the throne of the Majesty in the heavens;" who "hath obtained a more excellent ministry, by how much also He is the Mediator of a better covenant, which was established on better promises." Our High-priest has entered the heavens, the holiest of all. His body, the Church, is with us, but still stands in living union with its Head, and is thus the true medium of His mediatorial life to men. In it, because of His vital one-

263

ness with it, are the "heavenly places," the powers of the world to come, and the grace which bringeth salvation. It is the place, and the form, of His presence, the home of His Spirit, the bosom of His life, grace, and love.

In the Church, Christ carries forward His threefold office of Prophet, Priest, and King. Its sacred persons are "the ministers of Christ, and stewards of the mysteries of God." Its sacred places are its altars; its sacred times are its holy-days; its sacred things include all that it lays hold of and consecrates to its service.

As Christ is Head and centre of the Christian cultus, that is most central in cultus which is nearest to Him,—the Holy Sacraments. In the functions of the ministry that which is most central is the priestly office. The prophetic office directs men to Him; the kingly office excludes the un-worthy from Him; the priestly office offers Him, in all His fulness and grace, to men. The central service is the sacra-ment of the altar. The gospel calls to Baptism, and Baptism points to the Holy Supper as its own complete fulfilment. This is the central service. This is nearest Him. This is His body, His blood, the ultimate medium of union and communion with Him; where we have His death as the death of sin, and His life as the life of holiness. As the sacrifices of the old typical economy all looked to the one sacrifice of Christ,—as the atonement which He made in His death and resurrection was the central redeeming act, — as the cross of Calvary, on which He offered His body and blood, is the ruling symbol of Christianity,—so this sacrament of the altar, in which the significance of all this is exhibited and its virtue made over to us, is the central service in the cultus of the Church. This service irradiates and vivifies all others that lead to it, depend on it, or flow from it, even as the one sacrifice of Christ gave virtue to all before it that pointed to it, and life to all that followed, springing from it.

The central sacred time is the Easter Sunday, or Resur-rection day of Christ. It was the fact which created this day that set aside the old Sabbath day which came at the *end* of the week, creating a new Sunday, or Lord's Day, at the *beginning* of the week. The old rest, celebrating the *end* of creation, the end of work, reached its consummation at the close of the economy to which it belonged; and now, when a new creation begins, the old Sabbath is swallowed up in a new and higher beginning. The new fact also which originated the day has, by its very nature, delivered the day from its rigid legality and glorified it into a sacred festival; and the first Easter consecration of the day is transmitted to, and repeats itself in, all the Sundays of the year. Its prominence, as received from the event it celebrates, makes Easter properly the ruling day of the whole Church-year, determining, controlling, and regulating the whole cycle of the movable fasts and festivals commemorating the ruling acts and facts in Christ's life. The movable Holy-days are its satellites, and the fixed Festivals are the planets of the system of which it is the central sun. It holds this place not by fanciful assumption, but, as we have seen, by legitimate divine right, in accordance with the dignity of its origin. Easter day is the day of the new creation by resurrection, and all other Sundays of the year have their honor as they echo this central fact.

From this brief exhibition of the true nature of cultus, we see what are its centralities: the true high-priesthood of Christ in the Church, the mediation of the Church, the priestly character of the ministerial office, the altar in its true significance, the sacraments, the Church-year. These do not merely belong to cultus; they are fundamental and central, forming its starting-points, its basis and body, its vital organs, its indispensable supports and conservators. Cultus is mediation from Christ the Head to all His members; and these are the media through and by which the great mediation is realized for all God's worshipping people. Without these divine media, or without a believing sense of them on the part of the worshipper, let any one say how true Christian worship is possible. Let it be

W

shown how worship without the sense of these mediating mysteries is any thing different, in principle and essence, from the uncertain play of the religious instincts in natural religion, or the helpless and morbid dreams of anthropological sentimentality.

It would be possible, indeed, for any one approaching it with such mind and purpose, to point out some features in the Liturgy under examination which might seem inconsistent with these fundamental principles of Christian cultus:—its want of a full recognition of the altar in its outward form and position as the true conservator and representative of the essence of the priestly office, preferring the table; its lack of appreciation of the full circle of the Church-year; some wavering, accommodating, if not concealing and obscuring, phrases in regard to objective grace in the sacraments. But these are not of its essence, —only adherences; its weaknesses, not its strength. Underlying these, and reigning over them, are all the deeper elements of a true Christian cultus. It holds the priestly office in the holy ministry clearly and emphatically. It maintains the altar service in its true priestly form and spirit, not only as underlying its sacramental views, but as fully exhibited by the retention and use of the Confession and Absolution, as well as in its entire liturgical style of prayer. In the Baptismal and Eucharistic offices their objective and truly sacramental force, as grace-bearing mysteries, is clearly set forth as their essential character. It holds fast also to the reigning Festivals,—Christmas, Good Friday, Easter, Ascension day, and Whitsuntide,— which are the vital organs of the Church-year, the foundation and main pillars of the entire temple, calling for its full erection as the consistent carrying out of their own meaning.

That in this Liturgy the Lord's Supper is regarded not only as the most solemn service, but as the central and controlling service, to which all other services stood as subordinate and preparatory, is not only implied, but in various ways clearly revealed. A day was set apart, with its appropriate preparatory services, including special preaching and instruction, special examination, special profession of faith, confession of sin, associated with the special comforts of absolution. Special guards were thrown around this solemnity, designed to prevent its being profaned by such as led openly wicked lives. Besides, its celebration was connected with the ruling Holy-days of the Church-year; these high solemnities, as commemorating the central facts of redemption, having been regarded as best corresponding with this most solemn and central service.

Whatever may be found in this Liturgy not in full accordance with a true Christian cultus is easily seen, by one who will take in its scheme as a whole, to be foreign to its own inmost life and inconsistent with its reigning character. Nor is it difficult to point out the source of whatever unchurchly, unpriestly, and unsacramental adherences may incidentally and outwardly afflict its own deeper scheme. They will be found to result from whatever of the Calvinistic principle and element—the principle, namely, of the abstract and absolute decree of predestination—has entered into its constitution.

There are two principles which in the German Reformed Church, as also in other Reformed provincial Churches, have wrought powerfully toward a reduction of cultus from its churchly, priestly, sacramental, objective, and truly liturgical position and spirit, tending to make it unchurchly, unpriestly, unsacramental, unliturgical, subjective, individualistic, self-impelling, capricious, extemporaneous, bald, naked, weak, fitful, irreverent will-worship. Of these two principles, one began to work early in the Reformation, the other came in later, as a reaction from the first. Standing as extremes of one another, and both on unchurchly ground, the one starting in the will of God and the other in the will of man, in their influence on cultus they have both wrought toward the same end. These are Calvinism and Arminianism,—the first moulding all cultus prevailingly into the form of a rational intellectualism, the other diluting it into a natural emotionalism.

True cultus is the great benediction which mediates the *love* of God to us, through the *grace* of our Lord Jesus Christ, and the *communion* of the Holy Ghost, in and through the Church,—all these mediations being the history and historical channels of God's eternal love. In the Calvinistic principle* that love, starting out from an abstract eternal decree, extends itself direct, and without any mediation except that of the Holy Spirit, to each individual, selecting some to life. These are to be saved *by* Christ, not *through* Him. The existence of each one is presupposed before he exists. "The individual atoms emerge from unillumined darkness, and God makes acquaintance with them,"—with each one direct. The energy of saving love operates on each elect one as individual, and brings him to salvation; for all his ability to accept of the salvation of Christ—which salvation comes another way—must be wrought in him by the energy of the purposes of love direct on him. "We can only have part in the salvation which is in Christ by faith; but faithfulness and faith we cannot give to ourselves: we must obtain these of God by prayer. The last ground of our salvation is the eternal election, alone according to the purpose of His will."†

If the abstract will of God is the principle and last ground of salvation, then to believe in Christ for salvation was an ability which the virtue and energy of the decree of love alone could bestow; and, as no one could believe in Christ of himself, it was his duty to pray for ability to believe,

---

* By "the Calvinistic principle," as we shall use this expression, we mean only his doctrine of the decree of absolute abstract predestination,—which was the central and ruling principle of his system,—and not his views of the Sacraments.

† First edition of the Institutes, quoted in Herzog's Real-Encyk. vol. ii. 518.

which disposition to pray, again, God must give. This completes the circle of the abstract decree in its operations on the elect, making all dependent, again, upon the abstract and absolute will from which the decree proceeded at first direct to each individual of the elect. Thus all that is done to bring us to Christ is done in fact outside of Christ, through the channel of the decree of election. Christ is the Saviour as a means of grace, not as source and mediation; while the decree is saviour as source, operation, and end. Thus the apostolic benediction, which, with a deep significance, follows the true historical order of grace, thus, "The *grace* of our Lord Jesus Christ, and the *love* of God, and the *communion* of the Holy Ghost," ought in consistency to stand thus: The *love* of God, the *grace* of Christ, the *communion* of the Holy Ghost.

According to the principle of Calvinism, the Church is the *result* of the elective decree, not its medium. The Church does not bring the election to men; the election constructs the Church out of the elect. To the question, "What is the Church?" Calvin's Catechism replies: "The body and the communion of believers whom God has predestinated to eternal life." Not the body of Christ in the sense of organic production from Him, but the body of believers brought around Him by electing love to be saved. Christ does not bring men into union with Himself by the Church; the election brings them together as a Church, that they may be united with Him, and saved. It holds the elect as invisible Church, the reprobate as visible so far as they are in it, to whom also it is of no account. The invisible Church is realized decree. The visible Church is— what?—a means for hiding the decree?—a kind of deceptive revelation? When Calvin speaks, as he sometimes does, of the great importance of the Church, it is only as invisible Church; and whatever he attributes to the visible Church is mainly, if not wholly, because of its teaching and ruling powers: altogether his Church is not *saving* as from Christ, but merely *preparing* as facilitating the actual-

269

ization of the decree in behalf of the elect. His unity or oneness of the Church is merely in the invisible fellowship of the elect. So far as the visible Church operates on the elect, it only does so in its prophetic and kingly offices; and the priestly, so far as it has any real function, is shared alike by all believers,—the universal priesthood. The principle excludes a priestly mediation between the elect and the operative source of election. Christ's priestly mediation terminates on God, to whom His offering made satisfaction for the elect; and there it ends, continuing no perennial priestly mediation manward. "Christ sustains the character of a priest to render the Father favorable and propitious to us by an eternal law of reconciliation."* Hence it is deeply significant that Calvin uniformly gives the threefold office of Christ thus: Prophet, King, and Priest. In the discussion of these offices he uniformly places Him as Teacher first and highest, and as King next. "Doctrine is the soul of the Church; discipline is its nerves, mediating the fellowship of the different members, and keeping them together."† He depends far more on organization, rules, discipline, law, morals, than on cultus. Consistent with this was his habit of opening his service by sternly confronting the people with a repetition of the Decalogue from the altar. The prophetic and kingly offices,—these are the powers of his Church-culture. Even these are not absolutely necessary to realize for the elect the gracious potence of the decree, but are chosen of God for that end. "We see that though God could easily make His people perfect in a single moment, yet it was not His will that they should grow to mature age, but under the education of the Church. We see the means expressed: the *preaching* of the heavenly doctrine is assigned to the pastors. We see that all are placed under the same regulation, in order that they may submit themselves with gentleness and

---

* Institutes, vol. i. p. 453.
† Herzog's Real-Encyk. vol. ii. p. 519.

docility of mind to be *governed* by the pastors who are appointed for this purpose.''*

In the logical development of this principle, churchly cultus must disappear, as it also did so far as the system obtained sway, and in the process of its history more and more. The true and central significance of the priestly function in the ministry, and the priestly element in worship, disappeared. With it went the idea of the altar, and altar-service. With it went Holy-days. With it went the old liturgical formularies, and the anointed liturgical style and forms of devotional thought inherited from previous ages of the Church, so that the forms and prayers in his liturgy are in no way based no previous liturgical forms nor conformed to any laws of liturgical language. All is radical, subjective, new. Beginning in the abstract decree, and bringing its redeeming love down to reach individual men outside of history, instead of starting in the bosom of the Trinity, following the development of the divine redeeming grace through the Incarnation, and then through the Church down, not to man as individual, but to men as organically related, thus bringing the *love* of God to man through the *grace* of Jesus Christ, it sweeps away the entire basis, history, and nature of cultus, together with every detail as it stands in its true connections and relations to the whole.

In better words than we can use has Dr. Heppe exhibited the necessarily destructive sweep which this principle must take, and did take, in its development. "This powerful systematizer, making use of the ardent longing of the individual after a personal interest in redemption, proceeded in a manner altogether radical, *i.e.* he brought this principle of Protestantism to bear, not against isolated corruptions of the old Church, but *against its universal conception;* for to him the free, personal access of the believer to the personal Source of salvation only appeared possible by the entire

* Institutes, vol. ii. p. 225.

destruction of the Church as a communion which includes in itself a peculiar, historically conditioned life in the process of development, and conveys through its traditional organs and ordinances the gift of salvation to each of its members. But, since the gift of salvation could not be conveyed to each member through the historical and historically mediating life of the Church, *the absolute, unmediated will of God* remained *as the only condition of salvation.* The root of the Calvinistic principle, therefore, is a protest against every tradition of grace conveyed by the ordinances of a historical Church. Calvin tore the individual loose from the ground of history, in order to bring him into absolute unmediated dependence on the divine will."* Thus no mediating Church, and consequently no churchly cultus, remained possible.

Calvin's entire inward and outward life rendered him unapt for a churchly cultus. Here is the true key to his tastes and tendencies. He was early devoted to the Stoic philosophy. A keen conscience held his mind firmly and rigorously to duty, gave his spirit a legal tone, and powerfully cultivated his sense of personal responsibility. Hence he was averse to all foreign interference with the earnest, solemn sense of his personal mission. He felt himself called to freedom. His transition from Romanism was sudden. Neither his mind, heart, nor associations hung to any thing in it. This change, moreover, was not mediated, as in the case of Melanchthon, Zwingli, Erasmus, De Lasky, and some of the other Reformers, but immediate: "God led me in my course by the secret bridle of His providence." Speaking of his stiff neck whilst in the Roman Church, he says, "God brought me to obedience by a sudden conversion of my heart." The sovereign God, and his own personal relation to Him,—these were his all-control-

---

* The Character of the German Reformed Church, and its Relation to Lutheranism and Calvinism, by Dr. Heppe, Studien und Kritiken, Oct. 1850. See trans. in Mer. Review, April, 1853.

ling ideas. These ideas ran through and nerved his entire thinking, and are the key to his theological system. No human master, no earthly power, had taught him how to find out this sovereign God; and he acknowledged no human teacher, either present or past, except, later, St. Augustine, and him he honored because he found in him the central principle of his own system. This was the alembic in which he dissolved every thing that seemed to be in disharmony with God's sovereignty or proposed any mediation between the human will and the absolute divine will. This sundered him from the Roman Church; this sundered in his mind the present from the past,—the Bible from the Church,—the Church from the State; separated the Church into visible and invisible; divided the human race into elect and reprobate; sundered the mediation of Christ, the Head, from the mediation of the Church, His body; and brought to the whole problem of Christianity, from a new point, a power and principle of analysis before whose logical sequence nothing in Church and cultus can stand together as it stood before.

Calvin deeply felt the tendency of his principle, and the longer and later only more. He saw, more or less clearly, what must be surrendered to open the way for the logical development of his principle. Two principles struggle perpetually in the womb of his mind. Earnestly disposed to hold high views of the Church and sacraments, which he also again and again utters, he finds them sternly contradicted by the logical force of the ruling decretal principle. The two, he feels, cannot live together, and yet he knows not how to give up either. The principle from which his scheme starts is as firm in his mind as the decree itself. He cannot yield it. The church-system must yield. Hence, while he continues to utter high views of the Church, its sacraments and ordinances, yet, unconsciously deceiving his own mind by unfounded distinctions between visible and invisible Church, he ever weakens, or entirely explains away, his own teachings on these points. Hence

Calvin can be quoted as a witness to the strongest objective force of the Church and its sacraments, and at the same time also in favor of the most unchurchly and unsacramental subjectivism. Stand in which of these opposite systems we may, Calvin is equally tantalizing. Whilst we hear continually Jacob's voice, we see as certainly Esau's hands. "The Church order of the sacraments," to quote Dr. Heppe once more, "plays throughout a meaningless part in its historical transmission among those who are already predestined to eternal happiness or misery, and only becomes a *sign* of the communication of grace when it happens to meet with one of the elect, in which case the reception of the external elements coincides with the unmediated reception of the gifts of divine grace. In the prosecution of this fundamental view and its natural consequences, it came to pass that Calvin denied the participation of unbelievers in the Lord's Supper and the necessity of infant baptism,—abolished the specific distinction between the communication of grace in the *word* and in the *sacraments*,—regarded the relation of the *res externa* in the sacrament to the *res interna* as that of a sign to the thing signified,—founded worship in its simplicity, and public morals in their severity, on the letter of the word of holy writ (*i.e.* of the divine will delivered once for all), and in his form of church-government made great account of the rights of subjectivity over against every kind of churchly authority."

In the surrender, thus, of the idea of a historical, churchly mediation, and the consequent dropping away of the central priestly function in the Church, the Calvinistic cultus held fast only to the prophetic and kingly offices and their functions as the prominent means of Christian culture; thus plying an intellectual doctrinalism and a rigid moralism,— teaching and ruling being regarded as the main functions of the ministry. The prayers of Calvinism themselves, as they appear in liturgies of that type, are prevailingly doctrinal, calling more for intellectual than devotional exer-

274

cises in the worshipper; and the influence of this principle is clearly discernible in the Palatinate Liturgy, as we have already historically shown, and as may be learned by an examination of its devotional forms. These two—doctrinalism and regalism—are still the ruling elements in the Calvinistic cultus wherever that system prevails; only that the logical and historical developments of the system have more fully delivered its cultus from the traditional and churchly adherences from which in its earlier history it was not altogether free. As witnesses to this fact, we may respectfully, though properly, refer to Scotch Presbyterianism, and American Presbyterianism and Congregationalism.

The principle of Calvinism has also a deep and natural, if not necessary, tendency toward subjectivism. It has this affinity on account of the atomistic manner in which it regards the individual. In isolating him, it makes him restless and free. It sunders him from the old race by his sense of his election. It sunders him from history and traditional associations, by poising him on the absolute decree. At the same time, it fails to unite him by a power, except what comes through him, to his fellow-elect even in the Church, which is only to him an invisible, and withal between him and others an uncertain, bond. This fellowship, moreover, is only the more outward one of doctrine and government.

Besides this, Calvinism is always in danger of its own extreme,—Arminianism. From making the abstract divine will the *funis desperationis*, the turning-point of hope, it is most easy to swing to the other extreme of making the individual human the hinge on which salvation or damnation must turn. If the reaction is not toward the historical churchly mediation, this is its only refuge. "This fundamental protest against every sacramental meaning of the Church-order, handed down in history, revolves perpetually between two poles, one of which shows itself as the exclusive origin of salvation in the unchangeable will of God, and the other as absolute subjectivism."* How well Calvinism and Arminianism are able to stand on the same ground of unhistorical, untraditional, unchurchly subjectivism, later history has illustrated in Wesleyan and Whitefieldian Methodism—a historical fact worthy of profound study.

In the very nature of the Reformation there lay a temptation and a danger naturally adapted to weaken the historical conception and authority of the Church. Its nature as a historical manifestation, and a historical power in the world, though not ignored, was exposed to being overrun by the intense earnestness of reformatory zeal. This spirit and tendency of the age tended naturally and powerfully to create a bias toward the Calvinistic principle of an unmediated Christianity; for in that system of thinking it found a congenial and consistent home. Both in the sphere of doctrine and cultus the reforming spirit was unconsciously but strongly under the pressure of a creating spirit. In Calvin this tendency was strongest; and, whilst it was no doubt this that led him to find the decretal principle as the main principle of his system, the prevalence of this tendency in his own mind at the same time prepared him too far to follow its logical consequences. But the historical fact of the Church, and the fact of a historical Church, as the true mediation of Christ's life and redeeming grace, was always too deep and strong a power, especially in the *German* Reformed Church, to allow it to surrender itself to the logical tendencies of Calvinism, either in the sphere of doctrine or cultus. Hence in the period preceding the Synod of Dort, 1618–19, the doctrine of predestination did not reign in more than one-third of the continental Reformed Church. Its apparent triumph through that Synod was in fact a defeat. It proved, indeed, always a restless element which could not find a solid or peaceful home in its bosom. Various schools arose successively in the effort to find relief from it. From

---

* Dr. Heppe.

the Synod of Dort forward, its influence declined more and more. It was first modified, then treated with caution and lack of confidence, and at length passed out of the construction of Reformed' theological systems, at least in its original distinctive character.

That the outworking of the Calvinistic principle *must be* destructive of the genial bosom of a churchly cultus, we have shown to be a logical necessity of its own ruling principle; and that it *has done* so, will appear from an exhibition of the actual development of this same principle in subsequent history. That the bleakness into which this naked cultus carried the Church left the earnest instincts of a hearty piety unprovided for, and that this opened a ready field for the inauguration of a warm but wild, enthusiastic, subjective individualism, is in like manner historically certified.

This tendency, of which Calvinism was the occasion and the cause, wrought with equal force from a new principle —or rather from a new phase of the same principle—toward the destruction of a churchly cultus.

Through the last half of the seventeenth and the first half of the eighteenth centuries run two parallel tendencies: pietism with its unsteady subjective zeal for practical personal religion, and a subjective doctrinal criticism, tending to reduce all religious doctrines and mysteries to the measure of the rational understanding. This last was a co-ordinate protest against the first, and designed as its cure. Both together, and the first as the initiating element, formed the womb out of which rationalism more immediately had its birth. The subsequent periods of rationalism —as that of historical criticism, 1750–1800, that of philosophical criticism, 1780–1800, that of the vulgar rationalism, 1800–1814, and the latest philosophical rationalism—are only historical and logical developments of earnest endeavors at extrication from the same original subjective tendencies by what was supposed to be a steadier and safer subjectivism, but resting on substantially the same un-churchly, untraditional grounds. The felt wants of the age, rationalism attempted to cure, by the light of the best rational arbitration of truth through the native power of reason, unmediated by the traditionary monitions of a historical Church.

This twofold emancipation from traditional authority and life, from old forms and things sacred, produced, in the first several decades of the eighteenth century, a fermentation of enthusiasm which knew no restraint. It was a perfect storm of freedom from all traditional conservation in dogmas and cultus, to both of which prevailingly, if not only, subjective tests were applied. "The inward spark, the inward word," were exalted above all that is called authority. The heated conventicle with its "exercises" was more genial than the Church with its "services." Even Spener, the ruling spirit of the pietistic movement, was restless under confessional as well as under liturgical restraints, and declared it "too hard" that Christian ministers should be bound to received symbolic faith; and prominent spirits in the same movement could call symbolical books "Afterbibeln," and "Sektenbücher." Spener himself was a man of much piety, learning, and prudence. He continued also to the end of his life to adhere professedly to Lutheran orthodoxy, though, as we have seen, he limited somewhat the authority of its symbolical books and called into question some of its essential customs and practices in worship. Yet the subsequent history of the movement shows—running out as it did into various forms of self-righteous, censorious fanaticism and arrogant, self-assuming separatism—that it was, in its deepest heart, soul, and life, at war with orthodoxy and order, and had in it all those elements of subjectivity which ultimately waste themselves in the sediment of mere human vaporings, like waters in the sand.

Accordingly, in the outworking of these tendencies, both proved alike destructive of churchly cultus. Rationalism

278

corrupted liturgies, removing their unction, eviscerating them of their healthy doctrinal life, and flattening them down to a mere naturalistic level; while pietism more and more set them aside, substituting in their stead the extemporaneous "exercises" of individual taste, and the impulses of a capricious subjectivity. That the same subjective individualism evermore begets the same antagonism to an objective churchly cultus, the subsequent rise and history of Methodism, and of all fanatical sects, abundantly prove and illustrate.

The manner in which this tendency to subjectivity, both in the form of pietism and rationalism, destructively affected *all* the elements of a true objective Christian cultus, could easily be illustrated historically. It will, however, be sufficient to show how it wrought against the use of liturgical forms, and how, in this particular, the results of the movement at length historically ran together with Calvinism in its historical development, and how both systems ultimately manifested their aversion to the use of Liturgies, inaugurated free prayer in the conduct of public worship, and, generally, created and promoted a rigid and naked cultus.

Standing as we do in the midst of a prevailingly unliturgical mode of worship, and consciously or unconsciously biased by the short traditions of the Reformed cultus in America, where, as a fruit of the tendencies referred to, free prayer is the *rule* and liturgical prayer the *exception*, our attention is at once arrested by the fact that in the earlier practice of the Reformed Church no free prayer in public worship was allowed. It will have been noticed that in the Liturgy of the Palatinate, so long associated with the Heidelberg Catechism, not a single allusion is made to the use of free prayer. The directions for conducting the worship are all definitely given; the rubrics are all characterized by the positive *shall;* and every part of the service is distinctly and fully provided for. The weekday service, the Sunday afternoon catechetical service, the service for the regular monthly day of prayer, as well as for fast-days, and even the daily morning and evening services to be held in the churches, are all fully provided for by appropriate devotional Offices. No free prayer in public worship is thought of, or allowed.

This fact, evident from the Liturgy itself, is abundantly confirmed by co-ordinate historical notices. " The prayers in divine worship, and in the administration of the Sacraments, were by no means left free, but were conducted according to the Palatinate Liturgy which had been introduced. Strict watch was kept for the maintenance of unity, through uniformity in the use of the Liturgy; and hence the use of every Liturgy that had not been approved was prohibited, ' because nothing is more necessary than conformity, and a firm adherence to the Liturgy introduced, as all innovations are offensive.' (Clev. Syn., 1685.) For this reason also the General Synod of 1728 censured every departure of ministers from the liturgical formularies: 'that every dangerous disorder may be prevented, and also that inexperienced wavering minds may be warned and checked; since it does not become any individual minister, yea, not even a *synodo provinciali*, to make any changes in the administration of the word of God, the Holy Supper, Holy Baptism, and in the form of conducting worship, as handed down to us; but such changes must be undertaken, after mature consideration, in case it shall be found necessary and practicable, by the *reverendo synodo generali.*' Free prayers were therefore, in the beginning, not at all permitted, and were only allowed after 1677, having come in as a consequence of the introduction of Labadism."* Thus, during the first one hundred and ten years of the existence of the Reformed Church of the Heidelberg Catechism, its public worship was invariably bound to the full and exclusive use of its liturgical Offices and forms of prayer, to the entire exclusion of all extemporaneous worship.

---

* Max Göbel: Geschichte des Christlichen Lebens, &c., vol. ii. p. 121.

The fanatical leaven of Labadism,* having awakened in restless spirits a clamor for change, now began to open the

---

* LABADISM, a fanatical, separatistic sect or religious movement, the head of which was Jean de Labadie,—born 1610, died 1674.

Labadie was originally a Jesuit. After a vain endeavor to reform that society, he conceived the idea—a favorite with all fanatics—to "form a Church according to the apostolic model." Meeting unconquerable obstacles, he passed over into the Reformed Church at Montauban in 1650. He now found freer play for his ardent temperament, and labored as he could at his favorite scheme. In 1659 he came to Geneva, where his preaching produced great awakenings; and by the institution of "conferences," or private worship in families,—something like modern prayer-meetings,—he gathered around him a number of ardent young men, into whom he infused his own spirit, among whom was Philip James Spener, who afterward was the master-spirit of a movement in the Lutheran Church similar to that inaugurated by Labadie in the Reformed Church, commonly called pietism. By these young men, and through his numerous writings, the leaven spread into France, Germany, and Holland. His spirit having gone before him, he was in 1666 called as pastor of the Reformed Walloon congregation in Middelburg, having before his departure vowed before God, with three of his most intimate co-workers, to labor faithfully toward "the establishment of a community of goods,"—the germ of future separatism. In Middelburg he produced a lively sensation, which extended into the regions around, establishing as far as possible his favorite private meetings for edification, defending them by a book on the subject. Here, however, he soon got into trouble. Refusing, for trivial reasons, to sign the Belgic Confession, his arrogance, caprice, and dogmatical insubordination brought him into conflict with his Classis and Synod. He also refused to be bound to the prescribed liturgical prayers, which was then still an invariable custom in the Reformed Church, but offered in their stead his own free, extemporaneous prayers. He was finally suspended by the Synod for insubordination; after which, in 1668, he celebrated with his fanatical adherents, "in wicked blindness," the Lord's Supper privately, before the regular service, thus bringing his wild plant to the full bloom of sect, schism and fanatical separatism. He was, accordingly, excommunicated. He then made the attempt, first in a small town, Beere, and afterward in Amsterdam, after the fashion of the Donatists and all separatists, to form "a perfectly pure congregation to contain none but regenerated souls." Here they were at last broken up by the interference of the magistrate; when they—fifty in number, with five pastors—found an asylum in Herford, in the Palatinate. Here, whilst Labadie and others were only secretly married, they held the marriage of unbelievers as sinful, and regarded only the marriage of the holy ones as holy and right, and their children, born without pain, as holy members of the Church. The reigning inspiration and fanaticism here attained a terrible height, when after an ordinary love-feast there began a general revival, manifesting itself in "Christian shout

X   281

door for innovation. In 1677 the Synod of Cleves passed the following act, as quoted by Göbel:—"For the better edification and comfort of the ignorant, the customary formularies shall on ordinary occasions, in connection with preaching, be adhered to: still *freedom* shall be allowed, at *special* times and occasions, to *add* some things to the ordinary prayers, or even to form *other* prayers, agreeing with the Scriptures and the matter of the forms prescribed." The General Synod, held the same year (1677), fell in with this action; providing, however, that it should not be so construed "that the customary formularies should thereby be contemptuously set aside." "Nevertheless," says Göbel, "in consequence of this permission, the custom and caprice of free prayer began to prevail to such an extent in the following century, that the prescribed liturgical prayers were gradually altogether dislodged."

The same practice in the conduct of public worship prevailed also in the Reformed Church of Switzerland. "Great as the severity was with which the Roman ceremonies were opposed in the time of the Reformation, still the prayers were in no place left free; on the contrary, from the beginning, fixed forms of prayer, liturgies, and agenda were introduced, and in the process of time extended and improved. The Zurich Liturgy reigned for

---

ing, jumping, dancing, and kissing"! Nor could the decency of the civil law tolerate them here. In 1672 they went to the free city Altona, where Labadie died in 1674. After his death the movement, which had bloomed through twenty years, languished, in dying, forty years more. Some of the scattered seeds even took root in America, and a small community of the "new-born" grew up on the Hudson, in New York, previous to 1695, and one also in Maryland between 1721 and 1730. Some united with the Seventh-Day Baptists at Ephrata, Pa. Infant baptism was not practised; and the Lord's Supper, because they did not feel fit to celebrate it (the new-born!), was administered only three times between 1670 and 1703; after the latter date not at all! Wherever it was extended, "indifference to Church, sacraments, and hence separatism, were the bitter fruits of Labadism." For a full account of this sad but instructive phenomenon, see Herzog's Real-Encyk., vol. viii. pp. 150–155; also Göbel's "Geschichte des Christl. Lebens in der Rhein-Westph. evangel. Kirche," vol. ii. pp. 181–299.

a long time over the greater portion of Eastern Switzerland. At present every canton has its own liturgy, with the exception of Glarus, which is, however, at present engaged with a revision of the Zurich Liturgy. Much has been done in this sphere during late years."*

The early Liturgies of the Reformed of Holland were equally full with that of the Palatinate, in some points entering even more into the details of worship, and making provision for all the offices of public worship. Calvin, whose influence, as we have seen, was less friendly to the true liturgical spirit than that of any of the Reformers, nevertheless prepared, in 1543, a Liturgy with full circle of Offices, and "regarded it as most important, for the safety of the Church, to establish a durable order through uniformity in liturgical rites, and thereby to oppose effectually the wilfulness of individuals."†

Though these were the convictions of his mind and the sentiments of his heart, yet the system of Calvin cultivated a spirit which in the course of time, in circumstances where its logical effects were not, as they were in his own mind, hindered by traditional forms and associations, outrode all liturgical tastes and practices. Of this we have a historical illustration in the Reformed Church of Scotland. The Scotch Church at first made use of prepared prayers of the Calvinistic type, which Knox had brought with him from Geneva. In 1560–61, Knox and four others prepared a Book of Discipline for the Scotch Church. "In regard to worship, the Book of Discipline refers to the 'Order of Geneva, with its prayers and Catechism, which is in a number of places in use.' The Order here referred to is no doubt that of .the English Congregation of Geneva, whose minister Knox had been. That was formed after the pattern of Calvin's Liturgy, and was closely allied to that of the English Congregation of Re-

---

* Herzog's Real-Encyk., article Switzerland.
† Henry's Life and Times of Calvin, vol. i. p. 410.

fugees in Frankfort. The Book of Discipline allows the use of the prayers in the book to which it refers, yet discourages their use in the 'Sermon-Services,' that forms may not again become the occasion of superstition."*

If this cold treatment of liturgical formularies were not sufficient to dislodge them, the following rule in regard to the Lord's Supper and the Festivals which must ever underlie and give life and tone to liturgical worship, is abundantly sufficient in a short time to work them out of the way by logical, theological, and historical necessity:— " The Lord's Supper shall be positively received sitting; and it shall not be celebrated on the Festival days on which it has hitherto been customary to hold it, but on the first Sunday of March, June, September, and December; that no superstition may be practised by an observance of days. This was the end of the Festival days in the Scotch Church."† It must necessarily also prove, as it has in fact done, the end of all liturgical worship. In the " Directory for Public Worship" adopted in the Westminster Assembly, 1644, no fixed forms for the public prayers of the Church are given, but only extensive directions as to the contents which they should embody. Holydays are all abolished, only Sunday retained. More than two hundred years ago, the Scotch Church set aside all forms of prayer in the public service of the Church, and with them all use of Liturgies.‡

As we do not here discuss the merits of Calvinism itself as a system, and attempt no argument against it,— except so far as its necessary tendency to produce an unchurchly cultus may be regarded in the light of such argument,—so it is not necessary that we should here inquire whether at all, and, if at all, in how far, the Heidelberg Catechism is Calvinistic in that sense of Calvinism which makes the absolute decree the principle of salvation. If the system is not contained in it originally and legiti-

---

* Herzog's Real-Encyk., art. Scotland.   † Idem.   ‡ Idem.

mately, it is certain that it has been put into it, not only by many interpreters, but also by some entire provincial Reformed Churches.* All that our present discussion proposes is to show that wherever a strictly Calvinistic system of doctrine, in the sense just indicated, has been either found in it or been forced upon it, as the case may be, no such cultus as that originally connected with it in the Palatinate, and, indeed, no liturgical worship of a like tone and character, has ever been able long to maintain its place in a living way in its bosom or by its side.

That a cultus like that provided for by the Palatinate Liturgy, having so much of a churchly liturgical element in it, could be at home in the Reformed Church of the Palatinate, is itself sufficient to prove the absence of the influence of Calvinism in its distinctive character.† " So far as the Palatinate—the very heart of the German Reformed Church—was concerned," says Dr. Ebrard, " *Calvin had there only an indirect influence*, obtained partly by having been brought into more or less friendly relations with her

---

* It must, however, appear evident to any unbiased inquirer, from the face of the Catechism itself, that it eschews entirely that dogma of the absolute decree of predestination which constitutes the starting-point and centre of the system of Calvin. On depravity, sin, grace, the sacraments, and some other points, it is undoubtedly Calvinistic. But not only in the absence of all positive teaching in regard to the decrees, but also in some strong language which it employs in regard to the extent of the atonement, we may see that it does not rest in that principle. But most of all the Catechism has underlying it the churchly principle, and presupposes, in its entire scheme, genius, and teaching, a churchly mediation to which the decretal principle of Calvin is averse, against which his system in his own mind perpetually struggled, which in a measure he himself gradually more and more ignored, and which the logical and historical development of his system has demonstrated cannot coalesce with his system. For a discussion of this whole subject, see Mercersburg Review, vol. ix. 1857, pp. 83–107; also Dr. Nevin's Review of " Hodge on the Ephesians," Mer. Rev., vol. ix. pp. 46–83, and 192–245.

† " In no prayer or formulary of any Reformed Agenda, in any land, is there to be found a single reference to absolute predestination."—*Ebrard's Dogmatik*, vol. i. p. 53. " In the Palatinate the matter of predestination had not come under discussion."—*Ibid.* vol. i. p. 54.

eminent theologians during his residence in Germany in 1539–41, and partly by the acquaintance he made with German divines travelling in Switzerland." He shows that the Palatinate was "much more particularly under Melanchthon's influence than under that of either Calvin or Zwingli." His division of the Reformed into three classes of provincial Churches, distinguished as the *Zwinglian*, the *Calvinistic*, and the *Melanchthonian* or German Reformed, is fully approved by Dr. Daniel, in his article Kirchenagende in Herzog's Real-Encyklopädie. Both these eminent liturgists place the Palatinate in the last-named class. Dr. Heppe, Professor of Theology in the University of Marburg, from a strict study of the archival records of Cassel relating to the Church history of the Palatinate and Hesse,* comes to the same conclusion in regard to the Melanchthonian element in the Reformation of the Palatinate Church. Compared with the unbiased, comprehensive spirit in which this subject is handled by these eminent men, the opposition made to it, especially and with great zeal by Sudhoff,† betrays itself on its very face as special pleading. That both Lutheran and Calvinistic elements were consciously and unconsciously present in the Palatinate is most certain; but that both were subordinated to, and moulded by, another power may be gathered from the history of the times, from the ruling minds of the movement, and especially from the genius and characteristics of both the Catechism and the Liturgy.

It remains for us to show why Creed calls for its correlative Liturgy, and to inquire more particularly what kind of cultus is consistent with the Heidelberg Catechism,— whether that which we have exhibited as the true Christian cultus, and the fundamental features of which we have found in the Palatinate Liturgy, or that to which the Cal-

* See Mer. Rev., vol. v. pp. 181–207.
† In his Life of Olevianus and Ursinus. Also in the article on the Heidelberg Catechism in Herzog's Real-Encyk.

vinistic principle logically tends and leads, and which we have seen it has historically developed.

We may remark, in general, that Creed and Liturgy both require *language* and formularies of thought,—in the one of which we utter our faith, in the other our worship. It is at once clear that doctrine in Creed or Catechism cannot find expression in the language or formula of Holy Scripture. For the question .is, first, What is the true sense of Scripture? It is the answer to this question which the Creed of the Church is required to give. If it gave answer in the language of Scripture, it would in reality answer nothing as to the point in question. The Scriptures contain God's thoughts given to men through various human channels, in the form of history, biography, prophecy, poetry, precept, parable. Besides, these revelations are supernatural and superhuman, though clothed in natural and human forms. To be a revelation to man, it must be a revelation through man. The truths that thus lie before us must be taken up into the mind of the Church, moulded in forms objective to man, and re-uttered for man.

It is equally clear that no individual can interpret and utter these teachings, because no individual mind can be the full measure of revelation. His views of what the Scriptures teach are moulded by his own individual moods and tenses; and to pretend that his views of Scripture are *the* truth revealed in it, is to claim a wisdom and wideness greater than that of the whole Church of history! It is by the communion of minds, and even by their conflict, in the bosom of the Church, that the general consciousness of the Church is placed in full possession of the contents of revelation, and enabled to utter its creed. Thus, the history of doctrinal inquiry creates a doctrinal terminology and language by which it expresses its formularies of faith. This language and terminology, though allied to that of Scripture, is, nevertheless, different from it, containing even words and phrases, and those its ruling ones, which are not at all found in the word of God.

It is thus required of every individual to confess his faith, not in the language of Holy Scripture, nor yet in his own individual extemporaneous language, but in unison with the whole Church, in language and formularies born from her earnest inquiries, controversies, experiences, and decisions, brought down in her inward history and doctrinal traditions.

Now, the same holds true in all respects of the language of Church-devotion or public worship. By the same law, and in like manner, has the piety of the Church developed a liturgical language and liturgical formularies. Devotion has its peculiar style. Some words and phrases can never be made devotional. They fit neither the heart nor the mouth of the true worshipper. As in the case of doctrine, so in the case of devotion, its language is not that of Scripture, though perpetually calling it to mind. The oldest, purest, and best of prayers, those that have most of the unction and savor of devotion and best express it for all, have least of formal Scripture language. The devotion of the Scriptures has been taken up into the catholic consciousness of the Church, re-formed and re-uttered from its deepest heart and life of piety, and thus it furnishes to each one a power and appropriateness of utterance far beyond what he could himself extemporaneously attain. It is, therefore, a clear requirement of consistency that if the Church furnishes us the language and formularies of faith, to which it has itself attained by the process of historical development indicated, and requires us to utter our faith in its forms, it must, in like manner, furnish us with the language and formularies of devotion and worship which are its peculiar possession by similar blessed inheritance. Thus, the same necessity which urges the Church to furnish its children with a creed requires it also to provide for them a liturgy.

In regard to the *material* or *contents* of Creed and Liturgy, the same law holds good. The matter of Creed and Catechism, as objectively presented, cannot be drawn by the individual mind from the Bible direct. Eighteen centuries

288

of history mediate between us and the Bible. This history, under the perennial working of the Holy Spirit, has elicited the contents of the word of revelation and made them objective to us. We enter into the inheritance of the past. So the Heidelberg Catechism views this fact. Hence its heart of faith, the Apostles' Creed, is the creed of all ages. This it presents as the sense and measure of our faith. "What is then necessary for a Christian to believe? All that is promised us in the gospel, *which the articles of our catholic, undoubted Christian faith teach us in sum.*" "What are these articles?" This question it answers by presenting to us the Apostles' Creed. It does not send us to the Scripture direct, that we may measure its teachings in our own minds; it gives us its contents moulded and measured by the faith of the Church. It does not hold a dialogue with us, as placing us on the same level with itself, but presents to us a catechism ($\varkappa\alpha\tau\alpha$ and $\eta\chi\varepsilon\omega$), that we may be taught to echo back, in the way of personal confession, the truth divine which it has communicated to us. Why does not the Catechism call this faith scriptural? With a deep insight into the point just explained, it calls this faith catholic; because it is catholic, it is undoubted; and because it is catholic and undoubted, it is Christian; and because it is all these, it is truly faith, and not individual notion.

The Catechism is based throughout on what was from the first regarded as the proper catechetical matter,—the Creed, the Holy Sacraments, the doctrine of the Keys, the Commandments, and the Lord's Prayer. It is, indeed, only an expansion and connection of these. Now, does not consistency require that the same principle should underlie and determine the worship of the Church? Have not liturgical material forms, as well as liturgical language, the same mediating history? The Liturgy, therefore, which is consistent with the Catechism must be based substantially on liturgical materials created and brought down by the historical Church. This is the case in some degree in the Palatinate Liturgy; and so far as it is not, it stands inconsistent with the symbolical faith in which it rests and of which it is the correlative. Any such matter found in it is abnormal to its true life and position, inflicted upon it by cotemporaneous foreign inworkings; and there is, therefore, higher authority for their removal now than there was for incorporating them at the time of its formation. For is not that a legitimate right which the Church claims of going back into any period of its own renewal and advance, and, in the same surroundings in which those stood who then reformed, using the same sources which they used, but unembarrassed by the peculiar unsteady spirit of the times, and with the additional advantages furnished by the experience of subsequent history, to modify and perfect their work, by putting away some things which they retained, retaining some which they put away, and permeating all with that higher life of Christianity which we may believe its advance will ever more perfectly unfold?

The Catechism also has its *position* fully and firmly on churchly ground. It presupposes the existence of the Church as a divine constitution, having historical being, the mother of what it presents to be believed, as well as the mother of those who are to believe. Those to whom it proposes its faith, and whom it invites to learn and confess it, already stand in its bosom, are called Christians, are addressed as Christians, and are made to speak as Christians. It holds the view that grace comes to them mediated by the Church with its sacraments, ordinances, and entire cultus. Hence it regards and treats baptized children as in grace, and, believing, looks for their full preparation for heaven by the sanctifying grace of the Holy Spirit, through the Christian nurture of the Church. It does not regard the Church as merely a receptacle for those otherwise regenerated and prepared for admittance into it, either in consequence of a divine determination or by virtue of individual choice and will, but as bringing to men the new life in Christ by its sacrament of regeneration and renewal by the Holy Ghost, and as furnishing in its bosom all the nurturing and nourishing powers needed unto salvation. It exhibits the Holy Sacraments as God's gracious acts manward through Christ and His Church, and calls upon him to repent and believe and live, as that to which his position obliges, entitles, and enables him, seeing that the powers and the grace of the kingdom are thus for him at hand.

This calls for a cultus of like nature,—one which presupposes and rests in the Church. It calls for a worship that shall be directed to God in response to the gracious activities of God toward man,—a worship which depends on and rests in cultus, and springs forth from it as its true fruit; a worship, therefore, in which the sacramental, as being God's approach toward man, goes before the sacrificial, as being man's approach toward God,—the first being always before and higher and more controlling than the second, even as the divine is ever over the human. Such a cultus must have objective powers, must allow objective force to the Holy Sacraments, must include in it a real mediation; must, in a word, be to the worshipper more than he can himself furnish, and must itself afford to his faith gracious efficacies unto salvation,—a cultus which will make him feel that he is surrounded by gracious powers greater and stronger than himself, apprehending him whilst he seeks to apprehend, lifting up his spirit whilst he endeavors to lift it up; so that beholding, as in a glass, the glory of the Lord, he is changed into the same image from glory to glory as by the Spirit of the Lord.

In the organism of the Catechism, the *Holy Eucharist* is central. Assuming, as we have said, that the one called upon to utter his faith in its formula stands in a gracious covenant, it seeks, in its first part, to awaken him to a knowledge and sense of his sinfulness and misery. In the second part it begins to lead him to confess faith in God, Father, Son, and Holy Ghost, as these divine Persons have been historically manifested,—the Son manifesting the Father, the Holy Spirit manifesting the Father and the Son, in which successive manifestations God's love, Christ's

291

grace, and the Holy Spirit's communion are brought to man, by effecting a real atonement and union with man, all this leading to the founding on earth of the Church, in which the sacraments are instituted,—Holy Baptism as the sacrament of regeneration, in which the putting off the old and putting on the new, of burial and resurrection with Christ, is initially effected, whilst this sacrament directs and leads to the Holy Supper as the mystery and sanctuary of inmost union and communion with Christ, in which we " not only embrace with a believing heart all the sufferings and death of Christ, and thereby obtain the forgiveness of sin and life eternal; but also, besides that, to become more and more united to His sacred body by the Holy Ghost, who dwells both in Christ and in us; so that we, though Christ is in heaven, and we on earth, are, notwithstanding, flesh of His flesh, and bone of His bones, and that we live and are governed forever by one Spirit, as members of the same body are by one soul."*

Christian doctrine knows no mystery deeper than this to which it can lead. This is its innermost centre; and hence the Catechism here reaches its climax. Here it finds the turning-point in the work of redemption. All that follows flows from this, as all before lead to it. Next is the office of the Keys, which exhibit admission to the Eucharist and exclusion from it as the highest and most solemn power of the kingly office in the Church. All preceding the Holy Sacraments belongs to the prophetic function, pointing to them; all succeeding them is the function of the kingly office, ruling in the Church by word and discipline, in the conscience by the law, and in the heart by the high monitions of worship; while in the sacraments themselves, and in the Holy Eucharist, as the last and deepest sacramental sanctuary, the priestly function, as the central remedial office, exercises, as the Fathers would say, its tremendous mediation between a holy God and sinful men, in view of

---

* Heidelberg Catechism, Question 76.

which the very seraphim, we may believe, in meek awe and wonder exclaim, "Holy, holy, holy!"

A worship, therefore, which shall be consistent with the doctrinal system of the Catechism must consciously refer itself to this sacrament as its centre and ultimate bearer. As in the Jewish worship all service met at last in the high-priest, and through his mediation poured its oblations, "in the holiest of all," upon the mercy-seat, which was the shadow of the atonement, so does all truly Christian worship look to this sacrament, which holds forth the atonement fulfilled, and thus reaches Him acceptably who has taught our faith to discern in it His own body and blood. As to the prophetic element in cultus, the highest preaching is that which directs to this Christian altar, and cries, "Behold the Lamb of God, which taketh away the sin of the world." As to the kingly element in cultus, that is the most awful power which excludes from the altar sacrament. And that is the highest order of intercessory prayer which comes by this mercy-seat, presses through the rent vail of the Saviour's divine-human flesh, and presents itself in union with His sacrifice. That is the best penitence and confession which here looks upon Him who by sin has been pierced. That is the highest thanksgiving which embodies itself in the Eucharist,—a word which the Evangelist uses in connection with the Holy Supper,—and in which, with steady eye on His atoning death, we consecrate ourselves, "in soul and body, property and life, to His most blessed service and praise."

Finally, we must not undervalue the significance of the sacred power which the Heidelberg Catechism is adapted to exert upon religious *instincts* and *associations*. It is most sweetly destitute of cold abstractions. It lives,—in every question, line, and word. It has savorly treasures for the heart. It is full of beauty. Its very language and style is warm, glowing, even poetical; which characteristic, whilst it meets the sense of the beautiful, cultivates the mystical in the soul; and thus, like the Bible itself, its truths lead

293

us up perpetually to the very borders of mysterious devotional inspiration. Every earnest catechumen knows that it has the power of making all things sacred to the heart, by gathering fragrant memories around itself and all its teachings, and making the catechumenate period the enduring source of sacred associations, solemn monitions, and gracious refreshment for all after-life. It is in its whole nature and spirit adapted to provide for and cultivate that peculiarity of the human spirit which leads us to associate thoughts and feelings with objects and things, with instructions and warnings, with privileges and experiences, with persons, places, and times.

A worship that shall be consistent with it must honor, secure, and perpetuate for the religious instincts and associations this sacred power. Rigid didactic Calvinism, with its preference for bare, unornamented churches, with its love for an intellectual, reflective, unmystical worship, with its anti-festival spirit, does not provide for this want. As little is it found in the heated Arminian conventicle. That theory of worship which asks for naked churches, platform pulpits, bare altars, organless choirs, churches without steeples, or steeples without bells, bears this defect in cultus upon its face. The birds will not sing where there is no grove. The fruit-tree is known also by its blossoms. That which is ever produced anew in devotional exercises, either from reflection or emotion, cannot inspire reverence; and what does not inspire reverence cannot live sacredly in our associations, and thus leaves the highest and most beautiful part of our nature uncultivated.

The true spirit of worship cannot long live on originalities and generalities, even though these be called spiritualities. Home is location. As every home must have its old way-marks, its surroundings and belongings, its familiar scenes and things, its well-known rooms with pictures on the wall, its ticking clock and chirruping cricket, its weird moonlight through the window, its patter of rain upon the roof, its cradle and its graves, so must that home of the heart in the Church, which is formed by its cultus, have its sacred scenes and things, around which the religious home-feeling may learn to twine its hallowed affections. The tendrils of the heart must have something to cling to; and that must neither be devoid of mystery and the mystical, nor yet ever changing, ever moving. Variety may be the spice of life, but it is not the spice of devotion. Nor is spice a thing to live on. It may be pleasant and stimulating to the taste, but it brings no permanent strength to the system.

There must be in cultus a staff of life, which presents its steady support and nourishment,—its solid doctrines, its holy sacraments, its opening and shutting keys,—its creeds, prayers, hymns, and holy-days,—its altars and organs, its steeples and bells,—in short, all that is involved in the idea of sacred persons, places, times, and things, with all that constitutes the distinctive and peculiar scenery and atmosphere of the holy place of Jehovah's dwelling. The divine presence in the Church imparts to all these its own supernatural mystery of grace,—covers them, each in its degree and kind, with the soft and sacred aureola of its glory, and imbues them with something of its own heavenly nature. This is their consecration. This creates the mysteriously sacred scenery and atmosphere which, under the Holy Spirit and by His efficacious working, constitutes for our worship its mystical sustaining element. This touches the heart, and through the heart imbeds itself in the memory, and through the memory lives in the associations, and is for the spirit a heavenly presence and a perpetual benediction.

295

THE GENIUS AND MISSION

OF THE

GERMAN REFORMED CHURCH,

IN RELATION TO THE LUTHERAN CHURCH AND TO THOSE BRANCHES OF THE REFORMED CHURCH WHICH ARE NOT GERMAN.

By REV. PROF. THEODORE APPEL, A.M.
LANCASTER, PA.

THE GENIUS AND MISSION

OF THE

GERMAN REFORMED CHURCH,

IN RELATION TO THE LUTHERAN CHURCH AND TO THOSE BRANCHES
OF THE REFORMED CHURCH WHICH ARE NOT GERMAN.

By Reb. Prof. Theodore Appel, A. M., Lancaster, Pa.

WHILST the present occasion should be one of joy and
rejoicing, it should, at the same time, be one of profit and
edification throughout the church. To celebrate, as we
should, the formation of the Catechism, requires of us to
lay aside local prejudices and prepossessions; to pass over
centuries, and to commune with the good and great of
other days; to enter into their spirit, and to breathe in the
atmosphere in which they lived and died for the cause of
Christ; in a word, to sit at their feet and learn of them how
to believe and receive, how to work and how to pray. To
strengthen and confirm this communion with the saints of
other times, to awaken in our minds the consciousness of an
historical connection with the past, and thus to come into
union with the stream of living Church-tradition, must,
under the blessing of God, tend to quicken and refresh the
sensibilities of our church in a high degree, and to introduce us more fully into the communion of saints, and, as a
consequence, into communion with Christ and the Holy
Spirit. On this festival occasion we are called as a denomination to make a pilgrimage to the birthplace of the
church in the fatherland, and to commune with those who
took an active part in laying the foundations of that struc-

299

ture in which we now find our spiritual home. Our pilgrimage takes us back to the classic period of the Reformation, and places us in the very midst of those religious convulsions, which changed the current of history and stamped upon the modern era its distinguishing character. The great battle between German and Latin Christianity had been fought; the separation between the modern and the medieval church had been accomplished; the rent in the Saviour's body, owing to human weakness and folly, could not be avoided; the Latin Church was aroused from the fatal lethargy into which she had fallen, and called to watch and strengthen the things that remained, which were ready to die; whilst the Church of the Reformation, with youthful energy and enthusiasm, was just entering upon its career and preparing for its own specific work in the kingdom of God. Zwingli, Luther, and Melanchthon had fallen asleep in Jesus; whilst Calvin, who also belonged to the heroic period, was fast approaching the end of his course, and, as the brightest luminary in the spiritual firmament, continued to shed a brilliant light over Europe. The time in which the Heidelberg Catechism took its rise, A.D. 1563, was a period not so much of negative protestation against errors and abuses that had crept into the Church, as of positive reformation and evangelization within its pale. The results of the great conflict had become an actual possession, and it now became an object of concern to preserve and transmit them intact to the generations following. The Protestant principle, in its strength and weakness, had fully been unfolded, and the Church, conscious of itself and of its mission, was prepared to express in language and thought a proper sense of her own contents. Thirty-three years had elapsed from the time that the first Protestant confession had been made at Augsburg, a period which, as Schiller, the poet and historian, has remarked, was too early for a full and complete expression of the evangelical faith. Subsequent confessions, unfortunately for the unity of the

300

Church, were called for, which, though presenting an appearance of contradiction and antagonism toward each other, were, as essential parts of a general whole, necessary to present in its completeness the entire Protestant idea. The Heidelberg Catechism grew out of such a necessity, and received from it a distinct work to perform in the general movement of the Church during the modern period.

The relation of the Catechism to the Church may be viewed under two aspects. In the first place, it may be regarded as the proper expression of the life of the Church. This is the case, generally, with symbols of this kind. They originate in a period of earnest discussion, when as yet opinion is fluctuating and unsettled, and truth and error, with more or less of disorder and confusion, are struggling for the victory; but such periods cannot continue indefinitely: the elements of truth, separating themselves from the errors still clinging to them, seek to occupy their proper relation to each other, and, by a necessary law, embody themselves in some order or system. In this way we obtain catechisms and confessions of faith. They embody in an outward form the best life of the Church, with its peculiar character and tendencies. But, in the second place, they become a source of life and power to the Church, causing it to throw off foreign and incongruous elements, defining its general characteristics, and impressing upon it a peculiar stamp of piety. By studying the Catechism, consequently, we may learn what the spirit of the Church is, or, by making ourselves acquainted with the history and spirit of the Church, we may arrive at a correct knowledge of the Catechism. They thus mutually throw light upon each other. On the present occasion we shall endeavor to exhibit the spirit of our own church as it has impressed itself on the page of history. It is, indeed, impossible to arrive at a full and satisfactory understanding of the Catechism apart from the history, the church-life, and relations, in which it stands. Without, therefore, referring to it directly or in detail, we hope our contribution to this festal occasion may nevertheless tend in some degree to throw light upon its spirit and life.

Upon the general relation of our own church to the Church of Rome, we do not propose here to enter in detail. Nor is it necessary, in order to show its peculiar life and spirit. It is related to that church through the entire Protestant body, further removed in its spirit and animus than the Lutheran, on the one side, and not so far as other branches of the Reformed Church, on the other. The Protestant principle has different grades and degrees of intensity, from its just and normal use in protesting against palpable errors and abuses and unauthorized assumptions of authority, to the empty negations of rationalism and infidelity, in which it is shorn of all religious spirit and is simply a satanic caricature of the deeply earnest religious protest of the sixteenth century. In the Reformed churches it was carried to the highest degree of tension, consistent with its legitimate use,—in some churches, of course, more so than in others; in our own, as the most closely related to the Lutheran, not so much so as in the case of others. As a religious principle, one proceeding from a deeply-moved religious consciousness, in harmony with the word of God, it admits of no further extension, without destruction to the religious interests which originally called it forth. What with many is regarded as Protestantism is simply a negation of all church-authority and religious restraint, and is nothing better than infidelity, which carries its negations to the denial of all revelation. The Reformed churches, having made a more free use of the principle of protest, separated themselves to a larger extent from Roman Catholic tradition, but at the same time they came nearer the regions of infidelity and unbelief, than their Lutheran brethren,—a fact which it is well that we should bear in mind in considering their proper work and mission. A similar progress may be observed as it respects the principle of Reform as it lives and is active in

302

the Protestant communion. We observe here again, on the Reformed side, an intensity in its application which does not exist in the sister-church, which, to the great advantage of Protestantism, retained much more of Latin tradition in its purer and better form; and it is, perhaps, not at all something incidental that the term Reformed came to be applied almost exclusively to one side of the Reformation,—to those bodies which, in a more emphatic sense, were Reformed in spirit and tendency. A similar remark may be made as it regards the use of the term Evangelical, which adheres to the Protestant Church as such, but which has a much stronger affinity for the Lutheran than any other Protestant body. As originally used, it was intended to express the free, joyous, Christian consciousness of Protestantism, as mediated and set free by the gospel from the Jewish legalism which existed in the Church of Rome. When the Reformation first came home to the hearts and consciences of men, as salvation by pure grace, all alike rejoiced in the gospel, in their freedom from the curse of the law, and in their nearness of access to the throne of grace, and claimed this freedom as a common inheritance. But Lutheranism clung to it more intensely than the Reformed, and allowed its reformatory tendencies to divert its attention less from this, its first acquisition, than in the other church, so that, as a consequence, it may have less felt the magnitude and extent of the great Protestant call to go in and possess the land. In this way, we may again account for the more frequent use of the term Evangelical in a Lutheran than in a Reformed connection. The German Reformed Church, as closely allied to the Lutheran, and enjoying in common with it much of the fervor, depth, geniality, and freedom of German Christianity, still retains the epithet Evangelical in the fatherland; whereas in other Reformed churches its original distinctive use has in a great measure been forgotten: in its current use at present in this country, it is intended to express an antagonism to prelacy and high-churchism.

The peculiar spirit and tendency, however, of the Reformed Church, and of our own in particular, developed itself to a great extent in antagonism with the Lutheran Church, and can be best understood by viewing it in connection with that body. The old division of Protestantism into two grand divisions, embracing the Lutheran and the Reformed, the latter including all those originally Protestant churches, which were not distinctively Lutheran, is based on a correct principle; for the latter, though manifesting great variety and freedom in their development, in their confessions, their worship and piety, nevertheless exhibit a marked similarity of features, indicative of a common origin, and stand out in striking antithesis at almost every point to the Lutheran Confession. This distinction has been almost lost sight of in this country, and the more general opinion, we presume, is, that Lutheranism is simply a co-ordinate branch of Protestantism, on a level with others, and counting no more than any other in particular. But this is an historical error. It makes up fully one-half of Protestantism, with its own distinctive character, its immense vaults of theological literature, and its own distinctive work in the kingdom of God. It does not, therefore, stand exactly on a level with any single Reformed denomination, but rather over against them all, taken as a whole,— at particular times, in a position of uncompromising antagonism, but, according to its best representatives, in a position of friendly antithesis, as the necessary complement of the Reformed Church, the other half of the same Protestant movement.

Accordingly, we shall proceed to consider the spirit and tendency of the Reformed Church generally, as it developed itself in antagonism or friendly antithesis with the Lutheran Church, and, in the next place, show the distinctive character, which our own branch of the Reformed Church assumed in connection with other Reformed bodies. It will then appear that it has an historical necessity and an historical mission.

Various attempts have been made to comprehend in a single fundamental formula all the distinguishing characteristics of the Reformed Church,—to find some general principle from which its peculiar life, doctrine, and practice have been derived. Had this been discovered, and been clearly stated, the task assigned to us would have been comparatively an easy one. Then, as in the case of the exact sciences, the entire development of the church might be represented, in its unity and diversity, as a harmonious whole, derived from its life-giving principle. But it is not generally admitted that this has been accomplished in a satisfactory manner by any of the distinguished theologians, who have given the subject earnest study and attention. These efforts, however, that have been made to find some general thought or idea out of which the church took its rise, have resulted in bringing to light a number of very important points of difference between the two great branches of the Protestant family, more or less fundamental in their character, and of great importance to a correct understanding of the subject under consideration. All of these have their value, contain more or less truth in them, and, when combined, contribute materially in bringing into a clear light the peculiar life and genius of the Reformed Church as a whole. By proceeding in the course thus indicated, we will be under the necessity of adopting the analytic instead of the synthetic method; but we hope it will no less certainly lead us to the inmost seat of life in the church, or, at least, put us in a position, in which we may behold the working of that spirit which has given life and vitality to the Reformed Church for the last three hundred years.

Of course, in adverting to the points of difference between the two churches, we can in this place bring forward only such as are of a general or fundamental character. To produce all of them, as they show themselves in the minutiæ of theology and practical life, would require a volume; and we can only refer our readers to works on Comparative Dogmatics, for further information on the subject.*

One of the first points of difference, which manifested itself, leading to a division in the Protestant body, revealed itself in the different relative position of *Reason* in the interpretation of the word of God. Both churches based themselves on the supremacy of the Scriptures, as the source and normal authority of all truth pertaining to salvation. But, starting out on the same general principle, they soon discovered that they arrived at different results in their expositions of the Scripture. The Lutherans maintained that the Reformed made too free a use of reason, bringing down even its deepest mysteries to the comprehension of the mere understanding; whilst the Reformed justified themselves on the ground, that it is indispensable, as an instrumental guide, in arriving at the true sense of the word of God, and insinuated, on the other hand, that their Lutheran brethren allowed too much latitude for mystery, as it was employed in the old church. But it is plain to any one who has read the doctrinal controversies of the Reformation-period, that there is an element of truth on both sides in these mutual recriminations. Zwingli, breathing the free, bracing atmosphere of his Alpine home, could without difficulty set aside all mysteries that came in conflict with the results of his own transparent thinking; Luther, coming up out of great mental tribulation, bearing the marks of the severe discipline through which he had passed, still felt the power of authority, bowed reverently to the truth as it was revealed to him, and joyfully embraced it, whether it squared with the conclusions of his understanding or not. In these circumstances, it were strange if their followers should not imbibe their spirit. It

---

* As it regards the difference between the doctrines of the Lutheran and Reformed Church, *Die Vergleichende Darstellung des Lutherischen und Reformirten Lehrbegriffs von Dr. Schneckenburger*, is admirable in tone and execution. So also Dr. Ebrard's Dogmatik.

is, however, equally plain, when we consider the immense accessions which have been made to theology by the Lutherans, that they cannot be justly charged with the mistake of not having made a sufficiently free use of reason in the interpretation of the Bible. So, too, on the other hand, it would also be unjust to say that the Reformed Church, by its too free use of reason and common sense in theology, is chargeable with all the rationalism that has developed itself side by side with the progress of Protestant theology. Its most learned and powerful assaults against Christianity and the Bible have been made in the bosom of the Lutheran body, where also they have been successfully resisted and broken.

In close connection with the foregoing, the two churches soon experienced an antagonism as it regards the proper use of *Tradition*. Here, again, the contestants charged each other with making too much or too little use of it in their faith and practice. It is asserted that the Reformed rejected all traditions that were not based on the Bible; whilst the Lutherans rejected only those which were contrary to the word of God, retaining, therefore, many which were not opposed to it in spirit. This distinction is claimed as true without any limitation by D'Aubigné, though he speaks of Reformed traditions, which he would strenuously retain. It is no doubt true that tradition, all along, had more weight on the Lutheran than on the Reformed side. Ranke, in his profound History of the Reformation, says, "Lutheran doctrine is only the last form of Latin Christianity, the last link in the chain of Western church-tradition, spiritualized and purified by being brought once more in contact with the Scriptures; whilst the Reformed, as drawn directly from the Scriptures, characteristically breaks with tradition." But it would not be historically true to assert that the Reformed Church, at least in the beginning, broke off suddenly and violently from all connection with the life and tradition of the old church. This would have rendered it a purely radical body, with no historical basis to rest upon, and its dissolution must have been an historical necessity long ago. Equally with the sister-church it retained the decisions of the œcumenical councils; and its theologians, including Calvin himself, made a diligent use of the church-fathers, especially Augustine, in the reconstruction of the theology of the Church. Beza, in his disputation with the Catholic clergy at the convent of Poissy, 1563, after disclaiming all hostility to the episcopacy as such, says, "Our desire is to restore the broken-down walls of Jerusalem, to build up again the spiritual temple. We cherish no other wish but to restore the outward form of the Church again in its original purity and beauty, as it was in the days of the apostles. As it regards the *additions which have been made since then*, whilst every thing superstitious and contrary to the word of God must be abolished, whatever else, which, after a careful examination of the ancient canons and the authority of the church-fathers, is found to be of more real service to the pious and to the edification of the Church, should be retained, and, in God's name, observed." This, as well as the preceding distinction, shows that, as a general thing, the Reformed as compared with the Lutheran brethren are more biblical, are more strict constructionists of the Bible; but it does not explain the diversity of exegetical results, which, after all, was the real source of irritation between the contending parties. It must, therefore, be sought elsewhere, in some deeper source, in the religious consciousness, in the spirit and animus of the two communions. Where tradition confirms the results of Reformed thinking, its service and value have been always freely acknowledged; whilst reason, on the other side, has been called in just as freely where it has offered itself as an auxiliary in the support of any particular doctrine. Still it must be admitted that the historical continuity which exists between Catholic and Protestant Christianity starts with the Lutheran Church, which, on many accounts, is to it a source of strength and not reproach, and that it is carried forward by the Reformed at a more distant point.

Another point of difference has reference to the office of the *Church* in the salvation of the soul. It is said that the Lutheran comes to Christ through the Church, whilst the Reformed comes to Christ directly, and then to the Church. This is regarded by D'Aubigné with much favor, and without any word of caution or exception, as a real difference between the churches.* Like all other formulas, however, which seek to comprehend life and spirit in a brief, witty, striking sentence, it contains only an element of truth, but falls far short of the whole truth. The Lutheran Confession is more churchly than the Reformed, if we except the Church of England, which, with its reverence for antiquity and churchly authority, bears in its lineaments the marks of its Reformed origin. The office of the ministry occupies, relatively, in the congregation a much higher position, and the separation between the clergy and the laity is much greater, in Lutheran than in Reformed churches. An emphasis is also placed on the sacraments and the official acts of the ministry, which does not exist on the Reformed side,—with the single exception referred to, in the Episcopal Church of England and this country. On the other hand, in Reformed churches there is no such difference between the priesthood of the pastor and that of the people, and the Church does not exert such an immediate power and influence upon the individual believer. In strictly Calvinistic congregations more faith is placed in the divine decree than in the efficacy of the sacraments or the communion of saints. As in the sister-communion there is a tendency to rely on the mere outward connection with the Church for salvation, so, on the other side the tendency is ever manifesting itself either to set aside the Church altogether, or to overlook its educational, instrumental agency in bring-

---

* See his article on *Lutheranism and the Reform.*

ing the soul to Christ. In many cases the specific virtue of the sacraments and the means of grace is professedly ignored, and the unbaptized and unconfirmed penitent is directed to go immediately to Christ, and to give himself no further trouble as it respects any established order in the way of salvation. But neither of these tendencies is justified by the spirit or life of pure and genuine Protestantism, under either of its aspects. It is not true that the Reformed, when true to his original stand-point, seeks Christ in a purely direct and independent way, on the outside of the divinely established order. Standing in freer relation to the Church, and regarding more sensibly his responsibility as an individual on account of this enlargement of his freedom, he may feel a stronger impulse to exert himself, in working out the salvation of his soul with fear and trembling; but it is not a purely Reformed doctrine—certainly not a true practice—to seek salvation in any other way, except in accordance with God's own appointment, in the use of divinely appointed means of grace. As it regards the office of the Church, as a divine institute, in which the soul is brought into communion with Christ and prepared for heaven,* there is no essential difference between the two churches; but in their practical life this difference is manifest, and points us back again to some cause in their internal life.

Another characteristic difference between the two churches is found in the different degrees of emphasis which they place on Grace and the Law. With Luther, the grace of the gospel was truly the pearl of great price, which, when once found, became the absorbing object of

---

* It is well known that Calvin makes use of the strongest language in regard to the necessity of the Church. She is our mother. "There is no other entrance into life unless we are conceived by her, born of her, nourished at her breast, and continually preserved under her care till we are divested of this mortal flesh."—*Institutes*, book 4, chap. i. Many in our days would regard this view of the Church as an excrescence in his theological system which it has fully outlived.

his contemplation and joy. It was the balm of Gilead to his soul, and a certain cure for the maladies that afflict the race. With him the law was the stern, austere school-master which had brought him to Christ, but which might now be discarded, except as the remains of sin in his heart might tempt him to wander as a truant from the school of Christ. He made use of language, at times, in regard to the law, which would not now be regarded as scriptural in orthodox society, and he subsequently felt himself bound to soften it down and to modify it considerably. The posture of his own mind, with reference to the divine law, became the prevalent one in the Lutheran Church, so that even in the Form of Concord, it has only a negative use in refer-ence to the regenerated, only as it is needed to reprove them of their sins. It is urged that the Lutheran view is strictly evangelical, that it is more genial and profound than the view which is sometimes taken of it among the Reformed, and that it served powerfully to cut up by the roots all Jewish legalism,—which is no doubt true; but, on the other hand, it must be acknowledged that it was not sufficiently guarded to close the door against Anti-nomian tendencies, which soon made their appearance in the Church, and based themselves on Luther's word.

The Reformed, on the other side, whilst they also laid stress on grace as the weightier matter, regarded the law of God in close connection with it, not as something that had passed away with the regenerate, but as something yet to be fulfilled,—as something positive, binding the heart and conscience of the believer; not indeed as a Jewish burden, but as the divine will freely operating on the human, and imparting to it strength and vitality, as a lamp to his feet and a light to his path. In Luther's Cate-chism, the ten commandments are placed before faith and the Creed; whilst in the Heidelberg, they follow after, and obedience to them is regarded as a part of that gratitude which is due to God for redemption. The result of this emphasis placed on the moral law in the Reformed consciousness is manifest throughout the entire development of the church, impressing upon it—particularly in the hands of Calvin—a characteristically legal element, which has given its sterner piety a strong resemblance to that of the Catholic Church, though proceeding from an entirely different principle. Lutheran piety is quiet, calm, contemplative, mystical, absorbed in the contemplation of the mysteries of the kingdom of God; whilst the Reformed is restless, active, ever on the alert, and impelled forward by the spur of an unseen power. In the practice of piety, it inclines to the somewhat one-sided rule proposed by one of its practical writers:—"We should live as if there were no gospel, and die as if there were no law. In life we should work as if no one but Moses had the command over us." In the congregation all the members must be subject to wholesome rules and regulations, and where order is violated discipline must be exercised,—and, as we know, sometimes in a stern, Jewish sense. The congregation, again, with the pastor, are subject to the Classis or Presbytery, and this, again, to the Synod. As the individual and the Church must conform themselves to the divine law, so also must the State in Reformed countries; and, as history teaches us, so earnestly is this insisted on that disobedience to the law of God, on the part of civil rulers, is disloyalty, and must be renounced by a voluntary act, or involuntarily, by revolution or a change of government.

This legal element in the Reformed faith, if we may call it so, is no doubt one of the chief blessings involved in the Reformed faith; though, at times, when the positive Christianity underlying it has evaporated, it runs out into mechanical formalism or dry legalism, the sin which it rebukes in the Catholic Church. It tends to purify the Church, and, with its evangelic spirit, the moral atmosphere of society. In the greater freedom and latitude, which prevail in the Reformed Church, as compared with the Catholic and Lutheran, it is an indispensable curb to the

312

arbitrariness of opinion and the general licentiousness of manners, which must otherwise prevail; and as it is, more-over, one that is self-imposed, growing out of a strictly Christian consciousness, it stands in vital connection with the freedom of the gospel, its necessary condition or com-plement. No one, perhaps, better understood the danger to which the Reformed Church was exposed on account of its greater independence of the Christianity of the pre-vious ages than Calvin himself, and no one addressed him-self with such untiring zeal to the maintenance of law and order, in Church and State, against the infidel and radical tendencies of the times. A lawyer by profession, and of a Romanic nation by birth, he was just the instrument selected by Providence to give a decided character in this respect to the Reformed Church, and indeed, we may say, to the entire Protestant movement. As a Protestant law-giver he has exerted a wider and more beneficent influ-ence on history, than he has by the theological tenets called by his name. Apart from the legal element, which he impressed on the Reformed Church, it must have become helplessly radical in its tendencies, and, sooner or later, have fallen into a hopeless, discordant, chaotic mass. As it is, with its freer spirit, bounded at every point by the presence of law, it has, when fully organized, developed a talent for organization and an efficiency for action, which have left their impression wherever its influ-ence has been felt, whether in Church or State, whether in its own renovation and purification, or in the outward spread of the gospel in Christian and heathen lands.

The question might here be asked, whether its pre-vailingly practical tendency in morals and theology has resulted from its conception of the law in relation to grace, or *vice versa*. Most probably neither proposition by itself is entirely true. The legal has stimulated the practical element, whilst the practical has confirmed the legal, always more or less in harmony with the evan-gelical. So, too, it might be asked, whether other distin-

z

guishing characteristics of the Reformed faith—such as the sovereignty of God, the kingship of Christ, the freedom and equality of believers in the Church—are not derived from this original conception of the value and importance of the divine law. Here again, we say, we have no right to view them in such a connection, nor, indeed, to derive the development of the Church from any such general idea or thought. All those ideas, which are more Reformed than any thing else, are congenial, mutually support each other, and are no doubt simply co-ordinate or symmetrical parts of one general whole,—a spirit or animus out of which they naturally grew, and from which they received their form and place in one general conception of the kingdom of God. Thus it was not something accidental that the Reformed came to lay greater stress on the Scriptures as the word of God, and appropriated to themselves this, the formal principle of the Reformation, rather than the material one, justification by faith alone. The same remark may be made with regard to the sanctity of the Christian Sabbath, and to the political tendencies of the Reformed churches, which insist on their own autonomy and independence of the State, whilst at the same time, they just as strenuously seek to have the State penetrated with the leaven of the gospel.

In more recent times, the peculiar differences between the two Churches has been apprehended more profoundly, particularly in connection with the Union movement in Germany, in which the points of difference have been studied, not in the way of controversy, but with the view of finding the original principle of unity. Among the writers who have written with this object in view, we observe that the contributions of Dr. Schaff have been well received, and their value acknowledged.* He says

---

* Consisting of a series of articles, published in Berlin before he came to this country, which Dr. Schneckenburger regards as classic literature in reference to the subject here considered, but which he erroneously attributes to Dr. Dorner.

the two polar points, around which the common fundamental principle of the two evangelical churches revolves,
are the finite and the Infinite, God and man, the Creator
and creature: on the material side, divine grace and the
human will; on the formal side, the divine truth and the
human reason. The original harmony existing between
these antithetic ideas has been disturbed by sin, and the
contradiction cannot be removed by any human power;
but it is reconcilable by faith in the God-man. In the
Reformed Church the antithesis between the above-mentioned factors is more sharply defined; whilst in the Lutheran the separation is not so strenuously insisted on, and
they are allowed to flow more into each other. The Lutheran, in his view of God as a loving Father, brings the
divine love and mercy more prominently into view;
whilst the Reformed, in consistency with his conception
of God, looks upon Him more as his Sovereign, his
righteous and holy Lawgiver. According to the Lutheran stand-point, God created the world that it might
be the depository of His love; according to the Reformed,
it proceeded from His sovereign will, and was intended to
unfold His attributes and to show forth His praise: hence,
with the Reformed, the glory of God is the end of all
things,—of creation as a whole, as well as of human volition. According to the one view, the world is filled with
the presence of God, and calls for study and pious contemplation; according to the other, it is too abstractly
severed from God, and, involved as it is in sin, it appears
more hostile in its character, and becomes more an object
of horror to the pious consciousness. The believer
endures all this submissively, and, in the relation of a
servant, serves his Lord and Master, in strict obedience,
without regard to the promise of reward. The differences
here stated are much more far-reaching, and are traced
back to a more general ground; but, as in the cases
already mentioned, they are simply stated in their connection, and we do not suppose that their author intended

to state fully the reason or cause why they assumed the particular form in which we now find them.

The differences which have been thus far specified have more of the character of tendencies, which are so intimately related to each other, as to show a common origin in the general life of the Church. They are of much value, as they tend to exhibit in a greater or less degree its particular bias or animus. We now proceed to consider some of the points of difference based on the particular spheres of life, in reference to which the churches have been most active.

Thus it is said that, whilst Lutheranism seeks to promote the salvation of the intellectual nature of man, Calvinism has more to do with the active powers of man, with his will, with the government and control of men's actions. No one can have failed to observe an ideal and a real tendency in Protestantism: the one prevailingly theoretical, manifesting itself particularly in Lutheran Germany; the other intensely practical, manifesting itself in England, America, and other strictly Reformed countries, sustaining toward each other a polar relation, and serving as complements to each other in completing the one Christian idea. In close connection with this stands the view of Dr. Lange, according to which the peculiarities of the two churches are derived from the fact that the "Lutheran is the Church of theologians, the Reformed that of the believing congregation." All this is in harmony with what has been said of the prevailing tendencies of the churches; but it would be manifestly unjust, if it were carried so far as to withhold from the Reformed great credit for the theological works which it has produced. Calvin, even to this day, is hardly excelled as an objective, systematic theologian. The practical tendency of the church, however, has no doubt served as a restraint on her theologians, binding them down at times too much to the practical wants of the congregation, and at other times placing

316

too much of a curb on the free use of the speculative reason.

Again, the diversity as well as the spirit of the two churches has been sought in their origin and rise, in the first form of antagonism which they manifested toward the Church of Rome and the Christianity of the sixteenth century. With Luther, the Reformation was an accomplished fact in his own experience, when, after many struggles, he obtained peace of mind by saving faith in Christ. The principal obstacles, which he encountered in arriving at this experience, were the *legal Jewish elements,* which pervaded the Christianity of his times; and their removal from the Church and the pathway of pious, inquiring souls like himself became the object of his animadversions and the labors of his life. Zwingli, on the other hand, who had attained to peace of mind in the same manner as Luther, by faith, though, perhaps, not after such a sorrowful experience, directed his assaults, for the most part, against the *pagan elements* in the old church, against the existing church-organization, the forms of worship, and the prevailing state of morals in the Church and the world. These, with him, were as serious obstacles to the progress of the gospel as the legalism, which Luther felt himself called of God to resist. Here we observe a difference in the *direction,* which the life of the churches assumed at the start, but no real antagonism. It may be difficult for us to account for it in the religious consciousness in which it took its rise, and which gave it vigor; but it was no doubt facilitated by the individual temperaments of the first Reformers, by their educational training, and the political institutions of their respective countries. Luther rejoiced with joy unspeakable in the discovery of the doctrine of justification by faith, of salvation by grace without works; he was willing that the Church should rest upon it,—as if this were sufficient of itself to hold up a falling church; and he expected, as a matter of course, that its reception into the consciousness of believers would complete the work of reformation and renovation. He lived, moreover, in a despotic country, in which the people took no part in the control of the Church or the State, and, of course, with no talent for reconstruction or reorganization, they were not prepared to commence the work of building up outwardly what had been pulled down. Besides, the mind of Luther was so much occupied in establishing the doctrines of the gospel, that he had little time to attend to the outward organization of the Church. Zwingli, on the other hand, familiar with the humanistic culture of the times, which was in a great measure the revival of ancient classic heathenism, was the citizen of a free state, which centuries before had thrown off the despotic yoke and conferred upon the people their political rights. Under these circumstances, it became at once a plain, simple duty to the minds of the Swiss Reformers to carry out the reformation in the outward, objective church, and the more especially so, as it seemed to them that this necessity was not sufficiently felt in the sister-Church, where, with much Christian conservatism, there was also so much halting and hesitation in regard to outward changes. This more intense reformatory movement was inaugurated by Zwingli and his coadjutors, but it remained to be carried out not by a German, but by the French Reformer, John Calvin. It was no doubt providential that Zwingli was called off from the field early, in order that the work of reconstruction might fall into the hands of another master-mind, who was constitutionally better qualified to bring it to completion. A rigid discipline was introduced into the congregations; a regular form of church-government, republican in form, was established, and the old form of worship simplified, and cleansed of what were regarded as heathenish elements, oftentimes with iconoclastic zeal: thus it was supposed that the people would best grow in grace and knowledge with the greater freedom accorded to them, bounded on all sides by the presence of law and authority. This, in. fact, became the specific work of the Reformed Church as a whole; and it is remarkable that it gave no offence, but rather excited the admiration of the sister-church, showing that the peculiar direction of the spirit of reform involved no antagonism between them, but manifested rather a oneness in their religious life.

The two churches, thus directing their energies to the removal of the resident elements of paganism and Judaism still extant in the Church, initiated a truly reformatory movement. The enemies, which they had to encounter, were precisely those which, from the beginning, have done most to resist the free progress of Christianity in the world. Paganism is simply human nature in its highest and most cultivated form, always proud and hostile to grace, whilst Judaism, in a state of opposition to Christianity, is another phase of our common prostrate nature, with something more demoniacal in its spirit, akin to the pride and craft of an archangel fallen. These include, we may say, all the elements of opposition to the kingdom of God on earth,—the world, the flesh, and the devil. In the apostolic period the *Jew* and the *Greek* arrayed themselves in fierce opposition to the infant Church, and sought to strangle it in its cradle. In subsequent times, they directed their assaults more craftily, and with more or less success insinuated themselves into the faith and practice of believers; and the Church has been continuously called to struggle with them in mortal conflict. At the period of the Reformation no one would deny that they were actively present in the Church. The efforts to effect a reformation, which convulsed the Catholic Church previous to the rise of the Protestant movement, show beyond any doubt, how extensively foreign elements had entered the Church, and called for a reformation. A late Catholic writer freely admits this necessity, and goes so far as to acknowledge that there was a real reformation accomplished, though he confines it under its normal form to his own church. The Reformers, therefore, directed their weapons of assault upon the right points of attack in the stronghold of the enemy. They accom-

319

plished a herculean work for the Church of Christ, for which we this day are thankful and rejoice.

Assuming that what has now been said is, in the main, historically true, and of the facts, we presume, there can be no doubt, let us now consider, how the primitive points of attack conduced to give character, and to call forth the animus of the two grand divisions of Protestantism. Judaism in antagonism with Christianity, which is its fulfilment, the sum and substance of its rites and ceremonies, is reduced to a system of cold, lifeless forms and morals, in which God is an abstraction, removed far away from the homes and affections of men. It is a system of Deism, no better than Mohammedanism, and certainly not possessed of as much power and energy. Though not formally adopted by the Church in any age, its animus is ever lighting upon it as a blasting mildew. In the nature of the case, Luther must attack it with all the energy of his earnest soul, and conceive of God in an altogether different manner; not, as if he existed in a remote sphere of isolation from the world, but as the God-man dwelling in it, and filling the believer with His presence, causing all things to express the joyous emotions of his heart. Thus the *immanence* of the divine nature in the human became a distinguishing characteristic of Lutheran theology and piety.

With the Reformed, on the other hand, paganism in the Church being the point of attack, they met and encountered a different conception of God in His relation to the world: not in a deistic sense abstractly sundered from the creature, but one mixed up and confounded with the world in a polytheistic and pantheistic sense. Whilst they rejoiced also in the advent of Christ into the world and His abiding presence in the Church, they felt themselves impelled to insist on the *transcendence* of God, to separate and distinguish the creature from the Creator as far as possible; and both history and experience teach that they drew the line of demarcation to the highest degree of tension of which it was susceptible.*

Thus the two churches, starting from the same subjective religious consciousness, with one Faith, one Lord, and one Baptism, but directing their attention to different strongholds in the kingdom of Satan, amidst the noise and confusion of the conflict, owing to the infirmity of human nature and their own clashing nationalities, lost sight more and more of the original unity; the particular spirit of each branch was elicited and confirmed, directing and controlling it in its activities of willing and thinking, and giving to each its particular character and form.

The Immanence and the Transcendence of God came forward at an early day, in antagonistic relation to each other, in the disputes concerning the Lord's Supper. In the Lutheran doctrine the human and the divine elements in that sacrament are so closely related to each other as to be always offensive to Reformed ears; whilst in the view of the Reformed they are too much separated to satisfy the Lutheran feeling of the presence of Christ in the Church. From this it would appear that the two views, according to Dr. Ebrard, are complements to each other, and sustain to each other a polar relation. The Reformed, devoted to their own tactics and sharply distinguishing the divine from the human at every point, must necessarily be compelled to give an emphasis to every thing purely divine, on the one hand, and, on the other, to seek to lower the human, and, if not always putting it in the right place, at least, to prevent it from encroaching upon the functions of

---

* Dr. Schenkel says that there is no fundamental difference between the two churches, and that the only difference is of a theological or scientific character. The principle of this difference he finds in the Immanence and Transcendence of God as held by the two churches; and the principle of the Reformed Church, in the determining transcendence of the divine nature in relation to the human. To this Dr. Lücke objects, on the ground that it is too abstract and too far removed from the religious life of the Church; that it is rather dependent on the consciousness of the Church. Is it not rather the reflection of the Reformed Christian consciousness upon the sphere of thought?

the divine. Thus the Sacred Scriptures were regarded as the infallible word of God, all so purely inspired that no room was left for any difference in the degree of inspiration; the canon was adopted in its integrity, without demurring as to any single book, whilst the Apocrypha was no longer permitted to be bound up in the same volume with the in-spired books. The stress, which the Reformed have placed on the Scripture as the word of God, sometimes to the pre-judice of church-authority and of good and wholesome church-traditions, was doubtless promoted by other causes; but it is so fully in harmony with their conception of God, that it must, to a great extent, have been called forth by it; —at least, we cannot conceive of the two things as existing apart from each other.

The Transcendence of God gives a validity and authority to the word, the law and the will of God, which no other system of thinking can impart; and it is not, therefore, something accidental that the doctrine of predestination, even in its most rigorous form, came to play so important a part in Reformed theology. Though no doubt intended as a practical cure to the Pelagianizing tendencies of the times, —which had again made their appearance in the Church, though repressed by St. Augustine a thousand years be-fore,—as well as to promote individual piety, it was alto-gether in harmony with the Reformed mode of thinking, and the Reformed sense of the agency of God in the salva-tion of the soul. There was certainly ground for the old distinction, that the Reformed in his theology commences with God, whilst the Lutheran starts with himself,—that is, with his own subjective experience; but it is manifestly untrue, as it has been said, that the former comes to Christ through God, whilst the latter comes to God through Christ: Christ Himself says, "No man cometh to the Father, but by me." Dr. Schweizer, with much ability and truly Calvin-istic logic, maintains that the doctrine of absolute predesti-nation is the ground-principle of the Reformed theology, and the source of all its peculiarities,—to which, as German Reformed, we demur, because it was not universally received, certainly not in some of the Reformed churches, our own among the rest, and yet they remained distinctively Reformed.

Dr. Lücke, himself an old Lutheran, but a decided friend of the "Evangelical" or United Church in Germany, sees in the manner in which the two churches originally separated, as just stated, not only the principle of their difference, but also of their unity, and the ground of their reunion. He makes use of the following language, which, breathing so much of a truly Christian and catholic spirit, we cannot refrain from quoting on the present occasion. "In the Reformation-period, not only were the characters of the apostles reproduced according to their peculiar types, but the apostolic doctrine was also reproduced in its two different evolutions. The first is the Pauline, lying at the foundation, which is analogous to the Lutheran. In the former, as in the latter, the chief element is the essentially anti-Jewish doctrinal view of salvation by grace in Christ, and of justification by faith in the atoning death of Jesus Christ. From this the doctrinal system of the apostles was derived; and Luther was right in considering it as the inmost kernel of the sacred canon, upon which the Reformation in Germany, as well as elsewhere, rested. The second evolution of the apostolic doctrine I find in the catholic epistles, including that addressed to the Hebrews. Here the doctrines of Christ, of His person, of His office and work, of predestination, and of the absolute coming of the kingdom of grace, are more prominent. This second evolution already commences, in the way of transition, in the epistles of Paul. But it is to be remarked that the doctrine of Christ's person comes forward into a prominent light, for the first time, in the later epistles of the apostles; whilst the doctrine of predestination, as the boldest problem of the apostolic gnosis, forms only a kind of an epilogue to the Epistle to the Romans. Whilst Luther prevailingly relies on the Epistle to the Galatians and the first eight chapters of the

Epistle to the Romans, Calvin takes up the problem of predestination as contained in the Epistle to the Romans, in
connection with the catholic and the remaining Epistles of
Paul, and attempts, what Luther did not, systematically to
reconstruct as a whole the apostolic doctrine.

"As it regards the New Testament doctrine, there can
be no doubt that the problem, which it is necessary for us
to solve is, to distinguish properly the different types of
apostolic doctrine, to comprehend each in its peculiar character, then to embrace them in one and the same apostolic
doctrine, as the mutual completion of each other; and so to
place them, in their unity and diversity, into one organic
whole, that it may be seen how the different doctrines proceed from the same general ground-principle, and how,
without any contradiction, they are all reconciled in their
source. Is not this the problem the Biblical theology of
the present day is called to solve?"*

From what has now been said, we are enabled to form
some idea of the general spirit that pervades the Reformed
Church as a whole. The distinctions which have been
made, and others that might be brought forward, tend to
show how the Protestant life, after starting from a common
Protestant consciousness, gradually separated and formed
for itself two distinct channels of activity, pervaded by a
dominant spirit, which kept each within its own sphere
and gave it a distinct character and form. The one division is distinguished for its active, free, more Protestant
and reformed tendency, which, without the presence of the
other and the authority which it established for itself, must
have soon become hopelessly radical; the other, conservative and churchly, and intensely evangelical, is remarkable
for maintaining its connection with the past, amidst all the
storms and convulsions in which it took its rise, but which,
without the energetic watchword of the other wing of the

---

* Die Deutsche Zeitschrift for the year 1853, from the third to the seventh
numbers inclusive.

Protestant movement, must have been constantly in danger of turning backward toward Egypt. In the nature of the case, the Reformed side of the Reformation, as the progressive, freer movement, must exhibit a greater diversity within itself, and manifest a freer application of the Protestant principle. Accordingly, we find various Reformed churches, independent in their origin, distinguished from each other by some peculiarity of life or character, and pervaded by a spirit of their own. In order, therefore, to arrive at a definite conception of the genius or spirit of the German Reformed Church, or the Church of the Heidelberg Catechism, it is necessary that we should view it in connection with other Reformed churches, with which it agrees in its general life and tendency, but from which it is, again, distinguished by various important peculiarities.

In the first place, we observe that the German Reformed Church, in connection with German Christianity generally, is more historical, and breaks less violently with the Church of previous ages. As a distinct denomination, it took its rise in Germany, in a purely independent way, in strong sympathy, no doubt, with the Reformed churches of other lands, but just as much so with Lutheranism. At first, under Melanchthon, it appeared as if it was likely to carry all Germany in the direction of the Reformed stand-point; but a violent reaction ensued, which resulted in the establishment of the distinctively Lutheran principle, whilst the Reformed found a home and resting-place only in the Palatinate, in Hesse, in Prussia, and a few other countries, from which it could not be extirpated either by argument or more violent measures. In maintaining its ground, it did not for a moment suppose it was an intruder on German soil; nor was that its intention or purpose, though it freely professed a Christian sympathy for the churches of Christ in other lands. Frederick III., the Elector of the Palatinate, who, next to Melanchthon, was the founder of the church in Germany, could not believe that he was departing at all from the spirit of the Reformation or of German

Protestantism; rather, he was persuaded that he was entirely in harmony with it, and that, as prince, he was called
of God to bring, in this way, the great work to its proper
consummation. At every point he was assiduous in carrying out the Reformation in the spirit of Melanchthon, who
at that time stood at the head of the German Church and
gave the word for the times. He freely adopted the Augsburg Confession as explained by its author, and enforced
the same respect for it among his theologians and people.
The Reformed churches in other parts of Germany embraced the Reformation in the spirit of the Palatinate, and
followed in the footsteps of the pious Elector in his honest
adhesion to the Augsburg Confession. This, as an historical fact, is not without significance to our own church;
for, whilst other Reformed churches diverged more and
more from the Lutheran and the spirit of the first Protestant Confession, the German branch maintained its just
claim to this first legacy of the evangelical faith. Even
down to the treaty of Westphalia, at which the Reformed
churches, as such, were formally guarantied their equal
rights and privileges in the empire with the Lutheran, they
are still called the churches "addicted" to the Augsburg
Confession. So far as they were concerned, there was no
need of another German Confession, as there was for the
Helvetic, Gallic, Belgic, or Anglican Confessions: they
were already supplied with one in the Augustana, as interpreted in the Melanchthonian sense. This had proclaimed
the common consciousness of Protestantism in the first
bloom of its faith, through Melanchthon, the most catholic
of all the Reformers; it disclaimed all violent separation
from the past, professed that its " design was to show that
the evangelical estates remained throughout on the foundation of the old church," and that they called simply for its
reformation and restoration. Into this consciousness the
Reformed fully entered, and, without giving the same em-
phasis to the Confession as the Lutherans, who appropriated
to themselves what should have been the common legacy

326

of the Protestant world, they have been addicted to it to the present day. In this respect, the Reformation inaugurated in the Palatinate had a very different animus from that which Carlstadt attempted to initiate in Germany years before, but in which he so signally failed, and resembles more the Reformed movement in England.

In close connection with the peculiarity of our branch of the Reformed family just noticed, stands its relation to the strictly Calvinistic doctrines of predestination and election, as held by the French, Dutch, Scotch, and, to some extent, the Swiss Reformed Churches. Predestination was no new doctrine in the Church at the time of the Reformation; it had been maintained by St. Augustine long before, who gave it as a legacy to the Catholic Church, and it was embraced by Luther, Zwingli, and other Reformers as an established doctrine; but in the hands of Calvin, or at least of his disciples, it was not only carried to the highest degree of tension, including the "horrible degree" of the predestination of the wicked to the lower regions, but it became also the germinant *principle* of Calvinistic theology, and came to occupy a relation to the life of the Church and the believer, altogether disproportionate to its value and importance in the creed of Christianity. Dr. Schweizer, therefore, is not entirely without truth on his side, when he makes it the material principle of the Reformed theology. But it is to be remarked that, whilst it always met with more or less sympathy in the Reformed churches, always gained the victory in its contests, as at the Synod of Dort, and seemed to be exercising a supremacy as a cardinal doctrine in the Reformed Church, yet its claims were never universally accredited; its sharp points were rounded off, or so modified as to give less offence to the religious consciousness of the Church. In the Reformed Church of Germany, it never as such received any symbolical authority, and it was significantly left out of the Heidelberg Catechism and handed over to the schools and scientific theology. At the same time, it

327

was never rejected by the German Church, nor regarded with any thing like hostility; on the contrary, after the Synod of Dort attempted to give it general authority in the Reformed churches, it was regarded with favor in Germany; but here it was so qualified and modified as to deprive it in a great measure of its objectionable features; the fundamental truths which underlie it were honored and defended, whilst the doctrine itself was not regarded as of such cardinal importance as elsewhere, and it was held in subordination to other doctrines of the gospel, that had a more vital influence on the spread and increase of the evangelical faith.

This general posture of the Church, with reference to the doctrine of the divine decrees, serves to explain how it retained its churchly character and its reverence for the Creed, its faith in the Sacraments, and other churchly elements. The remark is no doubt true, that there are two elements in Calvin's theology, which it is difficult to reconcile so as to place them in their proper relation to each other,—his doctrine of the decrees, and his high views of the Church and the sacraments. Though both were upheld by him with equal fidelity, the former, among some of his followers, soon claimed altogether too much attention in theological discussion; whilst the latter, the questions connected with the sacraments, which were the life of the Protestant Church in the beginning, no longer gave character and tone to theology. It was a logical and necessary result of the undue stress placed on the doctrine of predestination, especially when carried out rigorously to all its supposed consequences. Luther was assured of his personal interest in Jesus Christ by means of the sacraments, and his own subjective faith as the only necessary condition of justification before God; but to the rigid Calvinist something more seemed to be necessary to complete his assurance, and this he thought he found in the eternal decree of God. Resting on this as something fixed and infallible, and constantly meditating on it as such, he

328

could not only be certain, but most certain, of his salvation, and soon, without perceiving it, he would no longer feel the necessity of an historical Church, which, by its channels and means of grace, confers on its members the gifts of salvation, keeps them in actual communion with Christ, and is ever awakening within them a hope that need not be ashamed. With Calvin this divorce of the one sphere of truth from the other never took place. He lived too near the Reformation-period, and felt himself too much drawn toward an historical Church and the sacramental views of German Reformers, to admit of such a separation in his own mind. It was after his time, when his theology fell into other hands, that Calvinism veered off farther and farther from the original doctrinal ground of the Reformed Church. This is most sensibly felt at the present day in our own country, where the Reformed Church appears so much in its diversity, that it is difficult any longer to see the point of original unity. In the Congregationalist, the Baptist, and the Methodist denominations, which constitute the extreme left wing of the Reformed Church, what has been said is not only admitted, but justified, on the ground that they are a reformation of the Reformation, and that the circumstances of the Protestant Church, when they took their rise, were such as to call for a new reformation. This justification, however, cannot be maintained on historical grounds, and, in the nature of the case, there could be no reformation of Protestantism, in the true sense of the term, except by a general return to its original doctrinal basis and life. Moreover, these denominations have originated no new theological principle, and bear on their exterior the features of their Reformed origin. The stress which they lay on discipline in the house of God, on the moral law in its application to the diversified relations of life, and especially to politics, show plainly their Calvinistic origin; whilst it is clear that these peculiarities no longer retain the same place as Calvin held them in connection with high sacramental views. The Puritans retain Calvin's

2 A

theology, but they have given up his idea of the Church; the Methodist brethren repudiate his theology, but enforce his rigor in the exercise of discipline.

As it regards the other Reformed churches, which are fully penetrated with the Calvinistic theology, consisting of the Reformed churches of Holland, of France, of Scotland, and, to some extent, that of Switzerland, the evidences of this departure from the original church-life of the Reformation show themselves in their theologies, as well as in the life of their congregations. No one can fail to observe the difference in the atmosphere, as he passes from the school of Jonathan Edwards to the study of the modern evangelical theology of Germany. In the one case the divine sovereignty in relation to human freedom is the salient point; in the other, the person of Christ in union with believers.

It was only a few years ago* that a most conservative divine, in the most conservative Calvinistic body in this country, freely admitted that the present Reformed view of the Lord's Supper differed from that of Calvin in a most important particular; that it did not admit that the worthy communicant partook of the Saviour's *humanity* as well as his divinity, and that, though this was Calvin's view, it was simply an excrescence on the original doctrine, which was thrown off in the regular development of the Church. We are here merely recording historical facts; and it is with no desire to undervalue the importance or mission of the Calvinistic Churches, when we say that they are not so near the fountain of the Reformation as they once were.† Rigid Calvinism had an important work

---

* Dr. Hodge *versus* Dr. Nevin. See Mercersburg Review, September number, 1850.

† Dr. Heppe has an interesting article on the "Character of the German Reformed Church in its relation to Lutheranism and Calvinism," in the October number of the "*Studien und Kritiken*" for 1850, and translated for the April number of the Mercersburg Review, 1853, by Rev. Prof. Porter. Whilst the learned author shows that the German Reformed Church is to be

to perform in its day, but this, it is believed, has passed away. According to Dr. Ebrard, it was on the wane already in the last century.* May we not hope that, as this tension is removed from the Calvinistic faith, there will be a return once more to the theology of the creed and more churchly principles?

As the German Reformed Church did not commit itself so fully to Calvinistic theology, it was the more easily enabled to retain its original historical and churchly position. It placed itself squarely on the Creed, and no particular interest or tenet diverted its attention from that solid foundation; that was the germinant point from which its theology was produced; the doctrines of the Creed claimed attention as the most vital parts of Christianity, and all others were held in subordination to them. Such a theology, of course, resting on the facts of Christianity, must be free and churchly, not bound by any particular tenet made predominant for the time. What was taught to the catechumens and the congregations for practical purposes was reproduced and taught in a more scientific form in the university for the benefit of candidates for the ministry. Much, indeed, of the theology of the Church is found in lectures and commentaries on the Heidelberg Catechism, a large portion of which is taken up in expositions of the Creed. In this Ursinus took the lead. The Church-year is closely connected with a heartfelt faith in the Apostles' Creed, and seems to be indispensable in order to a full and proper profession of it on the part of the con-

---

distinguished from Calvinism as such, and that it proceeded from the Calvino-Melanchthonian spirit in Germany, he asserts that it was simply the carrying out of the original, Protestant, evangelical consciousness of the Reformation, from which distinctive Lutheranism was a secession. This might be used, in the spirit of the old polemics, as an offset to the position, which has been sometimes assumed, that the Christianity of all previous ages found its full embodiment in the Form of Concord.

* See a translation, from Ebrard's Dogmatik, of the History of Reformed Dogmatics, by Rev. Dr. Wolff, in the Mercersburg Review, in the April number, 1857, and in the January number, 1858.

gregation. The Creed and the sacraments stand in close connection with each other in the Catechism, the one following the other, so that the Creed needs the sacraments as its necessary counterpart; for faith is receptive, and looks particularly to the sacraments as the means by which the blessings of salvation and eternal life are secured and sealed to believers. The Church of the Palatinate, though intimately allied to the Church of Switzerland, never for a moment was addicted to what were regarded as low Zwinglian views of the Lord's Supper. It took its rise after the Reformed Church had fully surmounted the Zwinglian platform, and adhered strenuously to the view held in common by Calvin and Melanchthon. It maintained also that it did not differ essentially from the Lutheran doctrine. The only difference had reference to the manner of the Saviour's presence, and the manner of His reception by the communicant. When the Elector Frederick was charged with heresy on this subject, he at once replied, that our union with Christ in the Holy Supper was not only with His divinity, but with the God-man, *ganz und gar*,—that is, with His entire life, human and divine. Proper views of the sacraments, again, as channels or means by which grace is communicated to believers, have their foundation in an outward objective Church, filled with the abiding presence of Christ, the God-man. When, therefore, we claim for the German Reformed Church a more churchly character than what inheres in the strictly Calvinistic Churches, we believe that we are fully sustained by history; and the language of a celebrated divine in our own communion is by no means too strong when he says, that the "proper historical relations of the Catechism, as they are presented to us in the *German Church, include the altar, the organ, and the gown; Church-lessons, and a Church-year, with its regular cycle of religious festivals; repetitions of the Lord's Prayer, and Creed; liturgical services; and an entire order of worship, in short, which to the nostrils of modern puri-*

tanism, it is to be feared, would carry no small stench of popery itself throughout."*

With the historical and churchly elements pervading our church, its catholicity has always been one of its prominent features. In this respect, as well as in those just mentioned, it is much more in sympathy with the Church of England, with which the ecclesiastical as well as the political relations of Protestant Germany have always been of the most friendly character. This sympathy, however, has never been allowed a full and free expression, owing, perhaps, to the insular and exclusive character of the English Church. As it regards doctrine, worship, and religious customs, there is nothing in the history of our own church, which should prevent it from continuing to cherish the sympathy, which existed at the period of the Reformation between the two churches. The most important point of difference has reference to the form of church-government, our own church placing less stress on it, right or wrong, than her Anglican sister. The late matrimonial union, which took place between a Reformed prince of Germany and an Episcopal princess of England, would, we presume, experience no let or hindrance, but be rather materially strengthened by their respective church-relations.

Thus, with an irenical reference to Lutheranism, already referred to, and to Calvinism, through Calvin himself, and to Anglicanism, the Church of the Heidelberg Catechism is bounded on all sides by powerful Protestant Churches and interests. With its Catholic basis in the Catechism and Creed, and its German, Melanchthonian tendency and spirit, it is in a condition to derive benefit from all its Protestant neighbors, whilst it exerts a beneficial influence on all of them in return. In Germany, it is in friendly union with the Lutheran Church, and, together with that body, is producing a new phase of Evangelical theology,

---

* The History and Genius of the Heidelberg Catechism, by J. W. Nevin, D.D.

which is destined to be felt as a leaven throughout all Protestant Churches, if not also in the Latin and Greek Churches. Its theoretical errors and shortcomings will, no doubt, be corrected in practical England and America, a respectable beginning, as it regards the church-question, having been made already in our own communion, in this country.

In regard to the peculiar work or mission of the German Reformed Church, the space allotted us will not permit us here to enlarge. From what has been said, it must be evident that, whilst it has a mission, in common with the Church universal, with Protestantism and the Reformed Church as a whole, it has also a work to perform as a distinct denomination. Having arisen from an historical necessity in the progress of the Reformation, it has a right to exist with its peculiar spirit until all true Christians shall see eye to eye, and the present divisions of Zion shall cease, in the consciousness of one universal, Christian Church. We shall endeavour to comprehend, briefly, our part of the work of bringing about this consummation, in a number of distinct points.

As the German branch of the Reformed Church occupies a *central* position in the Protestant body, with its sympathies extending in every direction, it is, no doubt, intended by Providence to serve, in some degree, as a *mediator* between the different conflicting interests. It is qualified for this by the irenical, Melanchthonian spirit which pervades it, as well as by its not having committed itself to any of the irritating tenets or peculiarities that have already caused so many rents in the Protestant Church. It can accomplish this best, however, not by sacrificing any of its principles, for the sake of peace and unity, but by remaining true to its historical ground and its catholic relation to the Apostles' Creed.

Inasmuch as unity among Christians can be promoted only as they see and feel, that they are one in Christ and His Church, which is His body, it is the duty of our Church

334

to hold up an outward, historical Church, possessed of supernatural powers, as our only refuge from the endless divisions to which Protestantism as a body is exposed. The original principle of unity having been in a great measure lost sight of in Protestant denominations, it must be sought for in the original life and Christian conscious-ness of the Reformation-period, and in the pure word of God. Our own communion, having diverged less from the common consciousness and original spirit of Protestantism, can with the greater consistency sound the note of alarm in regard to the dangers that beset us, urging our brethren everywhere to unite with us, in resisting all schismatical tendencies, and to insist on inward unity as a necessary preparation for that which is outward.

Whilst greater unity among Protestants is the first thing to be thought of, as the object of our immediate labors and prayers, it is not of itself the limit of the Saviour's prayer that His people may all be one; it is necessary, in all efforts to promote true Christian unity, to have some regard, at least, to the old Greek and Roman Churches, which also possess Christian elements, that are needed in order to realize the idea of one Holy, Apostolic, Catholic Church. The broad, catholic, Melanchthonian spirit which still pre-dominates in our church, and lives in the Catechism, will not allow us to leave them altogether out of consideration in our work and labor of love.

Inasmuch as our church retains many historical, churchly, and catholic elements, it should give them a special em-phasis at the present day, when radical and unchurchly tendencies are everywhere at work, threatening disintegra-tion in the Church and a dissolution of the bonds which hold civil society together. The principle of individual freedom has taken so wide a range, that it cannot be con-sidered safe and wholesome, except as the principle of authority and law is brought in to keep it within the free-dom of the gospel.

Whilst the Reformed Church, in the exercise of its large

335

degree of freedom, has guarded itself against lawlessness and radical tendencies, by placing so much greater stress on the moral law, yet experience goes to show that there is always danger of a one-sided application of the law, by which Christianity is reduced to a system of good morals, and the Church to an association for the promotion of good works and decent external conduct. It is, therefore, the mission, particularly, of the German Church, including our own, in which the tendency to an empty, moral formalism has never been carried so far, to mediate and to hold up the more vital elements of Christianity as contained in the Creed; that it consists not so much in good works or ortho-dox doctrines, as in a life of faith in God, of communion and fellowship with the God-man, our Saviour, through the Holy Ghost. Whilst good works are essential, they are of value only as they stand in connection with the principle of grace; and, whilst the sense of duty cannot be too keen and active, it ought not to interfere with the conscious enjoyment of our union with Christ through the Church, as a source of constant joy, admiration, and praise.

Protestantism having given free exercise to the intellec-tual nature of man, and thus produced much good fruit for the cause of humanity, experience has shown that serious evils have also resulted from this emancipation of the human intellect; that reason has been used as freely against the gospel as in its favor; and that along with the progress of the Protestant Reformation, the spirit of un-belief, skepticism, and infidelity has had free course, often justifying itself by the example of the first Reformers. As this evil has shown itself in fearful proportions in our days, it becomes the duty of all Protestant Churches, and espe-cially the more conservative, like our own, to give em-phasis to the mysteries of the gospel, to the Sacraments, to the Church and the Creed, and to resist all rationalistic tendencies and profane criticism.

Finally, the mission of the German Reformed Church is Protestant, Evangelical, and Reformed, but in no sense ultra or radical. It would seek peace and pursue it; it respects the inheritance which has come down to it from the fathers of the Reformation, and seeks to build up the kingdom of God on its original foundation. Under this view, the present celebration, this Jubilæum of the Catechism, as tending to bring us into communion with the life and theology of the Church in its beginning in the fatherland, is a contribution on our part to the cause of Protestant unity, and we would fain hope that our Protestant brethren, generally, may unite with us in seeking out and putting up again the ancient landmarks.

THE ORGANIC STRUCTURE

OF THE

HEIDELBERG CATECHISM.

By REV. THOMAS G. APPLE, A.M.
GREENCASTLE, PA.

THE ORGANIC STRUCTURE

OF THE

HEIDELBERG CATECHISM.

By Rev. Thomas G. Apple, A.M., Greencastle, Pa.

"It is the necessary condition of a book," says Trench, "which shall exert any great and effectual influence, which shall stamp itself with a deep impression upon the minds and hearts of men, that it must have a unity of purpose: one great idea must run through it all. There must be some single point in which all its different rays converge and meet. The common eye may fail to detect the unity, even while it unconsciously owns its power: yet this is necessary still; this growing out of a single root, this subordination of all the parts to a single aim, this returning of the end upon the beginning. . . . And it is hardly necessary to add, that, if the effects are to be deep and strong, this idea must be a great one: it must not be one which shall play lightly upon the surface of their minds that apprehend it, but rather one which shall reach far down to the dark foundations, out of sight, upon which reposes this awful being of ours."

These words, which were spoken in reference to the Bible, the inspired word of God, are applicable also, we think, to the Heidelberg Catechism, which professes to set forth in a condensed form the knowledge of salvation, as derived from this divine revelation. As the object of Holy Scripture is to present an inspired record of the history and nature of the work of redemption, as this centres in

341

Jesus Christ, so the leading object of the Catechism is to present so much of the knowledge of redemption as is necessary for salvation. Its general aim, therefore, is emiuently practical. It proposes to answer a highly important and practical question, viz.: How are we to be saved? Its object, therefore, is, not to furnish a scientific system of faith or theology, such as we find in works of divinity, nor a complete statement of every thing which the Church believes, as in a Confession of Faith; nor is it a mere compilation of the four essential parts of a Catechism,—the Apostles' Creed, the doctrine of the Sacraments, the Ten Commandments, and the Lord's Prayer. It is a work rather between a full scientific Confession and a Catechism of the kind referred to.

The general aim of the Catechism is presented in the first question:—"*What is thy only comfort in life and in death?*"

The answer to this question, which is noted for its simplicity and devotion, as well as for its truly sublime eloquence, is of vast importance, in view of the relation it bears to all that follows it in the Catechism. It is a response in beautiful language, which at once places the catechumen (who is supposed to be a baptized member of the Church) in proper relation to the scheme of redemption which it subsequently unfolds. This relation is that of one standing *in grace*, and therefore in real possession of the greatest comfort, but of one who is also to attain to the full enjoyment of this comfort by a willing and cordial assent to the truths and conditions of salvation as subsequently set forth.

It has, indeed, been made a question whether this first answer is descriptive of the present state of the catechumen, or intended as a summing up of the benefits to be attained by a proper study and use of the Catechism. We think it has special significance in its position at the beginning of the Catechism, as the first answer put into the mouth of the baptized member of the Church. It states an important fact in regard to the *status* of the catechumen.

342

The comfort here spoken of may be regarded as a most precious birthright, which, however, may be either embraced in faith and obedience, or wickedly sold and lost forever. This answer may be regarded as related to what follows in the Catechism, as the promise of redemption made to our first parents in Paradise immediately after the fall, to the historical development of the scheme of redemption, as carried forward in the old and new dispensations. This promise gave the full guarantee of salvation to all who would accept it and believe in it, yet the contents of that salvation could be made over to man in all their fulness only when the Son of God became incarnate. The comfort here spoken of is an objective gracious gift bestowed in Baptism, and it is to be appropriated in the way of subjective experience, by the faithful study and observance of the truths and means of grace pointed out in the Catechism.

This first question, therefore, is the beginning and the ending of the Catechism to the faithful catechumen, as it declares a comfort which is his in infancy and old age, in life and in death.

The central and formative principle of the Catechism, therefore, is, Jesus Christ in vital union with the baptized member of the Church. The sin and misery of man, his deliverance by a personal Redeemer, his faith, the holy sacraments, the power of the keys, his conversion, obedience, worship, all these are ruled continually by this relation,—by what Christ is and does toward the catechumen, and what the catechumen, as belonging to Him, is and does toward Christ.

After this introductory question, in which its general aim and ruling principle are stated, the Catechism proceeds to exhibit first that state or condition from which we are saved. Man must first be led to look upon his utter ruin, and be made to understand its nature, before he can understand and appreciate the gracious deliverance which God has provided for him. This ruin is viewed from a Christian stand-point. In the Lutheran catechisms the Ten Commandments are placed first, to be used, as they were used by the Jews, to lead to Christ. The Heidelberg Catechism differs here, not only in that it proclaims the gospel before the revelation of the law, in which respect it conforms to the Bible, where the promised redemption was revealed before the giving of the law; but also in this, that it uses the law to show man his natural condition of sin and misery, in its New Testament sense, as explained by Christ. It makes Christ our first teacher, and from His lips it furnishes us with that inward, spiritual interpretation of the law of God, as fulfilled in supreme love to God, and love to our fellow-men as to ourselves. From this centre of light in Jesus Christ, who came to reveal what man by nature is, as well as to save him, it surveys the wreck and ruin of a fallen world.

From this point, and with this light, it perceives the universal and organic sinfulness of the human race. Its survey is broader, and its scrutiny deeper, than could be afforded by the faint glimmering light of heathenism, or the twilight dawn of typical and prophetical Judaism.

If we ask the result of this survey and scrutiny, the answer is, that man's ruin is a total ruin. He is prone by nature to hate God and his neighbor. He is so corrupt that he is wholly incapable of doing any good, and prone to all wickedness.

In order to lead to a proper conception of the nature of man's ruin, the Catechism points to its ground or origin in the history of the race. Beyond that it does not go, because beyond that the question becomes theoretical and speculative. Man's ruin is organic, and holds in the life of the race, because it proceeds from the fall and disobedience of our first parents, Adam and Eve, in Paradise. The sin of the individual members of the race is only the fruit produced by an evil tree. Consequently, sin is a fact as broad and deep as humanity itself.

But it is an eternal law that sin produces misery and

death. Man, though fallen, is still under the law by the very constitution of his nature. In the awful experiment of disobedience he obtained or carried with him the knowledge of right and wrong, and, so long as his nature is not totally destroyed by the annihilation of his being, this knowledge of the right, while he pursues the wrong, must work out in his experience the bitter pangs of eternal death, as the penalty pronounced upon him by the righteous Judge. God's moral government in the universe, and man's nature as a reasonable and responsible being, both require, that sin must bring its own penalty. There is no hope of relief, in man, from this condition of misery, because the very foundations of moral rectitude in his nature have given way. The power that he allowed to subdue him in a state of innocency, which was then a power from without, has now become a power in his own life, and works as a law of depravity from within. It has become conjoined in life-union with his own will, and holds him, therefore, an eternally willing subject. There is no hope of relief in the interposition of any one attribute of God, in opposition to any other of His attributes, as, for instance, mercy against justice; for God cannot contradict Himself.

Such is the nature of man's ruin, as presented in the first Part of the Catechism. It is not a speculative or metaphysical treatment of the doctrine of sin, but a practical statement, for a practical end, of a ruin which is all the more dark and dreary when viewed through the light which Christ has shed upon it. What that practical end is, we are next to consider.

Between the first and second Parts there is a connecting-link. The transition from the one to the other is not abrupt. Indeed, it is characteristic of the Catechism that its different parts flow together as gracefully and readily as the branches of a stream unite their waters in one flow toward the ocean.

"What manner of mediator and redeemer, then, must we seek?" No help can come from man, for, instead of being able to make satisfaction to divine justice for himself, he daily increases his debt. No mere creature can make this satisfaction, for God will not punish any other creature for the sin which man hath committed, neither can any mere creature sustain the burden of God's eternal wrath against sin, so as to deliver others from it. Among all creatures man is the only one whom God will accept as a deliverer, yet man cannot make the satisfaction. The only alternative, then, is to seek for one who is very man and very God in one person. Such a Mediator is the Lord Jesus Christ, who of God is made unto us wisdom and righteousness and sanctification and redemption.

Thus we are conducted to the person of Christ as the fountain of life and salvation for a fallen world. When the tie which bound man to God was broken through the fall, it was necessary that the restoration should be made by a new living bond of union, and this union is effected in and by a personal Redeemer, even the Lord Jesus Christ. The person of Christ comes before the work which He performs. The constitution of His person, as God and man, comprehending two natures, is regarded as necessary in order that He may truly fill the place of a mediator between God and man. Thus the person of the second Adam is placed over against the first Adam. As the ruin of humanity is based on the organic relation which holds between Adam in his fallen state and all his descendants, so the restoration of man has its foundation in the organic union between Christ and those who are constituted members of Him by faith. *"Are all men, then, saved by Christ, as they have perished by Adam?* No; only such as by true faith are ingrafted into Him, and receive all His benefits." Here the redemption provided in Christ is regarded as an organic redemption, and as it was made *in* human nature, and not merely *for* individual men, it must be general in its character. It is potentially as broad and deep as humanity itself. There is no limitation of salvation in the person of Christ, and consequently there can be no limitation in His work. The limitation of salvation in the human race must be found, therefore, not in Christ, but in man. To say that Christ brought redemption for only a portion of the human family, is to misunderstand the constitution of His person and the nature of His work. We can find this limitation only in man. As the sin of Adam is a general fact, limited only by humanity itself, so the salvation in Christ is for all men. And yet it is just as true that all men are not saved, but only those who are made members of Christ by a true faith.

Here we have more specifically brought out what is implied in the first question,—that the whole idea of redemption centres in Christ in vital union with those who believe on His name.

We need now to know what true faith is, both in its subjective exercise and in its objective contents. As to the former, it is declared to be the gift of the Holy Ghost, and not the work of man; as to the latter, it is all that is promised us in the gospel, comprehended briefly in the *Apostles' Creed*. Christ is the object of faith, and in this faith the first Christians were baptized. The Creed, however, which was first limited to the single proposition, "believe in the Lord Jesus Christ, and thou shalt be saved," became extended afterward, in order to define it against rising error, until it became full and complete in the Apostles' Creed.

Christ, as He is presented to our faith in the Apostles' Creed, is made unto us *wisdom*. He is our prophet, to reveal to us the true knowledge of God. He reveals to us the Father; for "no man knoweth the Father save the Son, and he to whomsoever the Son will reveal Him." Hence we have in the Creed the knowledge of God the Father Almighty, Maker of heaven and earth, the Creator of all things visible and invisible, the Preserver and Governor of all things, the God and Father of our Lord Jesus Christ. Through Christ we know the Holy Ghost, the blessed Comforter, whom He sent into the world. Through

Christ we learn the nature of that kingdom of divine grace which He established on earth, the Church of the living God, the communion of saints, the remission of sins, the resurrection of the body, and the life everlasting.

Christ, as presented to our faith in the Creed, is made unto us *righteousness*. When the question is asked, at the close of the Creed, "What doth it help thee now that thou believest all this?" the terse and brief, yet comprehensive, answer is made, "That I am righteous in Christ before God, and an heir of eternal life." The justification here spoken of is represented as a real imparting of the merits of Christ to the believer. "Not that I am acceptable to God," it is said, "on account of the worthiness of my faith, but because only the satisfaction, righteousness, and holiness of Christ is my righteousness before God, and I can receive the same and make it my own in no other way than by faith alone."

Hence Christ, as presented for faith in the Creed, is also made unto us *sanctification* and *redemption*. In speaking of the necessity of bringing forth the fruits of righteousness in those who are justified, the Catechism declares, "it is impossible that those who are implanted into Christ by true faith should not bring forth fruits of thankfulness." The end of the Christian life, as it is continually nourished and fed by Christ in the Church, is the resurrection of the body, and life everlasting, or complete redemption.

It is easy to see, therefore, that, so far as the teaching of positive truth and doctrine is concerned, the Apostles' Creed occupies the central and principal place in the Catechism. It is for the catechumen "the faith once delivered to the saints." In the full and comprehensive explanation of its several articles, the Catechism furnishes all the knowledge which it considers necessary for the object it has in view in the instruction of the catechumen in reference to the Holy Trinity, Creation, Providence, the Atonement, the Holy Spirit, and the Church. Under this last may be included also the Holy Sacraments, the Keys, Obedience, and Prayer, as parts of the legitimate exercise of the functions, life, and worship of the Church.

But the Creed is presented as the principal part of the Catechism, not merely for the knowledge of Christian doctrine which it furnishes,—that is, truth for the intellect,—but to be adopted as the expression of the catechumen's faith.

It does not fall within the province of this article to follow the Catechism in its explanation of the Creed. Our object has been simply to endeavor to show why it stands where it does, and its relation to what goes before and what comes after it. We may add, however, in this connection, that, in adopting the Apostles' Creed as the form in which the facts and truths of redemption are presented, the Catechism exhibits its historical and churchly spirit. It presents the teachings of the gospel, the inspired word of God; but it presents these teachings as they have been understood, explained in, and believed by the Church from the beginning. This is not a system of faith drawn immediately and directly from the Bible, but it is the teaching of the Bible as it comes to us through the mind of the Church, which was established before the Bible was written, and to which the guardianship of the sacred oracles from the beginning was intrusted.

Next to the Apostles' Creed and the doctrine of justification by faith alone, the Catechism contains, in the second Part, the subject of the Holy Sacraments and the doctrine of the Keys, or the office of Christian Discipline.

In thus placing the Holy Sacraments next in order to the word of God, or the gospel, as set forth in the Apostles' Creed, the Catechism only follows the order usually observed. The meaning of this order may be at once perceived if we consider what a sacrament is, and what office it is appointed to perform in the work of man's salvation. In the Catechism a sacrament is defined to be a sign and seal of the promise of the gospel.

In order to assist and strengthen faith in His word, on account of human weakness and unbelief, God, from the beginning, associated with His promises certain outward signs. When He gave Noah the promise that He would never again destroy the world by a flood, He appointed the bow in the cloud as a sign of His promise. When He chose Abraham to be the father of the faithful, and promised that in his seed all the nations of the earth should be blessed, He gave him the sign of circumcision as a seal of the righteousness of his faith. In the language of Calvin, "there is never any sacrament without an antecedent promise of God, to which it is subjoined, in order to confirm and seal the promise itself, and to certify and ratify it to us; which means God foresees to be necessary, in the first place, on account of our ignorance and dulness, and, in the next place, on account of our weakness." The sign and seal, therefore, follow the promise or word which is declared for our faith.

Sacraments may be regarded as subserving two purposes, one of which is that they confirm and strengthen our faith. "Our faith, being slender and weak, unless it be supported on every side and sustained by every assistance, immediately shakes, fluctuates, totters, and falls. And as we are corporeal, always creeping on the ground, cleaving to terrestrial and carnal objects, and incapable of understanding or conceiving any thing of a spiritual nature, our merciful Lord, in His infinite indulgence, accommodates Himself to our capacity, condescending to lead us to Himself even by these earthly elements, and in the flesh itself to present to us a mirror of spiritual blessings. 'For if we were incorporeal,' Chrysostom says, 'He would have given us these things pure and incorporeal. Now, because we have souls enclosed in bodies, He gives us spiritual things under visible emblems; not because there are such qualities in the nature of the things presented to us in the sacraments, but because they have been designated by God to this signification.' "— CALVIN.

But another purpose sacraments subserve is, that they are *seals* impressed by the hand of God Himself, whereby He ratifies and establishes for us the gracious promises of His word. The word without the sacraments, now that God has instituted them, is like an official document or writing without the official seal. It is a mere statement, without force or validity. In this view we may see that the word must first be declared, the writing must first be produced, and afterward it receives the royal seal. But we may see also why the sacraments are made to follow the subject of faith both in its subjective character and its objective contents. The word declares certain good; faith is the receptive organ or faculty by which it is to be received; and the sacraments are the official seals by which a real conveyance of the promised good is made. The question is sometimes asked, whether the sacraments are essential to salvation. It is urged that the word alone is sufficient for this end. We need only ask, in reply, whether the seal of a charter or patent is essential to give it validity and force. The charter without the seal is useless; and the seal without the charter would be equally meaningless. Nor does this imply that the word of God is not in itself sufficiently unchangeable and true, any more than the official document of a king or ruler is not true without the seal. It means that God has taken this method to make over to us the blessings promised in His word.

As, therefore, the sacraments are God's royal seals affixed to His promise of redemption, and signs for the confirmation of our faith, they properly follow after the declaration of that promise and word, and the treatment of Christian faith.

Baptism is the sign and seal of the new birth, or " of initiation, by which we are admitted into the society of the

Church, in order that, being incorporated into Christ, we may be numbered among the children of God." The Lord's Supper is "a spiritual banquet, in which Christ testifies Himself to be the bread of life, to feed our souls for a blessed immortality." The beginning and the nourishing of the Christian life are thus made over to us by a faithful use of the sacraments.

It might be supposed that the way of man's deliverance is now complete. There is one other subject, however, necessary to complete our knowledge of the way of salvation.

The Church, which is "the body of Christ," to whom are given the oracles of inspired truth, and in whose bosom the holy sacraments are administered, has intrusted to her care the training or nurture of those who seek life and peace in her hallowed communion. As the Jerusalem from above, "the mother of us all," she has committed to her the prerogative of opening the kingdom of heaven to all believers and shutting it against all unbelievers. We say this is the prerogative of the Church; for it is expressly declared that this opening and shutting the kingdom of heaven is accomplished by the preaching of the gospel and Christian discipline. It is not the Bible, therefore, nor God immediately and directly, who pronounces the forgiveness of sin and retains the sins of those who are disobedient and without repentance, but it is the Church, whose office it is to preach the gospel, administer the sacraments, and maintain Christian discipline. "Go ye, therefore, into all the world, and preach my gospel." "Whosesoever sins ye remit, they are remitted; and whose-soever sins ye retain, they are retained."

Although there is not much said expressly of the Church in the second Part of the Catechism, the fact being simply stated, in explanation of the 9th article of the Creed, that God, from the beginning to the end of the world, gathers, preserves, and defends a Church chosen unto everlasting life, yet we may say its existence and important functions are implied in the whole system of truth taught. The theory of religion taught in the Catechism "assumes, throughout, that the Church is in a certain sense the medium and bearer of spiritual life for her own children; that while religion is a pre-eminently individual and subjective interest in one view, it is still, in another, conditioned and upheld, like all life, by an objective ground that lies without and beyond its particular subject altogether." (*Dr. Nevin's History and Genius of the Heidelberg Catechism.*)

This appears, now, in the doctrine of the Keys, with which the second Part of the Catechism closes. There is a power and authority here over and above the individual Christian. The Church is empowered to administer the sacraments, and this implies also that she is authorized to admit to and exclude from these sealing ordinances. On this account, the subject of the Keys is introduced immediately after the sacraments. These sacraments are holy mysteries, to be carefully guarded by the Church from abuse. As the tree of life was guarded after man was driven from Paradise, and as the ark of the covenant was shielded from all impertinent curiosity, so these are to be kept sacred. They are not for the impenitent, the irreverent, the profane.

We have now seen what God does for man in the work of redemption. Of His sovereign grace He provides a Saviour from sin and death, and through the Holy Spirit produces faith in this Saviour. He appoints for him holy sacraments, through which He makes over to him the things promised in the gospel,—the gift of a new life, and the nourishment of that life. What is the result or effect of this work of God toward man? It produces in him its legitimate effect. It inspires him with love and gratitude, and these reveal themselves in a life of obedience and consecration to the glory of God. As natural as it is for the fertile soil to produce fruit when the seed has been sown and the gentle showers and genial warmth have come upon it, so natural is it for man to respond in love and thankful obedience when God delivers him from sin and death.

In the third Part of the Catechism, which treats of *thankfulness*, we have set forth what man is moved to do toward God in return for his deliverance.

The first subject presented is that of conversion, or, as it is in the German, True Repentance. This presupposes the work of regeneration. Regeneration is the work which God performs in man when He creates within him a new heart, or implants within him the germ of a new life. It is the act of his incorporation into Christ. In this work God alone is active, man passive. Repentance, or conversion, is the effect of regeneration, and is the work man performs, not indeed in his own strength, but by the Holy Ghost. In his full and lucid argument on the subject of repentance, Calvin remarks "that repentance not only immediately follows faith, but is produced by it." And again he says, "those who imagine that repentance rather precedes faith than is produced by it, as fruit by a tree, have never been acquainted with its power, and are induced to adopt that sentiment by a very insufficient argument," —which argument he proceeds to review and satisfactorily refute. He concludes that "there is not the least appearance of reason in the notion of those who, in order to begin with repentance, prescribe to their young converts certain days during which they must exercise themselves in repentance; after the expiration of which they admit them to the communion of evangelical grace." His definition of repentance, too, corresponds entirely with that given in the Heidelberg Catechism. It is, he says, "a true conversion of our life to God, proceeding from a sincere and serious fear of God, and consisting in the mortification of our flesh and of the old man, and in the vivification of the Spirit."

This mortification of the old man and quickening of the new man is nothing else than the death and resurrection of Christ operating in the Christian. The calls to repentance generally in the Bible are addressed to those who are in covenant-relation with God. "Repent ye; for the kingdom of heaven is at hand," said John the Baptist, and the Saviour,—in which it is implied that repentance is possible only where the grace of the gospel kingdom comes to man. This order, we know, is the reverse of that frequently advocated, where repentance, or conversion, is made to precede regeneration. And if we regard the religion of Christ as only adapted to adults, as a missionary religion only addressed to the unbaptized, it might indeed be said that a certain preparation for regeneration is necessary for the reception of the grace of regeneration, though even this preparation would have to be the result also of grace. But the religion of the Bible, both in the old and new dispensations, is the result of God's covenant made not only with adults, but also with their children. If, then, repentance, or conversion, as a self-conscious process in the mind and heart, is a necessary condition of regeneration, we may well ask, how then are our children to be regenerated? To say they are not regenerated, is to shut them out of heaven if they die, and leave no basis for true Christian nurture if they live. The view of the Catechism manifestly regards conversion as following regeneration as its fruit; for how can the effects of Christ's death and resurrection be produced in the heart and life before we are made members of Christ and born into His gracious kingdom? "Know ye not that so many of us as were baptized into Jesus Christ were baptized into His death? Therefore we are buried with Him by baptism into death: that like as Christ was raised up from the dead by the glory of the Father, even so we also should walk in newness of life."

This point being established, we look for some rule or guide, not to produce obedience,—for this, in spirit at least, has already been produced,—but to regulate this obedience. This we find in the law of God, those divine commandments which comprehend the whole duty of man.

It may be said that in introducing the law in this third

Part of the Catechism there is a return to Jewish legalism, which St. Paul condemns. That apostle clearly teaches that the law is not the ground of man's justification; for in that view it brings only condemnation and death. He also teaches that the law is not the ground of our sanctification; for this he asserts to be the life of Christ in us.

But it must not be forgotten that the law still has a legitimate function to perform in the life of the Christian, considered, not as the voice which condemns, and as in this view being only a schoolmaster to lead us to Christ, but in its ethical character as a rule of life is the law employed in the third Part of the Catechism. We may say the Christian has within him the disposition to render obe- dience to God. This disposition or desire and the power to render obedience come from Christ, and so far he is not under the law, but under grace. Yet there is required an outward rule or model to aid him in carrying out this dis- position of his heart. "The third use of the law," says Calvin, "which is the principal one, and which is more nearly connected with the proper end of it, relates to the faithful, in whose hearts the Spirit of God already lives and reigns. For although the law is inscribed and engraven on their hearts by the finger of God,—that is, although they are so excited and animated by the direction of the Spirit that they desire to obey God,—yet they derive a twofold advantage from the law. For they find it an excellent instrument to give them, from day to day, a better and more certain understanding of the divine will to which they aspire, and to confirm them in the knowledge of it. As, though a servant be already influenced by the strongest desire of gaining the approbation of his master, yet it is necessary for him carefully to inquire and observe the orders of his master, in order to conform to them." A second benefit he states to be the excitement and stimu- lation to duty which the law aids in stirring up within the Christian.

It is here, indeed, that the law finds its full accordance

356

with the gospel. It did not stand opposed to the promise ✓ of salvation in the old dispensation, but was given to assist in leading the Jews to rest the more on the promise, and also to be unto them a rule of life. So in the new dispensation it is not opposed to grace, but becomes the measure of a perfect life to which the subjects of grace strive to attain.

That it is placed in the third Part of the Catechism as the rule of life for the Christian, therefore, shows us the profound view of the nature and use of the law which was held by the authors of the Catechism. It is in accordance with the many exhortations to obedience and good works found in the Epistles, especially in Paul's Epistle to the Romans, where these exhortations to obedience are made to follow the great doctrine of salvation by grace.

On this point the Heidelberg Catechism again differs in its organic structure from Luther's Catechism, in which the ten commandments are placed only in the first part, and employed, therefore, only to show the necessity of salvation by grace. It is known, too, that one of the weak points in the Lutheran system is its tendency, when not carefully guarded, toward antinomianism. And we are as free to grant also that one of the dangers to which the Reformed Church has been exposed is its tendency to legalism. This appeared to some extent in Calvin, and it has shown itself in later times in Puritanism and Methodism. But this danger lies not in the organic structure of the Heidelberg Catechism. It is a danger rather to which those expose themselves who part company with the churchly and sacramental features of the Reformed faith.

It seems proper in this place to notice also a peculiarity in the division of the Decalogue, in which the Reformed Church differs from the Roman Catholic and Lutheran. The Reformed churches, following the division of Origen and of Philo and Josephus, make the 3d verse of the 20th chapter of Exodus to contain the first commandment, and the 4th–6th verses to contain the second commandment; after which the remainder may be easily traced. The Lutheran Church, following the Augustinian method, makes the 2d–6th verses referred to contain but *one* commandment, and then to complete the number ten it makes the 17th verse contain two commandments. The former may be called the *Græco-Reformed*, the latter the *Latino-Lutheran*. Another method, still, agrees with the latter of the above in regard to the tenth commandment, but differs in regard to the first and second, making verse 2 in Exodus xx. to contain the first commandment, and 3–6 to contain the second. "Of these methods, the most ancient historical testimony is in favor of that adopted by the Reformed Church." A consideration of the internal structure of the Decalogue would also favor this method.*

The last subject introduced in the Catechism is *prayer*.

It is not to be inferred, of course, that the last thing a Christian does is to pray. Prayer is here represented as the perfection and crowning beauty of the Christian life. As the whole end of redemption is to bring man into

---

* Herzog's Encyclopædia, translated by Dr. Bomberger. Art. *Decalogue*, by Oehler.

We also quote here a note by Dr. Schaff, in his Catechism recently published:—

" . . . Besides the intrinsic evidence, which shows the ten commandments to be an indivisible unit, a comparison of Exod. xx. 17 with Deut. v. 21 settles the dispute in favor of the view of the Reformed churches, which is also admitted to be the correct one by many of the best Lutheran divines and commentators. For in Deut. v. 21 (as also in Exod. xx. 17 in the Greek translation of the Seventy) the order is transposed, and the neighbor's wife put before the neighbor's house. This would make what is the ninth commandment in Exodus to be the tenth commandment in Deuteronomy, if the Roman view were correct. St. Paul, moreover, in enumerating the commandments of the second table, Rom. xiii. 9 (compare also vii. 7), alludes to the tenth with the words, "Thou shalt not covet," without intimating any such division. The Roman Catechism indirectly refutes its own division, by treating the ninth and tenth commandments under one head (while all the others are treated separately), and by expressly admitting, " We have united these two commandments, because their object is the same, and the manner of treating them should be the same." Most of the modern commentators of Luther's Catechism (Stier, who adopts the Reformed division in full, the Würtemberg Catechism, Brieger, Caspari, Mann, Schmucker) likewise combine the two in the explanation.

358

living communion and fellowship with God, so that he may speak forth His praise and glorify Him forever, that exercise which is most concerned in praise and communion is placed last. According to the general order of the Catechism, prayer could not be placed in the first Part, which treats of man's sin and misery; neither could it well be placed in the second Part, which treats of man's deliverance. It belongs properly to the third Part, because, in the language of the Catechism, "it is that chief part of thankfulness which God requires of us," &c. The spirit of prayer, like the spirit of obedience, is begotten within us by the Holy Ghost. As the Christian is inwardly moved to obey the commandments by a desire to show his gratitude for favors and blessings received, so he is moved to pray by the same spirit of thankfulness and a longing desire after communion with God,—a desire that His glory may be promoted in the world. And as in the case of the commandments a guide is necessary for the development of the inner life, so the spirit of prayer also requires a model form of words. The Lord's Prayer is thus introduced, to teach us in what manner of expressions and petitions we should clothe those desires which are formed within us by the Holy Ghost. This, at last, is the great end of the Christian life. Man was originally created to be the mouthpiece of this lower creation, to speak forth the praise and glory of God. In his redemption he is more than restored to this original position; for now he shows forth not only the perfections of the natural creation, but the still higher glories of the new creation in Christ Jesus.

From this brief summary of the Heidelberg Catechism, in which an attempt has been made to follow up and trace out the connection of the different parts, these two things, we think, must be apparent:—

1. Viewing the Catechism as a book of Christian instruction for the young, it is ruled throughout by the relation of the baptized catechumen to Christ. The person to be instructed is in covenant-relation with God. He belongs

to his faithful Saviour Jesus Christ by his birth from Christian parents, and especially by his formal consecration to His service in Christian baptism. This relation is presupposed throughout the whole Catechism. When it treats of the sin and misery of man, it refers to it as a state and condition from which the catechumen has been delivered potentially, and from which he is to be delivered in his own life-experience. Hence it does not ask, "Whence knowest thou *man's* misery?" but, "Whence knowest thou *thy* misery?" So, also, in the explanation of the Creed it is continually regarded as the faith not merely of the Church, but of the catechumen. "What believest *thou* when thou sayest, I believe in God the Father Almighty, Maker of heaven and earth?" "That the eternal Father of our Lord Jesus Christ, &c., is, for the sake of Christ His Son, *my* God and *my* Father," &c. Other examples might be cited. This is the golden thread that runs through the whole Catechism from beginning to end.

2. Viewing the Catechism as a Church-confession or symbol of faith, it is ruled throughout in its construction by the Apostles' Creed. It does not go beyond this first of all creeds for its confession of faith. It stands in favorable contrast in this view, we think, with other confessions. They may give more full scientific definitions of many important points of Christian doctrine; they may give a more scientific definition of who God is, &c.; but we may submit whether much division and difficulty might not be avoided if the Confession proper of the Church of Christ were allowed to remain one and unaltered. Certain it is that all that is necessary to be known of God and the redemption He has provided for man is contained in the Apostles' Creed. We value the Heidelberg Catechism all the more because, in so far as it professes to be a confession of faith, it presents only that which has been believed by the saints of all ages, *the faith once delivered to the saints*. May it continue to be venerated and loved, as a precious legacy, by us and our children to the latest generation!

THE

THEOLOGICAL SYSTEM

IN WHICH

THE HEIDELBERG CATECHISM RESTS.

THE KIND OF RELIGIOUS LIFE IT CULTIVATES, AND THE THEORY OF PRACTICAL RELIGION WHICH IT ASSUMES.

———————

By PROF. M. KIEFFER, D.D.

TIFFIN, OHIO.

2 C

THE THEOLOGICAL SYSTEM

IN WHICH

THE HEIDELBERG CATECHISM RESTS,

THE KIND OF RELIGIOUS LIFE IT CULTIVATES, AND THE THEORY OF PRACTICAL RELIGION WHICH IT ASSUMES.

By Prof. M. Kieffer, D.D., Tiffin, Ohio.

THE relation of the Church's confessions of faith to the inspired Scriptures has come to be well understood, and is accurately defined. The Inspired Word, which takes its character from the *Incarnate* Word, is the *"norma credendi,"* and the confession is the *"forma credendi."* The one is the germ; the other is its development in the Christian consciousness. The one is more objective, and takes its peculiar character from the Absolute; it is divine: the other is more subjective, and takes its character from the relative, —the human. The one is the supernatural revelation of God through His only-begotten Son, by the Spirit; the other is the apprehension of this revelation by Christian faith.

But the relation of the Confession of Faith to *theology* is somewhat more difficult to determine, and at first view it might seem as though theology must rest in the Confession, and not the reverse. The Confession is more permanent and fixed, and hardly admits of any alteration or change. It stands like the towering mountain within the sphere of the new creation, as a symbol of the invisible, the eternal, the divine. No one would now think, for instance, of taking an article from, or adding to, the Apostles' Creed,—just as little as he would add to, or take from, the word of God. These articles stand as firm as the mountain upon its base,—as firm as the twelve apostolic pillars in the temple of the New Jerusalem.

But systems of theology are constantly changing. Nowhere is the law of change more visible than it is in the department of theological study. Here there is a constant growth and decay, a constant setting up and pulling down, a constant planting and supplanting, and a constant rising and going down of smaller and greater luminaries. As said by Dr. Ebrard in his *Dogmatik*, "No age can boast of having brought this science to its perfection." Its ideal is still far distant in the future; or, rather, it is high in the heavens, and will only be reached at the final consummation of all things.

It would seem, then, that the Confession of Faith, the symbol of Christian truth, should be the starting-point of theology; that this is the foundation upon which the scientific structure must rest. That which changes must rest in the unchangeable,—the living temple upon the pillars, and not the pillars upon the temple. Under one aspect, this is certainly correct; but there is a broader and a deeper view, according to which the statement of our theme will be found to be perfectly accurate. The Confession of Faith did not come into existence full grown, like Minerva from the head of Jupiter. Though it is now settled and fixed, it was brought to its present completion in the way of a process. Like every thing else that is human, it has its history. Here, as elsewhere, we have first the blade, then the ear, and afterward the full corn in the ear.

But we know that all history has two essential elements, the divine and human; and, indeed, all its truth and reality are derived from this divine element.

As all things consist in God, so human life especially has its being in Him, and without Him it cannot unfold its distinctive powers. God glorifies Himself in man. There is, then, a theology of history,—a divine idea underlying and pervading every thing that is human. Accordingly, all systems of human thought, all philosophy and all sciences, are theological in their ultimate ground. Without this divine idea, no system of thought can have any truth or meaning whatever. It can at best be only a cloud without water, a shadow without substance. It has long been conceded that there is an inspiration of poetry and of the fine arts generally: so we must also claim a divinity for the sciences, or deny to them all meaning and reality.

If, then, the truly human rests in the divine, and if *all* true systems of thought must have a theological basis, we may certainly, with the utmost propriety, speak of systems of belief, confessions of faith, resting in a theological system. They are related, it seems to me, as knowledge and faith; they rest the one in the other. It is true, according to Anselm, "we do not know that we may believe, but we believe that we may know;" yet it is equally true that Christian faith is intelligent,—it is not without knowledge. "And Simon Peter *answered and said*, Thou art the Christ, the Son of the living God. And Jesus answered and said unto him, Blessed art thou, Simon Barjona; for flesh and blood hath not *revealed* it unto thee, but my Father which is in heaven." (Matt. xvi. 16, 17.)

To place faith before knowledge in the order of time is evidently to do violence to both; they are twin graces, born at the same time by the same spirit. That which is believed is known; and our holy Christian religion, to be truly known, must be believed. Knowledge is intelligent faith, and faith is confiding knowledge. Thus *theology* is an intelligent and scientific confession of faith, and the confession of faith is confiding theology. This is strikingly illustrated by our venerable Heidelberg Catechism. It is a confession of faith, and it is at the same time a complete body of divinity. Hence it is not merely a suitable book for the instruction of the young, but it answers also the purposes of a text-book of theology in learned universities and seminaries. As said by Dr. Nevin (in the History and

Genius of the Heidelberg Catechism), "profound divines, such as Ursinus, Alting, Piscator, Cocceius, Schultens, &c., have made it the basis of their dogmatic, systems in this way. Innumerable pulpits and schools have lent their aid to give it voice and power in the world. It has been as the daily bread of the sanctuary to millions, generation after generation. Never was a Catechism more honored in the way of translations, commentaries, and expositions."

The general system of theology in which it rests may be designated as the *Orthodox*, or Trinitarian, as it was unfolded in the primitive period of dogmatic history over against the ancient heresies, and as it was again reproduced by the Reformers of the sixteenth century in opposition to the erroneous tendencies of their time.

It is the redeeming feature of the Church of the Reformation, that she does not ignore the history of the past; she does not introduce *new* confessions of faith in conflict with those of the primitive period; but, in humble reverence to the spirit and wisdom of the ancient Church, she adopts her creeds—the Apostolic, and those that grew out of it, such as the Nicene and Athanasian—as symbolic of all that is necessary for a Christian to believe. Our Reformed Zion, in celebrating the tercentenary of her Confession of Faith, does not offer devout thanks to God for a new gift; but she rejoices rather that the faith once delivered to the saints has been preserved and handed down to us in its present form. It follows as a corollary, therefore, from the preceding statements, that the theology of the Catechism is not new,—as a system, it is the living product of the past. It is the theology of the apostolic fathers revived, and that of the middle period reformed. For this science, like every other, in its upward struggle toward its ideal, necessarily produces from itself. Its exodus is in the way pointed out by Israel's pillar of cloud by day and pillar of fire by night. Beyond this it cannot go. Whilst it is constantly unfolding its own principle, it never loses its identity. The Christian theology of the sixteenth century, therefore, differs from that of the first, second, or third, only in the degree of its development.

Its essential elements are not so simple as to admit of being clothed in a formal sentence, or proposition. In their union they are rather the entire fulness of the Christian consciousness. God the Father is reconciling the world to Himself through the Son by the Holy Ghost. In Christ the Church knew in her earliest infancy her heavenly Father, her Redeemer and Comforter; she knew, farther, that redemption and reconciliation are of God, and not of men; for she knew full well the difference between the objectively real and subjective thought. She knew, also, that between God and man there is a real and essential difference. There was no room left in her consciousness for emanationism or pantheism. By faith she realized that the worlds were *made*. She knew that sin is sin, not an imperfection or defect belonging necessarily to the creature. Hence she knew, likewise, that a mere subjective reconciliation with God without an objective ground, or atonement, to rest upon, is a mere fancy or empty dream; for "whatever is born of the flesh is flesh;" hence self-redemption is impossible: on the contrary, God alone can bring in salvation to the children of men and reconcile them to Himself. It was a fact of consciousness, too, that through God alone the great salvation wrought out by the suffering Saviour could be made effectual in the single person,—that the Saviour had fulfilled His promise to send the Holy Spirit to illumine the understanding, to regenerate the heart, to sanctify the will, and comfort the mind. In the form of the Spirit the Saviour was believed to be present with His people, as He had promised: "Lo, I am with you always, even unto the end of the world."

These are the principal factors of the Trinitarian theology, as they were given in the New Testament canon, and as they were taken up in the consciousness of the Church. We cannot, in this brief essay, pursue the way of dogmatic history, and show how in the departments of apologetic, polemic, and didactic theology these momenta were carried out to their final results. This department of history, like that of the Church in general, has its periods and epochs. In the first period—reaching from the commencement to the time of Augustine, or perhaps more properly to the time of John of Damascus (confining our view to the East)— the Church came gradually to a consciousness of the momentous consequences of her faith. She overcomes Ebionism, Gnosticism, Arianism, &c., in one victory after another, until she finds the full truth in Athanasianism. This forms the first epoch of this period,—the first in the order of time, and the first in importance. Then, in the second, we have the exposition of this great drama, which presents its closing scene at the Synod of Constantinople. In the third, we find a more special effort to define the Trinitarian relation. God has revealed Himself as Father, Son, and Holy Ghost, and now this revelation is to be reconciled with His unity.

It is worthy of special notice that during this entire period the theology of the Church does not separate itself from her general life. In other words, the general interests of religion and those of theology are identical. The conception of theology, as we are aware, is derived from that of religion, and thus far this science lives and moves in its original element: it is eminently christological. To unfold the great plan of salvation, the great economy of grace, is its sole aim and design. Every canonical idea, every word, every sentence, and every doctrine sustains a living relation to Christ's person. "He is all, and in all." He is the revelation of God the Father; in the history of His person and work, all that was typified and foretold in the Old Testament dispensation comes to its fulfilment and meaning. "Of God He is made unto us wisdom, righteousness, sanctification, and complete redemption."

In the second great period of dogmatic history, from the time of Augustine to the Reformation, the Latin Church endeavored to apprehend the *Trinitarian theology* from the stand-point of the GOD-IDEA. As the Eastern Church passed over to the idea of the divine unity from that of the Trinity, so the Western Church would go from the conception of *unity* to that of the Trinity. But the effort does not succeed. The Pelagian element, though overcome by Augustanism, is revived, and comes to pervade the general life and influence the general practice of the Church. The interests of theology come to be separated more and more from the general interests of Christian life. Between the schools and the common people there is an unnatural divorce: they are regarded as two spheres of existence, entirely separate and distinct. The anthropological tendency gains the ascendency. We have the reign of scholasticism and mysticism,—the one degenerating into a cold intellectualism, and the other into blind fanaticism. Yet neither one is complete without the other. Theology, however, finds its principal expression in scholasticism. The most difficult problems are undertaken, but find no satisfactory solution; numberless questions are asked, but are not satisfactorily answered; difficulties are met with, but are only moved from one place to another, without being overcome or mastered. Help is sought in strict logical method,—in divisions and subdivisions, in distinctions and hair-breadth distinctions,—also in the Aristotelian philosophy. Very able and learned works make their appearance (for it must not be forgotten that there were intellectual giants in those days), but they do not divide themselves into branches, but rather into strata, which readily fall apart into numberless fragments. Thus the spirit of scholasticism degenerated into an empty subtilty, and dogmatic theology in this form lost its value. The effort to supply the defect from the side of mysticism is also a failure, the vital bond of union with the source of all truth being to a great extent wanting. To this general statement, however, there are some striking exceptions. About the end of the eleventh and the commencement of the twelfth century, Anselm of Canterbury, Roscelin, and Abelard labored with commendable zeal and with great ability to effect a recon-ciliation between Christian knowledge and faith. We here also think of Thomas Aquinas and his immediate co-laborers (1221–74), who were men of undoubted Christian earnestness. The light arising from such luminaries as these gives us the morning-dawn of the Reformation. Yet the entire surrounding field reminds us forcibly of Ezekiel's vision of dry bones: "Lo, they are very many, and they are very dry."

As said by Dr. Hagenbach (in his *Encyclopädie der theologischen Wissenschaften*), the REGENERATION of dogmatic theology commenced properly with the Reformation of the sixteenth century. Melanchthon (*preceptor Germaniæ*) re-laid the foundation of dogmatics as a science in his time-honored work, entitled the *Loci Communes*. At the same time, Luther, the mightiest preacher of his day, and also a mighty theologian, establishes the Protestant principle of justification by faith, and the supreme authority of the in-spired Scriptures. Independently of him, Zwingli at the same time carries on the work of the Reformation in Swit-zerland. Glarus, Einsiedeln, and Zurich are the immediate scenes of his activity. In this country no less than in Ger-many the earnest spirit of Christian theology is revived. In both countries, indeed, distinguished divines step upon the public stage in quick succession; sometimes they come for-ward simultaneously. Whilst in Germany the dogmatic ten-dency takes the lead, in Switzerland the exegetical tendency prevails. The richest treasures are found in the inspired Scriptures; they are the never-failing fountain of truth and wisdom, and come now to be regarded as the principal source of theology as a science. The work so auspiciously commenced in Switzerland, both the practical and scientific, is taken up and carried forward by John Calvin. In his "Institutes of the Christian Religion," a work more scien-tific and more comprehensive even than the "Loci Com-munes," we have unfolded the entire synthesis of the great fact of redemption through Christ, and man's need of the same. Under his influence, the Reformed Church assumes her distinctive character, over against the Church of Rome on the one hand and the rigidly Lutheran on the other.

Between the two great families of the Protestant Church there was, unfortunately, a difference of view concerning the Lord's Supper. The history of the controversy is well known. It is remarkable, however, that Melanchthon, the well-known author of the Augsburg Confession, was always in sympathy with the Reformed. He and his disciples generally co-operated with the Reformed divines with remarkable unanimity. The bond of union between them was only strengthened by the persecutions which they were made to suffer. Under their united influence, the interests of theological science are again, as in the beginning, identified with the general interests of Church-life. Its original momenta now assert their power with renewed force. Under the master-mind of Melanchthon especially, the main problem which scholasticism had failed to master, viz., the reconciliation of the *God-idea* with the scriptural doctrine of the Trinity, comes to a satisfactory solution. It is just in this, too, that he shows himself to be Reformed. For it is not, after all, the *abstract* doctrine of the sacrament that could bring the Church to a confessional difference, but this doctrine as it stands in living union with the TRINITY. From this broad ground, as given in the Scriptures, the Reformed theology, which we may now call the Melanchthonian-Calvinistic, unfolds the great economy of grace. Time would fail us to mention the difficulties to be overcome, the one-sided tendencies which here and there prevail for a time, and are then counteracted; how far scholasticism and mysticism maintain their ground upon Protestant soil, and to what extent the evangelical spirit prevails. The entire development shows that Christ, the great Teacher, is now, as He was in the beginning, with His people, leading them into all truth. To the end that theology may accomplish its Christian mission in the Church, establishing her in the faith, it readily takes the form of symbolism: indeed, the entire stream of theological life flows forward into this broad sea. In the Reformed Church especially, quite a number of confessions of faith soon make their appearance, some of a local and others of a more general influence. Already at the imperial diet of Augsburg four cities of Upper Germany, *Strasburg, Constance, Memmingen, and Lindau,* inclined to the Zwinglian faith, handed in their confession, which for this reason was called the Tetrapolitana, *i.e.* the Confession of the Four Cities. In the year 1534, the Church of Basel made a public profession of her evangelical faith in a written form; this was also adopted by the Church of Mühlhausen. And in the year 1536, under the influence of the peace-loving Bucer, who wished to bring the controversy concerning the sacrament to a close, the Second Confession of Basel, or the First Helvetic Confession, was adopted. The Churches of Zurich, and that of Geneva, came to a formal understanding in regard to the Lord's Supper, in the Consensus Figurinus (1549), whilst the doctrine of predestination, as farther carried out by Calvin, came to its formal expression in the Consensus Genevensis* (1552). But no one of these confessions, though of undoubted merit, grounding themselves, as they do, in the word of God and the ancient creeds, could, in the nature of the case, come to have œcumenical authority. As the Christian life of the time was not confined to any particular city or province, so no provincial confession could have force beyond its own geographical limits. Yet the general theological spirit of the time imperiously demanded a corresponding form of expression. It is felt more deeply now than ever that the Church should be one in reality as she is one in idea. It is not sufficient that the Churches of Zurich and Geneva be united in one common brotherhood. It is not enough that the Augsburg Confession, as interpreted by the Melanchthonian divines, agrees essentially with the Reformed faith

---

* See Hagenbach's Dogmengeschichte.

as distinguished from the Lutheran. A symbol is needed to unite, if possible, the entire Protestant family. The entire theological life of the time, flowing onward in different channels, seeks nevertheless to empty itself into the broad sea of peace and love. The theological spirit of the German Church (of the Melanchthonian type) finds a fit representative in the person of Dr. Ursinus, a disciple of the John-like Philip Melanchthon; and that of the Reformed faith generally finds its utterance through the conscious intelligence of Olevianus, a disciple of the Paul-like John Calvin.

Through these two distinguished divines, under the direction of Frederick the Pious, the theological life of the early Church, as now revived and reformed, finds its crowning expression in the form of the Heidelberg Catechism. Such is the broad and comprehensive system of theology in which it rests. We have called it the Melanchthonian-Calvinistic, not because it embodies the subjective views of these great divines in regard to this or that doctrine, but because their respective systems, resting upon the same common ground,—namely, the word of God,—reflect, in a representative way, the general life and spirit of theology as it reigns objectively in the Church.

To show the correctness of the view here expressed, it is not deemed necessary to enter into particulars. The essential factors of the primitive theology are so fully and comprehensively expressed in the introductory question and answer that we need but enter into their spirit and meaning to find ourselves in the theological communion of the apostolic fathers, as well as of the distinguished Reformers of the sixteenth century. In carrying out these factors to their ultimate consequences, the authors of the Catechism, as is generally known, pursue the general method of St. Paul in his Epistle to the Romans. First, we must learn " How great our sins and miseries are;" secondly, " How we may be redeemed from all our sin and misery;" and, thirdly, "How we are to be thankful to God for such redemption."

The depravity of man, who was created in the image of God in righteousness and true holiness, and who fell into sin by the instigation of the devil and his own wilful disobedience, is represented as *total*. Man is so depraved that he is wholly incapable of doing any good except he be regenerated by the Spirit of God. This, we perceive at once, is in direct opposition to the Pelagian tendency in the Church of Rome.

In the second part, which unfolds the great plan of salvation through Christ, or the economy of grace according to the venerable Apostolic Creed, we have brought to our view the Trinitarian relation as it came to be settled in the primitive Church over against the leading heresies already named. Christ is very God, over against every form of Ebionism and Arianism: He is very man, over against every species of Gnosticism: He is the God-man in *one* person, in direct opposition to Nestorianism. The Holy Ghost is God, yet personally *distinct* from the Father and the Son,—not a mere manifestation, not a mere influence,—in opposition to every form of ancient Sabellianism and modern Unitarianism.

Throughout, God is acknowledged to be the *sovereign* Creator and Preserver of the universe; His grace is *sovereign;* the doctrine of election, according to His *sovereign* purpose, must stand. To Him belong all the praise and all the glory of our salvation. Yet the doctrine of human accountability is not ignored. Man is responsible for his actions, and must in the last day give an account for all the deeds done in the body. It has been said by some that the doctrine of predestination, though taught in the Catechism, is kept in the background; and others have maintained that it does not contain this doctrine at all. Such difference of sentiment, however, is not surprising; for even the word of God has been differently interpreted in regard to the same point. Much depends upon the spectacles a man has on when he reads. Those who wear Arminian glasses find no predestination either in the Catechism or in the Epistles of St. Paul; whilst those of the opposite school find it in both. It must be said in commendation of the Catechism that it avoids all the knotty points of Calvinistic predestination, whilst at the same time it embodies the doctrine fully as it is contained in the Scriptures: in this respect it is strictly Pauline.*

The doctrine of justification by faith through grace, in opposition to the Jewish notion of justification by works, seems to be the point on which the whole system turns. With this every other doctrine here symbolized stands in living connection. Hence the Catechism, from beginning to end, proves itself to be decidedly Protestant.

In developing the doctrine of the Lord's Supper, it avoids the extreme of consubstantiation and transubstantiation on the one hand, and the shallow spiritualistic view, on the other hand, which makes the elements a mere commemoration of the Saviour's sufferings and death. The sacraments have an objective meaning; they are really grace-bearing. Baptism is the sign and *seal* of the grace of regeneration, and the holy supper is the sign and *seal* of the grace of communion. "The bread which we break, is it not the communion of the body of Christ? The cup of blessing which we bless, is it not the communion of the blood of Christ?" In regard to the real presence of Christ in the supper there was no difference of opinion really. The only question was, whether the communication is oral or by faith. The Calvinistic view in regard to this doctrine has now come to obtain in the entire Reformed Church.

These specifications, without naming any of the other doctrines contained in the Catechism, are sufficient to show that, whilst it grounds itself mainly upon, and is in harmony with, the Church's most ancient creed, *it has at the same time the word of God as its norm.* We retain it, there-

---

* See Dr. Nevin's Hist. and Gen. of the Heid. Cat., p. 131.

fore, as a most precious legacy, believing it to be, in the full sense of the expression,—

"A form of sound words."

Our symbol of faith, then, being the product of the Christian life of the Church, it must follow that the kind of religious life which it cultivates can be none other than the Christian, and that the theory of practical religion which it assumes can be none other than the churchly. The blessed fruits of the Christian life gathered up in such comprehensive form contain necessarily the vital germ of their own kind: "a good tree bringeth forth good fruit;" and the seed of this again will, under favoring conditions, unfold its own peculiar life in the form of other trees like the first. So the general life of the kind individualizes itself indefinitely. "And God said, Let the earth bring forth grass, the herb yielding seed, the fruit-tree yielding fruit after his kind, whose seed is in itself upon the earth; and it was so." We do not mean by this illustration to convey the idea that our Confession of Faith has produced literally other confessions of the same kind, —which is nevertheless true to some extent, as the history of the Second Helvetic, the Gallic and Scottish Confessions abundantly proves; but we mean to say that the Cate-chism reproduces the Christian life and spirit which it embodies in the hearts and lives of thousands and millions of people who are enabled by faith to apprehend its meaning. As it symbolizes the Christian life and doc-trine, these when taken up by the people must needs bring forth fruit of their own kind, namely, of righteous-ness and true holiness. Our holy Christian religion is something vastly more than mere doctrine and precept: it is life and power taking its character directly from its glorious Author. As He is the God-man, so His religion is the DIVINE-HUMAN; as His union with humanity is personal, so His union with believers is vital. Hence Christianity is the absolute religion over against Judaism and all forms

376

of paganism. This is more than intimated in the sublime language of the first question and answer of the Catechism: "What is thy only comfort in life and in death? *Ans.* That I, with body and soul, both in life and in death, am not my own, but belong to my faithful Saviour Jesus Christ, who, with His precious blood, has fully satisfied for all my sins, and redeemed me from all the power of the Devil; and so preserves me that, without the will of my Father in heaven, not a hair can fall from my head; yea, that all things must work together for my salvation; wherefore, by His Holy Spirit, He also assures me of eternal life, and makes me heartily willing and ready henceforth to live unto Him."

This certainly does not merely mean that we belong to our Saviour as property belongs to its owner, or as the servant belongs to his master; but we belong to Christ as the branches belong to the vine, and as the members belong to the body. He is the vine, and we are the branches; He is the head, and we are the members: and as the branches cannot bring forth fruit except they abide in the vine, no more can we, except we abide in Christ. It is by virtue of this inward life-union that God, in the gift of His Son, has with Him also freely given us all things. (Rom. viii. 32.)

The same vital truth is also brought clearly to view in the thirty-second question and answer: "Why art thou called a Christian? *Ans.* Because by faith I am a member of Christ, and thus a partaker of His anointing; that I also may confess His name; may present myself a living sacrifice of thankfulness to Him; and may with free conscience fight against sin and the Devil in this life, and hereafter in eternity reign with Him over all creatures." No language could well be employed to convey more forcibly the idea that the life of Christ is made over to His people, and that they are thus mystically united to His person: His life is their life, and their spirits are merged into His Spirit. The life of Christ as thus made over to

His people, though essentially *one*, unfolds itself in a three-fold form. As He is the absolute prophet, priest, and king, those who are baptized into His mystical body by the Holy Ghost are also in Him made prophets, priests, and kings unto God. As He is the Christ, so they are Christians. This statement, without carrying out these ideas in detail, gives us the true conception of the Christian religion. As said before, it is something more than knowledge and precept, and, it should be added here, it is something vastly more, too, than mere moral feeling and moral practice, though it unfolds itself in the form of feeling, knowledge, and practice: it is the life of God in man,—not the life of God in man, either, out of Christ,—not a life communicated by the Holy Ghost even apart from Christ,—but the life of God in *Christ* as He is formed in His people the hope of glory by the Holy Ghost. Such is Christianity, in distinction from Judaism and paganism, and in opposition also, we would here add, to every form of abstract spiritualism; and such is the kind of religious life which the Catechism cultivates. Christ Jesus is the life of all believers, and at the same time He is the heavenly bread by which this life is nourished. So the Catechism, which symbolizes Christ and the doctrines of His word, is the form also in which the heavenly manna is communicated for the nourishment of God's spiritual Israel whilst they sojourn upon the earth.

Hence we find that wherever the Catechism is faithfully used, whether in the instruction of the baptized children of the Church or in the further indoctrination of adult believers, there the cause of Zion prospers; there we find the membership of the Church rooted and grounded in the faith,—not easily blown about by adverse winds of doctrine, but usually steadfast, unmovable, always abounding in the work of the Lord, serving Him in reverence and humility. It is a fact sustained by observation that those members of our Church who are grounded in the doctrines of the Catechism are usually much more consistent and

378

efficient than those who have not been thus instructed. I
am glad to know that the number of those last named is
not large; yet there are some such in certain localities. It
is a fact, too, worthy of notice, that in those instances where
the indoctrinated youth of our Church have made a profession of faith by uniting with other denominations of Christians (as is often the case in the distant West), they are
generally among the most active and consistent, and,
whilst scores and hundreds of new converts fall away, they
maintain their integrity, for the obvious reason that they
know in whom they have believed.

The theory of practical religion which the Catechism
assumes may be readily inferred. It knows of no practical
religion excepting that which is the legitimate fruit of
Christianity as it exists in the form of the Church, "the
body of Christ, the fulness of Him that filleth all in all." As
there can be no Christian religion without the Christos, so
it cannot actualize itself practically in the world excepting
in the form ordained by its holy Author. This embraces
the entire complexity of those divinely ordained means of
grace which are always at hand in the sanctuary. This
conception of the Church as an organism of gracious means
involves, of course, the idea of a congregation or membership to whom the means are administered, and also the
idea of a ministry *ordained to dispense* these means of grace.
As the city must have its citizens and its office-bearers, as
well as its peculiar regulations and privileges, so the Christian Church, the City of the New Jerusalem, which cometh
down from above, must have its inhabitants, breathing its
heavenly air, obeying its laws, and enjoying its blessings.
In both relations all live and have their being in God; but
in both relations God sustains life, not immediately, but
mediately. He does not hold men in this *natural* sphere
of existence as in a prison, sending at intervals the food
convenient for them from the spirit-land, but He uses
nature itself as the general medium through which He
satisfies the wants of His creatures.

But what theory of practical life does the great symbolical book of nature assume? Does it assume the theory that human life can be sustained and unfold its powers in the absence of all means of subsistence and in the absence of all conditions? Does it assume the theory that it has the source of all life in itself, and that men will find the "*highest good*" in this world? Does it teach that the medium through which Jehovah sustains life *is the life?* No one in a Christian land would, certainly, so far stultify himself as to answer either one of these questions in the affirmative. Yet, strange to tell, the very errors here indicated prevail to an alarming extent in regard to the new creation in Christ Jesus. The Church is often defined to be "the collective body of believers," those using this language perhaps not dreaming at the time that the sentiment expressed is separatism of the purest water. According to this view, the Church is nothing more than a voluntary association, held together or separated into parties by considerations of interest or expediency. If it be deemed expedient for all to remain together in one organization, well; but if it be deemed expedient to divide into different denominations, or sects even, so let it be: all must be regarded then as the "different divisions of the same grand army going forth to fight the battles of the Lord." What a splendid illustration this! How often used, and how popular! What a romance gathers around the idea of the great Captain of our salvation, now entirely separated from the world of sense, nevertheless leading on the hosts of God (we dare not say sacramental hosts) to victory merely by the force of the example set before them more than eighteen hundred years ago! But, unfortunately, each party will only fight in its own way and with weapons of its own choosing. Great respect must also be had to the single person: he is an independent sovereign within himself. He has the right to interpret the example and the commands of his Lord for himself: God is a Spirit, and by an immediate influence He leads his people into all truth, though by

380

different ways. Thus the view here under consideration runs itself out into individualism and abstract spiritualism. The means of grace in the sanctuary are ignored or trampled under foot, and religion is nothing more than a gnostic dream. Of such a theory the Catechism knows nothing, except to condemn it. With the opposite extreme—the view, namely, that the Church is the mediatrix between Christ and His people—the Catechism has not the least sympathy, either. According to this view, the Church saves; her ministers have power to forgive sin; the sacraments are not holy visible signs of an invisible grace, but they are the grace. Baptism is regeneration, and the elevated host is Christ. The office-bearers have unlimited authority; the ideas of office and of the Church are identical; her authority is supreme, and her decisions are infallible. If she decides that the Virgin Mary is immaculate, then she *is* immaculate. If she canonizes saints, then they are saints indeed. If she works miracles, whether of healing the diseased or raising the dead, then the diseased are healed and the dead are restored to life.

Over against these opposite views the Catechism acknowledges a polar relation between the Church as nourishing mother, and the aggregate of her membership. According to Dr. Ebrard, "the Church comes from faith, and faith comes from the Church. She includes in her communion the assembly of believers, whilst she is at the same time the form in which the Saviour gathers those who are without into His kingdom. In truth the Church does not save, but she renders it possible to exercise saving faith; and in truth the Church is not saved, but she contains a membership who have the means at hand by which they may be saved." Hence "the articles of our undoubted Christian faith all sustain an organic relation to the person of Christ, and the article concerning the Church stands in immediate connection with the Holy Ghost, who proceeds from the Father and the Son." "I believe in the Holy Ghost, in the Holy Catholic Church;" *i.e.*, the Church is the sphere in which the Holy Ghost fulfils His office. By the means here ordained He convinces of sin, of righteousness, and a judgment to come. He regenerates by moving upon the waters of the baptismal fountain. As it is written, "Except a man be born of water and of the Spirit, he cannot enter the kingdom of God." Or, as it is expressed in the language of the Catechism, Question 54: "What dost thou believe concerning the Holy Catholic Church? *Ans.* That out of the whole human race, from the beginning to the end of the world, the Son of God, by His Spirit and word, gathers, defends, and preserves for Himself, unto everlasting life, a chosen communion, in the unity of true faith; and that I am and forever shall remain a living member of the same." We perceive that God does not gather and preserve the Church by His Spirit alone, but by the Spirit and word. Then, again, the word or preached gospel is confirmed by the sacraments, according to the 65th Question and Answer. "Since then we are made partakers of Christ and all His benefits by faith only, whence comes such faith? *Ans.* The Holy Ghost works the same in our hearts by the preaching of the holy gospel and confirms it by the use of the holy sacraments." Here we have the whole theory of practical religion which the Catechism assumes,—viz.: *the sacramental or churchly*, in opposition to separatism on the one hand and *"panchristism"* on the other. According to this view, Christ is not merely the life of His people, but He also permeates by His Spirit the entire organism of the Church as the institution of gracious means. He is the regenerating and sanctifying power which makes these means effectual by the Spirit. "He is the only mediator between God and man;" whilst the Church, not as mediatrix, but as "the mother of us all," is the form in which He carries on, by the Holy Ghost, His mediatorial work. From this it is sufficiently plain that the practical religion which is of the churchly order is altogether a different thing from the unchurchly piety of which we have so many specimens

382

at the present day. This last named is the religion merely of spiritual influences, of happy feelings and emotions, and of a tolerably decent and respectable morality. Its subjects are upright in their deportment, honest in their dealings, and liberal in their views. But they know nothing of erecting churches, neither do they go to church. They usually build splendid "meeting-houses," and place in them seats for the hearers and a stand for the speaker. They do not neglect the assembling of themselves together; they go in crowds to hear the eloquent Mr. Cicero or Demosthenes, but these are, of course, just men like other men, except that they are to be respected for their learning and their oratory. O God, is this the religion of thy dear Son? No, no! Christianity never has existed in the world, and never can exist, except in the form of the Church; it must, like all other forms of life, have its body. Hence Christ is not to be found at all, His Spirit does not regenerate or save at all, except in the Church. Hence the Christian religion moves its subjects to erect houses of worship; to place in them not only seats for the hearers, but an altar for the sacrament and a pulpit for the ambassador of Christ. They go to the sanctuary, to lay upon its altar, as the true priests of God, their offerings of thanksgiving and praise, i.e. to worship the Most High in spirit and in truth. They go there that they may hear the word of Christ from the lips of His ambassador, i.e. to hear the "minister of the true tabernacle which the Lord pitched, and not man." In short, the practical religious life of Christians is but the repetition of the Saviour's life, or its actualization, rather, in time. As He was conceived by the Holy Ghost, and born of the Virgin Mary, so He is reborn in His people by the same Spirit moving upon the waters of the sanctuary. As He led a righteous and blameless life, so they, being justified by faith in Him through grace, walk in the way of God's commandments. As He was the great Teacher, so they learn from Him as humble disciples, that they may in the spirit of true prophecy teach others the wonderful truth of God. As He, the great High-Priest, suffered and died upon the cross to atone for the world's sin, so they bear about His dying, and are crucified to the world more and more. And, finally, as He arose from the grave leading captivity captive, so by the power of His life they arise from the grave of spiritual death, and will ultimately triumph over the grave, to live and reign forever in heaven as priests and kings unto God.

384

THE

HEIDELBERG CATECHISM

IN ITS

RELATION TO OTHER CONFESSIONS.

By PROF. E. V. GERHART, D.D.
LANCASTER, PA.

HEIDELBERG CATECHISM

IN ITS RELATION TO OTHER CONFESSIONS.

By Prof. E. V. Gerhart, D.D., Lancaster, Pa.

THERE are two general methods which we may adopt in an endeavor to set forth the relation of the Heidelberg Catechism to other confessions. We may take up the principal characteristics of our symbol of faith in logical order, and compare them with corresponding characteristics of other confessions, in order to show the points of resemblance and difference. This method would lead us into details, and require a small volume in order to make the investigation complete, or, if compressed within narrow limits, would be incomplete and unsatisfactory.

According to the other method we seek to determine the ruling principle, or germ, of the Heidelberg Catechism, and, following the historical order, compare it with the ruling principle of other confessions,—either with that of each one singly, or with the ruling principle of classes or families of confessions. Thus we get a broad basis of judgment. We get an insight into the animating spirit of confessions relatively to each other. If the general comparison commend itself as sound, any one may, by reflection, enter into details for himself, and determine points of resemblance and difference.

We propose to pursue the latter method, as being, on the whole, better adapted to the circumstances and design of the occasion.

THE APOSTLES' CREED.

What is the theory of Christianity which underlies, pervades, and governs the Heidelberg Catechism? What place does the Apostles' Creed occupy, and what relation does it bear to the matter and form, or to the doctrine of the Catechism and the manner in which it is taught? These questions are but two ways of presenting the same idea; for the Creed answers to Christianity as the eye does to the light.

The Creed is the vision of faith. Faith beholds the eternal Son of God, the Father Almighty, becoming true man, living, teaching, suffering, dying, descending into the grave and into hades, rising, ascending on high, and sitting on the throne of glory. Faith beholds the outpouring of the Holy Ghost, the founding of the Church, and the forgiveness of sins, and the new life signified and sealed in holy sacraments. Turning from the past to the future, faith beholds the Son of Man coming again from heaven with all His holy angels, calling forth the dead from their graves, the just and the unjust, and consummating the new creation in the destruction of His enemies, the perfection and glorification of all His people, the burning up of the natural world under the law of sin, and the bringing in of the new heavens and the new earth under the law of life. The mystery of the new creation in time, in all its integral parts, past, present, and future, beginning and centring in the person of Jesus Christ, stands before the eye of faith a real, concrete, supernatural, imperishable order of spiritual being, which unfolds the fulness of its grace for man according to a law which is at the same time both divine and human.

The Creed *comprehends* those who say: I believe in God, and in Jesus Christ, and in the Holy Ghost. It is the language of a member of the kingdom of heaven; not of one who stands outside of its communion, and looks upon it with the eye of natural reason. To be in the kingdom is the condition of seeing the kingdom, its Head and King, its law, and order, and glory. The eye which is filled with light can see the light; no other. The individual is a member of the race which he sees, knows, and loves. The entire human race, in its historical development, its present division into nationalities, and future prospects, stands before his mind an organic whole; yet it has generated him and bears him in its bosom. The same relation the Creed bears to those who confess it, or Christianity to those who believe it and know it. The Creed is the immediate utterance or confession of the objective truth which those see and possess, who have become participants of the substance of Christianity by the sacraments and ordinances of the Church.

Christianity presupposes the fall of man, by transgression, from a state of original holiness and righteousness; a consequent general corruption of human nature, so radical and entire as to render salvation impossible by mere human power; and the dominion of sin unto death in all relations, social, civil, and moral. From this great misery we are delivered by Christ. Hence the Creed does not teach, but assumes, the fact of the fall; the presence of the principle of sin; the prevalence of transgression; the reign of death; and the consequent necessity of a Redeemer who is very God and very man. It does not include any thing that belongs to the kingdom of evil, the negative side of the world's life, but refers to it only by necessary implication. It includes only the positive side of the world's life,—that supernatural order of objects which counteracts and annuls the fall, supplants and destroys the principle of sin by the principle of life, takes away the guilt of. transgression, and transforms death into a glorious resurrection.

Nor does the Creed unfold the external life of believers. It teaches no moral precepts. It does not enforce the Decalogue. It does not describe the fruits of the Spirit. Not because the Decalogue and holy living are unimportant and unnecessary, but because they do not belong to the proper object of saving faith. The Decalogue does not introduce the necessity of redemption, nor does it redeem men. Christ alone, in all the acts of His mediatorial work, including His mystical body, the Church, with all its supernatural powers and triumphs, is the object on which the faith which saves can fasten. Love to the law of God, and obedience to His requirements, follow as a consequence, and as a certain consequence; the relation between true faith in Christ and holiness of life being the same as that which subsists between the germ of a tree and the fruit which grows on its branches.

THE CATECHISM AND THE CREED.

A comparison of these general characteristics of the Creed with the Heidelberg Catechism shows the relation which they sustain to each other. These general characteristics constitute the distinctive features of the Catechism. Or, rather, the peculiar character of the Catechism is derived from the peculiar character of the Creed. The Creed is in the Catechism not merely as a compend of divine truth which is to be expounded and illustrated. It is not employed as a means of communicating theological and religious knowledge to learners. Nor is it in the Catechism as one of its primary elements, co-ordinate with all the rest, but subordinate to some general truth, which, as a principle, forms its character and governs its general order. Nor does the Creed stand in the Catechism because logically demanded by a metaphysical theory of Christianity, operating as a force outside of the Catechism itself, and requiring, according to the laws of thought, the particular position which it occupies, to the exclusion of all others. Least of all is the Creed included from respect to the most ancient symbol of faith, as if, had the authors chosen to do so, it could have been omitted without affecting the integrity of the work. Neither of these hypotheses can solve the problem.

The Creed is the central, vital force in the Catechism. It
is the organic principle, and develops its idea both negatively and positively,—negatively, in ruling out a purely
logical arrangement, and a merely theoretical conception
of Christianity; positively, in determining the general character, spirit, and order of the work,—and thus makes the
Catechism the legitimate, though not the perfect actualization of itself. Hence the Catechism comes to be, from
beginning to end, the confession of the believer in Jesus
Christ. Not an acknowledgment of the nature of sin and
guilt in general; not a statement of what the person of
Christ and the work of redemption are; not an exposition
of the law and the believer's obligation to fulfil its demands.
But, like the Creed, it is a personal confession,—an act of
faith in the true object of faith. The Creed begins: I believe in God the Father Almighty; and so continues: I
believe in the Holy Ghost; assuming that he who utters its
sublime language does not repeat a series of truthful propositions in logical connection, but is putting forth an act
of faith of his own, from the bottom of his heart, which
holds him in immediate communion with God in the person
of His Son. Such an act of faith cannot proceed from one
who is in the state of nature and under the curse, but can
come only from one who is in the state of grace and under
the law of the Spirit.

In full accordance with this idea, the Catechism begins
with the question: "What is *thy* only comfort in life and in
death?" and answers: "That *I*, with body and soul, both in
life and in death, am not my own, but belong to my faithful
Saviour Jesus Christ." In like manner it concludes with
the question: "What is the meaning of the word, Amen?"
Answer: "Amen means, so shall it truly and surely be; for
my prayer is much more certainly heard of God, than *I* feel
in my heart that I desire of Him these things." This idea
governs the manner in which all the questions and answers
are framed. It is throughout a personal act,—the confession
of one who stands in the kingdom and with the eye of the

spirit beholds the objects of Christian faith as his own possession.

Accordingly, the first answer—which is neither a logical introduction nor a logical conclusion, but a summary confession coming from the bosom of the Christian state, and with wonderful skill unites conciseness of expression with fulness of matter—proceeds on a threefold assumption: namely, that there is among men a universal sense of sin and misery; that there is a complete redemption from sin and misery by Jesus Christ; and that the catechumen is not in his natural condition, but in the covenant of grace, and is a child of God. The same presumption underlies the language of the Catechism in all its parts.

Occupying this central place, the idea or organic force of the Creed determines the order in which the truth is unfolded. The Creed, as we have seen, presupposes a state of sin and guilt. Hence it requires reflection upon sin, its origin and consequences, to come in the first part of the Catechism. Here, accordingly, we have an inquiry into the essence of the divine law; the creation of man after the image of God; the fall by instigation of the devil; human depravity; and the displeasure of God with our inborn as well as actual sins.

As true faith in Christ is the bond of vital union to His person, the Creed involves the necessity of obedience as a consequence flowing from this inward relation. Hence the Catechism places the necessity of conversion or repentance, the Ten Commandments, and the Lord's Prayer, in the third, or last, part; repentance, good works or obedience, and worship, being the legitimate effect and consequence of the new creation in Christ.

The Creed is neither more nor less than an act of faith put forth in the divine-human person of Christ, who is the central fact on which hinges the whole work of redemption, the knowledge of sin, and everlasting righteousness and salvation. Hence in the Catechism the Creed is central. It is the ruling principle, and holds the central place. Going

392

before it we have the fall and sin, which the Creed presupposes; sin being seen as such in the light of the law of God, which, as to its essence, requires love to God and love to man. Connected with the fall and the curse we have portrayed also the constitution and character which are necessary in a Saviour who might be adapted to the deep wants of the human race in its abnormal state. Coming after the Creed we have the fruits or consequences of faith in Christ, which the Creed involves and produces. The Creed itself lies between its presuppositions and consequences, and thus constitutes the second and main part of the Catechism. In immediate connection with it come the *sacraments* and the *keys*, which the Creed includes by necessary implication as the efficacious means of the Holy Ghost, by which children of believers are incorporated into the Christian Church and qualified for the exercise of true faith, instructed in the truths of redemption, nourished unto eternal life by the body and blood of Christ, and protected and defended in the midst of temptations and dangers by the remedial power of Christian discipline. As the result of such faith and grace, the child of God turns from the world, sin, and self with a penitent heart, seeks to fulfil the commandments of God as the exponent of love to Christ and the rule of a holy life, and presents himself an offering of thankfulness to God in prayer and praise.

The order of the Catechism is thus determined by the Creed, as by the power of an organic force. The arrangement is not made on the basis of an abstract theory. The arrangement is not mechanical. It does not proceed from the will of the authors. In fact, there is no arrangement at all. The word does not express the true relation of the parts to each other. An arrangement is a relation and connection of parts which is originated by the human reason, and executed by the human will. The determinative force is not in the thing, but outside of it; not internal, but external. In no such sense is the Creed a force regulating the relative position of the different parts of the Catechism. But the Creed is in the Catechism as life is in the body, as the will is in the reason, as thought is in language. It is the life-principle, and moulds the character and order of the Catechism not so much through the reflective and dialectic faculty of its authors as by the law of spontaneous growth. Ursinus and Olevianus did not possess and master the Creed, but the spirit of the Creed possessed and mastered them; elevating them measurably above the system of thought in which each one stood by education, transferring them into the sphere of the primitive faith of the Church, putting them under the power of a grand old idea, and working in them spontaneously in the conjoint process of production, as a self-determining force, in a manner and to an extent of which they themselves were not fully conscious.

THE CATECHISM CHRISTOLOGICAL.

This life-principle, faith in the divine-human person of our Lord Jesus Christ in the sense of the Apostles' Creed, we may call, by way of distinction, *christological*. But it is not such theologically, or philosophically. The person of Christ is the ground on which Christianity as such rests, and from which the spiritual order of the new creation, objectively considered, is developed and perfected. A scientific system governed by this idea of Christ as its law, and answering at all points to the objective verity, would be christological. But the Catechism is not such a scientific system. It does not aim at exhibiting the new creation in Christ as it is in itself. It is objective, indeed, but in the sense in which the Creed is objective. The Catechism is a view of the supernatural mystery revealing itself in the order of time on earth from the conception and birth of Christ to His final glorification. But it is not purely objective. It includes the subject of salvation in his immediate relation to the supernatural mystery. Hence the principle of the Catechism is also subjective. But in this

394

respect, as before, it is ruled by the Creed. It is not purely subjective. It does not turn on faith as its pivot, as is the case in the method of thought peculiar to Luther. It does not grow out of a feeling of entire dependence on God, like the system of Schleiermacher. It does not unfold merely the spiritual exercises, the thoughts, feelings, purposes, and diversified experiences, of the new creature in Christ, as is done in the larger part of the current religious literature of the day; but it turns the mind and heart of the believer away from himself, his feelings, hopes, fears, joys, and sorrows, to Christ, His incarnation, life, death, resurrection, ascension, and glory, and holds him in this relation of dependence, faith, and adoration from the commencement to the end of life, in time and in eternity,—his penitence, peace, strength, consolation, and joy proceeding not from reflection on his experience, but from a believing contemplation of the great mystery of godliness, the Son of God manifested in the flesh.

The principle of the Catechism unites these two elements. It is both objective and subjective. These two elements, however, it unites in a third, namely, the reciprocal relation of the object and the subject of salvation. The principle is not Christ as He is in Himself, nor yet the believer, but the peculiar internal relation of Christ and the believer, which is expressed by the word *faith*. We have the entire principle embodied in the language, "I believe in Jesus Christ, His only begotten Son, our Lord." *Jesus Christ* is the object; and as the Catechism contemplates His person and work as the central truth of Christianity, it is objective. *I* is the subject; and as the Catechism does not exhibit truth in general terms, but in the form of a direct confession on the part of the individual, it is subjective. The word *believe* expresses the relation of the individual believer to Jesus Christ; and as the entire Catechism is an act of faith, not reflection upon the truths of supernatural revelation from a point of observation external to its peculiar sphere, but an intelligent response to the incarnate Redeemer, coming forth from the bosom of the Christian Church, it is neither objective exclusively nor subjective exclusively, but the union of these two forces in the character of a vital relation. Not Christ as such, nor. faith as such, but faith in Christ, or Christ apprehended and appropriated by faith, is the point on which the structure of the Heidelberg Catechism turns, and from which it derives its peculiar spirit and distinguishing characteristics.

The germ of the Creed and of the Catechism we have in the memorable confession of St. Peter:—" Thou art the. Christ, the Son of the living God." To which Jesus answered, " Blessed art thou, Simon Barjona; for flesh and blood hath not revealed it unto thee, but my Father which is in heaven. And I say also unto thee, that thou art Peter; and upon this rock I will build my Church, and the gates of hell shall not prevail against it." (Matt. xvi. 16–19.) It is not the person of Christ, separately considered, that conditions the perpetuity and strength of the Church; much less is it Peter, the individual man; nor yet is it the sublime confession of Peter, taken by itself or in an abstract sense; but it is the true apprehension and the real, vital appropriation by faith of the Christ. Peter was the first one in whom Christ, the ground and substance of Christianity, became the subjective principle of human life,—the first one in whom the mysterious relation, which before was only a latent, unconscious life-bond of fellowship, developed itself into such clear, full consciousness that it became a spontaneous and intelligent public confession, " Thou art the Christ, the Son of the living God," the principle of communion thus. completing itself in the act of the apostle. In virtue of this real life-connection with the Son of God, he who already was called *Rock* became in reality *the rock* on which the Church is built, the firm, immovable foundation of the kingdom of God actualized on the earth among men. For it is this apprehension and appropriation of the Son of God by faith, this life-union of man with the incarnate Logos, in which the Church comes to be a fact in space and time, in which it has stood throughout all the ages past, still stands in vigor and beauty, and will stand in all the ages to come. And the gates of hell shall not prevail against it.

The Creed is the development of Peter's confession, conditioned by the various forces, positive and negative, which influenced the life and consciousness of the Church in the first centuries of its history. The Heidelberg Catechism is the organic expansion of the Creed, grounded in its idea and determined in its articulate parts by its spirit. Peter's confession is the tap-root, the Creed is the trunk, and the Catechism is the mature organism.

We do not affirm that the Catechism is a perfect organism, true at all points to the idea and spirit of the Creed. Whilst it does not comport with our design to inquire into its supposed deficiencies, we may, nevertheless, instance the answer to the forty-fourth question, concerning the descent into hades. The Creed follows the historic order of facts. The article concerning the suffering of Christ under Pontius Pilate comes after the article concerning His birth of the Virgin Mary and before the article concerning His crucifixion and death, and must, therefore, mean something different from both. It must refer to something which succeeded His birth and preceded His death. So the article on the descent into hell comes after the burial of Christ and before His resurrection from the dead. Unless we would convict the Creed of violating its own order, this article must designate a part of the work of Christ, which at His death He had not yet done, and which constitutes the transition from His burial to His resurrection. But here the Heidelberg Catechism falters. Influenced by the exposition of Calvin, as given in the Genevan Catechism,* our beautiful formulary fails to

---

* We quote the entire passage. "M. Quod de ejus *ad inferos descensu* mox adjectum est, quem sensum habet?

"P. Eum non communem tantum mortem fuisse perpessum, quæ est animæ

represent any new act of Christ. It returns to the cross, and expounds the intermediate act between the burial and resurrection to be equivalent to the suffering of the most painful death; thus repeating, substantially, the answers given to the thirty-seventh and thirty-ninth questions. The defect, however, is negative rather than positive. The forty-fourth answer teaches truth, but not that objective fact which confronts the eye of the Creed.

Its deficiencies to the contrary notwithstanding, we affirm that the idea of the Creed actualizes itself as a vitalizing and form-giving principle in the order, proportions, and doctrines of the Heidelberg Catechism, and determines its peculiar characteristics in a degree that distinguishes it from all other Reformed Confessions. Among the numerous catechisms and confessions to which the Reformation gave birth in the sixteenth and seventeenth centuries, it is the glory of the Heidelberg Catechism that it is pre-eminently the confession of the Apostles' Creed.

●

THE NICENE AND ATHANASIAN CREEDS.

The Apostles' Creed connects the Heidelberg Catechism with the two other œcumenical creeds, the Nicene and the Athanasian. The one adopted by the œcumenical Synod of Nice, A.D. 325, and of Constantinople, A.D. 381, was necessitated by the extensive prevalence of Arianism, and develops the faith of the original symbol in opposition to the manifold perversions of that insinuating and destructive heresy, affirming the Lord Jesus Christ to be the only begotten Son of God, God of God, Light of Light, very God of very

---

a corpore separatio, sed etiam *dolores mortis*, sicut Petrus (Act. ii. 24) vocat. Hoc autem nomine horribiles angustias intelligo, quibus ejus anima constricta fuit.

"M. Cedo mihi hujus rei causam ac modum.

"P. Quia, ut pro peccatoribus satisfaceret, coram Dei tribunali se sistebat, torqueri hac anxietate ejus conscientiam oportebat, acsi derelictus a Deo esset: imo acsi Deum haberet infestum. In his angustiis erat, quum exclameret ad Patrem: (Matt. xxvii. 46.) Deus meus, Deus meus, ut quid dereliquisti me?"—(Cat. Ecc. Gen. I. De Fide.)

God, begotten of the Father before all worlds, begotten, not made, of one substance with the Father, by whom all things were made; and the Holy Ghost to be the Lord, the Giver of life, who proceedeth from the Father and the Son, who with the Father and the Son together is worshipped. The other, originating a century later, in the midst of the fierce controversies between Eutychianism and Nestorianism and various cognate heretical tendencies, defines the Catholic faith concerning the Unity and Trinity of the Godhead in its positive and negative relations, with unequalled clearness, logical consistency, and exhaustive fulness. Both are the legitimate expansion and determination of the original faith in its points of divergence from the false thinking of the fourth and fifth centuries. Rooted in the Apostolum Symbolicum, they are governed by the same principle and follow each other in logical order, the Nicene Creed being more definite and full than the original symbol, and the Athanasian more determinate, exclusive, and complete than its immediate predecessor, the Nicene.

The Heidelberg Catechism stands in the Apostles' Creed in the sense of the Nicene and Athanasian Creeds, especially as regards the unity of essence and the distinction and equality of the persons of the Godhead. "The Catholic faith is this: that we worship One God in Trinity, and Trinity in Unity; neither confounding the persons nor dividing the substance." "Such as the Father is, such is the Son, and such is the Holy Ghost." The Father, Son, and Holy Ghost are each uncreated, unlimited, eternal, almighty, and God, yet not three Gods, but one God,—the Son the only begotten of the Father, not made, nor created, and the Holy Ghost proceeding from the Father and the Son, neither made, nor created, nor begotten. The Lord Jesus Christ is God and man,—God, of the substance of the Father, begotten before the worlds; and man, of the substance of His mother, born in the world: yet He is not two, but one Christ; one, not by conversion of the Godhead into flesh, but by assumption of the manhood into

God; one altogether, not by confusion of substance, but by unity of person.

In perfect accordance with this primitive, apostolic, and catholic faith, the Heidelberg Catechism teaches that the Father is God, the Son is God, and the Holy Ghost is God (Q. 24); that there is but one divine essence; that these three distinct persons, Father, Son, and Holy Ghost, are the one true and eternal God (Q. 25); that Christ alone is the eternal natural Son of God (Q. 33); that the eternal Son of God, who is and continues true and eternal God, took upon Him the very nature of man of the flesh and blood of the Virgin Mary, by the operation of the Holy Ghost (Q. 35); that though Christ according to His human nature is now not upon earth, but in heaven, and there continues in behalf of His people, yet the two natures are not separated from one another; for, since the divine nature is incomprehensible and everywhere present, it must follow that the same is indeed beyond the limits of the human nature He assumed, and yet is none the less in it also, and remains personally united to it (Q. 47 and 48); and that the Holy Ghost is coeternal God with the Father and the Son. These lucid and unequivocal statements separate the Catechism from the Ebionitic, Gnostic, Arian, Manichean, Eutychian, and Nestorian heresies of the first five centuries of the Christian era, and demonstrate its organic connection with the fundamental articles of the faith held in all ages of the Church.

THE CATECHISM AND THE TRIDENTINE DECREES.

In as far as the Church of Rome has remained faithful to the œcumenical creeds, there is no conflict between its confessional dogmas, as formally settled by the Council of Trent, and the Heidelberg Catechism. But as regards the doctrines and customs which are peculiar to the Romish Church, and distinguish it from the catholic faith of the post-apostolical period, the Catechism dissents and protests. It protests in form against the adoration of the Virgin, praying to the saints, the use of images in the Church as helps to worship; against the doctrine of justification by works, the *opus operatum* theory of the sacraments, the doctrine of transubstantiation, and the adoration of the Host. By necessary implication, the Catechism stands opposed to the papal and hierarchical system; to the Romish view of the fall, of depravity, and tradition; the immaculate conception of the Virgin; to all ceremonies and forms of worship not warranted by the Holy Scriptures; to the false prominence of the priestly function of the ministry, the mutilation of the Ten Commandments, the administration of the Lord's Supper in one kind, the doctrine of purgatory, the exclusive use of the Latin language in public worship, the spirit of persecution, the infliction of civil penalties upon heretics, and all other doctrines and practices which are peculiar to the Roman Catholic Church and distinguish it from the faith and worship of original Protestantism.

THE CATECHISM AND OTHER REFORMED CONFESSIONS.

The Reformation of the sixteenth century, though beginning simultaneously in different places, is to be viewed as one great religious movement common . to Germany, Switzerland, France, the Netherlands, England, and Scotland. It was a revival of the original life and faith of the Church in opposition to the errors and abuses of the papacy. Of this great movement the first authoritative exponent was the Augsburg Confession, written by Melanchthon, signed by the rulers of the German States, and presented to the Emperor, in German and Latin, at the celebrated Diet of Augsburg, in 1530. It set forth the doctrines, not of one part of the representatives of the Reformation, but of the princes, theologians, and pastors generally, as prevailing at that time, in all portions of the German Empire where the authority of Rome had been cast off, and belongs, therefore, of right, not to the Lutherans exclusively, but to the entire Protestant Church. It was afterward signed by Calvin, the Elector Frederick IH., Ursinus, Olevianus, and other eminent princes and theologians of the Reformed Church, as well as by the coadjutors and followers of Luther.

Nevertheless, there were two antagonistic tendencies at work from the beginning,—the one represented first by Zwingli, the other first by Luther; the central point of divergency being the Sacrament of the Lord's Supper. Whilst Luther taught that the veritable body and blood of Christ were present under the form of the emblems, bread and wine, Zwingli asserted, in opposition to him, that the emblems, bread and wine, were only bread and wine, and as such the signs and seals of the body and blood of Christ. They agreed in rejecting the Romish dogma of transubstantiation as contrary to the Scriptures. In the progress of their development, these two different tendencies came into collision unavoidably, and gave rise to fierce theological conflicts, social convulsions, and terrible wars, which sometimes threatened to engulf both parties in common ruin. But God ruled in the midst of the storm. The two tendencies, like two streams, continued to flow on in deeper, broader, stronger, and more clearly defined channels. The one tendency terminated and became complete finally in the Heidelberg Catechism, 1563; the other in the Form of Concord, 1580. The progress of the Reformation, on the contrary, caused a powerful reaction in the Romish Church against both tendencies and in favor of its own peculiar dogmas, customs, and practices, and completed itself finally in the Decrees of the Council of Trent, 1545–1563. These three symbolical productions, the Tridentine Decrees, the Heidelberg Catechism, and the Form of Concord, are analogous, each one being in fact and by general acknowledgment the mature result of a life-force working in the bosom of the Church antagonistically to the others.

According to this view, the Heidelberg Catechism sustains a relation to Zwingli's Sixty-Seven Articles, his Confession of Faith and the Exposition of his Confession, the First and Second Confessions of Basel, the Genevan Catechism, the Zurich and Genevan Consensus, the Gallic, Scotch, and Belgic Confessions, such as ripe fruit bears to the life of the tree on which it grows. On the Lord's Supper the doctrine of Zwingli was negative rather than positive. Opposing the doctrine of a literal manducation of the body of Christ, as held in different forms by Luther and the Roman Catholics, he laid special stress on the commemorative aspect of the ordinance, which was held in abeyance by Luther* and suppressed by the Church of Rome. As a consequence, he failed to do full justice to the other side of the truth.† He did not emphasize the

---

* Lutheran symbols fail to recognize the commemorative aspect of the Holy Eucharist altogether. In his Small Catechism, Luther, in answer to the question : Was ist das Sacrament des Altars ? says : " Es ist der wahre Leib und Blut unsers Herrn Jesu Christi, unter dem Brot und Wein, uns Christen zu essen und zu trinken von Christo selbst eingesetzt." This is the keynote to all subsequent confessional statements. The Large Catechism repeats and expounds the same definition, without including the idea of a sign. The Augsburg Confession says in the tenth Article : "De cœna Domini docent, quod corpus et sanguis Christi vere adsint et distribuantur vescentibus in cœni Domini ; et improbant secus docentes." The Apology teaches the same dogma, but is more definite and full, and supports it with quotations from St. Paul ; but there is no reference to the commemoration of the sufferings and death of Christ. The Form of Concord is more full and explicit than any preceding Confession, incorporating the definitions of Luther, of the Augsburg Confession, the Apology and the Smalcald Articles, and vindicating them in opposition to the theory of Zwingli and of all who would not affirm : " Sub pane, cum pane, in pane adesse et exhiberi corpus Christi." Quoting from Luther, the Book says : " Ich rechne Sie alle in einen Kuchen, das ist, für Sacramentirer und Schwärmer, wie sie auch sind, die nicht glauben wollen, dass des Herrn Brod im Abendmahl sei sein rechter natürlicher Leib, welchen der Gottlose oder Judas eben sowohl mündlich empfahet, als S. Petrus und alle Heiligen." (Die Symb. Bücher d. Ev. Luth. K., von J. T. Müller, Stuttgart, pp. 653, 654.) The Lutheran Church, accordingly, lays stress only on one side or aspect of the truth. The Lord's Supper is a communion, thus ignoring its correlative element : " Do this in remembrance of me."

† In his Sixty-Seven Articles Zwingli says (18) : " Ex quo colligitur missam non esse sacrificium, sed sacrificii in cruce semel oblati commemo-

sacrament as a communion of the body and blood of Christ.
Nor did he clearly recognize the truth underlying the perversions of Rome and the one-sided view of Lutherans.
Yet the teachings of Zwingli were not incompatible with
the theory of communion as subsequently developed by
Calvin and established by later confessions. The Zwinglian conception did not contain positive error, but it was
wanting in a just apprehension of the humanity of Christ,
as essential in the communion of the Lord's Supper. This
defect was in a great degree regulative in Switzerland
and other countries. It is seen particularly in Zwingli's
Confession and Exposition of Faith, and in the Zurich
Consensus. From year to year, however, the defect was
more deeply felt, and greater stress was laid on the sacrament as a communion of the body and blood of Christ.
The powerful influence of Calvin and Melanchthon served
to carry the general mind of the Church steadily forward
toward a positive completion of the Zwinglian idea. Of
this positive tendency the Heidelberg Catechism was the
final culmination. It unites organically three kindred
tendencies, the Zwinglian, Calvinistic, and Melanchthonian.
The Lord's Supper is a sign and a seal; it is a commemoration and a communion. The Catechism completes two

---

rationem et quasi sigillum redemptiones per Christum exhibitæ." The presence of Christ in the Eucharist he explains thus: "Credo quod in sacra
Eucharistiæ, hoc est gratiarum actionis cœna, verum Christi corpus adsit,
fidei contemplatione: hoc est, quod ii qui gratias agunt Domino pro beneficio
nobis in filio suo collato, agnoscunt illum veram carnem adsumpsisse, vere in
illa passum esse, vere nostra peccata sanguine suo abluisse, et sic omnem
rem per Christum gestam illis fidei contemplatione velut presentem fieri."
(Zwinglii Fidei Ratio: De Eucharistia.) "Spiritualiter edere corpus Christi,
nihil est aliud quam spiritu ac mente niti misericordia et bonitate Dei per
Christum." * * * "Sacramentaliter autem edere corpus Christi, cum pro-
prie volumus loqui, est, adjuncto sacramento, mente ac spiritu corpus Christi
edere." (Zwinglii Exp. Chr. Fidei: Præsentia Corp. Christi in Cœna.) The
Lord's Supper, according to Zwingli, is a communion no less than a commemoration ; but the communion is resolved into a believing contemplation of the
incarnation and work of Christ, which are vividly brought before the mind in
the sacramental transaction.

apparently contradictory theories, that of Zwingli and that of the Augsburg Confession. It completes the theory of commemoration as held by Zwingli, by uniting with it the Calvino-Melanchthonian idea; and it completes the theory of communion as taught in the altered Augsburg Confession, by uniting with it the Zwinglian idea, the one being complemental to the other. Thus in it the common faith of the non-Lutheran part of the Protestant Church obtained full and satisfactory expression; and, as a consequence, it is distinguished from all previous confessions, and, indeed, from all particular Reformed Confessions, in this, that it became, like its formative principle, the Apostles' Creed, the symbol of the entire Reformed Church on the continent of Europe and elsewhere.

There is another important distinction to be made. No previous Reformed confession or catechism is an organic whole developed from the Creed as its formative principle. All acknowledge its authority, either in form or by implication. The Genevan Catechism, prepared by Calvin, includes and expounds it. But no one grows forth from the Creed as the central, plastic, vitalizing power, according to the law of life. No one is governed by it as to the ordering of constituent parts and the manner of setting forth truth. Though the doctrines are, in one view, substantially the same as those taught in the Heidelberg Catechism, yet they rest on a different basis and are pervaded by a different spirit.

We select the Genevan Catechism for comparison, since in point of authority and influence it stands next to our symbol. As already stated, the Genevan Catechism incorporates the Creed, but only as one part of a general plan; and the general plan springs from a conception of Christianity which differs from that of the Creed. Christianity, it is said, is the method of rightly honoring God. This is done by having true faith in God; by conforming our lives to the law of God; by prayer in the hour of need; by seeking salvation and all good in Him; and, finally, by

acknowledging Him from the heart and by the mouth.*
According to this theoretical arrangement, which turns not
upon the mediation of Christ, but upon a certain conception of duty toward God, Calvin divides his Catechism
into five parts. The Apostles' Creed becomes the theme of
the first part, the Ten Commandments the theme of the
second, the Lord's Prayer of the third, the Holy Scriptures
of the fourth, and the Sacraments of Baptism and the
Lord's Supper the theme of the fifth or last part. The
Creed is not the principle of the order in which the parts
follow each other. The principle is an abstract idea, to
which the Creed, the Decalogue, the Lord's Prayer, the
Bible, and the Sacraments stand in a subordinate relation,
each element being co-ordinate to the others. These
elements furnish matter and serve as means, each in its
own plâce, for the development, not of a concrete fact, but
of a metaphysical system based on an unchristological
thought. The Heidelberg Catechism rests on no abstract
idea. It grows forth from the idea of the mystical union,
a concrete fact. Hence, though the Genevan Catechism
is one of the principal sources from which the matter of our
symbol is drawn, yet the order and genius of the two are
totally dissimilar. In our symbol, the law, sacraments,
and the Lord's Prayer occupy a different relative position,
have a different meaning, and serve a different purpose.
The Holy Scriptures come to view here and there in
the body of the work, and numerous references to the Old
and New Testament support the doctrines which the Catechism teaches, but they nowhere receive special consider-

---

* We quote Calvin's language : " M. Porro, quænam vera est ac recta Dei
cognitio ?
" P. Ubi ita cognoscitur, ut suus illi ac debitus exhibeatur honor.
" M. Quænam vero ejus rite honorandi est ratio ?
" P. Si in eo sita sit tota nostra fiducia : si illum tota vita colere, voluntati
ejus obsequendo, studeamus : si eum, quoties aliqua nos urget necessitas,
invocemus ; salutem in eo quærentes, et quicquid expeti potest bonorum : si
postremo, tum corde, tum ore illum bonorum omnium solum auctorem agno-
scamus." (Cat. Ecc. Gen. I., De Fide.)

ation, and that for the reason that they are only the infallible record of divine revelation, but do not constitute a part of the object and substance of saving faith. For want of time, however, we cannot enter further into particulars.

CALVINISM AND ARMINIANISM.

These broad differences arise from the fact that our symbol is not a theoretical system, but an organic growth of which the Creed is the life-principle. This life-principle, faith in the divine-human person of our Lord Jesus Christ, excludes not only the particular theory which underlies the Catechism of Geneva, but all metaphysical conceptions of Christianity. We would mention particularly the two leading conceptions which have originated and perpetuated divergent systems of theological science and practical religion in the bosom both of the Catholic and Protestant Church, and now are commonly known as the Calvinistic and Arminian systems. The one starts in the sovereign will of God, which becomes the foundation of Christianity, whether considered as it is in itself or as a saving power working in the hearts and lives of men. The other starts in the free will of man, and generates a well-defined system which differs from Calvinism at all points throughout. Both are alike, however, in quietly assuming that the ground and law of Christianity are to be found not in Christ, but outside of Him. The Heidelberg Catechism, in virtue of its principle, excludes both systems. On the one hand, it excludes the supralapsarian theory of election and reprobation; the doctrine of a limited atonement; effectual calling by the Holy Ghost working according to the sovereign pleasure of God independently of the instituted means of grace; and the certain perseverance of the believer unto the end; in the sense in which these doctrines are developed from Calvin's theory of the decrees and exhibited in the Confession of Faith of the Westminster Assembly. On the other hand, it also excludes

407

the doctrine of free will; election unto life conditioned by God's foreknowledge of the sinner's repentance; the view of the atonement which makes it an exemplification of God's abhorrence of sin and love of sinners, or a necessary expedient to subserve the purposes of the moral government of God; and the moral ability of the sinner to turn from the world and submit to Christ at will; as these doctrines stand, with more or less consistency and fulness, in the theories of Pelagius, Socinus, Arminius, and in all cognate systems of theology and religion. The principle of our symbol belongs neither to Calvinism nor Arminianism, considered as the opposite extremes of abstract metaphysical theorizing concerning the nature of Christianity.

THE CATECHISM AND LUTHERAN CONFESSIONS.

The Heidelberg Catechism differs from the Confessions of the Lutheran Church both as regards its general character and the statement of particular doctrines. Luther's Smaller Catechism consists of six parts: the first explains the Ten Commandments; the second, the Apostles' Creed; the third, the Lord's Prayer; the fourth, Holy Baptism; the fifth, Confession; and the sixth, the Sacrament of the Lord's Supper. The Larger Catechism of Luther follows the same arrangement, but omits confession, and has, consequently, only five parts. It differs from the Smaller Catechism only in being a fuller and more extended exposition of these elements of the Christian religion. Both are a collocation of these several elements on the principle that the law is in order to grace; or that the knowledge of the law is preparatory to the knowledge of Christ and the exercise of saving faith. Ruled by the Creed as its vital principle, our Catechism places the law in the third part, assuming that grace is in order to the law; or that the possession of the life of grace by personal union to Christ qualifies us to know and keep the law, in accordance with the historical fact that the Decalogue was given on Mount

Sinai to the chosen people of God, who stood in covenant-relation with Him, and not to the uncircumcised nations of the world. The difference is broad and important. Is the law a branch of the plan of redemption,—a subordinate part of the order of grace? and is it revealed as a consequence following from the giving of the great original promise, and the institution of the Church? Or is the law given by God immediately,—that is, without the previous revelation of redemption? is it given before the promise, and as the great means of preparing the world for the reception of grace and the exercise of faith? The Heidelberg Catechism affirms the first proposition and denies the second; the Catechisms of Luther would, by their arrangement, deny the first and affirm the second.

Besides, it deserves to be noted that our symbol, like the Catechism of Geneva and other Reformed Catechisms and Confessions, adopts the Ten Commandments, without change, from the twentieth chapter of Exodus, whilst Luther transferred them, in their mutilated form, directly from the Roman Catholic Church, which omits the second commandment, substitutes the third for the second, the fourth for the third, and so on to the tenth, which is divided, the first clause being substituted for the ninth commandment, and the second clause standing for the tenth, thus completing the whole number. The Catechisms of Luther became a model in the Lutheran Church. The Form of Concord, the ultimate standard of the Lutheran faith, follows the same general arrangement, and, like other Lutheran Confessions, omits the second commandment.

CONCLUSION.

It would now be interesting and instructive to enter into further details. But it is the chief design of this essay to examine into the relation of our Formulary to other Confessions merely as to the general principles which govern their character respectively. Nor do we wish to occupy an undue proportion of the time of the Convention. Hence we hasten to conclude.

As among the earlier Reformed Confessions, so in the Catechisms of the Lutheran Church, and also in those of the Westminster Assembly, we look in vain for that immediate relation of the believer to our Lord Jesus Christ, the object of faith, which characterizes and distinguishes the Heidelberg Catechism. Luther's Catechisms proceed 'in general terms, and in the use of the third person. So does the Shorter Catechism of the Presbyterian Church. So do all the principal Catechisms of the Protestant Church. But, under the special direction of Divine Providence, our venerable symbol caught the genuine spirit of the Apostles' Creed. This spirit has given to it its extraordinary character. Like the loving John among the disciples of our Lord, like the Creed itself among the ancient symbols, the Heidelberg Catechism rises to view prominently among the Confessions of the Protestant Church, as uttering the faith of our Lord Jesus Christ in the language and catholic spirit of prophets and apostles, martyrs, confessors, and saints of all ages.

410

THE

HEIDELBERG CATECHISM

IN THE

REFORMED CHURCH OF HOLLAND AND AMERICA.

BY REV. THOMAS DE WITT, D.D.
NEW YORK.

THE HEIDELBERG CATECHISM IN THE REFORMED CHURCH OF HOLLAND AND AMERICA.

By Rev. Thomas De Witt, D.D,. New York.

THE Tricentenary of the Heidelberg Catechism, proposed to be observed by the German Reformed Church in North America, will prove an interesting event. It will be so to the Christian Church at large on account of the historical associations with which it stands connected, the character which it possesses, and the position which it occupies. To the Churches in which it has been the recognized standard during the three centuries of its existence it must be one replete with gratification and benefit.

I have been requested to contribute a short paper, to be added to those which are prepared, or are in preparation, to be submitted to the Convention which will assemble at Philadelphia on the 19th instant. I learn that various topics have been assigned to distinguished ministers, both in Germany and America, whose papers will prove exhaustive both as to the extent of investigation and as to the ability with which it is prosecuted. All that remains for me is to refer to the introduction of the Catechism into the Reformed Church of Holland, and the use which has continued to be made of it there and here in America. As the introduction of the Catechism into the Reformed Church of the Palatinate and into the Reformed Church of Holland was almost simultaneous,. it is proper to trace their previous affinity.

The northeastern and eastern portion of Holland, and the western part of Germany adjacent, were a favored field where the seed of evangelical truth was sown, which sprang up at the Reformation. "*The Brethren of the Common Lot*" took their rise in the fourteenth century, under the leading of Geert Groete, Radewyn, and others. They were natives of Holland. In the seminaries at Deventer and Zwolle large numbers of youth were trained, who went forth to promote practical piety and the cause of popular education. The *fraterhuysen*, or brethren-schools, were established in many parts of Eastern Netherlands and Western Germany. Thomas á Kempis was a pupil of Radewyn, and Erasmus of Hegius.

In the year 1366 the University of Heidelberg was founded. During the first century of its existence it did not excel others, but after that it made rapid advancement. This was greatly owing to the celebrated Hollander *Wessel* Gansevoort of Groningen, who was for a time at Cologne, and afterward Professor at Heidelberg, where he delivered lectures on philosophy and theology, bearing his testimony against the corruptions of the Church at Rome, and replete with evangelical sentiment. He was termed the "Morning Star" of the Reformation in Holland and Germany; and Luther remarked that if he had seen the works of Wessel before he had published his own it might have been supposed that he had drawn copiously from him. A full account of the life, labors, and writings of Gansevoort, as well as a sketch of the character and useful labors of the "Brethren of the Common Lot," are found in Ullman's valuable work "The Reformers before the Reformation." His successor was *Rudolph Agricola*, also of Groningen, who was a distinguished classical scholar, and followed in his footsteps in the advocacy and diffusion of evangelical doctrine and the exposure of the corruptions of the Church of Rome. John Reuchlin, another pupil of Gansevoort, officiated for some time at Heidelberg with great reputation and usefulness. These three, with doubtless others, exerted an influence in advancing the revival of letters and the diffusion of sound theology. In the University there were

414

received many youths who were afterward prominent in the work of the Reformation, as Melanchthon, Pelican, Bucer, &c. in Germany, and Junius and others, who became professors in the recently organized universities of Franeker and Leyden.

The country bordering on the eastern part of Holland and the western part of Germany became thus prepared to receive the influence of the Reformation, as already its principles had become planted and, to some degree, extended. From Embden in East Friesland, bordering on Holland, proceeded some of the earliest influences which led to the formation of the Reformed Church of Holland in the character it assumed; and so also of the Church of the Palatinate. In these and adjacent parts the Platte or Low German language prevailed, which is greatly assimilated to that used in Holland, and in their frequent intercourse characteristic customs were found. The oppression and persecution exerted by Spanish and Papal power under Charles V. and Philip II. over the Protestants in the Netherlands were in their severity almost exterminating, as will be found vividly exhibited in *Motley's Dutch Republic* and Watson's Philip II. The policy of Charles V. and his successor Ferdinand was to pursue a less severe and more conciliating course. In this state of things, many of the Protestants of the Netherlands fled to East Friesland and along the Rhine, in Westphalia, &c. Others sought refuge in England. The labors and writings of Luther exerted a strong influence. Toward the middle of the sixteenth century numerous refugees went to England, and received protection and privileges from the young King Edward. The main church organization was in London, in 1550, where the Austin Friars was furnished to them as a house of worship. John a Lasco, from Embden, was the superintendent, associated with three other ministers, who were originally Hollanders. The leading elder was John Uytenhuysen, distinguished for his character, acquirements, and the important service he rendered to the cause of the Reformation. The church in London, under the superintendence of A Lasco, mainly consisted of refugees from the Netherlands. There was a volume published a few years since in London, giving an account of the churches formed in England by the refugee Protestants in the sixteenth century,—Dutch, Huguenot, Swiss, &c.: quite a space is given to the Church of Austin Friars, furnishing a list of its members to the present time, its early statistics, &c. In 1553 the church numbered about eight hundred. After the death of King Edward, and the accession of bloody Queen Mary, the church became dispersed and weakened. After the accession of Queen Elizabeth it revived and increased, and remains at the present the Reformed Dutch Church at Austin Friars. It was formed under rules of church government and a liturgy which, on the return of A Lasco and Mikron, were introduced and incorporated into the Order and Liturgy of the Churches of the Palatinate and Holland. I lately met with a small volume in the Dutch language, printed in 1564, entitled, Christelike Ordinantien der Nederlandsche Gemeenten Christi die van de Christelike Prins Edward VI. te London opgestelt was (Christian Ordinances of the Netherlands Church of Christ, instituted by King Edward VI. at London). I found the liturgy comprised in it almost identically the same with that adopted by the Reformed Church of Holland, and, I believe, mainly so with the Liturgy of the Palatinate. The larger catechism by A Lasco, and the smaller by Mikron, prepared and used in London, were introduced and generally used in the Netherlands.

Owing to the severity of the raging persecution, the scattered Protestants in the Netherlands formed separate church organizations, necessitated to avoid publicity, and terming themselves Die Kerken Christi onder het Kruys (the Churches of Christ under the Cross). Their first General Synod was held at Antwerp in 1566. A few years after this they were under the dreadful power of the Duke of Alva, who remains infamously distinguished as exceeding the persecutors of all ages. In consequence, the next General Synod, in 1568, was held at Embden, in East Friesland, and that of 1571 at Wesel, on the Rhine, in Germany.

A colony of Refugee Protestant Hollanders was founded at Frankenthal, near Heidelberg, under the protection of the Elector Palatine, who held friendly and intimate communion with their German neighbors in the bonds of a common faith. Among the distinguished ministers who served at that time at Frankenthal were *Peter Dathenus* and Casper Vanderheyden (or Heidanus), afterwards noted among the Churches of Holland. After the preparation of the Catechism by Ursinus and Olevianus, under the authority of the pious Elector Frederick, it was submitted for inspection, and, if needed, revision, to the leading ministers, among whom are the above-named. In the very year of its publication, 1563, it was translated into Latin, and also by Dathenus into the Dutch language. Dathenus was the author of the version of the Psalms into Dutch, which version was used in the music of the Church until 1772. Very shortly after, he published the version of the Psalms set to music, and affixed thereto the Confession of Faith which was adopted in 1562, and the Liturgy. This soon gave wide currency to the Catechism among the Protestants of Holland. In the National Synod of 1568, and again of 1571, &c., the Catechism and the Belgic Confession of Faith were formally and authoritatively adopted as standards of doctrine, and so continued to be held and observed. At first ministers and professors of theology were required to sign a prescribed formula of assent to these standards, and afterward elders, schoolmasters, &c. were enjoined to do the same. The Remonstrants, at the opening of the seventeenth century, in connection with the controversies which had arisen, solicited a revision and amendment of the Heidelberg Catechism. When this matter was brought before the National Synod held at Dort in 1618 and 1619, after a careful examination and free discussion, the Catechism was unanimously approved without the least alteration, and the delegates from abroad (especially those from England) were earnest in their eulogy of its great merits. The delegates from the Palatinate were instructed to protest against any alteration. The delegates were of high distinction,—Abraham Scuttetus, Henry Alting, ministers, and Paul Tossanus, Professor in the University, an elder. David Paræus, the editor of the lectures of Ursinus on the Catechism, was appointed a delegate; but being unable to attend, on account of his advanced age and infirmity, he sent an admirable letter of some length, giving his views on the points before the Synod. John Ursinus, son of Zacharias Ursinus, author of the Catechism, was one of the early ministers of Amsterdam, filling his office with great acceptance. In the early part of the seventeenth century the Palatinate was brought under a new government, and new rules were adopted, hostile to the Protestant interest. As in the period of the Reformation, when the Netherlands were so sorely oppressed and crushed by persecution, Heidelberg supplied well-trained ministers for their churches "under the cross," so now the universities of Holland returned the benefit to the churches of the Palatinate and its vicinity.

The fact that this Catechism was in a short period translated into a number of the languages of Europe, bears strong testimony to its intrinsic merit. At what time it was translated into English I have no means of ascertaining. I have in my possession a translation of the notes, attached to the Dutch Bible, as prepared by the translators and revisers appointed by the Synod of Dort, in 1619, who, after great labor, caution, and care, finished it in 1637. This translation is considered to be one of the best to be found, and the accompanying notes are exceedingly judicious and comprehensive. The translation is by Theodore Haak, and is recommended by a large number of the prominent members of the Westminster Assembly, during the sessions of which it was published. I incidentally found in a note an allusion to an existing English translation, which doubtless was of an earlier date. It is probably the same with that in the books used in the English and Scotch Churches in Holland connected with the Classes and containing the standards and liturgy. The translation in the book used in our churches in America was prepared by a committee of the Consistory of New York, and published in 1767. English preaching was first introduced in 1764, by the call of Dr. Laidlie from Holland. He was born and educated in Scotland, and settled over the Scotch Church at Flushing, in Holland, for a number of years. As chairman of the committee, he was the reviser of the translation.

In Holland a small volume was early prepared, containing in two parallel columns the Latin and Greek translations of the Confession of Faith, Catechism, and Liturgy, to be used in the schools. *In usum scholarum* is broadly inscribed on it, and doubtless it was employed in teaching these languages in their schools and academies. The earliest Synods at the Reformation paid particular attention to measures for extending a system of religious education. This extended to religious education (1) in families; (2) in schools; and (3) in the ministrations of the Church. The principles applied, and the means to be employed in enforcing them, are most judicious. And happy would it have been if they had ever been faithfully employed and handed down to the present time.

The Heidelberg Catechism is divided into fifty-two Lord's-days, adapted to a series of discourses during the year. This course of preaching on the Catechism during the year has been observed in the Reformed Churches both of Holland and Germany. A large proportion of the religious publications in Holland consisted of lectures and expositions on the Heidelberg Catechism. In "Koecher's Catechetical History of the Reformed Church," edited by

Cramer, of Holland, and published in 1763, there is a catalogue of more than eighty works on the Catechism published in Holland at that time. The number since is very
largely increased. In the prescribed form of Calls, in our
Constitution, it is expressly stipulated that the minister
called is to preach in the afternoon from the Catechism.
In our revised Constitution four years are now allowed to
complete the course. The Classis annually institutes the
inquiry, "Has the Heidelberg Catechism been regularly
preached?"

There is an affinity in the rise, character, and onward
course of the German and Dutch Reformed Churches. The
Heidelberg Catechism is a standard common to both, their
original liturgies are very similar, while the Reformed
Dutch has in addition the Belgic Confession of Faith. The
respective Churches have adhered to their standards.
About 1614 the first settlement was made by Hollanders in
what is now the State of New York, and the colony, named
New Netherlands, remained subject to Holland till 1764,
when it was ceded to the British crown. After the cession
few emigrants came from Holland, and the churches formed
were mainly from the existing inhabitants and their descendants. They brought with them the faith of their
fathers, who had fought and died for its defence, and their
descendants have carefully adhered to it.

The emigration of the German Reformed commenced
early in the eighteenth century, about 1709, when the Palatinate was sorely oppressed under papal rule. One of the first
ministers, Rev. Mr. Boehm, was in regular correspondence
with the Reformed Dutch ministers in New York. About
1729, the Rev. Mr. Weiss went to Holland to solicit aid for
building houses of worship for two or three infant churches
now in Montgomery county. His visit created such an interest that the Classis of Rotterdam sent in a memorial to
the Synod of South Holland to take measures for systematically aiding the infant German settlements in Pennsylvania. Shortly afterward, during the meeting of the

Synod at Dordrecht, two ships passed by, carrying a large number of Palatine emigrants. The ships were visited by a committee of the Synod, who reported. The Synod then held religious service with the Palatines of a most interesting character, supplied them with temporal comforts and with Bibles and Testaments. They solemnly promised to bear them in remembrance from year to year, and to contribute to the promotion of Christ's kingdom in the Western world. This was the beginning of a series of measures for the benefit of the German Reformed in America, which only terminated with the independent organization after our Revolutionary war. Money was raised for the support of German Reformed youth in preparation for the missionary work in America, and for aiding feeble churches. In 1746, the Church of Holland sent out Michael Schlatter to visit the settlements in Pennsylvania and vicinity, as a general superintendent. In 1747, through his labors, a *coetus* or general Synod was formed, suoordinate to the Synod of North Holland. The care of these churches was specially intrusted to the committee *ad exteras* of the Classis of Amsterdam, who reported annually to the Synod of North Holland. The coetus of Pennsylvania regularly sent a copy of their minutes to the Synod with a letter. The minutes of the Synod of North Holland were doubtless annually sent both to the German and Dutch Reformed Churches here. It is to be regretted that they have not been better preserved. I have inspected several of these yearly minutes, and have been struck with the space occupied and the attention paid to the affairs of the German Reformed Church in this country. By direct authority of the Synods, collections were taken up in the churches, which amounted to a very considerable sum, which was appropriated to feeble churches and to the schools. The missionaries sent out were examined and commissioned by the Classis of Amsterdam.

We have a valuable document, sent over some years since by Professor Budding, of Delft. It is a report made

421

by a committee to the Synod of South Holland, in 1732, giving a view of the State of Pennsylvania in its geographical position, natural resources and advantages, then alludes to the German Reformed settlements, the population, the wants of education and ministry, and proposes a plan in detail for supplying these wants. It is a rare and interesting document.

I have alluded in this paper to the affinity between the German and Dutch Reformed Churches from their birth at the Reformation, as it would probably only incidentally be referred to in the papers which will be presented.

I anticipate and fervently pray that much benefit will result from the measures taken by the German Reformed Church to commemorate the Tercentenary of the Heidelberg Catechism.

THE

AUTHORITY

OF THE

HEIDELBERG CATECHISM.

By REV. G. B. RUSSEL, A.M.
PITTSBURGH, PA.

AUTHORITY

HEIDELBERG CATECHISM.

By Rev. Geo. B. Russell, A. M., Pittsburgh, Pa.

ONE great glory of the grand movement which forms the dividing line between our more modern period and the Middle Ages, is found in the fact that it is truly historical. This gives weight to its authority, force to its teachings, and value to the examples it furnishes for our use. All its great heart-throbs were in the bosom of history.

By this, the great Protestant Reformation is made a real and living part of catholic Christianity. In solving its great problem, it had a filial regard for what were the constituent elements of the Christian life, not only in the apostolic period, but also in its development and growth, through the periods of propagation, of persecution, and of authoritative councils for the settlement of doctrines over against the multiform heresies that afflicted the Church. So also it owned the Divine Presence with the body of Christ, during all its efforts to Christianize the barbarous nations of Europe, and in its subsequent contests with their emperors, down through the "Dark Ages," till the light of the new era dawned in the morning of the Reformation.

Christ's glorious promise, that the gates of hell should not prevail against the Church, the Reformers rightly regarded as still faithfully kept. Not only what the Church was at any given time, but also what it was to become, as they conceived, was bound historically to its divine life, as that was originally constituted and conditioned in the heavenly order of gracè, existing perennially at hand in the world. This shut out then, of course, the idea as well as the necessity for creating a new Church from any source whatever, not even from the Bible, as is falsely supposed by some, to take the place of that which, according to their own vain notion, has from time to time failed. A sorry thing, indeed, would the Reformation be, if it were made thus to stand isolated from all history and so be sundered from the living truth.

Not so did our fathers of the Reformed Church look upon Protestantism. And we also cherish it as an inheritance above the price of rubies, because whatever value attaches to it is to be found in the fact, that it flows legitimately in the life-stream of history. Its justification can only appear as it unites itself in this organic way with the fountain of life and truth, Jesus Christ, the same yesterday, to-day, and forever.

Anchored thus to the living faith of ages, it was necessary for the Reformed Church, holding its own peculiar stand-point, to provide for itself a normal confession, whose authority should be its guiding rule; so that in the element of this free law, its warm and genial life might unfold itself historically, with ever-vigorous growth, onward to the end of its high calling in the fulfilment of its heavenly mission.

This, as is known, gave occasion for the formation of the Heidelberg Catechism, whose three-hundredth anniversary we now celebrate. It was thus designed to become the authoritative symbol of doctrine and rule of faith, in which not only the Church, but the individual believer also, finds full freedom and normal liberty. It rests on the idea of the historical Church, which begets objective life from the conceptions of faith in the mysteries of the gospel, always efficaciously reached in the grace-bearing sacraments and ordinances of Christ's mystical body. Not, then, to new-form, or even reconstruct, the never-failing and never-

426

failed Church, was the problem that presented itself to the worthies of the sixteenth century.

Historical necessity in the form of development assigned to their epoch, the duty rather of Reformation. To them were given for this end, the results of all previous history, from which they were to unfold the covered, evolve the hidden, eliminate the corrupted, reject the erroneous, and reform the abuses then so notorious in the practices of the times.

Answering the main proposition: By what authority, and according to what rule, was this to be done? they were led to measure the problem by the only sure standard of truth. Jesus Christ, as the personal truth and only source of authority for the Church, furnishes all the conditions required; and from thence they sought the elements needed to satisfy the great demands of the age. He has not only revealed the living truth, but has also extended, in His commission to the holy apostles, the authority of the same, —which He also confirms by the continued operations of the Holy Spirit in the Church. From this is begotten the Holy Bible, the "more sure word of prophecy," embodying the "apostles' doctrine," the sum of the gospel of Christ.

Reduced to a system, this must take a definite type and form of expression. Hence there is early mention made of the "form of sound words," which is doubtless also "the faith once delivered to the saints." If it was necessary for the Reformers, in again setting free the course of this truth flowing from the pure fountain-head, but then dammed up with vain traditions and adulterated with the gathered refuse, drift, and abuses of centuries, to identify the newly clear-flowing current with the original outflowing truth; they did not, in order to do this, raise a question as to whether they should follow up the stream of history itself to its source, or dig for a new fountain. Their principle led them to set forth and establish the old primary truths; and of these the Holy Scriptures were to them the ultimate standard of authoritative record. They were always ready to go to them as to their last appeal. Armed with this weapon, they were willing to meet the champions of scholastic traditions; and the carnal teachings of the corrupt Romanists fell before it. Nor was the issue of such contests, when once fairly joined, ever long in doubt; for evangelical truth, the two-edged sword, vanquishes the subtlest forms of error. They accepted nothing that was in open contradiction to the plain truths of the Bible; or, at the very least, all that was not by them rejected must be in harmony with the Bible, and sanctioned by the letter or spirit of the sacred word.

They never contended, however, for the "Bible alone," in any such modern sect-notion of its sense as to make it in every man's hand a mere nose of wax, to be twisted to suit each one's passion or ignorant, selfish taste. They owned that the Bible alone contains the revealed truth in a fixed form; that it is given "for our learning;" that its truths make "wise unto salvation;" and that these "lively oracles" were committed to the sacred and faithful keeping of the Church, "the ground and pillar of the truth." And it is a remarkable fact that, whatever else may be truly charged upon the Church, so corrupt in the lives and practices of its members during the Middle Ages, it has not been indicted for wilfully corrupting, in the way of counterfeiting and falsifying, the recorded truth of divine revelation. The very fact, however, that the Romish Church did not encourage the general use of the whole Bible by the common people, and never supposed, indeed, that it was likely ever to come into such common use as it has since the Reformation, this fact itself may be a sufficient reason why party bigotry, passion, and prejudice, so notoriously bad, had no temptation then to corrupt the Bible when it was, humanly speaking, fully in its power so to do.

But while the Bible is all given by inspiration, and these things were written as profitable "ensamples" for us, yet it

428

does not claim to be a systematic arrangement or scheme of religious doctrine. It is more in the form of *life* than of *logic*. It is the authentic record of the divine, dealing with the human; it is the spiritual and invisible, manifesting truth to the visible and sensible. The whole body of divine truth is revealed in the incidents of the inspired history, age after age. Its sublime prophecy and heavenly precepts reach through our human life in all its varied forms. Through living men, divinely-inspired teachers, God brings His law and gospel, types and sacraments in the covenant of grace, to the sinful world. All this is scattered over ages of history before it comes to a full period.

Written truth, like all recorded enactments of right law, is, however, one with what was long before unwritten. The great body of revealed truth was, probably, for long ages not committed to writing. Even the truths of Christianity, as at first received from Christ and held and taught by the holy apostles, were as yet unwritten. The Church was founded, and disciples were made by its divine power, before the New Testament Scriptures were indited by the Holy Spirit, who moved the holy men of old to speak: so that, in this sense, the Church is older than the Bible. This is true, both as to its organization as well as to its norm or rule of faith. Hence the Bible is not the primary source of Christianity. As to time and order, the Bible grew out of the truth already at hand in the bosom of the Church, rather than, as some falsely teach, that the Church can be manufactured at any time, *de novo*, out of the Bible. God's divine order was to found the Church, the true "mother of us all," and from this life beget the history and experience, the exhortations and directions, which become a guiding rule, under the operations of the Holy Spirit, by which the saints are to walk.

"Steadfast," we read, the early Church remained after its Pentecostal birth, "in the apostles' doctrine and fellowship." They had, doubtless, been taught "the form of sound words," which they were exhorted to "hold fast," as containing all the fundamental truths of the gospel. This must have been more or less full, explicit, formal, definite, and positive,—a summary of Christian faith, substantially that of the Creed.

No man was expected or required, in the times of the apostles or afterward, when the claims of the gospel were presented to him, to go to the Bible and make up a correct creed at first hand for himself. But, on the contrary, this was done for him by the mind of the Church, which did produce from the revealed truth, what was essential for faith to hold; and, this her disciples were required to receive and confess. At first this was transmitted orally, doubtless, from one living teacher to another, and afterward also in written forms, so that those who were made ·disciples could all "walk by the same rule." As no one has ever, in point of fact, become a Christian without the divine teaching and mediation of the Church, with her means and ordinances, so no one can go to the Bible and construct, purely on private judgment at first hand, a system of faith equal in any respect to the Church's Creed.

More and more this grew into the symmetrical and completed form now known as the Apostles' Creed. In this, we have the conscious mind of the Church embodied and authenticated by all history, as the sense in which to use the truths of the Bible. How the truths of the sacred word are to constitute and regulate the faith of the disciples, is not left to mere individual judgment. The Bible, as we have seen, is the truth given in the life of history, and not in systematic forms; but, as such, it was committed to the keeping of the Church. Hence it is to be presumed that the Church can best understand and interpret, as well as teach, its meaning. Most especially is it not competent for those outside the bosom of the Church to determine just what the Holy Scriptures teach. Though so plain that "he may run that readeth," and even a "fool need not err"

430

therein; yet the carnal mind cannot perceive the things of the Spirit, for they are spiritually discerned.

So in nature, even, we find that no one is expected to construct, independent of the knowledge and labors of others, a full system for all the departments of science. Not so have the laws of nature,—as reduced to general systems and now taught in botany, chemistry, geology, mineralogy, or astronomy,—been discovered and arranged by the private judgment of a single brain. Rather do we find that only those who are in full sympathy with some particular part of nature may discover partial truths, and, by combining such results with what others have done, finally there is produced a system of tolerable perfection. All similar efforts in the history of the race are joined, by a common consciousness, to make the cycle of the natural sciences. The developments of science have always been in the general mind historically of the race of mankind.

Common Law, the general experience and consent of civilized nations, is begotten in the same generic sense. No barbarian or savage may, individually, either make laws or determine what is law for civilization. In order to this, they must stand first in the bosom of its life. But not even a citizen by pure private judgment, no matter what freedom he may be allowed to have, fixes the meaning of law and constitutional statute. Only as by the official declaration of the proper judge, in the bosom of general jurisprudence, can the law be expounded and declared. The imperfections of all such uttered interpretations, if there be any, will be readily accounted for in the want of full knowledge and harmony of the judge with the general element of law. The common citizens, in civilized communities, do not pretend to determine laws and give judgments for themselves. Yet every good citizen ought to know well the laws, and, in order to true freedom, must also obey them. So each one, to be a true Christian, must know, believe, and obey all that is required in the gospel. But just what that is, has not been left for each one to determine arbitrarily, or make to suit self-will, from the Bible alone. The true faith, the Church has reduced to form, from the living history of Christianity; and by the Holy Spirit teaches it, in living power and divine authority, to men.

.It will not be disputed that the early Church, with the holy apostles at the head of its affairs, and they under the special guidance and influence of the Holy Spirit, had certainly the ability to generate and beget, from all the divine truth revealed in the fact of Christianity itself, a system of common faith. What was this but the "apostles' doctrine," which they handed down to their immediate successors as the "form of sound words," and which, though as yet, perhaps, unwritten, these in turn committed to "other faithful men," who thereby could also teach others? It is not without ground, then, that it was held in all ages of the Church that there is such a common formula of doctrine for faith, called the Apostles' Creed. This teaches, as our Catechism affirms, in a brief and concise form, all that is necessary for each one to believe in order to be a Christian.

Here is the one true faith, in the right holding and living exercise of which is the sure pledge of salvation. Without it, all else is vain and valueless. Where it is wanting, God's abounding love in the rich provisions of grace fail, or become of none effect. Christ's humiliation, sufferings, bitter death, glorious resurrection, the ministrations of the Church, with all the means of grace, the preaching of.the gospel, the word, and the sacraments, do not save, except man believes. No mere general and undefined faith will do. It is, of course, required to believe all the revealed truth of God as given in the Bible. But there must be a formal confession from the mouth, as well as the holding of it in the heart. The formula must be definite and fixed in the same sense of the truth, to say the least, as it was apprehended and taught by the apostles and early Church before the Bible was finished. To hold this substantially,

432

in its true and proper conception, is historical Christianity; and none other is genuine.

Very difficult was then the work of reforming the Church, without destroying its historical life. In their efforts to set the Church free from the encumbering abuses coming down through the mediæval period, the Reformers seem to have fallen back, by divine guidance doubtless, upon the only ground of freedom and safety,—that of historical authority. Here they appeal to the record of truth, the Bible, as understood and honored by the general consciousness of the Church. To this law and testimony, they would have every thing held to a strict accountability.

Genuine Protestantism is now, as it has always been, anchored to the Bible in this sense as its only rule of faith, and its ultimate appeal in all controverted matters. Where this is plain, all else that contradicts cannot but be false and wrong.

But this does not require that nothing else shall regulate the order of our faith, but each one's private sense of the bare dead letter of the book. The Bible, as understood by the Church, which, led by the Spirit, is the best interpreter and judge, is to be the rule, not only for the general Creed of the Church, but also for the particular faith and confession of individual Christians. Whatever else found in Confessions, or taught in Catechisms, or held in private judgment, that contradicts any truth revealed in the Bible, must be given up. To this point the Reformers were ever willing to bring their adversaries, and in this was the secret of their strength and triumphs.

Let no one say now, that, having affirmed this much, the Reformers then left all the truth of the Bible to be settled and determined by individual judgment or private caprice. They were guilty of no such radical error, no such rank rationalism. In proof of this, we see that all branches of the Reformation soon found it necessary to have their own authorized Confessions and Catechisms, by the rule of which they could measure and declare their faith. But, in doing

433

this, they did by no means undervalue or set aside the precious Bible. They did not exalt Catechisms or Creeds as above the written word. They did not allow that any book or authority superseded the Bible. This is what they charged upon the Romanists. They permitted no formula, to claim independence of the inspired Book of books. It was just because they so highly honored the Holy Bible, that they framed a Catechism based so entirely on its truth, expressing its right teachings, as these were settled by the Holy Spirit—just as the canon of the Sacred Scriptures itself had been settled—in the Church. They stood in the light of this divine revelation; and, while they made no new light for the pathway of Christian pilgrims, they gathered for us, into our confessional symbol, the scattered rays of truth beaming on the track of history from the "faith once delivered to the saints." In this settled norm for our Church, we have "the true light" now guarded, as it were, by an impervious crystal shield, to make it forever safe against the winds and storms of fanatical heresy, while it continues to reflect the clear truth of God's word.

From this broad and general ground of history, grew out the Heidelberg Catechism. Its authority rests substantially, on the same sense of historical authority, that belongs to the Apostles' Creed. This appears from the fact, that the Creed itself holds the central place in the Catechism. On no other authority, could its authors construct a true symbol, which could be answerable at once to the life of the Church then, and for the three hundred years now gone, with much more yet, we trust, to come. Any thing less catholic could not have enabled them to join this effort of the Reformation in a living way, with all the ages of the Church gone before, nor give it a vitality which should preserve its true Christian life in the ages yet to follow.

In the ruling authority of the Creed, the Reformed Church fathers found the normal germ of their Catechism.

The mystic brooding power of the ancient Church-life pervades its spirit. Leading to repentance, faith, and love, its parts treat of sin and misery, of grace and redemption, and of Christian gratitude and saint-life. It rests on the "sure word of prophecy," and all its teachings are confirmed by proofs from the Bible, in the sense its truth held in the general mind of the Church, as this rests in the historical formula of the Christian creed. The Catechism has itself also been brought to the touchstone of truth, and has stood the test of trial by the word of God. Thus, speaking with the tongue of history, it utters the voice of the Holy Catholic Church, which only faithfully echoes the teaching of the Bible, while that itself is truly intoned by the Holy Spirit. His office is to take of the things of Christ, especially His words of truth, and show them in their full meaning to the believing discipleship.

On this ground alone have they a rule by which to reject the traditional abuses and corrupt practices of the Romish Church, and guard, at the same time, against the fanatical individualism of the Anabaptists and other forms of heresy. This saves the Reformed Church at once from the dangers of the sects, who leave this safe ground to follow the vague notions of their leaders, and from those also who fall blindly into the dark gulf of vain human traditions, and the bondage of absurd papal infallibility.

Steering clear of the dangers that beset on either hand, they differed in their work from the spirit of mere party or sect, whose radical error claims to find the truth fresh from the Bible for each individual whim; and yet our Reformers honor the Bible, by claiming for it in the Catechism the true spirit of divine light, which shines through it, in streaming rays, as concentrated by the lens of history. Not one pope, nor yet many; but they heed only the voice of Christ, the Good Shepherd.

Every private judgment, be it never so free, they did not think better than the rule of faith in the Creed of the Church, drawn from the divine administration of the Holy

435

Spirit in the body of Christ, the living revelation of the truth. Nor yet again, did they hold the truth to be lodged in any pretended infallible head, so that the Bible may be kept from the common people. Nay: the Bible is for the Church,—for the great body of believers,—for all Christians. The address of many of the epistles of the New Testament is plainly to the "Church," to "believers," to those "called to be saints;" not to priest, cardinal, or pope, to keep and explain, but clearly to all Christians, rather than to a hierarchy. Its true teachings are in the Church, and its right meanings are best understood and declared by the Church, led by the ever-present Spirit of truth.

"The Bible has no life of its own, no voice, save as the truth it reveals is brought to live and speak in those who receive it as God's word. To be a creed or rule, then, it must be reduced to some common understanding in the minds that embrace it and agree to follow it in such way. This may be written or unwritten, but in the end it amounts to the same thing: it is a standard of belief and practice,—in this respect a true church-symbol and constitution, supposed, of course, to be taken from the Bible, but still, as such, out of the Bible and beside it." It comes always to this, then, at last, that no pretending sect has, in point of fact, or indeed can have, the "Bible alone" for its authoritative creed. For, as a sect-creed, the Bible is only that particular sect's notion of it, whether by consent of few or many, and so may be something vastly different, after all, from the Bible.

A living branch of the "true vine" must, however, have in it also the real life of the vine, drawn from its native source. In order to this, it will not do to first put its own life into that vine, that the branch may draw it out again for itself. So the confessional life of the Reformed Church is not something newly put into the Bible, and then taken by individual judgment and put into the Catechism. Not from a new starting-point in the days of the Reformation does the Reformed branch of the Holy Catholic Church

436

draw its life-principle and rule of faith. It rests rather in the deep bosom of the divine order of grace, as that flows from the person of Jesus Christ, always present according to His promise.

Basing its claims to speak and to be heard, as worthy of respect and credit, on this ground, the Heidelberg Catechism comes to us as the full fruit of the Reformation, and not simply as the product of a few excellent Christian men. It was an organic outgrowth from the general life of Christianity, holding in the conscious experience of the saints in all ages of the Church,—this itself always produced from the life of the Lord Jesus, our divine Head.

From this historical stand-point, resting on the ground of the Creed of Christendom, embodying the true life of the Catholic Church, as that understood, honored, and obeyed the voice of the Sacred Scriptures, under the living teachings of the Holy Spirit, who unites to Christ's life, does the Heidelberg Catechism claim to speak to the Reformed Church. Only in such view are its teachings of more authoritative force than that of individuals or associations in the membership of the Church. In this sense it is of divine authority for the children of our spiritual mother; just as in the family, the parent is the divinely constituted authority for the child. It is for the Reformed Church the common bond of fellowship, the symbol of faith, and the rule of life,—the authoritative teacher of doctrinal truth, to which we all do well to give heed, as unto a light shining in a dark place.

If there was divine authority and historical necessity for the whole Reformation itself, it is to be presumed that the hand of God would so control it, by His providence and grace, as to fulfil the purpose of the great commission to the apostles, as to solve the problem of that age. The historical necessity for a Reformed symbol of faith, answerable to the wants of one whole side of that great movement, included also provision certainly for its production. The fact, too, that there was for this, the material already at hand in the Church, and authors also so peculiarly fitted to embody that in the needed confession, adds to the conviction that it was a work *then* to be accomplished. The ages since, not having been similarly prepared, could not have done that work as well. In fact, it has never been tried, or when attempted the efforts have always failed. For only in the epoch of a period can its genuine life be grasped and rightly unfolded,—not before nor afterwards as well, as the sad failures and grand successes in history most plainly show. So it appears, no age since the Reformation-epoch has been commissioned to reform symbols of faith. Other attempts made since have measurably failed; for even great minds, unsupported by history, produce abortive failures. But the problems of history, rightly solved, are greater than the human instruments themselves by which they are wrought out.

The Reformation, therefore, if it have any glory, finds it in this: that it is greater than the Reformers severally, or all together. It embraced them in its arms, enclosed them in its folds, while it towered higher, spread broader, and penetrated deeper than the personalities of its leading men, into whom it infused the life-powers of the age. So the Catechism, produced from the bosom of the Reform, is greater, as has been well said, than its framers. It has been shown to have more authority than was lodged in the Palatine Elector; it is more Christ-like than were the pious Frederick and his excellent professors, and is more learned than his renowned University. It has a life-spirit as universal as the Reformed Church, a religious fervor as holy as the Communion of Saints, and a system of doctrine as true as the teachings of the Holy Spirit. As no age before the Reformation was able to produce such a symbol, so neither has any since had the same mission to fulfil: hence none have produced any superior to the well-nigh universal symbol of the Palatinate Reformers.

Quite as strong is the evidence in favor also of this authority of the Catechism—as representing so truly the general

438

consciousness of the Church—drawn from the fact that it became so soon and so generally the standard under which rallied so large a portion of the Reformation. This ability to satisfy the general want, is a strong presumption in favor of the œcumenical authority of this Confession. In so far as the Reformed Church has remained true to itself in the spirit of the Catechism, this authoritative teacher and normal measure of its Christian life has blessed her with vigor and freshness. During the three hundred years now gathered to the bosom of the past, just in proportion as this has been held in honor, has the Church, in any given age, been flourishing in the true type of its own proper life. The converse of this, in the sad experience of the Church, has been found no less true. She is thus in absolute need, at every turn and in every age, of this guide to her faith. By this is marked and regulated the normal order of our Christian life.

God's order of grace requires that the children first be fed. This order of the covenant the Catechism owns. Where sin abounds, grace superabounds,—offering the blessings of the covenant to whomsoever will receive the faith. But it only brings saving power in the sacramental folds of the covenant of grace. Thus in the covenant, it is of authority for such teaching and nurture, bringing them into the Church for such purpose, but never outside of it first, in order to get them afterward within its folds.

Creeds and Catechisms grow from the life of the Church, —hence, as a rule, must be in the Church and for the Church, only to be used authoritatively by the Church. So the Creed and the Bible can only be rightly taught, received, apprehended, believed, and obeyed. As the Holy Spirit's operations are in the Church by means of the ordinances, the word, the sacraments, and the living teachers; so He brings grace, witnesses truth, and seals the promised salvation to such as hear and obey its conditions.

Uniformly is this the divine order in the New Testament

examples. For instance, Philip, a man ordained to the office, is called by the Spirit to teach the pious-minded eunuch who was reading the Bible. Though the man, being already a proselyte of the Jews, was hence partly in the covenant, yet the Holy Spirit did not, in even this case, honor the Bible alone as sufficient, to bring him to the full knowledge of the truth. The living preacher must approach him with the question, "Understandest thou what thou readest?" This fixes the attention of the reader to the truth, who willingly becomes a disciple, and replies, "How can I, except some *man* teach me?" The human teacher then brings him to faith and obedience, sealing the gospel grace in the holy sacrament of baptism; which having been received, the new-born happy soul goes on its way rejoicing.

Cornelius, too, was not regenerated by the Holy Ghost without the mediation of the Church, though his prayers and alms-deeds had gone up as a memorial before God. Though it required a vision to direct him to a human teacher, yet not until Peter came and preached the gospel to him in Christ's appointed way, did he receive the witness of the Spirit. In some particulars this case is peculiar, differing from all others given in the New Testament; yet in this one thing it conforms to the universal law in the order of grace, viz.: that no magic power, or immediate agent outside of Christ's apostolic commission to the Church, the home of the Spirit's presence and administrative operations, is allowed to interfere and meddle with the work of the sinner's salvation. In this order of redemption the Catechism teaches the way to be saved.

St. Paul was converted and brought into the Church in no other way. Miraculous as his case is in its surroundings, yet was he required to have Ananias come to him, under the authority of the Church by whom he had been ordained a living teacher, and, laying his hands upon him, command him to arise and be baptized, and wash away his sins, calling on the name of the Lord. Thus also the Cate-

440

chism teaches that souls are born to God in the Church, the mother of us all. Not outside of the mystical body, but in her, it shall be said of Zion, this and that man were born.

Nothing merely human and conventional is thus assumed for the authority of the Catechism. It presupposes the presence of the supernatural order of grace in the Church, which is here for the purpose of "making known" the mysteries of the gospel "unto principalities and powers," "revealing the grace of salvation," and teaching those who are made disciples to do all things commanded by our risen and glorified Lord. The objective existence of this divine order, representing in a truly historical life the prophetic, the priestly, and the kingly offices of Christ,—in the word, the sacraments, and the government of the Church,—is not only in full harmony and accord with the spirit of the Catechism, but also authenticates and establishes its claim to authority. At one with history, with the Church, with the Creed, with the Bible, with the Spirit of the Lord Jesus, the Catechism is a fit guide to our faith; and, in comparison, no individual, with the largest allowance of purely private judgment, never so pious and learned, could ever imagine or produce its equal for private Christians or the Church.

By its authority, derived not from united human consent, but from the Head of the Church, it infringes no rights of individuals when it comes to teach them its truths for faith, and to rule them by a power above their own will. For are not all the rights of private judgment, so often unduly exalted by some, only to believe and obey the truth,—not as they may fancy it or be disposed to make it from any source, but as God has revealed it in the gospel, which the Church is to teach to all nations?

Just as little could the authority of the Catechism grow out of a collection of subjective judgments, aggregated in one common consent. Not so do truth and grace come from individuals upwards, but from Jesus Christ downward. For instance, the separate persons who make up the vote of a synod, do not make the authority of that vote, which is something vastly more than just the united opinion of so many natural minds joining in one sentence by a majority or with one voice. The authority of Creeds and Catechisms, as made by the Church, is objective,—coming from Christ to His Church,—and so expressed, under the guidance of the Holy Spirit, to men, and yet through men.

Every such expression of authority is divine, and therefore carries with it a force above the collective opinion of any number of separate minds in the order of the merely natural. If in any real way there is faith in the promised presence of Christ even where two or three are assembled in His name, this must give force to Church acts. Not all decisions of Church courts have had the seal of the Spirit's authority; because some of these may have been more after the flesh than after the Spirit. But when we have the testimony of the Spirit bearing witness *with* our spirits, the authority of all such official decrees by the Church, lead into all truth, is divinely authenticated, and thus it becomes for us a binding rule.

From what has now been given, it would seem to appear:—

1. That the ground or basis of the authority of the Heidelberg Catechism is the word of God, in the sense of the Creed of Christendom ;

2. That the form or order of this same authority rests in the living consciousness of Christianity itself;

3. That the force or degree of this authority, in any proper sense, though expressed in the human, is yet truly divine.

Our Catechism comes to us, therefore, not simply as the mere subjective product of its pious authors. In the days of the Reformation the ground it held was broader and diviner; and now, at the end of three hundred years, it is even more firmly established on the truly historical life of the Church. For, if it grew organically from the bosom of the old Church-life, as that was found reigning in the Christian creed of all ages, which itself is in full harmony with the written word, whose living truth rests in the person of Jesus Christ, then have we verily an authority in the Heidelberg Catechism above that of any man, or any conventional agreement of the merely human. Here is, doubtless, the reason why its great authority has been "abiding in strength" for three hundred years. This will continue also till the Church reaches a new stadium of history; for, doubtless, not till then will there be provided for the Reformed Church a better symbol of faith than the Heidelberg Catechism.

During all the glorious history of our Reformed Church it has been the measure of its life, the standard of its faith, and the authority to govern private judgment and make it free, by regulating each one's creed and ruling the norm of his conceptions of Christianity. It is the gauge and index of all doctrine necessary to our salvation, and hence is the authoritative teacher of the Reformed faith for all willing disciples who come here to learn, and receive the kingdom of heaven, according to this norm, in the spirit of a little child baptized into grace.

Resting on the warm bosom of the common "mother of us all," the Catechism still continues to live in her spirit, and is thoroughly imbued with the general animus of the Christian Church of all ages. Breathing thus the saint-making atmosphere of the "communion of saints," the holy Catholic Church, it speaks to us in her name, teaches with her authority, and perpetuates her heavenly nurture. It apprehends the children of the covenant, and brings them by its teachings to her arms, as they are begotten and nourished by her sacraments and sanctified and confirmed unto the end by her spirit of truth. By this rule they are to be taught the revealed will of God. In this they are to be made wise unto salvation. It gives expression to the truth of Christianity in the light of the Bible. It says to all humble learners, "According to this rule study the Holy Scriptures." Its teaching, humbly followed, makes true disciples, and, rightly known and heartily obeyed, makes saints!

444

THE EDUCATIONAL SYSTEM OF RELIGION

UNDERLYING THE

HEIDELBERG CATECHISM.

By REV. D. GANS, A.M.

HARRISBURG, PA.

THE EDUCATIONAL SYSTEM OF RELIGION UNDER-
LYING THE HEIDELBERG CATECHISM.

By Reb. H. Gans, Harrisburg, Pa.

THE Heidelberg Catechism, which was the offspring of a definite, far-reaching, and significant theological movement in the Reformation-period, is properly no less distinguished for what it legitimately implies than for what it verbally expresses. In both views no symbolical book has been more highly regarded wherever it has come to be clearly understood in the circumstances of its origin and the respective elements which constitute its inward life. As there was a well-defined history preceding it, out of which it grew, so is there a substantial system underneath it, on which it rests. On this account it is always felt to have a life reaching farther back than its date and deeper down than its words; in view of which, as in the case of the Bible itself, notwithstanding its admirable simplicity, a certain indefinable mysteriousness permeates it, which invites to renewed study by discovering fresh depths at every effort.

This underlying and hence permeating system is practical rather than theoretical, forming the material womb of the Christian life rather than the basis of dogmas for the understanding; yet these last are also involved in such a form, however, as to make their appeal primarily to faith and not to reason. It ever rests in the central mystery of the Incarnation,—the real union of the divine and human natures in the person of Jesus Christ. This is its deepest idea, and constitutes the living factor by which all its other parts are ruled. In the true christological conception the deep voice of the heathen world, which has been trembling all through the ages, is fully met and substantially answered. Judaism also finds the true life of its divine being, and rises into the real dignity to which it was originally destined. In Christ heaven and earth are united in a most intimate and actual way, who on this account has become the centre of the world's life both as it respects the past, the present, and the future. He is God manifest in the flesh, the deepest and last sense of humanity, the true key to all the departments of the world under its physical form, and the only commensurate revelation of God to man. "No man knoweth the Son, but the Father; neither knoweth any man the Father, save the Son, and he to whomsoever the Son will reveal Him."* "I and my Father are one."† "He that hath seen me hath seen the Father."‡

We are not to be surprised, as all truth arises in and receives its legitimate form both for faith and reason from this divine-human centre, to find here also the prolific source of all fundamental error and heresy. The ruling errors arising at this point are fourfold:—Ebionism, which allows no real room at all for the divine, making the personality of Christ wholly human; Gnosticism, which degrades the human, making His personality wholly divine; Eutychianism, acknowledging both natures, but conceiving of them as confusedly flowing together in such a form as to lose their distinctive significance, constituting an unintelligible mixture; and Nestorianism, which also recognizes the two natures, but, denying the vital relation between them, results in dualism, in which there can be no organic activity, but only a moral co-operation in the work of atonement. The two last heresies are variously modified, according to the degree of degradation to which either nature is reduced, or their approximate union with or

---

* St. Matt. xi. 27.   † St. John x. 30.   ‡ St. John xiv. 9.

separation from each other, forming a full history of christological lights and shadows, each ending, however, at last in the same false system from which it arose. Nor have these false christological schemes affected merely the faith of the Christian world in regard to Christianity either as a whole or in its parts, but also the mind itself—the origin of thought—and every thing upon which it has been called to exert its powers.* Hence, corresponding with the four christological systems now mentioned, we find in philosophy Realism, Idealism, Absolutism, and Dualism, all modified, too, very much in the same way and to the same extent.

But though the true system in relation to the person of Christ, as the central formative fact in the history of the world, has been compelled to contend with manifold forms of error, it has never lost its deep hold upon the intuitive nature of man. The contest has rather served to develop the truth as it is in Jesus more fully and clearly, and thus given it a wider existence and a greater moral and real power.

As the truth, sundered into divergent and contradictory parts because of the absence of faith to grasp it in its mysterious totality, has resulted in error, so it is only in the bosom of faith and by its activity as a supernatural grace that these fragments can again be brought back and apprehended in their original union and truthful harmony. Error is manifold; truth is one,—but it is always the one in the many, involving a mystery, the necessity, beauty, and richness of which faith only can apprehend. Thus Christ is one person with two natures, divine and human, both realities, organically united, yet without mixture, very God and very man,—"Emmanuel, God with us." This is the christological truth in a mystery, to be received and

---

* Philosophy has followed in the wake of Christology, showing practically that Christ is the only key both to the meaning of our own being and that of the physical world by which we are surrounded.

rested in, by faith, as the central moulding fact of the whole world.

Here, now, must arise the true conception of the Christian Church, as His Body, the fulness of Him that filleth all in all.*   The Church resulting as it does from the christological law of Christ's nature, our idea of its character must, of course, take its cast from what we hold to be the truth in regard to Christ's person as now described. The Church can, therefore, be no mere outward association of believers brought together from abroad on any mere abstract principle, either human or divine.   This would contradict, in every view, the truth as we have already seen it to hold in the person of Christ.   No outward divine decree,—as held, for instance, by Calvin,— and no human purpose,—as was dreamed of by Arminius,— can in this way be the basis or the principle of the Church as such.   It arises not in any sense by accretion, but by growth; not from a doctrine, but from a fact, namely, Christ Himself, who is therefore its ground, its pervading life, and its beauty.

The first true conception which we can have of the nature of the Church is that which conceives of it as the body of Christ, immediately and personally, resulting directly from the mystery of the Incarnation under the Holy Ghost.   "A body hast Thou prepared me."†   This body, comprehended organically by His divinity, and thus sanctified and filled with grace, is the primary conception of the Church; a reality in the world, and yet invisible and intangible, and alike absolutely independent both of men and devils.   It is still the Church of Christ, organic and real, though not a single individual in all the millions of the race should be found to be actually connected with it. Subtraction here of individuals does not leave an abstraction as the result, but a reality only so much the more intensely real.   The humanity in Christ would still be a fact,

---

* Eph. i.   † Heb. x. 5.

and this fact would still be His body, the Church, as the objective bearer of salvation for our common fallen nature, —the pillar and ground of the truth. In this idea lies the essential unity of the Church, and likewise its proper and necessary diversity, both conceptions being involved in its *organic* nature.*

In the secondary sense, the Church as the organic body of Christ is viewed as taking up into itself, in view of its primary general relation to our nature, the individuals of the race, as members of His body. Hence the apostle says, "Now ye are the body of Christ, and members in particular."† The body is in order to the members, and never *vice versa*. We do not reach the conception of the Church under this form, by beginning with the members in their individual capacity, and ending with the aggregate, either in the way of the general number, or of the gifts which they may be supposed thus to bring together. The Church is still something vastly deeper and more than this, which we readily see when we begin with the body of Christ, which is the fulness of His own supernatural being, and then pass out to the members. However vast the number that may at any time belong to it and enjoy its life and grace, it still contains, in its deep fulness, life and grace sufficient for millions more. The *all* of the Church, which is the number belonging to it at a particular age, or through all the ages, can never be the measure of the *whole* of its life, which necessarily transcends all limitations. It grows from within out, as in the case of the human body, the family, or organic nature generally. First the vine, then the branches, and the branches not from without, but from within. Thus the Church is not something which we create, but which God creates for us in the Incarnation of His Son,—not something whose inward life we constitute by a voluntary association of ourselves on some general divine principle, and a yielding up of some individual

---

* See 1 Cor. xii. 12–31.   † 1 Cor. xii. 27.

Christian graces, forming thus a joint stock of spiritual powers, but something which existed before and independent of us,—not something to which we can give grace, but something from which we can only take grace. It is a supernatural objective creation from Jesus Christ, bearing His life, visible and invisible, which are the different sides only of the same inseparable inward organism, the womb in which we are spiritually born, and the storehouse from which we are fed and nourished unto eternal life.

In the same general way is the true sense of the Covenant also brought out to our faith. It is ruled entirely by the central christological mystery. It is an organic comprehension of our human life, beginning with the family, and completing itself in the Christian commonwealth,—the Church of Christ,—in which all the families become one. The covenant is not something which we do to God, as in the case of a vow, which can only bind the person vowing, and not God; nor is it a contract which God and man might be supposed to make in a mutual way. No such view can at all sound the depth of the covenant, or apprehend its full objective grace and glory. With the constitution of the covenant, its inward nature and moulding power, man can have no more to do than in constituting the person of Christ or the form and elemental powers of Christianity. All that man can do is to accept or reject it. In itself it is what God creates for, and in the mystery of the Incarnation brings to, man, with all the grace that is needful to his well-being here and hereafter.

Thus God made a covenant with Noah, when He placed the bow in the heavens, as an assurance by sign that He would not again destroy the earth by a flood.* Afterward He also made a covenant with Abram, who by it became separated. The same covenant comprehended, in an equally real way, the family that proceeded from his loins, and had the effect to separate them; and even when they had

---

* Gen. ix. 8–17.

grown into a great nation it still comprehended them, each and all, and constituted them a distinct and separate people. "And I will establish my covenant between me and thee, and thy seed after thee, in their generations, for an everlasting covenant, to be a God unto thee, and to thy seed after thee."* From the bosom of this covenant, which God made and called "my covenant," and whose practical boundaries widened as the pious seed expanded itself and increased in number, Christ arose, who, being the substantial end of the promise from the beginning, fulfilled, in His own person, all the prophecies respecting it, and became the embodiment, at the same time, of all the divine significance which it symbolized. Thus from Abel to Noah, through Seth, and from Noah across the flood to Abraham, and from Abraham through David to Christ, the blessing of God was made to descend organically, through a divine order in the bosom of nature. "Now to Abraham and his *seed* were the promises made. He saith not, And to *seeds*, as of many; but as of one, And to thy *seed*, which is Christ."† In Him the covenant, as it previously existed, met a real divine-human life, in view of which, by way of contrast, it is called a "new covenant." It is new and yet not new,—the old with a new grace, the old elevated, widened, and glorified, by being filled out by a new and supernatural life, the incarnate life of the Son of God. Christ came not to destroy, but to fulfil; and in thus taking up the old covenant and perpetuating it under a new form and with a new grace, He shows it to be, as was promised, an *everlasting* covenant. Just as circumcision, which was the sign and seal of the old covenant, was taken up and carried forward in the baptism of John, which was more directly preparatory to the richer kingdom of grace, imparting the power of repentance, so the baptism of John, in turn, was taken up organically in the baptism of Christ, which is the sign and seal, in the same way, of the new

---

* Gen. xvii. 7.   † Gal. iii. 16.

453

covenant. All these divine appointments stand in a grand organism, which rises as it advances through the ages, and completes itself in Him in whom all fulness dwells. There are therefore not two covenants, but only one, just as there is but one baptism as the sign and seal of this one covenant, bearing thus through all the past, in a true historical way, the sense of substantial *oneness* of all God's positive institutions.

This covenant, as it actualizes itself and becomes a practical fact in the world, may be contemplated in two general aspects: first in the light of the family, and second in the light of holy baptism. In the family we have the covenant as it were in its physiological and psychological nature. The family itself, under any circumstances, is no merely human, but a divine institution, the divine in the human, still after the christological idea, or the pattern in the mount; nor is the marriage relation a mere civil contract which may be formed by two equal contracting parties. The union which is constituted between man and woman under the law of marriage always carries in it forces which are deeper, more real and mysterious than any which the mere intelligence or arbitrary will of the parties could give to it. The christological idea expresses itself here plainly as, after all, the deepest and most controlling law of our life, even under its natural and lowest form.

"They twain shall be one flesh,"* are the divine creative words of the marriage institution. This is more than mere concert of wills or harmony of feeling. It is a mysterious oneness of nature, comprehending body, soul, and spirit, as in the case of Christ's person, with distinctive differences at the same time, and from it. Glimpses of this mystery are found already in the heathen world. "The soul of man and woman," says an ancient Greek fable, "was originally one; it was then divided by Jove into two portions, half to one body and half to the other; and hence the one soul,

---

* Gen. ii. 23, 24; Matt. xix. 5; Eph. v. 31.

with instinctive patience, seeks its lost half, and will wander over the world for it, and if united with it, shall be
happy, if not, miserable."* However grotesque the form
of thought as here expressed, the general oneness of husband and wife is still forcibly uttered.† Those that enter
the marriage relation pass, in that act, under powers or
laws which lie entirely beyond their wills, and which will
accomplish results in relation to each other, and the
children born from them, which they can neither prevent
nor materially modify. It will deeply condition the nature
of both parents, and the child will be made to receive,
embody, and reproduce the physical, moral, and intellectual peculiarities of both, through agencies which neither
it nor they can control. The family itself, in this way,
attests its divine origin, organic nature, and moulding
power.

Still more elevated, of course, is the family in the covenant and pervaded organically by the life-powers of the
Church. Here the significant parallelism which St. Paul
instituted between the relation of husband and wife and
that of Christ and the Church comes, we may say, to its
fullest meaning. As Christ is joined to the Church, so is
the husband joined to the wife; as the Church is Christ's
body, so is the wife the husband's own flesh. "This now,"
said Adam, "is bone of my bones, and flesh of my flesh."‡
"So ought men," says the apostle, "to love their wives as
their own bodies. He that loveth *his wife* loveth *himself.*
For no man ever yet hated his own flesh; but nourisheth
and cherisheth it, even as the Lord the Church: *for we are
members of His body, of His flesh, and of His bones.* For
this cause shall a man leave his father and mother, and
shall be joined to his wife, *and they two shall be one flesh.*
This is a great mystery; but I speak concerning Christ
and the Church."§ This affords the true conception of

---

* Adams, Elements of Christian Science, p. 273.
† Rauch's Psychology, p. 323.   ‡ Gen. ii. 24.   § Eph. v. 28–32.

the family constitution, especially under its substantially Christian character. It is pervaded by divine and mysterious forces. In its proper nature it rises infinitely above the idea of a mere human contract. It is a positive divine appointment; and, though it may not aspire to the dignity of a sacrament, it is nevertheless plainly sacramental in its nature and effect.

Children that are born from the constitution of such a family do not only inherit the physical, intellectual, and moral natures of the parents (for they do this where the family stands wholly in nature), but also, and in some peculiar sense, the gracious nature of the parents. Thus they "belong to the covenant and people of God," and, by baptism as a sign, are to "be distinguished from the children of unbelievers."* Were this not so, then substantially the covenant family would, as to its constitution, be no advance upon the natural. That Christianity carries in its own nature the purpose to lay hold inwardly upon the organic laws of the family, with a view to use them for the spiritual as well as physical welfare of the child, there can indeed be but little rational doubt. The incarnation of Christ is a reality for *nature*,—for the essential and vital forces of nature; and to suppose that physical laws and relations are not conditioned, and, in a certain sense, vitalized by it, would be to fall far short of its true organic sense. If the relation between grace and the laws of our natural constitution be not vital, then the parents, so far as they are Christian, have no organic relation to each other, or to the child, but only so far as they are natural beings. What is this but the same dualistic heresy which separates the divine from the human in Christ? But how, in view of such mechanical separation of grace from the physical constitution of the family, can it be said truly that "the unbelieving husband is sanctified by the wife, and the unbelieving wife is sanctified by the

---

* Question 74.

husband"? and, especially, how can the children of such families be called "holy"?* If grace enter not organically into the natural organism of the covenant family, then all this must be understood simply as a figure of speech, a play of words, without any substantial meaning. Taking our stand-point, however, in the christological law of Christ's nature, we are constrained to believe that parents, as Christians, stand no less organically related to their children than as natural beings. Nay, this spiritual relation is even more freely and intensely organic than the natural, because grace is stronger than nature. In this organic relation of husband and wife, parents and children, we can understand how the term "holy" may be truly applied to the latter in case the former be truly Christian: holy, not indeed as carrying in them a full and ripe Christian life, but as being in a gracious objective institution, as being open to heavenly powers, and as bearing the birthright to these through a higher ordinance of Christ.† They stand in what may be called a holy organic relation, and are thus constituted *receptive* in nature, waiting something more positive, to which they have a claim. It is the right relation, in other words, of the natural to the supernatural in the kingdom of God, with a view to a more full taking of the first in and by the last. Thus John Baptist is said to have been filled with the Holy Ghost from his mother's womb;‡ and this is the material ground of the invitation of Christ, "Suffer little children, and forbid them not, to come unto me; for of such is the kingdom of heaven."§ This position is secured to them, not from nature, but from Christ through nature, as this lies in the covenant and is pervaded by the Holy Ghost. "That which is born

---

* 1 Cor. vii. 14.

† "It takes for granted that the children of Christians were worthy of baptism, and were consequently baptized."—*Stier.* Such children "have a *historical* vocation to the kingdom of God."—*Nitzsch.* "They are members of the Christian community."—*De Wette.*

‡ St. Luke i. 15.　　　　§ St. Matt. xix. 20.

of the flesh is flesh; and that which is born of the Spirit is spirit."*

At this point, and thus conditioned, the children are met by Holy Baptism,† which has the effect not only to confirm and establish them in the gracious position which they already occupy, according to one theory on the subject, but to impart also a positive grace, corresponding with the capacity which has already been created, which they could, ordinarily, derive from no other source. As in the original creation of man, the process was of a twofold character, first from beneath up in the case of the body, and second from above down in the case of the soul, so also stand the facts in relation to the new creation in Christ Jesus. Through Holy Baptism God breathes into the lower covenanted being the breath of life, and a new spiritual creature is formed. Is the christological law, or the union of the two natures in Christ, allowed to be the preceding type and moulding power in the constitution of baptism itself? Then it can certainly be no empty form or idle ceremonial. The outward sign and the inward grace thereby signified must be most truly and vitally related. To conceive of dualism here would involve a destruction of the sacrament altogether. The very idea would be death; for, by its own nature, it is a mysterious union of an outward sign and an inward grace. Neither one in itself, nor both together, without any inward and necessary union, can satisfy the idea of this sacrament. Water is not baptism, any more than human nature in the Redeemer is Christ; neither is the Holy Spirit, any more than His divinity itself is Christ: nor are both of these together Christ, except as in the form of an organic union.

---

* St. John iii. 6.

† "Now, the true conception is, that baptism is applied to the child on the ground of its organic unity with the parents; imparting and pledging a grace to sanctify that unity and make it good in the field of religion."— *Christian Nurture*, by Horace Bushnell, p. 116. Ques. 74.

So water *and* Spirit, united organically by the mighty power of Him by whom it was ordained, constitutes baptism. "Except a man be born of water, *and* of the Spirit, he cannot enter into the kingdom of God."[*]

This sacrament, as thus constituted, looks symbolically always to the beginning of the Christian life under a positive form, just as the Holy Supper, in the same way, looks to the increase and expansion of this life. Nor can we, in view of the facts already adverted to, imagine that the grace itself falls below the symbol; and, the two being really united, we can conclude no otherwise than that baptism actually gives what it represents. Just as the sun symbolizes and *gives* light, so does baptism symbolize and *give* grace.[†] It not only imparts remission of sin, breaks the power of original depravity, but also gives a positive spiritual life, which relates the child really to the atonement of Jesus Christ, and through this to the quiescent, justifying will of God, to be exerted in an active way, in its case, at a more advanced stage of its maturity. "Know ye not," says the apostle, "that so many of us as were baptized into Jesus Christ were baptized into His *death?* Therefore"—because we have been baptized—"we are *buried* with Him *by* baptism into death," *i.e.* into the death of sin, "that, like as Christ was raised up from the dead by the glory of the Father, even so we should walk in *newness* of life."[‡] This is apparent also from the great

---

[*] St. John iii. 5. Compare 1 Cor. vi. 11; Ezek. xxxvi. 25–27. Ques. 73.

[†] "God really, that is, truly and *efficaciously*, gives us *whatever he there sacramentally shadows forth*, and therefore we annex to the signs the true *possession and fruition* of that thing which is thus offered us."—*Gallican Confession*, Art. 37, p. 338.

"But dost thou ascribe to the water nothing more than that it is a symbol of the washing away of sin? I believe that *it is a symbol in which, at the same time, there is reality contained.* For God deceiveth us not when He promises us His gifts."—*Geneva Catechism.*

[‡] Rom. vi. 3, 4. Olshausen here remarks, "Rückert's observation ad loc. is quite just; that the apostle is not saying here what Christians have done at their baptism, but what has *been done* to them in baptism."

commission which Christ gave to the apostles:—"All power is given unto me in heaven and in earth," said Christ: "Go ye, therefore, and *teach*" (μαθητεύσατε, *i.e.* disciple) "all nations, baptizing them in the name of the Father, and of the Son, and of the Holy Ghost; *teaching*" (διδασκοντες, *i.e.* educating) "them to observe all things whatsoever I have commanded you: and lo, I am with you alway, even unto the end of the world."* In the divine order, as here prescribed, the making of disciples by baptism is the first thing; then follows the duty of nurturing, teaching, educating. Baptism is also called the "washing of water by the word,"† the "washing of regeneration,"‡ a "putting on of Christ;"§ it is also said to be *saving*.|| This regenerating grace given to children in baptism, is clearly recognized in the Palatinate Liturgy, which grew up side by side with the Heidelberg Cate-chism, in the thanksgiving prayer which immediately

---

* St. Matt. xxviii. 18–20. "Μαϑητευσατε—βαπτιζοντες, *discipuliz,—baptizing.* The verb μαϑητευειν signifies *to make disciples;* it includes *baptism* and *teaching.*"—*Bengel's Gnomon.* "It is manifest that some persons have here quite misunderstood the passage by their understanding the μαϑητευσατε as what should precede baptism, just as if the meaning of the words had been, 'first instruct, then baptize them.' Even the grammatical construction does not warrant such a mode of statement; for the two participles βαπτιζοντες and διδασκοντες are precisely what constitute the μαϑητευειν. But, again, that view is contradicted by the apostolic practice, according to which instruction never preceded baptism."—*Olshausen's Commentaries.* This also is the interpretation of Lange: "Make all nations into disciples! And how is this to be accomplished? First by baptizing all who are to be taught in infancy,—and then by teaching the same." To insist upon μαϑητευσατε as involving a process of instruction preceding baptism, similar to that indicated in διδασκοντες as following baptism, would at once exclude all children from this sacrament, and establish in full the baptistic theory, which would break with the whole practice of the Apostolic Church, as well as confuse the order of plain language. Μαϑητευσατε refers rather to the *nature* of the children, being in the covenant by birth from pious parents, who on this account are open to the higher grace of baptism, and are, therefore, by the faith of parents, through this holy ordinance, to be dedicated to God, and thus made disciples, to be subsequently trained in the mysteries of grace which they hereby come to possess.

† Eph. v. 25, 26.   ‡ Titus iii. 5.   § Gal. iii. 27. || 1 Pet. iii. 21.

follows the baptismal transaction:—"Almighty, merciful God and Father, we render Thee praise and thanks, that, through the blood of Thy beloved Son Jesus Christ, Thou hast forgiven us and our children all our sins, and through Thy Holy Spirit hast received us as members of Thine only begotten Son, and thus also as Thy children, and hast sealed and confirmed all this by Holy Baptism," &c.* Thus the child comes to sustain, in Holy Baptism, an inward, mysterious, and vital relation to Jesus Christ, who is the fountain of all grace and salvation.

In the same way has baptism the effect also of relating the child to the Church. This does not mean, of course, the external and nominal Church only, as some take pleasure in thinking. Here again is found the old dualistic heresy, which if pushed to its legitimate consequences would not only result in two Churches, but also two Christs. Just as the two natures in Christ are united organically, without mixture, in one life, so the two aspects of the Church, as His body, the visible and the invisible, are but the different sides of a common organic whole, in which the sacraments stand immediately, and whose vital powers they take up, represent, and impart. The child, therefore, by baptism, is related, in a living way, to the one mystical body of Christ, so as to receive not only *through*, but also *from*, it, as a divine soil, the grace by which it grows, more and more, into Christ's image.† Thus the covenanted child is born in the Christian Church, from the life of Christ, through the operations of the Spirit, just as Christ Himself was born of the seed of Abraham, under the

---

* Dr. Daniel's Codex Liturgicus, p. 127.

† In regard to this Church relation of the catechumen the Heidelberg Catechism is clear and emphatic. To the question, "What dost thou believe concerning the Holy Catholic Church?" the catechumen is taught to answer: "I believe that, out of the whole human race from the beginning to the end of the world, the Son of God, by His Spirit and word, gathers, defends, and preserves for Himself, unto everlasting life, *a chosen communion* in the unity of the true faith; and that *I am, and forever shall remain, a living member of the same*." Ques. 54. English Church, 26th Article.

Holy Ghost, in the Jewish Church,* in which that seed was embodied and carried forward historically from age to age.

This idea is forcibly represented by the figures of *planting* and *grafting*. Indeed, the whole world of growth becomes a grand parable, in this view, pointing to this growing relation of the child to the kingdom of grace. "For," says the apostle, "if we have been *planted* together in the likeness of His death, we shall be also in the likeness of His resurrection."† The Church is pervaded both by the dying and rising life of Christ, and hence the child, planted into it, receives the benefits of both. Just as the old seed planted in the earth dies, will the new seed begin to live. So in baptism begins the death of the old nature of sin, and the new life of grace. Hence also, meeting the idea fairly, the Church is called a *garden*, a *vineyard*, a *field*, a *mother*, indicating the source of our new birth and growth from Christ in His Church. The beginning of this spiritual life in the Church is always in a small and hidden way, as the mustard-seed, "which indeed is the least of all seeds,"‡ as the leaven "which a woman took and hid in meal,"§ as the "new-born babe,"|| which is incapable of nourishing itself, but which must receive its nourishment from the mother, and that of the most delicate kind.

As the child cannot, in view of the organic relation of the Church to Christ, be in the latter without being at the same time in the former, so neither, for a similar reason, can we conceive of the child as being in the Church without possessing also the Holy Ghost. Where Christ and the Church are, there is the Holy Spirit. "Repent and be baptized," says the apostle, "in the name of Jesus Christ, for the remission of sins, *and ye shall receive the Holy Ghost.*" This language cannot be construed as limiting itself to adults, for in the following verse it is added, "*the promise is*

---

* St. John iv. 22.   † Rom. vi. 5.   ‡ St. Matt. xiii. 31, 32.
§ St. Matt. xiii. 33 || 1 Cor. iii. 1.

unto you and your children." Hence baptism is not only a "washing of regeneration," but also a *"renewing of the Holy Ghost."*† The Heidelberg Catechism recognizes the possession of the Holy Ghost by the catechumen, in express terms;‡ and the formula of baptism, specifying the three persons in the Trinity, Father, Son, and Holy Ghost, indicates no less clearly the threefold relationship which baptism gives its subjects.

The grace, then, which the covenanted child receives in the sacrament of Holy Baptism, is that which gives it a living relation to Christ, the Church, and the Holy Ghost.

The character of these several relations will be seen still more clearly by considering, in a more definite way, the relation which this baptismal grace holds to the nature of the child itself subjectively. What is the principle on which to determine, as far as may be, this relation inwardly to the child? We can conceive of none better for this purpose than the person of Christ itself. This is the pattern in the mount. There is plainly an inward parallelism between the mystery of the incarnation on the one hand, and that of regeneration on the other. These two supernatural facts can never be abstractly sundered. The last is derived from the first, not mechanically, but in a truly vital way; and although regeneration holds in a lower sphere and is altogether secondary, it still bears in it the supernatural forces of the incarnation. The last is not the shadow simply of the first,—it is rather the first itself projected in our personal human nature. In the bosom of this great fact the Christian life has its origin. Here lies its normal type, and hence arises the law according to which, from its

---

* Acts ii. 38, 39. † Titus iii. 5.

‡ *"What dost thou believe concerning the Holy Ghost?"* *Answer:* "First, that He is coeternal God with the Father and the Son: Secondly, that He is also given unto me, makes me by a true faith partaker of Christ and all His benefits, comforts me, and shall abide with me forever."—Ques. 53. And in the 76th Question the catechumens are taught to say, We "become more and more united to His sacred body by the Holy Ghost, who dwells *both in Christ and in us.*"

earliest beginnings to its most matured state, it is ruled and governed.

This relation of baptismal grace to the child subjectively is neither Ebionitic nor Gnostic; for, the one regarding the divinity of Christ as a myth, and the other His humanity as a deception, both will deny of course, on the same principle, the presence of such grace in the child altogether, and consequently are saved the trouble of determining its relations. Neither can the Eutychian blending or mixing of this grace with the nature of the child exhibit the true form of this mystery. Here is seen the fallacy of the *justitia infusa* doctrine, by which the child is supposed to be mechanically penetrated with grace, in such a way as not only to break the force of original depravity, but to destroy it altogether and make the child holy in nature. Baptism effects no such transubstantiation of the nature of the child into that of grace. The Nestorian view, which holds grace and nature entirely asunder, must be regarded, in like manner, as false in reference to the Christian child as it is in regard to the child Christ.

In the child Christ, as already seen, the relation is real and organic. The union deeply conditions both natures, but destroys the essential peculiarities of neither. His whole personality was the result, under the Holy Ghost, of this early, inward, living, and fundamental union. Even thus in the case of the Christian child. Its baptismal grace is neither sundered from nor identified with its own nature, but mysteriously united with it on the principle of life, under the same Holy Ghost, so that both, though distinct in nature, are yet really and truly one. Thus the grace of baptism is not infused into it immediately and generally, but is in its fulness rather turned over upon the central infantile life of the child organically, from which it may grow up a substantial Christian.

If it be objected here that this implies and requires a self-conscious condition on the part of the child, the objection is met by another parallelism, that, namely, which holds between the first and second Adam in their relation to the race, and the mode by which their lives, respectively, are communicated to man. "As in Adam all die, so in Christ shall all be made alive."* Wherever this analogy is contemplated in the Scriptures, it is set forth as complete at every point. Nay, the relation of Christ to the race is regarded as even more deep and real than that of Adam, for where sin abounded through the first, there hath grace much more abounded through the second.† It required no self-conscious condition on the part of the child, much less an intelligent volition, to connect it really with the corrupt life of the first Adam. This depravity has not passed directly or mechanically, but organically and through others, the race, the family, and is in every case strictly an unconscious inheritance. We can conceive of no moment, in the being of the child, at which this depravity was not present. Strict analogy now requires that we regard Christianity, as it arises in the incarnation, which is the organic assumption of the Headship of the race, as in no substantial respect inferior to the system of nature now described. Why should not the child, in these circumstances, begin life as well under the law of hereditary advantage as of hereditary damage? To allow that grace from Christ could not reach our nature at as early a point as depravity from Adam, and in as real a way, would not only break the analogy, but also argue an inferiority in the redemption itself, which true faith can never concede. Redemption, in the nature of the case, must be commensurate, in its own constitution, with the fall; and therefore

---

* 1 Cor. xv. 22. "*He* is the fountain of the whole Christian salvation (Question 18), having in Himself all the qualifications that are needed to constitute a perfect medium of reconciliation between the human nature and the divine (Questions 12–17); being in His own person in fact the fullest conjunction of both; so that 'the same human nature which hath sinned' is brought to make a full satisfaction for sin, and to become thus at the same time the righteousness of God, in Him as the second Adam."—*Nevin on the Catechism*, p. 134.

† Rom. v. 12–21.

it cannot allow any fraction of time, or any part of existence, left wholly in this way at the mercy of the evil life
from Adam, with a view to have it escape from it magically
at some future period. Just as divinity stood related to
the human nature of Christ, by the operation of the Holy
Ghost, in His unconscious childhood, so are we to suppose
that, through the covenant, comprehending Holy Baptism,
His righteousness is related to the unconscious child.
Why should this be thought more impossible than the
union of soul and body in the child; or the sign and thing
signified in the sacraments objectively; or than the communication of prophetic dreams when all the voluntary
faculties are suspended ; or than it is possible for any, old
or young, to be Christian at all while sleeping?* Although
the moral faculties of the child are not active consciously,
it nevertheless involves them all, and is, on this account, a
moral being. These, in the case of the covenanted child,
are all vitally united to the regenerating grace which·we
have already seen it to possess. To require personal faith
under an active form, on the part of the child, as a preceding condition of Baptism, would also be to go beyond
the analogy, by demanding more in the latter case, to
secure the end, than was needed in the former. Besides,
it would clearly involve the érror of Arminius, by implying that activity in the way of reaching salvation must first
arise in us, rather than in God to us. To say that a self-
conscious faith, personal with the child, is essential as a
condition of baptism, is to say also that it is essential to
salvation, and thus exclude the child from the last as well

---

* This is the reason why the Fathers generally laid such weighty stress upon
the childhood and youth of Jesus. Hear the words of one of them: "He
(Christ) came sanctifying every age *by its relation to Himself:* all, who by Him
are re-born to God: infants, and little ones, and children, and youths, and
elders. So He came in every age; and to infants was made an infant,
sanctifying infants ; among little children, a little child, sanctifying those of
this age, and made also to them an example of piety, and righteousness, and
subjection ; among young men, a young man, becoming an example to young
men, and sanctifying them to the Lord."—*Irenæus.*

466

as from the first. As the child by baptism is placed in an organic relation with Christ, the Church, and the Holy Ghost, the germ of faith must be regarded as already given herewith. In any case, and at any age, faith is a *gift* of God; and as such, why should it not be imparted by baptism as well, to say the least, as by any other means? and why not to the child as well as to the adult? Yea, why not even more readily to the child, since, as a child, it is less resistant, without wilfulness, and more passive? Thus God first turns to us, imparting all these gifts, in the case of childhood, unconsciously, and then, as these grow with our growth, we turn to God. The activity from God to us is regeneration, that resulting from this in us to God is conversion.

But active personal faith, in the sense in which this is necessary as a condition, is not wanting. The child in its constitution and covenant relations no more really represents the parents than the parents represent it. The relation of the parent to the child is, in a true sense, a vicarious relation. The child no less spiritually than physically exists in the parent, so that the faith of the parent, and the act of consecration to God in Holy Baptism, arising out of this faith, are, in a true sense, the faith and act of the child itself. This is the force of organic representation everywhere. Thus *Adam* sinned and *we* die; thus *Christ* died and *we* live. If the wicked acts of parents have real force for the children, why not also those that are good? Besides, the child when baptized is represented also by the faith of all others who, like the parents, stand in the covenant and form the communion of saints.* In this way, just as the effect of Adam's transgression enters the child through the family, so also does the result of Christ's

---

* "The faith of the Church, which consecrates infants to God in the spirit of love, takes the place of their own faith; and albeit they possess as yet no faith of their own, yet there is nothing in their thoughts to hinder the divine efficacy."—*Augustin.*

The sense of this, as rendered by *Neander*, is as follows: "that as the child, ere its corporeal and independent existence was fully developed, was

obedience pass to it through the family in covenant relation to Him. "If my sin cometh from another," says St. Bernard, "why should not my righteousness be granted me in the same manner?"*

Of course, the grace which is thus imparted cannot be regarded as completing the Christian character, any more than the depravity which the child bears in it completes, in the full sense, its wicked nature. Both are only germinally complete. They are the respective fountains from which flow the streams of sweet and bitter waters. Depravity itself is not condemning; it becomes condemning only when it becomes freely and intelligently endorsed and acted out. So grace, inherited in infancy, is itself not justifying, but becomes so also only when it is consciously chosen and actively accepted. Still, as original sin looks necessarily to actual, the child may indeed, in a certain sense, be regarded as condemned already. So, also, as covenant grace looks to actual good works, in the evangelical sense, the child may, in like manner, be looked upon as justified already. The ground, in both cases, is the law which connects the unconscious germ with its consciously developed state, but not this developed state of the germ itself, as a fact. When the child, therefore, becomes actually justified, it is not by any other grace than that which it already possesses, but this same grace intelligently endorsed and voluntarily made its own, just as the child becomes actually condemned by the power of its depravity assuming the form of actual transgression and thus involving the sense of personal guilt.

Now, from this condition of the covenanted child, which is brought about by the law of Christ's own mysterious being, and which is therefore in strict harmony with His own

---

supported by the vital forces of nature in its bodily mother, so, ere it came to the independent development of its spiritual being in its own consciousness, it is supported by the heightened vital forces of that spiritual mother, the Church."—*Church History*, vol. iv. p. 435.

* De Erroribus Abælardi.

experience, both as it regards the union between it and the parent, it and Christ, it and the Church, it and the Holy Ghost, it and the baptismal grace which the child embodies, we are led to the no less interesting and substantial subject of Christian Nurture. From this point of view the subject opens, not in a strained and arbitrary, but in a perfectly free and natural way. The nurture of the child, naturally, begins, not before but after its birth,—not with a nature which it does not possess, but with faculties which, however undeveloped, it yet really enshrines. The same must be true spiritually. Here is a real *Christian* child, possessed of a spiritual life, planted in the Church as a divine soil, and through this related inwardly and germinally to Christ and the Holy Ghost. Stier says: "If the Evangelical Church would begin diligently to point the baptized to the privileges and obligations of their baptism, and to take all pains with the fundamental religious education of those who are growing up; if institutions were to be established which should seek and strive to save those who are grovelling in sin and ignorance; then the original stamp (of Christian character from baptism) would shine out again distinctively in many who hardly exhibit it at all; then would it appear, far beyond expectation, how much of the germ of regeneration is still present among the people, derived from their baptism, and only waiting for discipline and nurture. This would be infinitely better and more correct than to blind ourselves, on account of general and flagrant perversion, to the actual grace of the Divine Institute." From this point, like the seed in the garden, it is expected to grow, not *into*, but *in*, grace, and in the knowledge of Jesus Christ.* Here the christological law of Christ's being is no less the ground-fact and moulding power than in the spheres already indicated. Thus the child Jesus *increased in wisdom and stature, and in favor with God and man.*† The covenanted child, in its advancement,

---

* 2 Peter iii. 18.   † St. Luke ii. 40, 52.

is not wholly at the mercy of the natural laws of growth, either physically or intellectually, but these laws are themselves permeated and conditioned by those of grace, which are deeper and stronger, and which, if the proper outward conditions are supplied, will always secure an inward and symmetrical growth in grace, as the body grows in size and the mind in intellectual power. In the absence of this grace there may indeed still be ground for nurture, but not *Christian* nurture, and for education, but not for *Educational Religion*, as these can only start in the *religious nature*, under a positive form, whose powers they are designed to nurture and educate.

Our moral nature, manifestly, is no more the entire work of the will than is our physical or mental. We may debase it,—we may ennoble it; but we cannot create it; nor is it developed purely by the conscious activity of our moral faculties. It involves original organic activities which necessitate progress even in the absence of mental consciousness and when the will is entirely quiescent. Cases are not rare where persons are inwardly advanced mentally and morally beyond any knowledge acquired by the force of mere will. We never wake in the morning at precisely the same point, either as it regards mental or moral being, or any of the laws or facts which these comprehend, where our intellectual or voluntary faculties were suspended by sleep on the previous evening. Our experience tells us that we are farther on,—that, however difficult to explain how, we have advanced. Nor does our spiritual nature form an exception to these facts, of which all have some experience more or less clear. Organic life, involving action, energy, whether we wake or sleep, preceding the will, forming its basis, and really independent of it, pervades every part of our being, and is equally operative at every age. But especially energetic is this life when, in addition to its own force, it enshrines the grace of Jesus Christ. "He giveth His beloved"—not "sleep,' as

470

rendered in the English Bible, but—*sleeping*,* *i.e.* communicates His gifts to His people while the active faculties are suspended by sleep. Now, this is the nature of the covenanted child no less than the adult or sire. In its after-consciousness it finds a progress which it cannot trace to its source, a progress which it had no intelligent mental, moral, or spiritual agency in accomplishing, which took place without its concurrence,—the result, therefore, purely of grace, given and governed according to the wisdom and good pleasure of God. In other words, the spiritual man does not create itself, any more than the mental and moral part of our nature does this, but is created by the mysterious agency of the Holy Ghost, without any aid from us, we "being dead in trespasses and in sins."†

The Apostle St. Paul meets the subject at this point with the most vigorous language. He takes for granted the presence of grace received in baptism at a previous period, and makes this the ground of an earnest exhortation in reference to its subsequent development under Christian nurture. "Knowing this," he says, "that our old man *is* crucified with Him, that the body of sin *might be destroyed*, that *henceforth* we should not serve sin. For he that is dead is *freed from sin*. Now, if we be *dead* with Christ, we believe that we shall also *live* with Him: knowing that Christ being raised from the dead dieth no more, death hath no more dominion over Him. For in that He *died*, He died unto sin once; but in that He *liveth*, He *liveth* unto God. *Likewise reckon ye also yourselves to be dead indeed unto sin, but alive unto God through Jesus Christ our Lord.* Let not sin

---

* Ps. cxxvii. 2. In the German translation this is rendered correctly: "Es ist unsanft, dasz ihr frühe aufstehet, und hernach lange sitzet, u. esset euer Brodt mit Sorgen; *denn seinen Freunden giebt Er es schlafend.*"

† It was by facts like these, brought up from the deeper experience of our nature and presented forcibly by St. Augustine, who was both theologian, philosopher, and logician, that the errors of Pelagius were driven from the field in the fifth century; and no less powerfully did they repel the same heresy, somewhat modified as to form by Arminius, in the sixteenth.

therefore reign in your mortal body, that ye should obey it in the lusts thereof. Neither yield ye your members as instruments of unrighteousness unto sin; but yield yourselves unto God, *as those that are alive from the dead,* and your members as instruments of righteousness unto God; for sin shall not have dominion over you; *for ye are not under the law, but under grāce."**

Moreover, Christian nurture not only starts in the organic relation of regenerating grace to the inward constitution of the child, but involves also in its own nature, as a system of education, a like union of intellectual and Christian elements. It is a system of training not heathen, not natural wholly, but natural and supernatural, which is plainly indicated by the respective spheres in which it arises and is expected to operate.

The first sphere in which this Christian nurture holds and is expected to exert itself in the case of the child, with a view to develop and expand its spiritual talent, is the family as already described. The necessity of the deeply organic nature already seen to belong to the Christian family is clearly apparent in view of the character of the work which here enlists its energies. A work is here to be accomplished in the child which precedes its consciousness, and which is to be the ground and form of that consciousness when it dawns. The nurturing forces, in the first stage, work not wilfully, but organically, upon the child. Just as the child grows physically, mentally, and morally *from* the physical, mental, and moral which lie organically in the family for it, so does it also grow spiritually *from* the spiritual, by which, in the same way, it is surrounded. In addition to the threefold natural relation, now indicated, which the parents sustain to the child, they sustain to it also another threefold relation, corresponding both with its nature and theirs, namely, that of prophet, priest, and king. This is the force of their anointing, according to

---

* Rom. vi. 6–14.

the Heidelberg Catechism.* "The character" of the parents, in this view, as well as in others, "is a stream, a river, flowing down upon the children hour by hour." In the covenant family the children see reflected, not in arbitrary or distorted form, but according to vital laws, the true constituent elements of their own being; and the parents, in the eyes of their children, may see their spiritual as well as natural likeness. Every meeting of this kind carries in it for the child a nurturing activity, which serves to draw out and unfold by the parent his image as it lies unconsciously in the child. The constitutional piety of the parent, standing itself in the living soil of the Church, is no mere autumn flower beautifully colored but destitute of fragrance. It forms a spiritual atmosphere, laden with silent nurturing forces, which penetrates the unconscious nature of the child from every point and quickens and moulds its inward life. The mere separate existence of the child from the mother does not indicate that its organic relation is broken, but rather that this same organic relation is now only broader and more free. It still lives from the parents and in the bosom of parental powers, which are as far beyond the mere volition of the father and mother as they are beyond the unconscious motions of the child's own moral nature.† No word, or

---

* Question 32.

† "We shall find that there is a law of connection, after birth, under which power over character is exerted without any design to do it. For a considerable time after birth the child has no capacity of will and choice developed, and therefore is not a subject of influence in the common sense of that term. He is not as yet a complete individual; he has only powers and capacities that prepare him to be, when they are unfolded. They are in him only as wings and a capacity to fly are in the egg. Meantime, he is open to *impressions* from every thing he sees. His character is forming under a principle, not of choice, but of nurture. The spirit of the house is breathed into his nature day by day. The anger and gentleness,—the fretfulness and patience,—the appetites, passions, and manners,—all the variant moods of feeling exhibited around him, pass into him as impressions, and become seeds of character in him; not because the parents will, but because it must be so, whether they will or not."—*Bushnell's Christian Nurture*, p. 100.

gesture, or expression of countenance, on the part of the mother particularly, is lost for the child at this formative period of the child's life. These all enter into and constitute the pabulum, so to speak, of its being, and energize the inward powers which are darkly struggling towards the light of full Christian consciousness :—

> "A pebble in the streamlet scant
> Has turn'd the course of many a river;
> A dew-drop on the infant plant
> Has warp'd the giant oak forever."

As ·the child advances under these mysterious forces, and begins consciously to open its eyes upon the world, it does this from the stand-point of a Christian character. Its nurture is continued, but, of course, under a higher and more intellectual form. Here the parents begin to *teach*, in the strict sense of this word as following baptism in the commission, always, however, in view still of the inward and gracious constitution of the child. Not lo, here, or lo, there, is Christ, but within thee; His life is formed there in germ, like the bud, to be unfolded into the beautiful flower, the full self-conscious hope of glory. With the Catechism in hand the parent meets the child as a prophet, at the family altar as a priest, and in the exercise of family authority, symbolized by the keys, he meets the child as a king, to lead it under God in the way in which it ought to go.* This is actively carrying out the injunction, "Ye fathers, provoke not your children to wrath, *but bring them up in the nurture and admonition of the* •*Lord.*"† · All this is foreshadowed in the words of the Almighty Himself in relation to Abraham, with whom He had made the covenant which comprehended his seed as well as himself: "I know him, that he will *command* his children and his household after him, that they shall *keep*"—not *seek*, as though they had not yet found it, or were not yet in it, but *keep*—"the way of the Lord, to do

---

* Prov. xxii. 6.   † Eph. vi. 4.

justice and judgment, that the Lord may bring upon Abraham that which He has spoken of him."*

The second sphere of Christian nurture, higher and wider, and according with the order in which the child came to possess its spiritual nature, is the Church in its own true and proper character. Hence the Church is called the *Lamb's Bride*, and the Christian's mother. She is the mother of us all.† In her we are born Christians;‡ and, just as the eagle stirreth up her nest, fluttereth over her young, spreadeth abroad her wings, thus drawing out their feeble powers, so the Church, as a faithful mother, teaches her children to arise on the strength of their inborn grace, and leads them, as by the hand,—

"Into the green pastures
And beside the still waters."

While the parents were thus made, for obvious reasons, the first catechists to their children, and the "Church in the house" was constituted the first nursery of piety and religious knowledge to baptized infant Christians, it is clear that the Church, as such, did not leave her families to depend upon their own energies in this work, but came to their aid as these young members advanced to an age at which they were capable of sharing in a fuller and freer communion with the Church.§ Here they are met by the pastor, in his properly official character, in the catechetical exposition of the word of God, who brings its truth, like rays of light and heat, to bear upon the seeds of grace already planted within them, with a view to prepare them for a fuller and more clearly conscious relation with the mystical body of Christ. Thus, under the word and by the silent operations of the Holy Ghost, who ever lives in the Church for this purpose, the germ of faith is expanded

---

* Gen. xviii. 19.   † Gal. iv. 26.   ‡ Ps. lxxxvii. 4, 6.

§ Vide Bingham's Antiq. vol. i. p. 431. Calvin's Institutes, book iv. chap. xix. 4.

and made to assume a direct and full relation to Jesus Christ.

Here also we meet the Parochial School in its true original character. Its necessity arises, first, from the inward demand of Christianity itself as connected with the mind, and, second, from the almost entire absence of Christianity, under any direct, positive educational form, in the schools of the State. Inferior as the most of these schools are in a strictly classical point of view to those which flourished in Roman Gaul between the fourth and fifth centuries, and which no doubt greatly aided, because of their purely pagan character, the decline and fall of the Empire,— namely, those of Treves, Bordeaux, Autun, Toulouse, Poitiers, Lyons, Narbonne, Arles, Marseilles, Vienne, Besançon, and others,—we can scarcely say that they are much superior to them in a positive Christian view. True, they have the Bible,—more, however, it is plain, in the way of compliment to it than of benefit from it to them: it is not allowed to enter the mental crucible, and hence forms no real part of the educational result. Nor can the Church expect the State to take the lead in this higher form of education, or furnish the facilities for its attainment. It could not, even if it felt so disposed. If Christianity, therefore, is to penetrate science, philosophy, literature, and art, condition the thinking of the young, and through them furnish the basis of true mental, moral, and even material progress, there must be a distinctive school,—that is to say, a school which in its origin and constitution involves the spiritual and the natural in vital union. This is the Parochial School. It claims no divine origin or nature, but is still closely associated with the Church, and made to meet her children in their Christian character and educate them on the Church principle. Its aim is to educate, in a joint way, both the spiritual and the natural faculties of the children, or rather their intellectual powers as conditioned by the principle of grace which they possess.

From the life of grace the children are made to wake up

to the world of scientific wonders. They are educated to see the presence of God in all His handiworks, and to hear His voice, born from the day, "uttering speech," and from the night, "showing knowledge." As the natural and supernatural are mysteriously joined in their own consciousness, so does this Christian education prepare them to behold their union also in history, philosophy, literature, and science; so that these, in this way, instead of leading from God, as they often do under their purely naturalistic character, constitute so many avenues through which they approach, with a more enlarged mind and heart, to the great Jehovah. Thus they are prepared to bow more humbly to Christ, and to adore Him more profoundly, as they are made to behold the law of His being giving shape and character to the world, causing it thus to meet and reflect the christological mould of their own minds. The harmony between science and revelation is in this way recognized as full and complete throughout. Thus also they see the elevated and spiritual purposes of the world, as well as those which are merely temporal and natural. It is all constituted a vast parable by the Incarnation of Christ, adumbrating from every point higher and more spiritual facts in the kingdom of grace.

The Sunday-school also, so far as it involves the baptized children of the Church, finds its legitimate work in developing this covenant grace, in cultivating the religious consciousness, and in strengthening the disposition on their part to claim the full advantage of the Church to which they have a good title. The Sunday-school was, however, originally designed for a very different class of children,—those who had none of the advantages which have now been described, but whose spiritual wants had been entirely neglected. To meet such and prepare them, as best it could, for the benefits of Christian baptism, the Sunday-school was originally designed. It was formed without an eye to grace in children; and, although the character of the children that are now brought under its educational control has at least prevailingly changed, the school itself still adheres extensively to its original nature,—regarding practically all children as in the same condition spiritually, out of Christ and destitute of grace. In so far as this proper discrimination is wanting in the practical operations of the school, it cannot be regarded as a genial nursery for the youthful members of the Church, but rather as a serious hindrance in their way. Instead of digging about the seed and watering it, it goes upon the assumption that the seed is not planted at all,—thus ignoring their true nature. Unlike the genial rays of the sun, which shine upon the plants in the garden, encouraging their growth, the influences of the school in this view are rather like the chilling autumnal winds and frosts, which soon strip them of their flowers, drive back their tender life, and cause them to wilt and die. Where, however, the Sunday-school has changed its system and made it to correspond with the covenanted children so far as these have been brought into it, and is seeking not to *give* but to *educate* the principle of spiritual life already at hand, it is a real aid both to the family and the Church; otherwise it is manifest that both the parents, the Church, and the children themselves would be far better off without it.

Now, under these several nurturing influences the children, planted in the Church by Holy Baptism, are expected to grow up Christians without ever knowing themselves to have been otherwise. This growth is gradual, quiet, and mysterious, as in all other forms of growth. "So is the 'kingdom of God, as if a man should cast *seed into the ground*, and should sleep, and rise night and day; and the *seed should spring and grow up, he knoweth not how*. For the earth *bringeth forth fruit of herself;* first the *blade*, then the *ear*, after that the *full corn in the ear*."* Here is an objective garden of plants pervaded by vital forces. From these forces the plants grow up, we know not how,—not, we do

---

* St. Mark iv. 26–29.

know, from merely designed personal effort, but from life-laws back of and deeper than the will. Such persons may never know when, or where, or how, they first began to love God. The time when they become conscious of this love is not the time when the love itself began to exist. Birth, naturally, always precedes the consciousness of it; and it were indeed a rather anomalous occurrence if, in the spiritual world, both should begin together. Regeneration is the beginning of the new creature in Christ Jesus, and to suppose that this new creature should come to any thing like consciousness of its existence, and of the constituent elements that compose its being, *immediately afterward*, would imply a rapidity or haste which would show it to be disconnected from all organic laws, to lie wholly on the outside of all analogy, and thus to be magical and not real. Many evidently deceive themselves by taking the sensible experience (quite vivid at times) which is felt when the mind wakes consciously to the presence of grace, for the beginning of this grace. This they call their new birth; whereas it is but the conscious recognition of it, and the point at which they voluntarily begin to turn or convert themselves to God. Here occurs the doctrine of conversion as it lies, not in the second, but in the third part of the Catechism, showing its order in the Christian experience.

In the case of the most of baptized children, however, under these silent educational forces, such is the gradual unfolding of the germ of regenerating grace, such is its quiet spread through their moral and mental being, that they are not able to point to any time or place at which they had any special or technical experience. To produce in such a consciousness of the divine favor, no quack apostle is needed to beat waves upon the emotional nature. There are no spasms in the normal evolution of grace from its germ to its fully developed maturity. Their life, from their baptism, arises under organic forces and by imperceptible degrees into the full drawing of the Christian character, so gently, amid such soft blendings of coloring, and with all, in the constant enjoyment—being children of God in fact—of so much real spiritual pleasure, that, like Baxter and others, they are utterly at a loss to tell where, at what time, or how they first became Christians in fact, or even to recognize themselves as such.

There is nothing better calculated than this true view to break that hardness and rudeness which have entered the piety of the present day, and to give it those softer charms which will attract rather than repel the mind. Activity is important; but all, nor yet the greater part, of the vast interest here involved, does not depend on our activity. To rest calmly in God's energies, which are active whether we wake or sleep, is no less a Christian grace. The humility arising from this objective view is essential to relieve those sharp features of piety which are produced by the impression that every thing depends upon direct individual effort. Calm hopefulness amid gentle energy in the bosom of divine powers is crowned more surely than the boldness that would take heaven by violence.*

This Christian nurture, under its direct character, completes itself, at least as to its first stage, in the sacred rite of Confirmation. Here the Christian bud comes to its first bloom. This rite involves more than a mere acknowledgment of the grace of baptism, accompanied with a solemn inward dedication to God of body, soul, and spirit, and a personal confession of faith in the great facts of the Christian salvation as embodied in the Creed. This is much on the subjective side; but, on the objective, it involves the "laying on of hands," the appropriation of God, the confirmation of the grace previously received, and a real leading on the part of God to a constantly nourishing and sustaining grace, without which, whatever is already at hand, must soon languish and perish. Here the way is open to the Lord's Supper, the "holiest of all," on which he feeds by faith, and by which he is carried forward—in

---

* Zech. iv. 6.

the use also of other divinely-appointed means—from strength to strength, until, at last, he shall be filled with all the fulness of God. This is to train a child in the way he should go; and, if no serious or substantial defect is found in the training itself, the promise annexed to it is absolute, " *When he is old, he will not depart from it.*"*

This now, in a very general way, is the outline of the educational system of religion which is supposed to underlie the Heidelberg Catechism. It is a religion which starts in the birth of the child in the covenant from pious parents, in view of which it is declared "holy,"—which rises to higher degrees of Christian perfection in Holy Baptism, where the grace from below is met by the grace from above,—is. carried forward in the bosom of the family and the Church under the vital forces of Christian nurture, and is made to bloom into conscious Christian character in the sacred rite of Confirmation and the Holy Sacrament of the body and blood of Jesus Christ. Underneath all, and as giving significance to every part and, finally, to the whole, lies the law of Christ's own person, mysteriously moulding that of the Christian into His own image, making him to repeat definitely the experience through which He passed in working out the great salvation and ascending, at last, to His throne in heaven.

That this *is* the underlying system of the Heidelberg Catechism will be manifest already by a mere casual glance at the first question.† Here the catechumen is evidently addressed as a personal Christian, and the answer which he is taught to return is just as clearly the answer of a personal Christian, for every word implies the presence of grace as its source. Whence did the catechumen derive this grace, but in his birth from pious parents and Holy Baptism? Thus the Catechism starts, and, in the way of detail, every subsequent part is made to form itself

---

* Prov. xxii. 6.

† The order of illustration and proof here adopted is that of Rev. Dr. Harbaugh's, published in the Mercersburg Review, vol. ix. p. 54.

harmoniously from this deep beginning. This question and answer can never be understood by those who stand outside of this system and in some other theory. Either they must rule out the meaning of this question altogether, or say that the Catechism in this particular tends to make "hypocrites," by placing words in the mouths of children for which they have no corresponding grace in their hearts. This charge were true, indeed, did the Catechism not stand in the substantial system of religion now described; but, recognized as holding in this system, no symbol can be further removed from the charge of favoring hypocrisy. Regarding the children of the covenant as possessing grace, the Catechism only teaches them to utter the language becoming their true nature and condition.

The order of the Catechism shows it no less to belong throughout to the system of religion now indicated. It is divided into three parts: the first concerns our misery; the second, our deliverance; and the third, our gratitude. Whatever things, institutions, or agencies these three parts comprehend respectively, are by the Catechism regarded as being necessary to accomplish the several Christian benefits which the parts themselves designate. Otherwise the book would be loose, unsystematic, and without either moral or logical force,—a jumble, rather than a system of facts. The Church and the Sacraments are placed not in the first, nor in the third, but in the second part. This is certainly significant as to the estimate in which these are held. They are regarded not only as a confirmation of grace already at hand, but as being concerned with the *origination* of our Christian life as well. Here arises the doctrine of *regeneration*, which those who stand in other systems fail altogether to recognize in the Catechism under any distinct form. Regeneration belongs to the second part of the Catechism just as conversion belongs to the third. Not to allow that the doctrine under its full and proper form occurs here, especially as connected with Holy Baptism, is indeed to be driven to the necessity of saying that it occurs nowhere in the Heidelberg Catechism, which would affect in a very radical way its hitherto supposed completeness as a system of Christian training. It would still be a symbol professedly Christian, but without Christianity,—as teaching the way of practical religion without defining where or how that way begins,—a sun without light or heat, a statue without heart or eye, a body without soul. Surely no such destructive negativism can be found in the Christian symbol which, of all others, has been most admired for its rich evangelical fulness and systematic theological completeness, if any thing like due force is allowed to its own form and order. Unchurchly systems invariably place the Church and Sacraments in the last part, implying thereby that they have no agency in the producing of the Christian life,—rather that they are privileges to be enjoyed after the new life of grace is obtained in some other way. The reverse order of the Catechism, however, shows conclusively a different order of system in which it moves, —a different mind altogether from that which sees no inward efficacy in the sacraments corresponding with their outward symbolical import.

The central position of the Apostles' Creed is no less significant in determining the same general fact. The Creed breathes the true christological spirit throughout, and, exhibiting the Church as an object of faith rather than of knowledge, clearly gives to it and its sacraments the mysterious life-giving and life-nourishing power which has now been described in part. The whole history of the Reformed Church previous to the formation of the Catechism confirms the point here made. Faith in the objective over against mere private individualism, and in the mysterious in contrast with the baldness which was afterward created by rationalism, was the deepest element of her life. Nothing but the Catechism of the Creed could properly meet this reigning spirit; and this must account also for its wonderful popularity and power from the beginning. This Creed itself grew organically in the consciousness of the

Church from the mystery of Christ's person; and no one can fail to perceive that the Heidelberg Catechism grew from it in very much the same way.

Nor can the idea of authority which, under the symbol of the keys, the Catechism gives to the Church, be explained satisfactorily on any other system. The authority which the Catechism accords to the Church involves the right of determining what is true and what is false doctrine, and what is regular and what irregular in the way of practice. It regards the acts of exclusion by the Church as being the acts of God, "whereby they are excluded from the Christian Church, and by God Himself from the kingdom of Christ."* Now, the Church, to wield such power, linking itself directly with that of God Himself and involving a real significance in heaven and on earth, cannot be a mere voluntary association from the human side simply, either on a human or divine principle. It must manifestly be *above* men,—must be a supernatural creation, as we have already seen,—His body, in the full mystical sense of the term, to whom all power is given both in heaven and in earth. But this is only to proclaim, in the most emphatic language, that the Catechism belongs to the Church system, which in the way of mystery involves the supernatural in the natural.

The place assigned to the *law* in its proper character determines, in the same clear way, the system of religion to which it belongs. It occurs, indeed, in the first part; but not in its strict character as law distinguished from gospel. At this place and in this character it is rather the "New Commandment," whose soul is filial love, which Christ gave to His "little children."† It is the law as lying in the Cross and as speaking from the richest life of the gospel, producing no slavish fear, but a deep evangelical sorrow. The idea of a legal drill, as fitting children for confirmation independently of baptismal grace, is

---

* Question 85.   † St. John xiii. 34.

entirely excluded by the nature of the law as it is made to speak from the first part of the Catechism. It is not found in the second part at all, under any distinct form; and we only see it in its full character in the third part, at which point the child is expected to meet it on the principle of grace consciously developed, and obey it on the ground of love. Here it becomes an educator, and, at the same time, a medium of gratitude for "such great deliverance" as is already wrought in the case of the baptized catechumen.

Finally, the Catechism itself determines the system of religion in which it moves by the stand-point from which it views the peculiarities both of Calvinism and Arminianism. While it has been charged as involving both, it may be said, with equal truth, to involve neither, — technically neither,—and yet, from its own peculiar genius, both. It is Calvinistic; but not in viewing the will of God, connected with election and reprobation, as something abstract, accomplishing its ends in an arbitrary and, at last, fatalistic way; or as making the incarnation of Christ a mere after-thought and an outward expedient, by which, as a means, the divine will, as the central causal principle, might secure its end. The Heidelberg Catechism views the will of God as embodying itself concretely in the person of Jesus Christ, who, as having all power in heaven and in earth, is the *source,* and not the means simply, of salvation. The person of Christ Himself is the origin of the decree for man. All the purposes of God actualize themselves in, and do not stand in front of, Christ, His Church and history; nor do they overleap these in an independent way in realizing themselves in the case of men. In Christ lies the decree of God; and in the Church it unfolds its power and grace. In the covenanted family we are called, in Confirmation we are chosen, and in the Holy Supper we are elected. A rejection of what is offered in these divine institutions is our reprobation. Nor does the Catechism endorse, in the high Calvinistic sense, the doctrine of perseverance, which is equally mechanical and arbitrary outside of the Church system. The nearest approach that is made to this idea is in the first question. Here, however, all is conditioned by the relation which we sustain to our "faithful Saviour Jesus Christ." Much depends upon our own fidelity to Christian duty on the ground of the grace which has already been planted within us by baptism. Although the catechumen has, in the way now described, reached new powers, he is still free in them and responsible for their proper use or abuse. The plant, however truly planted in the soil, may yet wither and die. The Jews, although they were the seed of Abraham, were yet by this fact not absolutely saved. Failure to comply practically with the duties involved in their position separated them from the promise of God no less than from their father Abraham, through whom it was made. So "we are made partakers of Christ, *if we hold the beginning of our confidence to the end.*"*

Here the Arminian also speaks from the Catechism; yet not from the Arminian, but Church basis. The Catechism, as already seen, implies gracious ability in those to whom it speaks, not, however, so as to deny the doctrine of total depravity, but so as to assert the presence at the same time of a spiritual factor,—derived, first, from the incarnation in a general way; second, and more specifically, from the incarnation through the constitution of the pious family; and third, and more specifically still, from ·the incarnation through the ordinance of Christian baptism. Here are three grades of spiritual ability, all falling back—not on nature, which is totally depraved, but —on Christ, who is the redeeming life of the world. Thus the Church system places the ground of salvation, not, with Calvin, in the abstract divine decree, nor, with Arminius, in the human purpose in an equally abstract way,—both uniting at last in making Christ a means, and not the

---

* Heb. iii. 14.

principle, of salvation,—but in the divine will as embodied in Jesus Christ and the Church, His body, by which we become first apprehended in the sacrament of Holy Baptism. All this indicates plainly enough that the Heidelberg Catechism lies at every point most fully and freely in the system of religion arising in the person of Christ, as we have now endeavored to set it forth. Its relation to this system is indeed like that of a plant to the soil, or fruit to the tree: it has grown out of it, taken its form from it, always rests in it, and, separated from it, can never be understood in its own true and deep genius.

As a corollary to the foregoing, we may yet remark that the two systems—the churchly, now described, and the unchurchly, carried along by implication—can never blend or in any real way unite with each other, either in whole or in part. By their own nature they are mutually exclusive. To endorse the one is to reject the other. Besides, the success of the German Reformed Church, both in Europe and in this country, has been plainly measured hitherto by her degree of fidelity to her own system of religion. The Catechism has had prominence, vigor, power, just in so far as in the consciousness of the people it has been made to move steadily on the law of true christology; but just as this underlying system has been lost sight of, or exchanged for another, has the Catechism itself been degraded and its power diminished. Where the Church has been most numerous, and the Christian graces most modest and humble, there has reigned the sacramental sense of religion; and where it has lost its power of growth, and in some cases died altogether, notwithstanding the greater boldness of the so-called spiritual virtues, there has the Church-system been superseded by the unchurchly and fanatic. May the German Reformed Church never hereafter lose sight of the history of her origin, nor the great christological law of life by which she is formed, nor yet of the sacramental sense of religion which she has been raised up to educate and promote. The signs in her midst are now even more favorable in this view than they have ever been heretofore. At this hour, the Church cleaves to her venerable symbol with an ardor which promises to increase with the increase of faith and knowledge,—rejoicing in it as the true key of her organization, and the bond also by which she will rise into new strength, and become fully compacted together as a holy temple unto the Lord.

488

CATECHETICS

AND

CATECHETICAL INSTRUCTION.

By REV. B. BAUSMAN, A.M.
CHAMBERSBURG, PA.

2 L

CATECHETICS AND CATECHETICAL INSTRUCTION.

By Reb. B. Bausman, A.M., Chambersburg, Pa.

CATECHETICS is the science of imparting religious instruction to the young. It is as old as the Christian Church. Jesus Christ was the ideal Catechist. How often He abruptly stops the flow of His discourse, and catechizes the multitude or His disciples! How apt, pointed, and well put are His questions! With what matchless skill He seizes upon the answers received, and improves them for the instruction of His hearers! And none of His questions were more solemn and penetrating than the three He put to Simon Peter after His resurrection: "Feed my sheep." "Feed my lambs."

Catechetics is nowhere mentioned in the Bible as a distinct office. In Ephesians iv. 11, five different offices are mentioned,—apostles, prophets, evangelists, pastors, and teachers. Whilst the word does not occur here, however, some of the offices specified substantially comprise duties which afterward were developed into the office of the catechist. The instruction which the apostles imparted. in the nature of the case, had to be mainly addressed to adults. In their addresses to the people they dwelt on the most general and essential topics of the gospel. Peter's sermon on Pentecost (Acts ii. 14–40), and his address to Cornelius (Acts x. 34–43), give us samples of the apostolic method of instruction. Their remarks were usually adapted to the character and capacities of their hearers. To the Jews they spoke of the Messianic promises, and showed how these were fulfilled in the person of Christ; to the Gentiles they showed how God's anointed was the "unknown God," whom for long ages they had ignorantly worshipped and blindly sought. But some instruction had to precede baptism. They must know something of Him in whom they are to believe; they must be taught to "observe all things whatsoever He has commanded."

It is no argument against catechization that it was not practised as a complete system by the apostles. Other offices of equal importance were then but in a formative state, in a state of becoming,—im Werden begriffen. Although the gospel was preached by the apostles, yet, as a distinct office, we do not find preaching until the middle of the third century. Up to this period, any member of the Church, by the permission of the bishop, could edify the congregation by preaching.

In the process of time the teaching functions of the Church were matured into more of a system. Multitudes knocked at her doors for admission. The most of these were from the lower and more ignorant classes. Many of them were Gentile converts, having their minds still tainted with a love for pagan rites and a lingering, superstitious reverence for idolatrous ceremonies. Their indiscriminate reception, without some preparatory training and doctrinal test, threatened to flood the different communities with a mass of crude, uncontrollable material. This led to the formation of the catechumenate, designed to furnish the needful preparatory instruction to applicants for baptism and church-membership. Persons were admitted among the catechumens by the laying on of the hands of the bishop. Sometimes he instructed them; at others the deacons and presbyters attended to this duty. In addition to these formal instructions, the catechumens derived much benefit from the intimate social intercourse cultivated among the early Christians. The doctrines of the gospel were topics of daily conversation. The heroic example of martyred saints, and the felt preciousness of grace, infinitely endeared by the support and comfort it yielded in seasons of trial, kindled and kept alive a fervid faith on the altar of their hearts. And out of the abundance of the heart the mouth spoke,—spoke in the simple, unadorned language of private life, which carried the truth to the hearts of those who were inquiring for the Saviour.

An important impulse was given to catechetics, in the middle of the second century, by the founding of the celebrated catechetical school in Alexandria in Egypt. Its origin dates still farther back; but, according to Eusebius, its existence only becomes historically certain about this time. Its teachers belong to the most celebrated scholars of the early Church. Toward the end of the second century, Pantänus, a Gentile convert, infused into it a Christian life. He was successively followed by Clemens of Alexandria, Origen, Heraklas, and Dionysius, who all received their catechetical training here. The instructions were imparted at the house of the catechist. Men and women flocked to hear them. Some came in search of truth, others to hear a literary celebrity. To those desiring it, instruction was also given in philosophy. But it is said that Clemens confined himself to the pure, simple " milk of the word," discarding metaphysical speculations on the being of God, the origin of the world, and kindred abstruse topics, in whose discussion the scholastics of a later age indulged so largely. Similar institutions were established, and flourished for a season, in Rome, Cesarea-Palestina, and Antioch. But the object of all these catechetical schools was to train and educate catechists and Christian philosophers rather than to impart catechetical instruction to the common masses. And in this way they wielded, for a season, an immense power. Their scholars were scattered over the Church, and, by their catechetical skill, became centres of influence. Some of them wrote works which have come down to us as monuments of patristic piety and learning.

The specimens of catechetical lectures which have been

preserved to us from the early Church are simple expositions of points of doctrine and practice. We do not find
catechization here in the modern sense of the term.
Cyril of Jerusalem delivered a course of lectures in the
Church of the Holy Sepulchre, in the middle of the fourth
century, to unbaptized catechumens and to some recently-
baptized converts. Gregory of Nyssa in his great Catechetical Discourse, and Augustine in his epistle to Deogratias on "The Catechizing of the Unlearned," have left
us samples of their catechetical efforts. But they are
simply lectures consisting of a continuous address, without
arresting the attention or inciting the learner's mind to
activity by means of questions.

This epistle of Augustine to Deogratias gives us a
glimpse at the difficulties which confronted the catechists
of the early Church. He was a deacon at Carthage, and
appeals to Augustine for advice. In replying to him,
Augustine says that persons were often brought to Deogratias "to receive instruction in the first rudiments of the
Christian faith, in consequence of his being judged to
possess a rich power of catechizing, the result both of
knowledge in the Faith and of sweetness of speech; but
that on almost every occasion he felt himself to be in a
strait, in what manner profitably to set forth that very
doctrine by the belief of which we are Christians; at
what point to commence, and up to what point to carry on
the narration; whether, when the narration is ended, we
ought to use any exhortation, or merely to add those
precepts by the future observance of which he whom we
are addressing may understand that the Christian life
and profession is maintained. Then again," Augustine
proceeds, "you have confessed and complained that it
hath often happened to you, that in a long and lukewarm discourse you grew to be worthless and weari-
some to yourself, much more to him whom you were by
your speech endeavoring to instruct, and to the rest who
were present as hearers." After giving Deogratias advice

as to the best method of catechization, he concludes with a specimen lecture, such as he would be likely to deliver to the persons described.

The Apostolical Constitutions (vii. 39) prescribe the following outline of doctrines: "Those that are catechized shall, previous to their baptism, be instructed in the doctrines of godliness, that is to say, in the knowledge of the only begotten Son of God, and in the conviction of the Holy Ghost. They shall learn the order of creation, of providence, and of the giving of the law. They shall be taught why the world was created, and why man became a citizen of the world. They shall learn the constitution of their own nature. They shall be taught how that God punishes the wicked with water and fire, but preserves the saints; and how, too, God in His providence has never deserted the human race." Moreover, they were to be instructed in the doctrine of the Trinity, of the Incarnation, of the forgiveness of sins, and of good works, of Baptism, the covenant with God and renunciation of the devil. From all this we learn that, although not in use in its present form, catechization was substantially practised in the early Church. Clemens of Alexandria, Irenæus, Tertullian, and the Clementine Homilies trace its origin to apostolic times. From the first founding of the catechumenate, catechists were held in high esteem. Their work was considered essential to the healthy growth of the Church. To reach females, and the more successfully to impress their minds with the truth, the instruction of their sex was assigned to the deaconesses, so long as their order continued.

The Middle Ages.—In the Middle Ages we notice a marked declension in catechization. The introduction of foreign elements, of untutored barbaric masses, which, under the circumstances, it was impossible always thoroughly to Christianize and practically to assimilate, impaired the educational activities of the Church. The wholesale and sometimes forced conversion of the barbarians seemed to leave no room for instruction prior to reception into her communion. When baptism was made a term of capitulation with a conquered foe,—when the Roman captives were the chief missionaries among their German conquerors,—when the marching of a vanquished army through a river was pronounced Christian baptism,—we need not be surprised that catechization should have gone out of practice. Deluged with a resistless restive tide of half-changed barbarians, it was but natural that the Church should in a measure lose her earlier catechetical zeal and activity. Efforts were made, here and there, to instruct a tribe of barbarians. Some of the convents made it their duty to instruct the young, but their endeavors were mainly confined to the children of wealthy and noble families. Occasionally the solitary voice of a bishop would be vainly raised in behalf of the young, perishing for lack of knowledge. Charlemagne and Louis the Pious issued general decrees, calling for a revival of religious instruction. The former called upon the convents to interest themselves in the religious education of the young in their neighborhoods, and admonished the priests to teach the children of their congregations the Lord's Prayer and the Creed. If they understood not the Latin, they should teach them in their mother-tongue. It is evident, however, that all their efforts resulted at best simply in a mechanical memorizing of the Creed and the Lord's Prayer.

In the eighth century, Kero, a monk of St. Gall, in Switzerland, published the first German Catechism. In the middle of the ninth century, *Rabanus Maurus*, afterwards Archbishop of Mentz, called the First Schoolman of Germany, published a method for the preparation of catechumens, and made earnest efforts to introduce catechetical instruction. As we approach the Reformation, the sense of want in this direction increases. Voices are heard at Church-councils, and occasionally from a bishop in his diocese, for a revival of catechization. But, as the Church adopted no formal and practicable measures to remedy the existing evil, earnest men began to work informally and without ecclesiastical sanction. As Palmer truly remarks (Evangelische Katechetik, p. 12): "The heretics of the Middle Ages inaugurated a new period for catechetics. And if we ask what they have rendered for this cause, it can be replied:—*a*. They accorded to the baptized youth the care and nurture of Christian instruction; *b*. They introduced catechisms into their communions, to give to their common faith a more fixed basis for the mind and memory; *c*. From early youth they sought to lead their people to the fountain of Scripture, which the Roman Catholic Church fails to do to this day." The Waldenses formed a catechism as early as A.D. 1100. The Jeromites or Gregorians, a sect founded by Gerhard Groote in 1384, likewise made great efforts to instruct the masses. For their zeal in this direction the mendicant monks tried their utmost to have them excommunicated. Thus, in the night of mediæval Catholicism, here and there an erratic ray darted above the horizon, heralding the dawn of returning day.

The Reformation.—The Reformers did not originate a new system of catechization, but simply developed the work of their predecessors. The doctrine of the universal priesthood of believers, and that of the Bible as the only rule of faith, would necessarily lead to a more general circulation of the Scriptures, and to the religious instruction of the common people. At this the Reformers aimed from the start. Having lost confidence in the magical efficacy of means, and in the blind mechanical memorizing of the Creed and the Lord's Prayer, they endeavored as far as possible to give an intelligible exposition of these, and to apply their truths practically to the heart and life. Catechetical institutions were founded. Their ecclesiastical regulations prescribe the duties of catechists and catechumens in detail,—when to catechize, how and how often, who and whom. Numerous catechisms were formed, —among others, our own Heidelberg Catechism, whose adoption the Reformed Church, after the expiration of an-

other hundred years, is, in the providence of God, permitted to commemorate.

But even in this period we do not yet find catechetics
developed into a distinct science. What we call catechization, by a free interchange of questions and answers, was
unknown even to the Reformers. The children committed
the catechism, and recited their lessons in the catechetical
meetings, all with a view, however, of assisting them to
understand the catechetical sermon. This consisted of a
simple explanation of portions of the catechism, for which
their previous lessons were but a preparation.

Despite the zeal of the Lutheran and Reformed branches
of Protestantism, catechization again declined. After the
death of the Reformers, the simple exercises held for the
young degenerated into a dry formal routine, without sap
or savor. In the hands of schoolmasters they were made
burdensome tasks, without religious unction, and repulsive
to the youthful mind. Ere long these exercises were
superseded by catechetical sermons, rendered pointless by
the abstruse speculations of Protestant scholastics.

Much as had been done for catechization in the previous
history of the Church, it was not until the seventeenth
century that it was developed and perfected into a distinct
science. The first work on catechetics was written by
Trotzendorf, toward the end of the sixteenth century, entitled *Methodium Doctrinæ Catecheticæ.* Again, as before,
catechetics received a reviving impulse from one in advance
of his age and who was persecuted for what was supposed his
unchurchly zeal. To Spener, the founder of the Pietist
school in Germany, more than to any other man, belongs
the credit of raising catechization to a science. His simple
expositions of doctrine, according to the order of Luther's
Smaller Catechism, kindled a new life in a large religious
circle, and gave a new impulse to Protestant Christianity
in Germany. What the rulers vainly endeavored to accomplish by royal edicts, Spener effected by his humble
personal efforts and influence. His instructions to the

young incited thousands earnestly to study the word of God. So unpopular had catechization become among the masses that when Spener was promoted by his ruler, they said of him, "In endeavoring to procure a court-preacher our Grand Duke has obtained a schoolmaster." His writings, lectures, and sermons form an epoch in the history of catechetics. From this on, it became a regular branch of study in some of the German universities. The first theory of catechetics was published by Mosheim, in his "Sittenlehre der heiligen Schrift," Halle, 1735. He was followed by Baumgarten and others. Thus the scientific groundwork of catechetics was laid. Others have continued to work at the superstructure. The building is still progressing. It is by no means completed. Much material and work are still needed to finish what has been so auspiciously begun. Notwithstanding the progress which has been made, however, leading writers on this subject regard the science of catechization as still in its infancy.

The Protestant Churches of Germany excel all others in their theory and practice of catechetics. The Lutheran, Reformed, Moravian, and United Evangelical bodies make the thorough and faithful instruction of the young a uniform practice. The German Reformed Church of the United States continues to practise the excellent usage inherited from the fatherland, as does also the main part of the Lutheran Church. The Dutch Reformed Church has from the start practised catechization. Holland has even surpassed Germany in furnishing valuable expositions of the Heidelberg Catechism.* The constitution of the Dutch Reformed Church in this country requires every one who takes a pastoral charge, to explain a portion of the Heidelberg Catechism on every Lord's day, so as to go over the whole of it, if possible, every year. The Church of England has practically retrograded in its catechetical zeal. In some parts of the Scotch Presbyterian Church the good old prac-

---

* Nevin on the Heidelberg Catechism, p. 98.

tice of family catechization is still retained. On every Lord's day, the father of the family, or one of the elders of the Church, catechizes the members of the household. So far as we can ascertain, however, this excellent custom has to a great extent gone out of use in the Presbyterian Churches of this country. Time will not allow us to give a detailed history of modern catechetics in the different branches of Protestantism.

It is conceded by standard Catholic writers that the revival of catechization by the Churches of the Reformation incited to a corresponding activity in the Roman Church. Roman Catholic catechisms were multiplied. Canisi's Catechism, published in 1554, is commended to general use by the Emperor Ferdinand and Philip, King of Spain. Both acknowledge that they found it necessary to oppose a catechism to the many works of this kind published by the errorists.* The same acknowledgment is made by the Council of Trent, which for this reason found it necessary to publish the catechism named after it. With all its catechisms, however, the Roman Catholic Church possesses a meagre system of catechization. As a general thing, its exercises simply consist of a memorizing and reciting of the lessons by rote.† In later times earnest men have made unauthorized efforts to improve their defective method. Some of these have been barely tolerated; others have been censured for their zeal.‡

The Greek Church published its first catechism in the middle of the seventeenth century. The multiplication of catechisms, and the zeal shown in their use, promised for a season a great improvement in her educational system; but she has relapsed into her former torpid state.

The history of catechization, like the history of the Church, is an alternating between light and darkness, be-

---

* Koecher's Kat. Gesch. der Päpstlichen Kirche, Jena, pp. 275–284.
† Pastoral Theologie, von Claus Harms, 1 Theil, p. 136.
‡ Palmer, Evangelische Katechetik, p. 48.

tween the revival and the decay of life. Like all vital growth, it has battled its way toward maturity through hindrances many and formidable. Like a good seed, it has fought its way through frost and thaw, through rain and drought, down to this present. It has steadily advanced. It will continue to grow. Ours is the honor to aid its progress.

The Method of Catechization.—It cannot be disguised that the prevailing educational spirit of this country is essentially uncatechetical. A notion is popular, that religion is not to be obtained by such means,—that it may be good enough in its place, but cannot be of any real effect in leading a soul to a saving knowledge of the truth, or in securing the renewing of the Holy Ghost. This, after all, it is supposed, must be produced by something else. Thus it has come to pass that, even in Churches which in former years practised catechization, the system has been emptied of its substantial significance and is now used only by way of compliment to a venerated custom.

In this country our classes of catechumens are often composed of baptized and unbaptized persons. Whatever may be our views of the objective power of baptism, it will be generally conceded that a baptized person sustains a different relation to Christ and the Holy Ghost from one that is unbaptized. So far as religious instruction is concerned, baptism predisposes the heart to gracious impressions. As the earth's surface in the spring of the year is turned toward the sun at an angle which will increase the life-giving heat of his rays, so baptism turns the heart to Christ, and to the Holy Ghost, at a renewing saving angle. A baptized person is no longer a natural man, in the sense of one unbaptized.* In the Church of St. Ouen, in France, there is a baptismal font, in whose water you can see reflected the whole grand architecture, pillar, arch, and roof of the building. It is a beautiful image of the relation of

---

* Ebrard, Praktische Theologie, p. 143.

baptism to the education and future character of the subject. The small font collects and concentrates in its mysterious mirror the possibilities of the future man.

The unbaptized are not as favorable subjects for catechization as the baptized. They require a different treatment. It would almost seem necessary to follow the example of the early Church, and adopt some special method to reach those outside of the covenant,—a mission-catechization to suit their peculiar case.

A proper family training is a necessary preparation for catechization. Christian nurture in the family is related to catechization as the law is to the gospel. It is a schoolmaster to bring them to the catechumenate. Christian education begins in the family, is continued in the school, completed in the catechetical class, and crowned by confirmation. Religious instruction in the family is, alas! too often neglected. Its training, in this country especially, is frequently but a passive influence, without the exercise of authority, restraint, or parental coercion. The child is allowed to grow up good or evil, moral or immoral, religious or irreligious, as it listeth. It is Rousseau's theory of human nature going to seed. Thus the minds of catechumens are preoccupied with a crop of evil. Good seed must be *sown* into the heart of childhood; it grows not native there. No field runs to wheat, but to weeds; and that left unweeded may render the future sowing of good seed but fruitless waste. Faithless family training is a bane to the catechist.

An efficient method of catechization assumes a good preparatory religious training. In Germany, and in other parts of Europe, the catechism is taught in the day-schools. The parents co-operate with the school-teachers in indoctrinating their children in the truths of the Bible. The catechism, Scripture verses, and hymns are committed to memory, and studied as regularly as any other part of their school lessons. This is done at an age when the memory is most retentive, the conscience unseared by sinful

502

habits, and the heart tenderly susceptible of religious impressions. In most places the pastor visits the school on certain days of the week and catechizes the children. Thus by the time he instructs them, preparatory to confirmation, their thorough knowledge of the catechism renders the work of catechization comparatively easy. As a rule, the schools of this country render no assistance of this sort.

It is sometimes asserted that the Sunday-school furnishes the religious instruction to the young which in some other countries is derived from the day-schools. This institution has been fitly named "the nursery of the Church." It has been a prolific source of good in these United States. It has scattered pages of truth as densely as the falling leaves of November days, which enrich the beds that offer them a place of repose. And yet institutions, like the men that found them, are fallible. That it has done so much good despite of its faults, shows how much more it might effect if these could be removed.

It cannot be denied that Sunday-schools, as the most of them are conducted, do not foster a love or cultivate a skill for catechetical exercises. There is a felt disagreement between the system of instruction pursued here, and that of catechization. It is true, the question-books used contain lessons explanatory of the Scriptures. But, instead of fixing in the minds of the children condensed crystallized truths which are complete in themselves, they are made to traverse chapter after chapter and book after book, studying hundreds of different subjects, simple and mysterious, as they may present themselves in the course of their lessons. Many commit Scripture verses, but at random, without any reference to the illustration or proof of a particular doctrine. Some are taught to lay all the stress on the largest number of verses, so as to secure a prize. The mind is filled with a chaotic mass of Scripture knowledge, instead of classifying it under doctrinal heads with a view of teaching and impressing upon the heart certain truths clearly stated and proven.

Thus it often happens that when persons are transferred from the Sunday-school into the catechetical class they feel themselves in a foreign element. The former should furnish a preparatory training for the latter. Just as in all preparatory institutions—and the Sunday-school should not claim to be any thing more than this—such text-books are studied as will best prepare the student for the examination he is required to undergo to enter college, so the books, especially the question-books used in the Sunday-school, should be selected with a view of preparing the young for a definite end,—for the completion of their religious instruction, which they receive by the final catechization of the pastor. The method and matter of instruction ought to be conformed as much as possible to that used and taught in the catechetical class. The chief question-book ought to be the catechism. The pastor should regularly visit the school on appointed days, just as the German Dorf-pastor visits the school of his parish, and catechize the children himself and impart such counsel as he may deem proper. This would, to some extent, make the Sunday-school in this country what the day-schools are in Germany,—a nursery of the Church and the handmaid of catechization.

METHODS OF CATECHIZATION.—There are three methods of catechization :—

1. *The Socratic Method,* purporting to have been derived from the celebrated Athenian philosopher. It is well known that Socrates instructed his disciples by means of wise and skilfully-framed questions. He alleged that his principal duty as an instructor of others was merely to assist them in giving birth to their ideas, assuming that, possessing these at least seminally, no teacher need impart them. His office, as he supposed, was not so much to sow seed, as to draw out that already in the mind, and make it germinate, sprout, grow, and ripen, as the rain and the sun do the seeds in the soil. As applied to catechization, this method requires the pupil to be purely active, the teacher simply

aiding him to understand and develop that which he inherently may possess in a latent form. This view was partly reproduced by Rousseau in his theory of human nature. He alleged that no child could recite its catechism without telling a falsehood. All that human nature needed, he thought, was fair play to develop that which it possesses,— that the best and only true system of education was that which put nothing into the mind and heart, granting a full liberty of development according to man's innate impulses. Hence he held that religious instruction, if imparted at all, should be deferred till old age. The Socratic method is partly false and partly true. It is false in that it makes the learner purely active. It assumes that man naturally possesses what can only be given him by another. It is true in that its method of questioning stimulates to thought and reflection, and trains the learner to reproduce the truth and make it his own by vital assimilation.

2. *The Akroamatic Method* is the opposite of this, in which the pupil is purely passive. The learner's mind is wholly receptive, into which the teacher pours the truth from without. The catechist lectures, without calling out the active mental energies of the catechumen by the use of questions. This method is true in so far as it regards the human mind as destitute of truth; but it runs to the other extreme, in that it treats it simply as a passive receptacle of truth, into which all must be poured from without; and in so far it is not true.

3. Between these two is the union of both,—the golden mean,—uniting the Socratic and Akroamatic in what is called the *Erotematic Method*. In this the learner is both passive and active, both receives and gives. He receives truth from the catechism and the catechist, which by a series of questions is linked to points of contact in the heart, and kindles into life latent powers that may lie innate in the soul. Here it will be proper to determine what the learner should receive, and what he should be made to give out of his own mind.

Giving and Receiving.—1. What should we give to the catechumen? Much depends here on his intelligence. If others have not done it, we must impart to him the facts of redemption, the leading essential doctrines of the Christian religion. These are not in the mind by nature, but are given to it by the word of God and through the ministry of the gospel.

2. *How much* should we give to the catechumen? Enough clearly to understand the way of life. Only this, and nothing more. The leading facts in sacred history, especially those in the life of Christ, should be imparted. The evil of giving too much is as great as that of giving too little. We live in an age when knowledge is measured by quantity rather than by quality. Men have a morbid appetite for aimless universal information. The world is full of literary inebriates, fast drinking themselves to madness and to death.

The ability of a teacher is often measured by his encyclopædiac pretensions. When learning degenerates into loquacity, it becomes like a shallow stream, possessing breadth without depth, noise without power. It has been said that in the American system of education "nothing less than too much is plenty of any thing." Alas! how often the minds of learners are made "to float on an ocean of talk"! Within a given space of ground five grains of wheat may produce hundreds, whereas five hundred will produce nothing, because there is too much seed for the strength of the soil. It is so with the mind. This morbid passion to know any thing and every thing, and more still, useful and useless,—these aspirings for multifarious knowing (Vielwisserei),—must be held in proper check. Apt truths and wisely put questions penetrate the rock, drop by drop; but sometimes the torrent carries it all off again. Give the learner facts, though few. Facts, like grains of wheat, are complete in themselves. Like the wheat found in Egyptian tombs, they may lie undeveloped for a long while, but, when the sun and rain reach them, at once they will sprout and grow up to a harvest. Like the pearls found in miry sea-beds, they are polished by the very impurities around them.

Beware of burdening the mind of the learner with ponderous and superfluous ballast. Discard needless amplification. Limit the lesson, the questions, the proof-texts, the words, to a minimum quantity. Too much blunts the mental perception. It dilutes the wine into insipidity. "The secret of a great mind is heroically to remain ignorant of many things which men take pride in knowing." 'Tis the secret, too, of a wise teacher. He will not make a parade of learning, or bury the pupil's mind beneath a heap of aptless information, however precious in itself. He will reject much that is good and true, because it is not to the point. Two apt proof-texts are better than twenty. "In der Beschränkung zeigt sich erst der Meister,"—Limitation is the mark of a master.* This, however, does not exclude explanation, illustration, exhortation, and warning. Points of doctrine should be illustrated and applied to practical life by historical examples and incidents from religious biography. These, too, are facts,—facts sprouted and sprung into fruit-bearing plants. In such illustrations theology teaches by example. *Verba docent, exempla trahunt.* (An excellent work of catechetical illustrations in the German is that of Caspari, *Altes und Neues zu Luther's Kleinem Katechismus.*)

3. What should be taken from the catechumen, or developed from his own mind? All that he can find by his own exertions. Like Socrates, the catechist should aid the learner to bring forth ideas. From what the catechumen knows he is to be taught what he does not know. The known forms the basis, the point of contact, for the unknown. Give him nothing which he can find or furnish himself. Half-forgotten instructions of years long gone should not be repeated: they should simply be called up

---

* Goethe.

by some question,—a question which will kindle them into life and light. Learners of the present day do not always like this so well. They wish to receive ideas without the pains of begetting them. But a better training will soon teach them a more excellent way. What we acquire by our own toil we prize more highly than the precious gifts of friends. We enjoy it more. Sweet is the taste of hard-earned bread! *"Eureka!"* exclaimed the ancient philosopher, in a frenzy of delight, when he found the long-sought truth. So there is joy in the heart of every earnest seeker of truth when he, and not another, finds the precious pearl. Give nothing to the catechumen which he knows, or can himself work out in his own mind with or without the aid of the catechist.

The Art of Questioning.—Of course the questions in the catechism will be used as they stand; but, in addition to these, the catechist will have to furnish others. He is not, as some suppose, simply to pour thoughts into *unthinking* minds. The learner must be stimulated and, if need be, goaded to mental action. And as good Pestalozzi, one of the masters of modern catechetics, says, "After all, in religion, as in other matters, *one only learns to think by thinking.*" But some one must point the way. The Greeks conquered the world by the strength they received in their athletic exercises. So mind gains strength by collision with mind. To excite to mental action, and not be a substitute for it, is the office of a catechist. Sir Isaac Newton said that he effected his discoveries "by thinking continually upon them." The disciple of Christ must be taught to "think on these things,"—TO THINK.

How should the questions be formed and asked?

1. No question should be simply affirmative or negative,— which admits of a simple *yes* or *no*,—except in rare cases. All the leading writers on pedagogics agree that the question and answer should be more than one word,—a sentence.

2. No question should admit of two or more answers.

It should not be vague and general, but definite and direct. "What is a comforter?" is a question that will admit of several answers, but which *one* you may desire will be difficult for the catechumen to determine. Hence the question should be compact and clear. The learner must be able distinctly to see what you want.

3. The question should be simple and short. "All great things are simple."* Goethe gives us a correct trait of the devil, when Mephistopheles counsels Faust to pay no attention to *things* in theology, but to dwell solely on *words*. This is the advice religious teachers usually receive from that quarter. And how many foolishly follow it! The question must not deal in empty words, but in words expressing things. The old Greeks only respected that method of mental cultivation which produced short sentences and brave men. It is the cultivation which the catechist needs. The question ask, and the question only, in one sentence, without complicated clauses, and as short as possible.

4. First address the question to the *whole* class, then name the person who is to answer. A question, no less than an explanation, belongs to *all*. Every learner should feel that it is addressed to him personally, even though another one should be called on for an answer.† In this way the questioner secures the attention of the whole class. Committing to memory is necessary for a good method of catechization. In some places memorizing has gone out of practice. It needs to be revived. The catechism, proof-passages, and good hymns, committed to memory, are a source of spiritual light through life. Truth thus treasured up in the mind becomes

> "A tower of strength,
> A trusty shield and weapon."

But the lessons should not be made too long, lest they

---

* Daniel Webster.   † Bormann, Unterrichtskunde, pp. 62–67.

become a dreaded task. Just enough should be assigned to enable the learner to commit it well, and no more. "A little well done is better than much half done."

The catechumen should not be made to commit that which is wholly unintelligible. For a man ignorant of the Latin, it is burdensome to commit one of Cicero's orations. Memorizing has been brought into reproach by the alleged magical efficacy which is sometimes claimed for it. All cannot be understandingly explained to the learner, but some idea of the lesson's meaning should be given him, to assist the memory in committing it. It is the dullest and dreariest burden imaginable, mechanically to commit a mass of unmeaning lumber. To give interest and attraction to the truth, therefore, and lighten the work of the memory, the question should be explained *before* it is committed.

We need scarcely remark that a catechetical exercise ought to be devotional. Singing and prayer, and an earnest practical application of the truth to the hearts of the catechumens, are of paramount importance. When a class is started, every member of it should procure a Bible, a catechism, and a hymn-book. The true aim and end of catechization is to bring the learner to the Lamb of God: if it produce not penitence and faith in his heart, its work has been poorly accomplished. To memorize the catechism and recite it well is already a great deal, but it is not enough. The heart of man must not be dealt with as a mummy, but as a garden,—a garden which needs weeding and good seed. To sink the seed into a fruitful earth-bed, is the aim of a wise farmer; to dig around the tree, dung it, and excite the bark-pores into action, is the aim of a wise gardener; it is likewise the aim of a wise catechist. To make the catechumen a devout worshipper of God and a faithful follower of His Son Jesus Christ, is the end of all catechization. A sympathizing, loving heart is needed no less than mind and method. But the best method, however skilfully plied, may prove fruitless. Its success depends much on the personality of the catechist. Not only a teacher, but a master, he should be. The former instructs, the latter moulds. He is authority to his catechumens, which gains power and respect by his faith and godly life. He must carry their souls on his heart. He must pray for them in his closet, and with them in the class. It must be seen that he loves their souls and earnestly desires their salvation. The genial piety and fervent zeal of a catechist give him a vantage-ground. As the ivy coils around the trunk of a strong tree, so they gradually work their hearts and habits heavenward by coiling around him. This is training: it is *Erziehung*. The catechumen raises his soul up toward faith and holiness by means of the pastor's personality. The young need a *human* teacher, too, in whom they can believe, whom they can obey and love. If he has the fire of God's Spirit in his heart, his speech and presence will help to kindle its light and warmth in their souls. He must live and love Christ, no less than proclaim and teach Him in language,—

> "He tries each art, reproves each dull delay,
> Allures to brighter worlds, and leads the way."

A man with a godly catechetical enthusiasm can do more with a bad method than one with a lukewarm heart can do with a good one.

At what age, and how long, persons should be catechized, it is not easy uniformly to determine. Among the Jews, eight months were required for religious instruction.* In the early Church, baptized persons were admitted as catechumens at the age of eight years, and continued learners from two to three years. Clemens, who was an exception to Gentile converts, was admitted to baptism after a preparation of three months. Jewish converts, who generally were well instructed in the Old Testament Scriptures, were admitted after a preparatory course of eight months. In

---

* Hueffell, Beruf des Geistlichen, Zweiter Band, p. 7.

Eastern countries, where the body and mind mature at an earlier period in life, ten years of age is equivalent to twelve and fourteen in Europe and America. We cannot fix a uniform time for all, as to *when* and *how long*. Some are as old at fourteen as others are at sixteen. Begin betimes. The younger the tenderer; the nearer their natural the more susceptible of their spiritual birth. The smallest planets are nearest the sun, as small children are nearest the Saviour, of whom He ever continues to say, "Suffer them to come unto me, and forbid them not." Much depends on previous training, as to the length of time required. Too great a hurry gives the exercises a careless cast, and the catechumen reason to despair of mastering his lessons. On the other hand, a course too much protracted becomes tedious and sometimes stale. Earnestness and vigor on the part of the catechist, and industry and devout zeal on the part of the catechumens, justify a course of not more than six months, where the services are held weekly. Care should be taken, however, that religious instruction comes in its proper order. Some favor a system of miscalled catechization after confirmation. This is like attempting to push the foundation under a building after the superstructure has been reared. Such persons, it would seem, need to be taught that the basis is the beginning and not the end of the building.

A diversity of temperament, training, and character requires the catechist to vary his mode of treatment. He must acquaint himself with the natural peculiarities of each learner. All persons are not constituted alike, and it is not always their fault that they are not. "No man could be anybody else." A person is not always to blame for not having what he has not. For his temperament and training we must not hold him too strictly responsible. A Peter, John, Nathanael, Timothy, Mary, Martha, and Magdalen, may all be in one and the same class. How differently each one thinks and feels from all the rest! Some treat new-born souls as the red Indian his offspring, who binds each new-born babe to the same board. They bandage and embalm them as did the old Egyptians their dead, and thus produce mummies instead of living moral beings. Nature casts no two souls over the same mould, and she allows no catechist to do it with impunity. Grace never subverts or destroys the natural temperament. It gives it a sanctified direction, and makes it tributary to the glory of God. Paul, Peter, and John, though regenerated, retained their psychological peculiarities to the end of life. Study your material. Michael Angelo saw in the rough unhewn mass of marble the future statue, and in each mass he saw a different statue. But it required many a cautious stroke of the chisel till all the parts were symmetrically developed. Steadily and hopefully stroke follows stroke, day after day and year after year, letting patience have her perfect work. Beware of ruining your material by endeavoring " to do at a blow what Providence does by degrees."

Angelo, too, master as he was, had his mishaps, showing that his immortal genius worked with a mortal hand. The catechist meets with some material which stubbornly resists his moulding efforts. A defective home-training and years of sinful habits have so wasted the vital energies, and given such a wrong bent to the mind and morals, as to defy the wisest remedies. A relapse into sin by the catechumen is not always a proof of a faithless catechist, or of the uselessness of catechization. A cut or scratch in the tender twig may heal over, but underneath remains a scar that may sink a rot to weaken the trunk of the oak, where the future storm will break it off. Catechumens sometimes bring hearts into the class, sore with parental neglect and sinful habits, or with concealed scars which absorb the diseased humors of the spiritual nature, forming the vulnerable part of the future Christian, against which Satan will direct his attacks with fatal success.

The diversity of mental capacity requires the catechist to vary his treatment. Some possess retentive memories, but are dull of apprehension; others grasp the truth

513

quickly, and just as quickly lose it. A German has always more in his head than he can get out; whilst a Frenchman gets out more than he has in. Catechists not unfrequently have German and French heads in the same class. The one has ideas without language, the other language without ideas. The one should be helped to an outlet for his ideas, the other should be helped to ideas for his mental outlet. In short, the catechist must study and learn many things not found in the books. A knowledge of human nature, and a sound and clear discrimination of character, are no less important than a thorough theological training. Like the physician, he can find general principles to guide him in his books, but when he comes to apply them to individual cases he is thrown upon his own judgment. Then his best counsellor is the Holy Ghost, his best means to procure direction is prayer.

It is not an easy matter to be a good catechist. We may say of our countrymen as Claus Harms said of his: "We lack skill and aptitude in catechization." (Es fehlt an Fettigkeir im Katechisiren.)* Earnestness and taste for it, too, are wanting. It is more difficult to catechize than to preach. But who devotes as much time, labor, and prayer to a catechetical exercise as to a sermon? A learned European author says, "There is nothing in the world whereby a servant of God can effect more good than by catechization." It has been the drilling-school of heroes, the mother of martyrs, the mysterious loom by which the Holy Spirit, through human agency, wove golden threads of undecaying truth into the woof of human hearts. It taught the Reformers before the Reformation courage to confess the truth in the face of fagots and flames, and to seal their faith by their blood. You can scarcely read a page in the life of Luther, Zwingli, Calvin, Melanchthon, or Knox, without seeing and feeling flashes of martyr-fire kindled by the thorough study of God's

* Pastoral Theologie, Erstes Buch, p. 136.

514

word. And what a noble concern these godly men evinced that these same principles, taught in the Holy Scriptures, should be early grafted into the minds of the young. The Reformed Church, too, has her martyrs, no less renowned than those who fell in earlier times. The soil of France, Holland, the Palatinate, and Switzerland is hallowed with the blood of saints. There were giants in those days, made strong by the early study and thorough knowledge of the word of God. Their piety was grounded on doctrine, sound doctrine, on truth that never lies and never dies. They had something to live for. They had principles to die for. There were doctrines at stake. Doctrines! They have strangely depreciated in modern times. We see the fatal fruits of a piety without doctrine, of faith without knowledge, of devotion without firmness. "It is a symptom of the wretched, flaccid, pulseless, condition of sundry in our day that they never speak of theology, of catechisms, of doctrinal sermons, but with a sneer. The religion which they would like, if indeed they have thought enough to know their own mind, would be all sentimentality and all softness. Their weakened mental organs reject the strong meat. Know ye that manly bone, sinew, and muscle do not form themselves on the emollient regimen of a Christianity without doctrine. The men who of old went to the stake went for doctrines. These doctrines they had learned in the Scriptures, elaborated in meditation, methodized in system, preached to listening thousands, digested in the succinct formulas of definition, and left for us, their children, in those permanent crystals of the Reformed Catechisms which are scoffed at by amiable wits and religious coxcombs. Men, MEN, who can stand fast in the faith, who can stand alone, who have vertebral columns, who can bear, who can forbear, who can advance, who, on due summons, can strike,—men armed with the armor of righteousness on the right hand and on the left,—that is, with sword and shield, —are bred in great study of God's word and great familiarity with those evangelic truths which are the motive powers of the spiritual universe."*

Such a training is the design of catechization. It seeks to root and ground the youthful mind on the basis of inspired truth; not to while away an occasional hour with an intellectual entertainment, but to teach the mind to see, grasp, and assimilate eternal principles. When Thucydides wrote the History of the Peloponnesian War, he said it should be "a possession forever" ($\varkappa\tau\eta\mu\alpha$ $\grave{\varepsilon}\varsigma$ $\grave{\alpha}\varepsilon\acute{\iota}$). Not for a day, a year, a lifetime, do we labor; but, in the highest sense, our work is to be the eternal possession of our catechumens. No monument which a man can rear is so imperishably glorious as a well-trained soul, and so eloquently proclaims and perpetuates the genius whose head and heart instrumentally gave it form and finish. "If we work upon marble, it will perish; if we work upon brass, time will efface it; if we rear temples, they will crumble into dust; but if we work on immortal minds,—if we imbue them with principles, with the just fear of God and our fellow-men,—we engrave on those tablets something that will brighten through all eternity."

The following points, then, claim our attention on this subject:—

1. We need a revival of family catechization, as it was practised among our Reformed ancestors. With this, of course, we also need a more faithful family training and nurture.

2. We need a modification of our Sunday-school system, to harmonize it with the system of instruction afterwards pursued in catechization. The pastor should have the general catechetical supervision and control of the school.

3. We need a professorship of Catechetics in our theological seminaries, to furnish our candidates for the ministry with a thorough catechetical discipline.

---

* Discourses, J. W. Alexander, D.D., p. 328.

THE

FORTUNES

OF THE

HEIDELBERG CATECHISM

IN THE

UNITED STATES.

By REV. J. H. A. BOMBERGER, D.D.

THE FORTUNES OF THE HEIDELBERG CATECHISM IN THE UNITED STATES.

By Rev. J. H. A. Bomberger, D.D.

THE intrinsic excellence and confessional importance of a symbolical book like the Heidelberg Catechism invests its transfer to America, and its influence among the American Churches, with deep and general interest. Greeted at its first appearance in the Palatinate, three hundred years ago, with devout joy by the thousands who longed for a united evangelical Protestantism, the genial, conciliatory spirit of the Catechism, no less than its profound and faithful exhibition of the gospel scheme of salvation, and its logical yet lucid and popular plan of construction, rapidly won for it the warmest admiration and very extraordinary honor. Bigotry, indeed, denounced it, and ecclesiastical haughtiness discarded it. But it was hailed with gratitude and most cordially welcomed by all who loved the grace and truth of the Lord Jesus Christ more than mere traditional churchism or partisan tenets. Its early triumphs on its native continent are, however, the theme of another essay designed for this commemorative festival, and need not be dwelt upon here.

But what fortunes attended it when, nearly a century after its first publication, it entered upon a new career in this country? How did it endure transplantation from the parent vineyard to the richer mould of cleared forests and reclaimed valleys on the great and almost unknown continent of the West? Did the change improve or hurt it, drive unnaturally forward or unhappily retard its growth?

519

Stimulated unduly by the richness and virgin vigor of the new soil, did it rapidly run out into rank but unsubstantial growths, like the exuberant vegetation of our vast alluvials, or, invigorated by the change and rendered more firm and hardy by the peculiar exposures incident to that change, has it been gathering greater inward strength and yielding even better fruits than in its native field?

These questions have been raised to indicate what we consider the import and bearings of the subject assigned for this essay. An attempt to answer them, according to the best sources of information at hand, shall be our task. At the outset, however, we cannot forbear expressing deep regret that the material necessary to a satisfactory investigation of such historical subjects is so exceedingly scanty among us, and that the little in existence is so scattered and inaccessible. The pioneer fathers of our Church in this country seem, for the most part, not to have realized the importance of the forests they were clearing, and the foundations they were laying, sufficiently to keep accurate diaries of their work. Either they were too intent upon their toils, too zealous in the faithful discharge of each day's responsibilities, too meek to attach sufficient importance to their labors, or too indifferent to what might be the wishes and wants of posterity, to write and preserve detailed narratives of the ecclesiastical events of their times. The real makers of the most important facts of history are rarely conscious of the part they are performing. If they were, they would be far less fitted for their work. Foundations are laid beneath the surface, and not with observation. And yet, when laid, and gradually made to support a building whose solidity and fair proportions draw all eyes towards it, who would not be glad to know what hands cut those foundation-stones out of the native quarry and laid them so wisely and securely upon the strong rock-bed below?

But the desirable records are wanting; and those upon whom is now devolved the duty of writing the history, or portions of the history, of those early times, must make the best use of the few and brief traditions preserved. They are but imperfect fragments, nor twelve basketsful at that, although thousands may have been fed at the original feast.

In the prosecution of the task before us, *the external fortunes of the Catechism in this country, or its history as a book*, claim the first attention.

For its earliest appearance in America we are indebted to the primitive Dutch settlers along the Hudson. Imbued from childhood with devout regard for the book from which at their parents' knees they had learned the doctrines of the grace of God in Jesus Christ, it seems to have been one of their chief cares to place a copy of the Catechism in their native language among the few treasures they brought with them from their Netherland homes to their new abodes. Uniformly it was bound in the same volume with their Psalm and Hymn book, as an appendix, and mostly with the Canons of Dort attached. Sometimes the Nicene and Athanasian Creeds were added. A copy now before us, published, by authority of the States-General and of the Classis of Leeuwarden, by Abraham Ferwerda, 1746 (a reprint of earlier editions), contains also the New Testament, forms for sacramental and other church-services, together with prayers for family and public use.

The first importation of the Catechism to this country may, therefore, be dated back as far as 1619 (or possibly even 1609), when the first Dutch Church was probably organized at Fort Amsterdam (New York). And the *earliest form* in which it existed here was that just described. No American edition of the Catechism in the Dutch language was ever printed. All that were used until the English language gained ascendency in the Reformed Dutch Church were imported from Holland in connection with the Psalm-book.

Nearly, or quite, a hundred years later than its first im-

2 N

portation by Hollanders in the Dutch language, the Catechism was brought over to America by members of the Reformed Church emigrating from the Palatinate and settling within the limits of the colony of Pennsylvania. In their case, too, it originally existed in combination with their Psalm and Hymn book, the principal services of the Palatinate Liturgy, and family prayers. Next to their Bible, this volume was their casket of choice jewels, their daily vade-mecum.

The earliest American edition of the Catechism in German was that printed and published in the Psalm and Hymn book of Christopher Saur, Germantown, Pennsylvania, 1752, 1753. An edition of the Hymn-Book, by the same publisher, 1744, does not contain the Catechism. A copy of this edition of 1744 is preserved in the Philadelphia Library. A copy of the edition of 1752–3 is in the writer's possession. The psalms of this edition are Ambrose Lobwasser's metrical version. The hymns, including Joachim Neander's Hymns of the Covenant, are a reprint of the Marburg Hymn-Book, published by John Henry Stock. These are followed by the Catechism and a compendium of the Catechism, morning and evening prayers, fast-day, penitential, and communion prayers, the gospels and epistles for the Church-year, a brief history of the destruction of Jerusalem, and, finally, devout private prayers for the Church. This volume was generally used by the German Reformed Churches of this country for many years, though we have no account of later editions.

Besides this form, the Catechism was also contained in the quarto copies of the Palatinate Agenda, in German, with which the first ministers of the Church in this country were supplied. These, however, were exclusively in the hands of the clergy.

Subsequently the Catechism, in German, was *published in a separate form*. The earliest edition with which we have met is that published by *Carl Cist*, on Second Street, near Race, Philadelphia, 1790. Its title is: "Catechismus, oder kurzer Unterricht Christlicher Lehre, für die angehende Jugend in der Churfürstlichen Pfalz und andern Reformirten Orten zu gebrauchen: sammt der Haus-Tafel mit und ohne Biblischen Sprüch-Buchlein. Alles zur Ehre und Lob Gottes." As an appendix it contains also the "Erste Wahrheits-Milch, für Säuglinge am Alter und Verstand;" and, "Ein kurzer Auszug aus dem Hrn. Doct. u. Prof. Lampens Heil. Brautschmuck, den rechten u. nützlichen Gebrauch des heil. Abendmahls betreffend; in Frag u. Antwort gestellt von J. Th. Schild, Ref. Pred. zu Oppenheim," &c. It is in small 18mo form. This same book was afterward republished by *Conrad Zentler*,* who seems to have been the successor of *Cist*. An edition before me, by Zentler, dated 1807, is an exact reprint of the edition above described. Zentler continued in business until 1845 or 1846. This *Cist-Zentler* Catechism may still be met with among our German members in great numbers.

Other, and later, editions of the Catechism in *German*, were published by G. W. Mentz, Philadelphia; by Gruber & May, Hagerstown, Md.; and finally by the Synod's Printing Establishment, Chambersburg, Pa., in 1840.

The first American edition of the Catechism separately in English was printed and published about 1820, by a Mrs. Schweitzer, at Fourth and Race Streets, Philadelphia. This edition appears to have subsequently passed over to the hands of Geo. W. Mentz, who commenced the publication of it about 1825, in Philadelphia.

Gruber & May of Hagerstown, and Smith of Chambersburg, published later editions; and finally the present authorized edition, with the Constitution of the Church, &c., was issued by the Synod's Printing Establishment, in 1840.

Parry's version of the Heidelberg Catechism in English, revised by L. H. Steiner, M.D., was published in the Mer-

---

* Zentler published the Minutes of Synod for 1821 and 1822.

cersburg Review in 1860, and issued in pamphlet form in the same year by M. Kieffer & Co., Chambersburg.

A Latin edition of the Catechism, carefully prepared and published under the eye of Dr. Steiner, has very recently appeared, for private circulation. It is printed in the finest style of typography. Baltimoriæ, Typis Joannis D. Toy, 1862.

Under this branch of our subject it is proper at least to notice a number of catechetical works which appeared from time to time in the Church, either as rivals or recruiting servants of our formal standard.

The earliest of these, a very rare little relic,* is entitled: "Kurzer Catechismus, vor etliche Gemeinen Jesu aus der Reformirten Religion, in Pennsylvania, Die sich zum alten Berner Synods halten: Herausgegeben von Johannes Bechteln, Diener des Worts Gottes. Philadelphia, Gedruckt bey Benjamin Franklin, 1742." On the second page we learn that the book was to be had: In Philadelphia, of Stephen Benezet; in Germantown, of J. Bechteln; in Falconer Swamp, of H. Antes; in Oley, of John Leinbach; in Lancaster town, of Daniel M. Quinet; in Skippack, of G. Merckeln; in Saucon, of Jacob Bachman; and in Forks (near Easton), of Eyreck.

It contains the "XII chief articles of the great Synod of Berne, Switzerland, held in January, 1532, published by the State authorities, and readopted in 1728. See p. 1 in the Hirten-Buchlein."

Then follows the Catechism proper. It was designed, in the full sense of the term, to be a rival of the Heidelberg Catechism, and a means of drawing the members of the Church away from the doctrinal basis of that confession of faith.†

The earliest *compendium* of the Heidelberg Catechism

---

* For the copy in my possession I am indebted to the kindness of the Rev. de Schweinitz, of the Moravian Church.

† See Harbaugh's "Fathers of the Reformed Church," vol. i. pp. 312–325, for an interesting sketch of Bechtel's life.

used in this country was that contained in the Palatinate Agenda brought over by the venerated missionary founders of our Church here. It is very brief, but comprehensive, and, after all our efforts to provide something better, may probably not be surpassed for its purpose. A translation of it may be found in the Mercersburg Review for 1850 (Vol. H.) pp. 266–268.

That valuable auxiliary to the Heidelberg Catechism, the so-called Palatinate Catechism, originally published in Heidelberg, September, 1684, was reprinted in this country, first in Philadelphia, 1777 (probably under the supervision of Weyberg, then pastor of this congregation), and again in Easton, 1829. Twenty years later it was translated by the Rev. J. H. Good and Rev. H. Harbaugh, and published by M. Kieffer & Co., Chambersburg. Its general excellence, and special fidelity to the genius and spirit of the original work of 1563, are too well known to need demonstration in this essay.

From the minutes of Synod for 1822, p. 12, we learn that a compendium of the Catechism, in German and English, was published in Carlisle, Pa., several years previously. Steps were taken for its improvement and reissue, but the instructions of Synod upon the subject seem never to have been fully carried out, although the chairman of the committee intrusted with the duty of its preparation, the Rev. A. Helfenstein, Jr., reported in 1823 that their work was nearly completed.

A number of compendiums, prepared by different clergymen, were subsequently published and used in the instruction of catechumens. Their use, however, was chiefly limited to the pastoral charges of those who prepared them.

The most important and widely circulated American contribution to the study and understanding of the Heidelberg Catechism is "The Exercises, &c., by the Rev. S. R. Fisher." This work first appeared in 1844, and was designed for use in Sunday schools and catechetical classes.

But little can be said in praise of the mechanical execution of most American editions of the Catechism. Some of them abound in typographical errors, and all are printed in rather plain style and on poor paper. The English translation in current use is said to be marred by many inaccuracies, some of which seriously affect the original sense. In this respect it is to be hoped that the tercentenary year will lead to improvements worthy of the work.

Turning from these bibliographical details, let us endeavor to *trace the internal fortunes of the Catechism, or its history as a text-book of religious instruction and a standard of theological doctrine* in the Reformed Church of this country. This branch of our subject will also require us to remark upon any *misfortunes* with which the Catechism may have met in its ecclesiastical course, and any dangers to which it may now be, or seem to be, exposed.

In the widest sense, the fortunes of the Catechism are most closely bound up with the entire inner life of the Church, and form the chief substance of her history. By the position it holds among us, it has had a double function to perform, and each one vital and pervasive. It is our confession of faith and standard of doctrine. It is also our text-book of practical religious instruction. It is our doctrinal symbol and our catechetical manual. And it is a peculiar glory of the book that it is so admirably adapted to both these purposes.

Assuming the necessity and importance of a formal creed or confession of faith as an explicit avowal of her cordial apprehension of the cardinal doctrines of Christianity and as a palladium of evangelical orthodoxy, the Reformed Church in this country from the first made the Heidelberg Catechism the actual or virtual standard of theological instruction and doctrinal belief. The liberal spirit, in regard to non-essential points, which animates the work was, indeed, cordially cherished. No trivial shibboleths were made a test of orthodoxy, or the condition of a welcome into the brotherhood. But, at the same time, an honest and hearty subscription to the Articles of Faith avowed in the Catechism was ever rigidly demanded. Most of the fathers of the Church in America had learned the doctrines of grace as they are set forth in this chief symbol of the Reformed Church; and, fully persuaded of their divine truth and their entire agreement with the faith of the primitive Church,—on which, as contained in the Apostles' Creed, they were based, and around which, as a living centre, they revolved,—those earnest and devoted men cast themselves upon the perils of the great deep, and encountered the trials of this new and desolate missionary field, that they might transplant and perpetuate on the growing continent of the West that system of evangelical truth which has been such a blessed bond of union and so strong a bulwark of orthodoxy among the Reformed Churches of their native land.

On minor points, and possibly on some even of more serious moment,—at least if their legitimate consequences were considered,—they might differ from each other. All had not been trained for the ministry in the same theological schools. All had not been nurtured under the same pious influences. Some were educated in Zurich, some in Heidelberg, some in Herborn, some in Basel, some in Halle, and some had learned the more rigid Calvinistic orthodoxy of the Dort school. According to the mode of thought and style of piety prevailing at the time of their education and during the earlier period of their ministry, they might severally be more or less stiffly orthodox, more or less pliantly pietistic. But in the main there was unanimity and union among them in regard to the peculiar doctrines of their Church, and they displayed common zeal for the maintenance of the doctrines of the Catechism of the Church *in their integrity*. The pietism of the previous period had largely yielded, in Europe, to the seductions of Illumination. Illumination· was drifting more and more rapidly into the dark and frigid zone of rationalistic skepticism and infidelity. Still it was mercifully ordered by the Head of the Church that our first missionaries of the Cross in this country should be men who had, in a good measure, been kept from the pernicious influences of what was becoming the ruling theology of the parent Church,—men of devout simplicity, evangelical integrity, and sincere personal piety. They were deeply imbued with the spirit of the doctrines of the Catechism, although it had almost entirely ceased to be a rule of faith in the theological schools in which they had been educated. ·The spirit of the Lobwasser metrical version of the Psalms, of Neander's Covenant Hymns, and of Freylinghausen's deeply spiritual songs still ruled in their hearts. Churchliness without the contractions of churchism, piety without the laxities of pietism, characterized their dogmas and their life. In this spirit they clung—theologically and ecclesiastically—to the Heidelberg Catechism, and even may be said to have revived and re-established its symbolical authority as the standard of doctrine in the Reformed Church of this country. Hence any attempt like that of John Bechtel of Germantown, in 1742, to set up another standard, not only failed to elicit co-operation, but excited so much opposition that the originator of it found it conducive to his comfort to seek a spiritual home in another Church. The piety of Zinzendorf and his brethren was not questioned. Their devoted and self-denying zeal was admired. The close and fraternal relations which had existed between the Bohemian Brethren and the Reformed Church of an earlier period were kindly remembered. But when their influence came in contact or ,conflict with the principles and genius of the acknowledged Reformed symbol, they were firmly, and sometimes even passionately, withstood. So that the zeal of the venerable John Philip Boehm in defending his position and that of his Church against the assaults made upon the faith of the Church* may be taken

---

* Fathers of the Reformed Church, p. i. p. 285.

as a fair index of the animus of our ministry during that early period.

To what extent the Catechism was made the basis of theological education in the case of candidates for the ministry, who, according to the prevailing custom of those days, pursued their studies under the direction of some private clergyman, we have no documentary means of ascertaining. But, from the traditional testimony of those aged fathers among us who form the living links between that early period and our own, we learn that a careful study of the Catechism constituted an important part of their otherwise irregular and defective course.

Indications of the theological authority of the Catechism for the fathers of our Church may be seen, we think, in such of their sermons as have been handed down to us. Few and rare as these are, they still serve as specimens not only of their style of preaching, but of the system of faith which ruled them. Such indications are furnished by the sermons of John Conrad Steiner, pastor of the very congregation in which we are now convened from 1751 to 1762, a volume of which was published by his intelligent and amiable widow in 1763. And that the eloquent and learned Christian Ludwig Becker of Baltimore—three of whose successors in the pastorate of the First Reformed Church of that city are members of this Convention—was animated by the same doctrinal faith, is satisfactorily attested by the volume of his sermons published in Leipsic shortly before his embarkation for this country.

Further proof of this interesting and important fact may also be derived, at least by fair inference, from the constant use made of the Catechism in the private and public instructions of the youth of the Church in the doctrines of the gospel. The reflex influence of this practice upon the views of the clergy must have been very great. In their faithful discharge of this part of their duty, to which so much importance was attached and so much time was annually devoted, the book was scarcely ever out of their hands. This continual rehearsal and explanation of its questions and answers would weave its doctrines, in all their shades of expression and peculiarities of statement, into the very web of their being. The familiar forms in which the truths of the Catechism are stated would thus not only become their habitual mode of expressing their views, but would, consciously or unconsciously to themselves, fashion and mould their thoughts and belief. In this way the hand-book of instruction would become a more dominant norm of their own faith than any system of theology in other form could well be. For, as good hymns in frequent use not only are vehicles of pious emotions, but serve to excite and modify those emotions, so a good catechism constantly used not only gives us words in which to avow our faith, but exerts a mighty moulding influence upon the character of that faith itself.

As our Church in this country progressed toward a more complete and perfect ecclesiastical organization, it also laid down, among other things, in more distinct and decided form, the authority of her doctrinal standard. Hence we find an explicit constitutional injunction—ordained by the proper judicatories of the Church in 1828— requiring those elected to professorships in the Theological Seminary of the Church to avow their hearty and full endorsement of the doctrines of the Catechism, not only as to their form, but as to their real substance and intention. Next to the Holy Scriptures, therefore, the Catechism was thus made the norm of all instructions in the training of candidates for the ministry. So far as it allowed of liberty in regard to less essential doctrines, those instructions were not bound to any rigidly defined dogmas. But where it took clear and decided ground it should be faithfully followed. And even in regard to adiaphoristic points no doctrine could be taught which conflicted, in its tenor or its tendencies, with the great doctrines of grace laid down.

This was indeed high, but only deserved, honor shown

530

to our old and noble symbolical book. It was restoring it, by solemn synodical action, to the dignity and authority with which it was originally invested on its native soil. Practically and virtually, it held such sway in the Church of, America before. But this was now, as it was meet it should be, strengthened and enforced by all the moral and spiritual power of the highest judicatory of our Church. This is significant; and its significance cannot readily be over-rated. It was applying the ecclesiastical power of the keys where the application of that power ought always to prove most effectual for the maintenance of truth and piety in a Church. It was throwing around the symbol of our faith the spiritual wall of a solemn compact, confirmed by oath, between the Church and the servants of the Church in the most influential office to which she could call any man. No man could make a breach in that wall without doing violence to his oath. No Pelagian, no Arian, no Papist, no rationalistic Puritan, could enter that office, and in contempt or distortion of the Catechism inculcate views and fancies peculiar to either of those theories of doctrinal belief. The Church stood firmly by the Catechism in its old Protestant evangelical sense, and with full and clear purpose determined that in that sense its influence and authority should be perpetuated.

All this was done, too, it deserves to be remembered, as the result of the experience of nearly a hundred years of the Church's history on this continent.

And it was well for the Church and the Catechism that this firm position in regard to it as a standard of doctrine was taken. We can now see a manifest Providence in the act. It seems as though under the influence of some pressing presentiment of coming evil the Church was girding up her loins with truth against approaching days of trial and conflict. As nature prepares the trees of the forest for the angry storms of winter by hardening the soil around their roots and hiding their vigor and life in the deep foundations of the earth, so the Church was led, though all

531

unconsciously, to fortify herself in her symbol for a season of agitations and tempests.

And the precaution had hardly been taken until special need of it became apparent, as it has, indeed, not yet ceased to exist. But, the better to understand and appreciate the nature and extent of the *perils* to which the Catechism now became exposed, it will be necessary to go back again chronologically, and advert to some antecedent facts connected with the *function performed by the Catechism as a text-book of catechetical instruction.*

Of the importance attached by the Palatinate Reformed Church to the thorough indoctrination of the people, and especially of youth, in the essential truths of Christianity, and of the reasons justifying her zeal in the matter, this essay is not the place to speak. It is the subject of another paper in this series. But the founders of the Church in the United States brought with them to this country strong and lively convictions of the wisdom of the course. Those convictions they put into zealous practice. They were heartily persuaded that if their people should enjoy true comfort in life and in death, they must *know* these three things: first, how great their sins and misery are; secondly, how to be delivered from their sins; and, thirdly, how to show their gratitude to God for such deliverance. Hence they set themselves diligently about instructing the people in these three chief points. This, indeed, made up a large part of their arduous labors. Not only did they devote to it a portion of their public Lord's days' ministrations; in most cases every day of the week, during half the year, was employed in catechetical instructions in the different congregations of their almost diocesan pastoral charges. Schools were scarce in those early days, and very often the schoolmaster was missing. So the catechetical class became even a sort of primary school for the education of youth. But the Catechism was the only text-book. And its solemn lessons were all the more deeply impressed on the minds of catechumens for being learned by laborious

school-like efforts. Those lessons were learned by heart.
And though in many instances the heart might be rude
and uncultivated, it became a treasury of precious truths.
The casket might be leaden, but the contents were pearls.
In those garden-spots of the Church's history and practice,
memories were planted which sprang up and flourished
after many days. Such labors excited but little observation, were prosecuted with no noise of trumpets. But
they produced solid and lasting effects. A religious system which can get such hold upon the mind and heart,
that what is wrought by the divine blessing in the boy is
remembered with tears of joy and gratitude by the hoary-
headed sire of threescore and ten, is a system whose power
and efficacy are not to be despised. There are sires now
living,—perhaps we have many in this jubilant Convention,
—aged fathers in Israel, who could· bear testimony to that
power and efficacy of the old catechetical system of the
Church,—nay, whose lives bear witness to it.

But the best wine may be adulterated, and the purest
stream may be rendered foul. And so the catechetical
system of instruction, though in itself so excellent, could
be perverted, misused, abused. And in many cases, over
large districts of the Church, it was so perverted and misused. What was prosecuted with hearty zeal by the fathers was done with frigid mechanical formality by the
sons. The Catechism was still used, but it was not taught
with spiritual earnestness. Young people continued to
have it put into their hands, and even into their heads, but
it did not get into their hearts. With all its warmth of
cordial piety, the minister was cold, and the catechumen
remained cold, unmoved, and dead. Or if there was occa-
sioual emotion it was excited by some sentimental appeals,
made in tender style, with reference to the external solemnity of their approaching confirmation. It was not the
deep, devout emotion of a heart glowing with the blessed
assurance, wrought by the Holy Ghost, that not only unto
others but unto it also were granted remission of sin,

everlasting righteousness, and salvation, through grace only, for the sake of the merits of Jesus Christ. Strange that a book setting forth truth and grace in the cordial, lively terms employed in our Catechism could ever become so powerless, dead a tool in the hands that held it! Strange that around so glowing a hearth as this any could be chilled into the coldness of a spiritual death! But as there is an intensity of cold which will extinguish even fire, so there is a kind of moral atmosphere which kills the glow even of such ardent piety as belongs to the inmost spirit of our honored symbol. Such is the fearful law of religious formalism. Even the "lively oracles of God" become a savor of death to those in whose hearts their facts and truths are not mixed with a living faith. How much more might this be the case with those oracles put forth at second hand!

This fall from the original life and energy with which the Catechism was used in the instruction of youth, this loss of the grace and unction with which it was once so vitally associated, could not fail to bring the whole system into temporary disrepute. It exposed the Catechism and the Church to the perils of some violent reaction, or fanatical assaults from without. We justly condemn religious fanaticism in all its forms and operations. But we cannot deny that there had come to be a state of piety, or rather impiety, in portions of our Church which justly exposed us to reproach and laid us open to the infliction of serious injury. A revival was needed,—if only it came in legitimate form, were wrought by legitimate means, and produced legitimate results. Might it but be a true revival of the genuine evangelical life of the Church, and not the radical destruction of that life with its proper conditions, and the violent, unnatural substitution for it of something seemingly better, but really worse!

The history of the brief storm of fanaticism through which our Church passed is fresh in the minds of all present. It need not be detailed. The Catechism did not, of course, escape the evils of that tumultuous but instructive period of our experience. It came in for its full share of reproach and contempt. With other old things, it was allowed to pass away. No pleading of its gray hairs could save it. The day of its glory had waned. Many were wild with joy that they had escaped its thraldom, and clapped their hands with pious merriment now that those hands were no longer shackled by its old, rusty chains. No longer should it furnish the tools for manufacturing church-members: the machine-shop was shut up. The fathers might have honored the book and the system as they pleased; their sprightlier sons were not to be duped by the doting affection of the ancients. So the Catechism was laid aside, and catechetical instruction was either wholly abolished or the term of it reduced to the briefest possible limits. In its place the mourner's bench, anxious meetings, and some other appliances of modern fanatical ingenuity were thought by many to be most happy, salutary, and efficient substitutes.

The season of that folly, however, has passed away, or nearly passed away. A few lingering after-clouds of the storm may still hover over us here and there, but for the most part we see clear sky again. And, oh, with what mildly bright and cheering radiance does it smile upon us to-day! The worst came, and it passed off again without spreading much desolation over the heritage of the Lord among us. Nay, has it not been marvellously overruled for good? So the hurricane is destructive in its course, but beneficial in its effects. The ploughshare plunged ruthlessly through the soil, and doubtless uprooted and destroyed many tender plants; but we must not forget what harvests the Lord has permitted us to gather since.

Not only did the Catechism suffer injury in this way, however, by being thrust aside as a text-book of instruction for the youth; it lost its authority also in the seminary and in the pulpit. There was no open war upon its doctrines,—no avowed rupture with them; but they were not made the standard of the preaching, and to a sad extent they were not preached. Repentance, conversion, faith, heaven, hell,—all these were indeed held forth, often with great earnestness and power. Even Christ was not forgotten. But they were not preached in the sense and spirit and conception of the Catechism and its deep christological apprehension of the gospel. That which was proclaimed was indeed, to a large extent, another gospel.

Treatment like this exposes a symbol of ecclesiastical faith to the greatest perils. Avowed hostility to it is less to be feared than such secret sappings of its foundations. It is not discarded in form, but dishonored in fact. It is not outwardly supplanted, but it is inwardly despoiled. None of its sacred doctrines are openly assailed, but their true original sense is utterly perverted. Laurel may be wreathed around its head, but hemlock is poured into its heart. And all this under pretences, possibly, of great devotion to its genius and spirit and of burning zeal to promote its honor and reputation.

The *banner* of the Cross was never lifted higher in the visible Church than by that visible Church which, more than any other, has caused the true life and gospel of the Cross to be blasphemed among the Gentiles. And who avowed greater zeal for Moses and the prophets than they who in the name of Moses and the prophets crucified the Lord of glory?

Nevertheless, perils like these have, from time to time, endangered all the chief symbols of the different evangelical Churches, and doubtless will continue to jeopardize, if not their life, yet their real influence in the future. The deadliest weapons ever used against them are forged out of metal taken from their own mine of truth; just as Absalom armed himself against his royal father with swords and spears purloined from the royal armory. And such, unhappily, is the pliancy or malleability of language, that wise or wily men disposed to its perversion may beat the most explicit definitions into foil for antagonistic tenets, or impale the most evangelical creed upon the very stakes with which the fathers sought securely to enclose it.

We repeat, then, and believe the fact full of admonition for us and for our day, that the Catechism of the Palatinate was never in greater danger in this country than when, though honored in form, it was ignored or perverted in fact.

How far the theological seminary of that period may be answerable for the dishonor thus done the Catechism, it were impossible to determine. Some responsibility undoubtedly attaches to it. But we do not think it merits any large degree of blame. The evil came rather from without, and with such irresistible force that scarcely any barriers of the school could have withstood it. And if for a short time the flag of the citadel was lowered as though for a surrender, it is just to remember that on the citadel first the banner was lifted up again, and with a bold, fearless hand: so that from it there was diffused a clearer and deeper sense of the excellence and superiority of the spirit and genius of the Heidelberg Catechism than the Church had possessed for many years before.

All this, however, proves the wise foresight of the Church in throwing around her symbol of faith the protection of special constitutional authority, to which reference has already been made. At the same time, it justifies the additional precaution taken in the revised Constitution of 1846, in requiring not only professors of theology formally to obligate themselves to conform their teachings to the doctrines of the Catechism, but all applicants for licensure and ordination to sign a declaration of their sincere adhesion to those doctrines and their purpose to conform their public ministrations thereto. Thus a double guard was placed around the acknowledged standard of the Church, and a reiterated pledge given by the highest judicatory of the Church and the most authoritative exponent of her views, that the Heidelberg Catechism should be made more than ever the norm of doctrine within her limits.

Many happy effects of the reaction thus brought about in favor of the Catechism have already begun to appear. In general it is receiving more earnest attention and is made the subject of deeper study. Its doctrines are more frequently woven into the body of our sermons and rule the style of thinking which characterizes them. This is especially true of its sacramental doctrine. The mere memorial and external covenant view of the sacraments, at least, has given way to the old Reformed conception of their significance and force. Their sealing efficacy through the operation of the Holy Ghost is again acknowledged. Baptism has generally ceased to be exhibited as but a solemn and impressive rite. The Lord's Supper is more than a solemn service of commemoration, and its outward elements serve another and higher purpose than that of significant impressive pictures of the tragedy on Calvary.

In the catechetical system of the Church the old Palatinate symbol is regaining its original ascendency. Pastors have been led to see and feel the value of the system as a means of grace for the youth of the Church. More time and attention are given to faithful and patient indoctrination. The fashion of the day and the frivolous temper of the times are, indeed, serious obstacles in the way of a full, immediate return to early usages. Parental neglects in regard to the religious training of their children increase the difficulty. A popular, flippant style of preaching, by which we are largely encompassed, has likewise tended to pervert the tastes of people, young and old, in regard to pulpit and pastoral instruction. Audiences are restive under the delivery of solid, substantial doctrinal sermons and lectures. The popular literature of the day aggravates the evil. Nevertheless, it seems to be felt that perseverance and the arts of heavenly wisdom may overcome these hindrances in due time, and abundantly reward any toils and patience demanded by the effort. And we have reason to rejoice that the effort is being made. So that it is probable that the Catechism is in more hands, and that its doctrines are lodged in more hearts, this day than for many years back.

There are, indeed, many pastors who, in the face of the proper constitutional requirements of the Church, still use, in the catechetical class, abstracts and compends of their own preparation. But this irregularity is gradually disappearing, and will, it may be hoped, be ere long wholly abolished.

It were a mistake, however, to feel secure in the belief that our symbol has now escaped all shoals and rocks and is sailing on a fair open sea, wholly free from perils. Why should the lessons of the past be lost upon us? Those experiences may, indeed, not recur in the same form. But as surely as the Catechism had to encounter dangers in that part of its course already traversed, so surely may we expect others to spring up in the future. It has escaped the whirlpool of unchurchliness: are we quite certain that it will not strike against the rock of churchism? It has gone through the shallow waters of a rationalistic dilution of the sacraments: is it beyond the reach of harm from a superstitious over-exaltation of them? It has been rescued from puritan perversions: should we not be jealous of other possible subversions of its great evangelical doctrines?

"Happy is the man that feareth always." "Be not highminded, but fear." "Watch and pray, that ye enter not into temptation." These are divine admonitions which apply to the case before us as really as to individual perils. Let us heed the admonitions in reference to the Heidelberg Catechism.

To the cherishing of such devout jealousy we may feel the more encouraged by the interesting occasion on which we are here assembled. This occasion is a monument of praise to God for the grace bestowed upon us, as a Church, through the Catechism. It is, therefore, also at the same time a solemn declaration of the Church's undiminished— nay, increased—regard for this old symbol of her faith in its proper Reformed sense. By the very appointment and observance of these festivities the German Reformed Church in the United States proclaims a solemn pledge of devotion to the work, and of her determination to cling more firmly than ever to this banner and keep it lifted up on high amidst all the tumults of the times. Rallying around it, as an ensign of spiritual peace, amidst the clangor of sanguinary political strifes, our hearts take comfort from its consoling truths. Uttering the promises of God in the language of men, it teaches us where to find a hiding-place until these calamities be overpast. With the memories of this occasion before us and the doctrines of this book within us, can we otherwise than thank God and take courage? The fortunes of the Heidelberg Catechism in America may be regarded as having reached a culminating point in this week's celebration. Such occasions are invested with solemn historical significance in the past. Often they are the turning-point of fortune. Not a few instances are on record in which they mark the commencement of a rapid decay for institutions which had prosperously reached them. But there are other more cheering instances in which they proved the starting-points of greater triumphs and nobler achievements. May these be the types and figures of what shall be the lot of our venerated symbol. But, that they may, let us not separate from this Convocation without vowing to God and to each other to be true and faithful to the high trust which has in this form been committed to our custody.

The review we have now made most clearly indicates wherein our true strength lies. It shows also where we may ever find, under God, the tower of our ecclesiastical safety. If we abandon that tower, we must stand exposed without defence to fierce assaults and bitter storms from every side. If we sap the foundations of that tower in the vain hope, or under the more vain pretence, of strengthening them, its walls will break and fall down in destruction upon our heads. But let us do neither the one nor the

540

other, and, by the favor of the God of our fathers, we shall be safe.

Woe be to the presumptuous hand which dares to disturb those old and tried foundations! And thrice woe to any who may impiously attempt to defile the fountain from which for three centuries the Church has been drawing waters of life!

541

THE

HISTORY OF THE THEOLOGICAL SEMINARY

OF THE

GERMAN REFORMED CHURCH

IN ITS RELATION TO THE HEIDELBERG CATECHISM.

By PROF. B. C. WOLFF, D.D.

MERCERSBURG, PA.

HISTORY OF THE THEOLOGICAL SEMINARY

OF THE

GERMAN REFORMED CHURCH

IN ITS RELATION TO THE HEIDELBERG CATECHISM.

By Professor B. C. Wolff, D.D., Mercersburg, Pa.

THE Church of the Heidelberg Catechism, in the British colonies of North America, traces its origin to the close of the seventeenth century. It consisted chiefly of emigrants from Switzerland and the Rhine provinces of Germany. Many of them were of Huguenot descent, whose fathers had fled from France to escape the persecution which followed the revocation of the Edict of Nantz. A better class of colonists never landed on these western shores. For the most part they were poor; but they were religiously educated, industrious and frugal in their habits. Their first ministers also were men of learning and sincere piety, who soon were aware of the importance of providing for the intellectual and moral culture of their people. But the difficulties in their way were very great. They were few in number, and their congregations were feeble and widely scattered. The people, too, debarred by their language and habits from many of the social advantages enjoyed by their more cultivated English neighbors, gradually became absorbed in worldly pursuits, and cared but little to engage in any special effort for their own spiritual improvement, or that of those who were to come after them. The consequence was that in a short time, in many places, they had neither public worship nor schools, bibles and devotional books were scarce, and often in pious families the children grew up without being baptized. When this state of things was made known in Europe, it awakened great sympathy, especially in Holland and Great Britain, and led to immediate measures of relief. In the Reformed Dutch churches, connected with the Synod of Amsterdam, the enthusiasm created by the representations of the missionary Schlatter was so great that the people literally ran together with their contributions of books and money for their destitute brethren in America; and in Scotland, at the instance of the Rev. Mr. Thompson, the pastor of a Presbyterian congregation in Amsterdam, who went to Glasgow for the purpose, the General Assembly, then in session, directed that collections for the same benevolent object should be taken up in all their congregations. In England, also, associations were formed, and large sums of money contributed by the nobility and higher classes, including the King and other members of the royal family, for educational purposes and for the distribution of the Scriptures and religious books among the German population of the colonies.* As the results of this enterprise, respectable foundations for public schools were laid at Lancaster, Easton, and other towns in Pennsylvania, and so arranged as to be under the joint control of the Lutheran and Reformed Churches in those places. The scheme, however, failed ultimately, in consequence of the political agitation which then already began to disturb the public mind and finally ended in the war of Independence. Nor was this the only difficulty. When peace was restored, and the country again began to prosper, the correspondence with the parent churches on the Continent was so frequently interrupted by the wars of the French Revolution, that it was at length broken off, and the German population in America was prematurely left to its own resources. This was very un-

---

* The appropriation and disbursement of these moneys were in the hands of a committee of distinguished gentlemen in the colonies, of whom we have the names of Benjamin Franklin, the first Judge Peters, and Conrad Weider, a wealthy German merchant.

fortunate. In their isolated and spiritually destitute condition, the dispersed congregations were often imposed upon, and obliged to put up with the ministrations of ecclesiastical adventurers from abroad, who engaged in preaching as a trade, and, instead of attempting any thing for the permanent advantage of the people, preferred, in most cases, that they should remain in their existing state of ignorance and religious indifference. Still there were ministers who at an early period proposed the establishment of a Theological Seminary for the training of a pious and efficient ministry for the German churches. It was first intended to connect it with Franklin College at Lancaster, an institution designed by its founders for the special benefit of the German population of the country, and for that purpose placed in the hands of trustees, two-thirds of whom were required to be of the Lutheran and Reformed persuasions. Owing, however, to denominational rivalry more than to confessional differences, it was never carried into effect. The fault, it is thought, was more on the side of the Reformed than on that of the Lutheran. The proposition was frequently renewed by the Lutheran Synod, but was as often evaded by the Reformed. The Reformed were disposed rather to cultivate friendly relations with the Reformed Dutch Church, whose ministers from the first had extended a fostering care to the destitute congregations of the German Church and were always willing to assist in promoting their interests. Among those most active in this way was the late venerable Dr. John P. Livingston, of the Theological Seminary at New Brunswick. He at his own expense, published "An Address to the Reformed German Churches in the United States," replete with valuable information and counsel, urging them to establish a Theological Seminary for themselves; and it was in a great measure owing to the influence of this wise and good man, exerted publicly and privately, upon the minds of prominent ministers in the German Reformed Church, that the project of a joint institution was abandoned in favor of one exclusively denominational. A pretty broad foundation, as far as expense was concerned, was laid for the contemplated Seminary; and, when the plan was matured, all eyes were turned to the Rev. Dr. Philip Milledoler, of the Reformed Dutch Church, but educated and ordained in the German Church, as the proper person to take charge of it. It was to have been located at Fredericktown, Maryland, and the citizens of the place had pledged themselves in various ways to give to it a liberal support. The prospect, indeed, was in every way encouraging. There was reason to believe that a personal friend of the Professor elect would have contributed largely to its endowment if it had gone into operation, and that the sister Church would have taken a generous interest in sustaining it. Unfortunately, the plan of the new institution was based upon mistaken premises. Preaching in English had been introduced in a few congregations in the Maryland Classis, and the success attending it led to the belief that in a short time it would be called for in most of the charges and take the place of the German altogether. The opinion was somewhat plausible, but altogether mistaken. The people continued to be prevailingly German in their language and habits, and the full tide of emigration from the fatherland, which not long after began to inundate the country, made it apparent that no material change of the kind could be expected. The effect upon the mind of the Church was very unfortunate. The people in the more German sections were alarmed, and made to believe that a plan had been concerted and was in progress to put down the German, and to introduce a state of things in America similar to that in the old countries, which in the end would lead to a union of Church and State and be utterly subversive of their religious and civil liberties. In the height of the excitement, meetings were held in many of the pastoral charges, and measures taken to arrest the dangerous movement. A number of ministers, with their congregations, seceded

548

from the Church; and matters assumed an aspect so serious that Dr. Milledoler was induced to decline the appointment tendered him, and the enterprise for the time fell through.

It was not, however, abandoned, but was again revived, a few years afterward, by its original friends.* Instead, however, of attempting it again upon the original foundation at Fredericktown, which had in view an establishment commensurate with the rapidly developing resources of the Church, it was thought best to commence upon a moderate scale and adapt it to its existing wants. In this, as great a mistake was made as the one committed at first. Instead of looking with hope and expectation to the future for improvement, the people were regarded as so fixed and stationary in their habits as to admit of no progress. They did not then need a thoroughly educated ministry, and there was no use in providing for succeeding generations. No great change could be brought about in a very short time, and the future would be able to take care of itself. It so happened, at the time, that Dickinson College, at Carlisle, had been resuscitated, with encouraging prospects of success; and, as it was situated in the midst of a population, a large portion of which was German, of increasing wealth and social influence, it occurred to its friends that it would be well to have the contemplated Theological Seminary in some way connected with it. Liberal offers of accommodation and assistance were accordingly made by the trustees to the Synod at its meeting in Bedford, in 1824; which were accepted, and a committee was appointed to make arrangements for the opening of the Seminary. They were instructed, first, to present a call to the Rev. Samuel Helfenstein, Senior, of Philadelphia, to become the professor, and, in case he declined, to offer the appointment

---

* The most active of these were the Rev. Messrs. William Hendell, Lewis Mayer, Jonathan Helfenstein, James R. Reily, Albert Helfenstein, Sr., and Frederick Rahauser.

to the Rev. Lewis Mayer, of York, Pa. The result was, that the Rev. L. Mayer yielded to the general wish, accepted the office, and opened the institution at Carlisle, on the 11th of March, 1825, with five students.

Soon after, the Rev. James R. Reily, one of the earliest and most zealous friends of the institution, proposed to visit Germany, to solicit aid in behalf of an enterprise so closely connected with the welfare of the emigrant population from the fatherland. He was well received, and collected a considerable amount for the endowment-fund, and a large number of books for the library. Still the revenue from the investments was not sufficient to meet the current expenses; and to depend upon occasional collections in the congregations was exceedingly precarious. This led to another effort to increase the endowment. The plan originated with a personal friend of the Professor, a lay member of the German Reformed congregation at Martinsburg, Virginia, of which Dr. Mayer had been the pastor, and was carried into effect by the Rev. Jacob Beecher, of Shepherdstown, Virginia, a young minister of devoted piety and great energy, just entered upon the sacred office, who was appointed by Synod for the purpose. The subscriptions were obtained without difficulty, and the scheme appeared to be an entire success, when a new trouble sprang up, growing out of the original feeling of opposition to the Seminary in the more German sections of the Church. The people were told that it was only another and more covert movement on the part of the ministers to bring them into spiritual bondage, and the one-half of the moneys was never paid. Other troubles also presented themselves at Carlisle, connected with the arrangements made by the congregation for the accommodation of the Seminary, and the condition of things there generally. The Professor became discouraged, and proposed its removal to the neighboring town of York, where, in the bosom of a larger congregation and a more German population, it would breathe a congenial atmosphere and acquire new life and vigor.

This proposition received the assent of the Synod at Lebanon, in 1829, and the removal was made.

At the same Synod the Rev. Daniel Young was elected Assistant Professor of Theology, and accepted the appointment. His health, however, failed, and he soon ceased from his labors, and entered into rest. Meanwhile the Seminary in its new location prospered; and as the number of students increased, and the labors of the Professor were multiplied,—owing, in some instances, to the deficient preparatory education of the young men under his care,—it was deemed expedient to connect with it a Classical school, at the head of which was placed Dr. Frederick Augustus Rauch, recently arrived from Germany. At the ensuing Synod at Fredericktown, in 1832, he was also elected to fill the vacancy in the Seminary created by the death of Professor Young. The prospect now for both institutions was very good.

But there were troubles ahead for the Seminary, and its course was not permitted to run smooth. The complications with the congregation at Carlisle resulted in a lawsuit which was brought to trial before the civil court at York; and the unfavorable effect of this, in connection with other embarrassments, rendered it expedient, as some thought, to seek for it another location. The question was brought before the Synod at Pittsburg, in 1834; and, after considerable discussion, it was determined that a circular should be issued, inviting proposals from the citizens of such places as might be disposed to compete for the advantages of having literary and theological institutions in their midst. The circular created considerable interest throughout the Church; and, at the next meeting of Synod in Chambersburg, propositions were submitted from the good people of that place, of Lancaster, and of Mercersburg. The proposals from Lancaster were at first regarded as most favorable. They were based upon the expediency of a connection with Franklin College, possessed as it was of a substantial endowment. But it involved also, so far as the Classical school was concerned, a joint control on the part of the Synods of the two Churches. In the course of discussion it was likewise ascertained that the union of the two literary institutions was the principal, if not the sole, object of the movement, and that in all probability the Theological Seminary would be permitted to remain at York without being benefited by the arrangement. This changed the mind of Synod altogether; and, as the proposals from Chambersburg, on account of alleged legal difficulties, were withdrawn, Mercersburg was fixed upon as the place for the permanent location of the Literary and Theological Institutions of the German Reformed Church.

The Classical school was at once removed to the place of its location. But when the Seminary was to follow, it was objected, by the Board of Trustees, that "by consenting to a removal the charter would be forfeited, the Board of Trustees would be dissolved, and a legal control of the funds be lost." For this reason, and because of affliction in his family, the Professor of theology was unwilling to leave York. The question was brought before the Synod of Baltimore in 1839; and, having obtained the opinion of eminent legal counsel to the effect that there was no ground for the fears expressed, it was decided that the seminary must be taken to Mercersburg, as was at first proposed. The domestic difficulty still continuing, the Professor of theology felt himself constrained to resign.

In the mean time, the Classical school at Mercersburg, under the care of Dr. Rauch, was so well sustained as to justify an application to the legislature for its incorporation as a College. The application was made, and a charter was obtained for the institution, under the style and title of Marshall College, together with a grant of $12,000 towards its endowment. For this the Church was mainly indebted to the enlightened zeal and perseverance of the late Rev. Henry L. Rice, then pastor of the German Reformed congregation at Chambersburg.

It now became necessary to fill the vacancy in the Seminary. This was done at the Synod of Lancaster by the re-election of the Rev. Dr. Mayer, who, as he said, "accepted the appointment, in the expectation that the Church, after some time, would be enabled to dispense with his services," and soon after entered upon its duties. In the course of the year, however, fresh troubles arose. In this instance they partook of a dogmatic character; and, although the Board of Visitors was persuaded that they were owing in great measure to misapprehension, the efforts made to adjust them satisfactorily were not successful. The consequence was that, at the ensuing meeting of Synod, at Philadelphia, Dr. Mayer availed himself of his conditional acceptance of the office, and resigned. Dr. Mayer was a truly pious and devoted minister, esteemed and venerated by all who knew him. He was an early and zealous friend of the Theological Seminary, and really did more for its establishment, and for the revival of evangelical piety in the Church, than any of the ministers in his day. It was at his instance, chiefly, after the project of a joint institution with the Lutherans had been abandoned, that an overture was prepared in the Maryland Classis, at its first meeting, and sent up to Synod, for the establishment of a Seminary of our own. He was a member of the committee* of Synod at Hagerstown, in 1828, that reported the "Plan of the Seminary," and was prominent in all the measures that were afterward taken to put it in operation. For this his name should ever be held in grateful remembrance. As a preacher, he was always instructive and edifying. It was the remark of an eminent and eloquent divine, who often heard him, that "he never preached an indifferent sermon." As a pastor, he was unsurpassed for truth and tenderness in the sick chamber, and in dealing

---

* The committee consisted of the Rev. Messrs. Hendell, Mayer, and S. Helfenstein, and the Elders Schnebly, Wolff, Teiss, and Hoffius.

with persons concerned on the subject of religion. His conversational powers were remarkable; and his rich, deep, thorough, personal experience as a Christian made him a safe and valuable counsellor. In debate there were few superior to him. His resources were always at command, and he well knew how to conduct an argument.

Although not extensively read in classic literature, his acquirements in the sphere of theology and its affiliated branches were by no means limited, and were highly respectable. He excelled in biblical criticism. With a mind acute, discriminating, and exact, he seldom failed to bring out the meaning of a text, and was equally successful, when he had done so, in exhibiting it in clear and explicit terms. As Professor, although his health was generally feeble, his labors were unwearied; and, as the fruit of them, the graduates of the Seminary, during his connection with it, were among the most efficient and useful ministers of the Church, many of whom remain to the present day, and are still active in every good word and work. His retirement from the sphere of active service in the Church was sincerely regretted by his numerous friends.

Thus, for the time being, both institutions were left under the care of Dr. Rauch, and so continued until, at a special meeting of the Synod at Chambersburg in 1840, the Rev. John W. Nevin, D.D., of the Theological Seminary of the Presbyterian Church at Alleghany, was elected to fill the vacancy in the Seminary. In every way, Dr. Nevin was well qualified to be the colleague and coadjutor of Dr. Rauch in building up a young and rising institution in the German Reformed Church. A profound thinker, possessed of great earnestness and depth of feeling, with decided independence and force of character, he was at the same time liberal in his views; and, equally animated by the spirit of self-sacrifice, he was prepared, in the prime of life, to devote his energies to the service of a people who, with their peculiar habits and in their fortunate geo-

554

graphical position in the country, only required to be properly trained to exert a wide-spread and happy influence upon its social and political destinies. Dr. Rauch's health, however, had begun to fail, and, wholly absorbed in the work to which he had given himself, he would take no repose, and in the course of a short time fell a martyr to the cause he had labored so assiduously to promote. His early death was universally lamented as a loss to the Church, to its institutions, and to the cause of philosophy and religion at large.

The chief control and care of the two institutions now devolved upon Dr. Nevin; and, as their interests were intimately blended, Synod readily consented to an arrangement by which he was temporarily placed at the head of the College. This was highly acceptable to the Church and the patrons of the institutions. The difficulty now was to find a successor to Dr. Rauch in the Seminary. There was no available man in the Church—none in the country—in all respects qualified to take his place. Admitting there were those who equalled him in learning and talents, it could not be expected that they would enter with the same zeal and ardor upon the work he had relinquished, or that they would be as well able to expose and correct the theological errors of the age, and exhibit and sustain the principles of a sound orthodoxy as they obtained in the Reformed Church. Upon this point the Church was exceedingly anxious, and, after much consultation, it was proposed to call some one of the eminent divines of Germany to fill the vacancy. The suggestion, it is believed, originated with the Rev. Dr. Zecharias, of Fredericktown. He had his mind fixed upon the Rev. Dr. Krummacher, then of Elberfeld. A General Synod, to consider the proposition, was called to meet at Lebanon, in the winter of 1843; and a commission* was appointed to

---

* The commission consisted of the Rev. Dr. Theodore L. Hoffeditz and the Rev. Dr. Benjamin S. Schneck.

proceed to Germany, and present him a call "to come over and help us." The Commissioners fulfilled their mission, and the mind of the Professor elect was deeply exercised in regard to his duty in the case; and "it was only after a prayerful review of the validity of his reasons, that he brought himself to the firm conviction that He alone, at the disposal of whose most holy will he had placed himself, had decided his cause, and commanded him to decline it." Failing to secure the services of Dr. Krummacher, the Commissioners, in accordance with their instructions, looked around for some other suitably qualified person to whom they might tender the appointment. Their attention was directed to the Rev. Philip Schaff, D.P., who was understood to be willing to accept it, if it were formally made to him by the authorities of the Church. This was done at the meeting of Synod at Winchester, in 1843; and in the course of the year following Dr. Schaff entered the Seminary as Professor of Exegetical and Historical Theology.

Dr. Schaff was qualified, in the most literal sense, to be the successor of Dr. Rauch. Dr. Rauch left Germany at the time, some of its greatest philosophers were feeling their way to the acknowledgment of evangelical truth. Dr. Schaff came to us after the triumph of orthodoxy, and the exhibition of its trophies, in the reassertion of the doctrines of the Reformation. If Dr. Rauch was the pious philosopher, able to detect and expose the neological fallacies of the day, beginning to set in as a reaction upon the false revivalism that had swept over the land, Dr. Schaff, with a mind equally cultivated and stored with various learning, was fitted to work reconstructively in the restoration of a sound orthodoxy. Alike generous in his impulses, he at once yielded to the inspiration of the new enterprise left to him as a legacy by his distinguished predecessor, and embarked in the work with all his energies. His inaugural address was an elaborate dissertation on "The Principle of Protestantism," in which he found occasion to give a frank expression of his views of the Church as the body of Christ, the appropriate sphere of His redeeming activity, and of the sacraments as means of grace, indicating clearly the course he would pursue in his doctrinal teachings. The views he presented were, however, so far in advance of, if not different from, those generally entertained, that many well-meaning persons thought there was something wrong in them. The impression was so strong, that a majority of the Philadelphia Classis felt it to be their duty to bring the published address to the notice of Synod. This was done at its meeting in York, 1845. An investigation was had, searching and thorough; and, after a protracted discussion, it was decided, with almost entire unanimity, that there was no just ground for the fears and suspicions expressed. The only persons dissenting were a minister and two elders, representing the majority of Classis, who by courtesy were allowed to vote.

The decision of Synod, however, did not allay the excitement abroad. The address and other writings of the Professors at Mercersburg continued to be severely criticized in the religious periodicals of the different Churches, and the charges which the Synod had pronounced groundless were virtually renewed before the ensuing Synod of the Reformed Dutch Church, at Albany, by one of its Corresponding Delegates, who was present at the investigation by the German Synod. The proceedings in the case were marked by courtesy and kindness, and nothing offensive was permitted to appear upon the published minutes. Still, the opposition to Mercersburg theology, as it came to be styled, was continued, and finally led to an abrogation of all correspondence between the two sister Churches of the Heidelberg Catechism. A course of action somewhat similar was also taken in the General Assembly of the Presbyterian Church. It was supposed, by some immediately interested, that the effect of these movements would be the dismemberment and breaking up of the German Church. The judgment of the supreme Councils of the Churches, thus solemnly pronounced, it was thought, would fall with crushing weight upon the feebler and less influential body, and produce general dissatisfaction among its members, and induce them to seek other connections. Such was the expectation; and plans in some instances were concerted to bring it to pass. " The wish, doubtless, was father to the thought;" but, though a considerable commotion was produced, the German Church suffered no permanent injury. Two or three ministers, educated in other confessions, left its communion, but the people held fast to their profession, and the principles of the " Address," sanctioned by subsequent decisions of Synod, were unfalteringly maintained. As has often been the case with speculative opinions in advance of prevailing theories upon subjects which in a measure had fallen out of the mind of the Church, or which claimed its attention in new aspects, the fierce opposition which " The Principle of Protestantism" at first provoked, gradually gave way, and the strange doctrines were regarded with greater favor. Nor was it the only instance in which the decrees of Councils solemnly expressed were corrected and set aside by the sober second thought of the Church. The discussions were continued in a better spirit and with happier results, and when the passions excited by the conflict had subsided, it was seen and confessed by many that the teachings of the Mercersburg divines involved no heresy, and were not at variance with the confessional writings of the Reformed Church; and there are those on both sides that now would gladly recall much that was said and done in the heat of the controversy.

That the people of the German Reformed Church, under the circumstances, adhered so steadfastly to the Professors of the Seminary, is remarkable. This was especially the case in the older sections of the Church, where, more than anywhere else, the people retained their original opinions and customs. With less cultivation than the people of the more English portions, their religious instincts seemed to assure them that the doctrines ascribed to the Professors were precisely those they had been accustomed to hear and were familiar with from their childhood; and never were they so cordially disposed to support the Church and its institutions, as during this period of opposition from without.

We have said that the institutions prospered. This was owing not just to the support they received from the Church and the public at large, but also to the disinterested zeal of the Professors themselves. For years the Professors of the Seminary discharged duties in the college equivalent to those of a professorship, without recompense. For nine years the whole burden and responsibility of the presidency of Marshall College rested upon Dr. Nevin, with no other reward than the consciousness of having performed a noble and generous part and of being held in affectionate remembrance by a grateful people. But it was not to be expected that such services would always be rendered gratuitously, or that the college could be sustained without an endowment. At the same time, the finances of the Theological Seminary became embarrassed, and were found to be insufficient to meet its current expenses. Dr. Nevin, in view of the existing state of things, announced his purpose to retire from the position in the Seminary which for eleven years he had so faithfully and acceptably filled, and finally submitted his resignation to the Synod at Lancaster, in 1851. Every effort was made to induce him to withdraw it; but he persisted in his determination, and Synod "with extreme reluctance yielded to his request for the present, but left the professorship vacant, in the hope that in the providence of God he might see his way clear to return to the same at no distant day." The vacancy still continuing, and there being no hope of a change in Dr. Nevin's mind, it was filled, at the next meeting of Synod in Baltimore, by the election of the Rev. Bernard C. Wolff, D.D., pastor of the Third German Reformed Church of that city.

In the mean time an arrangement had been made for the purchase by the Reformed Church of the Lutheran interest in Franklin College at Lancaster, with the understanding that Marshall College should be consolidated with it, and a new charter obtained under the style and title of Franklin Marshall College. The arrangement was completed, and Dr. Nevin was elected its president. He, however, could not be persuaded to leave his retirement. At a subsequent meeting of the Board of Trustees, the appointment was conferred upon Dr. Schaff. He expressed a willingness to accept it, provided he was permitted to retire from the Seminary. This the Synod, appreciating his services, was unwilling he should do. He then requested leave of absence for a year, to visit his friends in Germany, an object which for some time he had had at heart. The situation of affairs, as it regards the Seminary, was now sufficiently discouraging. Dr. Nevin having resigned, and Dr. Schaff being absent in Europe, its operations were necessarily suspended. Its financial embarrassments increased the difficulty, and, under the circumstances, the Professor elect hesitated to accept of his appointment. He was unwilling to assume alone the responsibility of conducting the institution, and could not think of adding to its difficulties by entering upon the office when the financial resources were not sufficient to pay the salaries of the Professors, to say nothing of other expenditures. He accordingly submitted the call he had received to the Synod of Philadelphia, with the request that he might be relieved from further responsibility in the premises. Synod, after due deliberation, declined to do this, and affectionately urged him to accept the trust presented to his consideration At this crisis of affairs, by a singular and striking providential coincidence, the embarrassed condition of the finances was relieved during the sessions of Synod, by the completion of the endowment of the two professorships in the Seminary, in the form of a legacy, available from the day of his death, from Mr. Daniel Keiffer, an aged father of the Church, from Berks county, and of a generous donation from Miss Ann E. Keller, of Huntingdon county, a young lady just come to the possession of her estate. This remarkable providence, in connection with the ascertained fact that the Professor elect would not have the responsibility of conducting the Seminary resting upon him alone, settled the question in his mind, and constrained him to accept the appointment tendered him for the second time by Synod. In the fall of '54, Dr. Schaff returned from Europe, and the Seminary was reopened with encouraging prospects. Since then the number of students has steadily increased, and at this time is greater than it has been at any previous period of its existence. A theological tutorship has also been created, at the suggestion, and in part endowed by the liberality, of Baron von Bethman Hollweg, a distinguished Christian gentleman of Berlin,—a member of the king's cabinet, in charge of the Department of Instruction and Public Worship. The plan proposes the appointment of two young men, graduates of our institution, who in succession are to complete their studies in Germany, and upon their return will be expected to teach two years in the Seminary. The first appointments made are the present incumbents, the licentiates Messrs. Wm. M. Reily, tutor, and Jacob R. Kershner, travelling in Germany.

In reviewing the history of the Theological Seminary, it will be seen that, like most enterprises which start from small beginnings and have to depend upon the good will of the public, it has had a constant succession of trials to pass through. This is uniformly the case when the movement is new and of magnitude and importance, and should create no surprise. All men do not see alike, and looking at objects from different points of view, they estimate them accordingly; and when they come to compare opinions, instead of allowing for this, and exercising a sound reflecting judgment, they suffer themselves to be controlled by prejudice and passion. In this way jealousies, suspicions, and strifes are engendered, even on the part of those who are upright and sincere and mean well. It was so with the Seminary. At first it was opposed on the ground, that the plan, upon which it was proposed to establish it, was not suited to the actual condition and wants of the Church, and that its reigning spirit would be foreign to its true character and design. Subsequently, the difficulties it had to contend with were owing chiefly to its financial embarrassments. Finally, the bitter opposition to it from without originated professedly in a concern for its orthodoxy. In all these conflicts and sore trials, the institution was remarkably sustained and encouraged. Good, indeed, in every instance, was brought out of evil; and this day the Seminary, the object of so many prayers and faithful self-denying labors, stands firm in the affections and confidence of the people, a monument of the piety and zeal of its founders, to endure, with the blessing of God, for ages to come.

It is obvious, also, to every reflecting mind acquainted with its history, that, notwithstanding the troubles it has had to contend with,—"fightings without and fears within,"—God, in His providence, has so graciously watched over and controlled all things in relation to it, that it has ever maintained its proper confessional position. This was remarkably the case in its relation to the Lutheran Church. At first it was proposed, as has been said, to establish a joint institution, in connection with Franklin College, for the benefit of both Confessions. If carried into effect, it was thought, it would be of great advantage to the whole German population of the country, and to the interests of religion at large. The simple fact that this people were from the same fatherland, were similarly educated, spoke the same language, lived in the same neighborhood, worshipped at the same altars, were distinguished by the same habits, and frequently were intermarried, was a powerful plea in favor of the measure proposed. But, after all, there is reason to believe that instead of advancing.the interests of sound scriptural truth and sincere piety, it would have been unfavorable to them. Either there would have been a commixture and modification of the elements of dogmatic truth, that would have divested it of its strength and fair proportions, or if the representatives of the two Confessions had continued true to their distinguishing principles, it would almost necessarily have resulted in divisions and strifes. The institute would have been based either upon dogmatic indifference, or it would have been influenced by the spirit of confessional rivalry. In the one case, the cause of truth would have suffered, and a shallow evangelism would have prepared the way, as in Germany, for more material error. In the other, we would have had on both sides a strict church orthodoxy, repellant and partial, that in the end would have been equally injurious to the teachings of the Bible. In the plan proposed, there was no calculation made for the play of human passion and the force of educational prejudices. It was taken for granted that all would go well and work harmoniously. But this is more than poor human nature would have permitted us to expect. It is better, therefore, that the plan did not succeed. The two denominations have gone forward, each in its own way, and have established institutions of their own, and taught their own views of truth. There have been no jealousies or jarrings, and, with the blessing of God, both have been instrumental in effecting good in their respective spheres of activity. In thus declining to unite in the establishment of a joint institution, the Reformed Church was influenced by no spirit of antagonism to the Lutheran. It has never been opposed to the theology of the Augsburg Confession. This is evident from the very design and contents of the Heidelberg Catechism. Its whole spirit is Melanchthonian. Its avowed object was to harmonize discordant views and to allay party strifes. It differs, on many points of great interest in theology, from the teachings of the Lutheran confessions. But the differences do not involve the substance of doctrine. They are frequently but different aspects of the same great truths, and may be said to complement each other. Whilst, then, they differ, there is no reason why the divines of the two Churches should dispute, and "fall out by the way." On the other hand, there is no special necessity for an absolute union. It is better that the two communions, representing as they do the different sides of Protestant Christianity, should remain apart, each maintaining its proper position, until at some more advanced period of exegetical and dogmatical theology they may, in the providence and by the grace of God, be brought to see eye to eye, and be merged together in the Church of Christ.

This same watchful providence and care in preserving the German Reformed Church and its institutions in their proper dogmatic position in relation to other denominations, are seen also even in the opposition that was made in the more German sections of the Church to the establishment of a Theological Seminary of her own at the time it was attempted at Fredericktown. It was not selfishness and sheer ignorance, as was alleged, that led to this opposition. Such motives to some extent may, here and there, have prevailed. But at the ground of them was a sound church feeling and concern for their peculiar customs and principles as a denomination. It was not just that it was feared that, in the course of time, the Church would be Anglicized, but it was apprehended—whether with good reason or not is another question—that with the introduction of English preaching in their congregations all that was peculiar in their doctrines and modes of worship would pass away, or be perverted. They had their own views of the Church and its ordinances. The Church with them was more than a congregation of the saints,—an assembly of pious people for the worship of God, presided over by a minister. It was the mother of the faithful, the dispenser of the means of grace in which they were "born of God," and with which were connected all their hopes of salvation. The sacraments, too, were actually channels and means of grace, possessed of supernatural efficacy, and, where the conditions were at hand, availed to that end. And that these sacred institutions should be stripped of their divine character and, in this sense, be made common and profane, was more than they could bear to think of. Nor were they disposed to receive the one-sided views of the divine sovereignty, as entertained by some, of which they had heard. They admitted the sovereignty of God. It was a doctrine traditionally dear to them. But they were inclined to think that, whilst God ordered all things according to the good pleasure of His own will, it was His good pleasure to allow a sphere of freedom to His intelligent creatures, in which there was room and place for the exercise of their own wills, and yet retain in His own hands the ability to overrule all their determinations and actions for His own glory in the accomplishment of His own wise and gracious purposes. In this way they thought the name of the Most High was magnified even more than by attributing to Him the arbitrary exercise of power in controlling the volitions of men. Many would not have been able thus to state their convictions,—some, perhaps, were not fully conscious of entertaining them; but such were the persuasions and impressions, more or less, at the ground of the opposition they made to the establishment of the Seminary under English auspices, and to the so-called evangelical operations of the day. There was nothing positively unfriendly to institutions of learning, or to living, active piety, in their minds. It was, in its fundamental principle, a holy jealousy and regard for the time-honored ordinances and customs which had descended to them from the days of the Reformation, and which they brought with them in their Liturgies and Hymn-books from the fatherland. A proof of this we have in the striking and affecting fact, that when a minister of the Presbyterian Church, of English education, and of whom they had never before heard, was placed at the head of their institutions with almost unlimited authority, and manifested a reverence for the ancient faith and worship of their Church, they received him gladly, and in his trials clung to him faithfully, and contributed freely to the very institutions they, under other circumstances, had fiercely opposed.

But most of all was this superintending providence, in keeping the German Reformed Church true to the Heidelberg Catechism and its proper confessional position, seen during the so-called Mercersburg theological controversies, which took place after the establishment of the Seminary. Dr. Rauch, in his day, exerted no particular positive influence upon the dogmatic character of our institutions. He was too much occupied with his philosophical studies, and too much interested in the vigorous life of American Christianity, to give much attention to dogmatic theology. Indirectly, however, his teachings were not without their effect upon the Church movement. They gave depth and power to the thinking of his students, and prepared the way for profounder views of religious truth. He may be said to have exerted an influence upon the reigning theological thinking of the Church somewhat similar to that of Schleiermacher upon the speculative theology of Germany. He was the bridge upon which others passed over to deeper views of important points of dogmatic inquiry. With all his willingness to fall in with American Christianity in its practical aspects, he was opposed to the fanatical features of the popular revivalism of the day. This was seen already in his sermons to the students of the college and in his lectures on the Heidelberg Catechism, which in its contents, as he thought, furnished a good answer to the question, "What must I do to be saved?" and again in the objections he made to the Liturgy, at that time submitted to the Church for its adoption. In his judgment it was too demonstrative and mechanical, and not at all answerable to the proper conception of worship as a Liturgy should be.

That his influence was felt in this way is seen also in the impression made by the publication of his Psychology. It was received by the public generally without opposition, for the reason in some measure, perhaps, that comparatively little attention had been given in this country to that department of science. Mental philosophy was known and had been cultivated, but the profounder and more comprehensive conception of man's spiritual nature, as expressed by the term "psychology," was not just familiar to every one's mind, and there were some symptoms of dissatisfaction and suspicion in reference to his book at the time of its appearance. His lamented death left the volume to fulfil its work silently upon the minds of those who studied it; and the effect was seen in the purpose of Synod to fill the vacancy in the Seminary by the appointment of a distinguished divine from abroad. This resulted in the selection of Dr. Schaff. The selection was singularly providential. As already remarked, he came to the Institutions bearing the first-fruits of the triumph of orthodoxy over the rationalism of the fatherland, and of the return of the Church to the doctrines of the Reformation. The views he brought with him and expressed in his public addresses served doubtless to stir up the mind of Dr. Nevin in reference to the Church and sacramental questions. But Dr. Nevin had been occupied with them before, as may be seen already in his sermon before the Triennial Convention at Harrisburg. Neither is there any thing new in these views, nor has this ever been claimed by the Mercersburg divines. The truths which they involve underlie the Heidelberg Catechism, and are exhibited in those admirable commentaries upon it published by the writers of the Federalist school in the latter half of the seventeenth century. They are contained, in fact, in organic connection, and may be developed from the Apostles' Creed. Owing, however, in some measure to the irenical spirit in which the Catechism was conceived,— the avowed object being the restoration of peace and harmony to the Church,—and the fact, also, that the Church

of the Reformation was so entirely taken up with the doctrine of justification by faith, in opposition to the Roman
Catholics, as to throw every other question connected with
the appropriation of salvation comparatively into the shade,
some of the doctrines involved were not brought out as
fully as could have been desired. This was especially the
case in regard to the doctrine of regeneration, and the
nature of religion as the principle of a new life implanted
in the soul, the centre of man's being, by the Holy Ghost,
in the use of the means of grace. Even in Calvin's great
work, the "Institutes of the Christian Religion,"—a work
the theological treasures of which the study of three centuries has not yet exhausted,—whilst he fully, and with
great clearness and force of argument, treats of justification
and sanctification, he merely mentions the doctrine of regeneration, without defining its nature or showing in what
it consists. He logically enough shows the transforming
power of faith, and the subjective holiness which flows from
it; but it is only in his doctrine of the Lord's Supper that
he unfolds the new birth in its objective form. Nor is it
treated in the Confessional writings of a later period under
a separate head. It is well, perhaps, that it was so. The
doctrine of regeneration involves questions of a profoundly
metaphysical character, and with an imperfect psychology
an attempt at satisfactory definitions would have been
rather hazardous. The Bible itself, although inspired and
possessed of all-saving knowledge, never pretends to define
formally in the sphere of pure science. Had this been
done by the sacred writers, it would have been necessary
to make the terms of their definitions intelligible to the
Church of all ages to accommodate them, from time to
time, to the measure of advancing knowledge. The teachings of the Bible, in fact, are not addressed to the logical
understanding, but to our faith, and thus verify the saying
of Anselm, that "to understand we must first believe," and
to believe, according to St. John,* we must be born of God.

---

* Πᾶς ὁ πιστεύων, ὅτι 'Ιησοῦς ἐστιν ὁ Χριστὸς, ἐκ τοῦ θεοῦ γεγέννηται.

But, whatever may be said upon this point, it will scarcely be denied that the Reformed Church of the nineteenth century, both of Europe and America, has been so exclusively occupied with the practical duties of religion, especially the evangelical enterprises of the age, that doctrinal questions came to be regarded as of minor importance. During this period, until recently, in Germany, there was no scientific work on dogmatic theology produced from the Reformed stand-point; and thus topics of great moment, as connected with religious experience, were permitted almost to pass away from the consciousness of the Church, the minds of Christians being completely taken up with the maintenance and spread of the gospel. So much was this the case with many, that they thought the best way to build up the Church at home was by the reflex influence of missions abroad, and that the most conclusive evidence of a sound faith and of Christian experience was an ardent zeal for the conversion of others, especially the heathen.

Under these circumstances, it is not surprising that the writings of the Mercersburg Professors—exhibiting, as they did, the more objective character of religion, as the principle of a new life imparted by the Holy Ghost, in contradistinction to the theory of it, either as a matter of mere feeling, or knowledge, or duty; and of the Church, as a divine constitution possessed of supernatural powers, in opposition to the conception of it as simply an association of pious individuals for religious purposes; and of its ordinances, as divinely-appointed means of grace and salvation, to the exclusion of all human inventions, however good in themselves—were regarded at first with suspicion and fear, as altogether wrong and at variance with the Confessions and the teachings of the Bible. And yet in all their teachings the Professors in the Seminary were true to the Catechism and other standard writings of the Reformed Church. They were somewhat in advance of them upon particular points, but in no respect at variance with them. They were built upon them, in connection with the Scriptures, as their proper basis. In this respect they were in harmony with the acknowledged spirit and principles of the Reformed Church itself. With all due deference to the Confessional writings as the standard of our teachings, we are not to forget that the Scriptures alone are the rule of our faith, and that we are not to consider the dogmas of the Church as so absolutely fixed and established as to preclude all further inquiry or investigation. So far from it, we may always feel at liberty, as occasion may require, to bring them to the Scriptures, as the only and all-sufficient norm and rule of saving knowledge. In doing this, there is no danger that the truth will be harmed. On the contrary, it will only be made to appear in brighter and fairer lines. In this way it will be purified and acquire beauty and strength. It is the stagnant pool that becomes putrid and foul. The flowing stream purges itself, gathering volume as it goes, and becomes deeper and broader and stronger, until it is lost in the vast ocean of waters. Just so with religious truth, as exhibited in the Church standards. The more frequently it is tested by the Bible in a becoming spirit of modesty and meekness, and in this way kept in constant flow, the more will it be understood and appreciated. It is believed this has been the experience in regard to the particular views expressed and advocated by the Mercersburg Professors. It is now pretty generally conceded that their teachings accord with the Scriptures and the standard writings of the Reformed Church. They only exhibit more distinctly and define more accurately, than the people were accustomed to have done for them in sermons and familiar theological treatises, the very truths contained in their catechisms and the Bible.

This fact, so interesting in itself,—that God in His providence has thus graciously sustained the Theological Seminary, and safely brought it through all its trials and conflicts, and so ordered all things in relation to it that, in a remarkable manner, it has been kept true to the proper

570

theological position of the German Reformed Church and the principles of the Heidelberg Catechism,*—should encourage her members to hope, at least, if not believe, that the Churches of the Palatinate and Switzerland have not been transplanted to this Western continent in vain, and that God in His wisdom has even yet some good object connected with the interests of His kingdom to accomplish through their agencies.

Nor has the happy effect of her theological position and dogmatic teachings been limited to her own people. Other denominations have felt their influence, and are not unwilling to acknowledge it. We have a striking instance of the fact in a recent movement in New England. Better-defined and juster views of the constitution and design of the Church, in its various aspects and relations, have come more generally to prevail, or are, at least, more distinctly impressed upon the public mind. The Church is regarded as—what it really is, according to the Scriptures—the body of Christ, the sphere of His official activity as the Prophet, Priest, and King of His people. In it He appears not simply as a mediator between God and man, but as the divinely constituted Redeemer of the world, and in whom alone we have a covenant-right and warrant for salvation. Religion, too, has come to be viewed, in greater measure, as an actual experience in man's inmost being, the principle and power of a new and endless life in Christ Jesus, manifesting itself in every part of his renewed existence, enabling him to keep his body under, influencing his feelings, his understanding, and his will. Thus man becomes a new creature, and is what he ought to be, and what at first he was intended to be, when, by the power of divine grace

---

* It is an interesting and suggestive fact, that in all the acts of Synod, in reference to Catechisms and Manuals of Instruction submitted from time to time by private individuals for the inspection and approval of Synod, it never in any way, or to any extent, committed itself to the prejudice or disparagement of the Heidelberg Catechism as the only standard and rule of teaching in the catechetical class, the Sunday-school, and the Church.

through the redemption which is in Jesus' blood, he is made holy and happy and wise. So also the ordinances of God's house are esteemed to be the means of grace appointed of God for the attainment of salvation, and most certainly efficacious for that end when the proper conditions are at hand,—as much so as any other means for the accomplishment of a special purpose in the natural world,—empty vessels and of no account, the savor of death unto death, without repentance and faith, but the savor of life unto life, the wisdom of God and the power of God to salvation, to every one who, with a sense of spiritual need upon his soul, looks believingly to the Son of God as the Saviour of mankind for His pardoning mercy and regenerating grace.

If, then, the Church of the Heidelberg Catechism and her Institutions, under the pressure of severe trials and great difficulties, have thus far been providentially kept true, to their proper Confessional principles, and at the same time have caused their influence to be felt in the promotion of a sound churchly orthodoxy, may we not venture to hope that, her Institutions firmly established upon a broad and liberal basis, and her spiritual resources unfolded, she will ever continue faithful to the principles she has avowed, and, taking her place meekly among the other denominations of our common Protestant faith, will fulfil her part in the work of ushering in the kingdom of God?

There may seem to be presumption in the thought, although it is uttered in no vainglorious spirit, that in bringing this final and most glorious consummation, so devoutly to be prayed for, to pass, the Church of the Heidelberg Catechism, in its several branches, may yet be allowed, in the good providence of God, to exert her influence as a peace-maker and mediatrix among the different Protestant Confessions. There are certainly indications to this effect on both sides of the Atlantic at the present time. Whilst in this country this admirable "form of sound words" is held in higher estimation every day by her own ministers and people, and is attracting more and more the attention of other denominations, in the fatherland, where all great religious movements have ever originated, there is a probability that the reaction against rationalism which has been in progress for the last thirty years will culminate in restoring this venerable symbol of our faith, originally intended to bring back peace and harmony to a distracted Church, to its proper position, and that its influence will be powerfully felt and cordially acknowledged. One thing is certain, and it is, that until the two great leading Confessions of the Protestant Church, the Lutheran and Reformed,—antithetic, and yet not necessarily antagonistic, but rather complementary to each other upon questions of vital interest in theology,—are thus reconciled and brought together, it is a vain imagination to suppose that other denominations, that have gone out and separated from each other upon points of comparative insignificance, but on that account do not the less fiercely maintain and adhere to them, can ever be brought into cordial union and co-operation; and it is equally certain, that if ever the different Confessions which now divide the Church are thus brought to unite, it must be upon some such common, conservative, churchly, scriptural ground as is furnished to them by the Church of the Heidelberg Catechism.

Let her people, then, rally to her support on this great Tercentenary occasion, that in all the departments of her activity she may be made efficient for usefulness. Let the people of the East and the West strike hands together, calling upon God for His blessing in building up their Institutions, theological and literary, and in carrying on their benevolent operations; and, whatever may befall us in these perilous times, when "the hearts of good men everywhere are failing them for fear of the evils that are coming upon the land," all in the end will be well: though the nation should disintegrate and the government be destroyed, the Church will survive and be safe. He whose right it is to reign will take to Himself His great power, and bring light out of darkness, order out of confusion, and cause prosperity to abound. "Come, Lord Jesus, come quickly," that the people may be glad and rejoice, "saying, Alleluia: for the Lord God omnipotent reigneth."

574

THE END.

STEREOTYPED BY L. JOHNSON & CO.,
PHILADELPHIA.

Lightning Source UK Ltd.
Milton Keynes UK
UKHW012315061118
331891UK00008B/253/P